Communism, Fascism, and Democracy

Communism, Fascism, and Democracy

The Theoretical Foundations

Edited by

C A R L   C O H E N

The University of Michigan

RANDOM HOUSE, NEW YORK

This Book is Dedicated
to My Mother and Father

Ninth Printing, June 1967

Library of Congress Catalog Card Number: 62-10779

Manufactured in the United States of America

INTRODUCTION

"If all communities aim at some good," Aristotle wrote, "the state, or political community, which is the highest of all, and which embraces all the rest, aims at good in a greater degree than any other, and at the highest good." More than two thousand years have elapsed since this was written, yet no single type of political organization, no set of fundamental principles has won universal acceptance. The proper goals of states, the best methods for the attainment of such goals, and the ideal constitution of political communities in general have been and remain the subjects of profound philosophical dispute.

The resolution of these disputes is of the highest importance. For although theoretical conflicts often bear on everyday life, none do so more far-reachingly and urgently than conflicts in the realm of politics. Political decisions may vitally affect almost every aspect of a society's life—from its level of economic welfare to its very existence as a community. And the basic ingredients of important public policies are the political philosophies subscribed to by the people concerned. Of course, the day-to-day decisions of individuals and governments are not normally made with sole or even prime reference to the largest principles of politics. But the most vital decisions, those which deeply affect the tenor of daily life and which give long-range direction to program and policy, are made with deliberate or unconscious regard for theory—for prior philosophical commitments concerning the nature of the person and the state.

In this century, these philosophical commitments have crystallized chiefly into three well-developed theories of community organization. We have witnessed, and continue to witness, the contrasts and conflicts of these political philosophies: communism, fascism, democracy—their

v

very names evoke powerful emotional reactions. The deepest meaning and highest aims of each may not be entirely clear to us; but the world has been largely divided among them, and so significant are the consequences of this division that the study of these political forms is among the most important we could undertake.

In spite of these contemporary political pressures, however, the philosophical underpinnings of communism, fascism and democracy are neither widely enough nor well enough understood. Lip service is easily given to a name or a slogan; it is no chore to make obedient reference to the "fatherland" or the "class-struggle of the proletariat" or the "democratic way of life." But whichever of these it is our aim to further and support, we are not greatly served by the cheap and easy use of expressions which, in the frequency of their repetition, have lost the largest part of their real significance. Whether it is our object to oppose or to defend communism or fascism or democracy, we cannot do so intelligently or effectively without the possession of a full understanding of the practical and theoretical operation of each, the works and aims of its supporters, and, perhaps most important, the philosophical foundations upon which the position ultimately rests.

A word about the selections that have been chosen for this volume and their arrangement is in order. The criteria employed in selecting appropriate authors and works must, of necessity, be complex; it is not to be expected that everyone will agree with the choices that have been made. Certain characteristics have been specially sought for, and do, I believe, regularly appear.

The first consideration has been the *representative* character of the author, as presenting, officially or unofficially, the true views of the position with which he is associated. In some cases this is not difficult, as when choosing Marx and Lenin to represent communism, or Locke and Mill to represent democracy. In other cases the matter is not so clear, as in selecting Hegel as contributing to the philosophy of fascism, or Robert Owen as contributing to that of communism. In such cases what must be kept in mind is not only the movement as a whole, but the special feature of its philosophy that is being presented. Thus Hegel can be clearly seen as a contributor to the political organicism later manifest in fascism, and Owen as an obvious representative of the utopian socialists from whom Marx learned a great deal. In regard to the particular works chosen, and the excerpts from them, I have also tried to make selections that are representative both of each author, and of the philosophical view to which he has chiefly contributed.

Second, I have sought to include those works and passages that are genuinely *fundamental* to the political philosophy concerned—the key works and their parts which disclose the foundational views of state, society, and the individual in each philosophy are the ones I have included. However, much material of this character necessarily has been passed over in view of the limitations of space.

Where possible, I have chosen *classical* works and authors, that is, statements that, over the years, have become accepted as the most authoritative within the context of the given political philosophy. This is much easier to do, of course, in the case of communism and fascism than in that of democracy, where, in the twentieth century, the question of who speaks with greatest authority is moot. Here too, however, I have tried to select only clear and profound statements of underlying philosophical principles that have been widely accepted and acclaimed.

It is always desirable, of course, to read an important philosophical work in its *entirety*. To that end, the complete text of a fair number of these philosophical essays is included. Frequently, where this was impossible, large segments of such works, retaining the essential integrity of the whole, represent them. In some instances, the limited space available necessitated the inclusion of relatively short excerpts; in such cases the intention is generally to display a specific feature of that philosophy, or a particularly influential passage.

Arrangement as well as selection sometimes must be arbitrary. In each of these three philosophies, the most influential contributing traditions have been distinguished, and a separate section devoted to each. For the most part, these sections follow one another in chronological order, but in some instances this order is impossible to maintain, as in the case of Sections I and II of Part One, and Sections III and IV of Part Three. Within each section chronological order again has been roughly followed, but abandoned when the substance of the selections has made it necessary. Thus in Section V of Part One, on the strategy and tactics of communism, excerpts from Stalin and Lenin follow one another alternately, and in Section II of Part Three certain passages from Mill and Calhoun precede the selection from de Tocqueville. Of course, the division into sections is itself a somewhat mechanical device that is inadequate to display the growth of an important philosophical view in all its complexity. These divisions are justified, however, by the increased ease of interpretation and interrelation that they make possible.

A short prefatory note begins each major part and section. These notes are intended neither as summaries nor as interpretations; their chief purpose is to set the scene for the selections that follow, to orient the reader by disclosing something of the character and substance of the philosophical views represented. Each selection, within the several sections, is headed by an introductory paragraph, the chief purpose of which is to identify the author and the work, and to orient the reader with reference to that author. Finally, there are brief headings interspersed within the selections themselves. Often, these are taken from the original text, but sometimes, when needed for purposes of clarification, they are supplied (and bracketed) by the editor.

It must be strongly emphasized that the arrangement of authors and works—and especially their inclusion under the general headings of communism, fascism, and democracy—should by no means be construed as a narrow labeling of the individual philosophers. Hegel, for example, appears as a contributor (however much he would have winced at the thought) to the foundations of both communism and fascism, and can himself be classified as neither. Hobbes and Bodin are no more properly called fascists than Feuerbach is properly called a communist. In short, the structure of the volume has been devised to disclose the development of philosophies, but assuredly not to encourage the mechanical classification of philosophers.

Any collection of readings of this kind must expect to be criticized for having omitted passages that should not have been omitted, or for including passages that need not have been included. It is my hope that it will be understood that such differences of opinion are inevitable, and that the selections I have chosen will serve as a reasonably adequate account of the theoretical foundations of communism, fascism, and democracy.

These three political philosophies are the ruling ones of our time. The force and effect of theory upon practice, the impact of philosophical speculation upon the course of human life, is nowhere clearer than in the realm of the political realities which they dominate. Upon our understanding of these political forms and their philosophical foundations depend not only the intelligent and just direction of our present affairs but our wisest preparations for the future.

Contents

Contents

Part One

COMMUNISM

The names of political philosophies are inevitably charged with high emotive content. The effects of politics upon our daily lives make this understandable, and it is therefore natural that, in the present serious conflicts between East and West, the terms "communism" and "democracy" should convey not only many meanings, but also intense feelings of reverence and enthusiasm or condemnation and hatred.

Yet most will agree that any adequate appraisal of a political philosophy requires, first of all, a clear understanding of what that philosophy is—what claims it makes with regard to the individual and the state, and what changes it demands for the future. Whatever our emotional reactions to communism may be, their justification must ultimately lie in accurate and cool-headed answers to questions of just this sort.

But what is the philosophy of communism? What claims does it make? What changes does it demand? And what are the underlying methodological and metaphysical principles upon which it rests? These are the issues to which the selections in this part are devoted. Of course, the term "communism" can refer to any system of social organization in which goods are held in common. As the term is most commonly used, however, it refers to a particular kind of communal organization—one that claims to arise out of the revolutionary movement begun by Karl Marx and Friedrich Engels in the nineteenth century. Its philosophical method is that of *dialectics;* its metaphysical principles are grounded in a strict *materialism;* and its philosophy is properly described, therefore, as *dialectical materialism.*

Section I

UTOPIAN SOCIALISM

The growth of socialism in the Western world began in earnest in the last quarter of the eighteenth century. It was a highly revolutionary period. Although the success of the American Revolution did promote the cause of human liberty, the recurring upheavals subsequent to the French Revolution seemed to disclose chronic ailments in European civilization. More fundamental than these, however, was the Industrial Revolution, rapidly sweeping over Western Europe, the impact of which was painfully felt yet only dimly understood.

The stupendous and far-reaching changes that the growth of indusry and mass production were to have upon human life and work could not then be foreseen. However, some of those consequences made an early appearance, often in the form of intense competition among growing industrial enterprises, and—because of the absence of regulation—in the resultant exploitation of the newly created mass of industrial workers. By the middle decades of the nineteenth century, the living and working conditions of the laborer in the industrial centers of Europe were so bad as to be almost beyond belief.

The extreme distress of these workers inevitably gave rise to many painful and moving humanitarian complaints. Among the most articulate critics of this period were those thinkers, chiefly French and English, who came to be known as utopian socialists. Witnessing extremes of poverty and degradation on the one hand, and luxury and leisure on the other, they came to believe that the only solution lay in reorganizing the structure of society and reapportioning its wealth. Although the schemes put forward varied greatly, all were alike in that they would result in a totally new order, in which everyone would work, goods would be owned

3

in common, and each would receive an equitable share of the wealth produced. The actual proposals of the utopians were often not only visionary, but far-fetched and unfeasible. Nevertheless, they constitute the background of social thought out of which Marxian communism arose. In articulating the plight of the exploited they opened a path that Marx and Engels were soon to follow, and their vigorous criticisms of the capitalist system were to contribute extensively to Marx's own critique.

Karl Marx himself was bitterly critical of the so-called foolishness, impracticality, and "utopianism" of these early socialists. Yet he defended them against the criticism of others, holding that because of their place in history they could not have done better than they did. In spite of their naïve optimism and wild dreams, he thought they were among the greatest social philosophers in history. Their socialism was *utopian;* what was needed, Marx thought, was a socialist theory of society that would be truly *scientific*. That, he believed, was destined to be provided by himself alone.

1. FRIEDRICH ENGELS

Friedrich Engels (1820-1895) was a life-long friend of, and frequent collaborator with, Karl Marx. Their names are linked as the founders of modern communism. The work from which the following selection is taken is made up of three chapters from a larger work, by Engels alone, Herr Eugen Dühring's Revolution in Science, *first published in 1878. These three chapters (the second and third of which appear later in this volume) comprise one of the clearest statements of communist theory. In this chapter Engels acknowledges his great debt to the utopian socialists and discusses the relation of their theories to the newer communism developed by Marx and himself.*

Socialism, Utopian and Scientific: Part I *

[The Utopians]

Modern socialism is, in its essence, the direct product of the recognition, on the one hand, of the class antagonisms, existing in the society of today, between proprietors and non-proprietors, between capitalists and wage workers; on the other hand, of the anarchy existing in production. But, in its theoretical form, modern socialism originally appears ostensibly as a more logical extension of the principles laid down by the great French philosophers of the eighteenth century. Like every new theory, modern socialism had, at first, to connect itself with the intellectual stock-in-trade ready to its hand, however deeply its roots lay in material economic facts.

The great men, who in France prepared men's minds for the coming revolution, were themselves extreme revolutionists. They recognized no external authority of any kind whatever. Religion, natural science, society, political institutions, everything, was subjected to the most unsparing criticism: everything must justify its existence before the judgment seat of reason, or give up existence. Reason became the sole measure of everything. It was the time when, as Hegel says, the world stood upon its head;† first, in the sense that the human head, and the principles arrived at by its thought, claimed to be the basis of all human action and association; but by and by,

---

* From F. Engels, *Socialism, Utopian and Scientific,* Swan Sonnenschein and Co., London, 1892.

† This is the passage on the French Revolution: "Thought, the concept of law, all at once made itself felt, and against this the old scaffolding of wrong could make no stand. In this conception of law, therefore, a constitution has now been established, and henceforth everything must be based upon this. Since the sun had been in the firmament, and the planets circled round him, the sight had never been seen of man standing upon his head—i.e., on the idea—and building reality after this image. Anaxagoras first said that the *Nous,* reason, rules the world; but now, for the first time, had man come to recognize that the Idea must rule the mental reality. And this was a magnificent sunrise. All thinking beings have participated in celebrating this holy day. A sublime emotion swayed men at that time, an enthusiasm of reason pervaded the world, as if now had come the reconciliation of the Divine Principle with the world." [Hegel: *Philosophy of History,* 1840, p. 535.] Is it not high time to set the Anti-Socialist Law in action against such teachings, subversive and to the common danger, by the late Professor Hegel?

also, in the wider sense that the reality which was in contradiction to these principles had, in fact, to be turned upside down. Every form of society and government then existing, every old traditional notion was flung into the lumber room as irrational; the world had hitherto allowed itself to be led solely by prejudices; everything in the past deserved only pity and contempt. Now, for the first time, appeared the light of day, the kingdom of reason; henceforth superstition, injustice, privilege, oppression, were to be superseded by eternal truth, eternal right, equality based on nature and the inalienable rights of man.

We know today that this kingdom of reason was nothing more than the idealized kingdom of the bourgeoisie; that this eternal right found its realization in bourgeois justice; that this equality reduced itself to bourgeois equality before the law; that bourgeois property was proclaimed as one of the essential rights of man; and that the government of reason, the *Contrat Social* of Rousseau, came into being, and only could come into being, as a democratic bourgeois republic. The great thinkers of the eighteenth century could, no more than their predecessors, go beyond the limits imposed upon them by their epoch.

But, side by side with the antagonism of the feudal nobility and the burghers, who claimed to represent all the rest of society, was the general antagonism of exploiters and exploited, of rich idlers and poor workers. It was this very circumstance that made it possible for the representatives of the bourgeoisie to put themselves forward as representing not one special class, but the whole of suffering humanity. Still further. From its origin, the bourgeoisie was saddled with its antithesis: capitalists cannot exist without wage workers, and, in the same proportion as the mediæval burgher of the guild developed into the modern bourgeois, the guild journeyman and the day laborer, outside the guilds, developed into the proletarian. And although, upon the whole, the bourgeoisie, in their struggle with the nobility, could claim to represent at the same time the interests of the different working classes of that period, yet in every great bourgeois movement there were independent outbursts of that class which was the forerunner, more or less developed, of the modern proletariat. For example, at the time of the German reformation and the peasants' war, the Anabaptists and Thomas Münzer; in the great English Revolution, the Levellers; in the great French Revolution, Babeuf.

There were theoretical enunciations corresponding with these revolutionary uprisings of a class not yet developed; in the sixteenth and seventeenth centuries, utopian pictures of ideal social conditions; in the eighteenth, actual communistic theories (Morelly and Mably). The demand for equality was no longer limited to political rights; it was extended also to the social conditions of individuals. It was not simply class privileges that were to be abolished, but class distinctions themselves. A communism, ascetic, denouncing all the pleasures of life, Spartan, was the first form of the new teaching. Then came the three great Utopians: Saint Simon, to whom the middle class movement, side by side with the proletarian, still had a certain significance; Fourier; and Owen, who in the country where capitalist production was most developed, and under the influence of the antagonisms begotten of this, worked out his proposals for the removal of class distinction systematically and in direct relation to French materialism.

One thing is common to all three. Not one of them appears as a representative of the interests of that proletariat, which historical development had in the meantime produced. Like the French philosophers, they do not claim to emancipate a particular class to begin with, but all humanity at once. Like them, they wish to bring in the kingdom of reason and eternal justice, but this kingdom, as they see it, is as far as heaven from earth from that of the French philosophers.

For, to our three social reformers, the bourgeois world, based upon the principles of these philosophers, is quite as irrational and unjust, and, therefore, finds its way to the dust hole quite as readily as feudalism and all the earlier stages of society. If pure reason and justice have not, hitherto, ruled the world, this has been the case only because men have not rightly understood them. What was wanted was the individual man of genius, who has now arisen and who understands the truth. That he has now arisen, that the truth has now been clearly understood, is not an inevitable event, following of necessity in the chain of historical development, but a mere happy accident. He might just as well have been born 500 years earlier, and might then have spared humanity 500 years of error, strife and suffering.

We saw how the French philosophers of the eighteenth century, the forerunners of the revolution, appealed to reason as the sole judge of all that is. A rational government, rational society, were to be founded; everything that ran counter to eternal reason was to be remorselessly done away with. We saw also that this eternal reason was in reality nothing but the idealized understanding of the eighteenth century citizen, just then evolving into the bourgeois. The French Revolution had realized this rational society and government. But the new order of things, rational enough as compared with earlier conditions, turned out to be by no means absolutely rational. The state based upon reason completely collapsed. Rousseau's *Contrat Social* had found its realization in the Reign of Terror, from which bourgeoisie, who had lost confidence in their own political capacity, had taken refuge first in the corruption of the Directorate, and, finally, under the wing of the Napoleonic despotism. The promised eternal peace was turned into an endless war of conquest. The society based upon reason had fared no better. The antagonism between rich and poor, instead of dissolving into general prosperity, had become intensified by the removal of the guild and other privileges, which had to some extent bridged it over, and by the removal of the charitable institutions of the Church. The "freedom of property" from feudal fetters, now veritably accomplished, turned out to be, for the small capitalists and small proprietors, the freedom to sell their small property, crushed under the overmastering competition of the large capitalists and landlords, to these great lords, and thus, as far as the small capitalists and peasant proprietors were concerned, became "freedom *from* property." The development of industry upon a capitalistic basis made poverty and misery of the working masses conditions of existence of society. Cash payment became more and more, in Carlyle's phrase, the sole nexus between man and man. The number of crimes increased from year to year. Formerly, the feudal vices had openly stalked about in broad daylight; though not eradicated, they were now at any rate thrust into the background. In their stead, the bourgeois vices, hitherto practiced in secret, began to blossom all the more luxuriantly. Trade became to a greater and greater extent cheating. The "fraternity" of the revolutionary motto was realized in the chicanery and rivalries of the battle of competition. Oppression by force was replaced by corruption; the sword, as the first social lever, by gold. The right of the first night was transferred from the feudal lords to the bourgeois manufacturers. Prostitution increased to an extent never heard of. Marriage itself remained, as before, the legally recognized form, the official cloak of prostitution, and, moreover, was supplemented by rich crops of adultery.

In a word, compared with the splendid promises of the philosophers, the social and political institutions born of the "triumph of reason" were bitterly disappointing caricatures. All that was wanting was the men to formulate this disappointment, and they came with the turn of the century. In 1802 Saint Simon's Geneva Letters appeared; in 1808 appeared Fourier's first work, although the groundwork of his theory dated from 1799; on January 1, 1800, Robert Owen undertook the direction of New Lanark.

At this time, however, the capitalist mode of production, and with it the antagonism between the bourgeoisie and the proletariat, was still very incompletely developed. Modern industry, which had just arisen in England, was still unknown in France. But modern in dustry develops, on the one hand, the conflicts which make absolutely necessary a revolution in the mode of production and the doing away with its capitalistic character—conflicts not only between the classes begotten of it, but also between the very productive forces and the forms of exchange created by it. And, on the other hand, it develops, in these very gigantic productive forces, the means of ending these conflicts. If, therefore, about the year 1800, the conflicts arising from the new social order were only just beginning to take shape, this holds still more fully as to the means of ending them. The "have-nothing" masses of Paris, during the Reign of Terror, were able for a moment to gain the mastery, and thus to lead the bourgeois revolution to vic tory in spite of the bourgeoisie themselves. But, in doing so, they only proved how impossible it was for their domination to last under the conditions then obtaining. The proletariat, which then for the first time evolved itself from these "have-nothing" masses as the nucleus of a new class, as yet quite incapable of independent political action, appeared as an oppressed, suffering order, to whom, in its incapacity to help itself, help could, at best, be brought in from without or down from above.

This historical situation also dominated the founders of socialism. To the crude conditions of capitalistic production and the crude class conditions corresponded crude theories. The solution of the social problems, which as yet lay hidden in undeveloped economic condi tions, the utopians attempted to evolve out of the human brain. Society presented nothing but wrongs; to remove these was the task of reason. It was necessary, then, to discover a new and more perfect system of social order and to impose this upon society from without by propaganda, and, wherever it was possible, by the example of model experiments. These new social systems were foredoomed as utopian; the more completely they were worked out in detail, the more they could not avoid drifting off into pure fantasies.

These facts once established, we need not dwell a moment longer upon this side of the question, now wholly belonging to the past. We can leave it to the literary small fry to solemnly quibble over these fantasies, which today only make us smile, and to crow over the superiority of their own bald reasoning, as compared with such "insanity." For ourselves, we delight in the stupendously grand thoughts and germs of thought that everywhere break out through their fantastic covering, and to which these philistines are blind.

Saint Simon was a son of the great French Revolution, at the outbreak of which he was not yet thirty. The revolution was the victory of the third estate, i.e., of the great masses of the nation, *working* in production and in trade over the privileged *idle* classes, the nobles and the priests. But the victory of the third estate soon revealed itself as exclusively the victory of a small part of this "estate," as the conquest of political power by the socially privileged section of it, i.e., the propertied bourgeoisie. And the bourgeoisie had certainly developed rapidly during the revolution, partly by speculation in the lands of the nobility and of the Church, confiscated and afterwards put up for sale, and partly by frauds upon the nation by means of army contracts. It was the domination of these swindlers that, under the Directorate, brought France to the verge of ruin, and thus gave Napoleon the pretext for his *coup d'état.*

Hence, to Saint Simon the antagonism between the third estate and the privileged classes took the form of an antagonism between "workers" and "idlers." The idlers were not merely the old privileged classes, but also all who, without taking any part in production or distribution, lived on their incomes. And the workers were not only the wage workers, but also the manufacturers, the merchants, the bankers. That the idlers had lost the capacity for intellectual leadership and political supremacy had been proved, and was by the revolution finally settled. That the non-possessing classes had not this capacity seemed to Saint Simon proved by the experiences of the Reign of Terror. Then, who was to lead and command? According to Saint Simon, science and industry, both united by a new religious bond, destined to restore that unity of religious ideas which had been lost since the time of the Reformation—a necessarily mystic and rigidly hierarchic "new Christianity." But science, that was the scholars; and industry, that was, in the first place, the working bourgeois, manufacturers, merchants, bankers. These bourgeoisie were, certainly, intended by Saint Simon to transform themselves into a kind of public officials, or social trustees; but they were still to hold, vis-à-vis of the workers, a commanding and economically privileged position. The bankers especially were to be called upon to direct the whole of social production by the regulation of credit. This conception was in' exact keeping with a time in which modern industry in France and, with it, the chasm between bourgeoisie and proletariat was only just coming into existence. But what Saint Simon especially lays stress upon is this: what interests him first, and above all other things, is the lot of the class that is the most numerous and the most poor (*"la classe la plus nombreuse et la plus pauvre"*).

Already, in his Geneva Letters, Saint Simon lays down the proposition that "all men ought to work." In the same work he recognizes also that the Reign of Terror was the reign of the non-possessing masses. "See," says he to them, "what happened in France at the time when your comrades held sway there; they brought about a famine." But to recognize the French Revolution as a class war, and not simply one between nobility and bourgeoisie, but between nobility, bourgeoisie and the non-possessors, was, in the year 1802, a most pregnant discovery. In 1816 he declares that politics is the science of production, and foretells the complete absorption of politics by economics. The knowledge that economic conditions are the basis of political institutions appears here only in embryo. Yet what is here already very plainly expressed is the idea of the future conversion of political rule over men into an administration of things and a direction of processes of production—that is to say, the "abolition of the state," about which recently there has been so much noise.

Saint Simon shows the same superiority over his contemporaries, when in 1814, immediately after the entry of the allies into Paris, and again in 1815, during the Hundred Days' War, he proclaims the alliance of France with England, and then of both these countries with Germany, as the only guarantee for the prosperous development and peace of Europe. To preach to the French in 1815 an alliance with the victors of Waterloo required as much courage as historical foresight.

If in Saint Simon we find a comprehensive breadth of view, by virtue of which almost all the ideas of later socialists, that are not strictly economic, are found in him in embryo, we find in Fourier a criticism of the existing conditions of society, genuinely French and witty, but not upon that account any the less thorough. Fourier takes the bourgeoisie, their inspired prophets before the revolution, and their interested eulogists after it, at their own word. He lays bare remorselessly the material and moral misery of the bourgeois world.

He confronts it with the earlier philosophers' dazzling promises of a society in which reason alone should reign, of a civilization in which happiness should be universal, of an illimitable human perfectibility, and with the rose-colored phraseology of the bourgeois ideologists of his time. He points out how everywhere the most pitiful reality corresponds with the most high-sounding phrases, and he overwhelms this hopeless fiasco of phrases with his mordant sarcasm.

Fourier is not only a critic; his imperturbably serene nature makes him a satirist and assuredly one of the greatest satirists of all time. He depicts, with equal power and charm, the swindling speculations that blossomed out upon the downfall of the revolution, and the shop-keeping spirit prevalent in, and characteristic of, French commerce at that time. Still more masterly is his criticism of the bourgeois form of the relations between the sexes, and the position of woman in bourgeois society. He was the first to declare that in any given society the degree of woman's emancipation is the natural measure of the general emancipation.

But Fourier is at his greatest in his conception of the history of society. He divides its whole course, thus far, into four stages of evolution—savagery, barbarism, the patriarchate, civilization. This last is identical with the so-called civil, or bourgeois society of today —i.e., with the social order that came in with the sixteenth century. He proves "that the civilized stage raises every vice practiced by barbarism in a simple fashion, into a form of existence, complex, ambiguous, equivocal, hypocritical"—that civilization moves in "a vicious circle," in contradictions which it constantly reproduces without being able to solve them; hence it constantly arrives at the very opposite to that which it wants to attain, or pretends to want to attain, so that, e.g., "under civilization poverty is born of superabundance itself."

Fourier, as we see, uses the dialectic method in the same masterly way as his contemporary, Hegel. Using these same dialectics, he argues against the talk about illimitable human perfectibility that every historical phase has its period of ascent and also its period of descent, and he applies this observation to the future of the whole human race. As Kant introduced into natural science the idea of the ultimate destruction of the earth, Fourier introduced into historical science that of the ultimate destruction of the human race.

While in France the hurricane of the revolution swept over the land, in England a quieter, but not on that account less tremendous, revolution was going on. Steam and the new tool-making machinery were transforming manufacture into modern industry, and thus revolutionizing the whole foundation of bourgeois society. The sluggish march of development of the manufacturing period changed into a veritable storm and stress period of production. With constantly increasing swiftness the splitting-up of society into large capitalists and non-possessing proletarians went on. Between these, instead of the former stable middle class, an unstable mass of artisans and small shopkeepers, the most fluctuating portion of the population, now led a precarious existence.

The new mode of production was, as yet, only at the beginning of its period of ascent; as yet it was the normal, regular method of production—the only one possible under existing conditions. Nevertheless, even then it was producing crying social abuses—the herding together of a homeless population in the worst quarters of the large town; the loosening of all traditional moral bonds, of patriarchal subordination, of family relations; overwork, especially of women and children, to a frightful extent; complete demoralization of the working class, suddenly flung into altogether new conditions, from the country into the town, from agriculture into modern industry, from stable conditions of existence into insecure ones that changed from day to day.

At this juncture there came forward as a reformer a manufacturer 29 years old—a man of almost sublime, childlike simplicity of character, and at the same time one of the few born leaders of men. Robert Owen had adopted the teaching of the materialistic philosophers: that man's character is the product, on the one hand, of heredity, on the other, of the environment of the individual during his lifetime, and especially during his period of development. In the industrial revolution most of his class saw only chaos and confusion, and the opportunity of fishing in these troubled waters and making large fortunes quickly. He saw in it the opportunity of putting into practice his favorite theory, and so of bringing order out of chaos. He had already tried it with success, as superintendent of more than five hundred men in a Manchester factory. From 1800 to 1829, he directed the great cotton mill at New Lanark, in Scotland, as managing partner, along the same lines, but with greater freedom of action and with a success that made him a European reputation. A population, originally consisting of the most diverse and, for the most part, very demoralized elements, a population that gradually grew to 2,500, he turned into a model colony, in which drunkenness, police, magistrates, lawsuits, poor laws, charity were unknown. And all this simply by placing the people in conditions worthy of human beings, and especially by carefully bringing up the rising generation. He was the founder of infant schools, and introduced them first at New Lanark. At the age of two the children came to school, where they enjoyed themselves so much that they could scarcely be got home again. While his competitors worked their people thirteen or fourteen hours a day, in New Lanark the working day was only ten and a half hours. When a crisis in cotton stopped work for four months, his workers received their full wages all the time. And with all this the business more than doubled in value, and to the last yielded large profits to its proprietors.

In spite of all this, Owen was not content. The existence which he secured for his workers was, in his eyes, still far from being worthy of human beings. "The people were slaves at my mercy." The relatively favorable conditions in which he had placed them were still far from allowing a rational development of the character and of the intellect in all directions, much less of the free exercise of all their faculties. "And yet, the working part of this population of 2,500 persons was daily producing as much real wealth for society as, less than half a century before, it would have required the working part of a population of 600,000 to create. I asked myself, what became of the difference between the wealth consumed by 2,500 persons and that which would have been consumed by 600,000?" *

The answer was clear. It had been used to pay the proprietors of the establishment 5 per cent on the capital they had laid out, in addition to over £300,000 clear profit. And that which held for New Lanark held to a still greater extent for all the factories in England. "If this new wealth had not been created by machinery, imperfectly as it has been applied, the wars of Europe, in opposition to Napoleon, and to support the aristocratic principles of society, could not have been maintained. And yet this new power was the creation of the working classes." † To them, therefore, the fruits of this new power belonged. The newly-created, gigantic productive

* From *The Revolution in Mind and Practice*, p. 21, a memorial addressed to all the "red republicans, communists and socialists of Europe," and sent to the provisional government of France, 1848, and also "to Queen Victoria and her responsible advisers."
† *Ibid.*

forces, hitherto used only to enrich individuals and to enslave the masses, offered to Owen the foundations for a reconstruction of society; they were destined, as the common property of all, to be worked for the common good of all.

Owen's communism was based upon this purely business foundation, the outcome, so to say, of commercial calculation. Throughout, it maintained this practical character. Thus, in 1823, Owen proposed the relief of the distress in Ireland by communist colonies, and drew up complete estimates of costs of founding them, yearly expenditure and probable revenue. And in his definite plan for the future, the technical working out of details is managed with such practical knowledge—ground plan, front and side and bird's-eye views all included—that the Owen method of social reform once accepted, there is from the practical point of view little to be said against the actual arrangement of details.

His advance in the direction of communism was the turning-point in Owen's life. As long as he was simply a philanthropist, he was rewarded with nothing but wealth, applause, honor and glory. He was the most popular man in Europe. Not only men of his own class, but statesmen and princes listened to him approvingly. But when he came out with his communist theories, that was quite another thing. Three great obstacles seemed to him especially to block the path to social reform: private property, religion, the present form of marriage. He knew what confronted him if he attacked these—outlawry, excommunication from official society, the loss of his whole social position. But nothing of this prevented him from attacking them without fear of consequences, and what he had foreseen happened. Banished from official society, with a conspiracy of silence against him in the press, ruined by his unsuccessful communist experiments in America, in which he sacrificed all his fortune, he turned directly to the working class and continued working in their midst for thirty years. Every social movement, every real advance in England on behalf of the workers links itself on to the name of Robert Owen. He forced through in 1819, after five years' fighting, the first law limiting the hours of labor of women and children in factories. He was president of the first congress at which all the trade unions of England united in a single great trade association. He introduced as transition measures to the complete communistic organization of society, on the one hand, co-operative societies for retail trade and production. These have since that time, at least, given practical proof that the merchant and the manufacturer are socially quite unnecessary. On the other hand, he introduced labor bazaars for the exchange of the products of labor through the medium of labor notes, whose unit was a single hour of work; institutions necessarily doomed to failure, but completely anticipating Proudhon's bank of exchange of a much later period, and differing entirely from this in that it did not claim to be the panacea for all social ills, but only a first step towards a much more radical revolution of society.

The Utopians' mode of thought has for a long time governed the socialist ideas of the nineteenth century, and still governs some of them. Until very recently all French and English socialists did homage to it. The earlier German communism, including that of Weitling, was of the same school. To all these, socialism is the expression of absolute truth, reason and justice, and has only to be discovered to conquer all the world by virtue of its own power. And as absolute truth is independent of time, space, and of the historical development of man, it is a mere accident when and where it is discovered. With all this, absolute truth, reason and justice are different with the founder of each different school. And as each one's special kind of absolute truth, reason and justice is again conditioned by his subjective understanding, his conditions of existence, the measure of his knowledge and his intellectual training, there is no other ending possible in this conflict of absolute truths than that they shall be mutually exclusive one of the other. Hence, from this nothing could come but a kind of eclectic, average socialism, which, as a matter of fact, has up to the present time dominated the minds of most of the socialist workers in France and England. Hence, a mish-mash allowing of the most manifold shades of opinion; a mish-mash of such critical statements, economic theories, pictures of future society by the founders of different sects, as excite a minimum of opposition; a mish-mash which is the more easily brewed the more the definite sharp edges of the individual constituents are rubbed down in the stream of debate, like rounded pebbles in a brook.

To make a science of socialism, it had first to be placed upon a real basis.

2. HENRI COMTE DE SAINT-SIMON

Henri de Saint-Simon (1760-1825) was a typical and influential representative of the group called "utopian socialists." Although his schemes were unrealistic and grandiose and his manner overweening, he was insistent upon the need for a science of social development (of which he conceived himself as founder), and placed great stress on the need to improve the lot of the poor. He believed that the new order which he proposed would revive a genuine Christianity and establish a golden age.

The New Christianity*

I conclude this first dialogue by declaring frankly what I think of the Christian revelation. We are certainly superior to our ancestors in the particular, applied sciences. It is only since the fifteenth century, and chiefly since the beginning of the last century, that we have made considerable progress in mathematics, physics, chemistry and physiology. But there is a science much more important for the community than physical and mathematical science—the science on which society is founded, namely ethics, the development of which has been completely different from that of the physical and mathematical sciences. It is more than eighteen centuries since its fundamental principle has been produced, and since then none of the researches of the men of the greatest genius has been able to discover a principle superior in universality or precision to that formulated by the Founder of Christianity. I will go further and say that when society has lost sight of this principle, and ceased to use it as a guide to its conduct, it has promptly relapsed under the despotism of Caesar, and the rule of brute force, which this principle of Christianity had subordinated to the rule of reason.

I therefore put the question whether the intelligence which pro-

* From *New Christianity*, 1825. This and the following passages are taken from *Selected Writings* of Henri Comte de Saint-Simon, translated and edited by F. M. Markham, 1952. Reprinted by permission of the publisher, Basil Blackwell, Oxford.

duced, eighteen centuries ago, the governing principle of the human race, and produced it fifteen centuries before any important progress was made in the physical and mathematical sciences, must not obviously be superhuman in character, and whether there can be any greater proof of the divine revelation of Christianity.

Yes, I believe that Christianity is divinely instituted, and I am persuaded that God extends a special protection to those who strive to subordinate all human institutions to the fundamental principle of this sublime doctrine. I am convinced that I am fulfilling a divine mission in recalling nations and kings to the true spirit of Christianity. Fully confident of the divine protection specially given me in my tasks, I feel emboldened to criticize the kings of Europe who are allied under the sacred name of the Holy Alliance. I address them directly, daring to say to them:

"Princes,

"What is the nature and character, in the eyes of God and of Christians, of the power which you wield?

"What is the basis of the social system which you endeavor to establish? What measures have you taken to improve the moral and physical condition of the poor?

"You call yourselves Christians, and yet you base your power on material force; you are still the successors of Caesar, and you forget that true Christians have as the final goal of their efforts the abolition of the power of the sword, the power of Caesar, which by its nature is essentially transitory.

"Yet this is the power on which you have undertaken to found the social order! According to you, to this power alone belongs the initiation in all improvements demanded by the progress of enlightenment. To support this monstrous system you keep two million men under arms, you compel all tribunals to adopt this principle, you oblige priests, whether Catholic, Protestant, or Orthodox, to preach the heresy that the power of Caesar is the governing principle of Christian society.

"In recalling the peoples to the Christian religion by the symbol of your union, in giving them peace which is their first need, you have nevertheless failed to win their gratitude: your personal interests are too prominent in the schemes which you claim to be in the common interest. The supreme authority in Europe which rests in your hands is far from being a Christian authority, as it should have been. As soon as you act, you display the character and signs of material power, of anti-Christian force.

"All the important measures which you have taken since your union in the Holy Alliance have had the effect of worsening the condition of the poor, not only for the present but for future generations. You have raised taxes, you raise them every year, in order to meet the mounting costs of your armies and the luxury of your courts. The class which you favor specially is that of the nobility—a class which, like yourselves, derives its rights from the sword.

"However, your blameworthy conduct can be excused in certain respects. If there is one thing which has led you into error, it is the praise which has been given to your united efforts to overthrow the power of the modern Caesar. In fighting against him you have acted in a truly Christian manner; but it is only because the authority of Caesar which was acquired by Napoleon through conquest had in his hands much greater power than in yours, where it came only through inheritance. Your conduct can also be excused, in that the churches which should have restrained you at the edge of the precipice, have joined you in throwing themselves over.

"Princes,

"Hearken to the voice of God which speaks through me. Return to the path of Christianity; no longer regard mercenary armies, the nobility, the heretical priests and perverse judges, as your principal support, but, united in the name of Christianity, understand how to carry out the duties which Christianity imposes on those who possess power. Remember that Christianity commands you to use all your powers to increase as rapidly as possible the social welfare of the poor!"

[A World Upside Down] *

Suppose that France suddenly lost fifty of her best physicists, chemists, physiologists, mathematicians, poets, painters, sculptors, musicians, writers; fifty of her best mechanical engineers, civil and military engineers, artillery experts, architects, doctors, surgeons, apothe- caries, seamen, clockmakers; fifty of her best bankers, two hundred of her best business men, two hundred of her best farmers, fifty of her best ironmasters, arms manufacturers, tanners, dyers, miners, cloth ·

* From Henri de Saint-Simon, *The Organizer,* 1819.

makers, cotton manufacturers, silk-makers, linen-makers, manufacturers of hardware, of pottery and china, of crystal and glass, ship chandlers, carriers, printers, engravers, goldsmiths, and other metal-workers; her fifty best masons, carpenters, joiners, farriers, locksmiths, cutlers, smelters, and a hundred other persons of various unspecified occupations, eminent in the sciences, fine arts, and professions; making in all the three thousand leading scientists, artists, and artisans of France.

These men are the Frenchmen who are the most essential producers, those who make the most important products, those who direct the enterprises most useful to the nation, those who contribute to its achievements in the sciences, fine arts and professions. They are in the most real sense the flower of French society; they are, above all Frenchman, the most useful to their country, contribute most to its glory, increasing its civilization and prosperity. The nation would become a lifeless corpse as soon as it lost them. It would immediately fall into a position of inferiority compared with the nations which it now rivals, and would continue to be inferior until this loss had been replaced, until it had grown another head. It would require at least a generation for France to repair this misfortune; for men who are distinguished in work of positive ability are exceptions, and nature is not prodigal of exceptions, particularly in this species.

Let us pass on to another assumption. Suppose that France preserves all the men of genius that she possesses in the sciences, fine arts and professions, but has the misfortune to lose in the same day Monsieur the King's brother, Monseigneur le duc d'Angoulême, Monseigneur le duc de Berry, Monseigneur le duc d'Orléans, Monseigneur le duc de Bourbon, Madame la duchesse d'Angoulême, Madame la duchesse de Berry, Madame la duchesse d'Orléans, Madame la duchesse de Bourbon, and Mademoiselle de Condé. Suppose that France loses at the same time all the great officers of the royal household, all the ministers (with or without portfolio), all the councillors of state, all the chief magistrates, marshals, cardinals, archbishops, bishops, vicars-general, and canons, all the prefects and sub-prefects, all the civil servants, and judges, and, in addition, ten thousand of the richest proprietors who live in the style of nobles.

This mischance would certainly distress the French, because they are kind-hearted, and could not see with indifference the sudden disappearance of such a large number of their compatriots. But this loss of thirty-thousand individuals, considered to be the most important in the State, would only grieve them for purely sentimental reasons and would result in no political evil for the State.

In the first place, it would be very easy to fill the vacancies which would be made available. There are plenty of Frenchmen who could fill the function of the King's brother as well as can Monsieur; plenty who could take the place of a Prince as appropriately as Monseigneur le duc d'Angoulême, or Monseigneur le duc d'Orléans, or Monseigneur le duc de Bourbon. There are plenty of Frenchwomen who would be as good princesses as Madame la duchesse d'Angoulême, or Madame la duchesse de Berry, or Mesdames d'Orléans, de Bourbon, and de Condé.

The ante-chambers of the palace are full of courtiers ready to take the place of the great household officials. The army has plenty of soldiers who would be as good leaders as our present Marshals. How many clerks there are who are as good as our ministers? How many administrators who are capable of managing the affairs of the departments better than the existing prefects and sub-prefects? How many barristers who are as good lawyers as our judges? How many vicars as expert as our cardinals, archbishops, bishops, vicars-general, and canons? As for the ten thousand aristocratic landowners, their heirs could need no apprenticeship to do the honors of their drawing-rooms as well as they.

The prosperity of France can only exist through the effects of the progress of the sciences, fine arts and professions. The Princes, the great household officials, the Bishops, Marshals of France, prefects and idle landowners contribute nothing directly to the progress of the sciences, fine arts and professions. Far from contributing they only hinder, since they strive to prolong the supremacy existing to this day of conjectural ideas over positive science. They inevitably harm the prosperity of the nation by depriving, as they do, the scientists, artists, and artisans of the high esteem to which they are properly entitled. They are harmful because they expend their wealth in a way which is of no direct use to the sciences, fine arts, and professions: they are harmful because they are a charge on the national taxation, to the amount of three or four hundred millions under the heading of appointments, pensions, gifts, compensations, for the upkeep of their activities which are useless to the nation.

These suppositions underline the most important fact of present politics: they provide a point of view from which we can see this fact in a flash in all its extent; they show clearly, though indirectly, that

our social organization is seriously defective: that men still allow themselves to be governed by violence and ruse, and that the human race
(politically speaking) is still sunk in immorality.

The scientists, artists, and artisans, the only men whose work is of
positive utility to society, and cost it practically nothing, are kept down
by the princes and other rulers who are simply more or less incapable
bureaucrats. Those who control honors and other national awards
owe, in general, the supremacy they enjoy, to the accident of birth,
to flattery, intrigue and other dubious methods.

Those who control public affairs share between them every year
one half of the taxes, and they do not even use a third of what they
do not pocket personally in a way which benefits the citizen.

These suppositions show that society is a world which is upside
down.

The nation holds as a fundamental principle that the poor should be
generous to the rich, and that therefore the poorer classes should daily
deprive themselves of necessities in order to increase the superfluous
luxury of the rich.

The most guilty men, the robbers on a grand scale, who oppress
the mass of the citizens, and extract from them three or four hundred
millions a year, are given the responsibility of punishing minor offenses
against society.

Ignorance, superstition, idleness and costly dissipation are the
privilege of the leaders of society, and men of ability, hard-working
and thrifty, are employed only as inferiors and instruments.

To sum up, in every sphere men of greater ability are subject to
the control of men who are incapable. From the point of view of
morality, the most immoral men have the responsibility of leading
the citizens towards virtue; from the point of view of distributive
justice, the most guilty men are appointed to punish minor delinquents.

[The Plan of a New Society] *

Let us return to the plan which I propose. If you adopt it and maintain it, you will place permanently in the hands of the twenty-one
most enlightened men the two great weapons of domination—prestige and wealth. The consequence will be, for many reasons, rapid

* From Henri de Saint-Simon, *Letters from an Inhabitant of Geneva*, 1803.

progress in the sciences. It is a fact that, with every advance in the sciences, discovery becomes easier; so that those who, like yourselves, can only devote little time to your education, will be able to learn more, and, as you become more educated, you will diminish the domination gained by the rich. You will soon see, my friends, excellent results. But I cannot spend more time on matters which are comparatively remote consequences of a course of action on which you have not yet embarked. Let us talk of what is immediately in view. You give your respect, that is to say, you voluntarily concede a degree of domination to men who perform services which you consider useful to you. The mistake which you make, in common with the whole of humanity, is in not distinguishing clearly enough between the immediate and more lasting benefits, between those of local and more general interest, between those which benefit a part of humanity at the expense of the rest, and those which promote the happiness of the whole of humanity. In short, you have not yet realized that there is but one interest common to the whole of humanity, the progress of the sciences.

If the mayor of your village obtains for you an advantage over your neighbors, you are pleased with him, you respect him. The inhabitants of the towns show the same desire to be superior to neighboring towns; the provinces are rivals, and between nations there are struggles, called wars, for their particular interests.

What part of the efforts of these fractions of the human race has a direct influence on the general interest? It is small, indeed; which is not surprising, considering that humanity has not yet taken steps collectively to reward those who do successful work in the general interest. To gather up and unite all these forces acting in different, and often contrary, directions; to direct them as far as possible to the single purpose of improving the lot of humanity—I do not think a better means can be found than the one I propose.

For the moment I have said enough of the scientists; let us speak of the artists.

On Sundays eloquence has charms for you: you take pleasure in reading a well-written book, in looking at beautiful pictures and statues, or in listening to music which holds your attention. A great deal of work is required to speak or write in a way which will amuse you, to create a picture or statue which pleases you, or to compose music which interests you. Is it not just, my friends, that you should reward the artists who fill your leisure hours with pleasures which develop your intelligence, by evoking the most delicate and subtle sensations?

My friends, let all of you subscribe, however little; you are so many that the total sum will be considerable. Moreover, the esteem which will accrue to those who are nominated, will give them an immeasurable force. You will see how the rich will strive to attain distinction in the sciences and arts, when this career leads to the highest positions of esteem. If you achieve nothing more from it than to distract them from quarrels caused by idleness, quarrels merely to decide how many of you shall be under their orders, quarrels which always involve yourselves, and in which you are the dupes, that will be a considerable gain.

If you are convinced by my plan, there will be one difficulty for you, that of selection. I will explain the way in which I should make my choice. I would ask all the mathematicians I know, who, in their opinion, are the three best mathematicians, and I would nominate the three who had the most votes of those whom I had consulted. I would do the same in the case of the physicists, etc.

Having divided humanity into three groups, and having put before each of them the reasons which should convince them, I shall now address my contemporaries as a whole, to put before them my reflections on the French Revolution.

The suppression of the privilege of birth required an effort which had ended by breaking up the old organization, and it was not in itself an obstacle to a re-organization of society. But the appeal which had been made to all members of society to fulfil frequently the functions of legislation, was unsuccessful. Apart from the fearful atrocities to which this application of the principle of equality led through the inevitable results of putting power in the hands of the ignorant, it ended by producing a form of government which was absolutely impracticable. The rulers, given salaries in order to include the have-nots, were so increased in number that the work of the governed was barely sufficient to support them. This was a result which was absolutely contrary to the most constant desire of the have-nots, which was to pay as few taxes as possible.

Here is an idea which seems to me sound. The elementary needs of life are the most imperative. The have-nots can only satisfy them inadequately. A physiologist can see clearly that their most constant desire must be to reduce taxation, or to increase wages, which comes to the same thing. I believe that all classes of society would benefit from an organization on these lines: the spiritual power in the hands of the scientists, the temporal power in the hands of the property-owners; the power to nominate those who should perform the functions of the leaders of humanity, in the hands of all; the reward of the rulers, esteem.

[The Golden Age] *

I have tried in this work to prove that the establishment of a political system in conformity with the present state of enlightenment, and the creation of a common power possessing force enough to repress the ambitions of peoples and kings, is the only means of producing a stable and peaceful order in Europe. In this respect the actual plan of organization which I have suggested is of secondary importance; if it were refuted, if it were found to be essentially faulty, I would still have done what I set out to do, provided some other plan were adopted.

From another point of view, the plan I have suggested is the most important part of my work. For a long time it has been agreed that the present political system is decayed to its very foundations, and that another system must be set up.

Yet in spite of the fact that this view is widespread, and that men's minds, wearied by revolutions and wars, are prepared to grasp at any means to recover order and repose, nobody has risen above the old routine. They have continued to act on the old principles, as if it was impossible to have any better ones; they have rung the changes on the old system in a thousand different ways, but nothing new has been thought of. The plan of organization which I have put forward is the first which is new and comprehensive.

Doubtless it would have been desirable that the plan of re-organization of the European community should have been thought out by one of the more powerful sovereigns, or at least by a statesman experienced in affairs and renowned for his political talent. Such a plan, backed by great power, or a great reputation, would have converted men's minds more quickly. The feebleness of human intelligence did not allow matters to follow this course. Was it possible for those who are engaged in the day-to-day conduct of affairs,

* From Henri de Saint-Simon, *The Reorganization of the European Community*, 1814.

and forced inevitably to reason according to the principles of the old system, which they maintain for lack of a better one, to pursue simultaneously two different courses? With their attention fixed on the old system and the old devices, could they conceive and keep before their eyes a new system and new methods?

With great effort and labor I have reached the standpoint of the common interest of the European peoples. This standpoint is the only one from which it is possible to perceive both the evils which threaten us, and the means of averting them. If those who are in charge of affairs can reach the same level as I have done, they will all be able to see what I have seen. The divisions of public opinion arise from the fact that each man has too narrow a view, and does not dare to free himself from this standpoint from which he persists in judging affairs.

For clear-thinking men there is only one method of reasoning, only one way of seeing things, if they are looking at them from the same point of view. If men who have the same nobility of sentiment, uprightness of judgment, desire for the public welfare, loyalty to the King, yet have such different opinions, it is because each has his own point of view which he will not abandon.

Let them rise above it, and put themselves in the position to which I have tried to elevate men's minds, and all these different opinions will merge into one.

Thus by a happy transformation, beneficial to the State, we shall see all the finest characters, the most enlightened minds, the Montesquious and the Raynouards, the d'Ambrais and the Lanjuinais, and all the others separated by their opinions but united by their feelings, aiming at the same goal and co-operating for the same purpose. There will come a time, without doubt, when all the peoples of Europe will feel that questions of common interest must be dealt with before coming down to national interests; then evils will begin to lessen, troubles abate, wars die out. That is the ultimate direction in which we are steadily progressing; it is there that the progress of the human mind will carry us. But which is more worthy of man's prudence—to hasten towards it, or to let ourselves be dragged there?

Poetic imagination has put the Golden Age in the cradle of the human race, amid the ignorance and brutishness of primitive times; it is rather the Iron Age which should be put there. The Golden Age of the human race is not behind us but before us; it lies in the perfection of the social order. Our ancestors never saw it; our children will one day arrive there; it is for us to clear the way.

3. F. M. CHARLES FOURIER

Charles Fourier (1772-1837) was another typically eccentric and unrealistic social thinker of this period. While he emphasized the fundamental importance of industry, which he called "the primordial function," and demanded its regulation in the new society, he is most famous for the utopian communities which he proposed. He described in meticulous detail the buildings, grounds, organization, and circumstances of life in the self-sufficient socialist societies, or phalanxes, which he envisioned. The following selections help to explain why this movement came to be called utopian.

[Of Association] *

It has been vaguely formulated as a principle that men are made for SOCIETY: it has not been noted that society may be of two orders, the *scattered* or *disjointed* (*morcelé*) and the *combined,* the non-associative and the associative condition. The difference between the one and the other is the difference between truth and falsehood, between riches and poverty, between light and darkness, between a comet and a planet, between a butterfly and a caterpillar.

The present age, with its presentiments of association, has pursued a hesitating advance; it has been afraid to trust to its inspirations which opened up hopes of a great discovery. It has dreamed of social union without daring to undertake the investigation of the means; it has never thought of speculating upon the following alternatives:

There can be but two methods in the exercise of industry, namely: the disjointed order or that of isolated families, such as we see, or the associative order.

God can choose for the prosecution of human labor only between GROUPS and INDIVIDUALS; *associative and combined* action, and *incoherent and disjointed* action.

***

* From C. Fourier, *The Theory of Universal Unity,* 1822. This and the following passages are from *Selections from the Works of Fourier,* translated by Julia Franklin, published by Swan Sonnenschein and Co., London, 1901.

As a wise dispenser, he could not have speculated upon the employment of isolated couples, working without union, according to the civilized method; for individual action carries within itself seven germs of disorganization, of which each one by itself would engender a multitude of disorders. We may judge by a list of these evils whether God could for an instant have hesitated to proscribe disjointed labor which engenders them all.

Evils of Individual Action in Industry*

Wage labor, indirect servitude.
1. Death of the functionary.
2. Personal inconstancy.
3. Contrast between the characters of the father and son.
4. Absence of mechanical economy.
5. Fraud, theft, and general mistrust.
6. Intermission of industry on account of lack of means.
7. Conflict of contradictory enterprises.
Opposition of individual and collective interest.
Absence of unity in plans and execution.
God would have adopted all these evils as a basis of the social system had he fixed upon the philosophic method or disjointed labor; can we suspect the Creator of such unreason? . . .

All the sophists agree in declaring that *man is made for society*: according to this principle ought man to aim for the smallest or the largest society possible? It is beyond doubt that it is in the largest that all the mechanical and economical advantages will be found: and since we have only attained the infinitely small, "family-labor" (*"travail familial"*), is any other indication required to verify the fact that civilization is the antipodes of destiny as well as of truth? . . .

To sum up, all our reformers feel and proclaim the necessity of uniting the working classes into masses or social phalanxes, but they do not wish to acknowledge that the associative process belongs to a science of which the economists have no conception, and of which I alone have formulated a regular theory, ample and without gaps, attacking, and solving all problems, boldly presenting those before

* From C. Fourier, *The Mistakes of Industry*, 1836.

which all economists have recoiled, such as the equilibrium of population, industry attractive and guaranteeing the good morals of the people.

[The Phalanstery] *

The announcement does, I acknowledge, sound very improbable, of a method for combining three hundred families unequal in fortune, and rewarding each person—man, woman, child—according to the three properties, *capital, labor, talent.* More than one reader will credit himself with humor when he remarks: "Let the author try to associate but three families, to reconcile three households in the same dwelling to social union, to arrangements of purchases and expenses, to perfect harmony in passions, character, and authority; when he shall have succeeded in reconciling three mistresses of associated households, we shall believe that he can succeed with thirty and with three hundred."

I have already replied with an argument which it is well to reproduce (for repetition will frequently be necessary here); I have observed *that as economy can spring only from large combinations, God had to create a social theory applicable to large masses and not to three or four families.*

An objection seemingly more reasonable, and which needs to be refuted more than once, is that of social discords. How conciliate the passions, the conflicting interests, the incompatible characters—in short, the innumerable disparities which engender so much discord?

It may easily have been surmised that I shall make use of a lever entirely unknown, and whose properties cannot be judged until I shall have explained them. The passional contrasted Series draws its nourishment solely from those disparities which bewilder civilized policy; it acts like the husbandman who from a mass of filth draws the germs of abundance; the refuse, the dirt, and impure matter which would serve only to defile and infect our dwellings, are for him the sources of wealth.

If social experiments have miscarried, it is because some fatality has impelled all speculators to work with bodies of poor people whom they subjected to a *monastic-industrial* discipline, chief obstacle to

* From C. Fourier, *The Theory of Universal Unity,* 1822, and *The New Industrial and Social World,* 1829.

the working of the series. Here, as in everything else, it is ever SIM-PLISM (*simplisme*) which misleads the civilized, obstinately sticking to experiments with combinations of the poor; they cannot elevate themselves to the conception of a trial with combinations of the rich. They are veritable Lemning rats (migrating rats of Lapland), preferring drowning in a pond to deviating from the route which they have decided upon.

It is necessary for a company of 1,500 to 1,600 persons to have a stretch of land comprising a good square league, say a surface of six million square *toises* (do not let us forget that a third of that would suffice for the simple mode).*

The land should be provided with a fine stream of water; it should be intersected by hills, and adapted to varied cultivation; it should be contiguous to a forest, and not far removed from a large city, but sufficiently so to escape intruders.

The experimental Phalanx standing alone, and without the support of neighboring phalanxes, will, in consequence of this isolation, have so many gaps in attraction, and so many passional calms to dread in its workings, that it will be necessary to provide it with the aid of a good location fitted for a variety of functions. A flat country such as Antwerp, Leipsic, Orleans, would be totally unsuitable, and would cause many Series to fail, owing to the uniformity of the land surface. It will, therefore, be necessary to select a diversified region, like the surroundings of Lausanne, or, at the very least, a fine valley provided with a stream of water and a forest, like the valley of Brussels or of Halle. A fine location near Paris would be the stretch of country lying between Poissy and Confleurs, Poissy and Meulan.

A company will be collected consisting of from 1,500 to 1,600 per-

---

* I had promised a very detailed article upon approximations to the associative mechanism: Companies with slender means might wish to start on a small scale; that is the favorite method of the French—to outline, to grope. The greater number would advocate a trial reduced to a half, to 900 persons, or to a third, 600 persons.

I call their attention to the fact that in reducing a mechanism, its system is perverted, unless all the parts are retained: we can reduce a huge belfry clock to proportions small enough to be enclosed in a minute case, to a watch an inch in diameter; but this watch contains all the parts of the large mechanism, even the arrangement for striking; hence, the system, though reduced, is not changed.

It is not so with a mechanism of the passions: in order to reduce it in the same proportions as the cathedral clock to a little watch, we should have to have miniature people, Lilliputians half a foot high, and animals and vegetables of proportionate dimensions.

sons of graduated degrees of fortune, age, character, of theoretical and practical knowledge; care will be taken to secure the greatest amount of variety possible, for the greater the number of variations either in the passions or the faculties of the members, the easier will it be to make them harmonize in a short space of time.

In this district devoted to experiment, there ought to be combined every species of practicable cultivation, including that in conservatories and hot-houses; in addition, there ought to be at least three accessory factories, to be used in winter and on rainy days; furthermore, various practical branches of science and the arts, independent of the schools.

Above all, it will be necessary to fix the valuation of the capital invested in shares; lands, materials, flocks, implements, etc. This point ought, it seems, to be among the first to receive attention; I think it best to dismiss it here. I shall limit myself to remarking that all these investments in transferable shares and stock-coupons will be represented.

A great difficulty to be overcome in the experimental Phalanx will be the formation of the ties of high mechanism or collective bonds of the Series, before the close of the first season. It will be necessary to accomplish the passional union of the mass of the members; to lead them to collective and individual devotion to the maintenance of the Phalanx, and, especially, to perfect harmony regarding the division of the profits, according to the three factors, *Capital, Labor, Talent*.

This difficulty will be greater in northern than in southern countries, owing to the difference between devoting eight months and five months to agricultural labor.

An experimental Phalanx, being obliged to start out with agricultural labor, will not be in full operation until the month of May (in a climate of 50 degrees, say in the region around London or Paris); and, since it will be necessary to form the bonds of general union, the harmonious ties of the Series, before the suspension of field labor, before the month of October, there will be barely five months of full practice in a region of 50 degrees: the work will have to be accomplished in that short space.

The trial would, therefore, be much more conveniently made in a temperate region, like Florence, Naples, Valencia, Lisbon, where they would have eight to nine months of full cultivation and a far better opportunity to consolidate the bonds of union, since there would be but two or three months of passional calm remaining to tide over till the advent of the second spring, a time when the Phalanx, resuming agricultural labor, would form its ties and cabals anew with much greater zeal, imbuing them with a degree of intensity far above that of the first year; it would thenceforth be in a state of complete consolidation, and strong enough to weather the passional calm of the second winter.

We shall see in the chapter on hiatuses of attraction, that the first Phalanx will, in consequence of its social isolation and other impediments inherent to the experimental canton, have twelve special obstacles to overcome, obstacles which the Phalanxes subsequently founded would not have to contend with. That is why it is so important that the experimental canton should have the assistance coming from field-work prolonged eight or nine months, like that in Naples and Lisbon.

As for the selection to be made among the candidates, rich and poor, various qualities which are accounted vicious or useless in civilization should be looked for; such are:

A good ear for music.
Good manners of families.
Aptitude for the fine arts.

And various rules which are contrary to philosophic ideas should be followed.

To prefer families having few children.
To have one-third of the organization consist of celibates.
To seek characters regarded as peculiar.
To establish a graduated scale respecting age, fortune, knowledge.

In view of the necessity of uniform education and fusion of the classes among children, I have advised, what I now reiterate, the selection, for the experimental Phalanx, of well-bred families, particularly in the lower class, since it will be necessary to have that class mingle in labor with the rich, and to make the latter find a charm in this amalgamation. That charm will be greatly dependent upon the good breeding of the inferiors; that is why the people in the environs of Paris, Blois, and Tours will be very suitable for the trial, provided, of course, that a proper selection is made.

Let us proceed with the details of composition. . . .

4. ROBERT OWEN

Robert Owen (1771-1858) is probably the most extraordinary and inspiring of the utopian socialists. From humble origins he rose to the position of an immensely successful industrialist and entrepreneur. In his own mills and plants in Scotland and England he proved that the reform of the living and working conditions of the laborer could be made feasible and highly profitable for all. His later attempts to incorporate these reforms into utopian communities, however (as in New Harmony, Indiana), proved abysmal failures. Highly critical of an economic order in which men were "merely trained to buy cheap and sell dear," he envisioned a wholly rational society in which, through the power of intelligence and education, a new and superior type of human character might be developed, and a new moral world brought into being.

[To the Nations of the World] *

You are now in the midst of a conflict which involves the deepest and dearest interest of every individual of the human race; and upon its result depends the misery or happiness of the present and future generations.

It is a contest between those who believe, that it is for their individual interest and happiness that man should continue to be kept in ignorance, and be governed, as heretofore, by force and fraud; and those who are convinced, that for his happiness, he should be henceforward governed by truth and justice only. The increase of knowledge renders the ultimate result of the contest no longer doubtful; but it is greatly to be desired that it should speedily terminate to the satisfaction of all parties: and it may now be made so to terminate, by the union of the six leading nations of the more civilized part of the

* Robert Owen, "An Address from the Association of All Classes of All Nations to the Governments and People of All Nations." This and the following selections are from *The Book of the New Moral World*, published by H. Robinson and Co., Glasgow, 1837.

world. For were they united to adopt simultaneously national measures, to give a wise direction to modern discoveries in the sciences of physics and of mind, they could accomplish the most magnificent results, for themselves and for the entire family of man.

The inexperienced will hastily conclude that these results are impracticable, or if practicable, that men are too ignorant, vicious, and selfish to promote a change which would ensure equal privileges to all, although the benefits, thereby arising to each, should far exceed the advantages which any one can enjoy, under the existing constitution of society. We believe, that through the self-interest of man, these objections may be overcome. For the experienced know, that all nations might, now, easily adopt arrangements to produce more of all kinds of wealth, essential to human happiness, than would satisfy all to the full extent of their desire, and also establish new institutions, in which the natural faculties and powers of each, might be cultivated from birth, to be greatly superior to any character ever formed, or that can be formed under any of the old institutions of the world. This vital change in the condition and character of the human race, may now be effected with only light, healthy, beneficial, and agreeable manual labour, combined with the most desirable and pleasant mental exercise: and this change may be effected in peace, with universal consent, without injury to the mind, body, or estate, of a single individual, in any rank or country.

This is the revolution which the progress of knowledge now requires from those who have hitherto ruled the destinies of nations; a revolution in the fundamental principles, and in the arrangement of society, which will essentially promote the interest, and secure the progressive happiness of all, from the highest to the lowest.

We undertake to explain the principles of nature, and to unfold the practical measures consequent upon them, by which this great revolution in human affairs, may be now effected, without disorder, or evil of any kind, not even disturbing existing private properties.

We proceed one step further; and consequently state, that the progress of knowledge now renders this revolution, in the general character of mankind, so irresistible, that no earthly power can prevent, or much retard its course; and it will be effected either by reason, or by violence forced upon society by the mental degradation of all, and the extreme misery of the many. We, therefore, as the disinterested friends of all Classes of all Nations, recommend to all Governments and People, that the old prejudices of the world, for or against class, sect, party, country, sex, and color, derived solely from ignorance, should be now allowed, by the common consent of all, to die their natural death; that standing armies of all nations should be disbanded, in order that the men may be employed in producing instead of destroying wealth; that the rising generation should be educated from birth to become superior, in character and conduct, to all past generations; that all should be trained to have as much enjoyment, in producing as in using or consuming wealth, which, through the progress of science, can be easily effected; that all should freely partake of it; and that, thus, the reign of peace, intelligence, and universal sympathy, or affection, may, for ever, supersede the reign of ignorance and oppression.

[From the Old World to the New]

The religious, moral, political, and commercial arrangements of society, throughout the world, have been based, from the commencement of history, upon an error respecting the nature of man; an error so grievous in its consequences, that it has deranged all the proceedings of society, made man irrational in his thoughts, feelings, and actions, and, consequently, more inconsistent, and perhaps more miserable, than any other animal.

This work is written to explain, first—the cause of this universal error, which has produced the derangement, degradation, and misery of the human race; and secondly—open to the present generation, a NEW MORAL WORLD founded on principles opposed to this error; and in which, the causes producing it will cease. In this NEW WORLD, the inhabitants will attain a state of existence, in which a spirit of charity and affection will pervade the whole human race, man will become spiritualized, and happy amidst a race of superior beings.

The knowledge which he will thus acquire of himself and of nature, will induce and enable him through his self-interest, or desire for happiness, to form such superior external arrangements as will place him within a terrestrial paradise.

As in this New World, all will know, that far more happiness can be obtained by union, than by disunion, all opposition and contention between man and man, and nation and nation, for individual or national advantages, of any kind, will cease.

The overwhelming power, which, through the progress of knowledge, may be now obtained by the external circumstances under the control of society, to form the general character of the human race, will become evident to all, and in consequence, no child will be permitted to grow up in ignorance, in superstition, or with inferior dispositions or habits; or without a knowledge of his own organization, of its laws, of the laws of nature generally, of the useful sciences, and of the practical arts of life.

The degradation, therefore, of mind and body, hitherto produced by a general training in error, regarding the organization or natural powers of man, and the innumerable errors thence arising, will be altogether unknown.

The evils, also, which are now produced by the desire ignorantly created to obtain individual superiority in wealth, privileges, and honours will not exist; but advantages much superior to these, will be secured to all, and feelings of a higher character than individual distinctions can create, will be universally experienced.

Scientific arrangements will be formed to make wealth everywhere, and at all times superabound beyond the wants or wishes of the human race, and all desire for individual accumulation, or any inequality of condition, will consequently cease.

The necessity for a never-ceasing supply of wealth for the use and enjoyment of all, and the right of each to produce and to enjoy his fair share of it, will be obvious and admitted. It will be equally evident that the unwrought materials to produce manufactured wealth, exist in superfluity, and that scientific aids may now be constructed to procure and work up these materials without any disagreeable, unhealthy, or premature manual labour, into every variety of the most useful and valuable productions.

With means thus ample to procure wealth with ease and pleasure to all, none will be so unwise as to desire to have the trouble and care of individual property. To divide riches among individuals in unequal proportions, or to hoard it for individual purposes, will be perceived to be as useless and as injurious as it would be to divide water or air into unequal quantities for different individuals, or that they should hoard them for their future use.

As more wealth will be produced through scientific aid, by healthy exercise, and as a gratifying amusement, than the population of the earth can require or advantageously use, no anxious thoughts, or care for a continued supply will perplex the mind, or injuriously occupy the time of any one. And as sufficient wealth will be so easily produced by scientific arrangements to effect whatever riches and knowledge can accomplish by the union of mankind, a far better education than any which has ever yet been proposed or conceived in the old world, will be given from birth to every one. In consequence of the ease with which wealth and scientific knowledge will be obtained, and made abundant for the most ample use and gratification of all, the inferior existing circumstances will be abandoned, and man will no longer live in crowded cities, or in seclusion from enlightened and superior society; but other arrangements will be formed to enable all, as soon as they shall be made rational, to live in superior habitations surrounded by gardens, pleasure-grounds, and scenery, far better designed and executed than any yet possessed by the monarchs of the most powerful, wealthy, and extended empires. The human race will also be surrounded by other very superior circumstances, which, now, by the progress of knowledge, can be placed for the first time under the control of man; circumstances of a far higher character than any which have yet existed in any part of the globe.

Ignorance therefore, and poverty, or the fear of it, now the fruitful causes of crime and misery, will no longer disunite man, and be the bane of his happiness. These evils will be known only in the history of the past, or of the irrational period of human existence.

Money, which has hitherto been the root, if not of *all* evil of great injustice, oppression and misery to the human race, making some slavish producers of wealth, and others its wasteful consumers or destroyers, will be no longer required to carry on the business of life: for as wealth of all kinds will be so delightfully created in greater abundance than will ever be required, no money price will be known, for happiness will not be purchaseable, except by a reciprocity of good actions and kind feelings.

Consequently, the present classification of society will be not only useless, but it will be discovered to be unjust and productive of every kind of evil; necessarily destructive of sincerity, honesty, and of all the finest feelings, and most valuable sympathies of our nature. This artificial and most injurious classification will be superseded by one derived immediately from nature—one that shall insure sincerity and honesty; that shall cultivate, foster, and encourage the finest feelings, and best sympathies, and continually calling into action the higher qualities of our nature, and that shall insure to every one the full amount of happiness that his original constitution, under the most favourable circumstances, shall be capable of receiving. These effects can be obtained, only, by a natural classification into employments according to age and capacity. All, at the same period of life, will pursue the same general occupations, for the public benefit, for which all, by their superior training and education, will be made more than competent; and all will have a large portion of each day to employ according to their peculiar capacities and individual inclinations, without interfering with the happiness of others.

By these arrangements, and this classification, all will become superior, physically, intellectually, and morally; each will know all the duties of life, and will have the greatest desire to execute them in the best manner. In this classification, however, none will be trained to teach incongruities or mysteries, which must derange the mental faculties and disorder all the transactions of mankind—none will be engaged in devising or administering laws in opposition to the laws of nature; or, in adjudging artificial rewards and punishments to counteract those of nature, which are all wise and efficient. It will be obvious, even to children, thus rationally educated, that all human laws must be either unnecessary, or in opposition to Nature's laws, they must create disunion, produce crime incessantly, and involve all transactions in inextricable confusion. None will be trained in idleness and uselessness to waste extravagantly the productions of others, to which no just law can give them a shadow of right or title; and no unjust law will be admitted into the code of the NEW MORAL WORLD. None will be trained and set apart to attack, plunder, and murder their fellow-men; this conduct will be known to be irrational, and the very essence of wickedness; nor, yet, will any be trained to bargain with, or even to attempt to take advantage of another, or to desire individual privileges or distinctions of any kind. The individual who is trained to buy cheap, sell dear, and seek for individual benefits above his fellows, is thereby degraded—is unfitted to acquire superior qualities—is deprived of the finest feelings of our nature, and rendered totally incompetent to experience the highest enjoyments of human existence. Nor will any be permitted, by society, to be trained in an *inferior manner,* or for *inferior purposes;* because one such example will be injurious to every one—but all will have the original powers and faculties of their nature directed and cultivated, in such a manner, as shall make it unavoidable, that each shall become, at maturity, superior in mind, manner, and conduct.

In this NEW WORLD, the sympathies of human nature will be

rightly directed from infancy, and will engender a spirit of benevolence, confidence, and affection, which will pervade mankind.

The impurities of the present system, arising from human laws opposed to nature's laws, will be unknown. The immense mass of degradation of character, and of heart-rending suffering, experienced by both sexes, but especially by women, will be altogether prevented —and the characters of all women will, by a superior, yet natural training, be elevated to become lovely, good, and intellectual. Of this state of purity and felicity few of the present generation have been trained to form any correct or rational conception.

In this *New World*, founded on universal and everlasting truths, no attempt will be made to falsify any of our physical or mental feelings; they will be known to be instincts given, as necessary parts of our nature, to be beneficially exercised and enjoyed.

Thus will be attained perfect truth, the great desideratum of human life, to prepare it for the enjoyment of happiness—truth, which, in this *New World*, will be, upon every subject, the sole language of man to the full extent of his knowledge.

There will, therefore, be an undeviating unity between all the thoughts, feelings, language, and actions of the human race. It will be distinctly perceived, that falsehood necessarily produces misery, and that truth necessarily produces happiness; consequently, no motives will arise among beings rationally educated, and possessing a knowledge of their own nature, to induce any one even to imagine a falsehood.

In this regenerated state of human existence, all will be trained from birth to attain physically, mentally, and morally, very superior qualities, and to have them regularly exercised up to the point of temperance, according to the constitution of each.

Thus will the well-being, the well-doing, and the happiness of each be insured, and permanently maintained.

It must now be evident, that the *New Moral World,* will have little in common with the old, excepting humanity as it comes into existence at birth, and the simple materials of nature; and even these will be made to receive forms and qualities so superior to those which have hitherto been given to them, that the inexperienced would scarcely believe their natures to be the same.

In this book the difference between the two states of existence, and also the mode by which the change from the one to the other will be effected, without injury to person or property, will be made so plain as easily to be understood.

The first part contains an explanation of the Constitution of Human Nature, and the Moral Science of Man, in order that a solid foundation may be laid at the commencement. In the succeeding parts of this book the Conditions requisite to insure the happiness of man, will be stated, with the reason for each Condition. Having considered what individual man is by nature, and what is necessary to the happiness of a being so constituted, an Explanation will be given of the arrangements which are necessary for his social condition, which will lead to the consideration of the best mode to *Produce and Distribute wealth—to Form the Character, and to Govern men in the aggregate, so as to insure their happiness.* The Religion and Morals of the NEW WORLD will then be explained, and their superiority shown over the mysteries and inconsistencies of the religions and morals of the old world. The principles on which to found a rational government for mankind will next follow, with its laws, the reasons for each law, and the consequences of such a government to the population of the world. To these will succeed an explanation of the practical arrangements by which *all* the conditions requisite to happiness may be obtained for, and *permanently* insured to, the human race; together with the mode of effecting the change from the Old to the New World.

[The Development of Superior Human Character]

A superior human being, or any one approaching a character deserving the name of rational, has not yet been known among mankind. A man intelligent and yet consistent in his feelings, thoughts, and actions, does not now exist even in the most civilized part of the world. Therefore, we know only from history or personal acquaintance, human beings who have been considered superior under the irrational system in which the human race has existed up to the present period; beings possessing comparatively superior organizations, and who have been placed through life amidst the least irrational circumstances. The most excellent of these characters, however, the most choice specimens that ever lived in the artificial and unnatural state which these circumstances have produced, have been but irrational beings—men who have been a little rational in a few points, while their fellow-men were made to be irrational in all their feelings, thoughts and actions.

Before a truly superior character can be formed among men, a new arrangement of external circumstances must be combined, all of which must be in unison with human nature, and calculated to produce rational impressions only upon the human organization. Every external circumstance, too, must be superior of its kind; and there must be also the absence of slavery and servitude, that no inferior impressions may be made upon any of our faculties.

Before this character can be given to the human race, a great change must occur in the whole proceedings of mankind; their feelings, thoughts, and actions must arise from principles altogether different from the vague and fanciful notions by which the mental part of the character of man has been hitherto formed; the whole external circumstances relative to the production and distribution of wealth, the formation of character, and the government of men, must be changed; the whole of these parts must be re-modeled and united into one system, in which each part shall contribute to the perfection of the whole; nothing must be left to the ignorance or inexperience of individuals or of individual families, whose apparent interests are made to oppose those of their fellows and neighbours; a false interest which diffuses a spirit of jealousy and competition among the members of every class, sect, and party, in every nation, city, town, and village, and too often in families.

No! a rational and superior character can be formed only by changing the whole of the existing irrational circumstances, now everywhere prevalent in the domestic, commercial, political, literary, and religious arrangements of mankind, for an entirely new and scientific combination of all these separate parts into one entire whole; and this so simplified and arranged, that all may be trained, even at an early period of life, to comprehend it, and also the reason for the formation of each part of this new and scientific machine of society. But this change can never be effected during the continuance of the laws, institutions, and customs of the world, which have arisen from the belief that the character of the individual is formed *by* himself; that he possesses within himself the power to form his own will, and the inclination or motives which induce him to act. These *errors* of the imagination have produced the most lamentable consequences in leading men to form institutions, codes of law, and customs in accordance with them; and, fatally for the happiness and improvement of mankind, in direct opposition to the laws of human nature, and to all the natural feelings of the human race. Ignorance, poverty, cruelty, injustice, crime, and misery were sure to follow from this opposition to the laws of that Power which pervades the universe, and gives man his nature, his feelings, and all his attributes. This opposition, however it may have arisen, is, in fact, a direct denial of wisdom, or design in the Cause which creates. That Cause gives man an organization or constitution with propensities, instincts, and faculties necessary for the well-doing, well-being, and happiness of the individual and of society; but inexperienced man, says, "No; these instincts, propensities, and faculties are bad; it is true, Nature has made them, but Nature is ignorant of the means to accomplish her own ends, we will instruct her better, and will therefore counteract her blind, or foolish, or injurious laws, by all the artificial and unnatural measures our wisdom can devise."

By these vain and futile attempts to oppose Nature, and improve himself, man is made the greatest obstacle in the way of his own happiness, and of the happiness of his race. . . .

[The Irrational Society]

These facts and laws make it evident that human nature is a compound of qualities, different from that which it has hitherto appeared to be; that these qualities have been misconceived, and that the true nature of man has been, to the present time, hidden from the human race; that this want of all knowledge of himself from which man has hitherto suffered, is now the great, and almost sole cause of all crime and misery. He has mistaken the most important instincts of his nature for the creations of his will, whereas facts now prove that his will is created by these instincts. This fundamental error respecting the qualities of the material of human nature, has, of necessity, deranged all the proceedings of mankind, and prevented the whole race from becoming rational. Man has imagined that he has been formed to believe and to feel as he likes, by the power of his will, and to be to a great extent, independent of external nature. All past society has been founded on these erroneous assumptions, and, in consequence, the human mind has been a chaos of perplexing inconsistencies, and all human affairs a compound of the most irrational transactions, individually, nationally, and universally.

The stronger members of every association have tyrannized over the weaker, and by open force or by fraud, made them their slaves— such is the state of society over the world at this moment. But tyrants and slaves are never rational; nor can such a condition of society ever produce intelligence, wealth, union, virtue, and happiness among mankind; or place man in a condition of permanent progressive improvement.

This division into tyrants and slaves, has produced a classification of society, which, however necessary in its early stages, is now creating every kind of evil over the earth, and prevents the possibility of any one attaining that high degree of excellence and happiness which, otherwise, might be so easily secured to the whole of the human race; a classification which must be destroyed before injustice and oppression—vice and misery, can be removed. For while men shall be divided into castes of employers and employee—masters and servants, sovereign and subject, tyrant and slave—ignorance, poverty, and disunion must pervade the world, and there must be an alternate advance and retrogression in all nations. The division of the inhabitants of the earth into tyrants and slaves has produced, not only the general classification which has been mentioned, but others subdividing these into Emperors, Kings, and Princes, into Legislators and Professors of divinity, law, medicine and arms; into producers and nonproducers of wealth and knowledge; into buyers and sellers of each other's powers, faculties, and products, and into the respective servants of all these divisions. Thus making a heterogeneous mass of contending interests among the whole human race, which, while these opposing feelings shall be created, must sever man from man, and nation from nation, to the incalculable injury of every individual of all nations.

It is now, therefore, evident that man has committed the same mistake from the beginning, respecting the power and faculties of his own nature, as he did for so long a period in relation to the laws of motion which govern the solar system; and from the same cause— the want of a sufficient number of facts accurately observed and systematically arranged, to enable him to draw sound deductions, and discover the truth. It is equally evident, that while these fundamental errors respecting the powers and faculties of human nature shall be entertained by, and shall control the conduct of those who govern the nations of the world, the same confusion of ideas, in the conception and direction of human affairs, must prevail, as existed in all minds respecting the solar system, when it was generally believed that the earth was the centre of the universe, and that the sun, stars, and planets moved round it.

Those who discovered the principles which now so beautifully explain the motions of the heavenly bodies, were deemed by the priest-hood of those days, infidels, because this knowledge of nature's laws was opposed to their superstitions and ignorance; and Galileo, to save his life, was compelled publicly to deny, in words, what he was forced, through the knowledge which he had acquired, to believe by an irresistible instinct of his nature. Thus the priesthood forced him to give a public denial to those truths which he was compelled to believe, in order to escape a death of excruciating torment.

In like manner, now, the promulgators of those divine principles of truth which must produce charity, kindness, and affection un-limited, and harmonize all minds as well as all human affairs, are called infidels by the priesthood of the present day; and the priests now desire to make them also deny the truth, by inflicting on them fines and imprisonment, or by using all the influence which they possess to destroy the only means of living within the power of these lovers of truth. Knowledge, however, progresses; the opinions of man-kind on these subjects are rapidly changing; the errors and evils of the priesthood are seen and felt by the intelligent over the world; and all the signs of the times make it evident that the era approaches when mental truth shall be as free as physical truth, and when the far greater benefits to be derived from the former will be experienced and universally acknowledged.

Men will then recur to the present state of mental imbecility, rela-tive to human nature, as we now do to the notions formerly entertained of the form of the earth, the solar movements, and the principles of mechanics and chemistry.

It seems extraordinary, at first, that the physical sciences, requiring so much accurate observation of external nature, so much profound thought and reflection, and often, such an extended, unbroken chain of close reasoning, should have made the advance the world now witnesses; and that so little progress should have been made in mental knowledge, which can alone insure happiness to the human race; this is, however, explained by the fact, that the priesthood in all countries, in all times, have opposed the barrier of their hitherto all-powerful influence, to stifle inquiries and prevent investigations, which they perceived would undermine their power over the human mind, and consequently, over the fortunes of men.

Thus the most intricate and important discoveries have been made in some of the physical sciences, while the mental and moral sciences have remained in total darkness. Even now, upon these latter subjects, the most erroneous assumptions, in opposition to all facts, are taught to the mass of mankind, who are, in consequence, made imbecile and mentally blind.

This injurious state of human affairs will remain as long as the authorized teachers of the people are made to believe that they (the teachers) have an interest in keeping the people in mental darkness. And the teachers will continue thus to instruct, until they shall be better instructed themselves with respect to their own interest and happiness.

Thus the errors of the world relative to these facts and laws of human nature, have kept past generations in the ignorance, poverty, disunion, crime, and misery which have hitherto pervaded all parts of the earth; and while these errors are retained, the evils must continue to increase. But it is, and always, without a single exception, has been the highest interest of all men, in all countries, that these errors should be removed; and happily men now begin to perceive this truth.

We have, in this chapter, stated a few only of the most obvious deductions from the facts and laws, or constitution of human nature; were we now to enter fully upon this wide field of new knowledge, a volume would be insufficient to contain that which might be advantageously written; but the subsequent parts of this book will afford a better opportunity to place the subject gradually before the mind, when it will be more habituated to follow this train of reasoning.

[The New Moral World]

These facts and laws of nature, whenever they shall be fully understood and generally adopted in practice, will become the means of forming a new character for the human race. Instead of being made irrational, as they have hitherto been, they will be made rational, they will be formed to become of necessity, CHARITABLE to their fellow-men of every clime, color, language, sentiment, and feeling;

and KIND to all that has life. When a knowledge of these facts and laws shall be taught to all from infancy, they will know that the clime, color, language, opinions, and feelings, are the necessary effects of causes over which the individuals, subject to their influence, have no control; they will not, therefore, be angry with their fellow-men for experiencing influences which are unavoidable. These different effects will be considered varieties of nature, useful for observation and reflection, for instruction and amusement. Such varieties in the character of man, as now produce opposing feelings and interests, and thence anger, violence, wars, and disunion, and all manner of oppression and injustice, crimes and misery, will, on the contrary, elicit knowledge, friendship, and pleasure. Hence characters the most opposite by nature will seek each other, unite and form intimate associations, in order that the most extended knowledge of human nature, and of nature generally, may be acquired, one interest formed, and affection made everywhere to abound.

The necessary result of unions of opposite varieties of character, will be, speedily to remove prejudices of every description, to dispel ignorance, root out all evil passions, destroy the very germs of disunion, and make men wise to their own happiness. Thus there will be no opposing interests or feelings among men in any part of the globe: the spirit of the world will be changed, and the selfishness of ignorance will be superseded by the self-interest, or, which is the same, the benevolence of intelligence.

The individuality of man, unavoidable by his nature, which is, now, through ignorance, a cause of so much of the disunion of the human race, will become the cause of the more intimate union, and of the increase of pleasure and enjoyment. Contrasts of feelings and opinions which have been hitherto causes of anger, hatred, and repulsion, will become sources of attraction, as being the most easy and direct mode to acquire an extended knowledge of our nature, and of the laws which govern it. The causes which produce these differences will be examined with affection by the parties, and solely with a view to discover the truth; for all will be lovers of truth, and no one will feel, or think of being ashamed of truth. They will know assuredly, and without a shadow of doubt, that truth is nature, and nature God; that "God is truth, and truth is God," as so generally expressed by the Mohammedans. And when men shall be made wise, by acquiring an accurate knowledge of the facts and laws of their nature, and can pursue a lengthened rational train of reasoning founded upon them;

no one will shrink from, or be ashamed of the discoveries which nature will thus unfold. It will be known to all, that our individual physical feelings, and mental convictions or feelings, are instincts of our nature; all will, therefore, express them as such—nature will be justified—man's false shame of declaring the truth will be removed, and all motive to falsehood will cease. As each human being will have the knowledge which will enable him accurately to express and explain the real power, state, and condition of his own mind, and will always speak the truth; his character will be fully known to every one. It is solely the want of an accurate acquaintance with the science of ᴊuman nature, or the individual and social character of man, that has given rise to the motives which have engendered falsehood, uncharitableness, and unkindness.

The effects which will be produced on society, by these facts and laws being known and publicly taught, are far too great to be comprehended by the faculties of men as they have been hitherto cultivated. When truth, in every department of human knowledge, shall supersede error and falsehood; when, by common consent, from conviction of the injury produced, men shall abandon falsehood, and speak the language of truth only, throughout all nations, then, indeed, will some conception be acquired of what human nature is, and what are its powers and capacities for improvement and enjoyment.

Under this change, man will appear to be a new-created being. The powers, capacities, and dispositions cultivated under a system of falsehood, arising from ignorance of the laws of his nature, will assume another character, when cultivated from infancy under a system of truth—a character so different in manner and spirit, that, could they now be seen in juxtaposition, they would appear to belong to opposite natures; the one irrational, actively engaged in measures to defeat its own happiness, and in making the earth a Pandemonium; the other rational, daily occupied in measures to promote and secure the happiness of all around, and in making the earth a paradise.

Thus will the present irrational arrangements of society give place to those which are rational. The existing classification of the population of the world will cease. One portion of mankind will not, as now, be trained and placed to oppress, by force or fraud, another portion, to the great disadvantage of both; neither will one portion be trained in idleness, to live in luxury on the industry of those whom they oppress, while the latter are made to labor daily and to live in poverty. Nor yet will some be trained to force falsehood into the human mind, and be paid extravagantly for so doing, while other parties are prevented from teaching the truth, or severely punished if they make the attempt. There will be no arrangements to give knowledge to a few, and to withhold it from the many; but, on the contrary, all will be taught to acquire knowledge of themselves, of nature generally, and of the principles and practice of society, in all its departments, which knowledge will be easily made familiar to every one. The whole business of life will be so simplified, that each will understand it, and will delight in its varied practice.

Thus, will the effects upon society, of a knowledge of these facts and laws, remove the causes of all evil, and establish the reign of good over the world.

Section II

DIALECTICS

While the theories of the utopian socialists constitute the critical background of communism, its positive character has complex and abstruse philosophical roots. Central among the ideas that Marx borrowed from earlier philosophers and incorporated into his own system was the concept of dialectical method, which virtually all post-Marxian communists believe is the only truly scientific approach to the course of history and the process of social development.

Dialectics, though part of a venerable philosophic tradition, does not become a paramount theme until its appearance in the philosophical and historical treatises of the German thinker, Georg Hegel. Although Marx became an active social theorist and revolutionary, it must never be forgotten that he began adult life as a serious student of academic philosophy, and particularly of the philosophy of Hegel. Marx eventually came to reject some of the principal elements of the Hegelian system, but he accepted as fundamental the dialectical interpretation of history that Hegel had emphasized. Orthodox communists still believe, as Marx maintained, that the dialectic of history makes inevitable the coming of the classless society to which they look forward.

The dialectical method is not easy to describe or understand. To put it as simply as possible, it views the logical and historical process of events as composed of opposing or conflicting elements or phases that must eventually be reconciled in some higher, more perfect union or synthesis. Out of this new synthesis, which may be a concept or an event, its own opposite arises in turn, and a new dialectical conflict appears, which must lead to yet another synthesis, and so on. The dialectician believes that only within the framework of this inexorable, spiral-like development can the course of past and present world events be fully understood.

In the following selections from Engels and Hegel, the nature of dialectics and the application of the dialectic to history are presented in the writings of its strongest advocates.

5. FRIEDRICH ENGELS

This, the second part of Socialism, Utopian and Scientific *(the first part appears in the preceding section), is the clearest description yet written of the communist conception of dialectical thinking, and the relation of the communist philosophy to the Hegelian system. Engels' argument, later to be spelled out more carefully, is that the Hegelian dialectic, while correct in essence, was not correctly applied. Correct application, he contends, was accomplished by Marx, and makes possible a truly scientific socialism.*

Socialism, Utopian and Scientific: Part II *

[Dialectical Philosophy]

In the meantime, along with and after the French philosophy of the eighteenth century had arisen the new German philosophy, culminating in Hegel. Its greatest merit was the taking up again of dialectics as the highest form of reasoning. The old Greek philosophers were all natural born dialecticians, and Aristotle, the most encyclopedic intellect of them, had already analyzed the most essential forms of dialectic thought. The newer philosophy, on the other hand, although in it also dialectics had brilliant exponents (e.g. Descartes and Spinoza), had, especially through English influence, become more and more rigidly fixed in the so-called metaphysical mode of reasoning, by which also the French of the eighteenth century were almost wholly dominated, at all events in their special philosophical work. Outside philosophy in the restricted sense, the French never-

* From F. Engels, *Socialism, Utopian and Scientific,* Swan Sonnenschein and Co., London, 1892.

theless produced masterpieces of dialectic. We need only call to mind Diderot's *Le Neveu de Rameau,* and Rousseau's *Discours sur l'origine et les fondements de l'inégalité parmi les hommes.* We give here, in brief, the essential character of these two modes of thought.

When we consider and reflect upon nature at large, or the history of mankind, or our own intellectual activity, at first we see the picture of an endless entanglement of relations and reactions, permutations and combinations, in which nothing remains what, where, and as it was, but everything moves, changes, comes into being and passes away. We see, therefore, at first the picture as a whole, with its individual parts still more or less kept in the background; we observe the movements, transitions, connections, rather than the things that move, combine, and are connected. This primitive, naïve, but intrinsically correct conception of the world is that of ancient Greek philosophy, and was first clearly formulated by Heraclitus: everything is and is not, for everything is fluid, is constantly changing, constantly coming into being and passing away.

But this conception, correctly as it expresses the general character of the picture of appearances as a whole, does not suffice to explain the details of which this picture is made up, and so long as we do not understand these, we have not a clear idea of the whole picture. In order to understand these details we must detach them from their natural or historical connection and examine each one separately, its nature, special causes, effects, etc. This is, primarily, the task of natural science and historical research; branches of science which the Greeks of classical times, on very good grounds, relegated to a subordinate position, because they had first of all to collect materials for these sciences to work upon. A certain amount of natural and historical material must be collected before there can be any critical analysis, comparison and arrangement in classes, orders and species. The foundations of the exact natural sciences were, therefore, first worked out by the Greeks of the Alexandrian period, and later, in the Middle Ages, by the Arabs. Real natural science dates from the second half of the fifteenth century, and thence onward it has advanced with constantly increasing rapidity. The analysis of nature into its individual parts, the grouping of the different natural processes and objects in definite classes, the study of the internal anatomy of organized bodies in their manifold forms—these were the fundamental conditions of the gigantic strides in our knowledge of nature that have been made during the last four hundred years. But this method of work has also left us as legacy the habit of observing natural objects and processes in isolation, apart from their connection with the vast whole; of observing them in repose, not in motion; as constants, not as essentially variables; in their death, not in their life. And when this way of looking at things was transferred by Bacon and Locke from natural science to philosophy, it begot the narrow, metaphysical mode of thought peculiar to the last century.

To the metaphysician, things and their mental reflexes, ideas, are isolated, are to be considered one after the other and apart from each other, are objects of investigation fixed, rigid, given once for all. He thinks in absolutely irreconcilable antitheses. "His communication is 'yea, yea; nay, nay'; for whatsoever is more than these cometh of evil." For him a thing either exists or does not exist; a thing cannot at the same time be itself and something else. Positive and negative absolutely exclude one another; cause and effect stand in a rigid antithesis one to the other.

At first sight this mode of thinking seems to us very luminous, because it is that so-called sound common sense. Only sound common sense, respectable fellow that he is, in the homely realm of his own four walls, has very wonderful adventures directly he ventures out into the wide world of research. And the metaphysical mode of thought, justifiable and necessary as it is in a number of domains whose extent varies according to the nature of the particular object of investigation, sooner or later reaches a limit, beyond which it becomes one-sided, restricted, abstract, lost in insoluble contradictions. In the contemplation of individual things, it forgets the connection between them; in the contemplation of their existence, it forgets the beginning and end of that existence; of their repose, it forgets their motion. It cannot see the wood for the trees.

For everyday purposes we know and can say, e.g., whether an animal is alive or not. But, upon closer inquiry, we find that this is, in many cases, a very complex question, as the jurists know very well. They have cudgeled their brains in vain to discover a rational limit beyond which the killing of the child in its mother's womb is murder. It is just as impossible to determine absolutely the moment of death, for physiology proves that death is not an instantaneous, momentary phenomenon, but a very protracted process.

In like manner, every organized being is every moment the same and not the same; every moment it assimilates matter supplied from without, and gets rid of other matter; every moment some cells of its body die and others build themselves anew; in a longer or shorter time the matter of its body is completely renewed, and is replaced by other molecules of matter, so that every organized being is always itself, and yet something other than itself.

Further, we find upon closer investigation that the two poles of an antithesis, positive and negative, e.g., are as inseparable as they are opposed, and that despite all their opposition, they mutually interpenetrate. And we find, in like manner, that cause and effect are conceptions which only hold good in their application to individual cases; but as soon as we consider the individual cases in their general connection with the universe as a whole, they run into each other, and they become confounded when we contemplate that universal action and reaction in which causes and effects are eternally changing places, so that what is effect here and now will be cause there and then, and vice versa.

None of these processes and modes of thought enters into the framework of metaphysical reasoning. Dialectics, on the other hand, comprehends things and their representations, ideas, in their essential connection, concatenation, motion, origin and ending. Such processes as those mentioned above are, therefore, so many corroborations of its own method of procedure.

Nature is the proof of dialectics, and it must be said for modern science that it has furnished this proof with very rich materials increasing daily, and thus has shown that, in the last resort, nature works dialectically and not metaphysically; that she does not move in the eternal oneness of a perpetually recurring circle, but goes through a real historical evolution. In this connection Darwin must be named before all others. He dealt the metaphysical conception of nature the heaviest blow by his proof that all organic beings, plants, animals and man himself, are the products of a process of evolution going on through millions of years. But the naturalists who have learned to think dialectically are few and far between, and this conflict of the results of discovery with preconceived modes of thinking explains the endless confusion now reigning in theoretical natural science, the despair of teachers as well as learners, of authors and readers alike.

An exact representation of the universe, of its evolution, of the development of mankind, and of the reflection of this evolution in the minds of men, can therefore only be obtained by the methods of dialectics, with its constant regard to the innumerable actions and reactions of life and death, of progressive or retrogressive changes.

And in this spirit the new German philosophy has worked. Kant began his career by resolving the stable solar system of Newton and its eternal duration, after the famous initial impulse had once been given, into the result of a historic process, the formation of the sun and all the planets out of a rotating nebulous mass. From this he at the same time drew the conclusion that, given this origin of the solar system, its future death followed of necessity. His theory half a century later was established mathematically by Laplace, and half a century after that the spectroscope proved the existence in space of such incandescent masses of gas in various stages of condensation.

This new German philosophy culminated in the Hegelian system. In this system—and herein is its great merit—for the first time the whole world, natural, historical, intellectual, is represented as a process, i.e., as in constant motion, change, transformation, development; and the attempt is made to trace out the internal connection that makes a continuous whole of all this movement and development. From this point of view the history of mankind no longer appeared as a wild whirl of senseless deeds of violence, all equally condemnable at the judgment seat of mature philosophic reason, and which are best forgotten as quickly as possible, but as the process of evolution of man himself. It was now the task of the intellect to follow the gradual march of this process through all its devious ways, and to trace out the inner law running through all its apparently accidental phenomena.

That the Hegelian system did not solve the problem it propounded is here immaterial. Its epoch-making merit was that it propounded the problem. This problem is one that no single individual will ever be able to solve. Although Hegel was—with Saint Simon—the most encyclopedic mind of his time, yet he was limited, first by the necessarily limited extent of his own knowledge, and, second, by the limited extent and depth of the knowledge and conceptions of his age. To these limits a third must be added. Hegel was an idealist. To him the thoughts within his brain were not the more or less abstract pictures of actual things and processes, but, conversely, things and their evolution were only the realized pictures of the "Idea," existing somewhere from eternity before the world was. This way of thinking turned everything upside down, and completely reversed the actual connection of things in the world. Correctly and ingeniously as many individual groups of facts were grasped by Hegel, yet, for the reasons just given, there is much that is botched, artificial, labored, in a word, wrong in point of detail. The Hegelian system, in itself, was a colossal miscarriage—but it was also the last of its kind. It was suffering, in fact, from an internal and incurable contradiction. Upon the one hand, its essential proposition was the conception that human history is a process of evolution, which, by its very nature, cannot find its intellectual final term in the discovery of any so-called absolute truth. But, on the other hand, it laid claim to being the very essence of this absolute truth. A system of natural and historical knowledge embracing everything, and final for all time, is a contradiction to the fundamental law of dialectic reasoning. This law, indeed, by no means excludes, but, on the contrary, includes the idea that the systematic knowledge of the external universe can make giant strides from age to age.

The perception of the fundamental contradiction in German idealism led necessarily back to materialism, but *nota bene,* not to the simply metaphysical, exclusively mechanical materialism of the eighteenth century. Old materialism looked upon all previous history as a crude heap of irrationality and violence; modern materialism sees in it the process of evolution of humanity, and aims at discovering the laws thereof. With the French of the eighteenth century, and even with Hegel, the conception obtained of nature as a whole, moving in narrow circles, and forever immutable, with its eternal celestial bodies, as Newton, and unalterable organic species, as Linnæus, taught. Modern materialism embraces the more recent discoveries of natural science according to which nature also has its history in time, the celestial bodies, like the organic species that, under favorable conditions, people them, being born and perishing. And even if nature, as a whole, must still be said to move in recurrent cycles, these cycles assume infinitely larger dimensions. In both aspects, modern materialism is essentially dialectic, and no longer requires the assistance of that sort of philosophy which, queen-like, pretended to rule the remaining mob of sciences. As soon as each special science is bound to make clear its position in the great totality of things and of our knowledge of things, a special science dealing with this totality is superfluous or unnecessary. That which still survives of all earlier philosophy is the science of thought and its laws—formal logic and dialectics. Everything else is subsumed in the positive science of nature and history.

While, however, the revolution in the conception of nature could only be made in proportion to the corresponding positive materials furnished by research, already much earlier certain historical facts had occurred which led to a decisive change in the conception of history. In 1831, the first working class rising took place in Lyons; between 1838 and 1842, the first national working class movement, that of the English Chartists, reached its height. The class struggle between proletariat and bourgeoisie came to the front in the history of the most advanced countries in Europe, in proportion to the development, upon the one hand, of modern industry, upon the other, of the newly-acquired political supremacy of the bourgeoisie. Facts more and more strenuously gave the lie to the teachings of bourgeois economy as to the identity of the interests of capital and labor, as to the universal harmony and universal prosperity that would be the consequence of unbridled competition. All these things could no longer be ignored, any more than the French and English socialism, which was their theoretical, though very imperfect, expression. But the old idealist conception of history, which was not yet dislodged, knew nothing of class struggles based upon economic interests, knew nothing of economic interests; production and all economic relations appeared in it only as incidental, subordinate elements in the "history of civilization."

The new facts made imperative a new examination of all past history. Then it was seen that *all* past history, with the exception of its primitive stages, was the history of class struggles; that these warring classes of society are always the products of the modes of production and of exchange—in a word, of the *economic* conditions of their time; that the economic structure of society always furnishes the real basis, starting from which we can alone work out the ultimate explanation of the whole superstructure of juridical and political institutions as well as of the religious, philosophical and other ideas of a given historical period. Hegel had freed history from metaphysics—he had made it dialectic; but his conception of history was essentially idealistic. But now idealism was driven from its last refuge, the philosophy of history; now a materialistic treatment of history was propounded, and a method found of explaining man's "knowing" by his "being," instead of, as heretofore, his "being" by his "knowing."

From that time forward socialism was no longer an accidental discovery of this or that ingenious brain, but the necessary outcome of the struggle between two historically developed classes—the proletariat and the bourgeoisie. Its task was no longer to manufacture a system of society as perfect as possible, but to examine the historico-economic succession of events from which these classes and their antagonisms had of necessity sprung, and to discover in the economic conditions thus created the means of ending the conflict. But the socialism of earlier days was as incompatible with this materialistic conception as the conception of nature of the French materialists was with dialectics and modern natural science. The socialism of earlier days certainly criticized the existing capitalistic mode of production and its consequences. But it could not explain them, and, therefore, could not get the mastery of them. It could only simply reject them as bad. The more strongly this earlier socialism denounced the exploitation of the working class, inevitable under capitalism, the less able was it clearly to show in what this exploitation consisted and how it arose. But for this it was necessary—1) to present the capitalistic method of production in its historical connection and its inevitableness during a particular historical period, and therefore, also, to present its inevitable downfall; and 2) to lay bare its essential character, which was still a secret. This was done by the discovery of *surplus value.* It was shown that the appropriation of unpaid labor is the basis of the capitalist mode of production and of the exploitation of the worker that occurs under it; that even if the capitalist buys the labor power of his laborer at its full value as a commodity on the market, he yet extracts more value from it than he paid for; and that in the ultimate analysis this surplus value forms those sums of value from which are heaped up the constantly increasing masses of capital in the hands of the possessing classes. The genesis of capitalist production and the production of capital were both explained.

These two great discoveries, the materialistic conception of history and the revelation of the secret of capitalistic production through surplus value, we owe to Marx. With these discoveries socialism became a science. The next thing was to work out all its details and relations.

6. GEORG WILHELM FRIEDRICH HEGEL

Georg Hegel (1770-1831) was one of the great philosophers of all time. He had not only an encyclopedic mind, as Engels said, but a grand synoptic vision, and he has exerted a powerful influence upon philosophers of every description. Except under communist regimes, his philosophical method is no longer commonly held in high repute; yet his contributions to the contemporary political philosophies of both extreme left and extreme right are extraordinary. He is a difficult, puzzling, and gigantic figure in the history of thought. The following selection, from The Philosophy of History, *illustrates the complexity of his views, and the way in which the dialectic serves him as an instrument of interpretation and comprehension. The whole of world history is to be understood, he claims, as the dialectical development of Spirit in time.*

[Dialectical History] *

Universal history—as already demonstrated—shows the development of the consciousness of Freedom on the part of Spirit, and of the consequent realization of that Freedom. This development implies a gradation—a series of increasingly adequate expressions or manifestations of Freedom, which result from its Idea. The logical, and—as still more prominent—the *dialectical* nature of the Idea in general, viz. that it is self-determined—that it assumes successive forms which it successively transcends; and by this very process of transcending its earlier stages, gains an affirmative, and, in fact, a richer and more concrete shape—this necessity of its nature, and the necessary series of pure abstract forms which the Idea successively assumes—is exhibited in the department of *Logic.* Here we need adopt only one of its results, viz. that every step in the process, as differing from any other, has its determinate peculiar principle. In history this principle is idiosyncrasy of Spirit—peculiar National Genius. It is within the limitations of this idiosyncrasy that the spirit of the nation, concretely manifested, expresses every aspect of its consciousness and will—the whole cycle of its realization. Its religion, its polity, its ethics, its legislation, and even its science, art, and mechanical skill, all bear its stamp. These special peculiarities find their key in that common peculiarity—the particular principle that characterizes a people; as, on the other hand, in the facts which History presents in detail, that common characteristic principle may be detected. That such or such a specific quality constitutes the peculiar genius of a people, is the

---

* From G. W. F. Hegel, *Lectures on the Philosophy of History.* These passages are from a translation by J. Sibree, published by Henry G. Bohn, London, 1861.

element of our inquiry which must be derived from experience, and historically proved. To accomplish this, pre-supposes not only a disciplined faculty of abstraction, but an intimate acquaintance with the Idea. The investigator must be familiar *à priori* (if we like to call it so), with the whole circle of conceptions to which the principles in question belong—just as Kepler (to name the most illustrious example in this mode of philosophizing) must have been familiar *à priori* with ellipses, with cubes and squares, and with ideas of their relations, before he could discover, from the empirical data, those immortal "Laws" of his, which are none other than forms of thought pertaining to those classes of conceptions. He who is unfamiliar with the science that embraces these abstract elementary conceptions, is as little capable—though he may have gazed on the firmament and the motions of the celestial bodies for a lifetime—of *understanding* those Laws, as of *discovering* them. From this want of acquaintance with the ideas that relate to the development of Freedom, proceed a part of those objections which are brought against the philosophical consideration of a science usually regarded as one of mere experience; the so-called *à priori* method, and the attempt to insinuate ideas into the empirical data of history, being the chief points in the indictment. Where this deficiency exists, such conceptions appear alien—not lying within the object of investigation. To minds whose training has been narrow and merely subjective—which have not an acquaintance and familiarity with ideas—they are something strange—not embraced in the notion and conception of the subject which their limited intellect forms. Hence the statement that Philosophy does not understand such sciences. It must, indeed, allow that it has not that kind of understanding which is the prevailing one in the domain of those sciences, that it does not proceed according to the categories of such Understanding, but according to the categories of *Reason*—though at the same time recognizing that Understanding, and its true value and position. It must be observed that in this very process of scientific *Understanding,* it is of importance that the essential should be distinguished and brought into relief in contrast with the so-called nonessential. But in order to render this possible, we must know what is *essential;* and that is—in view of the History of the World in general —the Consciousness of Freedom, and the phases which this consciousness assumes in developing itself. . . .

History in general is therefore the development of Spirit in *Time,* as Nature is the development of the Idea in *Space.*

If then we cast a glance over the World's-History generally, we see a vast picture of changes and transactions; of infinitely manifold forms of peoples, states, individuals, in unresting succession. Everything that can enter into and interest the soul of man—all our sensibility to *goodness, beauty, and greatness*—is called into play. On every hand aims are adopted and pursued, which we recognize, whose accomplishment we desire—we hope and fear for them. In all these occurrences and changes we behold human action and suffering predominant; everywhere something akin to ourselves, and therefore everywhere something that excites our interest for or against. Sometimes it attracts us by beauty, freedom, and rich variety, sometimes by energy such as enables even vice to make itself interesting. Sometimes we see the more comprehensive mass of some general interest advancing with comparative slowness, and subsequently sacrificed to an infinite complication of trifling circumstances, and so dissipated into atoms. Then, again, with a vast expenditure of power a trivial result is produced; while from what appears unimportant a tremendous issue proceeds. On every hand there is the motliest throng of events drawing us within the circle of its interest, and when one combination vanishes another immediately appears in its place.

The general thought—the category which first presents itself in this restless mutation of individuals and peoples, existing for a time and then vanishing—is that of *change* at large. The sight of the ruins of some ancient sovereignty directly leads us to contemplate this thought of change in its negative aspect. What traveler among the ruins of Carthage, of Palmyra, Persepolis, or Rome, has not been stimulated to reflections on the transiency of kingdoms and men, and to sadness at the thought of a vigorous and rich life now departed— a sadness which does not expend itself on personal losses and the uncertainty of one's own undertakings, but is a disinterested sorrow at the decay of a splendid and highly cultured national life! But the next consideration which allies itself with that of change, is, that change while it imports dissolution, involves at the same time the rise of a *new life*—that while death is the issue of life, life is also the issue of death. This is a grand conception; one which the Oriental thinkers attained, and which is perhaps the highest in their metaphysics. In the idea of *Metempsychosis* we find it evolved in its relation to individual existence; but a myth more generally known, is that of the *Phœnix* as a type of the Life of *Nature;* eternally preparing for itself its funeral pile, and consuming itself upon it; but so that from its ashes is produced the new, renovated, fresh life. But this image is also Asiatic; oriental not occidental. Spirit—consuming the envelope of its existence—does not merely pass into another envelope, nor rise rejuvenescent from the ashes of its previous form; it comes forth exalted, glorified, a purer spirit. It certainly makes war upon itself—consumes its own existence; but in this very destruction it works up that existence into a new form, and each successive phase becomes in its turn a material, working on which it exalts itself to a new grade.

If we consider Spirit in this aspect—regarding its changes not merely as rejuvenescent transitions, i.e., returns to the same form, but rather as manipulations of itself, by which it multiplies the material for future endeavors—we see it exerting itself in a variety of modes and directions; developing its powers and gratifying its desires in a variety which is inexhaustible; because every one of its creations, in which it has already found gratification, meets it anew as material, and is a new stimulus to plastic activity. The abstract conception of mere change gives place to the thought of spirit manifesting, developing, and perfecting its powers in every direction which its manifold nature can follow. What powers it inherently possesses we learn from the variety of products and formations which it originates. In this pleasurable activity, it has to do only with itself. As involved with the conditions of mere nature—internal and external—it will indeed meet in these not only opposition and hindrance, but will often see its endeavors thereby fail; often sink under the complications in which it is entangled either by Nature or by itself. But in such case it perishes in fulfilling its own destiny and proper function, and even thus exhibits the spectacle of self-demonstration as spiritual activity.

The very essence of Spirit is activity; it realizes its potentiality—makes itself its own deed, its own work—and thus it becomes an object to itself; contemplates itself as an objective existence. Thus is it with the Spirit of a people: it is a Spirit having strictly defined characteristics, which erects itself into an objective world, that exists and persists in a particular religious form of worship, customs, constitution, and political laws—in the whole complex of its institutions —in the events and transactions that make up its history. That is its work—that is what this particular Nation *is*. Nations are what their deeds are. Every Englishman will say: We are the men who navigate the ocean, and have the commerce of the world; to whom the East Indies belong and their riches; who have a parliament, juries, etc.— The relation of the individual to that Spirit is that he appropriates to himself this substantial existence; that it becomes his character and capability, enabling him to have a definite place in the world—to be *something*. For he finds the being of the people to which he belongs an already established, firm world—objectively present to him—with which he has to incorporate himself. In this its work, therefore—its world—the Spirit of the people enjoys its existence and finds its satisfaction.—A Nation is moral—virtuous—vigorous—while it is engaged in realizing its grand objects, and defends its work against external violence during the process of giving to its purposes an objective existence. The contradiction between its potential, subjective being—its inner aim and life—and its *actual* being is removed; it has attained full reality, has itself objectively present to it. But this having been attained, the activity displayed by the Spirit of the people in question is no longer needed; it has its desire. The Nation can still accomplish much in war and peace at home and abroad; but the living substantial soul itself may be said to have ceased its activity. The essential, supreme interest has consequently vanished from its life, for interest is present only where there is opposition. The nation lives the same kind of life as the individual when passing from maturity to old age—in the enjoyment of itself—in the satisfaction of being exactly what it desired and was able to attain. Although its imagination might have transcended that limit, it nevertheless abandoned any such aspirations as objects of *actual endeavor,* if the real world was less than favorable to their attainment—and restricted its aim by the conditions thus imposed. This mere *customary life* (the watch wound up and going on of itself) is that which brings on natural death. Custom is activity without opposition, for which there remains only a formal duration; in which the fulness and zest that originally characterized the aim of life are out of the question—a merely external sensuous existence which has ceased to throw itself enthusiastically into its object. Thus perish individuals, thus perish peoples by a natural death; and though the latter may continue in being, it is an existence without intellect or vitality; having no need of its institutions, because the need for them is satisfied—a political nullity and tedium. In order that a truly universal interest may arise, the Spirit of a People must advance to the adoption of some new purpose; but whence can this new purpose originate? It would be a higher, more comprehensive conception of itself—a transcending of its principle—but this very act would involve a principle of a new order, a new National Spirit.

Such a new principle does in fact enter into the Spirit of a people that has arrived at full development and self-realization; it dies not a simply natural death—for it is not a mere single individual, but a spiritual, generic life; in its case natural death appears to imply destruction through its own agency. The reason of this difference from the single natural individual, is that the Spirit of a people exists as a *genus,* and consequently carries within it its own negation, in the very generality which characterizes it. A people can only die a violent death when it has become naturally dead in itself, as, e.g., the German Imperial Cities, the German Imperial Constitution.

It is not of the nature of all-pervading Spirit to die this merely natural death; it does not simply sink into the senile life of mere custom, but—as being a National Spirit belonging to Universal History—attains to the consciousness of what its work is; it attains to a conception of itself. In fact it is world-historical only in so far as a *universal principle* has lain in its fundamental element—in its grand aim: only so far is the work which such a spirit produces, a moral, political organization. If it be mere desires that impel nations to activity, such deeds pass over without leaving a trace; or their traces are only ruin and destruction. Thus, it was first Chronos—Time—that ruled; the Golden Age, without moral products; and what was produced—the offspring of that Chronos—was devoured by it. It was Jupiter—from whose head Minerva sprang, and to whose circle of divinities belong Apollo and the Muses—that first put a constraint upon Time, and set a bound to its principle of decadence. He is the Political god, who produced a moral work—the State.

In the very element of an achievement the quality of generality, of thought, is contained; without thought it has no objectivity; that is its basis. The highest point in the development of a people is this— to have gained a conception of its life and condition—to have reduced its laws, its ideas of justice and morality to a science; for in this unity [of the objective and subjective] lies the most intimate unity that Spirit can attain to in and with itself. In its work it is employed in rendering itself an object of its own contemplation; but it cannot develop itself objectively in its essential nature, except in *thinking* itself.

At this point, then, Spirit is acquainted with its principles—the general character of its acts. But at the same time, in virtue of its very generality, this work of thought is different in point of form from the actual achievements of the national genius, and from the vital agency by which those achievements have been performed. We have then before us a *real* and an *ideal* existence of the Spirit of the Nation. If we wish to gain the general idea and conception of what the Greeks were, we find it in Sophocles and Aristophanes, in Thucydides and Plato. In these individuals the Greek spirit conceived and thought itself. This is the profounder kind of satisfaction which the Spirit of a people attains; but it is "ideal," and distinct from its "real" activity.

At such a time, therefore, we are sure to see a people finding satisfaction in the *idea* of virtue; putting *talk* about virtue partly side by side with actual virtue, but partly in the place of it. On the other hand pure, universal thought, since its nature is universality, is apt to bring the Special and Spontaneous—Belief, Trust, Customary Morality— to reflect upon itself, and its primitive simplicity; to show up the limitation with which it is fettered—partly suggesting reasons for renouncing duties, partly itself *demanding reasons,* and the connection of such requirements with Universal Thought; and not finding that connection, seeking to impeach the authority of duty generally, as destitute of a sound foundation.

At the same time the isolation of individuals from each other and from the Whole makes its appearance; their aggressive selfishness and vanity; their seeking personal advantage and consulting this at the expense of the State at large. That inward principle in transcending its outward manifestations is subjective also in *form*—viz., selfishness and corruption in the unbound passions and egotistic interests of men.

Zeus, therefore, who is represented as having put a limit to the devouring agency of Time, and stayed this transiency by having established something inherently and independently durable—Zeus and his race are themselves swallowed up, and that by the very power that produced them—the principle of thought, perception, reasoning, insight derived from rational grounds, and the requirement of such grounds.

Time is the negative element in the sensuous world. Thought is the same negativity, but it is the deepest, the infinite form of it, in which therefore all existence generally is dissolved; first *finite* existence—*determinate,* limited form: but existence *generally,* in its objective character, is limited; it appears therefore as a mere datum —something immediate—authority—and is either intrinsically finite and limited, or presents itself as a limit for the thinking subject, and its infinite reflection on itself [unlimited abstraction].

But first we must observe how the life which proceeds from death, is itself, on the other hand, only individual life; so that, regarding the species as the real and substantial in this vicissitude, the perishing of the individual is a regress of the species into individuality. The perpetuation of the race is, therefore, none other than the monotonous repetition of the same kind of existence. Further, we must remark how perception—the comprehension of being by thought—is the source and birthplace of a new, and in fact higher form, in a principle which while it preserves, dignifies its material. For Thought is that *Universal*—that *Species* which is immortal, which preserves identity with itself. The particular form of Spirit not merely passes away in the world by natural causes in Time, but is annulled in the automatic self-mirroring activity of consciousness. Because this annulling is an activity of thought, it is at the same time conservative and elevating in its operation. While then, on the one side, Spirit annuls the reality, the permanence of that which it *is,* it gains on the other side, the essence, the Thought, the Universal element of that which *it only was* [its transient conditions]. Its principle is no longer that immediate import and aim which it was previously, but the *essence* of that import and aim.

The result of this process is then that Spirit, in rendering itself objective and making this its being an object of thought, on the one hand destroys the determinate form of its being, on the other hand gains a comprehension of the universal element which it involves, and thereby gives a new form to its inherent principle. In virtue of this, the substantial character of the National Spirit has been altered —that is, its principle has risen into another, and in fact a higher principle.

It is of the highest importance in apprehending and comprehending History to have and to understand the thought involved in this transition. The individual traverses as a unity various grades of development, and remains the same individual; in like manner also does a people, till the Spirit which it embodies reaches the grade of universality. In this point lies the fundamental, the Ideal necessity of transition. This is the soul—the essential consideration—of the philosophical comprehension of History.

Spirit is essentially the result of its own activity: its activity is the transcending of immediate, simple, unreflected existence—the negation of that existence, and the returning into itself. We may compare it with the seed; for with this the plant begins, yet it is also the result of the plant's entire life. But the weak side of life is exhibited in the fact that the commencement and the result are disjoined from each other. Thus also is it in the life of individuals and peoples. The life of a people ripens a certain fruit; its activity aims at the complete manifestation of the principle which it embodies. But this fruit does not fall back into the bosom of the people that produced and matured it; on the contrary, it becomes a poison-draught to it. That poison-draught it cannot let alone, for it has an insatiable thirst for it: the taste of the draught is its annihilation, though at the same time the rise of a new principle.

We have already discussed the final aim of this progression. The principles of the successive phases of Spirit that animate the Nations in a necessitated gradation, are themselves only steps in the development of the one universal Spirit, which through them elevates and completes itself to a self-comprehending *totality*.

While we are thus concerned exclusively with the Idea of Spirit, and in the History of the World regard everything as only its manifestation, we have, in traversing the past—however extensive its periods—only to do with what is *present;* for philosophy, as occupying itself with the True, has to do with the *eternally present.* Nothing in the past is lost for it, for the Idea is ever present; Spirit is immortal; with it there is no past, no future, but an essential *now.* This necessarily implies that the present form of Spirit comprehends within it all earlier steps. These have indeed unfolded themselves in succession independently; but what Spirit is it has always been essentially; distinctions are only the development of this essential nature. The life of the ever present Spirit is a circle of progressive embodiments, which looked at in one aspect still exist beside each other, and only as looked at from another point of view appear as past. The grades which Spirit seems to have left behind it, it still possesses in the depths of its present.

7. FRIEDRICH ENGELS

The following brief letter, written to give assistance in reading Hegel, is equally valuable in presenting the essential character of the Hegelian dialectic, as Engels understood it.

Engels to Conrad Schmidt*
(London, 1 November 1891)

[On Understanding Hegel]

It is impossible, of course, to dispense with Hegel and the man also takes some time to digest. The shorter *Logic* in the Encyclopedia makes quite a good beginning. But you must take the edition in the sixth volume of the *Works*, not the separate edition by Rosenkranz (1845), because there are far more explanatory additions from the lectures in the former, even if that ass Henning has often not understood them himself.

In the Introduction you have the criticism, first (par. 26, etc.) of Wolf's version of Leibnitz (metaphysics *in the historical sense*), then of English-French empiricism (par. 37, etc.) then Kant (par. 40, seq.) and finally (par. 61) of Jacoby's mysticism. In the first section (Being) do not spend too long over Being and Nothing; the last paragraphs on Quality and then Quantity and Measure are much finer, but the theory of Essence is the main thing: the resolution of the abstract contradictions into their own instability, where one no sooner tries to hold on to one side alone than it is transformed unnoticed into the other, etc. At the same time you can always make the thing clear to yourself by concrete examples; for instance, you, as a bridegroom, have a striking example of the inseparability of identity and difference in yourself and your bride. It is absolutely impossible to decide whether sexual love is pleasure in the identity in difference or in the difference in identity. Take away the difference (in this case of sex) or the identity (the human nature of both) and what have you got left? I remember how much this very inseparability of identity and difference worried me at first, although we can never take a step without stumbling upon it.

But you ought on no account to read Hegel as Herr Barth has done, namely in order to discover the bad syllogisms and rotten dodges which served him as levers in construction. That is pure schoolboy's work. It is much more important to discover the truth and the genius which lie beneath the false form and within the artificial connections.

* From *Selected Correspondence of Marx and Engels,* 1942. Reprinted by permission of International Publishers, New York.

Thus the transitions from one category or from one contradiction to the next are nearly always arbitrary—often made through a pun, as when Positive and Negative (par. 120) *"zugrunde gehen"* [perish] in order that Hegel may arrive at the category of *"Grund"* [reason, ground]. To ponder over this much is waste of time.

Since with Hegel every category represents a stage in the history of philosophy (as he generally indicates), you would do well to compare the lectures on the history of philosophy (one of his most brilliant works). As relaxation, I can recommend the Aesthetic. When you have worked yourself into that a bit you will be amazed.

Hegel's dialectic is upside down because it is supposed to be the "self-development of thought," of which the dialectic of facts therefore is only a reflection, whereas really the dialectic in our heads is only the reflection of the actual development which is fulfilled in the world of nature and of human history in obedience to dialectical forms.

If you just compare the development of the commodity into capital in Marx with the development from Being to Essence in Hegel, you will get quite a good parallel for the concrete development which results from facts; there you have the abstract construction, in which the most brilliant ideas and often very important transmutations, like that of quality into quantity and vice versa, are reduced to the apparent self-development of one concept from another—one could have manufactured a dozen more of the same kind. . . .

Section III

MATERIALISM

To apply the dialectic, Marx believed, was not enough. It had to be applied correctly, and to the proper subject matter. The mistake that had been made with the dialectic heretofore, he maintained, was in applying it only to the realm of pure thought. Marx believed it should be applied to the hard facts of human life, to the concrete concerns of human needs and wants—in a word, to *matter*. Although they admitted their debt to the German materialist Ludwig Feuerbach, Marx and Engels believed that their philosophical materialism was new in that it was the first to view the world, not only as constituted of matter, but as organized in a dialectical framework. Only on these materialist premises, they claimed, could the dialectic be properly utilized, and world history understood. At the same time, only with this dialectical approach could materialism be truly scientific.

Because Marx and Engels were thoroughgoing materialists, they rejected all principles based on the supernatural or the divine. They rejected theism; they rejoiced in Feuerbach's atheistic account of the essence of Christianity. Marx's favorite myth was that of Prometheus bound to the rock yet defiant of the gods. On the basis of this materialism, communists since Marx have denied the truth or applicability of any ethical or religious principles founded on claims of divine or supernatural authority.

8. KARL MARX and FRIEDRICH ENGELS

Karl Marx (1818-1883) is the most important single figure in the development of the philosophy of modern communism. When the following selection, from The German Ideology, *was written, Marx was a young man of twenty-eight. His philosophical system was not yet fully developed, but he had grasped the issue concerning which he was to rebel against the Hegelian philosophy. "In direct contrast to German philosophy," he and Engels wrote, "which descends from heaven to earth, here we ascend from earth to heaven."*

[The Premises of Materialism] *

The premises from which we begin are not arbitrary ones, not dogmas, but real premises from which abstraction can only be made in the imagination. They are the real individuals, their activity and the material conditions under which they live, both those which they find already existing and those produced by their activity. These premises can thus be verified in a purely empirical way.

The first premise of all human history is, of course, the existence of living human individuals. Thus the first fact to be established is the physical organization of these individuals and their consequent relation to the rest of nature. . . .

The fact is, therefore, that definite individuals who are productively active in a definite way enter into these definite social and political relations. Empirical observation must in each separate instance bring out empirically, and without any mystification and speculation, the connection of the social and political structure with production. The social structure and the state are continually evolving out of the life process of definite individuals, but of individuals not as they may appear in their own or other people's imagination, but as they really

* From K. Marx and F. Engels, *The German Ideology*. Written in 1845-46, this work was first published almost a century later. These passages are reprinted by permission of International Publishers, New York.

are, i.e., as they are effective, produce materially, and are active under definite material limits, presuppositions, and conditions independent of their will.

The production of ideas, of conceptions, of consciousness is at first directly interwoven with the material activity and the material intercourse of men, the language of real life. Conceiving, thinking, the mental intercourse of men appear at this stage as the direct efflux of their material behavior. The same applies to mental production as expressed in the language of the politics, laws, morality, religion, metaphysics of a people. Men are the producers of their conceptions, ideas, etc.—real, active men, as they are conditioned by a definite development of their productive forces and of the intercourse corresponding to these, up to its furthest forms. Consciousness can never be anything else than conscious existence, and the existence of men is their actual life process. If in all ideology men and their circumstances appear upside down, as in a *camera obscura,* this phenomenon arises just as much from their historical life process as the inversion of objects on the retina does from their physical life process.

In direct contrast to German philosophy, which descends from heaven to earth, here we ascend from earth to heaven. That is to say, we do not set out from what men say, imagine, conceive, nor from men as narrated, thought of, imagined, conceived, in order to arrive at men in the flesh. We set out from real, active men, and on the basis of their real life process we demonstrate the development of the ideological reflexes and echoes of this life process. The phantoms formed in the human brain are also, necessarily, sublimates of their material life process, which is empirically verifiable and bound to material premises. Morality, religion, metaphysics, all the rest of ideology and their corresponding forms of consciousness, thus no longer retain the semblance of independence. They have no history, no development; but men, developing their material production and their material intercourse, alter, along with this, their real existence, their thinking, and the products of their thinking. Life is not determined by consciousness, but consciousness by life. In the first method of approach the starting point is consciousness taken as the living individual; in the second it is the real, living individuals themselves, as they are in actual life, and consciousness is considered solely as *their* consciousness.

This method of approach is not devoid of premises. It starts out from the real premises, and does not abandon them for a moment.

Its premises are men, not in any fantastic isolation or abstract definition, but in their actual, empirically perceptible process of development under definite conditions. As soon as this active life process is described, history ceases to be a collection of dead facts, as it is with the empiricists (themselves still abstract), or an imagined activity of imagined subjects, as with the idealists.

Where speculation ends—in real life—there real, positive science begins: the representation of the practical activity, of the practical process of development of men. Empty talk about consciousness ceases, and real knowledge has to take its place. When reality is depicted, philosophy as an independent branch of activity loses its medium of existence. At best, its place can be taken only by a summing up of the most general results, abstractions which arise from the observation of the historical development of men. Viewed apart from real history, these abstractions have in themselves no value whatsoever. They can only serve to facilitate the arrangement of historical material, to indicate the sequence of its separate strata. But they by no means afford a recipe or schema, as does philosophy, for neatly trimming the epochs of history. On the contrary, our difficulties begin only when we set about the observation and the arrangement—the real depiction—of our historical material, whether of a past epoch or of the present. The removal of these difficulties is governed by premises which it is quite impossible to state here, but which only the study of the actual life process and the activity of the individuals of each epoch will make evident. We shall select here some of these abstractions, which we use to refute the ideologists, and shall illustrate them by historical examples.

9. FRIEDRICH ENGELS

Late in his life Engels acknowledged the debt of the communist philosophy to the work of Ludwig Feuerbach, with a small volume named after that philosopher. In the following passage from that work, the impact of Feuerbach's materialism upon Marx and Engels is vividly described.

[Feuerbach and Hegel] *

. . . One can imagine what a tremendous effect this Hegelian system must have produced in the philosophy-tinged atmosphere of Germany. It was a triumphal procession which lasted for decades and which by no means came to a standstill on the death of Hegel. On the contrary, it was precisely from 1830 to 1840 that "Hegelianism" reigned most exclusively and, to a greater or lesser extent, infected even its opponents. It was precisely in this period that Hegelian views, consciously or unconsciously, most extensively penetrated the most diversified sciences and leavened even popular literature and the daily press, from which the average "educated consciousness" derives its mental pabulum. But this victory along the whole front was only the prelude to an internal struggle.

As we have seen, the doctrine of Hegel, taken as a whole, left plenty of room for giving shelter to the most diverse practical party views. And in the theoretical Germany of that time two things above all were practical: religion and politics. Whoever placed the chief emphasis on the Hegelian *system* could be fairly conservative in both spheres; whoever regarded the dialectical *method* as the main thing could belong to the most extreme opposition, both in politics and religion. Hegel himself, despite the fairly frequent outbursts of revolutionary wrath in his works, seemed on the whole to be more inclined to the conservative side. Indeed, his system had cost him much more "hard mental plugging" than his method. Towards the end of the thirties the cleavage in the school became more and more apparent. The left wing, the so-called Young Hegelians, in their fight with the pietist orthodox and the feudal reactionaries, abandoned bit by bit that philosophical-genteel reserve in regard to the burning questions of the day which up to that time had secured state toleration and even protection for their teachings. And when, in 1840, orthodox pietism and absolutist feudal reaction ascended the throne with Frederick William IV, open partisanship became unavoidable. The fight was still carried on with philosophical weapons, but no longer for abstract philosophical aims. It turned directly on the destruction of

* From F. Engels, *Ludwig Feuerbach and the End of Classical German Philosophy*. These passages are reprinted from *Basic Writings on Politics and Philosophy* by Marx and Engels, edited by L. S. Feuer, Doubleday and Company, Anchor Books; New York, 1959.

traditional religion and of the existing state. And while in the *Deutsche Jahrbücher* the practical ends were still predominantly put forward in philosophical disguise, in the *Rheinische Zeitung* of 1842 the Young Hegelian school revealed itself directly as the philosophy of the aspiring radical bourgeoisie and used the meager cloak of philosophy only to deceive the censorship. . . .

We will not go further into this side of the decomposition process of the Hegelian school. More important for us is the following: the main body of the most determined Young Hegelians was, by the practical necessities of its fight against positive religion, driven back to Anglo-French materialism. This brought them into conflict with their school system. While materialism conceives nature as the sole reality, nature in the Hegelian system represents merely the "alienation" of the Absolute Idea, so to say, a degradation of the Idea. At all events, thinking and its thought product, the Idea, is here the primary, nature the derivative, which exists at all only by the condescension of the Idea. And in this contradiction they floundered as well or as ill as they could.

Then came Feuerbach's *Essence of Christianity*. With one blow it pulverized the contradiction, in that without circumlocutions it placed materialism on the throne again. Nature exists independently of all philosophy. It is the foundation upon which we human beings, ourselves products of nature, have grown up. Nothing exists outside nature and man, and the higher beings our religious fantasies have created are only the fantastic reflection of our own essence. The spell was broken, the "system" was exploded and cast aside, and the contradiction, shown to exist only in our imagination, was dissolved. One must himself have experienced the liberating effect of this book to get an idea of it. Enthusiasm was general; we all became at once Feuerbachians. How enthusiastically Marx greeted the new conception and how much—in spite of all critical reservations—he was influenced by it, one may read in *The Holy Family*. . . .

The Hegelian school disintegrated, but Hegelian philosophy was not overcome through criticism. . . . Feuerbach broke through the system and simply discarded it. But a philosophy is not disposed of by the mere assertion that it is false. And so powerful a work as Hegelian philosophy, which had exercised so enormous an influence on the intellectual development of the nation, could not be disposed of by simply being ignored. It had to be "sublated" in its own sense, that is, in the sense that while its form had to be annihilated through criticism, the new content which had been won through it had to be saved. How this was brought about we shall see below.

10. LUDWIG ANDREAS FEUERBACH

Ludwig Feuerbach (1804-1872) was a popular German philosopher whose materialism was expressed in the famous epigram: Man is what he eats. (Der Mensch ist was er isst.) *In* The Essence of Christianity, *from the preface to which the following passage is taken, Feuerbach denies that God exists, except as an idealized object of human consciousness. "Let it be remembered," he remarks, "that atheism is the secret of religion itself."*

[Materialism and Atheism] *

The clamor excited by the present work has not surprised me and hence it has not in the least moved me from my position. On the contrary, I have once more, in all calmness, subjected my work to the severest scrutiny, both historical and philosophical; I have, as far as possible, freed it from its defects of form, and enriched it with new developments, illustrations and historical testimonies—testimonies in the highest degree striking and irrefragable. Now that I have thus verified my analysis by historical proofs, it is to be hoped that readers whose eyes are not sealed will be convinced and will admit, even though reluctantly, that my work contains a faithful, correct translation of the Christian religion out of the oriental language of imagery into plain speech. And it has no pretension to be anything more than a close translation, or, to speak literally, an empirical or historico-philosophical analysis, a solution of the enigma of the Christian religion. The general propositions which I premise in the Introduction are no *à priori,* excogitated propositions, no products of speculation; they have arisen out of the analysis of religion; they are only, as indeed

* From *The Essence of Christianity,* translated by Marian Evans. Published by John Chapman, London, 1854.

are all the fundamental ideas of the work, generalizations from the known manifestations of human nature, and in particular of the religious consciousness—facts converted into thoughts, i.e., expressed in general terms, and thus made the property of the understanding. The ideas of my work are only conclusions, *consequences,* drawn from premises which are not themselves mere ideas, but objective facts either actual or historical—facts which had not their place in my head simply in virtue of their ponderous existence in folio. I unconditionally repudiate *absolute,* immaterial, self-sufficing speculation—that speculation which draws its material from within. I differ *toto cœlo* from those philosophers who pluck out their eyes that they may see better; for *my* thought I require the senses, especially sight; I found my ideas on materials which can be appropriated only through the activity of the senses. I do not generate the object from the thought, but the thought from the object; and I hold *that* alone to be an object which has an existence beyond one's own brain. I am an idealist only in the region of *practical* philosophy, that is, I do not regard the limits of the past and present as the limits of humanity, of the future; on the contrary, I firmly believe that many things—yes, many things—which with the short-sighted, pusillanimous practical men of today, pass for flights of imagination, for ideas never to be realized, for mere chimeras, will tomorrow, i.e., in the next century— centuries in individual life are days in the life of humanity—exist in full reality. Briefly, the "Idea" is to me only faith in the historical future, in the triumph of truth and virtue; it has for me only a political and moral significance: for in the sphere of strictly theoretical philosophy, I attach myself, in direct opposition to the Hegelian philosophy, only to *realism,* to materialism in the sense above indicated. The maxim hitherto adopted by speculative philosophy: all that is mine I carry with me, the old *omnia mea mecum porto,* I cannot, alas! appropriate. I have many things outside myself, which I cannot convey either in my pocket or my head, but which nevertheless I look upon as belonging to me, not indeed as a mere man—a view not now in question—but as a philosopher. I am nothing but a *natural philosopher in the domain of mind;* and the natural philosopher can do nothing without instruments, without material means. In this character I have written the present work, which consequently contains nothing else than the principle of a new philosophy verified practically, i.e., *in concreto,* in application to a special object, but an object which has a universal significance: namely, to religion, in which this principle is exhibited, *developed* and thoroughly carried out. This philosophy is essentially distinguished from the systems hitherto prevalent, in that it corresponds to the real, complete nature of man; but for that very reason it is antagonistic to minds perverted and crippled by a super-human, i.e., anti-human, anti-natural religion and speculation. It does not, as I have already said elsewhere, regard the *pen* as the only fit organ for the revelation of truth, but the eye and ear, the hand and foot; it does not identify the idea of the fact with the fact itself, so as to reduce real existence to an existence on paper, but it separates the two, and precisely by this separation attains to the *fact itself;* it recognizes as the true thing, not the thing as it is an object of the abstract reason, but as it is an object of the real, complete man, and hence as it is itself a real, complete thing. This philosophy does not rest on an understanding *per se,* on an absolute, nameless under-standing, belonging one knows not to whom, but on the understanding of man—though not, I grant, on that of man enervated by specu-lation and dogma—and it speaks the language of men, not an empty, unknown tongue. Yes, both in substance and in speech, it places philosophy in *the negation of philosophy,* i.e., it declares *that* alone to be the true philosophy which is converted *in succum et sanguinem,* which is incarnate in Man; and hence it finds its highest triumph in the fact that to all dull and pedantic minds, which place the *essence* of philosophy in the *show* of philosophy, it appears to be no phi-losophy at all.

This philosophy has for its principle, not the Substance of Spinoza, not the *ego* of Kant and Fichte, not the Absolute Identity of Schel-ling, not the Absolute Mind of Hegel, in short, no abstract, merely conceptional being, but a *real* being, the true *Ens realissimum*—man; its principle, therefore, is in the highest degree positive and real. It generates thought from the *opposite* of thought, from Matter, from existence, from the senses; it has relation to its object first through the senses, i.e., passively, before defining it in thought. Hence my work, as a specimen of this philosophy, so far from being a production to be placed in the category of Speculation—although in another point of view it is the true, the incarnate result of prior philosophical sys-tems—is the direct opposite of speculation, nay, puts an end to it by explaining it. Speculation makes religion say only what it has *itself* thought, and expressed far better than religion; it assigns a meaning to religion without any reference to the *actual* meaning of religion; it does not look beyond itself. I, on the contrary, let religion itself speak; I constitute myself only its listener and interpreter, not its prompter. Not to invent, but to discover, "to unveil existence," has been my sole object; to *see* correctly, my sole endeavor. It is not I, but religion that worships man, although religion, or rather theology, denies this; it is not I, an insignificant individual, but religion itself that says: God is man, man is God; it is not I, but religion that denies the God who is *not* man, but only an *ens rationis*—since it makes God become man, and then constitutes this God, not distinguished from man, having a human form, human feelings and human thoughts, the object of its worship and veneration. I have only found the key to the cipher of the Christian religion, only extricated its true meaning from the web of contradictions and delusions called theology—but in doing so I have certainly committed a sacrilege. If therefore my work is negative, irreligious, atheistic, let it be remembered that atheism—at least in the sense of this work—is the secret of religion itself; that religion itself, not indeed on the surface, but fundamentally, not in intention or according to its own supposition, but in its heart, in its essence, believes in nothing else than the truth and divinity of human nature. . . .

11. KARL MARX

In the spring of 1845, Marx jotted down some notes on the philosophy of Ludwig Feuerbach, which were soon forgotten, and only came to light many years later. Called the Theses on Feuerbach, *these notes display Marx's activistic temper and the revolutionary direction of his thought.*

Theses on Feuerbach*

I

The chief defect of all hitherto existing materialism—that of Feuerbach included—is that the thing [*Gegenstand*], reality, sensuousness,

---

* Reprinted from *Basic Writings on Politics and Philosophy,* by Marx and Engels, edited by L. S. Feuer, Doubleday and Company, Anchor Books, New York, 1959.

is conceived only in the form of the *object* [*Objekt*] or of *contemplation* [*Anschauung*], but not as *human sensuous activity, practice*, not subjectively. Hence it happened that the *active* side, in contradistinction to materialism, was developed by idealism—but only abstractly, since, of course, idealism does not know real, sensuous activity as such. Feuerbach wants sensuous objects really differentiated from the thought objects, but he does not conceive human activity itself as *objective* [*gegenständliche*] activity. Hence, in the *Essence of Christianity*, he regards the theoretical attitude as the only genuinely human attitude, while practice is conceived and fixed only in its dirty-judaical form of appearance. Hence he does not grasp the significance of "revolutionary," of "practical-critical," activity.

II

The question whether objective [*gegenständliche*] truth can be attributed to human thinking is not a question of theory, but is a *practical* question. In practice man must prove the truth, that is, the reality and power, the this-sidedness [*Diesseitigkeit*] of his thinking. The dispute over the reality or non-reality of thinking which is isolated from practice is a purely *scholastic* question.

III

The materialist doctrine that men are products of circumstances and upbringing, and that, therefore, changed men are products of other circumstances and changed upbringing, forgets that it is men that change circumstances, and that the educator himself needs educating. Hence this doctrine necessarily arrives at dividing society into two parts, of which one is superior to society (in Robert Owen, for example).

The coincidence of the changing of circumstances and of human activity can be conceived and rationally understood only as *revolutionizing practice*.

IV

Feuerbach starts out from the fact of religious self-alienation, the duplication of the world into a religious, imaginary world and a real one. His work consists in the dissolution of the religious world into its secular basis. He overlooks the fact that after completing this work, the chief thing still remains to be done. For the fact that the secular foundation detaches itself from itself and establishes itself in the clouds as an independent realm is really to be explained only by the self-cleavage and self-contradictoriness of this secular basis. The latter must itself, therefore, first be understood in its contradiction and then, by the removal of the contradiction, revolutionized in practice. Thus, for instance, once the earthly family is discovered to be the secret of the holy family, the former must then itself be criticized in theory and revolutionized in practice. . . .

VII

Feuerbach, consequently, does not see that the "religious sentiment" is itself a *social product,* and that the abstract individual whom he analyzes belongs in reality to a particular form of society.

VIII

Social life is essentially *practical.* All mysteries which mislead theory to mysticism find their rational solution in human practice and in the comprehension of this practice.

IX

The highest point attained by *contemplative* materialism, that is, materialism which does not understand sensuousness as practical activity, is the contemplation of single individuals in "civil society."

X

The standpoint of the old materialism is *"civil"* society; the standpoint of the new is *human* society, or socialized humanity.

XI

The philosophers have only *interpreted* the world, in various ways; the point, however, is to *change* it.

12. FRIEDRICH ENGELS

The most powerful statement of the Marxist conception of the opposition of idealism and materialism is to be found in Engels' Ludwig Feuerbach. The following selection from that work presents a concise exposition of the materialistic presuppositions of the communist philosophy.

[Idealism and Materialism] *

The great basic question of all philosophy, especially of more recent philosophy, is that concerning the relation of thinking and being. From the very early times when men, still completely ignorant of the structure of their own bodies, under the stimulus of dream apparitions came to believe that their thinking and sensation were not activities of their bodies, but of a distinct soul which inhabits the body and leaves it at death—from this time men have been driven to reflect about the relation between this soul and the outside world. If upon death it took leave of the body and lived on, there was no occasion to invent yet another distinct death for it. Thus arose the idea of its immortality, which at that stage of development appeared not at all as a consolation, but as a fate against which it was no use fighting, and often enough, as among the Greeks, as a positive misfortune. Not religious desire for consolation, but the quandary arising from the common universal ignorance of what to do with this soul, once its existence had been accepted, after the death of the body led in a general way to the tedious notion of personal immortality. In an exactly similar manner the first gods arose through the personification of natural forces. And these gods in the further development of religions assumed more and more an extra-mundane form, until finally by a process of abstraction, I might almost say of distillation, oc-

* From F. Engels, *Ludwig Feuerbach and the End of Classical German Philosophy*. These passages are reprinted from *Basic Writings on Politics and Philosophy* by Marx and Engels, edited by L. S. Feuer, Doubleday and Company, Anchor Books, New York, 1959.

curring naturally in the course of man's intellectual development, out of the many more or less limited and mutually limiting gods there arose in the minds of men the idea of the one exclusive God of the monotheistic religions.

Thus the question of the relation of thinking to being, the relation of the spirit to nature—the paramount question of the whole of philosophy—has, no less than all religion, its roots in the narrow-minded and ignorant notions of savagery. But this question could for the first time be put forward in its whole acuteness, could achieve its full significance, only after humanity in Europe had awakened from the long hibernation of the Christian Middle Ages. The question of the position of thinking in relation to being, a question which, by the way, had played a great part also in the scholasticism of the Middle Ages, the question: Which is primary, spirit or nature?—that question, in relation to the Church, was sharpened into this: Did God create the world or has the world been in existence eternally?

The answers which the philosophers gave to this question split them into two great camps. Those who asserted the primacy of spirit to nature and, therefore, in the last instance, assumed world creation in some form or other—and among the philosophers, Hegel, for example, this creation often becomes still more intricate and impossible than in Christianity—comprised the camp of idealism. The others, who regarded nature as primary, belong to the various schools of materialism.

These two expressions, idealism and materialism, originally signify nothing else but this; and here, too, they are not used in any other sense. What confusion arises when some other meaning is put into them will be seen below.

But the question of the relation of thinking and being has yet another side: In what relation do our thoughts about the world surrounding us stand to this world itself? Is our thinking capable of the cognition of the real world? Are we able in our ideas and notions of the real world to produce a correct reflection of reality? In philosophical language this question is called the question of the identity of thinking and being, and the overwhelming majority of philosophers give an affirmative answer to this question. With Hegel, for example, its affirmation is self-evident; for what we cognize in the real world is precisely its thought content—that which makes the world a gradual realization of the Absolute Idea, which Absolute Idea has existed somewhere from eternity, independent of the world and before the world. But it is manifest without further proof that thought can know a content which is from the outset a thought content. It is equally manifest that what is to be proved here is already tacitly contained in the premises. But that in no way prevents Hegel from drawing the further conclusion from his proof of the identity of thinking and being that his philosophy, because it is correct for his thinking, is therefore the only correct one, and that the identity of thinking and being must prove its validity by mankind immediately translating his philosophy from theory into practice and transforming the whole world according to Hegelian principles. This is an illusion which he shares with well-nigh all philosophers.

In addition there is yet a set of different philosophers—those who question the possibility of any cognition, or at least of an exhaustive cognition, of the world. To them, among the more modern ones, belong Hume and Kant, and they have played a very important role in philosophical development. What is decisive in the refutation of this view has already been said by Hegel, in so far as this was possible from an idealist standpoint. The materialistic additions made by Feuerbach are more ingenious than profound. The most telling refutation of this, as of all other philosophical crotchets, is practice, namely, experiment and industry. If we are able to prove the correctness of our conception of a natural process by making it ourselves, bringing it into being out of its conditions and making it serve our own purposes into the bargain, then there is an end to the Kantian ungraspable "thing-in-itself." The chemical substances produced in the bodies of plants and animals remained just such things-in-themselves until organic chemistry began to produce them one after another, whereupon the thing-in-itself became a thing for us, as, for instance, alizarin, the coloring matter of the madder, which we no longer trouble to grow in the madder roots in the field, but produce much more cheaply and simply from coal tar. For three hundred years the Copernican solar system was a hypothesis with a hundred, a thousand, or ten thousand chances to one in its favor, but still always a hypothesis. But when Leverrier, by means of the data provided by this system, not only deduced the necessity of the existence of an unknown planet, but also calculated the position in the heavens which this planet must necessarily occupy, and when Galle really found this planet the Copernican system was proved. If, nevertheless, the Neo-Kantians are attempting to resurrect the Kantian conception in Germany and the agnostics that of Hume in England (where in fact

it never became extinct), this is, in view of their theoretical and practical refutation, accomplished long ago, scientifically a regression and
practically merely a shamefaced way of surreptitiously accepting
materialism while denying it before the world.

But during this long period from Descartes to Hegel and from
Hobbes to Feuerbach the philosophers were by no means impelled,
as they thought they were, solely by the force of pure reason. On the
contrary, what really pushed them forward most was the powerful and
ever more rapidly onrushing progress of natural science and industry.
Among the materialists this was plain on the surface, but the idealist
systems also filled themselves more and more with a materialist content, and attempted pantheistically to reconcile the antithesis between
mind and matter. Thus, ultimately, the Hegelian system represents
merely a materialism idealistically turned upside down in method and
content. . . .

The course of evolution of Feuerbach is that of a Hegelian—a
never quite orthodox Hegelian, it is true—into a materialist, an evolution which at a definite stage necessitates a complete rupture with
the idealist system of his predecessor. With irresistible force Feuerbach is finally driven to the realization that the Hegelian premun-
dane existence of the Absolute Idea, the "pre-existence of the logical
categories" before the world existed, is nothing more than the fantastic survival of the belief in the existence of an extramundane creator; that the material, sensuously perceptible world to which we ourselves belong is the only reality; and that our consciousness and
thinking, however suprasensuous they may seem, are the product of a
material, bodily organ, the brain. Matter is not a product of mind,
but mind itself is merely the highest product of matter. This is, of
course, pure materialism. But, having got so far, Feuerbach stops
short. He cannot overcome the customary philosophical prejudice,
prejudice not against the thing but against the name materialism.
He says: "To me materialism is the foundation of the edifice of human
essence and knowledge; but to me it is not what it is to the physiologist, to the natural scientists in the narrower sense, for example,
to Moleschott, and necessarily is from their standpoint and profession,
namely, the edifice itself. Backwards I fully agree with the materialists,
but not forwards."

Here Feuerbach lumps together the materialism that is a general
world outlook resting upon a definite conception of the relation between matter and mind and the special form in which this world out-

look was expressed at a definite historical stage, namely, in the eighteenth century. More than that, he lumps it with the shallow, vulgarized
form in which the materialism of the eighteenth century continues
to exist today in the heads of naturalists and physicians, the form
which was preached on their tours in the fifties by Büchner, Vogt, and
Moleschott. But just as idealism underwent a series of stages of
development, so also did materialism. With each epoch-making discovery even in the sphere of natural science it has to change its form,
and after history also was subjected to materialistic treatment a new
avenue of development has opened here, too.

The materialism of the last century was predominantly mechanical,
because at that time, of all natural sciences, only mechanics, and
indeed only the mechanics of solid bodies—celestial and terrestrial—
in short, the mechanics of gravity, had come to any definite close.
Chemistry at that time existed only in its infantile, phlogistic form.
Biology still lay in swaddling clothes; vegetable and animal organisms
had been only roughly examined, and were explained as the result
of purely mechanical cause. What the animal was to Descartes, man
was to the materialists of the eighteenth century—a machine. This
exclusive application of the standards of mechanics to processes of a
chemical and organic nature—in which processes the laws of mechanics are, indeed, also valid, but are pushed into the background
by other, higher laws—constitutes the first specific but at that time
inevitable limitation of classical French materialism.

The second specific limitation of this materialism lay in its inability
to comprehend the universe as a process, as matter undergoing uninterrupted historical development. This was in accordance with the
level of the natural science of that time, and with the metaphysical, that
is, anti-dialectical, manner of philosophizing connected with it. Nature
—so much was known—was in eternal motion. But according to the
ideas of that time, this motion turned, also eternally, in a circle and
therefore never moved from the spot; it produced the same results over
and over again. This conception was at that time inevitable. The
Kantian theory of the origin of the solar system had been put forward
but recently, and was still regarded merely as a curiosity. The history
of the development of the earth, geology, was still totally unknown,
and the conception that the animate natural beings of today are the
result of a long sequence of development from the simple to the complex could not at that time scientifically be put forward at all. The
unhistorical view of nature was therefore inevitable. We have the

less reason to reproach the philosophers of the eighteenth century on this account since the same thing is found in Hegel. According to him, nature, as a mere "alienation" of the Idea, is incapable of development in time—capable only of extending its manifoldness in space, so that it displays simultaneously and alongside of one another all the stages of development comprised in it, and is condemned to an eternal repetition of the same processes. This absurdity of a development in space, but outside of time—the fundamental condition of all development—Hegel imposes upon nature just at the very time when geology, embryology, the physiology of plants and animals, and organic chemistry were being built up, and when everywhere on the basis of these new sciences brilliant foreshadowings of the later theory of evolution were appearing (for instance, Goethe and Lamarck). But the system demanded it; hence the method, for the sake of the system, had to become untrue to itself.

This same unhistorical conception prevailed also in the domain of history. Here the struggle against the remnants of the Middle Ages blurred the view. The Middle Ages were regarded as a mere interruption of history by a thousand years of universal barbarism. The great progress made in the Middle Ages—the extension of the area of European culture, the viable great nations taking form there next to each other, and finally the enormous technical progress of the fourteenth and fifteenth centuries—all this was not seen. Thus a rational insight into the great historical interconnections was made impossible, and history served at best as a collection of examples and illustrations for the use of philosophers.

The vulgarizing peddlers, who in Germany in the fifties dabbled in materialism, by no means overcame this limitation of their teachers. All the advances of natural science which had been made in the meantime served them only as new proofs against the existence of a creator of the world; and, indeed, they did not in the least make it their business to develop the theory any further. Though idealism was at the end of its tether and was dealt a deathblow by the Revolution of 1848, it had the satisfaction of seeing that materialism had for the moment fallen lower still. Feuerbach was unquestionably right when he refused to take responsibility for this materialism, only he should not have confounded the doctrines of these itinerant preachers with materialism in general.

Here, however, there are two things to be pointed out. First, even during Feuerbach's lifetime natural science was still in that process of violent fermentation which only during the last fifteen years had reached a clarifying, relative conclusion. New scientific data were acquired to a hitherto unheard-of extent, but the establishing of interrelations, and thereby the bringing of order into this chaos of discoveries following closely upon each other's heels, has only quite recently become possible. It is true that Feuerbach had lived to see all three of the decisive discoveries—that of the cell, the transformation of energy, and the theory of evolution, named after Darwin. But how could the lonely philosopher, living in rural solitude, be able sufficiently to follow scientific developments in order to appreciate at their full value discoveries which natural scientists themselves at that time either still contested or did not know how to make adequate use of? The blame for this falls solely upon the wretched conditions in Germany, in consequence of which cobweb-spinning eclectic flea crackers had taken possession of the chairs of philosophy, while Feuerbach, who towered above them all, had to rusticate and grow sour in a little village. It is therefore not Feuerbach's fault that the historical conception of nature, which had now become possible and which removed all the one-sidedness of French materialism, remained inaccessible to him.

Second, Feuerbach is quite correct in asserting that exclusively natural-scientific materialism is indeed "the foundation of the edifice of human knowledge, but not the edifice itself." For we live not only in nature but also in human society, and this also no less than nature has its history of development and its science. It was therefore a question of bringing the science of society, that is, the sum total of the so-called historical and philosophical sciences, into harmony with the materialist foundation, and of reconstructing it thereupon. But it did not fall to Feuerbach's lot to do this. . . .

Section IV

THE THEORY OF DIALECTICAL AND HISTORICAL MATERIALISM

The dialectic applied to matter—correct philosophical method put to work on the real stuff of the world—provides the skeleton of dialectical materialism. What flesh was put on these bones? Marx and Engels believed that dialectical materialism applied to the course of world history could yield but one result, and the theory of history that they thus derived was called historical materialism.

In brief, historical materialism is the theory that history can only be understood as the development of human societies attempting in their several ways to meet the material needs of the different classes of which society is comprised. Since material and economic considerations are always paramount, the classes will always contend for control of the economic order. These class struggles will succeed one another in dialectical development, each dominant class necessarily giving rise to its own opposition, and to the new struggle that must lead to the next higher synthesis. "The history of all hitherto existing society," *The Communist Manifesto* begins, "is the history of class struggles."

The more detailed development of historical materialism will disclose the precise character of the present stage in the series of class struggles. Marx and Engels said that under the capitalist system, the current stage, dialectical conflict is concentrated in the clash of two great economic classes: the bourgeoisie, which controls the means of production and distribution, and the proletariat, or the mass of exploited industrial workers.

The selections in this section present the Marxist treatment of the background and character of this stage of world history and what Marxists think will be the following stage. Capitalism, Marx held, is but one of

88

a long series of phases through which the dialectic of history must move. Marx's economic treatise *Capital* is, as he subtitled it, "a critique of political economy," an attempt to describe and analyze the real character of the capitalist system, disclosing the essential contradictions contained within it. He believed that these internal contradictions, which dialectical materialism laid bare, must result in the downfall of the capitalist system and its eventual replacement by a new synthesis.

13. KARL MARX and FRIEDRICH ENGELS

In 1847 Marx was asked by a small group which called itself the International Communist League to prepare a statement of policy for the meeting of that group the coming year. He agreed to do so, and with Engels' help produced what is now known as the Communist Manifesto. *In this, their most famous and powerful work, Marx and Engels are consciously applying the principles of materialism and dialectical method to the problems of society. Into a pamphlet of only thirty-five pages, they compress a general theory of history, an analysis of the ills of European society, and a detailed program of revolutionary action. But the* Manifesto *is more than a program, more than an analytical and tightly woven argument: it is an impassioned plea for the union of the laboring classes. "Let the ruling classes tremble at a Communist revolution. The proletarians have nothing to lose but their chains. They have a world to win. Workingmen of all countries, unite!"*

Manifesto of the Communist Party*

A specter is haunting Europe—the specter of Communism. All the powers of old Europe have entered into a holy alliance to exorcise this specter: Pope and Czar, Metternich and Guizot, French Radicals and German police-spies.

Where is the party in opposition that has not been decried as communistic by its opponents in power? Where the Opposition that

* Reprinted here in its entirety, with the exception of Part III, a short diatribe against certain socialist groups of their time with whom Marx and Engels violently disagreed.

has not hurled back the branding reproach of Communism, against the more advanced opposition parties, as well as against its reactionary adversaries?

Two things result from this fact:

I. Communism is already acknowledged by all European powers to be itself a power.

II. It is high time that Communists should openly, in the face of the whole world, publish their views, their aims, their tendencies, and meet this nursery tale of the specter of Communism with a manifesto of the party itself.

To this end, Communists of various nationalities have assembled in London, and sketched the following manifesto, to be published in the English, French, German, Italian, Flemish and Danish languages.

I. Bourgeois and Proletarians

The history of all hitherto existing society is the history of class struggles.

Freeman and slave, patrician and plebeian, lord and serf, guildmaster and journeyman, in a word, oppressor and oppressed, stood in constant opposition to one another, carried on an uninterrupted, now hidden, now open fight, a fight that each time ended, either in a revolutionary reconstitution of society at large, or in the common ruin of the contending classes.

In the earlier epochs of history, we find almost everywhere a complicated arrangement of society into various orders, a manifold gradation of social rank. In ancient Rome we have patricians, knights, plebeians, slaves; in the Middle Ages, feudal lords, vassals, guild-masters, journeymen, apprentices, serfs; in almost all of these classes, again, subordinate gradations.

The modern bourgeois society that has sprouted from the ruins of feudal society, has not done away with class antagonisms. It has but established new classes, new conditions of oppression, new forms of struggle in place of the old ones.

Our epoch, the epoch of the bourgeoisie, possesses, however, this distinctive feature: It has simplified the class antagonisms. Society as a whole is more and more splitting up into two great hostile camps, into two great classes directly facing each other—bourgeoisie and proletariat.

From the serfs of the Middle Ages sprang the chartered burghers of the earliest towns. From these burgesses the first elements of the bourgeoisie were developed.

The discovery of America, the rounding of the Cape, opened up fresh ground for the rising bourgeoisie. The East-Indian and Chinese markets, the colonization of America, trade with the colonies, the increase in the means of exchange and in commodities generally, gave to commerce, to navigation, to industry, an impulse never before known, and thereby, to the revolutionary element in the tottering feudal society, a rapid development.

The feudal system of industry, in which industrial production was monopolized by closed guilds, now no longer sufficed for the growing wants of the new markets. The manufacturing system took its place. The guild-masters were pushed aside by the manufacturing middle class; division of labor between the different corporate guilds vanished in the face of division of labor in each single workshop.

Meantime the markets kept ever growing, the demand ever rising. Even manufacture no longer sufficed. Thereupon, steam and machinery revolutionized industrial production. The place of manufacture was taken by the giant, modern industry, the place of the industrial middle class, by industrial millionaires—the leaders of whole industrial armies, the modern bourgeois.

Modern industry has established the world market, for which the discovery of America paved the way. This market has given an immense development to commerce, to navigation, to communication by land. This development has, in its turn, reacted on the extension of industry; and in proportion as industry, commerce, navigation, railways extended, in the same proportion the bourgeoisie developed, increased its capital, and pushed into the background every class handed down from the Middle Ages.

We see, therefore, how the modern bourgeoisie is itself the product of a long course of development, of a series of revolutions in the modes of production and of exchange.

Each step in the development of the bourgeoisie was accompanied by a corresponding political advance of that class. An oppressed class under the sway of the feudal nobility, it became an armed and self-governing association in the medieval commune; here independent urban republic (as in Italy and Germany), there taxable "third estate" of the monarchy (as in France); afterwards, in the period of manufacture proper, serving either the semi-feudal or the absolute monarchy as a counterpoise against the nobility, and, in fact, corner-stone of the great monarchies in general—the bourgeoisie has at last, since the establishment of modern industry and of the world market, conquered for itself, in the modern representative state, exclusive political sway. The executive of the modern state is but a committee for managing the common affairs of the whole bourgeoisie.

The bourgeoisie has played a most revolutionary rôle in history.

The bourgeoisie, wherever it has got the upper hand, has put an end to all feudal, patriarchal, idyllic relations. It has pitilessly torn asunder the motley feudal ties that bound man to his "natural superiors," and has left no other bond between man and man than naked self-interest, than callous "cash payment." It has drowned the most heavenly ecstasies of religious fervor, of chivalrous enthusiasm, of philistine sentimentalism, in the icy water of egotistical calculation. It has resolved personal worth into exchange value, and in place of the numberless indefeasible chartered freedoms, has set up that single, unconscionable freedom—Free Trade. In one word, for exploitation, veiled by religious and political illusions, it has substituted naked, shameless, direct, brutal exploitation.

The bourgeoisie has stripped of its halo every occupation hitherto honored and looked up to with reverent awe. It has converted the physician, the lawyer, the priest, the poet, the man of science, into its paid wage-laborers.

The bourgeoisie has torn away from the family its sentimental veil, and has reduced the family relation to a mere money relation.

The bourgeoisie has disclosed how it came to pass that the brutal display of vigor in the Middle Ages, which reactionaries so much admire, found its fitting complement in the most slothful indolence. It has been the first to show what man's activity can bring about. It has accomplished wonders far surpassing Egyptian pyramids, Roman aqueducts, and Gothic cathedrals; it has conducted expeditions that put in the shade all former migrations of nations and crusades.

The bourgeoisie cannot exist without constantly revolutionizing the instruments of production, and thereby the relations of production, and with them the whole relations of society. Conservation of the old modes of production in unaltered form, was, on the contrary, the first condition of existence for all earlier industrial classes. Constant revolutionizing of production, uninterrupted disturbance of all social conditions, everlasting uncertainty and agitation distinguish the bourgeois epoch from all earlier ones. All fixed, fast-frozen relations, with their train of ancient and venerable prejudices and opinions, are swept away, all new-formed ones become antiquated before they can ossify. All that is solid melts into air, all that is holy is profaned, and man is at last compelled to face with sober senses his real conditions of life and his relations with his kind.

The need of a constantly expanding market for its products chases the bourgeoisie over the whole surface of the globe. It must nestle everywhere, settle everywhere, establish connections everywhere.

The bourgeoisie has through its exploitation of the world market given a cosmopolitan character to production and consumption in every country. To the great chagrin of reactionaries, it has drawn from under the feet of industry the national ground on which it stood. All old-established national industries have been destroyed or are daily being destroyed. They are dislodged by new industries, whose introduction becomes a life and death question for all civilized nations, by industries that no longer work up indigenous raw material, but raw material drawn from the remotest zones; industries whose products are consumed, not only at home, but in every quarter of the globe. In place of the old wants, satisfied by the production of the country, we find new wants, requiring for their satisfaction the products of distant lands and climes. In place of the old local and national seclusion and self-sufficiency, we have intercourse in every direction, universal inter-dependence of nations. And as in material, so also in intellectual production. The intellectual creations of individual nations become common property. National one-sidedness and narrow-mindedness become more and more impossible, and from the numerous national and local literatures there arises a world literature.

The bourgeoisie, by the rapid improvement of all instruments of production, by the immensely facilitated means of communication, draws all nations, even the most barbarian, into civilization. The cheap prices of its commodities are the heavy artillery with which it batters down all Chinese walls, with which it forces the barbarians' intensely obstinate hatred of foreigners to capitulate. It compels all nations, on pain of extinction, to adopt the bourgeois mode of production; it compels them to introduce what it calls civilization into their midst, i.e., to become bourgeois themselves. In a word, it creates a world after its own image.

The bourgeoisie has subjected the country to the rule of the towns. It has created enormous cities, has greatly increased the urban population as compared with the rural, and has thus rescued a considerable part of the population from the idiocy of rural life. Just as it has made the country dependent on the towns, so it has made barbarian and semi-barbarian countries dependent on the civilized ones, nations of peasants on nations of bourgeois, the East on the West.

More and more the bourgeoisie keeps doing away with the scattered state of the population, of the means of production, and of property. It has agglomerated population, centralized means of production, and has concentrated property in a few hands. The necessary consequence of this was political centralization. Independent, or but loosely connected provinces, with separate interests, laws, governments and systems of taxation, became lumped together into one nation, with one government, one code of laws, one national class interest, one frontier and one customs tariff.

The bourgeoisie, during its rule of scarce one hundred years, has created more massive and more colossal productive forces than have all preceding generations together. Subjection of nature's forces to man, machinery, application of chemistry to industry and agriculture, steam-navigation, railways, electric telegraphs, clearing of whole continents for cultivation, canalization of rivers, whole populations conjured out of the ground—what earlier century had even a presentiment that such productive forces slumbered in the lap of social labor?

We see then that the means of production and of exchange, which served as the foundation for the growth of the bourgeoisie, were generated in feudal society. At a certain stage in the development of these means of production and of exchange, the conditions under which feudal society produced and exchanged, the feudal organization of agriculture and manufacturing industry, in a word, the feudal relations of property became no longer compatible with the already developed productive forces; they became so many fetters. They had to be burst asunder; they were burst asunder.

Into their place stepped free competition, accompanied by a social and political constitution adapted to it, and by the economic and political sway of the bourgeois class.

A similar movement is going on before our own eyes. Modern bourgeois society with its relations of production, of exchange and of property, a society that has conjured up such gigantic means of production and of exchange, is like the sorcerer who is no longer able to control the powers of the nether world whom he has called up by his spells. For many a decade past the history of industry and commerce is but the history of the revolt of modern productive forces against modern conditions of production, against the property relations that are the conditions for the existence of the bourgeoisie and of its rule. It is enough to mention the commercial crises that by their periodical return put the existence of the entire bourgeois society on trial, each time more threateningly. In these crises a great part not only of the existing products, but also of the previously created productive forces, are periodically destroyed. In these crises there breaks out an epidemic that, in all earlier epochs, would have seemed an absurdity—the epidemic of over-production. Society suddenly finds itself put back into a state of momentary barbarism; it appears as if a famine, a universal war of devastation had cut off the supply of every means of subsistence; industry and commerce seem to be destroyed. And why? Because there is too much civilization, too much means of subsistence, too much industry, too much commerce. The productive forces at the disposal of society no longer tend to further the development of the conditions of bourgeois property; on the contrary, they have become too powerful for these conditions, by which they are fettered, and no sooner do they overcome these fetters than they bring disorder into the whole of bourgeois society, endanger the existence of bourgeois property. The conditions of bourgeois society are too narrow to comprise the wealth created by them. And how does the bourgeoisie get over these crises? On the one hand by enforced destruction of a mass of productive forces; on the other, by the conquest of new markets, and by the more thorough exploitation of the old ones. That is to say, by paving the way for more extensive and more destructive crises, and by diminishing the means whereby crises are prevented.

The weapons with which the bourgeoisie felled feudalism to the ground are now turned against the bourgeoisie itself.

But not only has the bourgeoisie forged the weapons that bring death to itself; it has also called into existence the men who are to wield those weapons—the modern working class—the proletarians.

In proportion as the bourgeoisie, i.e., capital, is developed, in the same proportion is the proletariat, the modern working class, developed—a class of laborers, who live only so long as they find work, and who find work only so long as their labor increases capital. These laborers, who must sell themselves piecemeal, are a commodity, like every other article of commerce, and are consequently exposed to all the vicissitudes of competition, to all the fluctuations of the market.

Owing to the extensive use of machinery and to division of labor, the work of the proletarians has lost all individual character, and, consequently, all charm for the workman. He becomes an appendage of the machine, and it is only the most simple, most monotonous, and most easily acquired knack, that is required of him. Hence, the cost of production of a workman is restricted, almost entirely, to the means of subsistence that he requires for his maintenance, and for the propagation of his race. But the price of a commodity, and there-fore also of labor, is equal to its cost of production. In proportion, therefore, as the repulsiveness of the work increases, the wage de-creases. Nay more, in proportion as the use of machinery and division of labor increases, in the same proportion the burden of toil also increases, whether by prolongation of the working hours, by increase of the work exacted in a given time, or by increased speed of the machinery, etc.

Modern industry has converted the little workshop of the patri-archal master into the great factory of the industrial capitalist. Masses of laborers, crowded into the factory, are organized like soldiers. As privates of the industrial army they are placed under the command of a perfect hierarchy of officers and sergeants. Not only are they slaves of the bourgeois class, and of the bourgeois state; they are daily and hourly enslaved by the machine, by the over-looker, and, above all, by the individual bourgeois manufacturer himself. The more openly this despotism proclaims gain to be its end and aim, the more petty, the more hateful and the more embittering it is.

The less the skill and exertion of strength implied in manual labor, in other words, the more modern industry develops, the more is the labor of men superseded by that of women. Differences of age and sex have no longer any distinctive social validity for the working class. All are instruments of labor, more or less expensive to use, according to their age and sex.

No sooner has the laborer received his wages in cash, for the mo-ment escaping exploitation by the manufacturer, than he is set upon by the other portions of the bourgeoisie, the landlord, the shop-keeper, the pawnbroker, etc.

The lower strata of the middle class—the small tradespeople, shopkeepers, and retired tradesmen generally, the handicraftsmen and peasants—all these sink gradually into the proletariat, partly because their diminutive capital does not suffice for the scale on which modern industry is carried on, and is swamped in the competition with the large capitalists, partly because their specialized skill is rendered worthless by new methods of production. Thus the proletariat is recruited from all classes of the population.

The proletariat goes through various stages of development. With its birth begins its struggle with the bourgeoisie. At first the contest is carried on by individual laborers, then by the work people of a factory, then by the operatives of one trade, in one locality, against the individual bourgeois who directly exploits them. They direct their attacks not against the bourgeois conditions of production, but against the instruments of production themselves; they destroy imported wares that compete with their labor, they smash machinery to pieces, they set factories ablaze, they seek to restore by force the vanished status of the workman of the Middle Ages.

At this stage the laborers still form an incoherent mass scattered over the whole country, and broken up by their mutual competition. If anywhere they unite to form more compact bodies, this is not yet the consequence of their own active union, but of the union of the bourgeoisie, which class, in order to attain its own political ends, is compelled to set the whole proletariat in motion, and is moreover still able to do so for a time. At this stage, therefore, the proletarians do not fight their enemies, but the enemies of their enemies, the remnants of absolute monarchy, the landowners, the non-industrial bourgeois, the petty bourgeoisie. Thus the whole historical movement is concentrated in the hands of the bourgeoisie; every victory so obtained is a victory for the bourgeoisie.

But with the development of industry the proletariat not only increases in number; it becomes concentrated in greater masses, its strength grows, and it feels that strength more. The various interests and conditions of life within the ranks of the proletariat are more and more equalized, in proportion as machinery obliterates all distinctions of labor and nearly everywhere reduces wages to the same low level. The growing competition among the bourgeois, and the resulting commercial crises, make the wages of the workers ever more fluctuating. The unceasing improvement of machinery, ever more rapidly developing, makes their livelihood more and more precarious; the collisions between individual workmen and individual bourgeois take more and more the character of collisions between two classes. Thereupon the workers begin to form combinations (trade unions) against the bourgeoisie; they club together in order to keep up the rate of wages; they found permanent associations in order to make provision beforehand for these occasional revolts. Here and there the contest breaks out into riots.

Now and then the workers are victorious, but only for a time. The real fruit of their battles lies, not in the immediate result, but in the ever expanding union of the workers. This union is furthered by the improved means of communication which are created by modern industry, and which place the workers of different localities in contact with one another. It was just this contact that was needed to centralize the numerous local struggles, all of the same character, into one national struggle between classes. But every class struggle is a political struggle. And that union, to attain which the burghers of the Middle Ages, with their miserable highways, required centuries, the modern proletarians, thanks to railways, achieve in a few years.

This organization of the proletarians into a class, and consequently into a political party, is continually being upset again by the competition between the workers themselves. But it ever rises up again, stronger, firmer, mightier. It compels legislative recognition of particular interests of the workers, by taking advantage of the divisions among the bourgeoisie itself. Thus the ten-hour bill in England was carried.

Altogether, collisions between the classes of the old society further the course of development of the proletariat in many ways. The bourgeoisie finds itself involved in a constant battle. At first with the aristocracy; later on, with those portions of the bourgeoisie itself whose interests have become antagonistic to the progress of industry; at all times with the bourgeoisie of foreign countries. In all these battles it sees itself compelled to appeal to the proletariat, to ask for its help, and thus, to drag it into the political arena. The bourgeoisie itself, therefore, supplies the proletariat with its own elements of political and general education, in other words, it furnishes the proletariat with weapons for fighting the bourgeoisie.

Further, as we have already seen, entire sections of the ruling classes are, by the advance of industry, precipitated into the proletariat, or are at least threatened in their conditions of existence. These also supply the proletariat with fresh elements of enlightenment and progress.

Finally, in times when the class struggle nears the decisive hour, the process of dissolution going on within the ruling class, in fact within the whole range of old society, assumes such a violent, glaring character, that a small section of the ruling class cuts itself adrift, and joins the revolutionary class, the class that holds the future in its hands. Just as, therefore, at an earlier period, a section of the nobility went over to the bourgeoisie, so now a portion of the bourgeoisie goes over to the proletariat, and in particular, a portion of the bourgeois ideologists, who have raised themselves to the level of comprehending theoretically the historical movement as a whole.

Of all the classes that stand face to face with the bourgeoisie today, the proletariat alone is a really revolutionary class. The other classes decay and finally disappear in the face of modern industry; the proletariat is its special and essential product.

The lower middle class, the small manufacturer, the shopkeeper, the artisan, the peasant, all these fight against the bourgeoisie, to save from extinction their existence as fractions of the middle class. They are therefore not revolutionary, but conservative. Nay more, they are reactionary, for they try to roll back the wheel of history. If by chance they are revolutionary, they are so only in view of their impending transfer into the proletariat; they thus defend not their present, but their future interests; they desert their own standpoint to adopt that of the proletariat.

The "dangerous class," the social scum (*Lumpenproletariat*), that passively rotting mass thrown off by the lowest layers of old society, may, here and there, be swept into the movement by a proletarian revolution; its conditions of life, however, prepare it far more for the part of a bribed tool of reactionary intrigue.

The social conditions of the old society no longer exist for the proletariat. The proletarian is without property; his relation to his wife and children has no longer anything in common with bourgeois family relations; modern industrial labor, modern subjection to capital, the same in England as in France, in America as in Germany, has stripped him of every trace of national character. Law, morality, religion, are to him so many bourgeois prejudices, behind which lurk in ambush just as many bourgeois interests.

All the preceding classes that got the upper hand, sought to fortify their already acquired status by subjecting society at large to their conditions of appropriation. The proletarians cannot become masters of the productive forces of society, except by abolishing their own previous mode of appropriation, and thereby also every other previous mode of appropriation. They have nothing of their own to secure and to fortify; their mission is to destroy all previous securities for, and insurances of, individual property.

All previous historical movements were movements of minorities, or in the interest of minorities. The proletarian movement is the self-conscious, independent movement of the immense majority, in the interest of the immense majority. The proletariat, the lowest stratum of our present society, cannot stir, cannot raise itself up, without the whole superincumbent strata of official society being sprung into the air.

Though not in substance, yet in form, the struggle of the proletariat with the bourgeoisie is at first a national struggle. The proletariat of each country must, of course, first of all settle matters with its own bourgeoisie.

In depicting the most general phases of the development of the proletariat, we traced the more or less veiled civil war, raging within existing society, up to the point where that war breaks out into open revolution, and where the violent overthrow of the bourgeoisie lays the foundation for the sway of the proletariat.

Hitherto, every form of society has been based, as we have already seen, on the antagonism of oppressing and oppressed classes. But in order to oppress a class, certain conditions must be assured to it under which it can, at least, continue its slavish existence. The serf, in the period of serfdom, raised himself to membership in the commune, just as the petty bourgeois, under the yoke of feudal absolutism, managed to develop into a bourgeois. The modern laborer, on the contrary, instead of rising with the progress of industry, sinks deeper and deeper below the conditions of existence of his own class. He becomes a pauper, and pauperism develops more rapidly than population and wealth. And here it becomes evident, that the bourgeoisie is unfit any longer to be the ruling class in society, and to impose its conditions of existence upon society as an over-riding law. It is unfit to rule because it is incompetent to assure an existence to its slave within his slavery, because it cannot help letting him sink into such a state, that it has to feed him, instead of being fed by him. Society can no longer live under this bourgeoisie, in other words, its existence is no longer compatible with society.

The essential condition for the existence and sway of the bourgeois class, is the formation and augmentation of capital; the condition for capital is wage-labor. Wage-labor rests exclusively on competition between the laborers. The advance of industry, whose involuntary promoter is the bourgeoisie, replaces the isolation of the laborers, due to competition, by their revolutionary combination, due to association. The development of modern industry, therefore, cuts from under its feet the very foundation on which the bourgeoisie produces and appropriates products. What the bourgeoisie therefore produces, above all, are its own grave-diggers. Its fall and the victory of the proletariat are equally inevitable.

II. Proletarians and Communists

In what relation do the Communists stand to the proletarians as a whole?

The Communists do not form a separate party opposed to other working class parties.

They have no interests separate and apart from those of the proletariat as a whole.

They do not set up any sectarian principles of their own, by which to shape and mold the proletarian movement.

The Communists are distinguished from the other working class parties by this only: 1. In the national struggles of the proletarians of the different countries, they point out and bring to the front the common interests of the entire proletariat, independently of all nationality. 2. In the various stages of development which the struggle of the working class against the bourgeoisie has to pass through, they always and everywhere represent the interests of the movement as a whole.

The Communists, therefore, are on the one hand, practically, the most advanced and resolute section of the working class parties of every country, that section which pushes forward all others; on the other hand, theoretically, they have over the great mass of the proletariat the advantage of clearly understanding the line of march, the conditions, and the ultimate general results of the proletarian movement.

The immediate aim of the Communists is the same as that of all the other proletarian parties: Formation of the proletariat into a class, overthrow of bourgeois supremacy, conquest of political power by the proletariat.

The theoretical conclusions of the Communists are in no way

based on ideas or principles that have been invented, or discovered, by this or that would-be universal reformer.

They merely express, in general terms, actual relations springing from an existing class struggle, from a historical movement going on under our very eyes. The abolition of existing property relations is not at all a distinctive feature of Communism.

All property relations in the past have continually been subject to historical change consequent upon the change in historical conditions. The French Revolution, for example, abolished feudal property in favor of bourgeois property.

The distinguishing feature of Communism is not the abolition of property generally, but the abolition of bourgeois property. But modern bourgeois private property is the final and most complete expression of the system of producing and appropriating products that is based on class antagonisms, on the exploitation of the many by the few.

In this sense, the theory of the Communists may be summed up in the single sentence: Abolition of private property.

We Communists have been reproached with the desire of abolishing the right of personally acquiring property as the fruit of a man's own labor, which property is alleged to be the groundwork of all personal freedom, activity and independence.

Hard-won, self-acquired, self-earned property! Do you mean the property of the petty artisan and of the small peasant, a form of property that preceded the bourgeois form? There is no need to abolish that; the development of industry has to a great extent already destroyed it, and is still destroying it daily.

Or do you mean modern bourgeois private property?

But does wage-labor create any property for the laborer? Not a bit. It creates capital, i.e., that kind of property which exploits wage-labor, and which cannot increase except upon condition of begetting a new supply of wage-labor for fresh exploitation. Property, in its present form, is based on the antagonism of capital and wage-labor. Let us examine both sides of this antagonism.

To be a capitalist, is to have not only a purely personal, but a social *status* in production. Capital is a collective product, and only by the united action of many members, nay, in the last resort, only by the united action of all members of society, can it be set in motion.

Capital is therefore not a personal, it is a social, power.

When, therefore, capital is converted into common property, into the property of all members of society, personal property is not thereby transformed into social property. It is only the social character of the property that is changed. It loses its class character. Let us now take wage-labor.

The average price of wage-labor is the minimum wage, i.e., that quantum of the means of subsistence which is absolutely requisite to keep the laborer in bare existence as a laborer. What, therefore, the wage-laborer appropriates by means of his labor, merely suffices to prolong and reproduce a bare existence. We by no means intend to abolish this personal appropriation of the products of labor, an appropriation that is made for the maintenance and reproduction of human life, and that leaves no surplus wherewith to command the labor of others. All that we want to do away with is the miserable character of this appropriation, under which the laborer lives merely to increase capital, and is allowed to live only insofar as the interest of the ruling class requires it.

In bourgeois society, living labor is but a means to increase accumulated labor. In Communist society, accumulated labor is but a means to widen, to enrich, to promote the existence of the laborer.

In bourgeois society, therefore, the past dominates the present; in Communist society, the present dominates the past. In bourgeois society capital is independent and has individuality, while the living person is dependent and has no individuality.

And the abolition of this state of things is called by the bourgeois, abolition of individuality and freedom! And rightly so. The abolition of bourgeois individuality, bourgeois independence, and bourgeois freedom is undoubtedly aimed at.

By freedom is meant, under the present bourgeois conditions of production, free trade, free selling and buying.

But if selling and buying disappears, free selling and buying disappears also. This talk about free selling and buying, and all the other "brave words" of our bourgeoisie about freedom in general, have a meaning, if any, only in contrast with restricted selling and buying, with the fettered traders of the Middle Ages, but have no meaning when opposed to the Communist abolition of buying and selling, of the bourgeois conditions of production, and of the bourgeoisie itself.

You are horrified at our intending to do away with private property. But in your existing society, private property is already done away with for nine-tenths of the population; its existence for the few is solely due to its non-existence in the hands of those nine-tenths. You reproach us, therefore, with intending to do away with a form of property, the necessary condition for whose existence is the non-existence of any property for the immense majority of society.

In a word, you reproach us with intending to do away with your property. Precisely so; that is just what we intend.

From the moment when labor can no longer be converted into capital, money, or rent, into a social power capable of being monopolized, i.e., from the moment when individual property can no longer be transformed into bourgeois property, into capital, from that moment, you say, individuality vanishes.

You must, therefore, confess that by "individual" you mean no other person than the bourgeois, than the middle class owner of property. This person must, indeed, be swept out of the way, and made impossible.

Communism deprives no man of the power to appropriate the products of society; all that it does is to deprive him of the power to subjugate the labor of others by means of such appropriation.

It has been objected, that upon the abolition of private property all work will cease, and universal laziness will overtake us.

According to this, bourgeois society ought long ago to have gone to the dogs through sheer idleness; for those of its members who work, acquire nothing, and those who acquire anything, do not work. The whole of this objection is but another expression of the tautology: There can no longer be any wage-labor when there is no longer any capital.

All objections urged against the Communist mode of producing and appropriating material products, have, in the same way, been urged against the Communist modes of producing and appropriating intellectual products. Just as, to the bourgeois, the disappearance of class property is the disappearance of production itself, so the disappearance of class culture is to him identical with the disappearance of all culture.

That culture, the loss of which he laments is, for the enormous majority, a mere training to act as a machine.

But don't wrangle with us so long as you apply, to our intended abolition of bourgeois property, the standard of your bourgeois notions of freedom, culture, law, etc. Your very ideas are but the outgrowth of the conditions of your bourgeois production and bourgeois property, just as your jurisprudence is but the will of your class made into a law for all, a will whose essential character and direction are determined by the economic conditions of existence of your class.

The selfish misconception that induces you to transform into eternal laws of nature and of reason, the social forms springing from your present mode of production and form of property—historical relations that rise and disappear in the progress of production—this misconception you share with every ruling class that has preceded you. What you see clearly in the case of ancient property, what you admit in the case of feudal property, you are of course forbidden to admit in the case of your own bourgeois form of property.

Abolition of the family! Even the most radical flare up at this infamous proposal of the Communists.

On what foundation is the present family, the bourgeois family, based? On capital, on private gain. In its completely developed form this family exists only among the bourgeoisie. But this state of things finds its complement in the practical absence of the family among the proletarians, and in public prostitution.

The bourgeois family will vanish as a matter of course when its complement vanishes, and both will vanish with the vanishing of capital.

Do you charge us with wanting to stop the exploitation of children by their parents? To this crime we plead guilty.

But, you will say, we destroy the most hallowed of relations, when we replace home education by social.

And your education! Is not that also social, and determined by the social conditions under which you educate, by the intervention of society, direct or indirect, by means of schools, etc.? The Communists have not invented the intervention of society in education; they do but seek to alter the character of that intervention, and to rescue education from the influence of the ruling class.

The bourgeois claptrap about the family and education, about the hallowed co-relation of parent and child, becomes all the more disgusting, the more, by the action of modern industry, all family ties among the proletarians are torn asunder, and their children transformed into simple articles of commerce and instruments of labor.

But you Communists would introduce community of women, screams the whole bourgeoisie in chorus.

The bourgeois sees in his wife a mere instrument of production.

He hears that the instruments of production are to be exploited in common, and, naturally, can come to no other conclusion than that the lot of being common to all will likewise fall to the women.

He has not even a suspicion that the real point aimed at is to do away with the status of women as mere instruments of production.

For the rest, nothing is more ridiculous than the virtuous indignation of our bourgeois at the community of women which, they pretend, is to be openly and officially established by the Communists. The Communists have no need to introduce community of women; it has existed almost from time immemorial.

Our bourgeois, not content with having the wives and daughters of their proletarians at their disposal, not to speak of common prostitutes, take the greatest pleasure in seducing each other's wives.

Bourgeois marriage is in reality a system of wives in common and thus, at the most, what the Communists might possibly be reproached with is that they desire to introduce, in substitution for a hypocritically concealed, an openly legalized community of women. For the rest, it is self-evident, that the abolition of the present system of production must bring with it the abolition of the community of women springing from that system, i.e., of prostitution both public and private.

The Communists are further reproached with desiring to abolish countries and nationality.

The workingmen have no country. We cannot take from them what they have not got. Since the proletariat must first of all acquire political supremacy, must rise to be the leading class of the nation, must constitute itself *the* nation, it is, so far, itself national, though not in the bourgeois sense of the word.

National differences and antagonisms between peoples are vanishing gradually from day to day, owing to the development of the bourgeoisie, to freedom of commerce, to the world market, to uniformity in the mode of production and in the conditions of life corresponding thereto.

The supremacy of the proletariat will cause them to vanish still faster. United action, of the leading civilized countries at least, is one of the first conditions for the emancipation of the proletariat.

In proportion as the exploitation of one individual by another is put an end to, the exploitation of one nation by another will also be put an end to. In proportion as the antagonism between classes within the nation vanishes, the hostility of one nation to another will come to an end.

The charges against Communism made from a religious, a philosophical, and, generally, from an ideological standpoint, are not deserving of serious examination.

Does it require deep intuition to comprehend that man's ideas, views, and conceptions, in one word, man's consciousness, changes with every change in the conditions of his material existence, in his social relations and in his social life?

What else does the history of ideas prove, than that intellectual production changes its character in proportion as material production is changed? The ruling ideas of each age have ever been the ideas of its ruling class.

When people speak of ideas that revolutionize society, they do but express the fact that within the old society the elements of a new one have been created, and that the dissolution of the old ideas keeps even pace with the dissolution of the old conditions of existence.

When the ancient world was in its last throes, the ancient religions were overcome by Christianity. When Christian ideas succumbed in the 18th century to rationalist ideas, feudal society fought its death-battle with the then revolutionary bourgeoisie. The ideas of religious liberty and freedom of conscience, merely gave expression to the sway of free competition within the domain of knowledge.

"Undoubtedly," it will be said, "religion, moral, philosophical and juridical ideas have been modified in the course of historical development. But religion, morality, philosophy, political science, and law, constantly survived this change.

"There are, besides, eternal truths, such as Freedom, Justice, etc., that are common to all states of society. But Communism abolishes eternal truths, it abolishes all religion, and all morality, instead of constituting them on a new basis; it therefore acts in contradiction to all past historical experience."

What does this accusation reduce itself to? The history of all past society has consisted in the development of class antagonisms, antagonisms that assumed different forms at different epochs.

But whatever form they may have taken, one fact is common to all past ages, viz., the exploitation of one part of society by the other. No wonder, then, that the social consciousness of past ages, despite all the multiplicity and variety it displays, moves within certain common forms, or general ideas, which cannot completely vanish except with the total disappearance of class antagonisms.

The Communist revolution is the most radical rupture with traditional property relations; no wonder that its development involves the most radical rupture with traditional ideas.

But let us have done with the bourgeois objections to Communism.

We have seen above, that the first step in the revolution by the working class, is to raise the proletariat to the position of ruling class, to establish democracy.

The proletariat will use its political supremacy to wrest, by degrees, all capital from the bourgeoisie, to centralize all instruments of production in the hands of the state, i.e., of the proletariat organized as the ruling class; and to increase the total of productive forces as rapidly as possible.

Of course, in the beginning, this cannot be effected except by means of despotic inroads on the rights of property, and on the conditions of bourgeois production; by means of measures, therefore, which appear economically insufficient and untenable, but which, in the course of the movement, outstrip themselves, necessitate further inroads upon the old social order, and are unavoidable as a means of entirely revolutionizing the mode of production.

These measures will of course be different in different countries. Nevertheless in the most advanced countries, the following will be pretty generally applicable.

1. Abolition of property in land and application of all rents of land to public purposes.

2. A heavy progressive or graduated income tax.

3. Abolition of all right of inheritance.

4. Confiscation of the property of all emigrants and rebels.

5. Centralization of credit in the hands of the state, by means of a national bank with state capital and an exclusive monopoly.

6. Centralization of the means of communication and transport in the hands of the state.

7. Extension of factories and instruments of production owned by the state; the bringing into cultivation of waste lands, and the improvement of the soil generally in accordance with a common plan.

8. Equal obligation of all to work. Establishment of industrial armies, especially for agriculture.

9. Combination of agriculture with manufacturing industries;

gradual abolition of the distinction between town and country, by a more equable distribution of the population over the country.

10. Free education for all children in public schools. Abolition of child factory labor in its present form. Combination of education with industrial production, etc.

When, in the course of development, class distinctions have disappeared, and all production has been concentrated in the hands of a vast association of the whole nation, the public power will lose its political character. Political power, properly so called, is merely the organized power of one class for oppressing another. If the proletariat during its contest with the bourgeoisie is compelled, by the force of circumstances, to organize itself as a class; if, by means of a revolution, it makes itself the ruling class, and, as such sweeps away by force the old conditions of production, then it will, along with these conditions, have swept away the conditions for the existence of class antagonisms, and of classes generally, and will thereby have abolished its own supremacy as a class.

In place of the old bourgeois society, with its classes and class antagonisms, we shall have an association, in which the free development of each is the condition for the free development of all. . . .

IV. Position of the Communists in Relation to the Various Existing Opposition Parties

Section II has made clear the relations of the Communists to the existing working class parties, such as the Chartists in England and the Agrarian Reformers in America.

The Communists fight for the attainment of the immediate aims, for the enforcement of the momentary interests of the working class; but in the movement of the present, they also represent and take care of the future of that movement. In France the Communists ally themselves with the Social-Democrats, against the conservative and radical bourgeoisie, reserving, however, the right to take up a critical position in regard to phrases and illusions traditionally handed down from the great Revolution.

In Switzerland they support the Radicals, without losing sight of the fact that this party consists of antagonistic elements, partly of Democratic Socialists, in the French sense, partly of radical bourgeois.

In Poland they support the party that insists on an agrarian revolution as the prime condition for national emancipation, that party which fomented the insurrection of Cracow in 1846.

In Germany they fight with the bourgeoisie whenever it acts in a revolutionary way, against the absolute monarchy, the feudal squire-archy, and the petty bourgeoisie.

But they never cease, for a single instant, to instil into the working class the clearest possible recognition of the hostile antagonism between bourgeoisie and proletariat, in order that the German workers may straightway use, as so many weapons against the bourgeoisie, the social and political conditions that the bourgeoisie must necessarily introduce along with its supremacy, and in order that, after the fall of the reactionary classes in Germany, the fight against the bourgeoisie itself may immediately begin.

The Communists turn their attention chiefly to Germany, because that country is on the eve of a bourgeois revolution that is bound to be carried out under more advanced conditions of European civilization and with a much more developed proletariat than what existed in England in the 17th and in France in the 18th century, and because the bourgeois revolution in Germany will be but the prelude to an immediately following proletarian revolution.

In short, the Communists everywhere support every revolutionary movement against the existing social and political order of things.

In all these movements they bring to the front, as the leading question in each case, the property question, no matter what its degree of development at the time.

Finally, they labor everywhere for the union and agreement of the democratic parties of all countries.

The Communists disdain to conceal their views and aims. They openly declare that their ends can be attained only by the forcible overthrow of all existing social conditions. Let the ruling classes tremble at a Communist revolution. The proletarians have nothing to lose but their chains. They have a world to win.

Workingmen of all countries, unite!

14. VLADIMIR I. LENIN *

V. I. Lenin (1870-1924) was the leader of the successful communist revolution in Russia in 1917, and the founder of the present Soviet Government. Some of his theoretical contributions to communist philosophy will appear in later sections of this volume. The Teachings of Karl Marx, from which the following selection is taken, was intended to be purely expository. Here Lenin presents a straightforward explanation of the concepts of value and surplus value as he understood them to be employed in Marx's economic writings.

Marx's Economic Doctrine†

"It is the ultimate aim of this work to reveal the economic law of motion of modern society" (that is to say, capitalist, bourgeois society), writes Marx in the preface to the first volume of *Capital.* The study of the production relationships in a given, historically determinate society, in their genesis, their development, and their decay—such is the content of Marx's economic teaching. In capitalist society the dominant feature is the production of *commodities,* and Marx's analysis therefore begins with an analysis of a commodity.

Value

A commodity is, firstly, something that satisfies a human need; and, secondly, it is something that is exchanged for something else. The utility of a thing gives it *use-value.* Exchange-value (or simply, value) presents itself first of all as the proportion, the ratio, in which a certain number of use-values of one kind are exchanged for a certain number of use-values of another kind. Daily experience shows

---

* Lenin's original name was Vladimir Ilyich Ulyanov, although he later came to be known as Nikolai Lenin. Following the most usual practice, however, he will be referred to here as Vladimir I. Lenin.—*Ed.*

† This and the following passages are from *The Teachings of Karl Marx.* Reprinted by permission of the Foreign Languages Publishing House, Moscow.

us that by millions upon millions of such exchanges, all and sundry use-values in themselves very different and not comparable one with another, are equated to one another. Now, what is common in these various things which are constantly weighed one against another in a definite system of social relationships? That which is common to them is that they are *products of labor*. In exchanging products, people equate to one another most diverse kinds of labor. The production of commodities is a system of social relationships in which different producers produce various products (the social division of labor), and in which all these products are equated to one another in exchange. Consequently, the element common to all commodities is not concrete labor in a definite branch of production, not labor of one particular kind, but *abstract* human labor—human labor in general. All the labor power of a given society, represented in the sum total of values of all commodities, is one and the same human labor power. Millions upon millions of acts of exchange prove this. Consequently, each particular commodity represents only a certain part of *socially necessary* labor time. The magnitude of the value is determined by the amount of socially necessary labor, or by the labor time that is socially requisite for the production of the given commodity of the given use-value. ". . . Exchanging labor products of different kinds one for another, they equate the values of the exchanged products; and in doing so they equate the different kinds of labor expended in production, treating them as homogeneous human labor. They do not know that they are doing this, but they do it." As one of the earlier economists said, value is a relationship between two persons, only he should have added that it is a relationship hidden beneath a material wrapping. We can only understand what value is when we consider it from the point of view of a system of social production relationships in one particular historical type of society; and, moreover, of relationships which present themselves in a mass form, the phenomenon of exchange repeating itself millions upon millions of times. "As values, all commodities are only definite quantities of congealed labor time." Having made a detailed analysis of the twofold character of the labor incorporated in commodities, Marx goes on to analyze the *form of value and of money*. His main task, then, is to study the *origin* of the money form of value, to study the *historical process* of the development of exchange, beginning with isolated and casual acts of exchange ("simple, isolated, or casual value form," in which a given quantity of one commodity is exchanged for a given quantity of another), passing on to the universal form of value, in which a number of different commodities are exchanged for one and the same particular commodity, and ending with the money form of value, when gold becomes this particular commodity, the universal equivalent. Being the highest product of the development of exchange and of commodity production, money masks the social character of individual labor, and hides the social tie between the various producers who come together in the market. Marx analyzes in great detail the various functions of money; and it is essential to note that here (as generally in the opening chapters of *Capital*) what appears to be an abstract and at times purely deductive mode of exposition in reality reproduces a gigantic collection of facts concerning the history of the development of exchange and commodity production.

> Money . . . presupposes a definite level of commodity exchange. The various forms of money (simple commodity equivalent or means of circulation, or means of payment, treasure, or international money) indicate, according to the different extent to which this or that function is put into application, and according to the comparative predominance of one or other of them, very different grades of the social process of production. [*Capital,* Vol. I.]

Surplus Value

At a particular stage in the development of commodity production, money becomes transformed into capital. The formula of commodity circulation was C-M-C (commodity—money—commodity); the sale of one commodity for the purpose of buying another. But the general formula of capital, on the contrary, is M-C-M (money—commodity —money); purchase for the purpose of selling—at a profit. The designation "surplus value" is given by Marx to the increase over the original value of money that is put into circulation. The fact of this "growth" of money in capitalist society is well known. Indeed, it is this "growth" which transforms money into *capital* as a special, historically defined, social relationship of production. Surplus value cannot arise out of the circulation of commodities, for this represents nothing more than the exchange of equivalents; it cannot arise out of an advance in prices, for the mutual losses and gains of buyers and sellers would equalize one another; and we are concerned here, not with what happens to individuals, but with a mass or average or social phenomenon. In order that he may be able to receive surplus value, "Moneybags must . . . find in the market a commodity whose use-value has the peculiar quality of being a source of value"—a commodity, the actual process of whose use is at the same time the process of the creation of value. Such a commodity exists. It is human labor power. Its use is labor, and labor creates value. The owner of money buys labor power at its value, which is determined, like the value of every other commodity, by the socially necessary labor time requisite for its production (that is to say, the cost of maintaining the worker and his family). Having bought labor power, the owner of money is entitled to use it, that is to set it to work for the whole day —twelve hours, let us suppose. Meanwhile, in the course of six hours ("necessary" labor time) the laborer produces sufficient to pay back the cost of his own maintenance; and in the course of the next six hours ("surplus" labor time), he produces a "surplus" product for which the capitalist does not pay him—surplus product or surplus value. In capital, therefore, from the viewpoint of the process of production, we have to distinguish between two parts: first, constant capital, expended for the means of production (machinery, tools, raw materials, etc.), the value of this being (all at once or part by part) transferred, unchanged, to the finished product; and, secondly, variable capital, expended for labor power. The value of this latter capital is not constant, but grows in the labor process, creating surplus value. To express the degree of exploitation of labor power by capital, we must therefore compare the surplus value, not with the whole capital, but only with the variable capital. Thus, in the example just given, the rate of surplus value, as Marx calls this relationship, will be 6:6, i.e., 100%.

There are two historical prerequisites to the genesis of capital: first, accumulation of a considerable sum of money in the hands of individuals living under conditions in which there is a comparatively high development of commodity production. Second, the existence of workers who are "free" in a double sense of the term: free from any constraint or restriction as regards the sale of their labor power; free from any bondage to the soil or to the means of production in general—i.e., of propertyless workers, of "proletarians" who cannot maintain their existence except by the sale of their labor power.

There are two fundamental ways in which surplus value can be increased: by an increase in the working day ("absolute surplus value"); and by a reduction in the necessary working day ("relative surplus value"). Analyzing the former method, Marx gives an impressive picture of the struggle of the working class for shorter hours and of government interference, first (from the fourteenth century to the seventeenth) in order to lengthen the working day, and subsequently (factory legislation of the nineteenth century) to shorten it. Since the appearance of *Capital,* the history of the working-class movement in all lands provides a wealth of new facts to amplify this picture. . . .

Of extreme importance and originality is Marx's analysis of the *accumulation of capital,* that is to say, the transformation of a portion of surplus value into capital and the applying of this portion to additional production, instead of using it to supply the personal needs or to gratify the whims of the capitalist. Marx pointed out the mistake made by earlier classical political economy (from Adam Smith on), which assumed that all the surplus value which was transformed into capital became variable capital. In actual fact, it is divided into *means of production* plus variable capital. The more rapid growth of constant capital as compared with variable capital in the sum total of capital is of immense importance in the process of development of capitalism and in that of the transformation of capitalism into Socialism.

The accumulation of capital, accelerating the replacement of workers by machinery, creating wealth at the one pole and poverty at the other, gives birth to the so-called "reserve army of labor," to a "relative over-abundance" of workers or to "capitalist over-population." This assumes the most diversified forms, and gives capital the possibility of expanding production at an exceptionally rapid rate. This possibility, in conjunction with enhanced facilities for credit and with the accumulation of capital in the means of production, furnishes, among other things the key to the understanding of the *crises* of overproduction that occur periodically in capitalist countries—first about every ten years, on an average, but subsequently in a more continuous form and with a less definite periodicity. From accumulation of capital upon a capitalist foundation we must distinguish the so-called "primitive accumulation": the forcible severance of the worker from the means of production, the driving of the peasants off the land, the stealing of the communal lands, the system of colonies and national debts, of protective tariffs, and the like. "Primitive accumulation" creates, at one pole, the "free" proletarian: at the other, the owner of money, the capitalist. . . .

15. KARL MARX

The last years of Marx's life were spent in an arduous attempt to give a definitive account of the principles, excesses, and contradictions of the capitalist economy. The result, never completed, was Capital (Das Kapital). *In Part VII of the first volume of* Capital, *from which the following passages are taken, several of Marx's laws of the behavior of capital are explained, and their effects described.*

[The Composition of Capital] *

In this chapter we consider the influence of the growth of capital on the lot of the laboring class. The most important factor in this inquiry, is the composition of capital and the changes it undergoes in the course of the process of accumulation.

The composition of capital is to be understood in a two-fold sense. On the side of value, it is determined by the proportion in which it is divided into constant capital or value of the means of production, and variable capital or value of labor-power, the sum total of wages. On the side of material, as it functions in the process of production, all capital is divided into means of production and living labor-power. This latter composition is determined by the relation between the mass of the means of production employed, on the one hand, and the mass of labor necessary for their employment on the other. I call the former the *value composition,* the latter the *technical composition* of capital. Between the two there is a strict correlation. To express this, I call the value-composition of capital, insofar as it is determined

* From K. Marx, *Capital.* This and the following selections are reprinted from the original English translation by Samuel Moore and Edward Aveling, edited by Friedrich Engels, and published by Swan Sonnenschein, Lowery, and Co., London, 1887.

by its technical composition and mirrors the changes of the latter, the *organic composition* of capital. Wherever I refer to the composition of capital, without further qualification, its organic composition is always understood.

The many individual capitals invested in a particular branch of production have, one with another, more or less different compositions. The average of their individual compositions gives us the composition of the total capital in this branch of production. Lastly, the average of these averages, in all branches of production, gives us the composition of the total social capital of a country, and with this alone are we, in the last resort, concerned in the following investigation.

[The Law of Capitalist Accumulation]

Growth of capital involves growth of its variable constituent or of the part invested in labor-power. A part of the surplus-value turned into additional capital must always be retransformed into variable capital, or additional labor-fund. If we suppose that, all other circumstances remaining the same, the composition of capital also remains constant (i.e., that a definite mass of means of production constantly needs the same mass of labor-power to set in motion), then the demand for labor and the subsistence-fund of the laborers clearly increase in the same proportion as the capital, and the more rapidly, the more rapidly the capital increases. . . . As simple reproduction constantly reproduces the capital-relation itself, i.e., the relation of capitalists on the one hand, and wage-workers on the other, so reproduction on a progressive scale, i.e., accumulation, reproduces the capital relation on a progressive scale, more capitalists or larger capitalists at this pole, more wage-workers at that. The reproduction of a mass of labor-power, which must incessantly reincorporate itself with capital for that capital's self-expansion; which cannot get free from capital, and whose enslavement to capital is only concealed by the variety of individual capitalists to whom it sells itself, this reproduction of labor-power forms, in fact, an essential of the reproduction of capital itself. Accumulation of capital is, therefore, increase of the proletariat. . . .

The law of capitalist production, that is at the bottom of the pretended "natural law of population," reduces itself simply to this: The correlation between accumulation of capital and rate of wages is nothing else than the correlation between the unpaid labor transformed into capital, and the additional paid labor necessary for the setting in motion of this additional capital. It is therefore in no way a relation between two magnitudes, independent one of the other: on the one hand, the magnitude of the capital; on the other, the number of the laboring population; it is rather, at bottom, only the relation between the unpaid and the paid labor of the same laboring population. If the quantity of unpaid labor supplied by the working-class, and accumulated by the capitalist class, increases so rapidly that its conversion into capital requires an extraordinary addition of paid labor, then wages rise, and, all other circumstances remaining equal, the unpaid labor diminishes in proportion. But as soon as this diminution touches the point at which the surplus-labor that nourishes capital is no longer supplied in normal quantity, a reaction sets in: a smaller part of revenue is capitalized, accumulation lags, and the movement of rise in wages receives a check. The rise of wages therefore is confined within limits that not only leave intact the foundations of the capitalistic system, but also secure its reproduction on a progressive scale. The law of capitalistic accumulation, metamorphosed by economists into a pretended law of nature, in reality merely states that the very nature of accumulation excludes every diminution in the degree of exploitation of labor, and every rise in the price of labor, which could seriously imperil the continual reproduction, on an ever enlarging scale, of the capitalistic relation. It cannot be otherwise in a mode of production in which the laborer exists to satisfy the needs of self-expansion of existing values, instead of on the contrary, material wealth existing to satisfy the needs of development on the part of the laborer. As, in religion, man is governed by the products of his own brain, so in capitalistic production, he is governed by the products of his own hand.

In Part IV * it was shown, how the development of the productiveness of social labor presupposes co-operation on a large scale; how it is only upon this supposition that division and combination of labor can be organized, and the means of production economized

---

* In Part IV, Marx explains that surplus value may be increased not only by increasing the length of the working day, but also by increasing the productivity of the worker. This reduces the time required for the laborer to produce the value needed for his own subsistence. By increasing productivity, therefore, the capitalist is enabled to take a larger *proportion* of the value created during the working day. This Marx calls "the production of relative surplus value."—*Ed.*

by concentration on a vast scale; how instruments of labor which, from their very nature, are only fit for use in common, such as a system of machinery, can be called into being; how huge natural forces can be pressed into the service of production; and how the transformation can be effected of the process of production into a technological application of science. On the basis of the production of commodities, where the means of production are the property of private persons, and where the artisan therefore either produces commodities, isolated from and independent of others, or sells his labor-power as a commodity, because he lacks the means for independent industry, co-operation on a large scale can realize itself only in the increase of individual capitals, only in proportion as the means of social production and the means of subsistence are transformed into the private property of capitalists. The basis of the production of commodities can admit of production on a large scale in the capitalistic form alone. A certain accumulation of capital, in the hands of individual producers of commodities, forms therefore the necessary preliminary of the specifically capitalistic mode of production. We had, therefore, to assume that this occurs during the transition from handicraft to capitalistic industry. It may be called primitive accumulation, because it is the historic basis, instead of the historic result of specifically capitalist production. How it itself originates, we need not here inquire as yet. It is enough that it forms the starting point. But all methods for raising the social productive power of labor that are developed on this basis, are at the same time methods for the increased production of surplus-value or surplus-product, which in its turn is the formative element of accumulation. They are, therefore, at the same time methods of the production of capital by capital, or methods of its accelerated accumulation. The continual retransformation of surplus-value into capital now appears in the shape of the increasing magnitude of the capital that enters into the process of production. This in turn is the basis of an extended scale of production, of the methods for raising the productive power of labor that accompany it, and of accelerated production of surplus-value. If, therefore, a certain degree of accumulation of capital appears as a condition of the specifically capitalist mode of production, the latter causes conversely an accelerated accumulation of capital. With the accumulation of capital, therefore, the specifically capitalistic mode of production develops, and with the capitalist mode of production the accumulation of capital. Both these economic factors bring about, in the compound ratio of the impulses they reciprocally give one another, that change in the technical composition of capital by which the variable constituent becomes always smaller and smaller as compared with the constant. . . .

[The Law of the Concentration of Capital]

Every individual capital is a larger or smaller concentration of means of production, with a corresponding command over a larger or smaller labor-army. Every accumulation becomes the means of new accumulation. With the increasing mass of wealth which functions as capital, accumulation increases the concentration of that wealth in the hands of individual capitalists, and thereby widens the basis of production on a large scale and of the specific methods of capitalist production. The growth of social capital is effected by the growth of many individual capitals. All other circumstances remaining the same, individual capitals, and with them the concentration of the means of production, increase in such proportion as they form aliquot parts of the total social capital. At the same time portions of the original capitals disengage themselves and function as new independent capitals. Besides other causes, the division of property, within capitalist families, plays a great part in this. With the accumulation of capital, therefore, the number of capitalists grows to a greater or lesser extent. Two points characterize this kind of concentration which grows directly out of, or rather is identical with, accumulation. First: The increasing concentration of the social means of production in the hands of individual capitalists is, other things remaining equal, limited by the degree of increase of social wealth. Second: The part of social capital domiciled in each particular sphere of production is divided among many capitalists who face one another as independent commodity-producers competing with each other. Accumulation and the concentration accompanying it are, therefore, not only scattered over many points, but the increase of each functioning capital is thwarted by the formation of new and the subdivision of old capitals. Accumulation, therefore, presents itself on the one hand as increasing concentration of the means of production, and of the command over labor; on the other, as repulsion of many individual capitals one from another.

This splitting-up of the total social capital into many individual capitals or the repulsion of its fractions one from another, is counteracted by their attraction. This last does not mean that simple concentration of the means of production and of the command over labor, which is identical with accumulation. It is concentration of capitals already formed, destruction of their individual independence, expropriation of capitalist by capitalist, transformation of many small into few large capitals. This process differs from the former in this, that it only presupposes a change in the distribution of capital already to hand, and functioning; its field of action is therefore not limited by the absolute growth of social wealth, by the absolute limits of accumulation. Capital grows in one place to a huge mass in a single hand, because it has in another place been lost by many. This is centralization proper, as distinct from accumulation and concentration.

The laws of this centralization of capitals, or of the attraction of capital by capital, cannot be developed here. A brief hint at a few facts must suffice. The battle of competition is fought by cheapening of commodities. The cheapness of commodities depends, *cæteris paribus,* on the productiveness of labor, and this again on the scale of production. Therefore, the larger capitals beat the smaller. It will further be remembered that, with the development of the capitalist mode of production, there is an increase in the minimum amount of individual capital necessary to carry on a business under its normal conditions. The smaller capitals, therefore, crowd into spheres of production which modern industry has only sporadically or incompletely got hold of. Here competition rages in direct proportion to the number, and in inverse proportion to the magnitudes, of the antagonistic capitals. It always ends in the ruin of many small capitalists, whose capitals partly pass into the hand of their conquerors, partly vanish. Apart from this, with capitalist production an altogether new force comes into play—the credit system. Not only is this itself a new and mighty weapon in the battle of competition. By unseen threads it, moreover, draws the disposable money, scattered in larger or smaller masses over the surface of society, into the hands of individual or associated capitalists. It is the specific machine for the centralization of capitals.

The centralization of capitals or the process of their attraction becomes more intense, in proportion as the specifically capitalist mode of production develops along with accumulation. In its turn, centralization becomes one of the greatest levers of this development. It shortens and quickens the transformation of separate processes of production into processes socially combined and carried out on a large scale.

The increasing bulk of individual masses of capital becomes the material basis of an uninterrupted revolution in the mode of production itself. Continually the capitalist mode of production conquers branches of industry not yet wholly, or only sporadically, or only formally, subjugated by it. At the same time there grow up on its soil new branches of industry, such as could not exist without it. Finally, in the branches of industry already carried on upon the capitalist basis, the productiveness of labor is made to ripen, as if in a hothouse. In all these cases, the number of laborers falls in proportion to the mass of the means of production worked up by them. An ever increasing part of the capital is turned into means of production, an ever decreasing one into labor-power. With the extent, the concentration and the technical efficiency of the means of production, the degree lessens progressively, in which the latter are means of employment for laborers. A steam plow is an incomparably more efficient means of production than an ordinary plow, but the capital-value laid out in it is an incomparably smaller means for employing men than if it were laid out in ordinary plows. At first, it is the mere adding of new capital to old, which allows of the expansion and technical revolution of the material conditions of the process of production. But soon the change of composition and the technical transformation get more or less completely hold of all old capital that has reached the term of its reproduction, and therefore has to be replaced. This metamorphosis of old capital is independent, to a certain extent, of the absolute growth of social capital, in the same way as its centralization. But this centralization which only redistributes the social capital already to hand, and melts into one a number of old capitals, works in its turn as a powerful agent in this metamorphosis of old capital.

On the one hand, therefore, the additional capital formed in the course of accumulation attracts fewer and fewer laborers in proportion to its magnitude. On the other hand, the old capital periodically reproduced with change of composition, repels more and more of the laborers formerly employed by it.

[The Law of Increasing Misery]

The greater the social wealth, the functioning capital, the extent and energy of its growth, and, therefore, also the absolute mass of the proletariat and the productiveness of its labor, the greater is the industrial reserve-army. The same causes which develop the expansive power of capital, develops also the labor-power at its disposal. The relative mass of the industrial reserve-army increases therefore with the potential energy of wealth. But the greater this reserve-army in proportion to the active labor-army, the greater is the mass of a consolidated surplus population, whose misery is in inverse ratio to its torment of labor. The more extensive, finally, the Lazarus-layers of the working-class, and the industrial reserve-army, the greater is official pauperism. *This is the absolute general law of capitalist accumulation.* Like all other laws it is modified in its working by many circumstances, the analysis of which does not concern us here.

The folly is now patent of the economic wisdom that preaches to the laborers the accommodation of their number to the requirements of capital. The mechanism of capitalist production and accumulation constantly effects this adjustment. The first word of this adaptation is the creation of a relative surplus population, or industrial reserve-army. Its last word is the misery of constantly extending strata of the active army of labor, and the dead weight of pauperism.

The law by which a constantly increasing quantity of means of production, thanks to the advance in the productiveness of social labor, may be set in movement by a progressively diminishing expenditure of human power, this law, in a capitalist society—where the laborer does not employ the means of production, but the means of production employ the laborer—undergoes a complete inversion and is expressed thus: the higher the productiveness of labor, the greater is the pressure of the laborers on the means of employment, the more precarious, therefore, becomes their condition of existence, viz., the sale of their own labor-power for the increasing of another's wealth, or for the self-expansion of capital. The fact that the means of production, and the productiveness of labor, increase more rapidly than the productive population, expresses itself, therefore, capitalistically in the inverse form that the laboring population always increases more rapidly than the conditions under which capital can employ this increase for its own self-expansion.

We saw in Part IV, when analyzing the production of relative surplus value: within the capitalist system all methods for raising the social productiveness of labor are brought about at the cost of the individual laborer; all means for the development of production transform themselves into means of domination over, and exploitation of, the producers; they mutilate the laborer into a fragment of a man, degrade him to the level of an appendage of a machine, destroy every remnant of charm in his work and turn it into a hated toil; they estrange from him the intellectual potentialities of the labor-process in the same proportion as science is incorporated in it as an independent power; they distort the conditions under which he works, subject him during the labor-process to a despotism the more hateful for its meanness; they transform his lifetime into working time, and drag his wife and child beneath the wheels of the juggernaut of capital. But all methods for the production of surplus value are at the same time methods of accumulation; and every extension of accumulation becomes again a means for the development of those methods. It follows therefore that in proportion as capital accumulates, the lot of the laborer, be his payment high or low, must grow worse. The law, finally, that always equilibrates the relative surplus population, or industrial reserve-army, to the extent and energy of accumulation, this law rivets the laborer to capital more firmly than the wedges of Vulcan did Prometheus to the rock. It establishes an accumulation of misery, corresponding with accumulation of capital. Accumulation of wealth at one pole is, therefore, at the same time accumulation of misery, agony of toil, slavery, ignorance, brutality, mental degradation, at the opposite pole, i.e., on the side of the class that produces its own product in the form of capital.

16. FRIEDRICH ENGELS

The following selection is the third Part of Engels' Socialism, Utopian and Scientific, *of which the two earlier Parts have been included in Part One, Sections I and II, of this volume. Even more clearly than* The Communist Manifesto, *this passage presents the general theory of historical materialism, as well as its conclusions about the future of capitalism and about the classless society which was, Engels believed, its inevitable successor. This is probably the best single short statement of the communist world view.*

[Scientific Socialism] *

The materialist conception of history starts from the proposition that the production of the means to support human life and, next to production, the exchange of things produced, is the basis of all social structure; that in every society that has appeared in history, the manner in which wealth is distributed and society divided into classes or orders is dependent upon what is produced, how it is produced, and how the products are exchanged. From this point of view the final causes of all social changes and political revolutions are to be sought, not in men's brains, not in man's better insight into eternal truth and justice, but in changes in the modes of production and exchange. They are to be sought, not in the *philosophy,* but in the *economics* of each particular epoch. The growing perception that existing social institutions are unreasonable and unjust, that reason has become un-reason, and right wrong, is only proof that in the modes of production and exchange changes have silently taken place, with which the social order, adapted to earlier economic conditions, is no longer in keeping. From this it also follows that the means of getting rid of the incon-gruities that have been brought to light must also be present, in a more or less developed condition, within the changed modes of production themselves. These means are not to be invented by de-duction from fundamental principles, but are to be discovered in the stubborn facts of the existing system of production.

What is, then, the position of modern socialism in this connection? The present structure of society—this is now pretty generally con-ceded—is the creation of the ruling class of today, of the bourgeoisie. The mode of production peculiar to the bourgeoisie, known, since Marx, as the capitalist mode of production, was incompatible with the feudal system, with the privileges it conferred upon individuals, entire social ranks and local corporations, as well as with the hereditary ties of subordination which constituted the framework of its social organization. The bourgeoisie broke up the feudal system and built upon its ruins the capitalist order of society, the kingdom of free competition, of personal liberty, of equality before the law of all commodity owners, and of all the rest of the capitalist blessings.

* From F. Engels, *Socialism, Utopian and Scientific,* Swan Sonnenschein and Co., London, 1892.

Thenceforward the capitalist mode of production could develop in freedom. Since steam, machinery and the making of machines by machinery transformed the older manufacture into modern industry, the productive forces evolved under the guidance of the bourgeoisie developed with a rapidity and in a degree unheard of before. But just as the older manufacture, in its time, and handicraft, becoming more developed under its influence, had come into collision with the feudal trammels of the guilds, so now modern industry, in its more complete development, comes into collision with the bounds within which the capitalistic mode of production holds it confined. The new productive forces have already outgrown the capitalistic mode of using them. And this conflict between productive forces and modes of production is not a conflict engendered in the mind of man, like that between original sin and divine justice. It exists, in fact, objectively, outside us, independently of the will and actions even of the men that have brought it on. Modern socialism is nothing but the reflex, in thought, of this conflict in fact; its ideal reflection in the minds, first, of the class directly suffering under it, the working class.

Now, in what does this conflict consist?

Before capitalistic production, i.e., in the Middle Ages, the system of petty industry obtained generally, based upon the private property of the laborers in their means of production; in the country, the agriculture of the small peasant, freeman or serf; in the towns, the handicrafts organized in guilds. The instruments of labor—land, agricultural implements, the workshop, the tool—were the instruments of labor of single individuals, adapted for the use of one worker, and, therefore, of necessity, small, dwarfish, circumscribed. But for this very reason they belonged, as a rule, to the producer himself. To concentrate these scattered, limited means of production, to enlarge them, to turn them into the powerful levers of production of the present day—this was precisely the historic rôle of capitalist production and of its upholder, the bourgeoisie. In Part IV of *Capital* Marx has explained in detail, how since the fifteenth century this has been historically worked out through the three phases of simple co-operation, manufacture and modern industry. But the bourgeoisie, as is also shown there, could not transform these puny means of production into mighty productive forces, without transforming them, at the same time, from means of production of the individual into *social* means of production only workable by a collectivity of men. The spinning-wheel, the hand-loom, the blacksmith's hammer were replaced by the spinning machine, the power-loom, the steam-hammer; the individual workshop, by the factory, implying the co-operation of hundreds and thousands of workmen. In like manner, production itself changed from a series of individual into a series of social acts, and the products from individual to social products. The yarn, the cloth, the metal articles that now came out of the factory were the joint product of many workers, through whose hands they had successively to pass before they were ready. No one person could say of them: "I made that; this is *my* product."

But where, in a given society, the fundamental form of production is that spontaneous division of labor which creeps in gradually and not upon any preconceived plan, there the products take on the form of *commodities,* whose mutual exchange, buying and selling, enable the individual producers to satisfy their manifold wants. And this was the case in the Middle Ages. The peasant, e.g., sold to the artisan agricultural products and bought from him the products of handicraft. Into this society of individual producers, of commodity producers, the new mode of production thrust itself. In the midst of the old division of labor, grown up spontaneously and upon *no definite plan,* which had governed the whole of society, now arose division of labor upon a *definite plan,* as organized in the factory; side by side with *individual* production appeared *social* production. The products of both were sold in the same market, and, therefore, at prices at least approximately equal. But organization upon a definite plan was stronger than spontaneous division of labor. The factories working with the combined social forces of a collectivity of individuals produced their commodities far more cheaply than the individual small producers. Individual production succumbed in one department after another. Socialized production revolutionized all the old methods of production. But its revolutionary character was, at the same time, so little recognized, that it was, on the contrary, introduced as a means of increasing and developing the production of commodities. When it arose, it found ready-made, and made liberal use of, certain machinery for the production and exchange of commodities; merchants' capital, handicraft, wage labor. Socialized production thus introducing itself as a new form of the production of commodities, it was a matter of course that under it the old forms of appropriation remained in full swing, and were applied to its products as well.

In the medieval stage of evolution of the production of commodities, the question as to the owner of the product of labor could not arise. The individual producer, as a rule, had, from raw material belonging to himself, and generally his own handiwork, produced it with his own tools, by the labor of his own hands or of his family. There was no need for him to appropriate the new product. It belonged wholly to him, as a matter of course. His property in the product was, therefore, based *upon his own labor*. Even where external help was used, this was, as a rule, of little importance, and very generally was compensated by something other than wages. The apprentices and journeymen of the guilds worked less for board and wages than for education, in order that they might become master craftsmen themselves.

Then came the concentration of the means of production and of the producers in large workshops and manufactories, their transformation into actual socialized means of production and socialized producers. But the socialized producers and means of production and their products were still treated, after this change, just as they had been before, i.e., as the means of production and the products of individuals. Hitherto, the owner of the instruments of labor had himself appropriated the product, because as a rule it was his own product and the assistance of others was the exception. Now the owner of the instruments of labor always appropriated to himself the product, although it was no longer *his* product but exclusively the product of the *labor of others*. Thus, the products now produced socially were not appropriated by those who had actually set in motion the means of production and actually produced the commodities, but by the *capitalists*. The means of production, and production itself, had become in essence socialized. But they were subjected to a form of appropriation which presupposes the private production of individuals, under which, therefore, everyone owns his own product and brings it to market. The mode of production is subjected to this form of appropriation, although it abolishes the conditions upon which the latter rests.*

* It is hardly necessary in this connection to point out, that, even if the form of appropriation remains the same, the *character* of the appropriation is just as much revolutionized as production is by the changes described above. It is, of course, a very different matter whether I appropriate to myself my own product or that of another. Note in passing that wage labor, which contains the whole capitalistic mode of production in embryo, is very ancient; in a sporadic, scattered form it existed for centuries alongside of slave labor. But the embryo could duly develop into the capitalistic mode of production only when the necessary historical pre-conditions had been furnished.

This contradiction, which gives to the new mode of production its capitalistic character, *contains the germ of the whole of the social antagonisms of today.* The greater the mastery obtained by the new mode of production over all important fields of production and in all manufacturing countries, the more it reduced individual production to an insignificant residuum, *the more clearly was brought out the incompatibility of socialized production with capitalistic appropriation.*

The first capitalists found, as we have said, alongside of other forms of labor, wage labor ready-made for them in the market. But it was exceptional, complimentary, necessary, transitory wage labor. The agricultural laborer, though, upon occasion, he hired himself out by the day, had a few acres of his own land on which he could at all events live at a pinch. The guilds were so organized that the journeyman of today became the master of tomorrow. But all this changed, as soon as the means of production became socialized and concentrated in the hands of capitalists. The means of production, as well as the product of the individual producer became more and more worthless; there was nothing left for him but to turn wage worker under the capitalist. Wage labor, aforetime the exception and accessory, now became the rule and basis of all production; aforetime complementary, it now became the sole remaining function of the worker. The wage worker for a time became a wage worker for life. The number of these permanent wage workers was further enormously increased by the breaking up of the feudal system that occurred at the same time, by the disbanding of the retainers of the feudal lords, the eviction of the peasants from their homesteads, etc. The separation was made complete between the means of production concentrated in the hands of the capitalists on the one side, and the producers, possessing nothing but their labor power, on the other. *The contradiction between socialized production and capitalistic appropriation manifested itself as the antagonism of proletariat and bourgeoisie.*

We have seen that the capitalistic mode of production thrust its way into a society of commodity producers, of individual producers, whose social bond was the exchange of their products. But every society, based upon the production of commodities, has this peculiarity: that the producers have lost control over their own social interrelations. Each man produces for himself with such means of production as he may happen to have, and for such exchange as he may require to satisfy his remaining wants. No one knows how much of his particular article is coming on the market, nor how much of it will be wanted. No one knows whether his individual product will meet an actual demand, whether he will be able to make good his cost of production or even to sell his commodity at all. Anarchy reigns in socialized production.

But the production of commodities, like every other form of production, has its peculiar inherent laws inseparable from it; and these laws work, despite anarchy, in and through anarchy. They reveal themselves in the only persistent form of social inter-relations, i.e., in exchange, and here they affect the individual producers as compulsory laws of competition. They are, at first, unknown to these producers themselves, and have to be discovered by them gradually and as the result of experience. They work themselves out, therefore, independently of the producers, and in antagonism to them, as inexorable natural laws of their particular form of production. The product governs the producers.

In medieval society, especially in the earlier centuries, production was essentially directed towards satisfying the wants of the individual. It satisfied, in the main, only the wants of the producer and his family. Where relations of personal dependence existed, as in the country, it also helped to satisfy the wants of the feudal lord. In all this there was, therefore, no exchange; the products, consequently, did not assume the character of commodities. The family of the peasant produced almost everything they wanted: clothes and furniture, as well as means of subsistence. Only when it began to produce more than was sufficient to supply its own wants and the payments in kind to the feudal lord, only then did it also produce commodities. This surplus, thrown into socialized exchange and offered for sale, became commodities.

The artisans of the towns, it is true, had from the first to produce for exchange. But they, also, themselves supplied the greatest part of their own individual wants. They had gardens and plots of land. They turned their cattle out into the communal forest, which, also, yielded them timber and firing. The women spun flax, wool, and so forth. Production for the purpose of exchange, production of commodities was only in its infancy. Hence, exchange was restricted, the market narrow, the methods of production stable; there was local exclusiveness without, local unity within; the mark in the country, in the town, the guild.

But with the extension of the production of commodities, and especially with the introduction of the capitalist mode of production, the laws of commodity production, hitherto latent, came into action more openly and with greater force. The old bonds were loosened, the old exclusive limits broken through, the producers were more and more turned into independent, isolated producers of commodities. It became apparent that the production of society at large was ruled by absence of plan, by accident, by anarchy; and this anarchy grew to greater and greater height. But the chief means by aid of which the capitalist mode of production intensified this anarchy of socialized production was the exact opposite of anarchy. It was the increasing organization of production, upon a social basis, in every individual productive establishment. By this, the old, peaceful, stable condition of things was ended. Wherever this organization of production was introduced into a branch of industry, it brooked no other method of production by its side. The field of labor became a battle ground. The great geographical discoveries, and the colonization following upon them, multiplied markets and quickened the transformation of handicraft into manufacture. The war did not simply break out between the individual producers of particular localities. The local struggles begat in their turn national conflicts, the commercial wars of the seventeenth and the eighteenth centuries.

Finally, modern industry and the opening of the world market made the struggle universal, and at the same time gave it an unheard-of virulence. Advantages in natural or artificial conditions of production now decide the existence or non-existence of individual capitalists, as well as of whole industries and countries. He that falls is remorselessly cast aside. It is the Darwinian struggle of the individual for existence transferred from nature to society with intensified violence. The conditions of existence natural to the animal appear as the final term of human development. The contradiction between socialized production and capitalistic appropriation now presents itself as *an antagonism between the organization of production in the individual workshop and the anarchy of production in society generally*.

The capitalistic mode of production moves in these two forms of the antagonism immanent to it from its very origin. It is never able to get out of that "vicious circle," which Fourier had already discovered. What Fourier could not, indeed, see in his time is: that this circle is gradually narrowing; that the movement becomes more and more a spiral, and must come to an end, like the movement of the planets, by collision with the center. It is the compelling force of anarchy in the production of society at large that more and more completely turns the great majority of men into proletarians; and it is the masses of the proletariat again who will finally put an end to anarchy in production. It is the compelling force of anarchy in social production that turns the limitless perfectibility of machinery under modern industry into a compulsory law by which every individual industrial capitalist must perfect his machinery more and more, under penalty of ruin.

But the perfecting of machinery is making human labor superfluous. If the introduction and increase of machinery means the displacement of millions of manual, by a few machine workers, improvement in machinery means the displacement of more and more of the machine workers themselves. It means, in the last instance, the production of a number of available wage workers in excess of the average needs of capital, the formation of a complete industrial reserve army, as I called it in 1845,* available at the times when industry is working at high pressure, to be cast out upon the street when the inevitable crash comes, a constant dead weight upon the limbs of the working class in its struggle for existence with capital, a regulator for the keeping of wages down to the low level that suits the interests of capital. Thus it comes about, to quote Marx, that machinery becomes the most powerful weapon in the war of capital against the working class; that the instruments of labor constantly tear the means of subsistence out of the hands of the laborer; that the very product of the worker is turned into an instrument for his subjugation. Thus it comes about that the economizing of the instruments of labor becomes at the same time, from the outset, the most reckless waste of labor power, and robbery based upon the normal conditions under which labor functions; that machinery, "the most powerful instrument for shortening labor time, becomes the most unfailing means for placing every moment of the laborer's time and that of his family at the disposal of the capitalist for the purpose of expanding the value of his capital." (*Capital,* p. 406, New York, 1939.) Thus it comes about that overwork of some becomes the preliminary condition for the idleness of others, and that modern industry, which hunts after new consumers over the whole world, forces the consumption of the masses at home down to a starvation minimum, and in doing thus destroys its own home market. "The law that always equilibrates the relative surplus

* *The Condition of the Working Class in England,* Sonnenschein and Co., p. 84.

population, or industrial reserve army, to the extent and energy of accumulation, this law rivets the laborer to capital more firmly than the wedges of Vulcan did Prometheus to the rock. It establishes an accumulation of misery, corresponding with accumulation of capital. Accumulation of wealth at one pole is, therefore, at the same time, accumulation of misery, agony of toil, slavery, ignorance, brutality, mental degradation, at the opposite pole, i.e., on the side of the class that produces *its own product in the form of capital.*" (Marx, *Capital,* p. 661, New York, 1939.) And to expect any other division of the products from the capitalistic mode of production is the same as expecting the electrodes of a battery not to decompose acidulated water, not to liberate oxygen at the positive, hydrogen at the negative pole, so long as they are connected with the battery.

We have seen that the ever-increasing perfectibility of modern machinery is, by the anarchy of social production, turned into a compulsory law that forces the individual industrial capitalist always to improve his machinery, always to increase its productive force. The bare possibility of extending the field of production is transformed for him into a similar compulsory law. The enormous expansive force of modern industry, compared with which that of gases is mere child's play, appears to us now as a *necessity* for expansion, both qualitative and quantitative, that laughs at all resistance. Such resistance is offered by consumption, by sales, by the markets for the products of modern industry. But the capacity for extension, extensive and intensive, of the markets is primarily governed by quite different laws, that work much less energetically. The extension of the markets cannot keep pace with the extension of production. The collision becomes inevitable, and as this cannot produce any real solution so long as it does not break in pieces the capitalist mode of production, the collisions become periodic. Capitalist production has begotten another "vicious circle."

As a matter of fact, since 1825, when the first general crisis broke out, the whole industrial and commercial world, production and exchange among all civilized peoples and their more or less barbaric hangers-on, are thrown out of joint about once every ten years. Commerce is at a standstill, the markets are glutted, products accumulate, as multitudinous as they are unsalable, hard cash disappears, credit vanishes, factories are closed, the mass of the workers are in want of the means of subsistence, because they have produced too much of the means of subsistence; bankruptcy follows upon bankruptcy, execution upon execution. The stagnation lasts for years; productive forces and products are wasted and destroyed wholesale, until the accumulated mass of commodities finally filter off, more or less depreciated in value, until production and exchange gradually begin to move again. Little by little the pace quickens. It becomes a trot. The industrial trot breaks into a canter, the canter in turn grows into the headlong gallop of a perfect steeplechase of industry, commercial credit and speculation, which finally, after breakneck leaps, ends where it began —in the ditch of a crisis. And so over and over again. We have now, since the year 1825, gone through this five times, and at the present moment (1877) we are going through it for the sixth time. And the character of these crises is so clearly defined that Fourier hit all of them off when he described the first as *"crise pléthorique,"* a crisis from plethora.

In these crises, the contradiction between socialized production and capitalist appropriation ends in a violent explosion. The circulation of commodities is, for the time being, stopped. Money, the means of circulation, becomes a hindrance to circulation. All the laws of production and circulation of commodities are turned upside down. The economic collision has reached its apogee. *The mode of production is in rebellion against the mode of exchange.*

The fact that the socialized organization of production within the factory has developed so far that it has become incompatible with the anarchy of production in society, which exists side by side with and dominates it, is brought home to the capitalists themselves by the violent concentration of capital that occurs during crises, through the ruin of many large, and a still greater number of small, capitalists. The whole mechanism of the capitalist mode of production breaks down under the pressure of the productive forces, its own creations. It is no longer able to turn all this mass of means of production into capital. They lie fallow, and for that very reason the industrial reserve army must also lie fallow. Means of production, means of subsistence, available laborers, all the elements of production and of general wealth, are present in abundance. But "abundance becomes the source of distress and want" (Fourier), because it is the very thing that prevents the transformation of the means of production and subsistence into capital. For in capitalistic society the means of production can only function when they have undergone a preliminary transformation into capital, into the means of exploiting human labor power. The necessity of this transformation into capital of the means of production and subsistence stands like a ghost between these and the workers. It alone prevents the coming together of the material and personal levers of production; it alone forbids the means of production to function, the workers to work and live. On the one hand, therefore, the capitalistic mode of production stands convicted of its own incapacity to further direct these productive forces. On the other, these productive forces themselves, with increasing energy, press forward to the removal of the existing contradiction, to the abolition of their quality as capital, to the *practical recognition of their character as social productive forces.*

This rebellion of the productive forces, as they grow more and more powerful, against their quality as capital, this stronger and stronger command that their social character shall be recognized, forces the capitalist class itself to treat them more and more as social productive forces, so far as this is possible under capitalist conditions. The period of industrial high pressure, with its unbounded inflation of credit, not less than the crash itself, by the collapse of great capitalist establishments, tends to bring about that form of the socialism of great masses of means of production, which we meet with in the different kinds of joint-stock companies. Many of these means of production and of distribution are, from the outset, so colossal, that, like the railroads, they exclude all other forms of capitalistic exploitation. At a further stage of evolution this form also becomes insufficient. The producers on a large scale in a particular branch of industry in a particular country unite in a "trust," a union for the purpose of regulating production. They determine the total amount to be produced, parcel it out among themselves, and thus enforce the selling price fixed beforehand. But trusts of this kind, as soon as business becomes bad, are generally liable to break up, and, on this very account, compel a yet greater concentration of association. The whole of the particular industry is turned into one gigantic joint-stock company; internal competition gives place to the internal monopoly of this one company. This has happened in 1890 with the English *alkali* production, which is now, after the fusion of 48 large works, in the hands of one company, conducted upon a single plan, and with a capital of £6,000,000.

In the trusts, freedom of competition changes into its very opposite—into monopoly; and the production without any definite plan of capitalistic society capitulates to the production upon a definite plan of the invading socialistic society. Certainly this is so far still to the benefit and advantage of the capitalists. But in this case the exploitation is so palpable that it must break down. No nation will put up with production conducted by trusts, with so barefaced an exploitation of the community by a small band of dividend mongers.

In any case, with trusts or without, the official representative of capitalist society—the state—will ultimately have to undertake the direction of production.* This necessity of conversion into state property is felt first in the great institutions for intercourse and communication—the post-office, the telegraphs, the railways.

If the crises demonstrate the incapacity of the bourgeoisie for managing any longer modern productive forces, the transformation of the great establishments for production and distribution into joint-stock companies, trusts and state property, show how unnecessary the bourgeoisie are for that purpose. All the social functions of the capitalist are now performed by salaried employees. The capitalist has no further social function than that of pocketing dividends, tearing off coupons, and gambling on the Stock Exchange, where the different capitalists despoil one another of their capital. At first the capitalistic mode of production forces out the workers. Now it forces out the capitalists, and reduces them, just as it reduced the workers, to the ranks of the surplus population, although not immediately into those of the industrial reserve army.

But the transformation, either into joint-stock companies and trusts,

---

* I say "have to." For only when the means of production and distribution have *actually* outgrown the form of management by joint-stock companies, and when, therefore, the taking them over by the state has become *economically* inevitable, only then—even if it is the state of today that effects this—is there an economic advance, the attainment of another step preliminary to the taking over of all productive forces by society itself. But of late, since Bismarck went in for state ownership of industrial establishments, a kind of spurious socialism has arisen, degenerating, now and again, into something of flunkeyism, that without more ado declares *all* state ownership, even of the Bismarckian sort, to be socialistic. Certainly, if the taking over by the state of the tobacco industry is socialistic, then Napoleon and Metternich must be numbered among the founders of socialism. If the Belgian state, for quite ordinary political and financial reasons, itself constructed its chief railway lines; if Bismarck, not under any economic compulsion, took over for the state the chief Prussian lines, simply to be the better able to have them in hand in case of war, to bring up the railway employees as voting cattle for the government, and especially to create for himself a new source of income independent of parliamentary votes—this was, in no sense, a socialistic measure, directly or indirectly, consciously or unconsciously. Otherwise, the Royal Maritime Company, the Royal porcelain manufacture, and even the regimental tailor of the army would also be socialistic institutions, or even, as was seriously proposed by a sly dog in Frederick William III's reign, the taking over by the state of the brothels.

or into state ownership, does not do away with the capitalistic nature of the productive forces. In the joint-stock companies and trusts this is obvious. And the modern state again, is only the organization that bourgeois society takes on in order to support the external conditions of the capitalist mode of production against the encroachments, as well of the workers as of individual capitalists. The modern state, no matter what its form, is essentially a capitalist machine, the state of the capitalists, the ideal personification of the total national capital. The more it proceeds to the taking over of productive forces, the more does it actually become the national capitalist, the more citizens does it exploit. The workers remain wage workers—proletarians. The capitalist relation is not done away with. It is rather brought to a head. But, brought to a head, it topples over. State ownership of the productive forces is not the solution of the conflict, but concealed within it are the technical conditions that form the elements of that solution.

This solution can only consist in the practical recognition of the social nature of the modern forces of production, and therefore in the harmonizing of the modes of production, appropriation and exchange with the socialized character of the means of production. And this can only come about by society openly and directly taking possession of the productive forces which have outgrown all control except that of society as a whole. The social character of the means of production and of the products today reacts against the producers, periodically disrupts all production and exchange, acts only like a law of nature working blindly, forcibly, destructively. But with the taking over by society of the productive forces, the social character of the means of production and of the products will be utilized by the producers with a perfect understanding of its nature, and instead of being a source of disturbance and periodical collapse, will become the most powerful lever of production itself.

Active social forces work exactly like natural forces; blindly, forcibly, destructively, so long as we do not understand and reckon with them. But when once we understand them, when once we grasp their action, their direction, their effects, it depends only upon ourselves to subject them more and more to our own will, and by means of them to reach our own ends. And this holds quite especially of the mighty productive forces of today. As long as we obstinately refuse to understand the nature of the character of these social means of action—and this understanding goes against the grain of the capitalist mode of production and its defenders—so long these forces are at work in spite of us, in opposition to us, so long they master us, as we have shown above in detail.

But when once their nature is understood, they can, in the hands of the producers working together, be transformed from master demons into willing servants. The difference is as that between the destructive force of electricity in the lightning of the storm, and electricity under command in the telegraph and the voltaic arc; the difference between a conflagration, and fire working in the service of man. With this recognition at last of the real nature of the productive forces of today, the social anarchy of production gives place to a social regulation of production upon a definite plan, according to the needs of the community and of each individual. Then the capitalist mode of appropriation, in which the product enslaves first the producer and then the appropriator, is replaced by the mode of appropriation of the products that is based upon the nature of the modern means of production; upon the one hand, direct social appropriation, as means to the maintenance and extension of production—on the other, direct individual appropriation, as means of subsistence and of enjoyment.

Whilst the capitalist mode of production more and more completely transforms the great majority of the population into proletarians, it creates the power which, under penalty of its own destruction, is forced to accomplish this revolution. Whilst it forces on more and more the transformation of the vast means of production, already socialized, into state property, it shows itself the way to accomplishing this revolution. *The proletariat seizes political power and turns the means of production into state property.*

But, in doing this, it abolishes itself as proletariat, abolishes all class distinctions and class antagonisms, abolishes also the state as state. Society thus far, based upon class antagonisms, had need of the state. That is, of an organization of the particular class which was *pro tempore* the exploiting class, an organization for the purpose of preventing any interference from without with the existing conditions of production, and therefore, especially, for the purpose of forcibly keeping the exploited classes in the condition of oppression corresponding with the given mode of production (slavery, serfdom, wage labor). The state was the official representative of society as a whole; the gathering of it together into a visible embodiment. But it was this only in so far as it was the state of that class which itself represented, for the time being, society as a whole; in ancient times, the state of slave-owning citizens; in the Middle Ages, the feudal lords; in our own time, the bourgeoisie. When at last it becomes the real representative of the whole of society, it renders itself unnecessary. As soon as there is no longer any social class to be held in subjection; as soon as class rule and the individual struggle for existence based upon our present anarchy in production, with the collisions and excesses arising from these, are removed, nothing more remains to be repressed, and a special repressive force, a state, is no longer necessary. The first act by virtue of which the state really constitutes itself the representative of the whole of society—the taking possession of the means of production in the name of society—this is, at the same time, its last independent act as a state. State interference in social relations becomes, in one domain after another, superfluous, and then dies out of itself; the government of persons is replaced by the administration of things, and by the conduct of processes of production. The state is not "abolished." *It dies out.* This gives the measure of the value of the phrase "a free state," both as to its justifiable use at times by agitators, and as to its ultimate scientific insufficiency; and also of the demands of the so-called anarchists for the abolition of the state out of hand.

Since the historical appearance of the capitalist mode of production, the appropriation by society of all the means of production has often been dreamed of, more or less vaguely, by individuals, as well as by sects, as the ideal of the future. But it could become possible, could become a historical necessity, only when the actual conditions for its realization were there. Like every other social advance, it becomes practicable, not by men understanding that the existence of classes is in contradiction to justice, equality, etc., not by the mere willingness to abolish these classes, but by virtue of certain new economic conditions. The separation of society into an exploiting and an exploited class, a ruling and an oppressed class, was the necessary consequence of the deficient and restricted development of production in former times. So long as the total social labor only yields a produce which but slightly exceeds that barely necessary for the existence of all; so long, therefore, as labor engages all or almost all the time of the great majority of the members of society—so long, of necessity, this society is divided into classes. Side by side with the great majority, exclusively bond slaves to labor, arises a class freed from directly productive labor, which looks after the general affairs of society, the direction of labor, state business, law, science, art, etc. It is, therefore, the law of division of labor that lies at the basis of the division into classes. But this does not prevent this division into classes from being carried out by means of violence and robbery, trickery and fraud. It does not prevent the ruling class, once having the upper hand, from consolidating its power at the expense of the working class, from turning their social leadership into an intensified exploitation of the masses.

But if, upon this showing, division into classes has a certain historical justification, it has this only for a given period, only under given social conditions. It was based upon the insufficiency of production. It will be swept away by the complete development of modern productive forces. And, in fact, the abolition of classes in society presupposes a degree of historical evolution, at which the existence, not simply of this or that particular ruling class, but of any ruling class at all, and, therefore, the existence of class distinction itself has become an obsolete anachronism. It presupposes, therefore, the development of production carried out to a degree at which appropriation of the means of production and of the products, and, with this, of political domination, of the monopoly of culture, and of intellectual leadership by a particular class of society, has become not only superfluous, but economically, politically, intellectually a hindrance to development.

This point is now reached. Their political and intellectual bankruptcy is scarcely any longer a secret to the bourgeoisie themselves. Their economic bankruptcy recurs regularly every ten years. In every crisis, society is suffocated beneath the weight of its own productive forces and products, which it cannot use, and stands helpless, face to face with the absurd contradiction that the producers have nothing to consume, because consumers are wanting. The expansive force of the means of production bursts the bonds that the capitalist mode of production had imposed upon them. Their deliverance from these bonds is the one precondition for an unbroken, constantly accelerated development of the productive forces, and therewith for a practically unlimited increase of production itself. Nor is this all. The socialized appropriation of the means of production does away not only with the present artificial restrictions upon production, but also with the positive waste and devastation of productive forces and products that are at the present time the inevitable concomitants of production, and that reach their height in the crises. Further, it sets free for the community at large a mass of means of production and of products, by doing away with the senseless extravagance of the ruling classes of today, and their political representatives. The possibility of securing for every member of society, by means of socialized production, an existence not only fully sufficient materially, and becoming day by day more full, but an existence guaranteeing to all the free development and exercise of their physical and mental faculties—this possibility is now for the first time here, but *it is here.*

With the seizing of the means of production by society, production of commodities is done away with, and, simultaneously, the mastery of the product over the producer. Anarchy in social production is replaced by systematic definite organization. The struggle for individual existence disappears. Then for the first time, man, in a certain sense, is finally marked off from the rest of the animal kingdom, and emerges from mere animal conditions of existence into really human ones. The whole sphere of the conditions of life which environ man, and which have hitherto ruled man, now comes under the dominion and control of man, who for the first time becomes the real, conscious lord of nature, because he has now become master of his own social organization. The laws of his own social action, hitherto standing face to face with man as laws of nature foreign to and dominating him, will then be used with full understanding, and so mastered by him. Man's own social organization, hitherto confronting him as a necessity imposed by nature and history, now becomes the result of his own free action. The extraneous objective forces that have hitherto governed history pass under the control of man himself. Only from that time will man himself, more and more consciously, make his own history—only from that time will the social causes set in movement by him have, in the main and in a constantly growing measure, the results intended by him. It is the ascent of man from the kingdom of necessity to the kingdom of freedom.

Let us briefly sum up our sketch of historical evolution.

I. *Medieval Society*—Individual production on a small scale. Means of production adapted for individual use; hence primitive, ungainly, petty, dwarfed in action. Production for immediate consumption, either of the producer himself or of his feudal lords. Only where an excess of production over this consumption occurs is such excess offered for sale, enters into exchange. Production of commodities therefore, is only in its infancy. But already it contains within itself, in embryo, *anarchy in the production of society at large.*

II. *Capitalist Revolution*—Transformation of industry, at first by means of simple co-operation and manufacture. Concentration of the means of production, hitherto scattered, into great workshops. As a consequence, their transformation from individual to social means of production—a transformation which does not, on the whole, affect the form of exchange. The old forms of appropriation remain in force. The capitalist appears. In his capacity as owner of the means of production, he also appropriates the products and turns them into commodities. Production has become a *social* act. Exchange and appropriation continue to be *individual* acts, the acts of individuals. *The social product is appropriated by the individual capitalist.* Fundamental contradiction, whence arise all the contradictions in which our present day society moves, and which modern industry brings to light.

A. Severance of the producer from the means of production. Condemnation of the worker to wage labor for life. *Antagonism between the proletariat and the bourgeoisie.*

B. Growing predominance and increasing effectiveness of the laws governing the production of commodities. Unbridled competition. *Contradiction between socialized organization in the individual factory and social anarchy in production as a whole.*

C. On the one hand, perfecting of machinery, made by competition compulsory for each individual manufacturer, and complemented by a constantly growing displacement of laborers. *Industrial reserve army.* On the other hand, unlimited extension of production, also compulsory under competition, for every manufacturer. On both sides, unheard of development of productive forces, excess of supply over demand, overproduction, glutting of the markets, crises every ten years, the vicious circle: excess here, of means of production and products—excess there, of laborers, without employment and without means of existence. But these two levers of production and of social well-being are unable to work together because the capitalist form of production prevents the productive forces from working and the products from circulating, unless they are first turned into capital—which their very superabundance prevents. The contradiction has grown into an absurdity. *The mode of production rises in rebellion against the form of exchange.* The bourgeoisie are convicted of incapacity further to manage their own social productive forces.

D. Partial recognition of the social character of the productive forces forced upon the capitalists themselves. Taking over of the great institutions for production and communication, first by joint-stock companies, later on by trusts, then by the state. The bourgeoisie demonstrated to be a superfluous class. All its social functions are now performed by salaried employees.

III. *Proletarian Revolution*—Solution of the contradictions. The proletariat seizes the public power, and by means of this transforms the socialized means of production, slipping from the hands of the bourgeoisie, into public property. By this act, the proletariat frees the means of production from the character of capital they have thus far borne, and gives their socialized character complete freedom to work itself out. Socialized production upon a predetermined plan becomes henceforth possible. The development of production makes the existence of different classes of society thenceforth an anachronism. In proportion as anarchy in social production vanishes, the political authority of the state dies out. Man, at last the master of his own form of social organization, becomes at the same time the lord over nature, his own master—free.

To accomplish this act of universal emancipation is the historical mission of the modern proletariat. To thoroughly comprehend the historical conditions and thus the very nature of this act, to impart to the now oppressed proletarian class a full knowledge of the conditions and of the meaning of the momentous act it is called upon to accomplish, this is the task of the theoretical expression of the proletarian movement, scientific socialism.

Section V

STATE, REVOLUTION, AND THE FUTURE

In 1917, the philosophy of communism entered a new phase of development. Previously its problems had been largely abstract, concerned with the interpretation of history, the analysis of the capitalist economy, and speculation about the classless society of the future and how it was to be brought to pass. With the successful completion of the revolution in Russia, Lenin and his associates assumed the responsibility of guiding, not only the destiny of the international proletarian class, but the policies of a large and powerful nation as well.

While this small group of revolutionary leaders claimed to be orthodox adherents of Marx's dialectical materialism, the problems of practical politics forced them to expand and reinterpret the doctrines of Marxism. Moreover, twentieth-century capitalism was not exactly what Marx's theories had led his followers to expect. The Russian communists were therefore obliged to explain anew the alleged contradictions within the capitalist system and the inevitability of its eventual breakdown.

There was, in addition, the problem of reconciling the actual political events of the first decades of the twentieth century with what, according to Marxist principles, was supposed to have taken place. For Marx had predicted the revolt of the oppressed industrial proletariat in the most advanced capitalist countries, but the revolution that Lenin directed took place in a relatively backward, agricultural land.

To make the facts and the theories fit together, and to do this within the framework of an orthodox dialectical materialism, was the task to which Lenin, Stalin, and their successors set themselves.

144

17. JOSEF STALIN *

Josef Stalin (1879-1953) was one of Lenin's closest associates in the November revolution, and an early leader in the new Soviet regime. The Foundations of Leninism, from which these and later selections in this volume are taken, consists of a series of lectures delivered in 1924, shortly after Lenin's death. It was at this time that Stalin became, as he remained until his death, the supreme power in Soviet Russia. These lectures were intended as a straightforward restatement of Lenin's own views, and in them he explains Lenin's attempted reconciliation of Marxist theory and actual events.

[What is Leninism?] †

And so, what is Leninism?

Some say that Leninism is the application of Marxism to the peculiar conditions of the situation in Russia. This definition contains a particle of truth, but not the whole truth by any means. Lenin, indeed, applied Marxism to Russian conditions, and applied it in a masterly way. But if Leninism were only the application of Marxism to the peculiar situation in Russia it would be a purely national and only a national, a purely Russian and only a Russian phenomenon. We know, however, that Leninism is not merely a Russian, but an international phenomenon rooted in the whole of international development. That is why I think this definition suffers from onesidedness.

Others say that Leninism is the revival of the revolutionary elements of Marxism of the forties of the nineteenth century, as distinct from the Marxism of subsequent years, when, it is alleged, it became moderate, non-revolutionary. If we disregard this foolish and vulgar division of the teachings of Marx into two parts, revolutionary and moderate, we must admit that even this totally inadequate and un-

---

* Stalin's original name was Iosif Viassarionovich Dzhugashvili.

† This and the following passages are from J. Stalin's *The Foundations of Leninism*, 1924. Reprinted by permission of the Foreign Languages Publishing House, Moscow.

satisfactory definition contains a particle of truth. That particle of truth is that Lenin did indeed restore the revolutionary content of Marxism, which had been immured by the opportunists of the Second International. Still, that is but a particle of the truth. The whole truth about Leninism is that Leninism not only restored Marxism, but also took a step forward, developing Marxism further under the new conditions of capitalism and of the class struggle of the proletariat.

What, then, in the last analysis, is Leninism?

Leninism is Marxism of the era of imperialism and of the proletarian revolution. To be more exact, Leninism is the theory and tactics of the proletarian revolution in general, the theory and tactics of the dictatorship of the proletariat in particular. Marx and Engels pursued their activities in the pre-revolutionary period (we have the proletarian revolution in mind), when developed imperialism did not yet exist, in the period of the proletarians' preparation for a revolution, in the period when the proletarian revolution was not yet a direct, practical inevitability. Lenin, however, the disciple of Marx and Engels, pursued his activities in the period of developed imperialism, in the period of the unfolding proletarian revolution, when the proletarian revolution had already triumphed in one country, had smashed bourgeois democracy and had ushered in the era of proletarian democracy, the era of the Soviets.

That is why Leninism is the further development of Marxism.

It is usual to point to the exceptionally militant and exceptionally revolutionary character of Leninism. This is quite correct. But this feature of Leninism is due to two causes: firstly, to the fact that Leninism emerged from the proletarian revolution, the imprint of which it cannot but bear; secondly, to the fact that it grew and became strong in contests with the opportunism of the Second International, the fight against which was and remains an essential preliminary condition for a successful fight against capitalism. It must not be forgotten that between Marx and Engels, on the one hand, and Lenin, on the other, there lies a whole period of undivided domination of the opportunism of the Second International, and the ruthless struggle against this opportunism could not but constitute one of the most important tasks of Leninism.

[The Roots of Leninism]

Leninism grew up and took shape under the conditions of imperialism, when the contradictions of capitalism had reached their extreme, when the proletarian revolution had become an immediate practical question, when the old period of preparation of the working class for the revolution had culminated in a new period, the period of the direct onslaught upon capitalism.

Lenin called imperialism "moribund capitalism." Why? Because imperialism carries the contradictions of capitalism to their last bounds, to the extreme limit, beyond which revolution begins. Of these contradictions, there are three which must be regarded as the most important.

The *first contradiction* is the contradiction between labor and capital. Imperialism is the omnipotence of the monopolist trusts and syndicates, of the banks and the financial oligarchy, in the industrial countries. In the fight against this omnipotence, the customary methods of the working class—trade unions and co-operative organizations, parliamentary parties and the parliamentary struggle—have proved to be totally inadequate. Either place yourself at the mercy of capital, linger in misery as of old and sink lower and lower, or adopt a new weapon—this is the alternative imperialism puts before the vast masses of the proletariat. Imperialism brings the working class to revolution.

The *second contradiction* is the contradiction among the various financial groups and imperialist powers in their struggle for sources of raw materials, for foreign territory. Imperialism is the export of capital to the sources of raw materials, the frenzied struggle for monopolist possession of these sources, the struggle for a redivision of the already divided world, a struggle waged with particular fury by new financial groups and powers seeking a "place in the sun" against the old groups and powers which cling tightly to what they have grabbed. This frenzied struggle among the various groups of capitalists is notable in that it includes as an inevitable element imperialist wars, wars for the annexation of foreign territories. This circumstance, in its turn, is notable in that it leads to the mutual weakening of the imperialists, to the weakening of the position of capitalism in general, to the acceleration of the advent of the proletarian revolution and to the practical inevitability of this revolution. The *third contradiction* is the contradiction between the handful of ruling "civilized" nations and the hundreds of millions of the colonial and dependent peoples of the world. Imperialism is the most barefaced exploitation and the most inhuman oppression of hundreds of millions of people inhabiting vast colonies and dependent countries. The purpose of this exploitation and of this oppression is to squeeze out super-profits. But in exploiting these countries imperialism is compelled to build railroads, factories and mills there, to create industrial and commercial centers. The appearance of a class of proletarians, the emergence of a native intelligentsia, the awakening of national consciousness, the growth of the movement for emancipation—such are the inevitable results of this "policy." The growth of the revolutionary movement in all colonies and dependent countries without exception clearly testifies to this fact. This circumstance is of importance for the proletariat in that it radically undermines the position of capitalism by converting the colonies and dependent countries from reserves of imperialism into reserves of the proletarian revolution.

Such, in general, are the principal contradictions of imperialism which have converted the old, "flourishing" capitalism into moribund capitalism.

The significance of the imperialist war which broke loose ten years ago lies, among other things, in the fact that it gathered all these contradictions into a single knot and threw them onto the scales, thereby accelerating and facilitating the revolutionary battles of the proletariat.

In other words, imperialism has brought it about, not only that revolution has become a practical inevitability, but also that favorable conditions have been created for a direct onslaught upon the citadels of capitalism.

Such is the international situation which gave birth to Leninism.

18. V. I. LENIN

The purpose of Imperialism: The Highest Stage of Capitalism *was to prove that the predictions of Marx and Engels were coming true in the early years of the twentieth century. Lenin argued that this was an era of industrial monopoly and finance capital, that the capitalist powers could only sustain themselves by combining and by controlling more and more of their markets and sources of raw materials, and that this leads to imperialism and the exploitation of colonial peoples. When the capitalist nations clash over the division of the spoils, as Lenin believed they inevitably must, they are forced to resort to armed conflict. Imperialism, he therefore maintained, was the underlying cause of the First World War.*

Concentration of Production and Monopolies*

Fifty years ago, when Marx was writing *Capital,* free competition appeared to most economists to be a "natural law." Official science tried, by a conspiracy of silence, to kill the works of Marx, which by a theoretical and historical analysis of capitalism showed that free competition gives rise to the concentration of production, which, in turn, at a certain stage of development, leads to monopoly. Today, monopoly has become a fact. The economists are writing mountains of books in which they describe the diverse manifestations of monopoly, and continue to declare in chorus that "Marxism is refuted." But facts are stubborn things, as the English proverb says, and they have to be reckoned with, whether we like it or not. The facts show that differences between capitalist countries, e.g., in the manner of protection or free trade, only give rise to insignificant variations in the form of monopolies or in the moment of their appearance; and that the rise of monopolies, as the result of the concentration of production, is a general and fundamental law of the present stage of development of capitalism.

For Europe, the time when the new capitalism *definitely* superseded the old can be established with fair precision: it was the beginning of the twentieth century. . . .

Thus, the principal stages in the history of monopolies are the following: 1) 1860-70, the highest stage, the apex of development of free competition; monopoly is in the barely discernible embryonic stage. 2) After the crisis of 1873, a wide zone of development of cartels; but they are still the exception. They are not yet durable. They are still a transitory phenomenon. 3) The boom at the end of

* This and the following passages are from V. I. Lenin, *Imperialism: The Highest Stage of Capitalism,* 1916. Reprinted by permission of the Foreign Languages Publishing House, Moscow.

the nineteenth century and the crisis of 1900-03. Cartels become one of the foundations of the whole of economic life. Capitalism has been transformed into imperialism.

Cartels come to an agreement on the conditions of sale, terms of payment, etc. They divide the markets among themselves. They fix the quantity of goods to be produced. They fix prices. They divide the profits among the various enterprises, etc. . . .

Competition becomes transformed into monopoly. The result is immense progress in the socialization of production. In particular, the process of technical invention and improvement becomes socialized.

This is no longer the old type of free competition between manufacturers, scattered and out of touch with one another, and producing for an unknown market. Concentration has reached the point at which it is possible to make an approximate estimate of all sources of raw materials (for example, the iron ore deposits) of a country and even, as we shall see, of several countries, or of the whole world. Not only are such estimates made, but these sources are captured by gigantic monopolist combines. An approximate estimate of the capacity of markets is also made, and the combines divide them up amongst themselves by agreement. Skilled labor is monopolized, the best engineers are engaged; the means of transport are captured; railways in America, shipping companies in Europe and America. Capitalism in its imperialist stage arrives at the threshold of the most complete socialization of production. In spite of themselves, the capitalists are dragged, as it were, into a new social order, a transitional social order from complete free competition to complete socialization.

Production becomes social, but appropriation remains private. The social means of production remain the private property of a few. The general framework of formally recognized free competition remains, but the yoke of a few monopolists on the rest of the population becomes a hundred times heavier, more burdensome and intolerable. . . .

Translated into ordinary human language this means that the development of capitalism has arrived at a stage when, although commodity production still "reigns" and continues to be regarded as the basis of economic life, it has in reality been undermined and the big profits go to the "geniuses" of financial manipulation. At the basis of these swindles and manipulations lies socialized production; but the immense progress of humanity, which achieved this socialization, goes to benefit the speculators. We shall see later how "on these grounds" reactionary, petty-bourgeois critics of capitalist imperialism dream of going *back* to "free," "peaceful" and "honest" competition. . . .

The statement that cartels can abolish crises is a fable spread by bourgeois economists who at all costs desire to place capitalism in a favorable light. On the contrary, when monopoly appears in *certain* branches of industry, it increases and intensifies the anarchy inherent in capitalist production *as a whole*. The disparity between the development of agriculture and that of industry, which is characteristic of capitalism, is increased. The privileged position of the most highly cartelized industry, so-called *heavy* industry, especially coal and iron, causes "a still greater lack of concerted organization" in other branches of production—as Jeidels, the author of one of the best works on the relationship of the German big banks to industry, puts it.*

"The more developed an economic system is," writes Liefmann, one of the most unblushing apologists of capitalism, "the more it resorts to risky enterprises, or enterprises abroad, to those which need a great deal of time to develop, or finally, to those which are only of local importance." †

The increased risk is connected in the long run with the prodigious increase of capital, which overflows the brim, as it were, flows abroad, etc. At the same time the extremely rapid rate of technical progress gives rise more and more to disturbances in the co-ordination between the various spheres of national economy, to anarchy and crisis. . . .

Crises of every kind—economic crises more frequently, but not only these—in their turn increase very considerably the tendency towards concentration and monopoly. . . .

Monopoly! This is the last word in the "latest phase of capitalist development." But we shall only have a very insufficient, incomplete, and poor notion of the real power and the significance of modern monopolies if we do not take into consideration the part played by the banks.

* Otto Jeidels, *The Relationship of the German Big Banks to Industry*, Leipzig, 1905, p. 271.
† Robert Liefmann, *Holding and Finance Companies*, p. 434.

The Export of Capital

Under the old capitalism, when free competition prevailed, the export of *goods* was the most typical feature. Under modern capitalism, when monopolies prevail, the export of *capital* has become the typical feature.

Capitalism is commodity production at the highest stage of development, when labor power itself becomes a commodity. The growth of internal exchange, and particularly of international exchange, is the characteristic distinguishing feature of capitalism. The uneven and spasmodic character of the development of individual enterprises, of individual branches of industry and individual countries, is inevitable under the capitalist system. England became a capitalist country before any other, and in the middle of the nineteenth century, having adopted free trade, claimed to be the "workshop of the world," the great purveyor of manufactured goods to all countries, which in exchange were to keep her supplied with raw materials. But in the last quarter of the nineteenth century, *this* monopoly was already undermined. Other countries, protecting themselves by tariff walls, had developed into independent capitalist states. On the threshold of the twentieth century, we see a new type of monopoly coming into existence. Firstly, there are monopolist capitalist combines in all advanced capitalist countries; secondly, a few rich countries, in which the accumulation of capital reaches gigantic proportions, occupy a monopolist position. An enormous "superabundance of capital" has accumulated in the advanced countries.

It goes without saying that if capitalism could develop agriculture, which today lags far behind industry everywhere, if it could raise the standard of living of the masses, who are everywhere still poverty-stricken and underfed, in spite of the amazing advance in technical knowledge, there could be no talk of a superabundance of capital. This "argument" the petty-bourgeois critics of capitalism advance on every occasion. But if capitalism did these things it would not be capitalism; for uneven development and wretched conditions of the masses are fundamental and inevitable conditions and premises of this mode of production. As long as capitalism remains what it is, surplus capital will never be utilized for the purpose of raising the standard of living of the masses in a given country, for this would mean a decline in profits for the capitalists; it will be used for the purpose of increasing those profits by exporting capital abroad to the backward countries. In these backward countries profits are usually high, for capital is scarce, the price of land is relatively low, wages are low, raw materials are cheap. The possibility of exporting capital is created by the fact that numerous backward countries have been drawn into international capitalist intercourse; main railways have either been built or are being built there; the elementary conditions for industrial development have been created, etc. The necessity for exporting capital arises from the fact that in a few countries capitalism has become "over-ripe" and (owing to the backward state of agriculture and the impoverished state of the masses) capital cannot find "profitable" investment. . . .

The export of capital greatly affects and accelerates the development of capitalism in those countries to which it is exported. While, therefore, the export of capital may tend to a certain extent to arrest development in the countries exporting capital, it can only do so by expanding and deepening the further development of capitalism throughout the world.

The countries which export capital are nearly always able to obtain "advantages," the character of which throws light on the peculiarities of the epoch of finance capital and monopoly. The following passage, for instance, occurred in the Berlin review, *Die Bank,* for October 1913:

> A comedy worthy of the pen of Aristophanes is being played just now on the international capital market. Numerous foreign countries, from Spain to the Balkan states, from Russia to the Argentine, Brazil and China, are openly or secretly approaching the big money markets demanding loans, some of which are very urgent. The money market is not at the moment very bright and the political outlook is not yet promising. But not a single money market dares to refuse a foreign loan for fear that its neighbor might first anticipate it and so secure some small reciprocal service. In these international transactions the creditor nearly always manages to get some special advantages: an advantage of a commercial-political nature, a coaling station, a contract to construct a harbor, a fat concession, or an order for guns.

Finance capital has created the epoch of monopolies, and monopolies introduce everywhere monopolist methods: the utilization of "connections" for profitable transactions takes the place of competition on the open market. The most usual thing is to stipulate that part of the loan that is granted shall be spent on purchases in the country of issue, particularly on orders for war materials, or for ships, etc. . . .

Thus, finance capital, almost literally, one might say, spreads its net over all countries of the world. Banks founded in the colonies, or their branches, play an important part in these operations. German imperialists look with envy on the "old" colonizing nations which are "well established" in this respect. In 1904, Great Britain had 50 colonial banks with 2,279 branches (in 1910 there were 72 banks with 5,449 branches); France had 20 with 136 branches; Holland 16 with 68 branches; and Germany had a "mere" 13 with 70 branches.* The American capitalists, in their turn, are jealous of the English and German: "In South America," they complained in 1915, "five German banks have forty branches and five English banks have seventy branches. . . . England and Germany have invested in Argentina, Brazil, and Uruguay in the last twenty-five years approximately four thousand million dollars, and as a result enjoy together 46 per cent of the total trade of these three countries." †

The capital exporting countries have divided the world among themselves in the figurative sense of the term. But finance capital has also led to the *actual* division of the world.

The Division of the World Among Capitalist Combines

Monopolist capitalist combines—cartels, syndicates, trusts—divide among themselves, first of all, the whole internal market of a country, and impose their control, more or less completely, upon the industry of that country. But under capitalism the home market is inevitably bound up with the foreign market. Capitalism long ago created a world market. As the export of capital increased, and as the foreign and colonial relations and the "spheres of influence" of the big monopolist combines expanded, things "naturally" gravitated towards an international agreement among these combines, and towards the formation of international cartels.

This is a new stage of world concentration of capital and produc-

---

* Dr. Riesser, *The German Big Banks and Their Concentration in Connection with the Development of the General Economy in Germany;* fourth ed., 1912, pp. 374-375.

† *The Annals of the American Academy of Political and Social Science,* Vol. LIX, May, 1915, p. 301.

tion, incomparably higher than the preceding stages. Let us see how this super-monopoly develops. . . .

Certain bourgeois writers (with whom K. Kautsky, who has completely abandoned the Marxist position he held, for example, in 1909, has now associated himself) express the opinion that international cartels are the most striking expressions of the internationalization of capital, and, therefore, give the hope of peace among nations under capitalism. Theoretically, this opinion is absurd, while in practice it is sophistry and a dishonest defense of the worst opportunism. International cartels show to what point capitalist monopolies have developed, and they *reveal the object* of the struggle between the various capitalist groups. This last circumstance is the most important; it alone shows us the historico-economic significance of events; for the *forms* of the struggle may and do constantly change in accordance with varying, relatively particular, and temporary causes, but the *essence* of the struggle, its class *content, cannot* change while classes exist. . . . The capitalists divide the world, not out of any particular malice, but because the degree of concentration which has been reached forces them to adopt this method in order to get profits. And they divide it in proportion to "capital," in proportion to "strength," because there cannot be any other system of division under commodity production and capitalism. But strength varies with the degree of economic and political development. In order to understand what takes place, it is necessary to know what questions are settled by this change of forces. The question as to whether these changes are "purely" economic or *non*-economic (e.g., military) is a secondary one, which does not in the least affect the fundamental view on the latest epoch of capitalism. To substitute for the question of the *content* of the struggle and agreements between capitalist combines the question of the *form* of these struggles and agreements (today peaceful, tomorrow war-like, the next day war-like again) is to sink to the role of a sophist.

The epoch of modern capitalism shows us that certain relations are established between capitalist alliances, *based* on the economic division of the world; while parallel with this fact and in connection with it, certain relations are established between political alliances, between states, on the basis of the territorial division of the world, of the struggle for colonies, of the "struggle for economic territory."

The Division of the World Among the Great Powers

In his book, *The Territorial Development of the European Colonies,* A. Supan, the geographer, gives the following brief summary of this development at the end of the nineteenth century:

PERCENTAGE OF TERRITORIES BELONGING TO THE
EUROPEAN COLONIAL POWERS (*Including United States*)

	1876	1900	INCREASE OR DECREASE
Africa	10.8	90.4	+79.6
Polynesia	56.8	98.9	+42.1
Asia	51.5	56.6	+ 5.1
Australia	100.0	100.0	—
America	27.5	27.2	— 0.3

"The characteristic feature of this period," he concludes, "is therefore, the division of Africa and Polynesia."

As there are no unoccupied territories—that is, territories that do not belong to any state—in Asia and America, Mr. Supan's conclusion must be carried further, and we must say that the characteristic feature of this period is the final partition of the globe—not in the sense that a *new* partition is impossible—on the contrary, new partitions are possible and inevitable—but in the sense that the colonial policy of the capitalist countries has *completed* the seizure of the unoccupied territories on our planet. For the first time the world is completely divided up, so that in the future *only* redivision is possible; territories can only pass from one "owner" to another, instead of passing as unowned territory to an "owner."

Hence, we are passing through a peculiar period of world colonial policy, which is closely associated with the "latest stage in the development of capitalism," with finance capital. . . .

The principal feature of modern capitalism is the domination of monopolist combines of the big capitalists. These monopolies are most firmly established when *all* the sources of raw materials are controlled by the one group. And we have seen with what zeal the international capitalist combines exert every effort to make it impossible for their rivals to compete with them; for example, by buying up mineral lands, oil fields, etc. Colonial possession alone gives complete guarantee of success to the monopolies against all the risks of the struggle with competitors, including the risk that the latter will defend themselves by means of a law establishing a state monopoly. The more capitalism is developed, the more the need for raw materials is felt, the more bitter competition becomes, and the more feverishly the hunt for raw materials proceeds throughout the whole world, the more desperate becomes the struggle for the acquisition of colonies. . . .

Finance capital is not only interested in the already known sources of raw materials; it is also interested in potential sources of raw materials, because present-day technical developments is extremely rapid, and because land which is useless today may be made fertile tomorrow if new methods are applied (to devise these new methods a big bank can equip a whole expedition of engineers, agricultural experts, etc.), and large amounts of capital are invested. This also applies to prospecting for minerals, to new methods of working up and utilizing raw materials, etc., etc. Hence, the inevitable striving of finance capital to extend its economic territory and even its territory in general. In the same way that the trusts capitalize their property by estimating it at two or three times its value, taking into account its "potential" (and not present) returns, and the further results of monopoly, so finance capital strives to seize the largest possible amount of land of all kinds and in any place it can, and by any means, counting on the possibilities of finding raw materials there, and fearing to be left behind in the insensate struggle for the last available scraps of undivided territory, or for the repartition of that which has been already divided. . . .

The necessity of exporting capital also gives an impetus to the conquest of colonies, for in the colonial market it is easier to eliminate competition, to make sure of orders, to strengthen the necessary "connections," etc., by monopolist methods (and sometimes it is the only possible way).

The non-economic superstructure which grows up on the basis of finance capital, its politics and its ideology, stimulates the striving for colonial conquest. "Finance capital does not want liberty, it wants domination," as Hilferding very truly says. . . .

Since we are speaking of colonial policy in the period of capitalist imperialism, it must be observed that finance capital and its corresponding foreign policy, which reduces itself to the struggle of the Great Powers for the economic and political division of the world, give rise to a number of *transitional* forms of national dependence.

The division of the world into two main groups—of colony-owning countries on the one hand and colonies on the other—is not the only typical feature of this period; there is also a variety of forms of dependent countries; countries which, officially, are politically independent, but which are, in fact, enmeshed in the net of financial and diplomatic dependence. We have already referred to one form of dependence—the semi-colony. Another example is provided by Argentina.

"South America, and especially Argentina," writes Schulze-Gaevernitz in his work on British imperialism, "is so dependent financially on London that it ought to be described as almost a British commercial colony."

Basing himself on the report of the Austro-Hungarian consul at Buenos Aires for 1909, Schilder estimates the amount of British capital invested in Argentina at 8,750,000,000 francs. It is not difficult to imagine the solid bonds that are thus created between British finance capital (and its faithful "friend," diplomacy) and the Argentine bourgeoisie, with the leading businessmen and politicians of that country. . . . Relations of this kind have always existed between big and little states. But during the period of capitalist imperialism they become a general system, they form part of the process of "dividing the world"; they become a link in the chain of operations of world finance capital.

Imperialism as a Special Stage of Capitalism

We must now try to sum up and put together what has been said above on the subject of imperialism. Imperialism emerged as the development and direct continuation of the fundamental attributes of capitalism in general. But capitalism only became capitalist imperialism at a definite and very high stage of its development, when certain of its fundamental attributes began to be transformed into their opposites, when the features of a period of transition from capitalism to a higher social and economic system began to take shape and reveal themselves all along the line. Economically, the main thing in this process is the substitution of capitalist monopolies for capitalist free competition. Free competition is the fundamental attribute of capitalism, and of commodity production generally. Monopoly is exactly the opposite of free competition; but we have seen the latter being transformed into monopoly before our very eyes, creating large-scale industry and eliminating small industry, replacing large-scale industry by still larger-scale industry, finally leading to such a concentration of production and capital that monopoly has been and is the result: cartels, syndicates and trusts, and merging with them, the capital of a dozen or so banks manipulating thousands of millions. At the same time monopoly, which has grown out of free competition, does not abolish the latter, but exists over it and alongside of it, and thereby gives rise to a number of very acute, intense antagonisms, friction and conflicts. Monopoly is the transition from capitalism to a higher system.

If it were necessary to give the briefest possible definition of imperialism we should have to say that imperialism is the monopoly stage of capitalism. Such a definition would include what is most important, for, on the one hand, finance capital is the bank capital of a few big monopolist banks, merged with the capital of the monopolist combines of manufacturers; and, on the other hand, the division of the world is the transition from a colonial policy which has extended without hindrance to territories unoccupied by any capitalist power, to a colonial policy of monopolistic possession of the territory of the world which has been completely divided up.

But very brief definitions, although convenient, for they sum up the main points, are nevertheless inadequate, because very important features of the phenomenon that has to be defined have to be specially deduced. And so, without forgetting the conditional and relative value of all definitions, which can never include all the concatenations of a phenomenon in its complete development, we must give a definition of imperialism that will embrace the following five essential features:

1) The concentration of production and capital developed to such a high stage that it created monopolies which play a decisive role in economic life.

2) The merging of bank capital with industrial capital, and the creation, on the basis of this "finance capital," of a "financial oligarchy."

3) The export of capital, which has become extremely important, as distinguished from the export of commodities.

4) The formation of international capitalist monopolies which share the world among themselves.

5) The territorial division of the whole world among the greatest capitalist powers is completed.

Imperialism is capitalism in that stage of development in which the dominance of monopolies and finance capital has established itself; in which the export of capital has acquired pronounced importance; in which the division of the world among the international trusts has begun; in which the division of all territories of the globe among the great capitalist powers has been completed.

We shall see later that imperialism can and must be defined differently if consideration is to be given, not only to the basic, purely economic factors—to which the above definition is limited—but also to the historical place of this stage of capitalism in relation to capitalism in general, or to the relations between imperialism and the two main trends in the working class movement. The point to be noted just now is that imperialism, as interpreted above, undoubtedly represents a special stage in the development of capitalism. In order to enable the reader to obtain as well grounded an idea of imperialism as possible, we deliberately quoted largely from *bourgeois* economists who are obliged to admit the particularly incontrovertible facts regarding modern capitalist economy. With the same object in view, we have produced detailed statistics which reveal the extent to which bank capital, etc., has developed, showing how the transformation of quantity into quality, of developed capitalism into imperialism, has expressed itself. Needless to say, all boundaries in nature and in society are conditional and changeable, and, consequently, it would be absurd to discuss the exact year or the decade in which imperialism "definitely" became established. . . .

The Parasitism and Decay of Capitalism

We have to examine yet another very important aspect of imperialism to which, usually, too little importance is attached in most of the arguments on this subject. . . . We refer to parasitism, which is a feature of imperialism. . . .

Imperialism is an immense accumulation of money capital in a few countries, which, as we have seen, amounts to 100-150 billion francs in various securities. Hence the extraordinary growth of a class, or rather of a category, of *bondholders* (*rentiers*), i.e., people who live by "clipping coupons," who take no part whatever in production, whose profession is idleness. The export of capital, one of the most essential economic bases of imperialism, still more completely isolates the *rentiers* from production and sets the seal of parasitism on the whole country that lives by the exploitation of the labor of several overseas countries and colonies. . . .

For that reason the term, "rentier state" (*Rentnerstaat*), or usurer state, is passing into current use in the economic literature that deals with imperialism. The world has become divided into a handful of usurer states on the one side, and a vast majority of debtor states on the other.

The Place of Imperialism in History

We have seen that the economic quintessence of imperialism is monopoly capitalism. This very fact determines its place in history, for monopoly that grew up on the basis of free competition, and precisely out of free competition, is the transition from the capitalist system to a higher social-economic order. We must take special note of the four principal forms of monopoly, or the four principal manifestations of monopoly capitalism, which are characteristic of the epoch under review.

Firstly, monopoly arose out of the concentration of production at a very advanced stage of development. This refers to the monopolist capitalist combines, cartels, syndicates and trusts. We have seen the important part that these play in modern economic life. At the beginning of the twentieth century, monopolies acquired complete supremacy in the advanced countries. And although the first steps towards the formation of the cartels were first taken by countries enjoying the protection of high tariffs (Germany, America), Great Britain, with her system of free trade, was not far behind in revealing the same basic phenomenon, namely, the birth of monopoly out of the concentration of production.

Secondly, monopolies have accelerated the capture of the most important sources of raw materials, especially for the coal and iron industries, which are the basic and most highly cartelized industries in capitalist society. The monopoly of the most important sources of raw materials has enormously increased the power of big capital, and has sharpened the antagonism between cartelized and non-cartelized industry.

Thirdly, monopoly has sprung from the banks. The banks have

developed from modest intermediary enterprises into the monopolists of finance capital. Some three or five of the biggest banks in each of the foremost capitalist countries have achieved the "personal union" of industrial and bank capital, and have concentrated in their hands the disposal of thousands upon thousands of millions which form the greater part of the capital and income of entire countries. A financial oligarchy, which throws a close net of relations of dependence over all the economic and political institutions of contemporary bourgeois society without exception—such is the most striking manifestation of this monopoly.

Fourthly, monopoly has grown out of colonial policy. To the numerous "old" motives of colonial policy, finance capital has added the struggle for the sources of raw materials, for the export of capital, for "spheres of influence," i.e., for spheres for profitable deals, concessions, monopolist profits and so on; in fine, for economic territory in general. When the colonies of the European powers in Africa, for instance, comprised only one-tenth of that territory (as was the case in 1876), colonial policy was able to develop by methods other than those of monopoly—by the "free grabbing" of territories, so to speak. But when nine-tenths of Africa had been seized (approximately by 1900), when the whole world had been divided up, there was inevitably ushered in a period of colonial monopoly and, consequently, a period of particularly intense struggle for the division and the redivision of the world.

The extent to which monopolist capital has intensified all the contradictions of capitalism is generally known. It is sufficient to mention the high cost of living and the oppression of the cartels. This intensification of contradictions constitutes the most powerful driving force of the transitional period of history, which began from the time of the definite victory of world finance capital.

Monopolies, oligarchy, the striving for domination instead of the striving for liberty, the exploitation of an increasing number of small or weak nations by an extremely small group of the richest or most powerful nations—all these have given birth to those distinctive characteristics of imperialism which compel us to define it as parasitic or decaying capitalism. More and more prominently there emerges, as one of the tendencies of imperialism, the creation of the "bondholding" (rentier) state, the usurer state, in which the bourgeoisie lives on the proceeds of capital exports and by "clipping coupons." It would be a mistake to believe that this tendency to decay precludes the possibility of the rapid growth of capitalism. It does not. In the epoch of imperialism, certain branches of industry, certain strata of the bourgeoisie and certain countries betray, to a more or less degree, one or other of these tendencies. On the whole, capitalism is growing far more rapidly than before. But this growth is not only becoming more and more uneven in general; its unevenness also manifests itself, in particular, in the decay of the countries which are richest in capital. . . .

The receipt of high monopoly profits by the capitalists in one of the numerous branches of industry, in one of numerous countries, etc., makes it economically possible for them to corrupt certain sections of the working class, and for a time a fairly considerable minority, and win them to the side of the bourgeoisie of a given industry or nation against all the others. The intensification of antagonisms between imperialist nations for the division of the world increases this striving. And so there is created that bond between imperialism and opportunism, which revealed itself first and most clearly in England, owing to the fact that certain features of imperialist development were observable there much earlier than in other countries.

From all that has been said in this book on the economic nature of imperialism, it follows that we must define it as capitalism in transition, or, more precisely, as moribund capitalism. It is very instructive in this respect to note that the bourgeois economists, in describing modern capitalism, frequently employ terms like "interlocking," "absence of isolation," etc.; "in conformity with their functions and course of development," banks are "not purely private business enterprises; they are more and more outgrowing the sphere of purely private business regulation." And this very Riesser, who uttered the words just quoted, declares with all seriousness that the "prophecy" of the Marxists concerning "socialization" has "not come true"!

What then does this word "interlocking" express? It merely expresses the most striking feature of the process going on before our eyes. It shows that the observer counts the separate trees, but cannot see the wood. It slavishly copies the superficial, the fortuitous, the chaotic. It reveals the observer as one who is overwhelmed by the mass of raw material and is utterly incapable of appreciating its meaning and importance. Ownership of shares and relations between owners of private property "interlock in a haphazard way." But the underlying factor of this interlocking, its very base, is the changing social relations of production. When a big enterprise assumes gigantic proportions, and, on the basis of exact computation of mass data, organizes according to plan the supply of primary raw materials to the extent of two-thirds, or three-fourths of all that is necessary for tens of millions of people; when the raw materials are transported to the most suitable place of production, sometimes hundreds or thousands of miles away, in a systematic and organized manner; when a single center directs all the successive stages of work right up to the manufacture of numerous varieties of finished articles; when these products are distributed according to a single plan among tens and hundreds of millions of consumers (as in the case of the distribution of oil in America and Germany by the American "oil trust")—then it becomes evident that we have socialization of production, and not mere "interlocking"; that private economic relations and private property relations constitute a shell which is no longer suitable for its contents, a shell which must inevitably begin to decay if its destruction be delayed by artificial means; a shell which may continue in a state of decay for a fairly long period (particularly if the cure of the opportunist abscess is protracted), but which will inevitably be removed.

19. JOSEF STALIN

The following selection from The Foundations of Leninism *provides a clear statement of how, as a result of the imperialistic development of capitalism, Lenin believed the proletarian revolution must take place. Stalin's account of the dictatorship of the proletariat as the proper continuation of the revolutionary movement remains authoritative, even though Stalin's reputation among orthodox communists has sharply declined.*

[Imperialism and the Proletarian Revolution] *

Formerly, the analysis of the conditions for the proletarian revolution was usually approached from the point of view of the economic

* This and the following passages are from J. Stalin, *The Foundations of Leninism*, 1924. Reprinted by permission of the Foreign Languages Publishing House, Moscow.

state of individual countries. Now, this approach is no longer adequate. Now the matter must be approached from the point of view of the economic state of all or the majority of countries, from the point of view of the state of world economy; for individual countries and individual national economies have ceased to be self-sufficient units, have become links in a single chain called world economy; for the old "cultured" capitalism has evolved into imperialism, and imperialism is a world system of financial enslavement and colonial oppression of the vast majority of the population of the earth by a handful of "advanced" countries.

Formerly, it was the accepted thing to speak of the existence or absence of objective conditions for the proletarian revolution in individual countries, or, to be more precise, in one or another developed country. Now this point of view is no longer adequate. Now we must speak of the existence of objective conditions for the revolution in the entire system of world imperialist economy as an integral unit; the existence within this system of some countries that are not sufficiently developed industrially cannot serve as an insurmountable obstacle to the revolution, *if* the system as a whole, or, more correctly, *because* the system as a whole is already ripe for revolution.

Formerly it was the accepted thing to speak of the proletarian revolution in one or another developed country as of something separate and self-sufficient, facing a separate national front of capital as its opposite. Now this point of view is no longer adequate. Now we must speak of the world proletarian revolution; for the separate national fronts of capital have become links in a single chain called the world front of imperialism, which must be opposed by a common front of the revolutionary movement in all countries.

Formerly, the proletarian revolution was regarded exclusively as the result of the internal development of a given country. Now this point of view is no longer adequate. Now the proletarian revolution must be regarded primarily as the result of the development of the contradictions within the world system of imperialism, as the result of the snapping of the chain of the imperialist world front in one country or another.

Where will the revolution begin? Where, in what country, can the front of capital be pierced first?

Where industry is more developed, where the proletariat constitutes the majority, where there is more culture, where there is more democracy—that was the reply usually given formerly.

No, objects the Leninist theory of revolution; *not necessarily where industry is more developed,* and so forth. The front of capital will be pierced where the chain of imperialism is weakest, for the proletarian revolution is the result of the breaking of the chain of the world imperialist front at its weakest link; and it may turn out that the country which has started the revolution, which has made a breach in the front of capital, is less developed in a capitalist sense than other, more developed, countries, which have, however, remained within the framework of capitalism.

In 1917 the chain of the imperialist world front proved to be weaker in Russia than in the other countries. It was there that the chain gave way and provided an outlet for the proletarian revolution. Why? Because in Russia a great popular revolution was unfolding, and at its head marched the revolutionary proletariat, which had such an important ally as the vast mass of the peasantry who were oppressed and exploited by the landlords. Because the revolution there was opposed by such a hideous representative of imperialism as tsarism, which lacked all moral prestige and was deservedly hated by the whole population. The chain proved to be weaker in Russia, although that country was less developed in a capitalist sense than, say, France or Germany, England or America.

Where will the chain break in the near future? Again, where it is weakest. It is not precluded that the chain may break, say, in India. Why? Because that country has a young, militant, revolutionary proletariat, which has such an ally as the national liberation movement—an undoubtedly powerful and undoubtedly important ally. Because there the revolution is opposed by such a well-known foe as foreign imperialism, which lacks all moral credit and is deservedly hated by the oppressed and exploited masses of India.

It is also quite possible that the chain will break in Germany. Why? Because the factors which are operating, say, in India are beginning to operate in Germany as well; but, of course, the enormous difference in the level of development between India and Germany cannot but leave its impress on the progress and outcome of a revolution in Germany.

That is why Lenin said that:

> The West-European capitalist countries are accomplishing their development towards socialism not by the even "ripening" of socialism, but by the exploitation of some countries by others, by the exploitation of the first of the countries to be vanquished in the imperialist war

combined with the exploitation of the whole of the East. On the other hand, precisely as a result of the first imperialist war, the East has been finally drawn into the revolutionary movement, has been drawn into the common maelstrom of the world revolutionary movement. (*Selected Works,* Vol. IX, p. 399.)

Briefly, the chain of the imperialist front must, as a rule, give way where the links are weaker and, at all events, not necessarily where capitalism is more developed, where there is such and such a percentage of proletarians and such and such a percentage of peasants, and so on.

This is why in deciding the question of proletarian revolution statistical calculations of the percentage of the proletarian population in a given country lose the exceptional importance so eagerly attached to them by the pedants of the Second International, who have not understood imperialism and who fear revolution like the plague.

[Revolution in One Country]

To proceed. Formerly, the victory of the revolution in one country was considered impossible, on the assumption that it would require the combined action of the proletarians of all or at least of a majority of the advanced countries to achieve victory over the bourgeoisie. Now this point of view no longer accords with the facts. Now we must proceed from the possibility of such a victory, for the uneven and spasmodic character of the development of the various capitalist countries under the conditions of imperialism, the development, within imperialism, of catastrophic contradictions leading to inevitable wars, the growth of the revolutionary movement in all countries of the world—all this leads, not only to the possibility, but also to the necessity of the victory of the proletariat in individual countries. The history of the Russian revolution is direct proof of this. At the same time, however, it must be borne in mind that the overthrow of the bourgeoisie can be successfully accomplished only when certain absolutely necessary conditions exist, in the absence of which there can be even no question of the proletariat taking power.

Here is what Lenin says about these conditions in his pamphlet *"Left-Wing" Communism, an Infantile Disorder:*

The fundamental law of revolution, which has been confirmed by all revolutions, and particularly by all three Russian revolutions in the twentieth century, consists in the following: it is not enough for revolution that the exploited and oppressed masses should understand the impossibility of living in the old way and demand changes; for revolution it is necessary that the exploiters should not be able to live and rule in the old way. Only when the "lower classes" *do not want* the old way, and when the "upper classes" *cannot carry on in the old way*—only then can revolution triumph. This truth may be expressed in other words: *Revolution is impossible without a nation-wide crisis (affecting both the exploited and the exploiters).** It follows that for revolution it is essential, first, that a majority of the workers (or at least a majority of the class conscious, thinking, politically active workers) should fully understand the necessity for revolution and be ready to sacrifice their lives for it; secondly, that the ruling classes should be passing through a governmental crisis which would draw even the most backward masses into politics . . . weaken the government and make it possible for the revolutionaries to overthrow it rapidly. (*Selected Works,* Vol. X, p. 127.)

But the overthrow of the power of the bourgeoisie and establishment of the power of the proletariat in one country still does not mean that the complete victory of socialism has been ensured. After consolidating its power and taking the peasantry in tow, the proletariat of the victorious country can and must build up a socialist society. But does this mean that it will thereby achieve the complete and final victory of socialism, i.e., does it mean that with the forces of only one country it can finally consolidate socialism and fully guarantee that country against intervention and, consequently, also against restoration? No, it does not. For this the victory of the revolution in at least several countries is needed. Therefore, the development and support of revolution in other countries is an essential task of the victorious revolution. Therefore, the revolution in the victorious country must regard itself not as a self-sufficient entity but as an aid, as a means of hastening the victory of the proletariat in other countries.

Lenin expressed this thought in a nutshell when he said that the task of the victorious revolution is to do "the utmost possible in one country *for* the development, support and awakening of the revolution *in all countries.*" (*Selected Works,* Vol. VII, p. 182.)

These, in general, are the characteristic features of Lenin's theory of proletarian revolution.

* My italics.—*J.S.*

The Dictatorship of the Proletariat as the Instrument of the Proletarian Revolution

The question of the proletarian dictatorship is above all a question of the main content of the proletarian revolution. The proletarian revolution, its movement, its scope and its achievements acquire flesh and blood only through the dictatorship of the proletariat. The dictatorship of the proletariat is the instrument of the proletarian revolution, its organ, its most important mainstay, brought into being for the purpose of, firstly, crushing the resistance of the overthrown exploiters and consolidating the achievements of the proletarian revolution, and, secondly, carrying the proletarian revolution to its completion, carrying the revolution to the complete victory of socialism. The revolution can vanquish the bourgeoisie, can overthrow its power, without the dictatorship of the proletariat. But the revolution will be unable to crush the resistance of the bourgeoisie, to maintain its victory and to push forward to the final victory of socialism unless, at a certain stage in its development, it creates a special organ in the form of the dictatorship of the proletariat as its principal mainstay.

"The fundamental question of revolution is the question of power." (*Lenin.*) Does this mean that all that is required is to assume power, to seize it? No, it does not mean that. The seizure of power is only the beginning. For many reasons the bourgeoisie that is overthrown in one country remains for a long time stronger than the proletariat which has overthrown it. Therefore, the whole point is to retain power, to consolidate it, to make it invincible. What is needed to attain this? To attain this it is necessary to carry out at least the three main tasks that confront the dictatorship of the proletariat "on the morrow" of victory:

(a) to break the resistance of the landlords and capitalists who have been overthrown and expropriated by the revolution, to liquidate every attempt on their part to restore the power of capital;

(b) to organize construction in such a way as to rally all the laboring people around the proletariat, and to carry on this work along the lines of preparing for the liquidation, the abolition of classes;

(c) to arm the revolution, to organize the army of the revolution for the struggle against foreign enemies, for the struggle against imperialism.

The dictatorship of the proletariat is needed to carry out, to fulfil these tasks.

The transition from capitalism to communism [says Lenin], represents an entire historical epoch. Until this epoch has terminated, the exploiters will inevitably cherish the hope of restoration, and this *hope* will be converted into *attempts* at restoration. And after their first serious defeat, the overthrown exploiters—who had not expected their overthrow, never believed it possible, never conceded the thought of it— will throw themselves with tenfold energy, with furious passion and hatred grown a hundredfold, into the battle for the recovery of their lost "paradise," on behalf of their families, who had been leading such a sweet and easy life and whom now the "common herd" is condemning to ruin and destitution (or to "common" work). . . . In the train of the capitalist exploiters will be found the broad masses of the petty bourgeoisie, with regard to whom the historical experience of every country for decades testifies that they vacillate and hesitate, one day marching behind the proletariat and the next day taking fright at the difficulties of the revolution; that they become panic-stricken at the first defeat or semi-defeat of the workers, grow nervous, run about aimlessly, snivel, and rush from one camp to the other. (*Selected Works*, Vol. VII, pp. 140-41.)

And the bourgeoisie has its grounds for making attempts at restoration, because for a long time after its overthrow it remains stronger than the proletariat which has overthrown it.

If the exploiters are defeated in one country only [says Lenin], and this, of course, is typical, since a simultaneous revolution in a number of countries is a rare exception, they *still* remain *stronger* than the exploited. (*Ibid.*, p. 140.)

Wherein lies the strength of the overthrown bourgeoisie?

Firstly, "in the strength of international capital, in the strength and durability of the international connections of the bourgeoisie." (Lenin, *Selected Works,* Vol. X, p. 60.)

Secondly, in the fact that:

for a long time after the revolution the exploiters inevitably continue to enjoy a number of great practical advantages: they still have money (since it is impossible to abolish money all at once), some movable property—often fairly considerable; they still have various connections, habits of organization and management, knowledge of all the "secrets" (customs, methods, means and possibilities) of management, superior education, close connections with the higher technical personnel (who live and think like the bourgeoisie), incomparably greater experience in the art of war (this is very important), and so on, and so forth. (Lenin, *Selected Works,* Vol. VII, p. 140.)

Thirdly,

in the *force of habit,* in the strength of *small-scale production.* For unfortunately, there is still very, very much of small-scale production left in the world, and small-scale production *engenders* capitalism and the bourgeoisie continuously, daily, hourly, spontaneously, and on a mass scale; . . . [for] the abolition of classes means not only driving out the landlords and capitalists—that we accomplished with comparative ease; it means also *getting rid of the small commodity producers,* and they *cannot be driven out,* they cannot be crushed, we must live *in harmony* with them; they can (and must) be remolded and re-educated only by very prolonged, slow, cautious organizational work. (Lenin, *Selected Works,* Vol. X, pp. 60, 83.)

That is why Lenin says:

The dictatorship of the proletariat is a most determined and most ruthless war waged by the new class against a *more powerful* enemy, the bourgeoisie, whose resistance is increased *tenfold* by its overthrow; [that] the dictatorship of the proletariat is a persistent struggle—sanguinary and bloodless, violent and peaceful, military and economic, educational and administrative—against the forces and traditions of the old society. (*Selected Works,* Vol. X, pp. 60, 84.)

It need hardly be proved that there is not the slightest possibility of carrying out these tasks in a short period, of doing all this in a few years. Therefore, the dictatorship of the proletariat, the transition from capitalism to communism, must not be regarded as a fleeting period of "super-revolutionary" acts and decrees, but as an entire historical era, replete with civil wars and external conflicts, with persistent organizational work and economic construction, with advances and retreats, victories and defeats. This historical era is needed not only to create the economic and cultural prerequisites for the complete victory of socialism, but also to enable the proletariat, first, to educate itself and become steeled as a force capable of governing the country, and, secondly, to re-educate and remold the petty-bourgeois strata along such lines as will assure the organization of socialist production.

Marx said to the workers:

> You will have to go through fifteen, twenty or fifty years of civil
> wars and international conflicts, not only to change existing conditions,
> but also to change yourselves and to make yourselves capable of wield-
> ing political power.

Continuing and developing Marx's idea still further, Lenin wrote
that: It will be necessary under the dictatorship of the proletariat to
re-educate:

> millions of peasants and small proprietors and hundreds of thousands
> of office employees, officials and bourgeois intellectuals, [to subordinate]
> all these to the proletarian state and to proletarian leadership, [to
> overcome] their bourgeois habits and traditions . . . [just as it will
> be necessary] to re-educate—in a protracted struggle, on the basis of
> the dictatorship of the proletariat—the proletarians themselves, who do
> not abandon their petty-bourgeois prejudices at one stroke, by a
> miracle, at the behest of the Virgin Mary, at the behest of a slogan,
> resolution or decree, but only in the course of a long and difficult mass
> struggle against mass petty-bourgeois influences. (*Selected Works,*
> Vol. X, pp. 157, 156.)

The Dictatorship of the Proletariat as the Domination of the Proletariat over the Bourgeoisie

From the foregoing it is evident that the dictatorship of the proletariat is not a mere change of personalities in the government, a
change of "cabinet," etc., leaving the old economic and political order
intact. The Mensheviks and opportunists of all countries, who fear
dictatorship like fire and in their fright substitute the concept "conquest of power" for the concept "dictatorship of the proletariat," usually reduce the meaning of "conquest of power" to a change of
"cabinet," to the accession to power of a new ministry made up of
people like Scheidemann and Noske, MacDonald and Henderson. It is
hardly necessary to explain that these and similar cabinet changes have
nothing in common with the dictatorship of the proletariat, with the
conquest of real power by the real proletariat. The MacDonalds and
Scheidemanns in power, while the old bourgeois order is allowed to
remain, their so-called governments cannot be anything else than an
apparatus serving the bourgeoisie, a screen to hide the ulcers of
imperialism, a weapon in the hands of the bourgeoisie against the
revolutionary movement of the oppressed and exploited masses.

Capital needs such governments as a screen when it finds it inconvenient, unprofitable, difficult to oppress and exploit the masses without the aid of a screen. Of course, the appearance of such governments is a symptom that "over there" (i.e., in the capitalist camp) "all is not quiet at the Shipka Pass"; nevertheless, governments of this kind necessarily remain governments of capital in disguise. The government of a MacDonald or a Scheidemann is as far removed from the conquest of power by the proletariat as the sky from the earth. The dictatorship of the proletariat is not a mere change of government, but a new state, with new organs of power, both central and local; it is the state of the proletariat, which has arisen on the ruins of the old state, the state of the bourgeoisie.

The dictatorship of the proletariat arises not on the basis of the bourgeois order, but in the process of the breaking up of this order after the overthrow of the bourgeoisie, in the process of the expropriation of the landlords and capitalists, in the principal instruments and means of production, in the process of violent proletarian revolution. The dictatorship of the proletariat is a revolutionary power based on the use of force against the bourgeoisie.

The state is a machine in the hands of the ruling class for suppressing the resistance of its class enemies. *In this respect* the dictatorship of the proletariat does not differ essentially from the dictatorship of any other class, for the proletarian state is a machine for the suppression of the bourgeoisie. But there is one *substantial* difference. This difference consists in the fact that all hitherto existing class states have been dictatorships of an exploiting minority over the exploited majority, whereas the dictatorship of the proletariat is the dictatorship of the exploited majority over the exploiting minority.

Briefly: *the dictatorship of the proletariat is the rule—unrestricted by law and based on force—of the proletariat over the bourgeoisie, a rule enjoying the sympathy and support of the laboring and exploited masses.* (*State and Revolution.*)

From this follow two main conclusions:

First conclusion: The dictatorship of the proletariat cannot be "complete" democracy, democracy for *all*, for the rich as well as for the poor; the dictatorship of the proletariat "must be a state that is democratic *in a new way—for** the proletarians and the propertyless in general—and dictatorial *in a new way—against** the bourgeoisie. . . ."

* My italics.—*J.S.*

(Lenin, *Selected Works,* Vol. VII, p. 34.) The talk of Kautsky and Co. about universal equality, about "pure" democracy, about "perfect" democracy, and the like, is but a bourgeois screen to conceal the indubitable fact that equality between exploited and exploiters is impossible. The theory of "pure" democracy is the theory of the upper stratum of the working class, which has been broken in and is being fed by the imperialist robbers. It was brought into being for the purpose of concealing the ulcers of capitalism, of touching up imperialism and lending it moral strength in the struggle against the exploited masses. Under capitalism there are no real "liberties" for the exploited, nor can there be, if for no other reason than that the premises, printing plants, paper supplies, etc., indispensable for the actual enjoyment of "liberties" are the privilege of the exploiters. Under capitalism the exploited masses do not, nor can they, really participate in the administration of the country, if for no other reason than that, even under the most democratic regime, governments, under the conditions of capitalism, are not set up by the people but by the Rothschilds and Stinneses, the Rockefellers and Morgans. Democracy under capitalism is *capitalist* democracy, the democracy of the exploiting minority, based on the restriction of the rights of the exploited majority and directed against this majority. Only under the dictatorship of the proletariat are real "liberties" for the exploited and real participation in the administration of the country by the proletarians and peasants possible. Under the dictatorship of the proletariat, democracy is *proletarian* democracy, the democracy of the exploited majority, based upon the restriction of the rights of the exploiting minority and directed against this minority.

Second conclusion: The dictatorship of the proletariat cannot arise as the result of the peaceful development of bourgeois society and of bourgeois democracy; it can arise only as the result of the smashing of the bourgeois state machine, the bourgeois army, the bourgeois bureaucratic machine, the bourgeois police.

In a preface to *The Communist Manifesto* Marx and Engels wrote, quoting from *The Civil War in France:*

> The working class cannot simply lay hold of the ready-made state machine and wield it for its own purposes. (Marx, *Selected Works,* Vol. I, p. 190.)

In a letter to Kugelmann (1871) Marx wrote that the task of the proletarian revolution is

> no longer as before, to transfer the bureaucratic military machine from one hand to another, but to *smash* it, and that is a preliminary condition for every real people's revolution on the Continent. (Marx, *Selected Works,* Vol. II, p. 528.)

Marx's qualifying phrase about the Continent gave the opportunists and Mensheviks of all countries a pretext for proclaiming that Marx had thus conceded the possibility of the peaceful evolution of bourgeois democracy into a proletarian democracy, at least in certain countries outside the European continent (England, America). Marx did in fact concede that possibility, and he had good grounds for conceding it in regard to England and America in the 'seventies of the last century, when monopoly capitalism, and imperialism did not yet exist, and when these countries, owing to the special conditions of their development, had as yet no developed militarism and bureaucracy. That was the situation before the appearance of developed imperialism. But later, after a lapse of thirty or forty years, when the situation in these countries had radically changed, when imperialism had developed and had embraced all capitalist countries without exception, when militarism and bureaucracy had appeared in England and America also, when the special conditions for peaceful development in England and the United States had disappeared—then the qualification in regard to these countries necessarily could no longer hold good.

> Today [said Lenin], in 1917, in the epoch of the first great imperialist war, this qualification made by Marx is no longer valid. Both England and America, the greatest and the last representatives—in the whole world—of Anglo-Saxon "liberty," in the sense that militarism and bureaucracy were absent, have slid down entirely into the all-European, filthy, bloody morass of military-bureaucratic institutions to which everything is subordinated and which trample everything underfoot. Today, both in England and in America, the "preliminary condition for every real people's revolution" is the smashing, the *destruction* of the "ready-made state machine" (brought in those countries, between 1914 and 1917, to general "European" imperialist perfection). (*Selected Works,* Vol. VII, p. 37.)

In other words, the law of violent proletarian revolution, the law of the smashing of the bourgeois state machine as a preliminary condition for such a revolution, is an inevitable law of the revolutionary movement in the imperialist countries of the world.

Of course, in the remote future, if the proletariat is victorious in the most important capitalist countries, and if the present capitalist encirclement is replaced by a socialist encirclement, a "peaceful" path of development is quite possible for certain capitalist countries, whose capitalists, in view of the "unfavorable" international situation, will consider it expedient "voluntarily" to make substantial concessions to the proletariat. But this supposition applies only to a remote and possible future. With regard to the immediate future, there is no ground whatsoever for this supposition.

Therefore, Lenin is right in saying:

> The proletarian revolution is impossible without the forcible destruction of the bourgeois state machine and the substitution for it of a *new one*. . . . (*Selected Works,* Vol. VII, p. 124.)

20. V. I. LENIN

State and Revolution *is one of Lenin's most important works: an attempt to give a detailed reinterpretation of the nature of the state, its downfall, and its replacement, according to Marxist theory. The following account of the state as an instrument of exploitation, and of the stages of the transition from capitalism to communism, is the best to be found anywhere.*

The theory presented here is explicitly reaffirmed by contemporary communist governments, who claim that their present stage of development is the dictatorship of the proletariat. It is worth noting that Lenin wrote this pamphlet during August and September of 1917 and never actually completed it, due to the occurrence of the political crisis, and the ensuing revolution which he directed. As a result of the success of that revolution Lenin remains today the greatest hero and the supreme authority of the orthodox communist movement.

The State as the Product of the Irreconcilability
of Class Antagonisms*

What is now happening to Marx's doctrine has, in the course of history, often happened to the doctrines of other revolutionary thinkers and leaders of oppressed classes struggling for emancipation. During the lifetime of great revolutionaries, the oppressing classes have visited relentless persecution on them and received their teaching with the most savage hostility, the most furious hatred, the most ruthless campaign of lies and slanders. After their death, attempts are made to turn them into harmless icons, canonize them, and surround their *names* with a certain halo for the "consolation" of the oppressed classes and with the object of duping them, while at the same time emasculating and vulgarizing the *real essence* of their revolutionary theories and blunting their revolutionary edge. At the present time, the bourgeoisie and the opportunists within the labor movement are co-operating in this work of adulterating Marxism. They omit, obliterate, and distort the revolutionary side of its teaching, its revolutionary soul. They push to the foreground and extol what is, or seems, acceptable to the bourgeoisie. All the social-chauvinists are now "Marxists"—joking aside! And more and more do German bourgeois professors, erstwhile specialists in the demolition of Marx, speak now of the "national-German" Marx, who, they aver, has educated the labor unions which are so splendidly organized for conducting the present predatory war!

In such circumstances, the distortion of Marxism being so widespread, it is our first task to *resuscitate* the real teachings of Marx on the state. For this purpose it will be necessary to quote at length from the works of Marx and Engels themselves. . . .

Summarizing his historical analysis Engels says:

> The state is therefore by no means a power imposed on society from the outside; just as little is it "the reality of the moral idea," "the image and reality of reason," as Hegel asserted. Rather, it is a product of society at a certain stage of development; it is the admission that this society has become entangled in an insoluble contradiction with itself, that it is cleft into irreconcilable antagonisms which it is power-

* This and the following passages are from V. I. Lenin, *State and Revolution,* 1917. Reprinted by permission of the Foreign Languages Publishing House, Moscow.

less to dispel. But in order that these antagonisms, classes with conflicting economic interests, may not consume themselves and society
in sterile struggle, a power apparently standing above society becomes
necessary, whose purpose is to moderate the conflict and keep it within
the bounds of "order"; and this power arising out of society, but
placing itself above it, and increasingly separating itself from it, is the
state.*

Here we have, expressed in all its clearness, the basic idea of Marxism on the question of the historical rôle and meaning of the state. The
state is the product and the manifestation of the *irreconcilability* of
class antagonisms. The state arises when, where, and to the extent
that the class antagonisms *cannot* be objectively reconciled. And,
conversely, the existence of the state proves that the class antagonisms
are irreconcilable.

The State as an Instrument for the Exploitation
of the Oppressed Class

For the maintenance of a special public force standing above society, taxes and state loans are needed.

Having at their disposal the public force and the right to exact taxes,
the officials now stand as organs of society *above* society. The free,
voluntary respect which was accorded to the organs of the gentilic form
of government does not satisfy them, even if they could have it. . . .

Special laws are enacted regarding the sanctity and the inviola-
bility of the officials. "The shabbiest police servant . . . has more
authority" than the representative of the clan, but even the head of
the military power of a civilized state "may well envy the least among
the chiefs of the clan the unconstrained and uncontested respect
which is paid to him."

Here the question regarding the privileged position of the officials
as organs of state power is clearly stated. The main point is indicated
as follows: what is it that places them *above* society? . . .

As the state arose out of the need to hold class antagonisms in check;
but as it, at the same time, arose in the midst of the conflict of these
classes, it is, as a rule, the state of the most powerful, economically

---

* Friedrich Engels, *The Origin of the Family, Private Property, and the
State.—Ed.*

dominant class, which by virtue thereof becomes also the dominant class politically, and thus acquires new means of holding down and exploiting the oppressed class. . . .

A general summary of his views is given by Engels in the most popular of his works in the following words:

> The state, therefore, has not existed from all eternity. There have been societies which managed without it, which had no conception of the state and state power. At a certain stage of economic development, which was necessarily bound up with the cleavage of society into classes, the state became a necessity owing to this cleavage. We are now rapidly approaching a stage in the development of production at which the existence of these classes has not only ceased to be a necessity, but is becoming a positive hindrance to production. They will disappear as inevitably as they arose at an earlier stage. Along with them, the state will inevitably disappear. The society that organizes production anew on the basis of a free and equal association of the producers will put the whole state machine where it will then belong: in the museum of antiquities, side by side with the spinning wheel and the bronze ax.*

It is not often that we find this passage quoted in the propaganda and agitation literature of contemporary Social-Democracy. But even when we do come across it, it is generally quoted in the same manner as one bows before an icon, i.e., it is done merely to show official respect for Engels, without any attempt to gauge the breadth and depth of revolutionary action presupposed by his relegating of "the whole state machine . . . to the museum of antiquities." In most cases we do not even find an understanding of what Engels calls the state machine.

The "Withering Away" of the State and Violent Revolution

Engels' words regarding the "withering away" of the state enjoy such popularity, they are so often quoted, and they show so clearly the essence of the usual adulteration by means of which Marxism is made to look like opportunism, that we must dwell on them in detail. Let us quote the whole passage from which they are taken.

> The proletariat seizes state power, and then transforms the means of production into state property. But in doing this, it puts an end to

* *Ibid.—Ed.*

itself as the proletariat, it puts an end to all class differences and class antagonisms, it puts an end also to the state as the state. Former society, moving in class antagonisms, had need of the state, that is, an organization of the exploiting class at each period for the maintenance of its external conditions of production; therefore, in particular, for the forcible holding down of the exploited class in the conditions of oppression (slavery, bondage or serfdom, wage-labor) determined by the existing mode of production. The state was the official representative of society as a whole, its embodiment in a visible corporate body; but it was this only in so far as it was the state of that class which itself, in its epoch, represented society as a whole: in ancient times, the state of the slave-owning citizens; in the Middle Ages, of the feudal nobility; in our epoch, of the bourgeoisie. When ultimately it becomes really representative of society as a whole, it makes itself superfluous. As soon as there is no longer any class of society to be held in subjection; as soon as, along with class domination and the struggle for individual existence based on the former anarchy of production, the collisions and excesses arising from these have also been abolished, there is nothing more to be repressed, and a special repressive force, a state, is no longer necessary. The first act in which the state really comes forward as the representative of society as a whole—the seizure of the means of production in the name of society—is at the same time its last independent act as a state. The interference of a state power in social relations becomes superfluous in one sphere after another, and then becomes dormant of itself. Government over persons is replaced by the administration of things and the direction of the processes of production. The state is not "abolished," *it withers away.* It is from this standpoint that we must appraise the phrase "people's free state"—both its justification at times for agitational purposes, and its ultimate scientific inadequacy —and also the demand of the so-called Anarchists that the state should be abolished overnight.*

Without fear of committing an error, it may be said that of this argument by Engels so singularly rich in ideas, only one point has become an integral part of Socialist thought among modern Socialist parties, namely, that, unlike the Anarchist doctrine of the "abolition" of the state, according to Marx the state "withers away." To emasculate Marxism in such a manner is to reduce it to opportunism, for such an "interpretation" only leaves the hazy conception of a slow, even, gradual change, free from leaps and storms, free from

* F. Engels, *Herr Eugen Dühring's Revolution in Science (Anti-Dühring).* For another translation of this famous passage see above, pp. 138-139, where it appears in the third part of *Socialism, Utopian and Scientific.*—*Ed.*

revolution. The current popular conception, if one may say so, of the "withering away" of the state undoubtedly means a slurring over, if not a negation, of revolution.

Yet, such an "interpretation" is the crudest distortion of Marxism, which is advantageous only to the bourgeoisie; in point of theory, it is based on a disregard for the most important circumstances and considerations pointed out in the very passage summarizing Engels' ideas, which we have just quoted in full.

In the first place, Engels at the very outset of his argument says that, in assuming state power, the proletariat by that very act "puts an end to the state as the state." One is "not accustomed" to reflect on what this really means. Generally, it is either ignored altogether, or it is considered as a piece of "Hegelian weakness" on Engels' part. As a matter of fact, however, these words express succinctly the experience of one of the greatest proletarian revolutions—the Paris Commune of 1871, of which we shall speak in greater detail in its proper place. As a matter of fact, Engels speaks here of the destruction of the bourgeois state by the proletarian revolution, while the words about its withering away refer to the remains of *proletarian* statehood *after* the Socialist revolution. The bourgeois state does not "wither away," according to Engels, but is "put an end to" by the proletariat in the course of the revolution. What withers away after the revolution is the proletarian state or semi-state.

Secondly, the state is a "special repressive force." This splendid and extremely profound definition of Engels' is given by him here with complete lucidity. It follows from this that the "special repressive force" of the bourgeoisie for the suppression of the proletariat, of the millions of workers by a handful of the rich, must be replaced by a "special repressive force" of the proletariat for the suppression of the bourgeoisie (the dictatorship of the proletariat). It is just this that constitutes the destruction of "the state as the state." It is just this that constitutes the "act" of "the seizure of the means of production in the name of society." And it is obvious that such a substitution of one (proletarian) "special repressive force" for another (bourgeois) "special repressive force" can in no way take place in the form of a "withering away."

Thirdly, as to the "withering away" or, more expressively and colorfully, as to the state "becoming dormant," Engels refers quite clearly and definitely to the period *after* "the seizure of the means of production [by the state] in the name of society," that is, *after* the Socialist revolution. We all know that the political form of the "state" at that time is complete democracy. But it never enters the head of any of the opportunists who shamelessly distort Marx that when Engels speaks here of the state "withering away," or "becoming dormant," he speaks of *democracy*. At first sight this seems very strange. But it is "unintelligible" only to one who has not reflected on the fact that democracy is *also* a state and that, consequently, democracy will *also* disappear when the state disappears. The bourgeois state can only be "put an end to" by a revolution. The state in general, i.e., most complete democracy, can only "wither away."

Fourthly, having formulated his famous proposition that "the state withers away," Engels at once explains concretely that this proposition is directed equally against the opportunists and the Anarchists. In doing this, however, Engels puts in the first place that conclusion from his proposition about the "withering away" of the state which is directed against the opportunists. . . .

Fifthly, in the same work of Engels, from which everyone remembers his argument on the "withering away" of the state, there is also a disquisition on the significance of a violent revolution. The historical analysis of its rôle becomes, with Engels, a veritable panegyric on violent revolution. This, of course, "no one remembers"; to talk or even to think of the importance of this idea is not considered good form by contemporary Socialist parties, and in the daily propaganda and agitation among the masses it plays no part whatever. Yet it is indissolubly bound up with the "withering away" of the state in one harmonious whole.

Here is Engels' argument:

. . . That force, however, plays another role (other than that of a diabolical power) in history, a revolutionary role; that, in the words of Marx, it is the midwife of every old society which is pregnant with the new; that it is the instrument with whose aid social movement forces its way through and shatters the dead, fossilized political forms—of this there is not a word in Herr Dühring. It is only with sighs and groans that he admits the possibility that force will perhaps be necessary for the overthrow of the economic system of exploitation—unfortunately! because all use of force, forsooth, demoralizes the person who uses it. And this in spite of the immense moral and spiritual impetus which has resulted from every victorious revolution! And this in Germany, where a violent collision—which indeed may be forced on the people—would at least have the advantage of wiping out the servility which has permeated the national consciousness as a result of the humiliation of the Thirty Years' War. And this parson's mode of thought—lifeless, insipid and impotent—claims to impose itself on the most revolutionary party which history has known? *

How can this panegyric on violent revolution, which Engels insistently brought to the attention of the German Social-Democrats between 1878 and 1894, i.e., right to the time of his death, be combined with the theory of the "withering away" of the state to form one doctrine?

Usually the two views are combined by means of eclecticism, by an unprincipled, sophistic, arbitrary selection (to oblige the powers that be) of either one or the other arguments, and in ninety-nine cases out of a hundred (if not more often), it is the idea of the "withering away" that is specially emphasized. Eclecticism is substituted for dialectics—this is the most usual, the most widespread phenomenon to be met with in the official Social-Democratic literature of our day in relation to Marxism. Such a substitution is, of course, nothing new; it may be observed even in the history of classic Greek philosophy. When Marxism is adulterated to become opportunism, the substitution of eclecticism for dialectics is the best method of deceiving masses; it gives an illusory satisfaction; it seems to take into account all sides of the process, all the tendencies of development, all the contradictory factors and so forth, whereas in reality it offers no consistent and revolutionary view of the process of social development at all.

We have already said above and shall show more fully later that the teaching of Marx and Engels regarding the inevitability of a violent revolution refers to the bourgeois state. It *cannot* be replaced by the proletarian state (the dictatorship of the proletariat) through "withering away," but, as a general rule, only through a violent revolution. The panegyric sung in its honor by Engels and fully corresponding to the repeated declarations of Marx (remember the concluding passages of the *Poverty of Philosophy* and the *Communist Manifesto,* with its proud and open declaration of the inevitability of a violent revolution; remember Marx's *Critique of the Gotha Programme* of 1875 in which, almost thirty years later, he mercilessly castigates the opportunist character of that programme)—this praise is by no means a mere "impulse," a mere declamation, or a polemical sally. The necessity of systematically fostering among the masses *this*

* *Ibid.* This passage appears in a passage of the *Anti-Dühring* which is not included within *Socialism, Utopian and Scientific.—Ed.*

and just this point of view about violent revolution lies at the root of the *whole* of Marx's and Engels' teaching. The neglect of such propaganda and agitation by both the present predominant social-chauvinist and the Kautskyist currents brings their betrayal of Marx's and Engels' teaching into prominent relief.

The replacement of the bourgeois by the proletarian state is impossible without a violent revolution. The abolition of the proletarian state, i.e., of all states, is only possible through "withering away."

The Transition from Capitalism to Communism

It is clear that there can be no question of defining the exact moment of the *future* withering away—the more so as it must obviously be a rather lengthy process. . . .

The whole theory of Marx is an application of the theory of evolution—in its most consistent, complete, well considered and fruitful form—to modern capitalism. It was natural for Marx to raise the question of applying this theory both to the *coming* collapse of capitalism and to the *future* evolution of *future* Communism.

On the basis of what *data* can the future evolution of future Communism be considered?

On the basis of the fact that *it has its origin* in capitalism, that it develops historically from capitalism, that it is the result of the action of a social force to which capitalism *has given birth*. There is no shadow of an attempt on Marx's part to conjure up a Utopia, to make idle guesses about that which cannot be known. Marx treats the question of Communism in the same way as a naturalist would treat the question of the evolution of, say, a new biological species, if he knew that such and such was its origin, and such and such the direction in which it changed.

Marx, first of all, brushes aside the confusion the Gotha Programme brings into the question of the interrelation between state and society.

"Contemporary society" is the capitalist society—he writes—which exists in all civilized countries, more or less free of medieval admixture, more or less modified by each country's particular historical development, more or less developed. In contrast with this, the "contemporary state" varies with every state boundary. It is different in the

Prusso-German Empire from what it is in Switzerland, and different in England from what it is in the United States. The "contemporary state" is therefore a fiction.

Nevertheless, in spite of the motley variety of their forms, the different states of the various civilized countries all have this in common: they are all based on modern bourgeois society, only a little more or less capitalistically developed. Consequently, they also have certain essential characteristics in common. In this sense, it is possible to speak of the "contemporary state" in contrast to the future, when its present root, bourgeois society, will have perished.

Then the question arises: what transformation will the state undergo in a Communist society? In other words, what social functions analogous to the present functions of the state will then still survive? This question can only be answered scientifically, and however many thousand times the word people is combined with the word state, we get not a flea-jump closer to the problem. . . .*

Having thus ridiculed all talk about a "people's state," Marx formulates the question and warns us, as it were, that to arrive at a scientific answer one must rely only on firmly established scientific data.

The first fact that has been established with complete exactness by the whole theory of evolution, by science as a whole—a fact which the Utopians forgot, and which is forgotten by the present-day opportunists who are afraid of the Socialist revolution—is that, historically, there must undoubtedly be a special stage or epoch of *transition* from capitalism to Communism. . . .

Between capitalist and Communist society—Marx continues—lies the period of the revolutionary transformation of the former into the latter. To this also corresponds a political transition period, in which the state can be no other than *the revolutionary dictatorship of the proletariat.*†

This conclusion Marx bases on an analysis of the role played by the proletariat in modern capitalist society, on the data concerning the evolution of this society, and on the irreconcilability of the opposing interests of the proletariat and the bourgeoisie.

Earlier the question was put thus: to attain its emancipation, the proletariat must overthrow the bourgeoisie, conquer political power and establish its own revolutionary dictatorship.

* K. Marx, *Critique of the Gotha Programme.—Ed.*
† *Ibid.—Ed.*

Now the question is put somewhat differently: the transition from capitalist society, developing towards Communism, towards a Communist society, is impossible without a "political transition period," and the state in this period can only be the revolutionary dictatorship of the proletariat.

What, then, is the relation of this dictatorship to democracy?

We have seen that the *Communist Manifesto* simply places side by side the two ideas: the "transformation of the proletariat into the ruling class" and the "establishment of democracy." On the basis of all that has been said above, one can define more exactly how democracy changes in the transition from capitalism to Communism.

In capitalist society, under the conditions most favorable to its development, we have more or less complete democracy in the democratic republic. But this democracy is always bound by the narrow framework of capitalist exploitation, and consequently always remains, in reality, a democracy for the minority, only for the possessing classes, only for the rich. Freedom in capitalist society always remains just about the same as it was in the ancient Greek republics: freedom for the slave-owners. The modern wage-slaves, owing to the conditions of capitalist exploitation, are so much crushed by want and poverty that "democracy is nothing to them," "politics is nothing to them"; that, in the ordinary peaceful course of events, the majority of the population is debarred from participating in social and political life. . . .

Democracy for an insignificant minority, democracy for the rich— that is the democracy of capitalist society. If we look more closely into the mechanism of capitalist democracy, everywhere, both in the "petty"—so-called petty—details of the suffrage (residential qualification, exclusion of women, etc.), and in the technique of the representative institutions, in the actual obstacles to the right of assembly (public buildings are not for "beggars"!), in the purely capitalist organization of the daily press, etc., etc.—on all sides we see restriction after restriction upon democracy. These restrictions, exceptions, exclusions, obstacles for the poor, seem slight, especially in the eyes of one who has himself never known want and has never been in close contact with the oppressed classes in their mass life (and nine-tenths, if not ninety-nine hundredths, of the bourgeois publicists and politicians are of this class), but in their sum total these restrictions exclude and squeeze out the poor from politics and from an active share in democracy.

Marx splendidly grasped this *essence* of capitalist democracy, when, in analyzing the experience of the Commune, he said that the oppressed were allowed, once every few years, to decide which particular representatives of the oppressing class should be in parliament to represent and repress them!

But from this capitalist democracy—inevitably narrow, subtly rejecting the poor, and therefore hypocritical and false to the core—progress does not march onward, simply, smoothly, and directly, to "greater and greater democracy," as the liberal professors and petty-bourgeois opportunists would have us believe. No, progress marches onward, i.e., towards Communism, through the dictatorship of the proletariat; it cannot do otherwise, for there is no one else and no other way to *break the resistance* of the capitalist exploiters.

But the dictatorship of the proletariat—i.e., the organization of the vanguard of the oppressed as the ruling class for the purpose of crushing the oppressors—cannot produce merely an expansion of democracy. *Together* with an immense expansion of democracy which *for the first time* becomes democracy for the poor, democracy for the people, and not democracy for the rich folk, the dictatorship of the proletariat produces a series of restrictions of liberty in the case of the oppressors, the exploiters, the capitalists. We must crush them in order to free humanity from wage-slavery; their resistance must be broken by force; it is clear that where there is suppression there is also violence, there is no liberty, no democracy.

Engels expressed this splendidly in his letter to Bebel when he said, as the reader will remember, that "as long as the proletariat still *needs* the state, it needs it not in the interests of freedom, but for the purpose of crushing its antagonists; and as soon as it becomes possible to speak of freedom, then the state, as such, ceases to exist."

Democracy for the vast majority of the people, and suppression by force, i.e., exclusion from democracy, of the exploiters and oppressors of the people—this is the modification of democracy during the *transition* from capitalism to Communism.

Only in Communist society, when the resistance of the capitalists has been completely broken, when the capitalists have disappeared, when there are no classes (i.e., there is no difference between the members of society in their relation to the social means of production), *only then* "the state ceases to exist," and *"it becomes possible to speak of freedom."* Only then a really full democracy, a democracy without any exceptions, will be possible and will be realized. And only then will democracy itself begin to *wither away* due to the simple fact that, freed from capitalist slavery, from the untold horrors, savagery, absurdities and infamies of capitalist exploitation, people will gradually *become accustomed* to the observance of the elementary rules of social life that have been known for centuries and repeated for thousands of years in all school books; they will become accustomed to observing them without force, without compulsion, without subordination, without the *special apparatus* for compulsion which is called the state.

The expression "the state *withers away*," is very well chosen, for it indicates both the gradual and the elemental nature of the process. Only habit can, and undoubtedly will, have such an effect; for we see around us millions of times how readily people get accustomed to observe the necessary rules of life in common, if there is no exploitation, if there is nothing that causes indignation, that calls forth protest and revolt and has to be *suppressed*.

Thus, in capitalist society, we have a democracy that is curtailed, poor, false; a democracy only for the rich, for the minority. The dictatorship of the proletariat, the period of transition to Communism, will, for the first time, produce democracy for the people, for the majority, side by side with the necessary suppression of the minority—the exploiters. Communism alone is capable of giving a really complete democracy, and the more complete it is the more quickly will it become unnecessary and wither away of itself.

In other words: under capitalism we have a state in the proper sense of the word, that is, special machinery for the suppression of one class by another, and of the majority by the minority at that. Naturally, for the successful discharge of such a task as the systematic suppression by the exploiting minority of the exploited majority, the greatest ferocity and savagery of suppression are required, seas of blood are required, through which mankind is marching in slavery, serfdom, and wage-labor.

Again, during the *transition* from capitalism to Communism, suppression is *still* necessary; but it is the suppression of the minority of exploiters by the majority of exploited. A special apparatus, special machinery for suppression, the "state," is *still* necessary, but this is now a transitional state, no longer a state in the usual sense, for the suppression of the minority of exploiters, by the majority of the wage slaves *of yesterday,* is a matter comparatively so easy, simple and natural that it will cost far less bloodshed than the suppression of the risings of slaves, serfs or wage laborers, and will cost mankind far less. This is compatible with the diffusion of democracy among such an overwhelming majority of the population, that the need for *special machinery* of suppression will begin to disappear. The exploiters are, naturally, unable to suppress the people without a most complex machinery for performing this task; but *the people* can suppress the exploiters even with very simple "machinery," almost without any "machinery," without any special apparatus, by the simple *organization of the armed masses* (such as the Soviets of Workers' and Soldiers' Deputies, we may remark, anticipating a little).

Finally, only Communism renders the state absolutely unnecessary, for there is *no one* to be suppressed—"no one" in the sense of a *class,* in the sense of a systematic struggle with a definite section of the population. We are not Utopians, and we do not in the least deny the possibility and inevitability of excesses on the part of *individual persons,* nor the need to suppress *such* excesses. But, in the first place, no special machinery, no special apparatus of repression is needed for this; this will be done by the armed people itself, as simply and as readily as any crowd of civilized people, even in modern society, parts a pair of combatants or does not allow a woman to be outraged. And, secondly, we know that the fundamental social cause of excesses which consist in violating the rules of social life is the exploitation of the masses, their want and their poverty. With the removal of this chief cause, excesses will inevitably begin to *"wither away."* We do not know how quickly and in what succession, but we know that they will wither away. With their withering away, the state will also *wither away.*

Without going into Utopias, Marx defined more fully what can *now* be defined regarding this future, namely, the difference between the lower and higher phases (degrees, stages) of Communist society.

First Phase of Communist Society

In the *Critique of the Gotha Programme,* Marx goes into some detail to disprove the Lassallean idea of the workers' receiving under

Socialism the "undiminished" or "full product of their labor." Marx
shows that out of the whole of the social labor of society, it is necessary to deduct a reserve fund, a fund for the expansion of production,
for the replacement of worn-out machinery, and so on; then, also,
out of the means of consumption must be deducted a fund for the
expenses of management, for schools, hospitals, homes for the aged,
and so on.

Instead of the hazy, obscure, general phrase of Lassalle's—"the
full product of his labor for the worker"—Marx gives a sober estimate of exactly how a Socialist society will have to manage its affairs.
Marx undertakes a *concrete* analysis of the conditions of life of a
society in which there is no capitalism, and says:

> What we are dealing with here [analyzing the programme of the
> party] is not a Communist society which has *developed* on its own
> foundations, but, on the contrary, one which is just *emerging* from
> capitalist society, and which therefore in all respects—economic, moral
> and intellectual—still bears the birthmarks of the old society from
> whose womb it sprung.*

And it is this Communist society—a society which has just come
into the world out of the womb of capitalism, and which, in all
respects, bears the stamp of the old society—that Marx terms the
"first," or lower, phase of Communist society.

The means of production are no longer the private property of
individuals. The means of production belong to the whole of society.
Every member of society, performing a certain part of socially-neces-
sary work, receives a certificate from society to the effect that he has
done such and such a quantity of work. According to this certificate,
he receives from the public warehouses, where articles of consumption are stored, a corresponding quantity of products. Deducting that
proportion of labor which goes to the public fund, every worker,
therefore, receives from society as much as he has given it.

"Equality" seems to reign supreme.

But when Lassalle, having in view such a social order (generally
called Socialism, but termed by Marx the first phase of Communism),
speaks of this as "just distribution," and says that this is "the equal
right of each to an equal product of labor," Lassalle is mistaken, and
Marx exposes his error.

* *Ibid.—Ed.*

"Equal right," says Marx, we indeed have here; but it is *still* a "bourgeois right," which, like every right, *presupposes inequality*. Every right is an application of the *same* measure to *different* people who, in fact, are not the same and are not equal to one another; this is why "equal right" is really a violation of equality, and an injustice. In effect, every man having done as much social labor as every other, receives an equal share of the social products (with the above-mentioned deductions).

But different people are not alike: one is strong, another is weak; one is married, the other is not; one has more children, another has less, and so on.

. . . With equal labor—Marx concludes—and therefore an equal share in the social consumption fund, one man in fact receives more than the other, one is richer than the other, and so forth. In order to avoid all these defects, rights, instead of being equal, must be unequal.*

The first phase of Communism, therefore, still cannot produce justice and equality; differences, and unjust differences, in wealth will still exist, but the *exploitation* of man by man will have become impossible, because it will be impossible to seize as private property the *means of production,* the factories, machines, land, and so on. In tearing down Lassalle's petty-bourgeois, confused phrase about "equality" and "justice" *in general,* Marx shows the *course of development* of Communist society, which is forced at first to destroy *only* the "injustice" that consists in the means of production having been seized by private individuals, and which *is not capable* of destroying at once the further injustice consisting in the distribution of the articles of consumption "according to work performed" (and not according to need).

The vulgar economists, including the bourgeois professors and also "our" Tugan-Baranovsky, constantly reproach the Socialists with forgetting the inequality of people and with "dreaming" of destroying this inequality. Such a reproach, as we see, only proves the extreme ignorance of the gentlemen propounding bourgeois ideology.

Marx not only takes into account with the greatest accuracy the inevitable inequality of men; he also takes into account the fact that the mere conversion of the means of production into the common property of the whole of society ("Socialism" in the generally ac-

* *Ibid.—Ed.*

cepted sense of the word) *does not remove* the defects of distribution
and the inequality of "bourgeois right" which *continue to rule* as long
as the products are divided "according to work performed."

But these defects—Marx continues—are unavoidable in the first
phase of Communist society, when, after long travail, it first emerges
from capitalist society. Justice can never rise superior to the economic
conditions of society and the cultural development conditioned by them.*

And so, in the first phase of Communist society (generally called
Socialism) "bourgeois right" is *not* abolished in its entirety, but only
in part, only in proportion to the economic transformation so far
attained, i.e., only in respect of the means of production. "Bourgeois
right" recognizes them as the private property of separate individuals.
Socialism converts them into common property. *To that extent,* and
to that extent alone, does "bourgeois right" disappear.

However, it continues to exist as far as its other part is concerned;
it remains in the capacity of regulator (determining factor) distributing the products and allotting labor among the members of society.
"He who does not work, shall not eat"—this Socialist principle is *already* realized; "for an equal quantity of labor, an equal quantity of
products"—this Socialist principle is also *already* realized. However,
this is not yet Communism, and this does not abolish "bourgeois
right," which gives to unequal individuals, in return for an unequal (in
reality unequal) amount of work, an equal quantity of products.

This is a "defect," says Marx, but it is unavoidable during the
first phase of Communism; for, if we are not to fall into Utopianism,
we cannot imagine that, having overthrown capitalism, people will
at once learn to work for society *without any standards of right;* indeed, the abolition of capitalism *does not immediately lay* the economic foundations for *such* a change.

And there is no other standard yet than that of "bourgeois right."
To this extent, therefore, a form of state is still necessary, which, while
maintaining public ownership of the means of production, would
preserve the equality of labor and equality in the distribution of
products.

The state is withering away in so far as there are no longer any
capitalists, any classes, and, consequently, no *class* can be suppressed.

But the state has not yet altogether withered away, since there still
remains the protection of "bourgeois right" which sanctifies actual

* *Ibid.—Ed.*

inequality. For the complete extinction of the state, complete Communism is necessary.

Higher Phase of Communist Society

Marx continues:

> In a higher phase of Communist society, when the enslaving subordination of individuals in the division of labor has disappeared, and with it also the antagonism between mental and physical labor; when labor has become not only a means of living, but itself the first necessity of life; when, along with the all-round development of individuals, the productive forces too have grown, and all the springs of social wealth are flowing more freely—it is only at that stage that it will be possible to pass completely beyond the narrow horizon of bourgeois rights, and for society to inscribe on its banners: from each according to his ability; to each according to his needs! *

Only now can we appreciate the full correctness of Engels' remarks in which he mercilessly ridiculed all the absurdity of combining the words "freedom" and "state." While the state exists there is no freedom. When there is freedom, there will be no state.

The economic basis for the complete withering away of the state is that high stage of development of Communism when the antagonism between mental and physical labor disappears, that is to say, when one of the principal sources of modern *social* inequality disappears—a source, moreover, which it is impossible to remove immediately by the mere conversion of the means of production into public property, by the mere expropriation of the capitalists.

This expropriation will make a gigantic development of the productive forces *possible*. And seeing how incredibly, even now, capitalism *retards* this development, how much progress could be made even on the basis of modern technique at the level it has reached, we have a right to say, with the fullest confidence, that the expropriation of the capitalists will inevitably result in a gigantic development of the productive forces of human society. But how rapidly this development will go forward, how soon it will reach the point of breaking away from the division of labor, of removing the antagonism between mental and physical labor, of transforming work into the "first necessity of life"—this we do not and *cannot* know.

* *Ibid.—Ed.*

Consequently, we have a right to speak solely of the inevitable withering away of the state, emphasizing the protracted nature of this process and its dependence upon the rapidity of development of the *higher phase* of Communism; leaving quite open the question of lengths of time, or the concrete forms of withering away, since material for the solution of such questions is *not available.*

The state will be able to wither away completely when society has realized the rule: "From each according to his ability; to each according to his needs," i.e., when people have become accustomed to observe the fundamental rules of social life, and their labor is so productive, that they voluntarily work *according to their ability.* "The narrow horizon of bourgeois rights," which compels one to calculate, with the hard-heartedness of a Shylock, whether he has not worked half an hour more than another, whether he is not getting less pay than another—this narrow horizon will then be left behind. There will then be no need for any exact calculation by society of the quantity of products to be distributed to each of its members; each will take freely "according to his needs."

From the bourgeois point of view, it is easy to declare such a social order "a pure Utopia," and to sneer at the Socialists for promising each the right to receive from society, without any control of the labor of the individual citizen, any quantity of truffles, automobiles, pianos, etc. Even now, most bouregois "savants" deliver themselves of such sneers, thereby displaying at once their ignorance and their self-seeking defense of capitalism.

Ignorance—for it has never entered the head of any Socialist to "promise" that the highest phase of Communism will arrive; while the great Socialists, in *foreseeing* its arrival, presupposed both a productivity of labor unlike the present and a person not like the present man in the street, capable of spoiling, without reflection, like the seminary students in Pomyalovsky's book, the stores of social wealth, and of demanding the impossible.

Until the "higher" phase of Communism arrives, the Socialists demand the *strictest* control, *by society and by the state,* of the quantity of labor and the quantity of consumption; only this control must *start* with the expropriation of the capitalists, with the control of the workers over the capitalists, and must be carried out, not by a state of bureaucrats, but by a state of *armed workers.*

Self-seeking defense of capitalism by the bourgeois ideologists (and their hangers-on like Tsereteli, Chernov and Co.) consists in that they *substitute* disputes and discussions about the distant future for the essential imperative questions of present-day policy: the expropriation of the capitalists, the conversion of *all* citizens into workers and employees of *one* huge "syndicate"—the whole state—and the complete subordination of the whole of the work of this syndicate to the really democratic state of the *Soviets of Workers' and Soldiers' Deputies.*

In reality, when a learned professor, and following him some philistine, and following the latter Messrs. Tsereteli and Chernov, talk of the unreasonable Utopias, of the demagogic promises of the Bolsheviks, of the impossibility of "introducing" Socialism, it is the higher stage or phase of Communism which they have in mind, and which no one has ever promised, or even thought of "introducing," for the reason that, generally speaking, it cannot be "introduced."

And here we come to that question of the scientific difference between Socialism and Communism, upon which Engels touched in his above-quoted discussion on the incorrectness of the name "Social-Democrat." The political difference between the first, or lower, and the higher phase of Communism will in time, no doubt, be tremendous; but it would be ridiculous to emphasize it now, under capitalism, and only, perhaps, some isolated Anarchist could invest it with primary importance. . . .

But the scientific difference between Socialism and Communism is clear. What is generally called Socialism was termed by Marx the "first" or lower phase of Communist society. In so far as the means of production become *public* property, the word "Communism" is also applicable here, providing we do not forget that it is *not* full Communism. The great significance of Marx's elucidations consists in this: that here, too, he consistently applies materialist dialectics, the doctrine of evolution, looking upon Communism as something which evolves *out of* capitalism. Instead of artificial, "elaborate," scholastic definitions and profitless disquisitions on the meaning of words (what Socialism is, what Communism is), Marx gives an analysis of what may be called stages in the economic ripeness of Communism.

In its first phase or first stage Communism *cannot* as yet be economically ripe and entirely free of all tradition and of all taint of capitalism. Hence the interesting phenomenon of Communism retaining, in its first phase, "the narrow horizon of bourgeois rights." Bourgeois rights, with respect to distribution of articles of *consump-*

tion, inevitably presupposes, of course, the existence of the *bourgeois state,* for rights are nothing without an apparatus capable of *enforcing* the observance of the rights.

Consequently, for a certain time not only bourgeois rights, but even the bourgeois state remains under Communism, without the bourgeoisie!

This may look like a paradox, or simply a dialectical puzzle for which Marxism is often blamed by people who would not make the least effort to study its extraordinarily profound content.

But, as a matter of fact, the old surviving in the new confronts us in life at every step, in nature as well as in society. Marx did not smuggle a scrap of "bourgeois" rights into Communism of his own accord; he indicated what is economically and politically inevitable in a society issuing *from the womb* of capitalism.

Democracy is of great importance for the working class in its struggle for freedom against the capitalists. But democracy is by no means a limit one may not overstep; it is only one of the stages in the course of development from feudalism to capitalism, and from capitalism to Communism.

Democracy means equality. The great significance of the struggle of the proletariat for equality, and the significance of equality as a slogan, are apparent, if we correctly interpret it as meaning the abolition of *classes.* But democracy means only *formal* equality. Immediately after the attainment of equality for all members of society *in respect of* the ownership of the means of production, that is, of equality of labor and equality of wages, there will inevitably arise before humanity the question of going further from formal equality to real equality, i.e., to realizing the rule, "From each according to his ability; to each according to his needs." By what stages, by means of what practical measures humanity will proceed to this higher aim— this we do not and cannot know. But it is important to realize how infinitely mendacious is the usual bourgeois presentation of Socialism as something lifeless, petrified, fixed once for all, whereas in reality, it is *only* with Socialism that there will commence a rapid, genuine, real mass advance, in which first the *majority* and then the whole of the population will take part—an advance in all domains of social and individual life.

Democracy is a form of the state—one of its varieties. Consequently, like every state, it consists in organized, systematic application of force against human beings. This on the one hand. On the other hand, however, it signifies the formal recognition of the equality of all citizens, the equal right of all to determine the structure and administration of the state. This, in turn, is connected with the fact that, at a certain stage in the development of democracy, it first rallies the proletariat as a revolutionary class against capitalism, and gives it an opportunity to crush, to smash to bits, to wipe off the face of the earth the bourgeois state machinery—even its republican variety: the standing army, the police, and bureaucracy; then it substitutes for all this a *more* democratic, but still a state machinery in the shape of armed masses of workers, which becomes transformed into universal participation of the people in the militia.

Here "quantity turns into quality": *such* a degree of democracy is bound up with the abandonment of the framework of bourgeois society, and the beginning of its Socialist reconstruction. If *everyone* really takes part in the administration of the state, capitalism cannot retain its hold. In its turn, capitalism, as it develops, itself creates *prerequisites* for "everyone" *to be able* really to take part in the administration of the state. Among such prerequisites are: universal literacy, already realized in most of the advanced capitalist countries, then the "training and disciplining" of millions of workers by the huge, complex, and socialized apparatus of the post-office, the railways, the big factories, large-scale commerce, banking, etc., etc.

With such *economic* prerequisites it is perfectly possible, immediately, within twenty-four hours after the overthrow of the capitalists and bureaucrats, to replace them, in the control of production and distribution, in the business of *control* of labor and products, by the armed workers, by the whole people in arms. (The question of control and accounting must not be confused with the question of the scientifically educated staff of engineers, agronomists and so on. These gentlemen work today, obeying the capitalists; they will work even better tomorrow, obeying the armed workers.)

Accounting and control—these are the *chief* things necessary for the organizing and correct functioning of the *first phase* of Communist society. *All* citizens are here transformed into hired employees of the state, which is made up of the armed workers. *All* citizens become employees and workers of *one* national state "syndicate." All that is required is that they should work equally, should regularly do their share of work, and should receive equal pay. The accounting and control necessary for this have been *simplified* by capitalism to the utmost, till they have become the extraordinarily simple operations of watching, recording and issuing receipts, within the reach of anybody who can read and write and knows the first four rules of arithmetic.*

When the *majority* of the people begin everywhere to keep such accounts and maintain such control over the capitalists (now converted into employees) and over the intellectual gentry, who still retain capitalist habits, this control will really become universal, general, national; and there will be no way of getting away from it, there will be "nowhere to go."

The whole of society will have become one office and one factory, with equal work and equal pay.

But this "factory" discipline, which the proletariat will extend to the whole of society after the defeat of the capitalists and the overthrow of the exploiters, is by no means our ideal, or our final aim. It is but a *foothold* necessary for the radical cleansing of society of all the hideousness and foulness of capitalist exploitation, *in order to advance further.*

From the moment when all members of society, or even only the overwhelming majority, have learned how to govern the state *themselves,* have taken this business into their own hands, have "established" control over the insignificant minority of capitalists, over the gentry with capitalist leanings, and the workers thoroughly demoralized by capitalism—from this moment the need for any government begins to disappear. The more complete the democracy, the nearer the moment when it begins to be unnecessary. The more democratic the "state" consisting of armed workers, which is "no longer a state in the proper sense of the word," the more rapidly does *every* state begin to wither away.

For when *all* have learned to manage, and independently are actually managing by themselves social production, keeping accounts, controlling the idlers, the gentlefolk, the swindlers and similar "guardians of capitalist traditions," then the escape from this national accounting and control will inevitably become so increasingly difficult, such a rare exception, and will probably be accompanied by such swift and severe punishment (for the armed workers are men of practical life, not sentimental intellectuals, and they will scarcely allow anyone to trifle with them), that very soon the *necessity* of observing

* When most of the functions of the state are reduced to this accounting and control by the workers themselves, then it ceases to be a "political state," and the "public functions will lose their political character and be transformed into simple administrative functions" [Engels, *Neue Zeit,* 1913, Vol. 32, p. 39—*Ed.*].

the simple, fundamental rules of everyday social life in common will have become a *habit*.

The door will then be wide open for the transition from the first phase of Communist society to its higher phase, and along with it to the complete withering away of the state.

21. PROGRAMME OF THE COMMUNIST INTERNATIONAL

The Third Communist International (or Comintern), established by Lenin in 1919, held its Sixth World Congress in September, 1928. The programme which it adopted was the best statement of the objectives of international communism since the Communist Manifesto *in 1848.*

The Ultimate Aim of the Communist International— World Communism*

The ultimate aim of the Communist International is to replace world capitalist economy by a world system of Communism. Communist society, the basis for which has been prepared by the whole course of historical development, is mankind's only way out, for it alone can abolish the contradictions of the capitalist system which threaten to degrade and destroy the human race.

Communist society will abolish the class division of society, i.e., simultaneously with the abolition of anarchy in production, it will abolish all forces of exploitation and oppression of man by man. Society will no longer consist of antagonistic classes in conflict with each other, but will represent a united commonwealth of labor. For the first time in its history mankind will take its fate into its own hands. Instead of destroying innumerable human lives and incalculable wealth in struggles between classes and nations, mankind will devote

* From *The Programme of the Communist International*, 1928. Reprinted from *The Strategy and Tactics of World Communism*, Supplement I, United States Government Printing Office, Washington, 1948.

all its energy to the struggle against the forces of nature, to the development and strengthening of its own collective might.

After abolishing private ownership in the means of production and converting them into social property, the world system of Communism will replace the elemental forces of the world market, of competition and the blind process of social production, by consciously organized and planned production for the purpose of satisfying rapidly growing social needs. With the abolition of competition and anarchy in production, devastating crises and still more devastating wars will disappear. Instead of colossal waste of productive forces and spasmodic development of society—there will be planned utilization of all material resources and painless economic development on the basis of unrestricted, smooth and rapid development of productive forces.

The abolition of private property and the disappearance of classes will do away with the exploitation of man by man. Work will cease to be toiling for the benefit of a class enemy: instead of being merely a means of livelihood it will become a necessity of life: want and economic inequality, the misery of enslaved classes, and a wretched standard of life generally will disappear; the hierarchy created in the division of labor system will be abolished together with the antagonism between mental and manual labor; and the last vestige of the social inequality of sexes will be removed. At the same time, the organs of class domination, and the State in the first place, will disappear also. The State, being the embodiment of class domination, will die out insofar as classes die out, and with it all measures of coercion will expire.

With the disappearance of classes the monopoly of education in every form will be abolished. Culture will become the acquirement of all and the class ideologies of the past will give place to scientific materialist philosophy. Under such circumstances the domination of man over man, in any form, becomes impossible, and a great field will be opened for the social selection and the harmonious development of all the talents inherent in humanity.

In Communist society no social restrictions will be imposed upon the growth of the forces of production. Private ownership in the means of production, the selfish lust for profits, the artificial retention of the masses in a state of ignorance, poverty—which retards technical progress in capitalist society, and unproductive expenditures will have no place in a Communist society. The most expedient utilization of the forces of nature and of the natural conditions of production in the various parts of the world; the removal of the antagonism between town and country, that under capitalism results from the low technical level of agriculture and its systematic lagging behind industry; the closest possible cooperation between science and technics; the utmost encouragement of research work and the practical application of its results on the widest possible social scale; planned organization of scientific work; the application of the most perfect methods of statistical accounting and planned regulation of economy; the rapidly growing social need, which is the most powerful internal driving force of the whole system—all these will secure the maximum productivity of social labor, which in turn will release human energy for the powerful development of science and art.

The development of the productive forces of world Communist society will make it possible to raise the well-being of the whole of humanity and to reduce to a minimum the time devoted to material production and, consequently, will enable culture to flourish as never before in history. This new culture of a humanity that is united for the first time in history, and has abolished all State boundaries, will, unlike capitalist culture, be based upon clear and transparent human relationships. Hence, it will bury forever all mysticism, religion, prejudice and superstition and will give a powerful impetus to the development of all-conquering scientific knowledge.

This higher stage of Communism, the stage in which Communist society has already developed on its own foundation, in which an enormous growth of social productive forces has accompanied the manifold development of man, in which humanity has already inscribed on its banner: "From each according to his abilities to each according to his needs!"—presupposes, as an historical condition precedent, a lower stage of development, the stage of Socialism. At this lower stage, Communist society only just emerges from capitalist society and bears all the economic, ethical and intellectual birthmarks it has inherited from the society from whose womb it is just emerging. The productive forces of Socialism are not yet sufficiently developed to assure a distribution of the products of labor according to needs: these are distributed according to the amount of labor expended. Division of labor, i.e., the system whereby certain groups perform certain labor functions, and especially the distinction between mental and manual labor, still exists. Although classes are abolished, traces of the old class division of society and, consequently, remnants of the

Proletarian State power, coercion, laws, still exist. Consequently, certain traces of inequality, which have not yet managed to die out altogether, still remain. The antagonism between town and country has not yet been entirely removed. But none of these survivals of former society is protected or defended by any social force. Being the product of a definite level of development of productive forces, they will disappear as rapidly as mankind, freed from the fetters of the capitalist system, subjugates the forces of nature, re-educates itself in the spirit of Communism, and passes from Socialism to complete Communism.

22. NIKITA S. KHRUSHCHEV

Nikita Khrushchev (1894-   ) is First Secretary of the Communist Party, and Premier of the Soviet Union. After a generation of ruthless but successful rule, Stalin died in 1953, leaving no obvious successor. By mid-1957 Khrushchev emerged as the dominant figure in the Soviet regime. In the fall of 1959, during a visit to the United States for talks with President Eisenhower, Khrushchev gave a press conference in Washington, part of which appears below. His statements clearly indicate the orthodox communist philosophy of his government, and his retention of the dialectical principles of Marx and Engels.

"We Will Bury You" *

Mr. Lawrence: A number of questions reflect a great interest in another remark once attributed to you, Mr. Khrushchev, to a diplomat at a reception, that you would bury us.

If you didn't say it, say so, and if you did say it, could you explain what you meant?

Premier Khrushchev: Present here is only a very small portion of the American people. But if I were to start to try to bury even this group, one life would not be enough. I believe I did use that expres-

* From replies to questions at a press conference at the National Press Club, Washington, D.C., as reported by *The Washington Post*, September 17, 1959. Reprinted by permission of *The Washington Post*.

sion once, and if I did, I will try to explain why and what it means. To put it more precisely, the expression I used was distorted, and on purpose, because what was meant was not the physical burial of any people but the question of the historical force of development.

It is well known that at the present time no one social or economic system is dominant throughout the world, but that there are different systems, social systems in different countries. And those systems change. At one time the most widespread system of society in the world was feudalism.

Then capitalism took its place. Why was that? Because capitalism was a more progressive kind of a system than was feudalism.

As compared to feudalism capitalism provided better opportunities to develop the productive forces of society. We believe that now capitalism has developed so far that it has given birth to certain fundamental differences within itself, and each society gives birth to the kind of society that will follow it. We believe that Karl Marx, Engels and Lenin gave scientific proof of the fact that the system, the social system of socialism would take the place of capitalism.

We believe in that. You do not, not all of you. I am sure there are people, many people under your form, system of society, who believe in that, and that is why I said that looking at the matter from the historical point of view, socialism, communism, would take the place of capitalism and capitalism thereby would be, so to speak, buried. You will say that that cannot be. But it will be recalled that in the ages past, feudals used to burn people who said that feudalism would disappear. Yet capitalism came to take the place of feudalism.

Now, capitalism is struggling, fighting against communism. I personally am convinced that communism will be victorious, as a system of society which provides better possibilities for the development of a country's productive forces; which enables every person to develop his capacities best; and insures full freedom of a person in that society. Many of you will not agree with that, but that means that I cannot agree with you either.

What is to be done? Let us each of us live under the system which we prefer, you under capitalism, and we will continue to build under communism.

All that is not progressive will die away someday, because if capitalism, the capitalist society, is a better form of society and gives better opportunities to develop a country's productive forces, then certainly it will win. But we think that the short history of the existence of our state does not speak in your favor. What place did our country hold in economics before the revolution, and in the development in the world? It was an illiterate country. Today the rate of literacy in our country is higher than anywhere else. We now have 160,000 engineers graduate from our universities each year, which is three times more than this country. Some say that the more scientists we have, the sooner will communism collapse. Then we seem to be working to our own end, but that is not the case. We regard communism as a science.

Thank you, ladies and gentlemen.

23. MAO TSE-TUNG

Mao Tse-Tung (1893-   ) was one of the founders of the Communist Party of China in 1921, and its unquestioned leader at the time of this important statement in 1949. On People's Democratic Dictatorship is the official doctrine of the Chinese People's Republic and forms the basis for the revolutionary legislation and political action of the present regime. As the foremost spokesman and theoretician of the communist movement in the world's most populous country, Mao symbolizes the growing strength of communism outside the Soviet Union. These passages illustrate the way in which historical materialism, with Leninist emendations, remains the rigid framework for his communist thought.

On People's Democratic Dictatorship*

This day, the first of July, 1949, bears witness that the Communist Party of China has already run a course of twenty-eight years. Like a human being, it has its childhood, youth, manhood, and old age. The Communist Party of China is no longer a child or a lad in his teens. It has reached manhood. When a man grows old, he will die; the same is true of political parties. When classes disappear, all

* From Mao Tse-Tung, *On People's Democratic Dictatorship*, 1949. These passages are from an official translation, published by the Foreign Languages Press, Peking, as the revised fifth edition, 1952.

instruments of class struggle—political parties and the state machine —will also lose their reason for existence, become unnecessary and gradually wither away. They will have fulfilled their historical mission, and human society will move to a higher stage.

Our Party forms the precise opposite to the political parties of the bourgeoisie. They are afraid to speak of the disappearance of classes, state power, and parties. We, on the contrary, openly declare that we are striving with all our might precisely to create the conditions that will hasten the end of these things. The Communist Party and the state power of the people's dictatorship constitute such conditions.

Anyone who does not recognize this truth is not a Communist. Perhaps it is not yet grasped by young comrades who have only recently joined the Party and have not studied Marxism-Leninism. They must understand this truth before they can form a correct world outlook. They have to understand that all mankind must go through the process of eliminating classes, state power, and parties; it is only a question of time and conditions.

Everywhere in the world Communists know much better than the bourgeoisie. They understand the laws governing the existence and development of things; they understand dialectics; they can see further ahead.

The bourgeoisie does not welcome this truth because it does not want to be overthrown by the people. It is painful and intolerable to those to be overthrown as the Kuomintang is now being overthrown by us, or as the Japanese imperialists were overthrown by us in cooperation with the peoples of other countries.

For the working class, the laboring people, and the Communists, the problem of being overthrown simply does not exist. Theirs is the problem of working hard to create the conditions for the natural disappearance of classes, state power, and political parties so that mankind can advance to universal harmony.

We have here touched briefly upon the distant prospect of human progress in order to clarify the problems which follow.

Our Party has already run a course of twenty-eight years. As we all know, the course has not been a peaceful one, but beset with difficulties. We have had to fight foreign and domestic enemies, as well as enemies inside and outside the Party. We are indebted to Marx, Engels, Lenin, and Stalin for our weapon. This weapon is not a machine gun, but Marxism-Leninism. . . .

It was through the Russians that the Chinese were introduced to Marxism. Before the October Revolution, the Chinese were not only unaware of Lenin and Stalin but did not even know of Marx or Engels. The salvos of the October Revolution awoke us to Marxism-Leninism. The October Revolution helped the progressives of China and of the whole world to adopt the proletarian world outlook as an instrument for foreseeing a nation's future and considering anew one's own problems. "Follow the path of the Russians" was the conclusion.

In 1919, the May Fourth Movement took place in China. In 1921, the Communist Party of China was founded. Sun Yat-sen, then in the depths of despair, encountered the October Revolution and the Chinese Communist Party. He welcomed the October Revolution, welcomed Russian aid to the Chinese, and welcomed the co-operation of the Chinese Communist Party.

Sun Yat-sen died and Chiang Kai-shek rose to power. In the course of the long period of twenty-two years, Chiang Kai-shek dragged China into helpless straits.

Within this period there occurred the anti-fascist Second World War, with the Soviet Union as its main force. This resulted in the downfall of three great imperialist powers and the weakening of two others. Only one great imperialist power came out unscathed, the United States. However, the domestic crisis in the United States is very grave; she wants to enslave the world, and by supplying Chiang Kai-shek with arms, has helped slaughter several million Chinese. Under the leadership of the Chinese Communist Party, the Chinese people, after driving out Japanese imperialism, have carried on the War of Liberation for three years and have basically gained victory.

That is how it happened that Western bourgeois civilization, bourgeois democracy, and the bourgeois pattern of republic all went bankrupt in the eyes of the Chinese people. Bourgeois democracy gives way to the people's democracy under the leadership of the working class, and the bourgeois republic gives way to the people's republic. This creates the possibility of passing through a people's republic to Socialism and Communism, to the disappearance of classes and the attainment of universal harmony. . . .

Internationally we belong to the side of the anti-imperialist front, headed by the Soviet Union. We can only turn to this side for genuine and friendly help, not to the side of the imperialist front.

"You are dictatorial." My dear sirs, just as you say. That is just what we are. All the experiences of the Chinese people, accumulated in the course of several decades, tell us to put into effect a people's democratic dictatorship. This means that the reactionaries must be deprived of the right to voice their opinions; only the people have that right.

Who are the "people"? At the present stage in China, they are the working class, the peasantry, the petty bourgeoisie, and the national bourgeoisie.

Under the leadership of the working class and the Communist Party these classes unite to create their own state and elect their own government so as to enforce their dictatorship over the henchmen of imperialism—the landlord class and bureaucratic capitalist class, as well as the reactionary clique of the Kuomintang, which represents these classes, and their accomplices. The people's government will suppress such individuals. It will only tolerate them if they behave themselves, but not if they prove intractable in speech or action. If they are intractable, they will be instantly curbed and punished. Within the ranks of the people, the democratic system is carried out by giving freedom of speech, assembly, and association. The right to vote is given only to the people, not to the reactionaries.

These two aspects, democracy for the people and dictatorship for the reactionaries, when combined, constitute the people's democratic dictatorship.

Why must things be done in this way? Everyone is clear on this point. If things were not done in this way, the revolution would fail, the people would suffer, and the state would perish.

"Don't you want to abolish state power?" Yes, we do, but not at the present time. We cannot yet afford to. Why not? Because imperialism still exists, and within our country reactionaries and classes still exist.

Our present task is to strengthen the people's state machine— meaning principally the people's army, the people's police, and the people's courts—so that national defense can be made secure and the people's interests protected. Given these conditions, China, under the leadership of the working class and the Communist Party, can develop steadily from an agricultural into an industrial country and from a New Democratic into a Socialist and, eventually, a Communist society, when all classes will disappear and universal harmony become a reality. . . .

Summarizing our experiences and putting them in a nutshell: the people's democratic dictatorship is led by the working class through the Communist Party and based upon the alliance of the workers and peasants. This dictatorship must unite with all international revolutionary forces. Such then is our formula, our main experience, our main program.

During the long period of its twenty-eight years' existence, our Party has done just one thing, that is, it has achieved basic victory in the revolutionary war. This is worth celebrating because it is a people's victory, and because it is a victory in such a large country as China.

But much work still lies ahead of us. If we think of ourselves as walking down a road, the distance so far covered would seem little more than the first step in a ten thousand *li* march. Remnants of the enemy have still to be wiped out. A serious task of economic construction lies before us. We shall soon lay aside some of the things we have learned to do with ease, and we shall be compelled to take up things we are not familiar with. This means difficulties. The imperialists count upon our inability to tackle our economic problems. They are looking on, waiting for our failure.

We must overcome all the difficulties and learn the things we do not understand. We must learn to do economic work from all who know the ropes, no matter who they are. We must respect them as teachers, learning from them respectfully and earnestly. We must not pretend to know when we do not know. We must not put on bureaucratic airs. If one bores into a subject for several months, for a year or two, or perhaps even three or five years, one will eventually master it.

At first some Communists in the Soviet Union were also unable to handle economic matters, and the imperialists then also looked forward to their failure. But the Communist Party of the U.S.S.R. emerged victorious. Under Lenin's and Stalin's leadership, the Soviet Communists have been able not only to conduct a revolution but also to carry out construction. They have already built up a great and glorious Socialist state.

The Communist Party of the U.S.S.R. is our very best teacher, and we must learn from it. The situation at home and abroad is in our favor. We can rely entirely upon the weapon of the people's democratic dictatorship, unite all the people throughout the country, except the reactionaries, and march steadily towards our goal.

Section VI

THE STRATEGY AND TACTICS OF COMMUNISM

More than a philosophy, communism has become, under the leadership of Lenin, Stalin, Khrushchev, Mao, and others, an effective, militant, and extremely powerful international movement. Today roughly one third of the world's population live under communist regimes. The successes of the communist movement have been due largely to shrewd and careful analysis by its leaders of the problems of military and political strategy and tactics which they have faced.

Chief among the instruments in their international struggles has been a highly organized and well disciplined Communist Party. It is the Party which, Lenin said, made the revolution in Russia possible, and it is the Party which must be used to penetrate the bastions of a hostile capitalism; to educate the masses along Marxist lines; and to prepare the way for the international revolution of the proletarian class.

24. V. I. LENIN

Precisely at the turn of the twentieth century Lenin returned from Siberian exile and began immediately to stir the fires of revolution in Russia. Most famous among the series of vigorous works which ensued was that from which these passages are taken, in which he insisted upon a return to orthodox revolutionary Marxism, and attacked the "revision-ists" and "opportunistic trade-unionists." Ceaseless propaganda on the largest possible scale, directed by a centralized party according to care-fully prepared plans, was the core of his demands. The party must con-sist of members "who shall devote to the revolution not only their spare evenings, but the whole of their lives."

What Is To Be Done? *

We are marching in a compact group along a precipitous and difficult path, firmly holding each other by the hand. We are sur-rounded on all sides by enemies, and are under their almost constant fire. We have combined voluntarily, especially for the purpose of fighting the enemy and not to retreat into the adjacent marsh, the inhabitants of which, right from the very outset, have reproached us with having separated ourselves into an exclusive group, and with having chosen the path of struggle instead of the path of conciliation. And now several in our crowd begin to cry out: Let us go into this marsh! And when we begin to shame them, they retort: How con-servative you are! Are you not ashamed to deny us the right to invite you to take a better road!

Oh yes, gentlemen! You are free, not only to invite us, but to go yourselves wherever you will, even into the marsh. In fact, we think that the marsh is your proper place, and we are prepared to render *you* every assistance to get there. Only, let go of our hands, don't clutch at us, and don't besmirch the grand word "freedom"; for we too are "free" to go where we please, free, not only to fight against the marsh, but also those who are turning towards the marsh.

Revolutionary Theory and the Social-Democratic Movement in Russia

"Dogmatism, doctrinairism," "ossification of the party—the inevi-table retribution that follows the violent strait-lacing of thought," these are the enemies against which the kindly champions of "free-dom of criticism" are allying their forces in *Rabocheye Dyelo*. We

* This and the following passages are from V. I. Lenin, *What Is To Be Done?*, 1902. Reprinted by permission of the Foreign Languages Publishing House, Moscow.

are very glad that this question has been brought up and we would propose only to add to it another question:

Who are to be the judges? . . .

We see that high-sounding phrases against the ossification of thought, etc., conceal carelessness and helplessness in the development of theoretical ideas. The case of the Russian Social-Democrats strikingly illustrates the fact observed in the whole of Europe (and long ago observed in German Marxism) that the notorious freedom of criticism implies, not the substitution of one theory by another, but freedom from every complete and thought-out theory; it implies eclecticism and absence of principle. Those who are in the least acquainted with the actual state of our movement cannot but see that the spread of Marxism was accompanied by a certain deterioration of theoretical standards. Quite a number of people, with very little, and even totally lacking in, theoretical training, joined the movement for the sake of its practical significance and its practical successes. We can judge, therefore, how tactless *Rabocheye Dyelo* is when, with an air of invincibility, it quotes the statement of Marx that: "A single step of the real movement is worth a dozen programmes." To repeat these words in the epoch of theoretical chaos is sheer mockery. Moreover, these words of Marx are taken from his letter on the Gotha Programme, in which he *sharply condemns* eclecticism in the formulation of principles: "If you must combine," Marx wrote to the party leaders, "then enter into agreements to satisfy the practical aims of the movement, but do not haggle over principles, do not make 'concessions' in theory." This was Marx's idea, and yet there are people among us who strive—in his name!—to belittle the significance of theory.

Without a revolutionary theory there can be no revolutionary movement. This cannot be insisted upon too strongly at a time when the fashionable preaching of opportunism is combined with absorption in the narrowest forms of practical activity. The importance of theory for Russian Social-Democrats is still greater for three reasons, which are often forgotten:

The first is that our party is only in the process of formation, its features are only just becoming outlined, and it has not yet completely settled its reckoning with other tendencies in revolutionary thought which threaten to divert the movement from the proper path. . . .

The second reason is that the Social-Democratic movement is

essentially an international movement. This does not mean merely that we must combat national chauvinism. It means also that a movement that is starting in a young country can be successful only on the condition that it assimilates the experience of other countries. In order to assimilate this experience, it is not sufficient merely to be acquainted with it, or simply to transcribe the latest resolutions. A critical attitude is required towards this experience, and ability to subject it to independent tests. Only those who realize how much the modern labor movement has grown in strength will understand what a reserve of theoretical forces and political (as well as revolutionary) experience is required to fulfill this task.

The third reason is that the national tasks of Russian Social-Democracy are such as have never confronted any other Socialist party in the world. Farther on we shall deal with the political and organizational duties which the task of emancipating the whole people from the yoke of autocracy imposes upon us. At the moment, we wish merely to state that the *rôle of vanguard can be fulfilled only by a party that is guided by an advanced theory*. . . . The Russian workers . . . will have to take up the fight against a monster, compared with which anti-Socialist laws in a constitutional country are but pigmies. History has now confronted us with an immediate task which is *more revolutionary than all the immediate tasks* that confront the proletariat of any other country. The fulfillment of this task, the destruction of the most powerful bulwark, not only of European, but also (it may now be said) of Asiatic reaction, places the Russian proletariat in the vanguard of the international revolutionary proletariat. We shall have the right to count upon acquiring the honorable title already earned by our predecessors, the revolutionists of the seventies, if we succeed in inspiring our movement—which is a thousand times wider and deeper—with the same devoted determination and vigor. . . .

Since there can be no talk of an independent ideology being developed by the masses of the workers in the process of their movement then *the only choice is:* Either bourgeois, or Socialist ideology. There is no middle course (for humanity has not created a "third" ideology, and, moreover, in a society torn by class antagonisms there can never be a non-class or above-class ideology). Hence, to belittle Socialist ideology *in any way,* to *deviate from it in the slightest degree* means strengthening bourgeois ideology. There is a lot of talk about spontaneity, but the *spontaneous* development of the labor movement leads to its becoming subordinated to bourgeois ideology, it means developing *according to the programme* of the *Credo,* for the spontaneous labor movement is pure and simple trade unionism, is *Nur-Gewerkschaftlerei,* and trade unionism means the ideological subordination of the workers to the bourgeoisie. Hence, our task, the task of Social-Democracy, is to *combat spontaneity,* to *divert* the labor movement, with its spontaneous trade-unionist striving, from under the wing of the bourgeoisie, and to bring it under the wing of revolutionary Social-Democracy. . . .

The Working Class as Champion of Democracy

We have seen that the organization of wide political agitation, and consequently, of all-sided political exposures are an absolutely necessary *and paramount* task of activity, that is, if that activity is to be truly Social-Democratic. We arrived at this conclusion *solely* on the grounds of the pressing needs of the working class for political knowledge and political training. But this ground by itself is too narrow for the presentation of the question, for it ignores the general democratic tasks of Social-Democracy as a whole, and of modern, Russian Social-Democracy in particular. In order to explain the situation more concretely we shall approach the subject from an aspect that is "nearer" to the Economists, namely, from the practical aspect. "Everyone agrees" that it is necessary to develop the political consciousness of the working class. But the question arises, How is that to be done? What must be done to bring this about? The economic struggle merely brings the workers "up against" questions concerning the attitude of the government towards the working class. Consequently, *however, much we may try* to "give to the economic struggle itself a political character" *we shall never be able* to develop the political consciousness of the workers (to the degree of Social-Democratic consciousness) by confining ourselves to the economic struggle, for *the limits of this task are too narrow.* . . .

The workers can acquire class political consciousness *only from without,* that is, only outside of the economic struggle, outside of the sphere of relations between workers and employers. The sphere from which alone it is possible to obtain this knowledge is the sphere of relationships between *all* classes and the state and the government

—the sphere of the inter-relations between *all* classes. For that reason, the reply to the question: What must be done in order that the workers may acquire political knowledge? cannot be merely the one which, in the majority of cases, the practical workers, especially those who are inclined towards Economism, usually content themselves with, i.e., "go among the workers." To bring political knowledge to the workers the Social-Democrats must *go among all classes of the population,* must dispatch units of their army *in all directions.*

We deliberately select this awkward formula, we deliberately express ourselves in a simple, forcible way, not because we desire to indulge in paradoxes, but in order to "stimulate" the Economists to take up their tasks which they unpardonably ignore, to make them understand the difference between trade-union and Social-Democratic politics, which they refuse to understand. Therefore, we beg the reader not to get excited, but to hear us patiently to the end.

Take the type of Social-Democratic circle that has been most widespread during the past few years, and examine its work. It has "contact with the workers," it issues leaflets—in which abuses in the factories, the government's partiality towards the capitalists, and the tyranny of the police are strongly condemned—and rests content with this. At meetings of workers, there are either no discussions or they do not extend beyond such subjects. Lectures and discussions on the history of the revolutionary movement, on questions of the home and foreign policy of our government, on questions of the economic evolution of Russia and of Europe, and the position of the various classes in modern society, etc., are extremely rare. Of systematically acquiring and extending contact with other classes of society, no one even dreams. The ideal leader, as the majority of the members of such circles picture him, is something more in the nature of a trade-union secretary than a Socialist political leader. Any trade-union secretary, an English one, for instance, helps the workers to conduct the economic struggle, helps to expose factory abuses, explains the injustice of the laws and of measures which hamper the freedom of strikes and the freedom to picket, to warn all and sundry that a strike is proceeding at a certain factory, explains the partiality of arbitration courts which are in the hands of the bourgeois classes, etc., etc. In a word, every trade-union secretary conducts and helps to conduct "the economic struggle against the employers and the government." It cannot be too strongly insisted that *this is not* enough to constitute Social-Democracy. The Social-Democrat's ideal should not be a trade-union secretary, but a *tribune of the people,* able to react to every manifestation of tyranny and oppression, no matter where it takes place, no matter what stratum or class of the people it affects; he must be able to group all these manifestations into a single picture of police violence and capitalist exploitation; he must be able to take advantage of every petty event in order to explain his Socialistic convictions and his Social-Democratic demands *to all,* in order to explain to *all* and everyone the world historical significance of the struggle for the emancipation of the proletariat. . . .

We said that a Social-Democrat, if he really believes it is necessary to develop the political consciousness of the proletariat, must "go among all classes of the people." This gives rise to the questions: How is this to be done? Have we enough forces to do this? Is there a base for such work among all the other classes? Will this not mean a retreat, or lead to a retreat from the class point-of-view? We shall deal with these questions.

We must "go among all classes of the people" as theoreticians, as propagandists, as agitators, and as organizers. No one doubts that the theoretical work of Social-Democrats should be directed towards studying all the features of the social and political position of the various classes. But extremely little is done in this direction compared with the work that is done in studying the features of factory life. In the committees and circles, you will meet men who are immersed say in the study of some special branch of the metal industry, but you will hardly ever find members of organizations (obliged, as often happens, for some reason or other to give up practical work) especially engaged in the collection of material concerning some pressing question of social and political life which could serve as a means for conducting Social-Democratic work among other strata of the population. In speaking of the lack of training of the majority of present-day leaders of the labor movement, we cannot refrain from mentioning the point about training in this connection also, for it is also bound up with the "economic" conception of "close organic contact with the proletarian struggle." The principal thing, of course, is *propaganda and agitation* among all strata of the people. The Western-European Social-Democrats find their work in this field facilitated by the calling of public meetings, to which *all* are free to go, and by the parliament, in which they speak to the representatives of *all* classes. We have neither a parliament, nor the freedom to call meetings, nevertheless we are able to arrange meetings of workers who desire to listen to *a Social-Democrat*. We must also find ways and means of calling meetings of representatives of all and every other class of the population that desire to listen to a *Democrat;* for he who forgets that "the Communists support every revolutionary movement," that we are obliged for that reason to emphasize *general democratic tasks before the whole people,* without for a moment concealing our Socialistic convictions, is not a Social-Democrat. He who forgets his obligation to *be in advance of everybody* in bringing up, sharpening and solving *every* general democratic question, is not a Social-Democrat. . . .

Is there scope for activity among all classes of the population? Those who fail to see this also lag intellectually behind the spontaneous awakening of the masses. The labor movement has aroused and is continuing to arouse discontent in some, hopes for support for the opposition in others, and the consciousness of the intolerableness and inevitable downfall of autocracy in still others. We would be "politicians" and Social-Democrats only in name (as very often happens), if we failed to realize that our task is to utilize every manifestation of discontent, and to collect and utilize every grain of even rudimentary protest. . . .

Only a party that will *organize* real all-national exposures can become the vanguard of the revolutionary forces in our time. The word "all-national" has a very profound meaning. The overwhelming majority of the non-working class exposers (and in order to become the vanguard, we must attract other classes) are sober politicians and cool business men. They know perfectly well how dangerous it is to "complain" even against a minor official, let alone against the "omnipotent" Russian government. And they will come to us with their complaints only when they see that these complaints really have effect, and when they see that we represent a *political* force. In order to become this political force in the eyes of outsiders, much persistent and stubborn work is required to *increase* our own consciousness, initiative and energy. . . .

25. JOSEF STALIN

The following passages from The Foundations of Leninism *present a concise and forthright statement of the strategic and tactical principles of the communist movement.*

[The Strategy of the Revolution] *

Strategy is the determination of the direction of the main blow of the proletariat at a given stage of the revolution, the elaboration of a corresponding plan for the disposition of the revolutionary forces (the main and secondary reserves), the fight to carry out this plan throughout the given stage of the revolution.

Our revolution already passed through two stages, and after the October Revolution it has entered a third stage. Our strategy changed accordingly.

First stage. 1903 to February 1917. Objective: to overthrow tsarism and completely wipe out the survivals of medievalism. The main force of the revolution: the proletariat. Immediate reserves: the peasantry. Direction of the main blow: the isolation of the liberal-monarchist bourgeoisie, which was striving to win over the peasantry and liquidate the revolution by *compromising* with tsarism. Plan for the disposition of forces: alliance of the working class with the peasantry.

The proletariat must carry to completion the democratic revolution, by allying to itself the mass of the peasantry in order to crush by force the resistance of the autocracy and to paralyze the instability of the bourgeoisie. (Lenin, *Selected Works,* Vol. III, p. 110.)

* This and the following passages are from J. Stalin, *The Foundations of Leninism,* 1924. Reprinted by permission of the Foreign Languages Publishing House, Moscow.

Second stage. March 1917 to October 1917. Objective: to over-throw imperialism in Russia and to withdraw from the imperialist war. The main force of the revolution: the proletariat. Immediate reserves: the poor peasantry. The proletariat of neighboring countries as probable reserves. The protracted war and the crisis of imperialism as the favorable factor. Direction of the main blow: isolation of the petty-bourgeois democrats (Mensheviks and Socialist-Revolutiona-ries), who were striving to win over the toiling masses of the peasantry and to terminate the revolution by *compromising* with imperialism. Plan for the disposition of forces: alliance of the proletariat with the poor peasantry.

> The proletariat must accomplish the socialist revolution by allying to itself the mass of the semi-proletarian elements of the population in order to crush by force the resistance of the bourgeoisie and to paralyze the instability of the peasantry and the petty bourgeoisie. (*Ibid.*, p. 111.)

Third stage. Commenced after the October Revolution. Objective: to consolidate the dictatorship of the proletariat in one country, using it as a base for the overthrow of imperialism in all countries. The revolution is spreading beyond the confines of one country; the period of world revolution has commenced. The main forces of the revolution: the dictatorship of the proletariat in one country, the revolutionary movement of the proletariat in all countries. Main reserves: the semi-proletarian and small-peasant masses in the de-veloped countries, the liberation movement in the colonies and dependent countries. Direction of the main blow: isolation of the petty-bourgeois democrats, isolation of the parties of the Second International, which constitute the main support of the policy of *compromise* with imperialism. Plan for the disposition of forces: alliance of the proletarian revolution with the liberation movement in the colonies and the dependent countries.

Strategy deals with the main forces of the revolution and their reserves. It changes with the passing of the revolution from one stage to another, but remains essentially unchanged throughout a given stage. . . .

[The Tactics of the Revolution]

Tactics are the determination of the line of conduct of the proletariat in the comparatively short period of the flow or ebb of the movement, of the rise or decline of the revolution, the fight to carry out this line by means of replacing old forms of struggle and organization by new ones, old slogans by new ones, by combining these forms, etc. While the object of strategy is to win the war against tsarism, let us say, or against the bourgeoisie, to carry the struggle against tsarism or against the bourgeoisie to its end, tactics concern themselves with less important objects, for they aim not at winning the war as a whole, but at winning a particular engagement, or a particular battle, at carrying through successfully a particular campaign or a particular action corresponding to the concrete circumstances in the given period of rise or decline of the revolution. Tactics are a part of strategy, subordinate to it and serving it.

Tactics change according to flow and ebb. While the strategic plan remained unchanged during the first stage of the revolution (1903 to February 1917) tactics changed several times during that period. In the period from 1903 to 1905 the Party pursued offensive tactics, for the tide of the revolution was rising, the movement was on the upgrade, and tactics had to proceed from this fact. Accordingly, the forms of struggle were revolutionary, corresponding to the requirements of the rising tide of the revolution. Local political strikes, political demonstrations, the general political strike, boycott of the Duma, insurrection, revolutionary fighting slogans—such were the successive forms of the struggle during that period. These changes in the forms of struggle were accompanied by corresponding changes in the forms of organization. Factory committees, revolutionary peasant committees, strike committees, Soviets of workers' deputies, a workers' party operating more or less openly—such were the forms of organization during that period.

In the period from 1907 to 1912 the Party was compelled to resort to tactics of retreat; for we then experienced a decline in the revolutionary movement, the ebb of the revolution, and tactics necessarily had to take this fact into consideration. The forms of struggle, as well as the forms of organization, changed accordingly: Instead of boycott of the Duma there was participation in the Duma; instead

of open, direct revolutionary action outside the Duma, there were
parliamentary speeches and work in the Duma; instead of general
political strikes, there were partial economic strikes, or simply a
lull in activities. Of course, the Party had to go underground during
that period, while the revolutionary mass organizations were superseded by cultural, educational, cooperative, insurance and other legal
organizations.

The same must be said of the second and third stages of the
revolution, during which tactics changed dozens of times, whereas
the strategical plans remained unchanged.

Tactics deal with the forms of struggle and the forms of organization of the proletariat, with their changes and combinations. During
a given stage of the revolution tactics may change several times,
depending on the flow and ebb, the rise and decline, of the revolution.

26. V. I. LENIN

*While ethics have never been a primary concern of the Marxist philoso-
phers, the following passage from one of Lenin's speeches presents an
outline of the ethical principles they employ.*

[On Communist Morality] *

. . . This brings me to the question of how we should teach
Communism and what are the specific features of our methods.

Here, first of all, I will deal with the question of Communist ethics.

You must train yourselves to become Communists. The task of the
Young Communist League is to organize its practical activities in
such a way that, in learning, organizing, uniting and fighting, it shall

* From *The Tasks of the Youth Leagues,* an address delivered to the Third
All-Russian Congress of the Russian Young Communist League, October 2,
1920. Reprinted from *The Strategy and Tactics of World Communism,* Supplement I, United States Government Printing Office, Washington, 1948.

train its members and all those who look upon it as their leader, train them to become Communists. The whole object of the training, education and tuition of the youth of today should be to imbue them with Communist ethics.

But is there such a thing as Communist ethics? Is there such a thing as Communist morality? Of course there is. Often it is made to appear that we have no ethics of our own; and very often the bourgeoisie accuse us Communists of repudiating all ethics. This is a method of shuffling concepts, of throwing dust in the eyes of the workers and peasants.

In what sense do we repudiate ethics and morality?

In the sense that they were preached by the bourgeoisie, who declared that ethics were God's commandments. We, of course, say that we do not believe in God, and that we know perfectly well that the clergy, the landlords and the bourgeoisie spoke in the name of God in order to pursue their own exploiters' interests. Or, instead of deducing these ethics from the commandments of morality, from the commandments of God, they deduced them from idealistic or semi-idealistic phrases, which were always very similar to God's commandments.

We repudiate all morality that is taken outside of human, class concepts. We say that this is deception, a fraud, which clogs the brains of the workers and peasants in the interests of the landlords and capitalists.

We say that our morality is entirely subordinated to the interests of the class struggle of the proletariat. Our morality is deduced from the class struggle of the proletariat.

The old society was based on the oppression of all the workers and peasants by the landlords and capitalists. We had to destroy this, we had to overthrow this; but for this we had to create unity. God will not create such unity.

This unity could be created only by the factories and works, only by the proletariat, trained, and roused from its age-long slumber; only when that class was formed did the mass movement begin which led to what we see now—the victory of the proletariat revolution in one of the weakest countries in the world, a country which for three years has repelled the attacks of the bourgeoisie of the whole world. And we see that the proletarian revolution is growing all over the world. We now say, on the basis of experience, that the proletariat alone could create the compact force that could take the lead of the disunited and scattered peasantry, that could withstand all the attacks of the exploiters. This class alone can help the toiling masses to unite, to rally and completely withstand all attacks upon, completely consolidate and completely build up, Communist society.

That is why we say that for us there is no such thing as morality taken outside of human society; such a morality is a fraud. For us, morality is subordinated to the interests of the class struggle of the proletariat.

27. V. I. LENIN

Rigid internal discipline, combined with the utmost flexibility in external arrangements, were the key elements of the Communist Party strategy which Lenin adopted. In "Left Wing" Communism, *Lenin supplements these general principles with specific tactical directives concerning the infiltration of trade unions and parliaments and the making of compromises. "There are," he points out, "compromises and compromises."*

[Party Discipline] *

Certainly nearly everyone now realizes that the Bolsheviks could not have maintained themselves in power for two and a half months, let alone for two and a half years, unless the strictest, truly iron discipline prevailed in our Party, and unless the latter had been rendered the fullest and unreserved support of the whole mass of the working class, that is, of all its thinking, honest, self-sacrificing and influential elements who are capable of leading or of attracting the backward strata.

The dictatorship of the proletariat is a most determined and most ruthless war waged by the new class against a *more powerful* enemy, the bourgeoisie, whose resistance is increased *tenfold* by its overthrow (even if only in one country), and whose power lies not only

* This and the following passages are from V. I. Lenin, *"Left Wing" Communism: An Infantile Disorder*, 1920. Reprinted by permission of the Foreign Languages Publishing House, Moscow.

in the strength of international capital, in the strength and durability of the international connections of the bourgeoisie, but also in the *force of habit,* in the strength of *small production.* For, unfortunately, small production is still very, very widespread in the world, and small production *engenders* capitalism and the bourgeoisie continuously, daily, hourly, spontaneously, and on a mass scale. For all these reasons the dictatorship of the proletariat is essential, and victory over the bourgeoisie is impossible without a long, stubborn and desperate war of life and death, a war demanding perseverance, discipline, firmness, indomitableness and unity of will.

I repeat, the experience of the victorious dictatorship of the proletariat in Russia has clearly shown even to those who are unable to think, or who have not had occasion to ponder over this question, that absolute centralization and the strictest discipline of the proletariat constitute one of the fundamental conditions for victory over the bourgeoisie.

This is often discussed. But far from enough thought is given to what it means, and to the conditions that make it possible. Would it not be better if greetings to the Soviet power and the Bolsheviks were *more frequently* accompanied by a *profound analysis* of the reasons *why* the Bolsheviks were able to build up the discipline the revolutionary proletariat needs?

As a trend of political thought as a political party, Bolshevism exists since 1903. Only the history of Bolshevism during the *whole* period of its existence can satisfactorily explain why it was able to build up and to maintain under the most difficult conditions the iron discipline that is needed for the victory of the proletariat.

And first of all the question arises: how is the discipline of the revolutionary party of the proletariat maintained? How is it tested? How is it reinforced? First, by the class consciousness of the proletarian vanguard and by its devotion to the revolution, by its perseverance, self-sacrifice and heroism. Secondly, by its ability to link itself, to keep in close touch with, and to a certain extent, if you like, to merge itself with the broadest masses of the toilers—primarily with the proletarian, *but also with the non-proletarian* toiling masses. Thirdly, by the correctness of the political leadership exercised by this vanguard and of its political strategy and tactics, provided that the broadest masses have been convinced *by their own experiences* that they are correct. Without these conditions, discipline in a revolutionary party that is really capable of being a party of the advanced class, whose mission it is to overthrow the bourgeoisie and transform the whole of society, cannot be achieved. Without these conditions, all attempts to establish discipline inevitably fall flat and end in phrasemongering and grimacing. On the other hand, these conditions cannot arise all at once. They are created only by prolonged effort and hard-won experience. Their creation is facilitated by correct revolutionary theory, which, in its turn, is not a dogma but assumes final shape only in close connection with the practical activity of a truly mass and truly revolutionary movement.

That Bolshevism was able in 1917-20, under unprecedentedly difficult conditions, to build up and successfully maintain the strictest centralization and iron discipline was simply due to a number of historical peculiarities of Russia.

On the one hand, Bolshevism arose in 1903 on the very firm foundation of the theory of Marxism. And the correctness of this— and only this—revolutionary theory has been proved not only by the experience of all countries throughout the nineteenth century, but particularly by the experience of the wanderings and vacillations, the mistakes and disappointments of revolutionary thought in Russia. For nearly half a century—approximately from the 'forties to the 'nineties—advanced thinkers in Russia, under the oppression of an unprecedented, savage and reactionary tsardom, eagerly sought for the correct revolutionary theory and followed each and every "last word" in Europe and America in this sphere with astonishing diligence and thoroughness. Russia achieved Marxism, the only correct revolutionary theory, virtually through *suffering,* by a half century of unprecedented torment and sacrifice, of unprecedented revolutionary heroism, incredible energy, devoted searching, study, testing in practice, disappointment, verification and comparison with European experience. Thanks to the enforced emigration caused by tsardom, revolutionary Russia in the second half of the nineteenth century possessed a wealth of international connections and excellent information about world forms and theories of the revolutionary movement such as no other country in the world possessed.

On the other hand, having arisen on this granite theoretical basis, Bolshevism passed through fifteen years (1903-17) of practical history which in wealth of experience has had no equal anywhere else in the world. For no other country during these fifteen years had anything even approximating to this revolutionary experience, this rapid and varied succession of different forms of the movement—

legal and illegal, peaceful and stormy, underground and open, circles and mass movements, parliamentary and terrorist. In no other country was there concentrated during so short a time such a wealth of forms, shades, and methods of struggle involving *all* classes of modern society, and moreover, a struggle which, owing to the backwardness of the country and the heaviness of the yoke of tsardom, matured with exceptional rapidity and assimilated most eagerly and successfully the appropriate "last word" of American and European political experience.

[Compromises]

. . . The conclusion to be drawn is clear: to reject compromises "on principle," to reject the admissibility of compromises in general, no matter of what kind, is childishness which it is difficult even to take seriously. A political leader who desires to be useful to the revolutionary proletariat must know how to single out *concrete* cases of such compromises as are inadmissible, as express opportunism and *treachery,* and direct all the force of his criticism, the edge of his merciless exposure and relentless war, against *those concrete* compromises, and not allow the highly experienced "practical" Socialists and parliamentary Jesuits to dodge and wriggle out of responsibility by resorting to arguments about "compromises in general." It is precisely in this way that Messieurs the "leaders" of the British trade unions, as well as of the Fabian Society and the "Independent" Labour Party, dodge responsibility *for the treachery they have perpetrated,* for the commission of a compromise that *really* expresses the worst kind of opportunism, treachery and betrayal.

There are compromises and compromises. One must be able to analyze the situation and the concrete conditions of each compromise, or of each variety of compromise. One must learn to distinguish between a man who gave the bandits money and firearms in order to lessen the evil committed by them and to facilitate the task of getting them captured and shot, and a man who gives bandits money and firearms in order to share in the loot. In politics this is not always as easy as in this childishly simple example. But anyone who set out to invent a recipe for the workers that would provide ready-made solutions for all cases in life, or who promised that the politics of the revolutionary proletariat would never encounter difficult or intricate situations, would be simply a charlatan. . . .

. . . Of course, to very young and inexperienced revolutionaries, as well as to petty-bourgeois revolutionaries of even a very respectable age and very experienced, it seems exceedingly "dangerous," incomprehensible and incorrect to "allow compromises." And many sophists (being super-experienced or excessively "experienced" politicians) reason exactly in the same way as the British leaders of opportunism mentioned by Comrade Lansbury: "If it is permissible for the Bolsheviks to make such and such a compromise, then why should we not be allowed to make any compromise?" But proletarians schooled in numerous strikes (to take only this manifestation of the class struggle) usually understand quite well the very profound (philosophical, historical, political and psychological) truth expounded by Engels. Every proletarian has been through strikes and has experienced "compromises" with the hated oppressors and exploiters, when the workers had to go back to work either without having achieved anything or consenting to a partial satisfaction of their demands. Every proletarian—owing to the conditions of the mass struggle and the sharp intensification of class antagonisms in which he lives—notices the difference between a compromise enforced by objective conditions (such as lack of strike funds, no outside support, extreme hunger and exhaustion), a compromise which in no way diminishes the revolutionary devotion and readiness for further struggle on the part of the workers who have agreed to such a compromise, and a compromise by traitors who try to ascribe to outside causes their own selfishness (strikebreakers also effect "compromises"!), cowardice, desire to toady to the capitalists and readiness to yield to intimidation, sometimes to persuasion, sometimes to sops, and sometimes to flattery on the part of the capitalists. (Such cases of traitors' compromises by trade union leaders are particularly plentiful in the history of the British labor movement; but in one form or another nearly all workers in all countries have witnessed the same sort of thing.)

Of course, individual cases of exceptional difficulty and intricacy occur when it is possible to determine the real character of this or that "compromise" only with the greatest difficulty; just as there are cases of homicide where it is very difficult to decide whether the homicide was fully justified and even essential (as, for example, legitimate self-defense), or due to unpardonable negligence, or even to a cunningly executed plan. Of course, in politics, in which extremely complicated—national and international—relations between classes and parties have sometimes to be dealt with, very many cases will arise that will be much more difficult than a legitimate "compromise" during a strike, or the treacherous "compromise" of a strikebreaker, or of a treacherous leader, etc. It would be absurd to concoct a recipe or general rule ("No Compromise!") to serve all cases. One must have the brains to analyze the situation in each separate case. Incidentally, the significance of a party organization and of party leaders worthy of the name lies precisely in the fact that they help by means of the prolonged, persistent, varied and all-round efforts of all thinking representatives of the given class,* in the acquisition of the necessary knowledge, the necessary experience and—apart from knowledge and experience—the necessary political instinct for the speedy and correct solution of intricate political problems.

Naïve and utterly inexperienced people imagine that it is sufficient to admit the permissibility of compromises *in general* in order to obliterate the dividing line between opportunism, against which we wage and must wage an irreconcilable struggle, and revolutionary Marxism, or Communism. But if such people do not yet know that *all* dividing lines in nature and in society are mutable and to a certain extent conventional—they cannot be assisted otherwise than by a long process of training, education, enlightenment, and by political and everyday experience. It is important to single out from the practical questions of the politics of each separate or specific historical moment those which reveal the principal type of impermissible, treacherous compromises embodying the opportunism that is fatal to the revolutionary class, and to exert all efforts to explain them and combat them. During the imperialist war of 1914-18 between two groups of equally predatory and rapacious countries, the principal, fundamental type of opportunism was social-chauvinism, that is, the support of "defense of the fatherland," which, in *such* a war, was really equivalent to defense of the predatory interests of "one's own" bourgeoisie. After the war, the defense of the robber "League of Nations," the defense of direct or indirect alliances with the bourgeoisie of one's own country against the revolutionary proletariat

* In every class, even in the most enlightened countries, even in the case of the most advanced class, placed by the circumstances of the moment in a state of exceptional elevation of all spiritual forces, there always are—and as long as classes exist, as long as classless society has not fully entrenched and consolidated itself, and has not developed on its own foundation, there inevitably *will be*—representatives of the class who do *not* think and are incapable of thinking. Were this not so, capitalism would not be the oppressor of the masses it is.

and the "Soviet" movement, and the defense of bourgeois democracy
and bourgeois parliamentarism against the "Soviet power" became
the principal manifestations of those impermissible and treacherous
compromises, the sum total of which constituted the opportunism
that is fatal to the revolutionary proletariat and its cause.

". . . to reject most emphatically all compromises with other
parties . . . all policy of maneuvering and compromise," write the
German "Lefts" in the Frankfurt pamphlet.

It is a wonder that, holding such views, these "Lefts" do not emphatically condemn Bolshevism! For, the German "Lefts" must know
that the whole history of Bolshevism, both before and after the October Revolution, is *full* of instances of maneuvering, temporizing
and compromising with other parties, bourgeois parties included!

To carry on a war for the overthrow of the international bourgeoisie, a war which is a hundred times more difficult, prolonged
and complicated than the most stubborn of ordinary wars between
states, and to refuse beforehand to maneuver, to utilize the conflict
of interests (even though temporary) among one's enemies, to refuse
to temporize and compromise with possible (even though transitory,
unstable, vacillating and conditional) allies—is not this ridiculous
in the extreme? Is it not as though, when making a difficult ascent
of an unexplored and hitherto inaccessible mountain, we were to
refuse beforehand ever to move in zigzags, ever to retrace our steps,
ever to abandon the course once selected to try others? . . .

[Communism and Trade Unions]

And we cannot but regard as equally ridiculous and childish nonsense the ponderous, very learned, and frightfully revolutionary disquisitions of the German Lefts to the effect that Communists cannot
and should not work in reactionary trade unions, that it is permissible to refuse to do such work, that it is necessary to leave the trade
unions and to create an absolutely brand-new, immaculate "Workers'
Union" invented by very nice (and for the most part, probably, very
youthful) Communists, etc., etc.

Capitalism inevitably bequeaths to Socialism, on the one hand,
old trade and craft distinctions among the workers, distinctions
evolved in the course of centuries, and, on the other, trade unions
which only very slowly, in the course of years and years, can and

will develop into broader, industrial unions with less of the craft union about them (embracing whole industries, and not only crafts, trades and occupations), and later proceed, through these industrial unions, to the abolition of the division of labor among people, to the education, schooling and training of people with *an all-round development and an all-round* training, people *able to do everything.* Communism is marching and must march towards this goal, and *will reach it,* but only after very many years. To attempt in practice today to anticipate this future result of a fully developed, fully stabilized and formed, fully expanded and mature Communism would be like trying to teach higher mathematics to a four year old child.

We can (and must) begin to build Socialism not with imaginary human material, not with human material invented by us, but with the human material bequeathed to us by capitalism. That is very "difficult," it goes without saying, but no other approach to this task is serious enough to warrant discussion.

The trade unions were a tremendous progressive step for the working class at the beginning of the development of capitalism, inasmuch as they represented a transition from the disunity and helplessness of the workers to the *rudiments* of class organization. When the *highest* form of proletarian class organization began to arise, viz., the *revolutionary party of the proletariat* (which will not deserve the name until it learns to bind the leaders with the class and the masses into one single indissoluble whole), the trade unions inevitably began to reveal *certain* reactionary features, a certain craft narrowness, a certain tendency to be non-political, a certain inertness, etc. But the development of the proletariat did not, and could not, proceed anywhere in the world otherwise than through the trade unions, through their interaction with the party of the working class. The conquest of political power by the proletariat is a gigantic forward step for the proletariat as a class, and the Party must more than ever, and not merely in the old way but in a new way, educate and guide the trade unions, at the same time not forgetting that they are and will long remain an indispensable "school of Communism" and a preparatory school for training the proletarians to exercise their dictatorship, an indispensable organization of the workers for the gradual transfer of the management of the whole economic life of the country to the working *class* (and not to the separate trades), and later to all the toilers.

A *certain* amount of "reactionariness" in trade unions, in the sense mentioned, is *inevitable* under the dictatorship of the proletariat. He who does not understand this utterly fails to understand the fundamental conditions of the *transition* from capitalism to Socialism. To fear *this* "reactionariness," to try to *avoid* it, to skip it, would be the greatest folly, for it would mean fearing that function of the proletarian vanguard which consists in training, educating, enlightening and drawing into the new life the most backward strata and masses of the working class and the peasantry. On the other hand, to postpone the achievement of the dictatorship of the proletariat until a time when not a single worker with a narrow craft outlook, not a single worker with craft and craft-union prejudices is left, would be a still greater mistake. The art of politics (and the Communist's correct understanding of his tasks) lies in correctly gauging the conditions and the moment when the vanguard of the proletariat can successfully seize power, when it is able, during and after the seizure of power, to obtain adequate support from adequately broad strata of the working class and of the non-proletarian toiling masses, and when it is able thereafter to maintain, consolidate and extend its rule by educating, training and attracting ever broader masses of the toilers. . . .

But we wage the struggle against the "labor aristocracy" in the name of the masses of the workers and in order to attract them to our side; we wage the struggle against the opportunist and social-chauvinist leaders in order to attract the working class to our side. To forget this most elementary and self-evident truth would be stupid. But it is just this stupidity the German "Left" Communists are guilty of when, *because* of the reactionary and counter-revolutionary character of the *heads* of the trade unions, they jump to the conclusion that . . . we must leave the trade unions!! that we must refuse to work in them!! that we must create new and *artificial* forms of labor organization!! This is such an unpardonable blunder as to be equivalent to the greatest service the Communists could render the bourgeoisie. For our Mensheviks, like all the opportunist, social-chauvinist, Kautskian trade union leaders, are nothing but "agents of the bourgeoisie in the labor movement" (as we have always said the Mensheviks were), or "labor lieutenants of the capitalist class," to use the splendid and absolutely true expression of the followers of Daniel DeLeon in America. To refuse to work in the reactionary trade unions means leaving the insufficiently developed or backward masses of the workers under the influence of the reactionary leaders, the agents of the bourgeoisie, the labor aristocrats, or the workers who have "become completely bourgeois" (*cf.* Engels' letter to Marx in 1852 on the British workers) [*Selected Correspondence* of Marx and Engels, p. 60].

It is just this absurd "theory" that the Communists must not belong to reactionary trade unions that most clearly shows how frivolous is the attitude of the "Left" Communists towards the question of influencing "the masses," and how they abuse their vociferations about "the masses." If you want to help "the masses" and to win the sympathy, confidence and support of "the masses," you must not fear difficulties, you must not fear the pin-pricks, chicanery, insults and persecution of the "leaders" (who, being opportunists and social-chauvinist, are in most cases directly or indirectly connected with the bourgeoisie and the police), but must imperatively *work wherever the masses are to be found.* You must be capable of every sacrifice, of overcoming the greatest obstacles in order to carry on agitation and propaganda systematically, perseveringly, persistently and patiently precisely in those institutions, societies and associations— even the most reactionary—in which proletarian or semi-proletarian masses are to be found. And the trade unions and workers' co-operatives (the latter at least sometimes) are precisely the organizations where the masses are to be found. . . .

There can be no doubt that people like Gompers, Henderson, Jouhaux and Legien are very grateful to "Left" revolutionaries who, like the German opposition "on principle" (heaven preserve us from such "principles"!) or like some of the revolutionaries in the American Industrial Workers of the World, advocate leaving the reactionary trade unions and refusing to work in them. There can be no doubt that those gentlemen, the "leaders" of opportunism, will resort to every trick of bourgeois diplomacy, to the aid of bourgeois governments, the priests, the police and the courts, to prevent Communists joining the trade unions, to force them out by every means, to make their work in the trade unions as unpleasant as possible, to insult, bait and persecute them. We must be able to withstand all this, to agree to any sacrifice, and even—if need be—to resort to all sorts of stratagems, artifices, illegal methods, to evasions and subterfuges, only so as to get into the trade unions, to remain in them, and to carry on Communist work within them at all costs. . . . Of course, in Western Europe, where legalistic, constitutionalist, bourgeois-democratic prejudices are very deeply ingrained, it is more difficult to carry on such work. But it can and should be carried on, and carried on systematically. . . .

[Communism and Parliaments]

The German "Left" Communists, with the greatest contempt—and with the greatest frivolity—reply to the question [of a parliament] in the negative. Their arguments? . . .

> . . . One must emphatically reject . . . all reversion to parliamentary forms of struggle, which have become historically and politically obsolete. . . .

This is said with absurd pretentiousness, and is obviously incorrect. "Reversion" to parliamentarism! Perhaps there is already a Soviet republic in Germany? It does not look like it! How, then, is it possible to speak of "reversion"? Is it not an empty phrase?

Parliamentarism has become "historically obsolete." That is true as regards propaganda. But everyone knows that this is still a long way from overcoming it *practically*. Capitalism could have been declared, and quite rightly, to be "historically obsolete" many decades ago, but that does not at all remove the need for a very long and very persistent struggle *on the soil* of capitalism. Parliamentarism is "historically obsolete" from the standpoint of *world history,* that is to say, the *epoch* of bourgeois parliamentarism has come to an end and the *epoch* of the proletarian dictatorship has *begun*. That is incontestable. But when dealing with world *history* one counts in decades. Ten or twenty years sooner or later makes no difference when measured by the scale of world history; from the standpoint of world history it is a trifle that cannot be calculated even approximately. But that is precisely why it is a howling theoretical blunder to measure questions of practical politics with the scale of world history.

Is parliamentarism "politically obsolete"? That is quite another matter. . . . How can one say that "parliamentarism is politically obsolete," when "millions" and "legions" of *proletarians* are not only still in favour of parliamentarism in general, but are downright "counter-revolutionary"!? Clearly, parliamentarism in Germany is *not yet* politically obsolete. Clearly, the "Lefts" in Germany have mistaken *their desire,* their ideological-political attitude, for actual fact. That is the most dangerous mistake revolutionaries can make. In Russia—where the extremely fierce and savage yoke of tsardom for a very long time and in very varied forms produced revolutionaries of diverse shades, revolutionaries who displayed astonishing devotion, enthusiasm, heroism and strength of will—we observed this mistake of the revolutionaries very closely, we studied it very attentively and are very well acquainted with it, and we can therefore notice it very clearly in others. Parliamentarism, of course, is "politically obsolete" for the Communists in Germany; but—and that is the whole point—we must not regard what is obsolete *for us* as being obsolete *for the class,* as being obsolete *for the masses.* Here again we find that the "Lefts" do not know how to reason, do not know how to conduct themselves as the party of the *class,* as the party of the *masses.* You must not sink to the level of the masses, to the level of the backward strata of the class. That is incontestable. You must tell them the bitter truth. You must call their bourgeois-democratic and parliamentary prejudices—prejudices. But at the same time you must *soberly* observe the *actual* state of class consciousness and preparedness of the whole class (not only of its Communist vanguard), of all the toiling *masses* (not only of its advanced elements). . . .

[The Task of the Communist Parties]

The whole point now is that the Communists of every country should quite consciously take into account both the main fundamental tasks of the struggle against opportunism and "Left" doctrinairism and the *specific features* which this struggle assumes and inevitably must assume in each separate country in conformity with the peculiar features of its economics, politics, culture, national composition (Ireland, etc.), its colonies, religious divisions, etc. Everywhere we observe that dissatisfaction with the Second International is spreading and growing, both because of its opportunism and because of its inability, or incapacity, to create a really centralized, a really leading center that would be capable of directing the international tactics of the revolutionary proletariat in its struggle for a world Soviet republic. We must clearly realize that such a leading center cannot under any circumstances be built up on stereotyped, mechanically equalized and identical tactical rules of struggle. As long as national and state differences exist among peoples and countries—and these differences will continue to exist for a very long time even after the dictatorship of the proletariat has been established on a world scale—the unity of international tactics of the Communist working class movement of all countries demands, not the elimination of variety, not the abolition of national differences (that is a foolish dream at the present moment), but such an application of the *fundamental* principles of Communism (Soviet power and the dictatorship of the proletariat) as will *correctly modify* these principles in *certain particulars,* correctly adapt and apply them to national and national-state differences. The main task of the historical period through which all the advanced countries (and not only the advanced countries) are now passing is to investigate, study, seek, divine, grasp that which is peculiarly national, specifically national in the *concrete manner* in which each country *approaches* the fulfillment of the *single* international task, the victory over opportunism and "Left" doctrinairism within the working class movement, the overthrow of the bourgeoisie, and the establishment of a Soviet republic and a proletarian dictatorship. The main thing— not everything by a very long way, of course, but the main thing— has already been achieved in that the vanguard of the working class has been won over, in that it has ranged itself on the side of the Soviet power against parliamentarism, on the side of the dictatorship of the proletariat against bourgeois democracy. Now all efforts, all attention, must be concentrated on the *next* step—which seems, and from a certain standpoint really is, less fundamental, but which, on the other hand, is actually much closer to the practical carrying out of the task —namely, on seeking the forms of *transition* or *approach* to the proletarian revolution.

The proletarian vanguard has been ideologically won over. That is the main thing. Without it not even the first step towards victory can be made. But it is still a fairly long way from victory. Victory cannot be won with the vanguard alone. To throw the vanguard alone into the decisive battle, before the whole class, before the broad masses have taken up a position either of direct support of the vanguard, or at least of benevolent neutrality towards it and one in which they cannot possibly support the enemy, would be not merely folly but a crime. And in order that actually the whole class, that actually the broad masses of toilers and those oppressed by capital may take up such a position, propaganda and agitation alone are not enough. For this the masses must have their own political experience. Such is the fundamental law of all great revolutions. . . .

The immediate task that confronts the class-conscious vanguard of the international labor movement, i.e., the Communist Parties, groups and trends, is to be able to *lead* the broad masses (now, for the most part, slumbering, apathetic, hidebound, inert and dormant) to their new position, or, rather, to be able to lead *not only* their own party, but also these masses in their approach, their transition to the new position. While the first historical task (viz., that of winning over the class-conscious vanguard of the proletariat to the side of the Soviet power and the dictatorship of the working class) could not be accomplished without a complete ideological and political victory over opportunism and social-chauvinism, the second task, which now becomes the immediate task, and which consists in being able to lead *the masses* to the new position that will ensure the victory of the vanguard in the revolution. . . .

The Communists in Western Europe and America must learn to create a new, unusual, non-opportunist, non-careerist parliamentarism; the Communist Parties must issue their slogans; real proletarians, with the help of the unorganized and downtrodden poor, should scatter and distribute leaflets, canvass workers' houses and the cottages of the rural proletarians and peasants in the remote villages (fortunately there are not nearly so many remote villages in Europe as there are in Russia, and in England there are very few); they should go into the most common taverns, penetrate into the unions, societies and casual meetings where the common people gather, and talk to the people, not in scientific (and not in very parliamentary) language, they should not at all strive to "get seats" in parliament, but should everywhere strive to rouse the minds of the masses and to draw them into the struggle, to catch the bourgeois on their own statements, to utilize the aparatus they have set up, the elections they have appointed, the appeals to the country they have made, and to tell the people what Bolshevism is in a way that has never been possible (under bourgeois rule) outside of election times (not counting, of course, times of big strikes, when, in Russia, a *similar* apparatus for widespread popular agitation worked even more intensively). It is very difficult to do this in Western Europe and America, very, very difficult; but it can and must be done, because the tasks of Communism cannot be fulfilled without effort; and every effort must be made to fulfill *practical* tasks, ever more varied, ever more closely connected with all branches of social life, *winning* branch after branch and sphere after sphere *from the bourgeoisie.* . . .

After the proletarian revolution in Russia and its victories on an international scale, which the bourgeoisie and the philistines did not expect, the whole world has changed, and everywhere the bourgeoisie has also changed. It is terrified by "Bolshevism," incensed with it almost to the point of frenzy, and precisely for that reason it is, on the one hand, accelerating the progress of events and, on the other, concentrating attention on the suppression of Bolshevism by force, and thereby weakening its position in a number of other fields. The Communists in all advanced countries should make allowances for both these circumstances in their tactics.

When the Russian Cadets and Kerensky raised a furious hue-and-cry against the Bolsheviks—especially after April 1917, and more particularly in June and July 1917—they "overdid" it. Millions of copies of bourgeois papers, shrieking in every key against the Bolsheviks, helped to induce the masses to appraise Bolshevism; and, apart from the newspapers, all public life was thoroughly permeated with discussions about Bolshevism just because of the "zeal" of the bourgeoisie. The millionaires of all countries are now behaving on an international scale in a way that deserves our heartiest thanks. They are hunting Bolshevism with the same zeal as did Kerensky and Co.; they are, moreover, "overdoing" it and *helping* us just as Kerensky did. When the French bourgeoisie makes Bolshevism the central issue at the elections, and abuses the comparatively moderate or vacillating Socialists for being Bolsheviks; when the American bourgeoisie, having completely lost its head, seizes thousands and thousands of people on suspicion of Bolshevism, creates an atmosphere of panic and broadcasts stories of Bolshevik plots; when the British bourgeoisie —the most "solid" in the world—despite all its wisdom and experience, commits acts of incredible stupidity, founds richly endowed "anti-Bolshevik societies," creates a special literature on Bolshevism, and hires an extra number of scientists, agitators and priests to combat it—we must bow and thank the capitalist gentlemen. They are working for us. They are helping us to get the masses interested in the nature and significance of Bolshevism. And they cannot act otherwise; for they have *already* failed to stifle Bolshevism by "silence." . . .

But in all cases and in all countries Communism is becoming steeled and is growing; its roots are so deep that persecution does not weaken it, does not debilitate it, but strengthens it. Only one thing is lacking to enable us to march forward more confidently and firmly to victory, namely, the universal and thoroughly thought-out appreciation by all Communists in all countries of the necessity of displaying the utmost *flexibility* in their tactics. . . .

28. JOSEF STALIN

The following passages from The Foundations of Leninism *contain the classical statement of the nature and role of the Communist Party in the accomplishment of world communism.*

The Party as the Vanguard of the Working Class*

The Party must be, first of all, the *vanguard* of the working class. The Party must absorb all the best elements of the working class, their experience, their revolutionary spirit, their selfless devotion to the cause of the proletariat. But in order that it may really be the vanguard, the Party must be armed with revolutionary theory, with a knowledge of the laws of the movement, with a knowledge of the laws of revolution. Without this it will be incapable of directing the struggle of the proletariat, of leading the proletariat. The Party cannot be a real party if it limits itself to registering what the masses of the working class feel and think, if it follows in the tail of the spontaneous movements, if it is unable to overcome the inertness and the political indifference of the spontaneous movement, if it is unable to rise above the momentary interests of the proletariat, if it is unable to elevate the masses to the level of the class interests of the proletariat. The Party must stand at the head of the working class; it must see farther than the working class; it must lead the proletariat, and not follow in the tail of the spontaneous movement. The parties of the Second International, which preach "khvostism," are vehicles of bourgeois policy, which condemns the proletariat to the role of a tool in the hands of the bourgeoisie. Only a party which

* From J. Stalin, *The Foundations of Leninism,* 1924. Reprinted by permission of the Foreign Languages Publishing House, Moscow.

takes the standpoint of the vanguard of the proletariat and is able
to elevate the masses to the level of the class interests of the proletariat
—only such a party can divert the working class from the path of trade
unionism and convert it into an independent political force. The Party
is the political leader of the working class.

I have spoken of the difficulties of the struggle of the working class,
of the complicated conditions of the struggle, of strategy and tactics,
of reserves and maneuvering, of attack and retreat. These conditions
are no less complicated, if not more so, than the conditions of war.
Who can find his bearings in these conditions, who can give correct
guidance to the proletarian millions? No army at war can dispense
with an experienced General Staff if it does not want to court certain
defeat. Is it not clear that the proletariat can still less dispense with
such a General Staff if it does not want to give itself up to be devoured by its mortal enemies? But where is this General Staff? Only
the revolutionary party of the proletariat can serve as this General
Staff. The working class without a revolutionary party is an army
without a General Staff. The Party is the General Staff of the proletariat.

But the Party cannot be only a *vanguard* detachment. It must at the
same time be a detachment of the *class,* part of the class, closely
bound up with it by all the fibers of its being. The distinction between
the vanguard and the main body of the working class, between
Party members and non-Party people, cannot disappear until classes
disappear; it will exist as long as the ranks of the proletariat continue
to be replenished with newcomers from other classes, as long as
the working class as a whole lacks the possibility of rising to the
level of the vanguard. But the Party would cease to be a party if this
distinction were widened into a gap, if it shut itself up in its own
shell and became divorced from the non-Party masses. The Party
cannot lead the class if it is not connected with the non-Party masses,
if there is no bond between the Party and the non-Party masses, if
these masses do not accept its leadership, if the Party enjoys no moral
and political credit among the masses. Recently two hundred thousand
new members from the ranks of the workers were admitted into our
Party. The remarkable thing about this is the fact that these people
did not merely join the Party themselves, but were rather sent there
by the main body of non-Party workers, who took an active part in
the work of accepting the new members, and without whose approval
no new member was accepted. This fact proves that the broad masses

of non-Party workers regard our Party as *their* Party, as a Party *near and dear* to them, in whose expansion and consolidation they are vitally interested and to whose leadership they voluntarily entrust their destiny. It need hardly be proved that without these intangible moral threads which connect the Party with the non-Party masses, the Party could not have become the decisive force of its class. The Party is an inseparable part of the working class.

We are the Party of a class [says Lenin], and therefore *almost the entire class* (and in times of war, in the period of civil war, the entire class) should act under the leadership of our Party, should adhere to our Party as closely as possible. But it would be Manilovism and "khvostism" to think that at any time under capitalism the entire class, or almost the entire class, would be able to rise to the level of consciousness and activity of its vanguard, of its socialist party. No sensible socialist has ever yet doubted that under capitalism even the trade union organizations (which are more primitive and more comprehensible to the undeveloped strata) are unable to embrace the entire, or almost the entire, working class. To forget the distinction between the vanguard and the whole of the masses which gravitate towards it, to forget the constant duty of the vanguard to *raise* ever wider strata to this most advanced level, means merely to deceive oneself, to shut one's eyes to the immensity of our tasks, and to narrow down these tasks. (*Collected Works,* Russian edition, Vol. VI, pp. 205-6.)

The Party as the Organized Detachment of the Working Class

The Party is not only the *vanguard* of the working class. If it desires really to direct the struggle of the class it must at the same time be the *organized* detachment of its class. The Party's tasks under the conditions of capitalism are extremely serious and varied. The Party must direct the struggle of the proletariat under the exceptionally difficult conditions of internal and external development; it must lead the proletariat in the offensive when the situation calls for an offensive; it must lead the proletariat in retreat when the situation calls for retreat in order to ward off the blows of a powerful enemy; it must imbue the millions of unorganized non-Party workers with the spirit of discipline and system in the struggle, with the spirit of organization and endurance. But the Party can fulfill these tasks only if it is itself the embodiment of discipline and organization, if it is itself the *organized* detachment of the proletariat. Without these conditions there can be no talk of the Party really leading the proletarian millions. The Party is the organized detachment of the working class.

The conception of the Party as an organized whole is embodied in Lenin's well-known formulation of the first paragraph of our Party Rules, in which the Party is regarded as the *sum* of its organizations, and the Party member as a member of one of the organizations of the Party. The Mensheviks, who objected to this formulation as early as 1903, proposed to substitute for it a "system" of self-enrollment in the Party, a "system" of conferring the "title" of Party member upon every "professor" and "high school student," upon every "sympathizer" and "striker" who supported the Party in one way or another, but who did not join and did not desire to join any one of the Party organizations. It need hardly be proved that had this singular "system" become firmly entrenched in our Party it would inevitably have led to our Party becoming inundated with professors and high school students and to its degeneration into a loose, amorphous, disorganized "formation," lost in a sea of "sympathizers," that would have obliterated the dividing line between the Party and the class and would have upset the Party's task of elevating the unorganized masses to the level of the vanguard. Needless to say, under such an opportunist "system" our Party would have been unable to fulfill the role of the organizing nucleus of the working class in the course of our revolution.

> From Martov's point of view [says Lenin], the boundary line of the Party remains entirely undefined, for "every striker" can "declare himself a member of the Party." What advantage is there in this looseness? The widespread dissemination of an "appellation." Its harmfulness lies in that it introduces the *disorganizing* idea of confusing the class with the Party. (*Collected Works,* Russian edition, Vol. VI, p. 211.)

But the Party is not merely the *sum* of Party organizations. The Party at the same time represents a single *system* of these organizations, their formal amalgamation into a single whole, with higher and lower leading bodies, with subordination of the minority to the majority, with practical decisions binding on all members of the Party. Without these conditions the Party cannot be a single organized whole capable of exercising systematic and organized leadership in the struggle of the working class.

> *Formerly* [says Lenin], our Party was not a formally organized whole, but only the sum of separate groups, and therefore no other

relations except those of ideological influence were possible between these groups. *Now* we have become an organized Party, and this implies the establishment of authority, the transformation of the power of ideas into the power of authority, the subordination of lower Party bodies to higher Party bodies. (*Ibid.*, p. 291.)

The principle of the minority submitting to the majority, the principle of directing Party work from a center, not infrequently gives rise to attacks on the part of wavering elements, to accusations of "bureaucracy," "formalism," etc. It need hardly be proved that systematic work by the Party, as one whole, and the directing of the struggle of the working class would have been impossible if these principles had not been adhered to. Leninism in the organizational question means unswerving application of these principles. Lenin terms the fight against these principles "Russian nihilism" and "aristocratic anarchism," deserving only of being ridiculed and swept aside.

Here is what Lenin has to say about these wavering elements in his book *One Step Forward, Two Steps Back:*

> This aristocratic anarchism is particularly characteristic of the Russian nihilist. He thinks of the Party organization as a monstrous "factory"; he regards the subordination of the part to the whole and of the minority to the majority as "serfdom" . . . division of labor under the direction of a center evokes from him a tragi-comical outcry against people being transformed into "wheels and cogs" . . . mention of the organizational rules of the Party calls forth a contemptuous grimace and the disdainful remark . . . that one can very well dispense with rules altogether. . . . It is clear, I think, that the outcries against the much talked of bureaucracy are simply a screen to conceal dissatisfaction with the personnel of these centers, a fig leaf. . . . You are a bureaucrat, because you were appointed by the Congress not in accordance with my wishes but in spite of them; you are a formalist, because you base yourself on the formal decisions of the Congress and not on my consent; you act in a crudely mechanical way, because your authority is the "mechanical" majority of the Party Congress and you do not consult my desire to be co-opted; you are an autocrat, because you do not want to deliver power into the hands of the old gang.* (*Collected Works,* Russian edition, Vol. VI, pp. 310, 287.)

* The "old gang" here referred to is that of Axelrod, Martov, Potresov and others, who would not submit to the decisions of the Second Congress and who accused Lenin of being a "bureaucrat."—*J.S.*

The Party as the Highest Form of Class Organization of the Proletariat

The Party is the organized detachment of the working class. But the Party is not the only organization of the working class. The proletariat has also a number of other organizations, without which it cannot properly wage the struggle against capital: trade unions, cooperative societies, factory and works organizations, parliamentary groups, non-Party women's associations, the press, cultural and educational organizations, youth leagues, revolutionary fighting organizations (in times of open revolutionary action), Soviets of deputies as the form of state organization (if the proletariat is in power), etc. The overwhelming majority of these organizations are non-Party, and only a certain part of them adhere directly to the Party, or represent its offshoots. All these organizations, under certain conditions, are absolutely necessary for the working class, for without them it would be impossible to consolidate the class positions of the proletariat in the diverse spheres of struggle; for without them it would be impossible to steel the proletariat as the force whose mission it is to replace the bourgeois order by the socialist order. But how can single leadership be exercised with such an abundance of organizations? What guarantee is there that this multiplicity of organizations will not lead to divergency in leadership? It might be argued that each of these organizations carries on its work in its own special field, and that therefore these organizations cannot hinder one another. This, of course, is true. But it is also true that all these organizations should work in one direction, for they serve *one* class, the class of the proletarians. The question then arises: who is to determine the line, the general direction, along which the work of all these organizations is to be conducted? Where is that central organization which is not only able, because it has the necessary experience, to work out such a general line, but, in addition, is in a position, because it has sufficient prestige for that, to induce all these organizations to carry out this line, so as to attain unity of leadership and to preclude the possibility of working at cross purposes?

This organization is the Party of the proletariat.

The Party possesses all the necessary qualifications for this because, in the first place, it is the rallying center of the finest elements in the working class, who have direct connections with the non-Party organizations of the proletariat and very frequently lead them; because, secondly, the Party, as the rallying center for the finest members of the working class, is the best school for training leaders of the working class, capable of directing every form of organization of their class; because, thirdly, the Party, as the best school for training leaders of the working class, is by reason of its experience and prestige the only organization capable of centralizing the leadership of the struggle of the proletariat, thus transforming each and every non-Party organization of the working class into an auxiliary body and transmission belt linking the Party with the class. The Party is the highest form of class organization of the proletariat.

This does not mean, of course, that non-Party organizations, trade unions, cooperative societies, etc., should be officially subordinated to the Party leadership. It only means that the members of the Party who belong to these organizations and are doubtlessly influential in them, should do all they can to persuade these non-Party organizations to draw nearer to the Party of the proletariat in their work and to accept voluntarily its political guidance.

That is why Lenin says that "the Party is the *highest* form of class association of the proletarians," whose political leadership must extend to every other form of organization of the proletariat. (*Selected Works,* Vol. X, p. 91.)

That is why the opportunist theory of the "independence" and "neutrality" of the non-Party organizations, which breeds *independent* members of parliament and journalists *isolated* from the Party, *narrow-minded* trade unionists and cooperative society officials *grown smug and philistine,* is wholly incompatible with the theory and practice of Leninism.

The Party as the Instrument of the Dictatorship of the Proletariat

The Party is the highest form of organization of the proletariat. The Party is the principal guiding force within the class of the proletarians and among the organizations of that class. But it does not by any means follow from this that the Party can be regarded as an end in itself, as a self-sufficient force. The Party is not only the highest form of class association of the proletarians; it is at the same time an *instrument* in the hands of the proletariat *for* achieving the dictatorship where that has not yet been achieved and *for* consolidating and expanding the dictatorship where it has already been achieved. The Party could not have risen so high in importance and could not have overshadowed all other forms of organization of the proletariat, if the latter were not confronted with the problem of power, if the conditions of imperialism, the inevitability of wars, and the existence of a crisis did not demand the concentration of all the forces of the proletariat at one point, the gathering of all the threads of the revolutionary movement into one spot in order to overthrow the bourgeoisie and to achieve the dictatorship of the proletariat. The proletariat needs the Party first of all as its General Staff, which it must have for the successful seizure of power. It need hardly be proved that without a Party capable of rallying around itself the mass organizations of the proletariat, and of centralizing the leadership of the entire movement during the progress of the struggle, the proletariat in Russia could never have established its revolutionary dictatorship.

But the proletariat needs the Party not only to achieve the dictatorship; it needs it still more to maintain the dictatorship, to consolidate and expand it in order to achieve the complete victory of socialism.

> Certainly almost everyone now realizes [says Lenin] that the Bolsheviks could not have maintained themselves in power for two and a half months, let alone for two and a half years, without the strictest and truly iron discipline in our Party, and without the fullest and most unreserved support rendered it by the whole mass of the working class, that is, by all thinking, honest, self-sacrificing and influential elements in it who are capable of leading or of attracting the backward strata. (*Selected Works,* Vol. X, p. 60.)

Now, what does it mean to "maintain" and "expand" the dictatorship? It means imbuing the millions of proletarians with the spirit of discipline and organization; it means creating among the proletarian masses a cementing force and a bulwark against the corrosive influences of the petty-bourgeois elements and petty-bourgeois habits; it means enhancing the organizing work of the proletarians in reeducating and re-molding the petty-bourgeois strata; it means helping the masses of the proletarians to educate themselves as a force capable of abolishing classes and of preparing the conditions for the organization of socialist production. But it is impossible to accomplish all this without a Party which is strong by reason of its solidarity and discipline.

The dictatorship of the proletariat [says Lenin] is a persistent struggle—sanguinary and bloodless, violent and peaceful, military and economic, educational and administrative—against the forces and traditions of the old society. The force of habit of millions and tens of millions is a most terrible force. Without an iron party tempered in the struggle, without a party enjoying the confidence of all that is honest in the given class, without a party capable of watching and influencing the mood of the masses, it is impossible to conduct such a struggle successfully. (*Selected Works*, Vol. X, p. 84.)

The proletariat needs the Party for the purpose of achieving and maintaining the dictatorship. The Party is an instrument of the dictatorship of the proletariat.

But from this it follows that when classes disappear and the dictatorship of the proletariat withers away, the Party will also wither away.

The Party as the Embodiment of Unity of Will, Incompatible with the Existence of Factions

The achievement and maintenance of the dictatorship of the proletariat is impossible without a party which is strong by reason of its solidarity and iron discipline. But iron discipline in the Party is inconceivable without unity of will, without complete and absolute unity of action on the part of all members of the Party. This does not mean, of course, that the possibility of contests of opinion within the Party is thereby precluded. On the contrary, iron discipline does not preclude but presupposes criticism and contest of opinion within the Party. Least of all does it mean that discipline must be "blind." On the contrary, iron discipline does not preclude but presupposes conscious and voluntary submission, for only conscious discipline can be truly iron discipline. But after a contest of opinion has been closed, after criticism has been exhausted and a decision has been arrived at, unity of will and unity of action of all Party members are the necessary condition without which neither Party unity nor iron discipline in the Party is conceivable.

In the present epoch of acute civil war [says Lenin], a Communist Party will be able to perform its duty only if it is organized in the most centralized manner, only if iron discipline bordering on military discipline prevails in it, and if its Party center is a powerful and authoritative organ, wielding wide powers and enjoying the universal confidence of the members of the Party. (*Selected Works,* Vol. X, p. 204.)

This is the position in regard to discipline in the Party in the period of struggle preceding the achievement of the dictatorship.

The same, but to an even greater degree, must be said about discipline in the Party after the dictatorship has been achieved.

> Whoever in the least [says Lenin] weakens the iron discipline of the Party of the proletariat (especially during its dictatorship) actually aids the bourgeoisie against the proletariat. (*Selected Works,* Vol. X, p. 84.)

But from this it follows that the existence of factions is incompatible either with the Party's unity or with its iron discipline. It need hardly be proved that the existence of factions leads to the existence of a number of centers, and the existence of a number of centers connotes the absence of one common center in the Party, the breaking up of the unity of will, the weakening and disintegration of discipline, the weakening and disintegration of the dictatorship. Of course, the parties of the Second International, which are fighting against the dictatorship of the proletariat and have no desire to lead the proletarians to power, can afford such liberalism as freedom of factions, for they have no need at all for iron discipline. But the parties of the Communist International, which base their activities on the task of achieving and consolidating the dictatorship of the proletariat, cannot afford to be "liberal" or to permit freedom of factions. The Party represents unity of will, which precludes all factionalism and division of authority in the Party.

Hence Lenin's warning about the "danger of factionalism from the point of view of Party unity and of effecting the unity of will of the vanguard of the proletariat as the fundamental condition for the success of the dictatorship of the proletariat," which is embodied in the special resolution of the Tenth Congress of our Party "On Party Unity." (Lenin, *Selected Works,* Vol. IX, p. 132.)

Hence Lenin's demand for the "complete elimination of all factionalism" and the "immediate dissolution of all groups, without exception, that had been formed on the basis of various platforms," on pain of "unconditional and immediate expulsion from the Party." (*Ibid.,* pp. 133-34.)

29. JOSEF STALIN

The clash of capitalism and communism as the two great centers of world power was predicted by Stalin in 1927.

[Two World Centers] *

. . . With regard to the international conditions necessary for the complete triumph of communist society, these will develop and grow in proportion as revolutionary crises and revolutionary outbreaks of the working class in capitalist countries grow. It must not be imagined that the working class in one country, or in several countries, will march towards socialism, and still more to communism, and that the capitalists of other countries will sit still with folded arms and look on with indifference. Still less must it be imagined that the working class in capitalist countries will agree to be mere spectators of the victorious development of socialism in one or another country. As a matter of fact, the capitalists will do all in their power to crush such countries. As a matter of fact, every important step taken towards socialism, and still more towards communism, in any country will be inevitably accompanied by the unrestrained efforts of the working class in capitalist countries to achieve the dictatorship and socialism in those countries. Thus, in the further progress of development of the international revolution, two world centers will be formed the socialist center, attracting to itself all the countries gravitating towards socialism, and the capitalist center attracting to itself all the countries gravitating towards capitalism. The fight between these two centers for the conquest of world economy will decide the fate of capitalism and communism throughout the whole world, for the final defeat of world capitalism means the victory of socialism in the arena of world economy. . . .

* From an interview with J. Stalin by the first American labor delegation, on Sept. 9, 1927. Reprinted from *The Strategy and Tactics of World Communism* Supplement I, United States Government Printing Office, Washington, 1948.

30. NIKITA S. KHRUSHCHEV

In a world-shaking speech in 1956 Khrushchev destroyed the reputation of one of the two great Soviet heroes. Not made public for a long time after its delivery, this address vigorously condemned the "cult of the individual" and the crimes of the Stalin era. Khrushchev claimed to be reviving the older theory of "collective leadership."

[The Cult of the Individual] *

Comrades! In the report of the Central Committee of the party at the 20th Congress, in a number of speeches by delegates to the Congress, as also formerly during the plenary CC/CPSU [Central Committee of the Communist Party of the Soviet Union] sessions, quite a lot has been said about the cult of the individual and about its harmful consequences.

After Stalin's death the Central Committee of the party began to implement a policy of explaining concisely and consistently that it is impermissible and foreign to the spirit of Marxism-Leninism to elevate one person, to transform him into a superman possessing supernatural characteristics, akin to those of a god. Such a man supposedly knows everything, sees everything, thinks for everyone, can do anything, is infallible in his behavior.

Such a belief about a man, and specifically about Stalin, was cultivated among us for many years.

The objective of the present report is not a thorough evaluation of Stalin's life and activity. Concerning Stalin's merits, an entirely sufficient number of books, pamphlets and studies had already been written in his lifetime. The role of Stalin in the preparation and execution of the Socialist Revolution, in the Civil War, and in the fight

* From N. Khrushchev, *Crimes of the Stalin Era; a Special Report to the 20th Congress of the Communist Party of the Soviet Union,* Closed Session, February 24-25, 1956. Reprinted by permission of *The New Leader.*

for the construction of socialism in our country, is universally known. Everyone knows this well.

At present, we are concerned with a question which has immense importance for the party now and for the future—with how the cult of the person of Stalin has been gradually growing, the cult which became at a certain specific stage the source of a whole series of exceedingly serious and grave perversions of party principles, of party democracy, of revolutionary legality.

Because of the fact that not all as yet realize fully the practical consequences resulting from the cult of the individual, the great harm caused by the violation of the principle of collective direction of the party and because of the accumulation of immense and limitless power in the hands of one person, the Central Committee of the party considers it absolutely necessary to make the material pertaining to this matter available to the 20th Congress of the Communist Party of the Soviet Union.

Allow me first of all to remind you how severely the classics of Marxism-Leninism denounced every manifestation of the cult of the individual. In a letter to the German political worker, Wilhelm Bloss, Marx stated: "From my antipathy to any cult of the individual, I never made public during the existence of the International the numerous addresses from various countries which recognized my merits and which annoyed me. I did not even reply to them, except sometimes to rebuke their authors. Engels and I first joined the secret society of Communists on the condition that everything making for superstitious worship of authority would be deleted from its statute. Lassalle subsequently did quite the opposite."

Sometime later Engels wrote: "Both Marx and I have always been against any public manifestation with regard to individuals, with the exception of cases when it had an important purpose; and we most strongly opposed such manifestations which during our lifetime concerned us personally."

The great modesty of the genius of the Revolution, Vladimir Ilyich Lenin, is known. Lenin had always stressed the role of the people as the creator of history, the directing and organizational role of the party as a living and creative organism, and also the role of the Central Committee.

Marxism does not negate the role of the leaders of the working class in directing the revolutionary liberation movement.

While ascribing great importance to the role of the leaders and

organizers of the masses, Lenin at the same time mercilessly stigma-
tized every manifestation of the cult of the individual, inexorably
combated the foreign-to-Marxism views about a "hero" and a
"crowd," and countered all efforts to oppose a "hero" to the masses
and to the people.

Lenin taught that the party's strength depends on its indissoluble
unity with the masses, on the fact that behind the party follows the
people—workers, peasants and intelligentsia. "Only he will win and
retain the power," said Lenin, "who believes in the people, who sub-
merges himself in the fountain of the living creativeness of the
people."

Lenin spoke with pride about the Bolshevik Communist party as
the leader and teacher of the people; he called for the presentation of
all the most important questions before the opinion of knowledgeable
workers, before the opinion of their party; he said: "We believe in it,
we see in it the wisdom, the honor, and the conscience of our epoch."

Lenin resolutely stood against every attempt aimed at belittling or
weakening the directing role of the party in the structure of the Soviet
state. He worked out Bolshevik principles of party direction and
norms of party life, stressing that the guiding principle of party
leadership is its collegiality. Already during the pre-Revolutionary
years, Lenin called the Central Committee of the party a collective
of leaders and the guardian and interpreter of party principles. "During the period between congresses," pointed out Lenin, "the Central
Committee guards and interprets the principles of the party."

Underlining the role of the Central Committee of the party and its
authority, Vladimir Ilyich pointed out: "Our Central Committee constituted itself as a closely centralized and highly authoritative group."

During Lenin's life the Central Committee of the party was a real
expression of collective leadership of the party and of the nation.
Being a militant Marxist-revolutionist, always unyielding in matters
of principle, Lenin never imposed by force his views upon his co-
workers. He tried to convince; he patiently explained his opinions to
others. Lenin always diligently observed that the norms of party life
were realized, that the party statute was enforced, that the party congress and the plenary sessions of the Central Committee took place
at the proper intervals.

In addition to the great accomplishments of V. I. Lenin for the
victory of the working class and of the working peasants, for the
victory of our party and for the application of the ideas of scientific

Communism to life, his acute mind expressed itself also in this—
that he detected in Stalin in time those negative characteristics which
resulted later in grave consequences. Fearing the future fate of the
party and of the Soviet nation, V. I. Lenin made a completely correct
characterization of Stalin, pointing out that it was necessary to consider the question of transferring Stalin from the position of the
Secretary General because of the fact that Stalin is excessively rude,
that he does not have a proper attitude toward his comrades, that he
is capricious and abuses his power.

In December 1922, in a letter to the Party Congress, Vladimir
Ilyich wrote: "After taking over the position of Secretary General,
Comrade Stalin accumulated in his hands immeasurable power and I
am not certain whether he will be always able to use this power with
the required care."

This letter—a political document of tremendous importance, known
in the party history as Lenin's "testament"—was distributed among
the delegates to the 20th Party Congress. You have read it and will
undoubtedly read it again more than once. You might reflect on
Lenin's plain words, in which expression is given to Vladimir Ilyich's
anxiety concerning the party, the people, the state, and the future
direction of party policy.

Vladimir Ilyich said: "Stalin is excessively rude, and this defect,
which can be freely tolerated in our midst and in contacts among us
Communists, becomes a defect which cannot be tolerated in one
holding the position of the Secretary General. Because of this, I
propose that the comrades consider the method by which Stalin would
be removed from this position and by which another man would be
selected for it, a man who, above all, would differ from Stalin in
only one quality, namely, greater tolerance, greater loyalty, greater
kindness and more considerate attitude toward the comrades, a less
capricious temper, etc." . . .

As later events have proven, Lenin's anxiety was justified: In the
first period after Lenin's death, Stalin still paid attention to his advice, but later he began to disregard the serious admonitions of Vladimir Ilyich.

When we analyze the practice of Stalin in regard to the direction
of the party and of the country, when we pause to consider everything
which Stalin perpetrated, we must be convinced that Lenin's fears
were justified. The negative characteristics of Stalin, which, in Lenin's
time, were only incipient, transformed themselves during the last years

into a grave abuse of power by Stalin, which caused untold harm to our party.

We have to consider seriously and analyze correctly this matter in order that we may preclude any possibility of a repetition in any form whatever of what took place during the life of Stalin, who absolutely did not tolerate collegiality in leadership and in work, and who practiced brutal violence, not only toward everything which opposed him, but also toward that which seemed, to his capricious and despotic character, contrary to his concepts.

Stalin acted not through persuasion, explanation and patient co-operation with people, but by imposing his concepts and demanding absolute submission to his opinion. Whoever opposed this concept or tried to prove his viewpoint and the correctness of his position was doomed to removal from the leading collective and to subsequent moral and physical annihilation. This was especially true during the period following the 17th Party Congress, when many prominent party leaders and rank-and-file party workers, honest and dedicated to the cause of Communism, fell victim to Stalin's despotism. . . .

We should, in all seriousness, consider the question of the cult of the individual. We cannot let this matter get out of the party, especially not to the press. It is for this reason that we are considering it here at a closed Congress session. We should know the limits; we should not give ammunition to the enemy; we should not wash our dirty linen before their eyes. I think that the delegates to the Congress will understand and assess properly all these proposals. (Tumultuous applause.)

Comrades! We must abolish the cult of the individual decisively, once and for all; we must draw the proper conclusions concerning both ideological-theoretical and practical work. It is necessary for this purpose:

First, in a Bolshevik manner to condemn and to eradicate the cult of the individual as alien to Marxism-Leninism and not consonant with the principles of party leadership and the norms of party life, and to fight inexorably all attempts at bringing back this practice in one form or another.

To return to and actually practice in all our ideological work the most important theses of Marxist-Leninist science about the people as the creator of history and as the creator of all material and spiritual good of humanity, about the decisive role of the Marxist party in the revolutionary fight for the transformation of society, about the victory of communism.

In this connection we will be forced to do much work in order to examine critically from the Marxist-Leninist viewpoint and to correct the widely spread erroneous views connected with the cult of the individual in the sphere of history, philosophy, economy and of other sciences, as well as in literature and the fine arts. It is especially necessary that in the immediate future we compile a serious textbook of the history of our party which will be edited in accordance with scientific Marxist objectivism, a textbook of the history of Soviet society, a book pertaining to the events of the Civil War and the Great Patriotic War.

Secondly, to continue systematically and consistently the work done by the party's Central Committee during the last years, a work characterized by minute observation in all party organizations, from the bottom to the top, of the Leninist principles of party leadership, characterized, above all, by the main principle of collective leadership, characterized by the observance of the norms of party life described in the statutes of our party, and, finally, characterized by the wide practice of criticism and self-criticism.

Thirdly, to restore completely the Leninist principles of Soviet socialist democracy, expressed in the Constitution of the Soviet Union, to fight willfulness of individuals abusing their power. The evil caused by acts violating revolutionary socialist legality which have accumulated during a long time as a result of the negative influence of the cult of the individual has to be completely corrected.

Comrades! The 20th Congress of the Communist Party of the Soviet Union has manifested with a new strength the unshakable unity of our party, its cohesiveness around the Central Committee, its resolute will to accomplish the great task of building communism. (Tumultuous applause.)

And the fact that we present in all their ramifications the basic problems of overcoming the cult of the individual which is alien to Marxism-Leninism, as well as the problem of liquidating its burdensome consequences, is an evidence of the great moral and political strength of our party. (Prolonged applause.)

We are absolutely certain that our party, armed with the historical resolutions of the 20th Congress, will lead the Soviet people along the Leninist path to new successes, to new victories. (Tumultuous, prolonged applause.)

Long live the victorious banner of our party—Leninism! (Tumultuous, prolonged applause ending in ovation. All rise.)

3¹. MAO TSE-TUNG

Although intended to encourage intellectual criticism, this speech of the "hundred blossoms" is carefully worded to permit criticism only within a Marxist framework. Rigorous political criteria are suggested for the judgment of right action, and, "As far as unmistakable counterrevolutionaries . . . are concerned, the matter is easy; we simply deprive them of their freedom of speech."

[Let a Hundred Schools of Thought Contend] *

"Let a hundred flowers blossom" and "let a hundred schools of thought contend," "long-term coexistence and mutual supervision"—how did these slogans come to be put forward?

They were put forward in the light of the specific conditions existing in China, on the basis of the recognition that various kinds of contradictions still exist in a socialist society, and in response to the country's urgent need to speed up its economic and cultural development.

The policy of letting a hundred flowers blossom and a hundred schools of thought contend is designed to promote the flourishing f the arts and the progress of science; it is designed to enable a socialist culture to thrive in our land. Different forms and styles in art can develop freely, and different schools in science can contend freely. We think that it is harmful to the growth of art and science if administrative measures are used to impose one particular style of art or school of thought and to ban another. Questions of right and wrong in the arts and sciences should be settled through free discussions in artistic and scientific circles and in the course of practical work in the arts and sciences. They should not be settled in summary fashion.

---

* From Mao Tse-Tung, *On the Correct Handling of Contradictions Among the People,* a speech delivered to the Supreme State Conference, Peiping, February 27, 1957. Reprinted by permission of *The New Leader.*

A period of trial is often needed to determine whether something is right or wrong. In the past, new and correct things often failed at the outset to win recognition from the majority of people and had to develop by twists and turns in struggle. Correct and good things have often at first been looked upon not as fragrant flowers but as poisonous weeds; Copernicus's theory of the solar system and Darwin's theory of evolution were once dismissed as erroneous and had to win through over bitter opposition. Chinese history offers many similar examples. In socialist society, conditions for the growth of new things are radically different from and far superior to those in the old society. Nevertheless, it still often happens that new, rising forces are held back and reasonable suggestions smothered.

The growth of new things can also be hindered, not because of deliberate suppression but because of lack of discernment. That is why we should take a cautious attitude in regard to questions of right and wrong in the arts and sciences, encourage free discussion, and avoid hasty conclusions. We believe that this attitude will facilitate the growth of the arts and sciences.

Marxism has also developed through struggle. At the beginning, Marxism was subjected to all kinds of attack and regarded as a poisonous weed. It is still being attacked and regarded as a poisonous weed in many parts of the world. However, it enjoys a different position in the socialist countries. But, even in these countries, there are non-Marxist as well as anti-Marxist ideologies. It is true that in China socialist transformation, insofar as a change in the system of ownership is concerned, has in the main been completed, and the turbulent, large-scale, mass class struggles characteristic of the revolutionary periods have in the main concluded. But remnants of the overthrown landlord and comprador classes still exist, the bourgeoisie still exists, and the petty bourgeoisie has only just begun to remold itself. Class struggle is not yet over. The class struggle between the proletariat and the bourgeoisie, the class struggle between various political forces, and the class struggle in the ideological field between the proletariat and the bourgeoisie will still be long and devious and at times may even become very acute. The proletariat seeks to transform the world according to its own world outlook; so does the bourgeoisie. In this respect, the question of whether socialism or capitalism will win is still not really settled. Marxists are still a minority of the entire population as well as of the intellectuals. Marxism therefore must still develop through struggle. Marxism can only develop through struggle—this is true not only in the past and present, it is necessarily true in the future also. What is correct always develops in the course of struggle with what is wrong. The true, the good and the beautiful always exist in comparison with the false, the evil and the ugly, and grow in struggle with the latter. As mankind in general rejects an untruth and accepts a truth, a new truth will begin struggling with new erroneous ideas. Such struggles will never end. This is the law of development of truth, and it is certainly also the law of development of Marxism. . . .

Although there are defects and mistakes in our work, every fair-minded person can see that we are loyal to the people, that we are both determined and able to build up our country together with the people, and that we have achieved great successes and will achieve still greater ones. The vast majority of the bourgeoisie and intellectuals who come from the old society are patriotic; they are willing to serve their flourishing socialist motherland, and they know that, if they turn away from the socialist cause and the working people led by the Communist party, they will have no one to rely on and no bright future to look forward to.

People may ask: Since Marxism is accepted by the majority of the people in our country as the guiding ideology, can it be criticized? Certainly it can. As a scientific truth, Marxism fears no criticism. If it did and could be defeated in argument, it would be worthless. In fact, are not the idealists criticizing Marxism every day and in all sorts of ways? As for those who harbor bourgeois and petty-bourgeois ideas and do not wish to change, are not they also criticizing Marxism in all sorts of ways? Marxists should not be afraid of criticism from any quarter. Quite the contrary, they need to steel and improve themselves and win new positions in the teeth of criticism and the storm and stress of struggle. Fighting against wrong ideas is like being vaccinated—a man develops greater immunity from disease after the vaccine takes effect. Plants raised in hot-houses are not likely to be robust. Carrying out the policy of letting a hundred flowers blossom and a hundred schools of thought contend will not weaken but strengthen the leading position of Marxism in the ideological field.

What should our policy be toward non-Marxist ideas? As far as unmistakable counter-revolutionaries and wreckers of the socialist cause are concerned, the matter is easy; we simply deprive them of their freedom of speech. But it is quite a different matter when we are faced with incorrect ideas among the people. Will it do to ban such ideas and give them no opportunity to express themselves? Certainly not. It is not only futile but very harmful to use crude and summary methods to deal with ideological questions among the people, with questions relating to the spiritual life of man. You may ban the expression of wrong ideas, but the ideas will still be there. On the other hand, correct ideas, if pampered in hot-houses without being exposed to the elements or immunized against disease, will not win out against wrong ones. That is why it is only by employing methods of discussion, criticism and reasoning that we can really foster correct ideas, overcome wrong ideas and really settle issues.

The bourgeoisie and petty bourgeoisie are bound to give expression to their ideologies. It is inevitable that they should stubbornly persist in expressing themselves in every way possible on political and ideological questions. You cannot expect them not to do so. We should not use methods of suppression to prevent them from expressing themselves, but should allow them to do so and at the same time argue with them and direct well-considered criticism at them.

There can be no doubt that we should criticize all kinds of wrong ideas. It certainly would not do to refrain from criticism and look on while wrong ideas spread unchecked and acquire their market. Mistakes should be criticized and poisonous weeds fought against wherever they crop up. But such criticism should not be doctrinaire. We should not use the metaphysical method, but strive to employ the dialectical method. What is needed is scientific analysis and fully convincing arguments. Doctrinaire criticism settles nothing. We do not want any kind of poisonous weeds, but we should carefully distinguish between what is really a poisonous weed and what is really a fragrant flower. We must learn together with the masses of the people how to make this careful distinction and use the correct methods to fight poisonous weeds.

While criticizing doctrinairism, we should at the same time direct our attention to criticizing revisionism. Revisionism, or rightist opportunism, is a bourgeois trend of thought which is even more dangerous than doctrinairism. The revisionists or right opportunists pay lip-service to Marxism and also attack "doctrinairism." But the real target of their attack is actually the most fundamental elements of Marxism. They oppose or distort materialism and dialectics, oppose or try to weaken the people's democratic dictatorship and the leading role of the Communist party, oppose or try to weaken socialist transformation and socialist construction. Even after the basic victory of the socialist revolution in our country, there are still a number of people who vainly hope for a restoration of the capitalist system. They wage a struggle against the working class on every front, including the ideological front. In this struggle, their right-hand men are the revisionists.

On the surface, these two slogans—let a hundred flowers blossom and a hundred schools of thought contend—have no class character; the proletariat can turn them to account, and so can the bourgeoisie and other people. But different classes, strata and social groups each have their own views on what are fragrant flowers and what are poisonous weeds. So what, from the point of view of the broad masses of the people, should be a criterion today for distinguishing between fragrant flowers and poisonous weeds?

In the political life of our country, how are our people to determine what is right and what is wrong in our words and actions? Basing ourselves on the principles of our constitution, the will of the overwhelming majority of our people and the political programs jointly proclaimed on various occasions by our political parties and groups, we believe that, broadly speaking, words and actions can be judged right if they:

1. Help to unite the people of our various nationalities and do not divide them.

2. Are beneficial, not harmful, to socialist transformation and socialist construction.

3. Help to consolidate, not undermine or weaken, the people's democratic dictatorship.

4. Help to consolidate, not undermine or weaken, democratic centralism.

5. Tend to strengthen, not to cast off or weaken, the leadership of the Communist party.

6. Are beneficial, not harmful, to international socialist solidarity and the solidarity of the peace-loving peoples of the world.

Of these six criteria, the most important are the socialist path and the leadership of the Party. These criteria are put forward in order to foster, and not hinder, the free discussion of various questions among the people. Those who do not approve of these criteria can still put forward their own views and argue their cases. When the majority of the people have clear-cut criteria to go by, criticism and self-criticism can be conducted along proper lines, and these criteria can be applied to people's words and actions to determine whether they are fragrant flowers or poisonous weeds. These are political criteria. Naturally, in judging the truthfulness of scientific theories or assessing the esthetic value of works of art, other pertinent criteria are needed, but these six political criteria are also applicable to all activities in the arts or sciences. In a socialist country like ours, can there possibly be any useful scientific or artistic activity which runs counter to these political criteria? . . .

We all know that supervision over the Communist party is mainly exercised by the working people and Party membership. But we will benefit even more if the other democratic parties do this as well. Of course, advice and criticism exchanged between the Communist party and the other democratic parties will play a positive role in mutual supervision only when they conform to the six political criteria given above. That is why we hope that the other democratic parties will all pay attention to ideological remolding and strive for long-term coexistence and mutual supervision with the Communist party so as to meet the needs of the new society.

Part Two

FASCISM

"Fascism" is the Italian name for the twentieth-century manifestation of certain trends in political philosophy that are probably as old as politics itself. The distinguishing features of recent fascism have not been the profundity of its thought or the novelty of its elements, but the flair and efficiency with which these elements have been united, and the extreme lengths to which its doctrines have been carried.

The political philosophy called fascism is difficult to define, not so much because of its intrinsic complexity, as because of its eclectic and irrational character. Fascist thinkers borrowed freely from both ancients and moderns and emerged with a potpourri of doctrine virtually impossible to present as a coherent political system. This extensive borrowing from older thinkers makes it necessary to include within this part selections from philosophers such as Machiavelli, Hobbes, and Bodin who, although not fascists, provided important materials of which recent and contemporary fascists have made much use.

Out of this mixture of past and present, of principles and dogmas and expedients, three predominant streams of thought may be delineated. Perhaps fascism can best be understood as the contemporary blending of these three philosophical traditions.

The first is the absolutist tradition. This is the view that the power of government, to be successful in its chief goal of maintaining and expanding itself, must lie in the hands of one powerful and intelligent leader— the prince or sovereign, *Il Duce* or *Der Führer*. This absolutism has many ramifications. It helps determine the principles of organization within the state, which will be authoritarian and generally molded on military lines.

Since the leader is all-powerful, all authority and rights within the state will stem from him, while the virtues of the lower echelons will be chiefly those of responsibility and obedience. Again, since the leader is the source of the law, he himself will be above the law. Therefore the standards of conduct that apply to him will not be those of the private citizen; as leader of the state he can be judged only by his success in maintaining and extending his power and the power of his state. The result has rightly been called Machiavellianism, for fascist dictators have generally acted under the old principle that "if the act accuse him, the result will excuse him."

The second leading element in fascism is organicism, or the theory that a nation is an organic unity like a human being, having many separate organs that contribute to the general welfare, and a larger interest, or general will, that is superior to, and more important than, the interest or will of any particular member or members. There is some plausibility in this organic approach to the nature of states, and fascists are not the only theorists who have developed it. Organicism, however, when carried to extremes, can lead to the conclusion that the state is not only a real person, but a superperson whose reality is greater than that of any individual within it, and whose will is always the true will of its members, whether they think so or not. The state, or superorganism, will then be fully justified in liquidating those elements within it that interfere with its larger good. Some such views have even endowed the state with supernatural or divine power. Hegel said: "The march of God in the world, that is what the State is." One serious problem for this theory is that of determining what the will of the state really is and how it is to be known. This kind of problem is resolved, though often painfully, when the theories of organicism and absolutism are combined. The general will of the state is thus identified with the will of its leader. This identification is one of the distinguishing marks of recent German and Italian fascism.

Acting as a catalyst in combining the two characteristics already mentioned is a third, no less important: the attitude, and sometimes even the methodology, of deliberate irrationalism. Although many varieties of philosophic irrationalism became popular during the nineteenth century through the works of Schopenhauer, Nietzsche, and others, it was only at the beginning of the twentieth century that this approach was seriously applied to politics. Armed with this defense against rational criticism, the philosophy of fascism could proceed with the manufacture of effective social myths, attaching them to a latent but powerful nationalistic sentiment.

It is perhaps overly simple, but not incorrect, to describe fascism as no more than the philosophical commingling of these traditions of absolutism, organicism, and irrationalism. Unlike communism, whose classical statement is found in the philosophy of the nineteenth century, fascism received its full formulation much more recently. Like communism, however, the hard realities of its practice, including many ramifications that may not have been foreseen, have become clear only in the past half century.

Section I

ABSOLUTISM

The theory that absolute power in the hands of the sovereign is a necessary condition for a well-ordered state is very old. Its exemplifications in the Oriental societies of antiquity, as in the tyrannies of classical Greece and Rome, are too many and too well known to detail. Yet it was only with the rise of modern absolutism in Europe during the fifteenth and sixteenth centuries that this theory of political organization received its clear philosophical statement.

During that period the national state was becoming the typical and paramount political institution in Western Europe. The monarch was coming to be viewed as the supreme earthly power, divinely instituted as ruler, and representing in his person the will and interest of the state. Actual political tensions most frequently took the form of conflicts between the governing power of the sovereign, on the one side, and the several individuals and institutions within the nation, on the other. In France, England, and Spain, this process of national unification, and the triumph of monarchy, came at a relatively early date. Italy and Germany, on the other hand, were not to experience full unity under one powerful leader for some centuries.

The political philosophers represented in this section all belong to this period of early modern European history. Each, in his way, was presenting the case for national unity and the placement of absolute power in the hands of the sovereign. Are they then to be considered fascists? Clearly not. For each had philosophical views that were, in other respects, inconsistent with modern fascism. Yet, in developing the theoretical foundation of sovereign power and absolute rule, they contributed mightily to this movement, and directly or indirectly, modern fascists have borrowed a great deal from them.

32. NICCOLO MACHIAVELLI

Niccolo Machiavelli (1469-1527) was one of the most remarkable and influential political philosophers of early modern Europe. A patriot who wished above all for the unity and glory of the Italian state, he was at the same time a practical man, and an honest observer of the political circumstances of his time. Although his ideals were sometimes noble, he had no illusions about the immediate needs of Italy, in which unity could be achieved and maintained, he believed, only through the vigorous and ruthless rule of a strong man—The Prince—after whom he named his most famous work. This book, from which the following passages are taken, was dedicated to Lorenzo de Medici, of Florence, and can be construed as a manual for the successful despot.

Concerning the Things for which Men, and Especially Princes, are Praised or Blamed *

It remains now to see what ought to be the rules of conduct for a prince towards subject and friends. And as I know that many have written on this point, I expect I shall be considered presumptuous in mentioning it again, especially as in discussing it I shall depart from the methods of other people. But, it being my intention to write a thing which shall be useful to him who apprehends it, it appears to me more appropriate to follow up the real truth of a matter than the imagination of it; for many have pictured republics and principalities which in fact have never been known or seen, because how one lives is so far distant from how one ought to live, that he who neglects what is done for what ought to be done, sooner effects his ruin than his preservation; for a man who wishes to act entirely up to his professions of virtue soon meets with what destroys him among so much that is evil.

Hence it is necessary for a prince wishing to hold his own to know

---

* From N. Machiavelli, *The Prince,* 1513. These passages are reprinted from a translation by W. K. Marriott by permission of E. P. Dutton & Co., New York, and of J. M. Dent and Sons, Ltd., London.

how to do wrong, and to make use of it or not according to necessity. Therefore, putting on one side imaginary things concerning a prince, and discussing those which are real, I say that all men when they are spoken of, and chiefly princes for being more highly placed, are remarkable for some of those qualities which bring them either blame or praise; and thus it is that one is reputed liberal, another miserly, using a Tuscan term (because an avaricious person in our language is still he who desires to possess by robbery, while we call one miserly who deprives himself too much of the use of his own); one is reputed generous, one rapacious; one cruel, one compassionate; one faithless, another faithful; one effeminate and cowardly, another bold and brave; one affable, another haughty; one lascivious, another chaste; one sincere, another cunning; one hard, another easy; one grave, another frivolous; one religious, another unbelieving, and the like. And I know that everyone will confess that it would be most praiseworthy in a prince to exhibit all the above qualities that are considered good; but because they can neither be entirely possessed nor observed, for human conditions do not permit it, it is necessary for him to be sufficiently prudent that he may know how to avoid the reproach of those vices which would lose him his state; and also to keep himself, if it be possible, from those which would not lose him it; but this not being possible, he may with less hesitation abandon himself to them. And again, he need not make himself uneasy at incurring a reproach for those vices without which the state can only be saved with difficulty, for if everything is considered carefully, it will be found that something which looks like virtue, if followed, would be his ruin; while something else, which looks like vice, yet followed brings him security and prosperity.

Concerning Liberality and Meanness

Commencing then with the first of the above-named characteristics, I say that it would be well to be reputed liberal. Nevertheless, liberality exercised in a way that does not bring you the reputation for it, injures you; for if one exercises it honestly and as it should be exercised, it may not become known, and you will not avoid the reproach of its opposite. Therefore, any one wishing to maintain among men the name of liberal is obliged to avoid no attribute of magnificence; so that a prince thus inclined will consume in such acts all his property, and will be compelled in the end, if he wish to maintain the name of liberal, to unduly weigh down his people, and tax them, and do everything he can to get money. This will soon make him odious to his subjects, and becoming poor he will be little valued by anyone; thus, with his liberality, having offended many and rewarded few, he is affected by the very first trouble and imperiled by whatever may be the first danger; recognizing this himself, and wishing to draw back from it, he runs at once into the reproach of being miserly.

Therefore, a prince, not being able to exercise this virtue of liberality in such a way that it is recognized, except to his cost, if he is wise he ought not to fear the reputation of being mean, for in time he will come to be more considered than if liberal, seeing that with his economy his revenues are enough, that he can defend himself against all attacks, and is able to engage in enterprises without burdening his people; thus it comes to pass that he exercises liberality towards all from whom he does not take, who are numberless, and meanness towards those to whom he does not give, who are few. . . .

A prince, therefore, provided that he has not to rob his subjects, that he can defend himself, that he does not become poor and abject, that he is not forced to become rapacious, ought to hold of little account a reputation for being mean, for it is one of those vices which will enable him to govern.

And if anyone should say: Caesar obtained empire by liberality, and many others have reached the highest positions by having been liberal, and by being considered so, I answer: Either you are a prince in fact, or in a way to become one. In the first case this liberality is dangerous, in the second it is very necessary to be considered liberal; and Caesar was one of those who wished to become pre-eminent in Rome; but if he had survived after becoming so, and had not moderated his expenses, he would have destroyed his government. And if anyone should reply: Many have been princes, and have done great things with armies, who have been considered very liberal, I reply: Either a prince spends that which is his own or his subjects' or else that of others. In the first case he ought to be sparing, in the second he ought not to neglect any opportunity for liberality. And to the prince who goes forth with his army, supporting it by pillage, sack, and extortion, handling that which belongs to others, this liberality is necessary, otherwise he would not be followed by soldiers. And of that which is neither yours nor your subjects' you can be a ready giver, as were Cyrus, Caesar, and Alexander; because it does not take away your reputation if you squander that of others, but adds to it; it is only squandering your own that injures you.

And there is nothing wastes so rapidly as liberality, for even while you exercise it you lose the power to do so, and so become either poor or despised, or else, in avoiding poverty, rapacious and hated. And a prince should guard himself, above all things, against being despised and hated; and liberality leads you to both. Therefore it is wiser to have a reputation for meanness which brings reproach without hatred, than to be compelled through seeking a reputation for liberality to incur a name for rapacity which begets reproach with hatred.

Concerning Cruelty and Clemency, and Whether it is Better to be Loved than Feared

Coming now to the other qualities mentioned above, I say that every prince ought to desire to be considered clement and not cruel. Nevertheless he ought to take care not to misuse this clemency. Cesare Borgia was considered cruel; notwithstanding, his cruelty reconciled the Romagna, unified it, and restored it to peace and loyalty. And if this be rightly considered, he will be seen to have been much more merciful than the Florentine people, who, to avoid a reputation for cruelty, permitted Pistoia to be destroyed. Therefore a prince, so long as he keeps his subjects united and loyal, ought not to mind the reproach of cruelty; because with a few examples he will be more merciful than those who, through too much mercy, allow disorders to arise, from which follow murder or robbery; for these are wont to injure the whole people, while those executions which originate with a prince offend the individual only.

And of all princes, it is impossible for the new prince to avoid the imputation of cruelty, owing to new states being full of dangers. . . . Nevertheless he ought to be slow to believe and to act, nor should he himself show fear, but proceed in a temperate manner with prudence and humanity, so that too much confidence may not make him incautious and too much distrust render him intolerable.

Upon this a question arises: whether it be better to be loved than feared or feared than loved? It may be answered that one should wish to be both, but, because it is difficult to unite them in one person, it is much safer to be feared than loved, when, of the two, either must be dispensed with. Because this is to be asserted in general of men, that they are ungrateful, fickle, false, cowards, covetous, and as long as you succeed they are yours entirely; they will offer you their blood, property, life, and children, as is said above, when the need is far distant; but when it approaches they turn against you. And that prince who, relying entirely on their promises, has neglected other precautions, is ruined; because friendships that are obtained by payments, and not by greatness or nobility of mind, may indeed be earned, but they are not secured, and in time of need cannot be relied upon; and men have less scruple in offending one who is beloved than one who is feared, for love is preserved by the link of obligation which, owing to the baseness of men, is broken at every opportunity for their advantage; but fear preserves you by a dread of punishment which never fails.

Nevertheless a prince ought to inspire fear in such a way that, if he does not win love, he avoids hatred; because he can endure very well being feared while he is not hated, which will always be as long as he abstains from the property of his citizens and subjects and from their women. But when it is necessary for him to proceed against the life of someone, he must do it on proper justification and for manifest cause, but above all things he must keep his hands off the property of others, because men more quickly forget the death of their father than the loss of their patrimony. Besides, pretexts for taking away the property are never wanting; for he who has once begun to live by robbery will always find pretexts for seizing what belongs to others; but reasons for taking life, on the contrary, are more difficult to find and sooner lapse. But when a prince is with his army, and has under control a multitude of soldiers, then it is quite necessary for him to disregard the reputation of cruelty, for without it he would never hold his army united or disposed to its duties.

Among the wonderful deeds of Hannibal this one is enumerated: that having led an enormous army, composed of many various races of men. to fight in foreign lands, no dissensions arose either among them or against the prince, whether in his bad or in his good fortune. This arose from nothing else than his inhuman cruelty, which, with his boundless valor, made him revered and terrible in the sight of his soldiers. but without that cruelty, his other virtues were not sufficient to produce this effect. And short-sighted writers admire his deeds from one point of view and from another condemn the principal cause of them. . . .

Returning to the question of being feared or loved, I come to the conclusion that, men loving according to their own will and fearing according to that of the prince, a wise prince should establish himself on that which is in his own control and not in that of others; he must endeavor only to avoid hatred, as is noted.

Concerning the Way in which Princes Should Keep Faith

Every one admits how praiseworthy it is in a prince to keep faith, and to live with integrity and not with craft. Nevertheless our experience has been that those princes who have done great things have held good faith of little account, and have known how to circumvent the intellect of men by craft, and in the end have overcome those who have relied on their word. You must know there are two ways of contesting, the one by the law, the other by force; the first method is proper to men, the second to beasts; but because the first is frequently not sufficient, it is necessary to have recourse to the second. Therefore it is necessary for a prince to understand how to avail himself of the beast and the man. This has been figuratively taught to princes by ancient writers, who describe how Achilles and many other princes of old were given to the Centaur Chiron to nurse, who brought them up in his discipline; which means solely that, as they had for a teacher one who was half beast and half man, so it is necessary for a prince to know how to make use of both natures, and that one without the other is not durable. A prince, therefore, being compelled knowingly to adopt the beast, ought to choose the fox and the lion; because the lion cannot defend himself against snares and the fox cannot defend himself against wolves. Therefore, it is necessary to be a fox to discover the snares and a lion to terrify the wolves. Those who rely simply on the lion do not understand what they are about. Therefore a wise lord cannot, nor ought he to, keep faith when such observance may be turned against him, and when the reasons that caused him to pledge it exist no longer. If men were entirely good this precept would not hold, but because they are bad, and will not keep faith with you, you too are not bound to observe it with them. Nor will there ever be wanting to a prince legitimate reasons to excuse this non-observance. Of this endless modern examples could be given, showing how many treaties and engagements have been made void and of no effect through the faithlessness of princes; and he who has known best how to employ the fox has succeeded best.

But it is necessary to know well how to disguise this characteristic, and to be a great pretender and dissembler; and men are so simple, and so subject to present necessities, that he who seeks to deceive will always find someone who will allow himself to be deceived. One recent example I cannot pass over in silence. Alexander the Sixth did nothing else but deceive men, nor ever thought of doing otherwise, and he always found victims; for there never was a man who had greater power in asserting, or who with greater oaths would affirm a thing, yet would observe it less; nevertheless his deceits always succeeded according to his wishes, because he well understood this side of mankind.

Therefore it is unnecessary for a prince to have all the good qualities I have enumerated, but it is very necessary to appear to have them. And I shall dare to say this also, that to have them and always to observe them is injurious, and that to appear to have them is useful; to appear merciful, faithful, humane, religious, upright, and to be so, but with a mind so framed that should you require not to be so, you may be able and know how to change to the opposite.

And you have to understand this, that a prince, especially a new one, cannot observe all those things for which men are esteemed, being often forced, in order to maintain the state, to act contrary to fidelity, friendship, humanity, and religion. Therefore it is necessary for him to have a mind ready to turn itself accordingly as the winds and variations of fortune force it, yet, as I have said above, not to diverge from the good if he can avoid doing so, but, if compelled, then to know how to set about it.

For this reason a prince ought to take care that he never lets anything slip from his lips that is not replete with the above-named five qualities, that he may appear to him who sees and hears him altogether merciful, faithful, humane, upright, and religious. There is nothing more necessary to appear to have than this last quality, inasmuch as men judge generally more by the eye than by the hand, because it belongs to everybody to see you, to few to come in touch with you. Everyone sees what you appear to be, few really know what you are, and those few dare not oppose themselves to the opinion of the many, who have the majesty of the state to defend them; and in the actions of all men, and especially of princes, which it is not prudent to challenge, one judges by the result.

For that reason, let a prince have the credit of conquering and holding his state, the means will always be considered honest, and he will be praised by everybody; because the vulgar are always taken by what a thing seems to be and by what comes of it; and in the world there are only the vulgar, for the few find a place there only when the many have no ground to rest on.

One prince of the present time, whom it is not well to name, never preaches anything else but peace and good faith, and to both he is most hostile, and either, if he had kept it, would have deprived him of reputation and kingdom many a time.

That One Should Avoid Being Despised and Hated

Now, concerning the characteristics of which mention is made above, I have spoken of the more important ones, the others I wish to discuss briefly under this generality, that the prince must consider, as has been in part said before, how to avoid those things which will make him hated or contemptible; and as often as he shall have succeeded he will have fulfilled his part, and he need not fear any danger in other reproaches.

It makes him hated above all things, as I have said, to be rapacious, and to be a violator of the property and women of his subjects, from both of which he must abstain. And when neither their property nor honor is touched, the majority of men live content, and he has only to contend with the ambition of a few, whom he can curb with ease in many ways.

It makes him contemptible to be considered fickle, frivolous, effeminate, mean-spirited, irresolute, from all of which a prince should guard himself as from a rock; and he should endeavour to show in his actions greatness, courage, gravity, and fortitude; and in his private dealings with his subjects let him show that his judgments are irrevocable, and maintain himself in such reputation that no one can hope either to deceive him or to get round him.

That prince is highly esteemed who conveys this impression of himself, and he who is highly esteemed is not easily conspired against; for, provided it is well known that he is an excellent man and revered by his people, he can only be attacked with difficulty. For this reason a prince ought to have two fears, one from within, on account of his subjects, the other from without, on account of external powers. From the latter he is defended by being well armed and having good allies, and if he is well armed he will have good friends, and affairs will always remain quiet within when they are quiet without, unless they should have been already disturbed by conspiracy; and even should affairs outside be disturbed, if he has carried out his preparations and has lived as I have said, as long as he does not despair, he will resist every attack, as I said Nabis the Spartan did.

But concerning his subjects, when affairs outside are disturbed he has only to fear that they will conspire secretly, from which a prince can easily secure himself by avoiding being hated and despised, and by keeping the people satisfied with him, which it is most necessary for him to accomplish, as I said above at length. And one of the most efficacious remedies that a prince can have against conspiracies is not to be hated and despised by the people, for he who conspires against a prince always expects to please them by his removal; but when the conspirator can only look forward to offending them, he will not have the courage to take such a course, for the difficulties that confront a conspirator are infinite. And as experience shows, many have been the conspiracies, but few have been successful; because he who conspires cannot act alone, nor can he take a companion except from those whom he believes to be malcontents, and as soon as you have opened your mind to a malcontent you have given him the material with which to content himself, for by denouncing you he can look for every advantage; so that, seeing the gain from this course to be assured, and seeing the other to be doubtful and full of dangers, he must be a very rare friend, or a thoroughly obstinate enemy of the prince, to keep faith with you. . . .

For this reason I consider that a prince ought to reckon conspiracies of little account when his people hold him in esteem; but when it is hostile to him, and bears hatred towards him, he ought to fear everything and everybody. And well-ordered states and wise princes have taken every care not to drive the nobles to desperation, and to keep the people satisfied and contented, for this is one of the most important objects a prince can have

The Art of War

A prince ought to have no other aim or thought, nor select anything else for his study, than war and its rules and discipline; for this is the sole art that belongs to him who rules, and it is of such force that it not only upholds those who are born princes, but it often enables men to rise from a private station to that rank. And, on the contrary, it is seen that when princes have thought more of ease than of arms they have lost their states. And the first cause of your losing it is to neglect this art; and what enables you to acquire a state is to be master of the art. Francesco Sforza, through being martial, from a private person became Duke of Milan; and the sons, through avoiding the hardships and troubles of arms, from dukes became private persons. For among other evils which being unarmed brings you, it causes you to be despised, and this is one of those ignominies against which a prince ought to guard himself, as is shown later on. Because there is nothing proportionate between the armed and the unarmed; and it is not reasonable that he who is armed should yield obedience willingly to him who is unarmed, or that the unarmed man should be secure among armed servants. Because, there being in the one disdain and in the other suspicion, it is not possible for them to work well together. And therefore a prince who does not understand the art of war, over and above the other misfortunes already mentioned, cannot be respected by his soldiers, nor can he rely on them. He ought never, therefore, to have out of his thoughts this subject of war, and in peace he should addict himself more to its exercise than in war . . .

An Exhortation to Liberate Italy from the Barbarians

Having carefully considered the subject of the above discourses, and wondering within myself whether the present times were propitious to a new prince, and whether there were the elements that would give an opportunity to a wise and virtuous one to introduce a new order of things which would do honor to him and good to the people of this country, it appears to me that so many things concur to favor a new prince that I never knew a time more fit than the present.

And if, as I said, it was necessary that the people of Israel should be captive so as to make manifest the ability of Moses; that the Persians should be oppressed by the Medes so as to discover the greatness of the soul of Cyrus; and that the Athenians should be dispersed to illustrate the capabilities of Theseus: then at the present time, in order to discover the virtue of an Italian spirit, it was necessary that Italy should be reduced to the extremity she is now in, that she should be more enslaved than the Hebrews, more oppressed than the Persians, more scattered than the Athenians; without head, without order, beaten, despoiled, torn, overrun; and to have endured every kind of desolation.

Although lately some spark may have been shown by one, which made us think he was ordained by God for our redemption, nevertheless it was afterwards seen, in the height of his career, that fortune rejected him; so that Italy, left as without life, waits for him who shall yet heal her wounds and put an end to the ravaging and plundering of Lombardy, to the swindling and taxing of the Kingdom and of Tuscany, and cleanse those sores that for long have festered. It is seen how she entreats God to send some one who shall deliver her from these wrongs and barbarous insolencies. It is seen also that she is ready and willing to follow a banner if only someone will raise it.

Nor is there to be seen at present one in whom she can place more hope than in your illustrious house, with its valor and fortune, favored by God and by the Church of which it is now the chief, and which could be made the head of this redemption. This will not be difficult if you will recall to yourself the actions and lives of the men I have named. And although they were great and wonderful men, yet they were men, and each one of them had no more opportunity than the present offers, for their enterprises were neither more just nor easier than this, nor was God more their friend than He is yours.

With us there is great justice, because that war is just which is necessary, and arms are hallowed when there is no other hope but in them. Here there is the greatest willingness, and where the willingness is great the difficulties cannot be great if you will only follow those men to whom I have directed your attention. Further than this, how extraordinarily the ways of God have been manifested beyond example: the sea is divided, a cloud has led the way, the rock has poured forth water, it has rained manna, everything has contributed to your greatness; you ought to do the rest. God is not willing to do everything, and thus take away our free will and that share of glory which belongs to us.

And it is not to be wondered as if none of the above-named Italians have been able to accomplish all that is expected from your illustrious house; and if in so many revolutions in Italy, and in so many campaigns, it has always appeared as if military virtue were exhausted, this has happened because the old order of things was not good, and none of us have known how to find a new one. And nothing honors a man more than to establish new laws and new ordinances when he himself has newly risen. Such things when they are well founded and dignified will make him revered and admired, and in Italy there are not wanting opportunities to bring such into use in every form.

Here there is great valor in the limbs while it fails in the head. Look attentively at the duels and the hand-to-hand combats, how superior the Italians are in strength, dexterity, and subtlety. But when it comes to armies they do not bear comparison, and this springs entirely from the insufficiency of the leaders, since those who are capable are not obedient, and each one seems to himself to know, there having never been anyone so distinguished above the rest, either by valor or fortune, that others would yield to him. Hence it is that for so long a time, and during so much fighting in the past twenty years, whenever there has been an army wholly Italian, it has always given a poor account of itself.

This opportunity, therefore, ought not to be allowed to pass for letting Italy at last see her liberator appear. Nor can one express the love with which he would be received in all those provinces which have suffered so much from these foreign scourings, with what thirst for revenge, with what stubborn faith, with what devotion, with what tears. What door would be closed to him? Who would refuse obedience to him? What envy would hinder him? What Italian would refuse him homage? To all of us this barbarous dominion stinks. Let, therefore, your illustrious house take up this charge with that courage and hope with which all just enterprises are undertaken, so that under its standard our native country may be ennobled, and under its auspices may be verified that saying of Petrarch:

Virtue against violence will take up arms;
    And be the combat quickly sped!
For the ancient valor of Italian hearts
    Is not yet dead.

33. JEAN BODIN

Jean Bodin (1530-1596) wrote the Six Books of the Commonwealth *with the specific intention of strengthening the authority of the French monarch. In it he undertook a complete discussion of politics and the state; but the most influential part of the work was its philosophical treatment of sovereignty—"power supreme and perpetual, absolute, and subject to no law"—and all its necessary attributes. It is, he claims, that majesty which alone can be "the distinguishing mark of a state."*

[Concerning Sovereignty] *

Sovereignty is that absolute and perpetual power vested in a commonwealth which in Latin is termed *majestas* . . . The term needs careful definition, because although it is the distinguishing mark of a commonwealth, and an understanding of its nature fundamental to any treatment of politics, no jurist or political philosopher has in fact attempted to define it. . . .

I have described it as *perpetual* because one can give absolute power to a person or group of persons for a period of time, but that time expired they become subjects once more. Therefore even while they enjoy power, they cannot properly be regarded as sovereign rulers, but only as the lieutenants and agents of the sovereign ruler, till the moment comes when it pleases the prince or the people to revoke the gift. The true sovereign remains always seized of his power. Just as a feudal lord who grants lands to another retains his eminent domain over them, so the ruler who delegates authority to judge and command, whether it be for a short period, or during pleasure, remains seized of those rights of jurisdiction actually exercised by another in the form of a revocable grant, or precarious tenancy. For this reason the law requires the governor of a province,

* From J. Bodin, *Six Books of the Commonwealth*, 1576. These passages are from a translation by M. J. Tooley, reprinted by permission of the publisher, Basil Blackwell, Oxford, 1955.

or the prince's lieutenant, to make a formal surrender of the authority committed to him, at the expiration of his term of office. In this respect there is no difference between the highest officer of state and his humblest subordinate. If it were otherwise, and the absolute authority delegated by the prince to a lieutenant was regarded as itself sovereign power, the latter could use it against his prince who would thereby forfeit his eminence, and the subject could command his lord, the servant his master. This is a manifest absurdity, considering that the sovereign is always excepted personally, as a matter of right, in all delegations of authority, however extensive. However much he gives there always remains a reserve of right in his own person, whereby he may command, or intervene by way of prevention, confirmation, evocation, or any other way he thinks fit, in all matters delegated to a subject, whether in virtue of an office or a commission. Any authority exercised in virtue of an office or a commission can be revoked, or made tenable for as long or short a period as the sovereign wills. . . .

But supposing the king grants absolute power to a lieutenant for the term of his life, is not that a perpetual sovereign power? For if one confines *perpetual* to that which has no termination whatever, then sovereignity cannot subsist save in aristocracies and popular states, which never die. If one is to include monarchy too, sovereignty must be vested not in the king alone, but in the king and the heirs of his body, which supposes a strictly hereditary monarchy. In that case there can be very few sovereign kings, since there are only a very few strictly hereditary monarchies. Those especially who come to the throne by election could not be included.

A perpetual authority therefore must be understood to mean one that lasts for the lifetime of him who exercises it. If a sovereign magistrate is given office for one year, or for any other predetermined period, and continues to exercise the authority bestowed on him after the conclusion of his term, he does so either by consent or by force and violence. If he does so by force, it is manifest tyranny. The tyrant is a true sovereign for all that. The robber's possession by violence is true and natural possession although contrary to the law, for those who were formerly in possession have been disseized. But if the magistrate continues in office by consent, he is not a sovereign prince, seeing that he only exercises power on sufferance. Still less is he a sovereign if the term of his office is not fixed, for in that case he has no more than a precarious commission. . . .

What bearing have these considerations on the case of the man to whom the people has given absolute power for the term of his natural life? One must distinguish. If such absolute power is given him simply and unconditionally, and not in virtue of some office or commission, nor in the form of a revocable grant, the recipient certainly is, and should be acknowledged to be, a sovereign. The people has renounced and alienated its sovereign power in order to invest him with it and put him in possession, and it thereby transfers to him all its powers, authority, and sovereign rights, just as does the man who gives to another possessory and proprietary rights over what he formerly owned. The civil law expresses this in the phrase "all power is conveyed to him and vested in him." *

But if the people gives such power for the term of his natural life to anyone as its official or lieutenant, or only gives the exercise of such power, in such a case he is not a sovereign, but simply an officer, lieutenant, regent, governor, or agent, and as such has the exercise only of a power inhering in another. When a magistrate institutes a perpetual lieutenant, even if he abandons all his rights of jurisdiction and leaves their exercise entirely to his lieutenant, the authority to command and to judge nevertheless does not reside in the lieutenant, nor the action and force of the law derive from him. If he exceeds his authority his acts have no validity, unless approved and confirmed by him from whom he draws his authority. For this reason King John, after his return from captivity in England, solemnly ratified all the acts of his son Charles, who had acted in his name as regent, in order, as was necessary, to regularize the position.

Whether then one exercises the power of another by commission, by institution, or by delegation, or whether such exercise is for a set term, or in perpetuity, such a power is not a sovereign power, even if there is no mention of such words as representative, lieutenant, governor, or regent, in the letters of appointment, or even if such powers are a consequence of the normal working of the laws of the country. In ancient times in Scotland, for instance, the law vested the entire governance of the realm in the next of kin, if the king should be a minor, on condition that everything that was done, was done in the king's name. But this law was later altered because of its inconvenient consequences.

Let us now turn to the other term of our definition and consider

* Ei et in eum omnem potestatem contulit.

the force of the word *absolute*. The people or the magnates of a commonwealth can bestow simply and unconditionally upon some-one of their choice a sovereign and perpetual power to dispose of their property and persons, to govern the state as he thinks fit, and to order the succession, in the same way that any proprietor, out of his liberality, can freely and unconditionally make a gift of his property to another. Such a form of gift, not being qualified in any way, is the only true gift, being at once unconditional and irrevocable. Gifts burdened with obligations and hedged with conditions are not true gifts. Similarly sovereign power given to a prince charged with conditions is neither properly sovereign, nor absolute, unless the con-ditions of appointment are only such as are inherent in the laws of God and of nature. . . .

On the other hand it is the distinguishing mark of the sovereign that he cannot in any way be subject to the commands of another, for it is he who makes law for the subject, abrogates law already made, and amends obsolete law. No one who is subject either to the law or to some other person can do this. That is why it is laid down in the civil law that the prince is above the law, for the word *law* in Latin implies the command of him who is invested with sovereign power. Therefore we find in all statutes the phrase "not-withstanding all edicts and ordinances to the contrary that we have infringed, or do infringe by these present." This clause applies both to former acts of the prince himself, and to those of his predecessors. For all laws, ordinances, letters patent, privileges, and grants what-soever issued by the prince, have force only during his own lifetime, and must be expressly, or at least tacitly, confirmed by the reigning prince who has cognizance of them . . . In proof of which, it is the custom of this realm for all corporations and corporate bodies to ask for the confirmation of their privileges, rights, and jurisdic-tions, on the accession of a new king. Even Parlements and high courts do this, as well as individual officers of the crown.

If the prince is not bound by the laws of his predecessors, still less can he be bound by his own laws. One may be subject to laws made by another, but it is impossible to bind oneself in any matter which is the subject of one's own free exercise of will. As the law says, "there can be no obligation in any matter which proceeds from the free will of the undertaker." * It follows of necessity that the king

---

* Nulla obligatio consistere potest, quae a voluntate promittentis statum capit.

cannot be subject to his own laws. Just as, according to the canonists, the Pope can never tie his own hands, so the sovereign prince cannot bind himself, even if he wishes. For this reason edicts and ordinances conclude with the formula "for such is our good pleasure," thus intimating that the laws of a sovereign prince, even when founded on truth and right reason, proceed simply from his own free will. . . .

From all this it is clear that the principal mark of sovereign majesty and absolute power is the right to impose laws generally on all subjects regardless of their consent . . . And if it is expedient that if he is to govern his state well, a sovereign prince must be above the law, it is even more expedient that the ruling class in an aristocracy should be so, and inevitable in a popular state. A monarch in a kingdom is set apart from his subjects, and the ruling class from the people in an aristocracy. There are therefore in each case two parties, those that rule on the one hand, and those that are ruled on the other. . . .

[The True Attributes of Sovereignty]

Because there are none on earth, after God, greater than sovereign princes, whom God establishes as His lieutenants to command the rest of mankind, we must enquire carefully into their estate, that we may respect and revere their majesty in all due obedience, speak and think of them with all due honor. He who contemns his sovereign prince, contemns God whose image he is. . . .

Before going any further, one must consider what is meant by *law*. The word law signifies the right command of that person, or those persons, who have absolute authority over all the rest without exception, saving only the law-giver himself, whether the command touches all subjects in general or only some in particular. To put it another way, the law is the rightful command of the sovereign touching all his subjects in general, or matters of general application . . .

The first attribute of the sovereign prince therefore is the power to make law binding on all his subjects in general and on each in particular. But to avoid any ambiguity one must add that he does so without the consent of any superior, equal, or inferior being necessary. If the prince can only make law with the consent of a superior he is a subject; if of an equal he shares his sovereignty; if of an inferior, whether it be a council of magnates or the people, it is not he who is sovereign. . . .

It may be objected however that not only have magistrates the power of issuing edicts and ordinances, each according to his competence and within his own sphere of jurisdiction, but private citizens can make law in the form of general or local custom. It is agreed that customary law is as binding as statute law. But if the sovereign prince is author of the law, his subjects are the authors of custom. But there is a difference between law and custom. Custom establishes itself gradually over a long period of years, and by common consent, or at any rate the consent of the greater part. Law is made on the instant and draws its force from him who has the right to bind all the rest. Custom is established imperceptibly and without any exercise of compulsion. Law is promulgated and imposed by authority, and often against the wishes of the subject. For this reason Dion Chrysostom compared custom to the king and law to the tyrant. Moreover law can break custom, but custom cannot derogate from the law, nor can the magistrate, or any other responsible for the administration of law, use his discretion about the enforcement of law as he can about custom. Law, unless it is permissive and relaxes the severity of another law, always carries penalties for its breach. Custom only has binding force by the sufferance and during the good pleasure of the sovereign prince, and so far as he is willing to authorize it. Thus the force of both statutes and customary law derives from the authorization of the prince . . . Included in the power of making and unmaking law is that of promulgating it and amending it when it is obscure, or when the magistrates find contradictions and absurdities. . . .

All the other attributes and rights of sovereignty are included in this power of making and unmaking law, so that strictly speaking this is the unique attribute of sovereign power. It includes all other rights of sovereignty, that is to say of making peace and war, of hearing appeals from the sentences of all courts whatsoever, of appointing and dismissing the great officers of state; of taxing, or granting privileges of exemption to all subjects, of appreciating or depreciating the value and weight of the coinage, of receiving oaths of fidelity from subjects and liege-vassals alike, without exception of any other to whom faith is due. . . .

34. THOMAS HOBBES

*Thomas Hobbes (1588-1679) was a vigorous defender of the roya.
prerogative in England. He is distinguished from his contemporaries in
that he justifies his support of absolute sovereignty with a complete theory
of human nature and the state. The monarch, he argues, is that person
into whose hands all power has been placed for the purpose of maintaining peace and order. Royal authority is the only means of avoiding
what, in his view, is infinitely worse, the "war of each against all" which
must constantly be waged in a state of nature. As a thoroughgoing individualist, Hobbes was surely no fascist; yet he did play a significant part
in the development of the theory of absolute rule.*

[The Origin and Nature of the State] *

Of the Causes, Generation, and Definition of a Commonwealth.

The final cause, end, or design of men, who naturally love liberty,
and dominion over others, in the introduction of that restraint upon
themselves, in which we see them live in commonwealths, is the
foresight of their own preservation, and of a more contented life
thereby; that is to say, of getting themselves out from that miserable
condition of war, which is necessarily consequent, as hath been
shown in chapter xiii, to the natural passions of men, when there is
no visible power to keep them in awe, and tie them by fear of punishment to the performance of their covenants, and observation of those
laws of nature set down in the fourteenth and fifteenth chapters.

For the laws of nature, as "justice," "equity," "modesty," "mercy,"
and, in sum, "doing to others as we would be done to," of themselves, without the terror of some power to cause them to be observed, are contrary to our natural passions, that carry us to partiality, pride, revenge, and the like. And covenants, without the sword,

* From T. Hobbes, *Leviathan,* 1651. These passages are from a modernized
edition edited by Michael Oakeshott and published by Basil Blackwell, Oxford.
1946.

are but words, and of no strength to secure a man at all. Therefore notwithstanding the laws of nature, which everyone hath then kept, when he has the will to keep them, when he can do it safely, if there be no power erected, or not great enough for our security, every man will and may lawfully rely on his own strength and art, for caution against all other men. And in all places where men have lived by small families, to rob and spoil one another has been a trade, and so far from being reputed against the law of nature, that the greater spoils they gained, the greater was their honor; and men observed no other laws therein, but the laws of honor; that is, to abstain from cruelty, leaving to men their lives, and instruments of husbandry. And as small families did then, so now do cities and kingdoms, which are but greater families, for their own security, enlarge their dominions, upon all pretenses of danger, and fear of invasion, or assistance that may be given to invaders, and endeavor as much as they can to subdue or weaken their neighbors, by open force and secret arts, for want of other caution, justly; and are remembered for it in after ages with honor.

Nor is it the joining together of a small number of men that gives them this security; because in small numbers, small additions on the one side or the other make the advantage of strength so great as is sufficient to carry the victory; and therefore gives encouragement to an invasion. The multitude sufficient to confide in for our security is not determined by any certain number, but by comparison with the enemy we fear; and is then sufficient, when the odds of the enemy is not of so visible and conspicuous moment to determine the event of war, as to move him to attempt.

And be there never so great a multitude; yet if their actions be directed according to their particular judgments and particular appetites, they can expect thereby no defense, nor protection, neither against a common enemy, nor against the injuries of one another. For being distracted in opinions concerning the best use and application of their strength, they do not help but hinder one another; and reduce their strength by mutual opposition to nothing: whereby they are easily, not only subdued by a very few that agree together; but also when there is no common enemy, they make war upon each other, for their particular interests. For if we could suppose a great multitude of men to consent in the observation of justice, and other laws of nature, without a common power to keep them all in awe, we might as well suppose all mankind to do the same; and then there neither would be nor need to be any civil government or common-wealth at all; because there would be peace without subjection.

Nor is it enough for the security, which men desire should last all the time of their life, that they be governed and directed by one judgment, for a limited time: as in one battle, or one war. For though they obtain a victory by their unanimous endeavor against a foreign enemy; yet afterwards, when either they have no common enemy, or he that by one part is held for an enemy is by another part held for a friend, they must needs by the difference of their interests dissolve, and fall again into a war among themselves. . . .

The only way to erect such a common power as may be able to defend them from the invasion of foreigners and the injuries of one another, and thereby to secure them in such sort as that by their own industry, and by the fruits of the earth, they may nourish themselves and live contentedly, is to confer all their power and strength upon one man, or upon one assembly of men, that may reduce all their wills, by plurality of voices, unto one will: which is as much as to say, to appoint one man, or assembly of men, to bear their person; and everyone to own and acknowledge himself to be author of whatsoever he that so beareth their person shall act, or cause to be acted, in those things which concern the common peace and safety; and therein to submit their wills, every one to his will, and their judgments to his judgment. This is more than consent, or concord; it is a real unity of them all in one and the same person, made by covenant of every man with every man, in such manner as if every man should say to every man, "I authorize and give up my right of governing myself, to this man or to this assembly of men, on this condition, that thou give up thy right to him and authorize all his actions in like manner." This done, the multitude so united in one person is called a "commonwealth," in Latin *civitas*. This is the generation of that great leviathan, or rather, to speak more reve-rently, of that mortal god, to which we owe under the immortal God, our peace and defense. For by this authority, given him by every particular man in the commonwealth, he hath the use of so much power and strength conferred on him, that by terror thereof, he is enabled to perform the wills of them all, to peace at home, and mutual aid against their enemies abroad. And in him consisteth the essence of the commonwealth; which, to define it, is "one person, of whose acts a great multitude, by mutual covenants one with an-other, have made themselves every one the author, to the end he may use the strength and means of them all, as he shall think expedient, for their peace and common defense."

And he that carrieth this person is called sovereign, and said to have sovereign power; and everyone besides, his subject.

The attaining to this sovereign power is by two ways. One, by natural force; as when a man maketh his children to submit themselves, and their children, to his government, as being able to destroy them if they refuse; or by war subdueth his enemies to his will, giving them their lives on that condition. The other is when men agree among themselves to submit to some man, or assembly of men, voluntarily, on confidence to be protected by him against all others. This latter may be called a political commonwealth, or commonwealth by institution; and the former, a commonwealth by acquisition. And first, I shall speak of a commonwealth by institution.

[Sovereignty]

Of the Rights of Sovereigns by Institution.

A commonwealth is said to be instituted when a multitude of men do agree and convenant, everyone with everyone, that to whatsoever man or assembly of men shall be given by the major part the right to present the person of them all, that is to say, to be their representative; everyone, as well he that voted for it as he that voted against it, shall authorize all the actions and judgments of that man or assembly of men in the same manner as if they were his own, to the end to live peaceably among themselves and be protected against other men.

From this institution of a commonwealth are derived all the rights and faculties of him, or them, on whom sovereign power is conferred by the consent of the people assembled.

First, because they covenant, it is to be understood, they are not obliged by former covenant to anything repugnant hereunto. And consequently that they have already instituted a commonwealth, being thereby bound by covenant to own the actions and judgments of one, cannot lawfully make a new covenant among themselves to be obedient to any other in anything whatsoever, without his permission. And therefore, they that are subjects to a monarch, cannot without his leave cast off monarchy, and return to the confusion of a disunited multitude; nor transfer their person from him that beareth it, to another man, or other assembly of men: for they are bound, every man to every man, to own and be reputed author of all that he that already is their sovereign shall do, and judge fit to be done: so that any one man dissenting, all the rest should break their covenant made to that man, which is injustice: and they have also every man given the sovereignty to him that beareth their person; and therefore if they depose him, they take from him that which is his own, and so again it is injustice. Besides, if he that attempteth to depose his sovereign be killed, or punished by him for such attempt, he is author of his own punishment, as being by the institution author of all his sovereign shall do: and because it is injustice for a man to do anything for which he may be punished by his own authority, he is also upon that title unjust. And whereas some men have pretended for their disobedience to their sovereign, a new covenant, made not with men, but with God, this also is unjust: for there is no covenant with God but by mediation of somebody that representeth God's person; which none doth but God's lieutenant, who hath the sovereignty under God. But this pretense of covenant with God is so evident a lie, even in the pretenders' own consciences, that it is not only an act of an unjust, but also of a vile and unmanly disposition.

Secondly, because the right of bearing the person of them all is given to him they make sovereign, by covenant only of one to another, and not of him to any of them, there can happen no breach of covenant on the part of the sovereign: and consequently none of his subjects, by any pretense of forfeiture, can be freed from his subjection. That he which is made sovereign maketh no covenant with his subjects beforehand, is manifest; because either he must make it with the whole multitude, as one party to the covenant, or he must make a several covenant with every man. With the whole, as one party, it is impossible; because as yet they are not one person; and if he make so many several covenants as there be men, those covenants after he hath the sovereignty are void; because what act soever can be pretended by any one of them for breach thereof, is the act both of himself and of all the rest, because done in the person and by the right of every one of them in particular. Besides, if any one or more of them pretend a breach of the covenant made by the sovereign at his institution; and others, or one other of his subjects, or himself alone, pretend there was no such breach, there is in this case no judge to decide the controversy; it returns therefore to the sword again, and every man recovereth the right of protecting him-self by his own strength, contrary to the design they had in the institution. It is therefore in vain to grant sovereignty by way of precedent covenant. The opinion that any monarch receiveth his power by covenant, that is to say, on condition, proceedeth from want of understanding this easy truth, that covenants being but words and breath, have no force to oblige, contain, constrain, or protect any man, but what they have from the public sword; that is, from the united hands of that man or assembly of men that hath the sovereignty, and whose actions are avouched by them all, and per-formed by the strength of them all, in him united. But when an assembly of men is made sovereign, then no man imagineth any such covenant to have passed in the institution; for no man is so dull as to say, for example, the people of Rome made a covenant with the Romans to hold the sovereignty on such or such conditions; which not performed, the Romans might lawfully depose the Roman people. That men see not the reason to be alike in a monarchy and in a popular government, proceedeth from the ambition of some that are kinder to the government of an assembly, whereof they may hope to participate, than of monarchy, which they despair to enjoy.

Thirdly, because the major part hath by consenting voices de-clared a sovereign, he that dissented must now consent with the rest, that is, be contented to avow all the actions he shall do, or else justly be destroyed by the rest. For if he voluntarily entered into the congregation of them that were assembled, he sufficiently de-clared thereby his will, and therefore tacitly covenanted to stand to what the major part should ordain: and therefore if he refuse to stand thereto, or make protestation against any of their decrees, he does contrary to his covenant, and therefore unjustly. And whether he be of the congregation or not, and whether his consent be asked or not, he must either submit to their decrees, or be left in the con-dition of war he was in before; wherein he might without injustice be destroyed by any man whatsoever.

Fourthly, because every subject is by this institution author of all the actions and judgments of the sovereign instituted, it follows that whatsoever he doth it can be no injury to any of his subjects, nor ought he to be by any of them accused of injustice. For he that doth anything by authority from another doth therein no injury to him by whose authority he acteth: but by this institution of a common-wealth every particular man is author of all the sovereign doth; and consequently, he that complaineth of injury from his sovereign complaineth of that whereof he himself is author, and therefore ought not to accuse any man but himself; no, nor himself of injury, because to do injury to one's self is impossible. It is true that they that have sovereign power may commit iniquity, but not injustice or injury in the proper signification.

Fifthly, and consequently to that which was said last, no man that hath sovereign power can justly be put to death, or otherwise in any manner by his subjects punished. For seeing every subject is author of the actions of his sovereign, he punisheth another for the actions committed by himself.

And because the end of this institution is the peace and defense of them all, and whosoever has right to the end has right to the means, it belongeth of right to whatsoever man or assembly that hath the sovereignty to be judge both of the means of peace and defense, and also of the hindrances and disturbances of the same, and to do whatsoever he shall think necessary to be done, both beforehand, for the preserving of peace and security, by prevention of discord at home and hostility from abroad; and, when peace and security are lost, for the recovery of the same. And therefore,

Sixthly, it is annexed to the sovereignty to be judge of what opinions and doctrines are averse and what conducing to peace; and consequently, on what occasions, how far, and what men are to be trusted withal, in speaking to multitudes of people, and who shall examine the doctrines of all books before they be published. For the actions of men proceed from their opinions, and in the well governing of opinions consisteth the well governing of men's actions, in order to their peace and concord. And though in matter of doctrine nothing ought to be regarded but the truth; yet this is not repugnant to regulating the same by peace. For doctrine repugnant to peace can be no more true than peace and concord can be against the law of nature. It is true that in a commonwealth, where, by the negligence or unskilfulness of governors and teachers, false doctrines are by time generally received, the contrary truths may be generally offensive. Yet the most sudden and rough bursting in of a new truth that can be, does never break the peace, but only sometimes awake the war. For those men that are so remissly governed, that they dare take up arms to defend or introduce an opinion, are still in war; and their condition not peace, but only a cessation of arms for fear of one another; and they live, as it were, in the precincts of battle continually. It belongeth therefore to him that hath the sovereign power to be judge, or constitute all judges, of opinions and doctrines, as a thing necessary to peace, thereby to prevent discord and civil war.

Seventhly, is annexed to the sovereignty, the whole power of prescribing the rules whereby every man may know what goods he may enjoy and what actions he may do, without being molested by any of his fellow-subjects; and this is it men call "propriety." For before constitution of sovereign power, as hath already been shown, all men had right to all things, which necessarily causeth war: and therefore this propriety, being necessary to peace, and depending on sovereign power, is the act of that power, in order to the public peace. These rules of propriety, or *meum* and *tuum,* and of good, evil, lawful, and unlawful in the actions of subjects, are the civil laws; that is to say, the laws of each commonwealth in particular; though the name of civil law be now restrained to the ancient civil laws of the city of Rome, which being the head of a great part of the world, her laws at that time were in these parts the civil law.

Eighthly, is annexed to the sovereignty, the right of judicature, that is to say, of hearing and deciding all controversies which may arise concerning law, either civil or natural, or concerning fact. For without the decision of controversies, there is no protection of one subject against the injuries of another; the laws concerning *meum* and *tuum* are in vain, and to every man remaineth, from the natural and necessary appetite of his own conservation, the right of protecting himself by his private strength, which is the condition of war, and contrary to the end for which every commonwealth is instituted.

Ninthly, is annexed to the sovereignty, the right of making war and peace with other nations and commonwealths, that is to say, of judging when it is for the public good, and how great forces are to be assembled, armed, and paid for that end, and to levy money upon the subjects to defray the expenses thereof. For the power by which the people are to be defended consisteth in their armies, and the strength of an army, in the union of their strength under one command, which command the sovereign instituted, therefore hath; because the command of the "militia," without other institution, maketh him that hath it sovereign. And therefore whosoever is made general of an army, he that hath the sovereign power is always generalissimo.

Tenthly, is annexed to the sovereignty, the choosing of all counsellors, ministers, magistrates, and officers, both in peace and war. For seeing the sovereign is charged with the end, which is the common peace and defense, he is understood to have power to use such means as he shall think most fit for his discharge.

Eleventhly, to the sovereign is committed the power of rewarding with riches or honor, and of punishing with corporal or pecuniary punishment, or with ignominy, every subject according to the law he hath formerly made; or if there be no law made, according as he shall judge most to conduce to the encouraging of men to serve the commonwealth, or deterring of them from doing disservice to the same.

Lastly, considering what value men are naturally apt to set upon themselves, what respect they look for from others, and how little they value other men, from whence continually arise amongst them, emulation, quarrels, factions, and at last war, to the destroying of one another, and diminution of their strength against a common enemy, it is necessary that there be laws of honor, and a public rate of the worth of such men as have deserved or are able to deserve well of the commonwealth; and that there be force in the hands of some or other, to put those laws in execution. But it hath already been shown that not only the whole "militia," or forces of the commonwealth, but also the judicature of all controversies, is annexed to the sovereignty. To the sovereign therefore it belongeth also to give titles of honor; and to appoint what order of place and dignity each man shall hold; and what signs of respect, in public or private meetings, they shall give to one another.

These are the rights which make the essence of sovereignty, and which are the marks whereby a man may discern in what man, or assembly of men, the sovereign power is placed and resideth. For these are incommunicable, and inseparable. The power to coin money, to dispose of the estate and persons of infant heirs, to have preëmption in markets, and all other statute prerogatives, may be transferred by the sovereign, and yet the power to protect his subjects be retained. But if he transfer the "militia," he retains the judicature in vain, for want of execution of the laws: or if he grant away the power of raising money, the "militia" is in vain; or if he give away the government of doctrines, men will be frighted into rebellion with the fear of spirits. And so if we consider any one of the said rights, we shall presently see that the holding of all the rest will produce no effect in the conservation of peace and justice, the end for which all commonwealths are instituted. And this division is it whereof it is said, "a kingdom divided in itself cannot stand": for unless this division

precede, division into opposite armies can never happen. If there had
not first been an opinion received of the greatest part of England that
these powers were divided between the King, and the Lords, and the
House of Commons, the people had never been divided and fallen into
this civil war, first between those that disagreed in politics, and after
between the dissenters about the liberty of religion; which have so
instructed men in this point of sovereign right, that there be few now
in England that do not see that these rights are inseparable, and will
be so generally acknowledged at the next return of peace, and so
continue, till their miseries are forgotten; and no longer, except the
vulgar be better taught than they have hitherto been.

And because they are essential and inseparable rights, it follows
necessarily that in whatsoever words any of them seem to be granted
away, yet if the sovereign power itself be not in direct terms renounced, and the name of sovereign no more given by the grantees
to him that grants them, the grant is void: for when he has granted
all he can, if we grant back the sovereignty, all is restored, as inseparably annexed thereunto.

This great authority being indivisible and inseparably annexed to
the sovereignty, there is little ground for the opinion of them that
say of sovereign kings, though they be *singulis majores,* of greater
power than every one of their subjects, yet they be *universis minores,*
of less power than them all together. For if by "all together" they
mean not the collective body as one person, then "all together" and
"every one" signify the same; and the speech is absurd. But if by "all
together," they understand them as one person, which person the
sovereign bears, then the power of all together is the same with the
sovereign's power; and so again the speech is absurd: which absurdity
they see well enough, when the sovereignty is in an assembly of the
people; but in a monarch they see it not; and yet the power of
sovereignty is the same in whomsoever it be placed.

And as the power, so also the honor of the sovereign, ought to be
greater than that of any or all the subjects. For in the sovereignty is
the fountain of honor. The dignities of lord, earl, duke, and prince
are his creatures. As in the presence of the master the servants are
equal, and without any honor at all; so are the subjects in the
presence of the sovereign. And though they shine some more, some
less, when they are out of his sight; yet in his presence, they shine
no more than the stars in the presence of the sun.

But a man may here object that the condition of subjects is very miserable; as being obnoxious to the lusts, and other irregular passions of him or them that have so unlimited a power in their hands. And commonly they that live under a monarch, think it the fault of monarchy; and they that live under the government of democracy, or other sovereign assembly, attribute all the inconvenience to that form of commonwealth; whereas the power in all forms, if they be perfect enough to protect them, is the same: not considering that the state of man can never be without some incommodity or other; and that the greatest, that in any form of government can possibly happen to the people in general, is scarce sensible, in respect of the miseries and horrible calamities that accompany a civil war, or that dissolute condition of masterless men, without subjection to laws and a coercive power to tie their hands from rapine and revenge: nor considering that the greatest pressure of sovereign governors proceedeth not from any delight or profit they can expect in the damage or weakening of their subjects, in whose vigor consisteth their own strength and glory; but in the restiveness of themselves, that unwillingly contributing to their own defense, make it necessary for their governors to draw from them what they can in time of peace, that they may have means on any emergent occasion, or sudden need, to resist, or take advantage on their enemies. For all men are by nature provided of notable multiplying glasses, that is their passions and self-love, through which every little payment appeareth a great grievance; but are destitute of those prospective glasses, namely, moral and civil science, to see afar off the miseries that hang over them, and cannot without such payments be avoided.

Section II

ORGANICISM

The organic theory of the state rose to prominence in Germany during the nineteenth century. This emphasis on the integral unity of the state and on the organic interrelation of its members was largely an effort to provide a philosophical foundation for political unity among the numerous German principalities—a national unity that was finally attained under "the man of blood and iron," Bismarck, who became the first Chancellor of the German Empire in 1871.

"Germany is no longer a state," Hegel said in his essay on *The Constitution of Germany,* in 1802. The immediate political problem was that of creating throughout Germany a strong state government; the philosophical task was to provide the theory on which this national unification could be based. Hegel and his followers were thus motivated by factors similar to those that had influenced Machiavelli and Bodin so many years before—and, indeed, Hegel refers to Machiavelli as a true political genius. The organicists differed from the early defenders of absolute sovereignty, however, in directing their attention chiefly to problems of Germany and in developing a theory of the state as an actual person, through whose will and conduct the dialectic of human history is worked out. As the superorganic unity in which the divine spirit is manifested, the state is held to be the only institution in which human freedom can be realized. It is the most purely rational representation of the interests of its individual organs. Since the state is on a level of reality higher than that of any single human being, and since its will is every member's real will, the organicist recognizes no possible conflict of interest between individual and state. The will of the state is always supreme, and its members shall, if necessary, "be forced to be free."

35. GEORG W. F. HEGEL

Elements of the philosophy of Hegel were borrowed by both communists and fascists. The Marxist use of the Hegelian dialectic has been discussed earlier in this volume.* The fascist philosophers utilized not the dialectical methodology, but the Hegelian idealization of the national state, and the Hegelian arguments against any individuality opposed to, or outside of, state organization.

Idea and Aim of the State†

The State is the realization of the ethical idea. It is the ethical spirit as revealed, self-conscious, substantial will. It is the will which thinks and knows itself, and carries out what it knows, and in so far as it knows. The unreflected existence of the State rests on custom, and its reflected existence on the self-consciousness of the individual, on his knowledge and activity. The individual, in return, has his substantial freedom in the State, as the essence, purpose, and product of his activity.

The true State is the ethical whole and the realization of freedom. It is the absolute purpose of reason that freedom should be realized. The State is the spirit, which lives in the world and there realizes itself consciously; while in nature it is actual only as its own other or as dormant spirit. Only as present in consciousness, knowing itself as an existing object, is it the State. The State is the march of God through the world, its ground is the power of reason realizing itself as will. The idea of the State should not denote any particular State, or particular institution; one must rather consider the Idea only, this actual God, by itself. Because it is more easy to find defects than to grasp the positive meaning, one readily falls into the mistake of

* See above, pp. 49 ff.

† G. Hegel, *The Philosophy of Law*, 1821. These passages are reprinted with the permission of Charles Scribner's Sons from *Hegel: Selections*, edited by J. Loewenberg, Modern Student's Library copyright 1929; renewal copyright 1956.

emphasizing so much the particular nature of the State as to over-look its inner organic essence. The State is no work of art. It exists in the world, and thus in the realm of caprice, accident, and error. Evil behavior toward it may disfigure it on many sides. But the ugliest man, the criminal, the invalid, and the cripple, are still living human beings. The affirmative, life, persists in spite of defects, and it is this affirmative which alone is here in question.

In the State, everything depends upon the unity of the universal and the particular. In the ancient States the subjective purpose was absolutely one with the will of the State. In modern times, on the contrary, we demand an individual opinion, an individual will and conscience. The ancients had none of these in the modern sense; the final thing for them was the will of the State. While in Asiatic despo-tisms the individual had no inner self and no self-justification, in the modern world man demands to be honored for the sake of his sub-jective individuality.

The union of duty and right has the twofold aspect that what the State demands as duty should directly be the right of the individual, since the State is nothing but the organization of the concept of freedom. The determinations of the individual will are given by the State objectivity, and it is through the State alone that they attain truth and realization. The State is the sole condition of the attainment of the particular end and good.

Political disposition, called patriotism—the assurance resting in truth and the will which has become a custom—is simply the result of the institutions subsisting in the State, institutions in which reason is actually present.

Under patriotism one frequently understands a mere willingness to perform extraordinary acts and sacrifices. But patriotism is essentially the sentiment of regarding, in the ordinary circumstances and ways of life, the weal of the community as the substantial basis and the final end. It is upon this consciousness, present in the ordinary course of life and under all circumstances, that the disposition to heroic effort is founded. But as people are often rather magnanimous than just, they easily persuade themselves that they possess the heroic kind of patriotism, in order to save themselves the trouble of having the truly patriotic sentiment, or to excuse the lack of it.

Political sentiment, as appearance, must be distinguished from what people truly will. What they at bottom will is the real cause, but they cling to particular interests and delight in the vain contemplation of improvements. The conviction of the necessary stability of the State in which alone the particular interests can be realized, people indeed possess, but custom makes invisible that upon which our whole existence rests; it does not occur to anyone, when he safely passes through the streets at night, that it could be otherwise. The habit of safety has become a second nature, and we do not reflect that it is the result of the activity of special institutions. It is through force—this is frequently the superficial opinion—that the State coheres, but what alone holds it together is the fundamental sense of order, which is possessed by all.

The State is an organism or the development of the idea into its differences. These different sides are the different powers of the State with their functions and activities, by means of which the universal is constantly and necessarily producing itself, and, being presupposed in its own productive function, it is thus always actively present. This organism is the political constitution. It eternally springs from the State, just as the State in turn maintains itself through the constitution. If these two things fall asunder, if both different sides become independent of each other, then the unity which the constitution produces is no longer operative; the fable of the stomach and the other organs may be applied to it. It is the nature of an organism that all its parts must constitute a certain unity; if one part asserts its independence the other parts must go to destruction. No predicates, principles, and the like suffice to express the nature of the State; it must be comprehended as an organism.

The State is real, and its reality consists in the interest of the whole being realized in particular ends. Actuality is always the unity of universality and particularity, and the differentiation of the universal into particular ends. These particular ends seem independent, though they are borne and sustained by the whole only. In so far as this unity is absent, no thing is real, though it may exist. A bad State is one which merely exists. A sick body also exists, but it has no true reality. A hand, which is cut off, still looks like a hand and exists, but it has no reality. True reality is necessity. What is real is eternally necessary.

To the complete State belongs, essentially, consciousness and thought. The State knows thus what it wills, and it knows it under the form of thought.

The essential difference between the State and religion consists in that the commands of the State have the form of legal duty, irrespec-

tive of the feelings accompanying their performance; the sphere of
religion, on the other hand, is in the inner life. Just as the State, were
it to frame its commands as religion does, would endanger the right
of the inner life, so the church, if it acts as a State and imposes
punishment, degenerates into a tyrannical religion.

In the State one must want nothing which is not an expression of
rationality. The State is the world which the spirit has made for itself;
it has therefore a determinate and self-conscious course. One often
speaks of the wisdom of God in nature, but one must not believe that
the physical world of nature is higher than the world of spirit. Just
as spirit is superior to nature, so is the State superior to the physical
life. We must therefore worship the State as the manifestation of
the divine on earth, and consider that, if it is difficult to comprehend
nature, it is infinitely harder to grasp the essence of the State. . . .

The Constitution

The constitution is rational, in so far as the State defines and
differentiates its functions according to the nature of its concept.

Who shall make the constitution? This question seems intelligible,
yet on closer examination reveals itself as meaningless, for it presupposes the existence of no constitution, but only a mere mass of
atomic individuals. How a mass of individuals is to come by a
constitution, whether by its own efforts or by those of others, whether
by goodness, thought, or force, it must decide for itself, for with
a disorganized mob the concept of the State has nothing to do. But
if the question does presuppose an already existing constitution, then
to make a constitution means only to change it. The presupposition of
a constitution implies, however, at once, that any modification in it
must take place constitutionally. It is absolutely essential that the
constitution, though having a temporal origin, should not be regarded
as made. It (the principle of constitution) is rather to be conceived as
absolutely perpetual and rational, and therefore as divine, substantial,
and above and beyond the sphere of what is made. . . .

Since spirit is real only in what it knows itself to be, and since the
State, as the nation's spirit, is the law permeating all its affairs, its
ethical code, and the consciousness of its individuals, the constitution
of a people chiefly depends upon the kind and the character of its

self-consciousness. In it lies both its subjective freedom and the reality of the constitution.

To think of giving people a constitution *a priori,* though according to its content a more or less rational one—such a whim would precisely overlook that element which renders a constitution more than a mere abstract object. Every nation, therefore, has the constitution which is appropriate to it and belongs to it.

The State must, in its constitution, permeate all situations. A constitution is not a thing just made; it is the work of centuries, the idea and the consciousness of what is rational, in so far as it is developed in a people. No constitution, therefore, is merely created by the subjects of the State. The nation must feel that its constitution embodies its right and its status, otherwise the constitution may exist externally, but has no meaning or value. . . .

The Power of the Prince

Because sovereignty contains in ideal all special privileges, the common misconception is quite natural, which takes it to be mere force, empty caprice, and synonymous with despotism. But despotism means a state of lawlessness, in which the particular will as such, whether that of monarch or people (*ochlocracy*), is the law, or rather instead of the law. Sovereignty, on the contrary, constitutes the element of ideality of particular spheres and functions under lawful and constitutional conditions.

The sovereignty of the people, conceived in opposition to the sovereignty residing in the monarch, stands for the common view of democracy, which has come to prevail in modern times. The idea of the sovereignty of the people, taken in this opposition, belongs to a confused idea of what is commonly and crudely understood by "the people." The people without its monarch and without that whole organization necessarily and directly connected with him is a formless mass, which is no longer a State. In a people, not conceived in a lawless and unorganized condition, but as a self-developed and truly organic totality—in such a people sovereignty is the personality of the whole, and this is represented in reality by the person of the monarch.

The State must be regarded as a great architectonic edifice, a hieroglyph of reason, manifesting itself in reality. Everything referring merely to utility, externality, and the like, must be excluded from its philosophic treatment. That the State is the self-determining and the completely sovereign will, the final decision being necessarily referred to it—that is easy to comprehend. The difficulty lies in grasping this "I will" as a person. By this it is not meant that the monarch can act arbitrarily. He is bound, in truth, by the concrete content of the deliberations of his council, and, when the constitution is stable, he has often nothing more to do than sign his name—but this name is important; it is the point than which there is nothing higher.

It may be said that an organic State has already existed in the beautiful democracy of Athens. The Greeks, however, derived the final decision from entirely external phenomena, from oracles, entrails of sacrificed animals, and from the flight of birds. Nature they considered as a power which in this wise made known and gave expression to what was good for the people. Self-consciousness had at that time not yet attained to the abstraction of subjectivity; it had not yet come to the realization that an "I will" must be pronounced by man himself concerning the decisions of the State. This "I will" constitutes the great difference between the ancient and the modern world, and must therefore have its peculiar place in the great edifice of the State. Unfortunately this modern characteristic is regarded as merely external and arbitrary.

It is often maintained against the monarch that since he may be ill-educated or unworthy to stand at the helm, it is therefore absurd to assume the rationality of the institution of the monarch. The presupposition, however, that the fortunes of the State depend upon the particular character of the monarch is false. In the perfect organization of the State the important thing is only the finality of formal decision and the stability against passion. One must not therefore demand objective qualification of the monarch; he has but to say "yes" and to put the dot upon the "i." The crown shall be of such a nature that the particular character of its bearer is of no significance. Beyond his function of administering the final decision, the monarch is a particular being who is of no concern. Situations may indeed arise in which his particularity alone asserts itself, but in that case the State is not yet fully developed, or else is ill constructed. In a well-ordered monarchy the law alone has objective power to which the monarch has but to affix the subjective "I will."

Monarchs do not excel in bodily strength or intellect, and yet millions permit themselves to be ruled by them. To say that the people permit themselves to be governed contrary to their interests, aims, and intentions is preposterous, for people are not so stupid. It is their need, it is the inner power of the idea, which, in opposition to their apparent consciousness, urges them to this situation and retains them therein. . . .

The Meaning of War

There is an ethical element in war. It must not be regarded as an absolute ill, or as merely an external calamity which is accidentally based upon the passions of despotic individuals or nations, upon acts of injustice, and, in general, upon what ought not to be. The recognition of the finite, such as property and life, as accidental, is necessary. This necessity is at first wont to appear under the form of a force of nature, for all things finite are mortal and transient. In the ethical order, in the State, however, nature is robbed of its force, and the necessity is exalted to a work of freedom, to an ethical law. The transient and negative nature of all things is transformed in the State into an expression of the ethical will. War, often painted by edifying speech as a state in which the vanity of temporal things is demonstrated, now becomes an element whereby the ideal character of the particular receives its right and reality. War has the deep meaning that by it the ethical health of the nations is preserved and their finite aims uprooted. And as the winds which sweep over the ocean prevent the decay that would result from its perpetual calm, so war protects the people from the corruption which an everlasting peace would bring upon it. History shows phases which illustrate how successful wars have checked internal unrest and have strengthened the entire stability of the State.

In peace, civic life becomes more extended, every sphere is hedged in and grows immobile, and at last all men stagnate, their particular nature becoming more and more hardened and ossified. Only in the unity of a body is health, and, where the organs become still, there is death. Eternal peace is often demanded as an ideal toward which mankind should move. Thus Kant proposed an alliance of princes, which should settle the controversies of States, and the Holy Alliance probably aspired to be an institution of this kind. The State, however, is individual, and in individuality negation is essentially contained. A number of States may constitute themselves into a family, but this confederation, as an individuality, must create an opposition and so beget an enemy. Not only do nations issue forth invigorated from their wars, but those nations torn by internal strife win peace at home as a result of war abroad. War indeed causes insecurity in property, but this real insecurity is only a necessary commotion. From the pulpits much is preached concerning the insecurity, vanity, and instability of temporal things, and yet everyone, though he may be touched by his own words, thinks that he, at least, will manage to hold on to his possessions. Let the insecurity finally come, in the form of Hussars with glistening sabers, and show its earnest activity, and that touching edification which foresaw all this now turns upon the enemy with curses. In spite of this, wars will break out whenever necessity demands them; but the seeds spring up anew, and speech is silenced before the grave repetitions of history.

The military class is the class of universality. The defense of the State is its privilege, and its duty is to realize the ideality contained in it, which consists in self-sacrifice. There are different kinds of bravery. The courage of the animal, or the robber, the bravery which arises from a sense of honor, the chivalrous bravery, are not yet the true forms of bravery. In civilized nations true bravery consists in the readiness to give oneself wholly to the service of the State, so that the individual counts but as one among many. Not personal valor alone is significant; the important aspect of it lies in self-subordination to the universal cause. . . .

International Relations

Just as the individual is not a real person unless related to other persons, so the State is no real individuality unless related to other States. The legitimate power of a State, and more especially its princely power, is, from the point of view of its foreign relations, a wholly internal affair. A State shall, therefore, not interfere with the internal affairs of another State. On the other hand, for a complete State, it is essential that it be recognized by others; but this recognition demands as a guarantee that it shall recognize those States which recognize it, and shall respect their independence. Hence its internal affairs cannot be a matter of indifference to them.

When Napoleon, before the peace of Campoformio, said, "The French Republic requires recognition as little as the sun needs to be recognized," his words suggest nothing but the strength of existence, which already carries with it the guarantee of recognition, without needing to be expressed.

When the particular wills of the State can come to no agreement their controversy can be decided only by war. What offense shall be regarded as a breach of treaty, or as a violation of respect and honor, must remain indefinite, since many and various injuries can easily accrue from the wide range of the interests of the States and from the complex relations of their citizens. The State may identify its infinitude and honor with every one of its single aspects. And if a State, as a strong individuality, has experienced an unduly protracted internal rest, it will naturally be more inclined to irritability, in order to find an occasion and field for intense activity.

The nations of Europe form a family according to the universal principle of their legislation, their ethical code, and their civilization. But the relation among States fluctuates, and no judge exists to adjust their differences. The higher judge is the universal and absolute Spirit alone—the World-Spirit.

The relation of one particular State to another presents, on the largest possible scale, the most shifting play of individual passions, interests, aims, talents, virtues, power, injustice, vice, and mere external chance. It is a play in which even the ethical whole, the independence of the State, is exposed to accident. The principles which control the many national spirits are limited. Each nation as an existing individuality is guided by its particular principles, and only as a particular individuality can each national spirit win objectivity and self-consciousness; but the fortunes and deeds of States in their relation to one another reveal the dialectic of the finite nature of these spirits. Out of this dialectic rises the universal Spirit, the unlimited World-Spirit, pronouncing its judgment—and its judgment is the highest—upon the finite nations of the world's history; for the history of the world is the world's court of justice.

36. JOHANN G. FICHTE

Johann G. Fichte (1762-1814) gave an impassioned and effective plea for German unity, based upon what he claimed to be the internal and

*eternal reality of the German nation. His Addresses to the German Nation
have inspired a patriotic zeal and willingness to sacrifice in the interests
of the nation which remain strong to the present. "Love of fatherland must
itself govern the State and be the supreme, final, and absolute authority."*

[The Unity of the German Nation] *

I speak for Germans simply, of Germans simply, not recognizing,
but setting aside completely and rejecting, all the dissociating distinctions which for centuries unhappy events have caused in this single
nation. You, gentlemen, are indeed to my outward eye the first and
immediate representatives who bring before my mind the beloved
national characteristics, and are the visible spark at which the flame
of my address is kindled. But my spirit gathers round it the educated
part of the whole German nation, from all the lands in which they
are scattered. It thinks of and considers our common position and
relations; it longs that part of the living force, with which these addresses may chance to grip you, may also remain in and breathe
from the dumb printed page which alone will come to the eyes of
the absent, and may in all places kindle German hearts to decision
and action. Only of Germans and simply for Germans, I said. In due
course we shall show that any other mark of unity or any other
national bond either never had truth and meaning or, if it had, that
owing to our present position these bonds of union have been
destroyed and torn from us and can never recur; it is only by means
of the common characteristic of being German that we can avert the
downfall of our nation which is threatened by its fusion with foreign
peoples, and win back again an individuality that is self-supporting
and quite incapable of any dependence upon others. . . .

To begin with and before all things: the first, original, and truly
natural boundaries of States are beyond doubt their internal boundaries. Those who speak the same language are joined to each other
by a multitude of invisible bonds by nature herself, long before any
human art begins; they understand each other and have the power
of continuing to make themselves understood more and more
clearly; they belong together and are by nature one and an inseparable whole. Such a whole, if it wishes to absorb and mingle with

---

* From J. Fichte, *Addresses to the German Nation,* 1808. These passages
are from a translation by R. F. Jones and G. H. Turnbull, 1922, and are reprinted by permission of the Open Court Publishing Company, Chicago.

itself any other people of different descent and language, cannot do so without itself becoming confused, in the beginning at any rate, and violently disturbing the even progress of its culture. From this internal boundary, which is drawn by the spiritual nature of man himself, the marking of the external boundary by dwelling-place results as a consequence; and in the natural view of things it is not because men dwell between certain mountains and rivers that they are a people, but, on the contrary, men dwell together—and, if their luck has so arranged it, are protected by rivers and mountains—because they were a people already by a law of nature which is much higher.

Thus was the German nation placed . . .

[The Love of Fatherland]

The noble-minded man's belief in the eternal continuance of his influence even on this earth is thus founded on the hope of the eternal continuance of the people from which he has developed, and on the characteristic of that people as indicated in the hidden law of which we have spoken, without admixture of, or corruption by, any alien element which does not belong to the totality of the functions of that law. This characteristic is the eternal thing to which he entrusts the eternity of himself and of his continuing influence, the eternal order of things in which he places his portion of eternity; he must will its continuance, for it alone is to him the means by which the short span of his life here below is extended into continuous life here below. His belief and his struggle to plant what is permanent, his conception in which he comprehends his own life as an eternal life, is the bond which unites first his own nation, and then, through his nation, the whole human race, in a most intimate fashion with himself, and brings all their needs within his widened sympathy until the end of time. This is his love for his people, respecting, trusting, and rejoicing in it, and feeling honored by descent from it. The divine has appeared in it, and that which is original has deemed this people worthy to be made its vesture and its means of directly influencing the world; for this reason there will be further manifestations of the divine in it. Hence, the noble-minded man will be active and effective, and will sacrifice himself for his people. Life merely as such, the mere continuance of changing existence, has in any case never had any value for him; he has wished for it only as the source of what is permanent. But this permanence is promised to him only by the continuous and independent existence of his nation. In order to save his nation he must be ready even to die that it may live, and that he may live in it the only life for which he has ever wished.

So it is. Love that is truly love, and not a mere transitory lust, never clings to what is transient; only in the eternal does it awaken and become kindled, and there alone does it rest. Man is not able to love even himself unless he conceives himself as eternal; apart from that he cannot even respect, much less approve of, himself. Still less can he love anything outside himself without taking it up into the eternity of his faith and of his soul and binding it thereto. He who does not first regard himself as eternal has in him no love of any kind, and, moreover, cannot love a fatherland, a thing which for him does not exist. He who regards his invisible life as eternal, but not his visible life as similarly eternal, may perhaps have a heaven and therein a fatherland, but here below he has no fatherland, for this, too, is regarded only in the image of eternity—eternity visible and made sensuous—and for this reason also he is unable to love his fatherland. If none has been handed down to such a man, he is to be pitied. But he to whom a fatherland has been handed down, and in whose soul heaven and earth, visible and invisible meet and mingle, and thus, and only thus, create a true and enduring heaven—such a man fights to the last drop of his blood to hand on the precious possession unimpaired to his posterity.

So it always has been, although it has not always been expressed in such general terms and so clearly as we express it here. What inspired the men of noble mind among the Romans, whose frame of mind and way of thinking still live and breathe among us in their works of art, to struggles and sacrifices, to patience and endurance for the fatherland? They themselves express it often and distinctly. It was their firm belief in the eternal continuance of their Roma, and their confident expectation that they themselves would eternally continue to live in this eternity in the stream of time. In so far as this belief was well founded, and they themselves would have comprehended it if they had been entirely clear in their own minds, it did not deceive them. To this very day there still lives in our midst what was truly eternal in their eternal Roma; they themselves live with it, and its consequences will continue to live to the very end of time.

People and fatherland in this sense, as a support and guarantee of eternity on earth and as that which can be eternal here below, far transcend the State in the ordinary sense of the word, viz., the social order as comprehended by mere intellectual conception and as established and maintained under the guidance of this conception. The aim of the State is positive law, internal peace, and a condition of affairs in which everyone may by diligence earn his daily bread and satisfy the needs of his material existence, so long as God permits him to live. All this is only a means, a condition, and a framework for what love of fatherland really wants, viz., that the eternal and the divine may blossom in the world and never cease to become more and more pure, perfect, and excellent. That is why this love of fatherland must itself govern the State and be the supreme, final, and absolute authority. . . .

Then, too, it must be love of fatherland that governs the State by placing before it a higher object than the usual one of maintaining internal peace, property, personal freedom, and the life and wellbeing of all. For this higher object alone, and with no other intention, does the State assemble an armed force. When the question arises of making use of this, when the call comes to stake everything that the State, in the narrow conception of the word, sets before itself as object, viz., property, personal freedom, life, and well-being, nay, even the continued existence of the State itself; when the call comes to make an original decision with responsibility to God alone, and without a clear and reasonable idea that what is intended will surely be attained—for this is never possible in such matters—then, and then only, does there live at the helm of the State a truly original and primary life, and at this point, and not before, the true sovereign rights of government enter, like God, to hazard the lower life for the sake of the higher. In the maintenance of the traditional constitution, the laws, and civil prosperity there is absolutely no real true life and no original decision. Conditions and circumstances, and legislators perhaps long since dead, have created these things; succeeding ages go on faithfully in the paths marked out, and so in fact they have no public life of their own; they merely repeat a life that once existed. In such times there is no need of any real government. But, when this regular course is endangered, and it is a question of making decisions in new and unprecedented cases, then there is need of a life that lives of itself. What spirit is it that in such cases may place itself at the helm, that can make its own decisions with sureness and certainty, untroubled by any hesitation? What spirit has an undisputed right to summon and to order everyone concerned, whether he himself be willing or not, and to compel anyone who resists, to risk everything including his life? Not the spirit of the peaceful citizen's love for the constitution and the laws, but the devouring flame of higher patriotism, which embraces the nation as the vesture of the eternal, for which the noble-minded man joyfully sacrifices himself, and the ignoble man, who only exists for the sake of the other, must likewise sacrifice himself. It is not that love of the citizen for the constitution; that love is quite unable to achieve this, so long as it remains on the level of the understanding. Whatever turn events may take, since it pays to govern they will always have a ruler over them. Suppose the new ruler even wants to introduce slavery (and what is slavery if not the disregard for, and suppression of, the characteristic of an original people?—but to that way of thinking such qualities do not exist), suppose he wants to introduce slavery. Then, since it is profitable to preserve the life of slaves, to maintain their numbers and even their well-being, slavery under him will turn out to be bearable if he is anything of a calculator. Their life and their keep, at any rate, they will always find. Then what is there left that they should fight for? After those two things it is peace which they value more than anything. But peace will only be disturbed by the continuance of the struggle. They will, therefore, do anything just to put an end to the fighting, and the sooner the better; they will submit, they will yield; and why should they not? All they have ever been concerned about, and all they have ever hoped from life, has been the continuation of the habit of existing under tolerable conditions. The promise of a life here on earth extending beyond the period of life here on earth—that alone it is which can inspire men even unto death for the fatherland. . . .

In this belief our earliest common forefathers, the original stock of the new culture, the Germans, as the Romans called them, bravely resisted the on-coming world-dominion of the Romans. Did they not have before their eyes the greater brilliance of the Roman provinces next to them and the more refined enjoyments in those provinces, to say nothing of laws and judges' seats and lictors' axes and rods in superfluity? Were not the Romans willing enough to let them share in all these blessings? In the case of several of their own princes, who did no more than intimate that war against such benefactors of mankind was rebellion, did they not experience proofs of the belauded Roman clemency? To those who submitted the Romans gave marks of distinction in the form of kingly titles, high commands in their armies, and Roman fillets; and if they were driven out by their countrymen, did not the Romans provide for them a place of refuge and a means of subsistence in their colonies? Had they no appreciation of the advantages of Roman civilization, e.g., of the superior organization of their armies, in which even an Arminius did not disdain to learn the trade of war? They cannot be charged with ignorance or lack of consideration of any one of these things. Their descendants, as soon as they could do so without losing their freedom, even assimilated Roman culture, so far as this was possible without losing their individuality. Why, then, did they fight for several generations in bloody wars, that broke out again and again with ever renewed force? A Roman writer puts the following expression into the mouth of their leaders: "What was left for them to do, except to maintain their freedom or else to die before they became slaves." Freedom to them meant just this: remaining Germans and continuing to settle their own affairs independently and in accordance with the original spirit of their race, going on with their development in accordance with the same spirit, and propagating this independence in their posterity. All those blessings which the Romans offered them meant slavery to them, because then they would have to become something that was not German, they would have to become half Roman. They assumed as a matter of course that every man would rather die than become half a Roman, and that a true German could only want to live in order to be, and to remain, just a German and to bring up his children as Germans.

They did not all die; they did not see slavery; they bequeathed freedom to their children. It is their unyielding resistance which the whole modern world has to thank for being what it now is. Had the Romans succeeded in bringing them also under the yoke and in destroying them as a nation, which the Roman did in every case, the whole development of the human race would have taken a different course, a course that one cannot think would have been more satisfactory. It is they whom we must thank—we, the immediate heirs of their soil, their language, and their way of thinking—for being Germans still, for being still borne along on the stream of original and independent life. It is they whom we must thank for everything that we have been as a nation since those days, and to them we shall be indebted for everything that we shall be in the future, unless things have come to an end with us now and the last drop of blood inherited from them has dried up in our veins. To them the other branches of the race, whom we now look upon as foreigners, but who by descent from them are our brothers, are indebted for their very existence. When our ancestors triumphed over Roma the eternal, not one of all these peoples was in existence, but the possibility of their existence in the future was won for them in the same fight. . . .

From all this it follows that the State, merely as the government of human life in its progress along the ordinary peaceful path, is not something which is primary and which exists for its own sake, but is merely the means to the higher purpose of the eternal, regular, and continuous development of what is purely human in this nation. It follows, too, that the vision and the love of this eternal development, and nothing else, should have the higher supervision of State administration at all times, not excluding periods of peace, and that this alone is able to save the people's independence when it is endangered. In the case of the Germans, among whom as an original people this love of fatherland was possible and, as we firmly believe, did actually exist up to the present time, it has been able up to now to reckon with great confidence on the security of what was most vital to it. As was the case with the ancient Greeks alone, with the Germans the State and the nation were actually separated from each other, and each was represented for itself, the former in the separate German realms and principalities, the latter represented visibly in the imperial connection and invisibly—by virtue of a law, not written, but living and valid in the minds of all, a law whose results struck the eye everywhere—in a mass of customs and institutions. Wherever the German language was spoken, everyone who had first seen the light of day in its domain could consider himself as in a double sense a citizen, on the one hand, of the State where he was born and to whose care he was in the first instance commended, and, on the other hand, of the whole common fatherland of the German nation. . . .

These addresses lay before you the sole remaining means, now that the others have been tried in vain, of preventing this annihilation of every nobler impulse that may break out among us in the future, and of preventing this degradation of our whole nation. They propose that you establish deeply and indelibly in the hearts of all, by means of education, the true and all-powerful love of fatherland, the conception of our people as an eternal people and as the security for our own eternity. What kind of education can do this, and how it is to be done, we shall see in the following addresses. . . .

37. HEINRICH VON TREITSCHKE

Heinrich von Treitschke (1834-1896) was a Prussian historian and philosopher, and was a vigorous advocate of German national unity. His work embodies the philosophic culmination of the Hegelian theory of the state. The state is a real personality; it is identified with power; it is "the necessary outward form which the inner life of a people bestows upon itself."

The State Idea*

The State is the people, legally united as an independent entity. By the word "people" we understand briefly a number of families permanently living side by side. This definition implies that the State is primordial and necessary, that it is as enduring as history, and no less essential to mankind than speech. History, however, begins for us with the art of writing; earlier than this men's conscious recollection of the past cannot be reckoned with. Therefore everything which lies beyond this limit is rightly judged to be prehistoric. We, on the other hand, must deal here with man as a historical being, and we can only say that creative political genius is inherent in him, and that the State, like him, subsists from the beginning. The attempt to present it as something artificial, following upon a natural condition, has fallen completely into discredit. We lack all historical knowledge of a nation without a constitution. Wherever Europeans have penetrated they have found some form of State organization, rude though it may have been. This recognition of the primordial character of the State is very widespread at the present day, but was in fact discovered in the eighteenth century. Eichhorn, Niebuhr, and Savigny were the first to show that the State is the constituted people. It was indeed a familiar fact to the Ancients in their great and simple Age. For them

* H. Treitschke, *Politics*, Vol. I, 1870. These passages are from a translation by B. Dugdale and T. de Bille, 1916, and are reprinted by permission of Michael Dugdale and the publisher, Constable and Company, Ltd., London.

the State was a divinely appointed order, the origins of which were not subject to inquiry. The constitutional doctrines of the Philosophers were in complete accord with the naïveté of the popular beliefs. For them the citizen was in his very nature no more than a fragment of the State; it therefore followed that the whole must have been anterior to the parts. . . .

The human race was once for all created with certain innate qualities among which speech and political genius must undoubtedly be counted. Aristotle says truly that man is φύσει, that is to say in his very nature and essence a ζῷον πολιτικόν. A being who feels no need for a constitution, he proceeds, must either be a god, and thus superior to man, or a beast, and his inferior. . . .

If, then, political capacity is innate in man, and is to be further developed, it is quite inaccurate to call the State a necessary evil. We have to deal with it as a lofty necessity of Nature. Even as the possibility of building up a civilization is dependent upon the limitation of our powers combined with the gift of reason, so also the State depends upon our inability to live alone. This Aristotle has already demonstrated. The State, says he, arose in order to make life possible; it endured to make good life possible.

This natural necessity of a constituted order is further displayed by the fact that the political institutions of a people, broadly speaking, appear to be the external forms which are the inevitable outcome of its inner life. Just as its language is not the product of caprice but the immediate expression of its most deep-rooted attitude towards the world, so also its political institutions regarded as a whole, and the whole spirit of its jurisprudence, are the symbols of its political genius and of the outside destinies which have helped to shape the gifts which Nature bestowed. . . .

We may say with certainty that the evolution of the State is, broadly speaking, nothing but the necessary outward form which the inner life of a people bestows upon itself, and that peoples attain to that form of government which their moral capacity enables them to reach. Nothing can be more inverted than the opinion that constitutional laws were artificially evolved in opposition to the conception of a Natural Law. Ultramontanes and Jacobins both start with the assumption that the legislation of a modern State is the work of sinful man. They thus display their total lack of reverence for the objectively revealed Will of God, as unfolded in the life of the State.

When we assert the evolution of the State to be something inherently necessary, we do not thereby deny the power of genius or of creative Will in history. For it is of the essence of political genius to be national. There has never been an example of the contrary. The summit of historical fame was never attained by Wallenstein because he was never a national hero, but a Czech who played the German for the sake of expediency. He was, like Napoleon, a splendid Adventurer of history. The truly great maker of history always stands upon a national basis. This applies equally to men of letters. He only is a great writer who so writes that all his countrymen respond, "Thus it must be. Thus we all feel"—who is in fact a microcosm of his nation.

If we have grasped that the State is the people legally constituted we thereby imply that it aims at establishing a permanent tradition throughout the Ages. A people does not only comprise the individuals living side by side, but also the successive generations of the same stock. This is one of the truths which Materialists dismiss as a mystical doctrine, and yet it is an obvious truth. Only the continuity of human history makes man a ζῷον πολιτικόν. He alone stands upon the achievements of his forebears, and deliberately continues their work in order to transmit it more perfect to his children and children's children. Only a creature like man, needing aid and endowed with reason, can have a history, and it is one of the ineptitudes of the Materialists to speak of animal States. It is just a play upon words to talk of a bee State. Beasts merely reproduce unconsciously what has been from all time, and none but human beings can possess a form of government which is calculated to endure. There never was a form of Constitution without a law of inheritance. The rational basis for this is obvious, for by far the largest part of a nation's wealth was not created by the contemporary generation. The continuous legalized intention of the past, exemplified in the law of inheritance, must remain a factor in the distribution of property among posterity. In a nation's continuity with bygone generations lies the specific dignity of the State. It is consequently a contradiction to say that a distribution of property should be regulated by the deserts of the existing generation. Who would respect the banners of a State if the power of memory had fled? There are cases when the shadows of the past are invoked against the perverted will of the present, and prove more potent. Today in Alsace we appeal from the distorted opinions of the Francophobes to Geiler von Kaisersberg and expect to see his spirit revive again. No one who does not recognize the continued action of the past upon the present can ever understand the nature and necessity of War. Gibbon calls Patriotism "the living sense of my own interest in society"; but if we simply look upon the State as intended to secure life and property to the individual, how comes it that the individual will also sacrifice life and property to the State? It is a false conclusion that wars are waged for the sake of material advantage. Modern wars are not fought for the sake of booty. Here the high moral ideal of national honor is a factor handed down from one generation to another, enshrining something positively sacred, and compelling the individual to sacrifice himself to it. This ideal is above all price and cannot be reduced to pounds, shillings, and pence. Kant says, "Where a price can be paid, an equivalent can be substituted. It is that which is above price and which consequently admits of no equivalent, that possesses real value." Genuine patriotism is the consciousness of co-operating with the body-politic, of being rooted in ancestral achievements and of transmitting them to descendants. Fichte has finely said, "Individual man sees in his country the realization of his earthly immortality."

[The State as Person]

This involves that the State has a personality, primarily in the juridical, and secondly in the politico-moral sense. Every man who is able to exercise his will in law has a legal personality. Now it is quite clear that the State possesses this deliberate will; nay more, that it has the juridical personality in the most complete sense. In State treaties it is the will of the State which is expressed, not the personal desires of the individuals who conclude them, and the treaty is binding as long as the contracting State exists. When a State is incapable of enforcing its will, or of maintaining law and order at home and prestige abroad, it becomes an anomaly and falls a prey either to anarchy or a foreign enemy. The State therefore must have the most emphatic will that can be imagined. Roman Law was not fortunate in its development of the conception of legal personality, for in spite of their marvelous legal acuteness the Romans lacked the talent for philosophical speculation, and this is most disastrously displayed in their doctrine of legal personality. Roman Law assumes that a person in the legal sense must be merely an individual citizen.

That is crude materialism. Rather should all associations possessed of legal will be considered as legal persons. Now it was laid down by the Romans, who also felt this imperfection, that the State should attribute this juridical personality to monasteries, churches, etc., to enable them to transact legal business, and to stand in legal relationship with individuals. Thus the preposterous assertion is made that a human being has a legal personality because he has two legs, while the State has to acquire it, not having it by nature. But the will of the State is not fictitious. It is the most real of all. Moreover, what is the meaning of attributing to the State a personality which is not inherent in it? The aim of knowledge is truth. Knowledge must not invent facts but must state them. A legal fiction is therefore not scientific. It is not scientific for me to pretend, when the State fixes a prescriptive period for certain offenses, that no offense has been committed, for there has actually been one, and the State acts thus on grounds of expediency only. How is it possible, in treating of the fundamental fact of all constitutional and political life, to assert, and to act upon, this legal fiction, that the great collective person, the State—the most supremely real person, in the literal sense of the word, that exists—is first of all obliged to endow itself with a personality? How can we deny this attribute to the very source of all authority?

As our Germanic public life was always very rich in all manner of corporations, our German jurisprudence was the first to abandon the theory of Roman Law which regarded the conception of personality as bound up with the individual, and it defined legal personality by competence to act in law. In this way the dictum becomes applicable to the State as well, for the State is the people's collective will. This does not imply that it is the mere mechanical total of all individual wills, for the individual is able to belong to several corporate bodies at the same time. Rousseau has aptly said, in one of the few maintainable passages of his *Contrat Social, "La volonté générale n'est pas la volonté de tous."*

The State, then, has from all time been a legal person. It appears to be so still more clearly in the historico-moral sense. States must be conceived as the great collective personalities of history, thoroughly capable of bearing responsibility and blame. We may even speak of their legal guilt, and still more accurately of their individuality. Even as certain people have certain traits, which they cannot alter however much they try, so also the State has characteristics which cannot be obliterated. Pindar's warning words apply as much to the State as to the individual: "Pawn all thy goods to one, and debt will overtake thee."

We cannot imagine the Roman State humane, or encouraging Art and Science. It would be an implicit contradiction. Who cannot discern, in the course of German history, that excess of individual strength and violence whose centrifugal tendencies have made it so hard for us to establish a central authority? The State would no longer be what it has been and is, did it not stand visibly girt about with armed might. Sallust said truly that there is nothing more dangerous for a State founded by arms than to discard this essential principle of its strength. . . .

[The State as Power]

Treat the State as a person, and the necessary and rational multiplicity of States follows. Just as in individual life the ego implies the existence of the non-ego, so it does in the State. The State is power, precisely in order to assert itself as against other equally independent powers. War and the administration of justice are the chief tasks of even the most barbaric States. But these tasks are only conceivable where a plurality of States are found existing side by side. Thus the idea of one universal empire is odious—the ideal of a State co-extensive with humanity is no ideal at all. In a single State the whole range of culture could never be fully spanned; no single people could unite the virtues of aristocracy and democracy. All nations, like all individuals, have their limitations, but it is exactly in the abundance of these limited qualities that the genius of humanity is exhibited. The rays of the Divine light are manifested, broken by countless facets among the separate peoples, each one exhibiting another picture and another idea of the whole. Every people has a right to believe that certain attributes of the Divine reason are exhibited in it to their fullest perfection. No people ever attains to national consciousness without overrating itself. The Germans are always in danger of enervating their nationality through possessing too little of this rugged pride. The average German has very little political pride; but even our Philistines generally revel in the intellectual boast of the freedom and universality of the German spirit, and this is well, for such a sentiment is necessary if a people is to maintain and assert itself. . . .

The features of history are virile, unsuited to sentimental or feminine natures. Brave peoples alone have an existence, an evolution or a future; the weak and cowardly perish, and perish justly. The grandeur of history lies in the perpetual conflict of nations, and it is simply foolish to desire the suppression of their rivalry. Mankind has ever found it to be so. . . .

Further, if we examine our definition of the State as "the people legally united as an independent entity," we find that it can be more briefly put thus: "The State is the public force for Offense and Defense." It is, above all, Power which makes its will to prevail, it is not the totality of the people as Hegel assumes in his deification of it. The nation is not entirely comprised in the State, but the State protects and embraces the people's life, regulating its external aspects on every side. It does not ask primarily for opinion, but demands obedience, and its laws must be obeyed, whether willingly or no.

A step forward has been taken when the mute obedience of the citizens is transformed into a rational inward assent, but it cannot be said that this is absolutely necessary. Powerful, highly-developed Empires have stood for centuries without its aid. Submission is what the State primarily requires; it insists upon acquiescence; its very essence is the accomplishment of its will. The terrible words βία βία βιάζεται permeate the history of all governments. A State which can no longer carry out its purpose collapses in anarchy. What a contrast to the life of the Church. We may say that power is the vital principle of the State, as faith is that of the Church, and love that of the family. The Church is an essentially spiritual force, having also an external life, but appealing first of all to conscience, insisting above all upon the willing mind, and standing high in proportion to its ability to give profound and intense expression to this its vital principle. Therefore it is said, "He that eateth and drinketh unworthily eateth and drinketh judgment to himself." But if the State were to hold this view, or, for instance, to require from its soldiers more than the fulfillment of their military duties, it would be unbearable. "It does not matter," says the State, "what you think, so long as you obey." It is for this reason that gentle characters find it so hard to understand its nature. It may be said roughly that the normal woman first obtains an insight into justice and government through men's eyes, just as the normal man has no natural aptitude for petty questions of household management. This is easily understood, for undoubtedly power is a stern idea, and its enforcement is here the highest and only aim. For this reason the ruling nations are not so much the races rich in mental endowment, but rather those whose peculiar gift is force of character. In this the thoughtful student of the world's history perceives the awful nature of justice. The sentimentalist may bewail the overthrow of cultured Athens by Sparta, or of Hellas by Rome, but the serious thinker must recognize its necessity, and understand why Florence for all her refinement could not withstand the rivalry of Venice. All these cases took their inevitable course.

The State is not an Academy of Arts. If it neglects its strength in order to promote the idealistic aspirations of man, it repudiates its own nature and perishes. This is in truth for the State equivalent to the sin against the Holy Ghost, for it is indeed a mortal error in the State to subordinate itself for sentimental reasons to a foreign Power, as we Germans have often done to England. . . .

[The State as Sovereign]

We have described the State as an independent force. This pregnant theory of independence implies firstly so absolute a moral supremacy that the State cannot legitimately tolerate any power above its own, and secondly a temporal freedom entailing a variety of material resources adequate to its protection against hostile influences. Legal sovereignty, the State's complete independence of any other earthly power, is so rooted in its nature that it may be said to be its very standard and criterion.

The State is born in a community whenever a group or an individual has achieved sovereignty by imposing its will upon the whole body. . . .

Human communities do exist which in their own fashion pursue aims no less lofty than those of the State, but which must be legally subject to it in their outward relations with the world. It is obvious that contradictions must arise, and that two such authorities, morally but not legally equal, must sometimes collide with each other. Nor is it to be wished that the conflicts between Church and State should wholly cease, for if they did one party or the other would be soulless and dead, like the Russian Church for example. Sovereignty, however, which is the peculiar attribute of the State, is of necessity supreme, and it is a ridiculous inconsistency to speak of a superior and inferior authority within it. The truth remains that the essence of the State consists in its incompatibility with any power over it.

How proudly and truly statesmanlike is Gustavus Adolphus' exclamation, "I recognize no power over me but God and the conqueror's sword." This is so unconditionally true that we see at once that it cannot be the destiny of mankind to form a single State, but that the ideal towards which we strive is a harmonious comity of nations, who, concluding treaties of their own free will, admit restrictions upon their sovereignty without abrogating it.

For the notion of sovereignty must not be rigid, but flexible and relative, like all political conceptions. Every State, in treaty making, will limit its power in certain directions for its own sake. States which conclude treaties with each other thereby curtail their absolute authority to some extent. But the rule still stands, for every treaty is a voluntary curb upon the power of each, and all international agreements are prefaced by the clause *"Rebus sic stantibus."* No State can pledge its future to another. It knows no arbiter, and draws up all its treaties with this implied reservation. This is supported by the axiom that so long as international law exists all treaties lose their force at the very moment when war is declared between the contracting parties; moreover, every sovereign State has the undoubted right to declare war at its pleasure, and is consequently entitled to repudiate its treaties. Upon this constantly recurring alteration of treaties the progress of history depends; every State must take care that its treaties do not survive their effective value, lest another Power should denounce them by a declaration of war; for antiquated treaties must necessarily be denounced and replaced by others more consonant with circumstances.

It is clear that the international agreements which limit the power of a State are not absolute, but voluntary self-restrictions. Hence, it follows that the establishment of a permanent international Arbitration Court is incompatible with the nature of the State, which could at all events only accept the decision of such a tribunal in cases of second- or third-rate importance. When a nation's existence is at stake there is no outside Power whose impartiality can be trusted. Were we to commit the folly of treating the Alsace-Lorraine problem as an open question, by submitting it to arbitration, who would seriously believe that the award could be impartial? It is, moreover, a point of honor for a State to solve such difficulties for itself. International treaties may indeed become more frequent, but a finally decisive tribunal of the nations is an impossibility. The appeal to arms will be valid until the end of history, and therein lies the sacredness of war.

Section III

IRRATIONALISM

The irrational tradition in political philosophy must, by its nature, defy any systematic analysis or description. It is the outcome of the abandonment of intellect as the ideal ruling faculty in political affairs and its replacement by some nonintellectual function. "Sentiment," "inspiration," "passion," "intuition," "force," "will"—all have served as names for the dynamic but nonrational director of political activity in this school of thought.

The clearest expression of political irrationalism is found in the works of Georges Sorel, whose doctrine of the social myth has had great influence, not only upon the syndicalist movement of which he was a part, but especially upon fascist philosophy in the twentieth century. A true myth, said Sorel, was not a rational conception of a future society, but a vision, a dream, a great emotional force that could inspire violent revolutionary activity. Such myths are not subject to scientific analysis or rational discussion. Their nature renders analysis inappropriate, and their advocates must refuse to engage in any intellectual discussion of their virtues. The function of a myth is mass inspiration; "the myths are not descriptions of things," Sorel said, "but determinations to act."

He believed that the Marxist conception of the classless society was successful only insofar as it functioned as a myth of this sort. He held the Christian doctrine of the Second Coming to be equally irrational, and therefore effective, and Sorel himself proposed the myth of the general strike. Following this line of thought the Italian and German fascists have developed effective myths of their own: the myth of eternal Roman power—and that of the Aryan master race.

38. GEORGES SOREL

Georges Sorel (1847-1922) stated his theory of social myths most clearly in a letter to Daniel Halevy, from which the following passages are excerpted. Sorel was a socialist, a syndicalist, and after 1917, a vigorous admirer of Lenin. His philosophic irrationalism, however, was most influential in shaping the direction of twentieth-century fascism.

[The Social Myth] *

In the course of this study one thing has always been present in my mind, which seemed to me so evident that I did not think it worth while to lay much stress on it—that men who are participating in a great social movement always picture their coming action as a battle in which their cause is certain to triumph. These constructions, knowledge of which is so important for historians, I propose to call myths; the syndicalist "general strike" and Marx's catastrophic revolution are such myths. As remarkable examples of such myths, I have given those which were constructed by primitive Christianity, by the Reformation, by the Revolution and by the followers of Mazzini. I now wish to show that we should not attempt to analyze such groups of images in the way that we analyze a thing into its elements, but that they must be taken as a whole, as historical forces, and that we should be especially careful not to make any comparison between accomplished fact and the picture people had formed for themselves before action.

I could have given one more example which is perhaps still more striking: Catholics have never been discouraged even in the hardest trials, because they have always pictured the history of the Church as a series of battles between Satan and the hierarchy supported by Christ; every new difficulty which arises is only an episode in a war which must finally end in the victory of Catholicism.

At the beginning of the nineteenth century the revolutionary per-

---

* G. Sorel, *Letter to Daniel Halevy*. These passages are from an edition of *Reflections on Violence*, 1950, translated by T. E. Hulme and J. Roth, and are reprinted by permission of The Free Press, Glencoe, Illinois.

secution revived this myth of the struggle with Satan, which inspired so many of the eloquent pages in Joseph de Maistre; this rejuvenation explains to a large extent the religious renascence which took place at that epoch. If Catholicism is in danger at the present time, it is to a great extent owing to the fact that the myth of the Church militant tends to disappear. . . .

In employing the term myth I believed that I had made a happy choice, because I thus put myself in a position to refuse any discussion whatever with the people who wish to submit the idea of a general strike to a detailed criticism, and who accumulate objections against its practical possibility. It appears, on the contrary, that I had made a most unfortunate choice, for while some told me that myths were only suitable to a primitive state of society, others imagined that I thought the modern world might be moved by illusions analogous in nature to those which Renan thought might usefully replace religion. But there has been a worse misunderstanding than this even, for it has been asserted that my theory of myths was only a kind of lawyer's plea, a falsification of the real opinions of the revolutionaries, the *sophistry of an intellectualist.*

If this were true, I should not have been exactly fortunate, for I have always tried to escape the influence of that intellectualist philosophy, which seems to me a great hindrance to the historian who allows himself to be dominated by it. . . .

The whole of this philosophy can be summed up in the following phrase of Renan's: "Human affairs are always an approximation lacking gravity and precision"; and as a matter of fact, for an intellectualist, what lacks precision must also lack gravity. But in Renan the conscientious historian was never entirely asleep, and he at once adds as a corrective: "To have realized this truth is a great result obtained by philosophy; but it is an abdication of any active rôle. The future lies in the hands of those who are not disillusioned." * From this we may conclude that the intellectualist philosophy is entirely' unable to explain the great movements of history.

The intellectualist philosophy would have vainly endeavored to convince the ardent Catholics, who for so long struggled successfully against the revolutionary traditions, that the myth of the Church militant was not in harmony with the scientific theories formulated by the most learned authors according to the best rules of criticism; it would never have succeeded in persuading them. It would not have

* Renan, *Histoire du peuple d'Israël,* vol. iii. p. 497.

been possible to shake the faith that these men had in the promises made to the Church by any argument; and so long as this faith remained, the myth was, in their eyes, incontestable. Similarly, the objections urged by philosophy against the revolutionary myths would have made an impression only on those men who were anxious to find a pretext for abandoning any active rôle, for remaining revolutionary in words only.

I can understand the fear that this myth of the general strike inspires in many *worthy progressives,** on account of its character of *infinity;*† the world of today is very much inclined to return to the opinions of the ancients and to subordinate ethics to the smooth working of public affairs, which results in a definition of virtue as the golden mean; as long as socialism remains a *doctrine expressed only in words,* it is very easy to deflect it towards this doctrine of the golden mean; but this transformation is manifestly impossible when the myth of the "general strike" is introduced, as this implies an absolute revolution. You know as well as I do that all that is best in the modern mind is derived from this "torment of the infinite"; you are not one of those people who look upon the tricks by means of which readers can be deceived by words, as happy discoveries. That is why you will not condemn me for having attached great worth to a myth which gives to socialism such high moral value and such great sincerity. It is because the theory of myths tends to produce such fine results that so many seek to dispute it. . . .

As long as there are no myths accepted by the masses, one may go on talking of revolts indefinitely, without ever provoking any revolutionary movement; this is what gives such importance to the general strike and renders it so odious to socialists who are afraid of a revolution; they do all they can to shake the confidence felt by the workers in the preparations they are making for the revolution; and in order to succeed in this they cast ridicule on the idea of the general strike—the only idea that could have any value as a motive force.

---

* Translator's Note.—In French, *"braves gens."* Sorel is using the words ironically to indicate those naïve, philanthropically disposed people who believe that they have discovered the solution to the problem of social reform—whose attitude, however, is often complicated by a good deal of hypocrisy, they being frequently rapacious when their own personal interests are at stake.

† Parties, as a rule, *define* the reforms that they wish to bring about; but the general strike has a character of *infinity,* because it puts on one side all discussion of definite reforms and confronts men with a catastrophe. People who pride themselves on their practical wisdom are very much upset by such a conception, which puts forward no definite project of future social organization.

One of the chief means employed by them is to represent it as a Utopia; this is easy enough, because there are very few myths which are perfectly free from any Utopian element.

The revolutionary myths which exist at the present time are almost free from any such mixture; by means of them it is possible to understand the activity, the feelings and the ideas of the masses preparing themselves to enter on a decisive struggle: the myths are not descriptions of things, but expressions of a determination to act. A Utopia is, on the contrary, an intellectual product; it is the work of theorists who, after observing and discussing the known facts, seek to establish a model to which they can compare existing society in order to estimate the amount of good and evil it contains. It is a combination of imaginary institutions having sufficient analogies to real institutions for the jurist to be able to reason about them; it is a construction which can be taken to pieces, and certain parts of it have been shaped in such a way that they can (with a few alterations by way of adjustment) be fitted into approaching legislation. While contemporary myths lead men to prepare themselves for a combat which will destroy the existing state of things, the effect of Utopias has always been to direct men's minds towards reforms which can be brought about by patching up the existing system; it is not surprising, then, that so many makers of Utopias were able to develop into able statesmen when they had acquired a greater experience of political life. A myth cannot be refuted, since it is, at bottom, identical with the convictions of a group, being the expression of these convictions in the language of movement; and it is, in consequence, unanalyzable into parts which could be placed on the plane of historical descriptions. A Utopia, on the contrary, can be discussed like any other social constitution; the spontaneous movements it presupposes can be compared with the movements actually observed in the course of history, and we can in this way evaluate its verisimilitude; it is possible to refute Utopias by showing that the economic system on which they have been made to rest is incompatible with the necessary conditions of modern production.

Liberal political economy is one of the best examples of a Utopia that could be given. A state of society was imagined which could contain only the types produced by commerce, and which would exist under the law of the fullest competition; it is recognized today that this kind of ideal society would be as difficult to realize as that of Plato; but several great statesmen of modern times have owed their fame to the efforts they made to introduce something of this ideal of commercial liberty into industrial legislation.

We have here a Utopia free from any mixture of myth; the history of French democracy, however, presents a very remarkable combination of Utopias and myths. The theories that inspired the authors of our first constitutions are regarded today as extremely chimerical; indeed, people are often loth to concede them the value which they have been so long recognized to possess—that of an ideal on which legislators, magistrates, and administrators should constantly fix their eyes, in order to secure for men a little more justice. With these Utopias were mixed up the myths which represented the struggle against the ancient regime; so long as the myths survived, all the refutations of liberal Utopias could produce no result; the myth safeguarded the Utopia with which it was mixed.

For a long time Socialism was scarcely anything but a Utopia; the Marxists were right in claiming for their master the honor of bringing about a change in this state of things; Socialism has now become the preparation of the masses employed in great industries for the suppression of the State and property; and it is no longer necessary, therefore, to discuss how men must organize themselves in order to enjoy future happiness; everything is reduced to the *revolutionary apprenticeship* of the proletariat. Unfortunately Marx was not acquainted with facts which have now become familiar to us; we know better than he did what strikes are, because we have been able to observe economic conflicts of considerable extent and duration; the myth of the "general strike" has become popular, and is now firmly established in the minds of the workers; we possess ideas about violence that it would have been difficult for him to have formed; we can then complete his doctrine, instead of making commentaries on his text, as his unfortunate disciples have done for so long.

In this way Utopias tend to disappear completely from Socialism; Socialism has no longer any need to concern itself with the organization of industry since capitalism does that. I think, moreover, that I have shown that the general strike corresponds to a kind of feeling which is so closely related to those which are necessary to promote production in any very progressive state of industry, that a revolutionary apprenticeship may at the same time be considered as an apprenticeship which will enable the workman to occupy a high rank among the best workmen of his own trade.

People who are living in this world of "myths," are secure from all refutation; this has led many to assert that Socialism is a kind of religion. For a long time people have been struck by the fact that religious convictions are unaffected by criticism, and from that they have concluded that everything which claims to be beyond science must be a religion. It has been observed also that Christianity tends at the present day to be less a system of dogmas than a Christian life, i.e. a moral reform penetrating to the roots of one's being; consequently, a new analogy has been discovered between religion and the revolutionary Socialism which aims at the apprenticeship, preparation, and even reconstruction of the individual—a gigantic task. But Bergson has taught us that it is not only religion which occupies the profounder region of our mental life; revolutionary myths have their place there equally with religion. The arguments which Yves Guyot urges against Socialism on the ground that it is a religion, seem to me, then, to be founded on an imperfect acquaintance with the new psychology.

Renan was very surprised to discover that Socialists are beyond discouragement. "After each abortive experiment they recommence their work: the solution is not yet found, but it will be. The idea that no solution exists never occurs to them, and in this lies their strength." The explanation given by Renan is superficial; it regards Socialism as a Utopia, that is, as a thing which can be compared to observed realities; if this were true, it would be scarcely possible to understand how confidence can survive so many failures. But by the side of the Utopias there have always been myths capable of urging on the workers to revolt. For a long time these myths were founded on the legends of the Revolution, and they preserved all their value as long as these legends remained unshaken. Today the confidence of the Socialists is greater than ever since the myth of the general strike dominates all the truly working-class movement. No failure proves anything against Socialism since the latter has become a work of preparation (for revolution); if they are checked, it merely proves that the apprenticeship has been insufficient; they must set to work again with more courage, persistence, and confidence than before; their experience of labor has taught workmen that it is by means of patient apprenticeship that a man may become a true comrade, and it is also the only way of becoming a true revolutionary.

39. HOUSTON S. CHAMBERLAIN

Houston S. Chamberlain (1855-1927) was an Anglo-German writer on music and literature who was the author of a powerful early statement of the myth of the superiority of the Germanic people. His Foundations of the Nineteenth Century *is a massive and fanatical work in which it is lengthily argued that the Aryans are "by right . . . the lords of the world."*

The Entrance of the Germanic People into the History of the World *

The entrance of the Jew into European history had, as Herder said, signified the entrance of an alien element—alien to that which Europe had already achieved, alien to all it was still to accomplish; but it was the very reverse with the Germanic peoples. This barbarian, who would rush naked to battle, this savage, who suddenly sprang out of woods and marshes to inspire into a civilized and cultivated world the terrors of a violent conquest won by the strong hand alone, was nevertheless the lawful heir of the Hellene and the Roman, blood of their blood and spirit of their spirit. It was his own property which he, unwitting, snatched from the alien hand. But for him the sun of the Indo-European must have set. The Asiatic and African slave had by assassination wormed his way to the very throne of the Roman Empire, the Syrian mongrel had made himself master of the law, the Jew was using the library at Alexandria to adapt Hellenic philosophy to the Mosaic law, the Egyptian to embalm and bury for boundless ages the fresh bloom of natural science in the ostentatious pyramids of scientific systematization; soon, too, the beautiful flowers of old Aryan life—Indian thought, Indian poetry—were to be trodden under foot by the savage blood-

* From H. S. Chamberlain, *Foundations of the Nineteenth Century,* Vol. I, 1899. These passages are reprinted from a translation by John Lees, 1911, by permission of Dodd Mead and Co., New York, and of The Bodley Head, London.

thirsty Mongolian, and the Bedouin, with his mad delusions bred of
the desert, was to reduce to an everlasting wilderness that garden of
Eden, Erania, in which for centuries all the symbolism of the world
had grown; art had long since vanished; there were nothing but
replicas for the rich, and for the poor the circus: accordingly, to use
that expression of Schiller which I quoted at the beginning of the
first chapter, there were no longer men but only creatures. It is high
time for the Saviour to appear. He certainly did not enter into history in the form in which combining, constructive reason, if consulted, would have chosen for the guardian angel, the harbinger of
a new day of humanity; but today, when a glance back over past
centuries teaches us wisdom, we have only one thing to regret, that
the Teuton did not destroy with more thoroughness, wherever his
victorious arm penetrated, and that as a consequence of his moderation the so-called "Latinizing," that is, the fusion with the chaos
of peoples, once more gradually robbed wide districts of the one
quickening influence of pure blood and unbroken youthful vigor,
and at the same time deprived them of the rule of those who possessed the highest talents. At any rate it is only shameful indolence
of thought, or disgraceful historical falsehood, that can fail to see
in the entrance of the Germanic tribes into the history of the world
the rescuing of agonizing humanity from the clutches of the ever-
lastingly bestial.

Freedom and Loyalty

Let us attempt a glance into the depths of the soul. What are the
specific intellectual and moral characteristics of this Germanic race?
Certain anthropologists would fain teach us that all races are equally
gifted; we point to history and answer: that is a lie! The races of
mankind are markedly different in the nature and also in the extent
of their gifts, and the Germanic races belong to the most highly
gifted group, the group usually termed Aryan. Is this human family
united and uniform by bonds of blood? Do these stems really all
spring from the same root? I do not know and I do not much care;
no affinity binds more closely than elective affinity, and in this sense
the Indo-European Aryans certainly form a family. In his *Politics*
Aristotle writes (i.5): "If there were men who in physical stature
alone were so pre-eminent as the representatives of the Gods, then

everyone would admit that other men by right must be subject unto them. If this, however, is true in reference to the body, then there is still greater justification for distinguishing between pre-eminent and commonplace souls." Physically and mentally the Aryans are pre-eminent among all peoples; for that reason they are by right, as the Stagirite expresses it, the lords of the world. Aristotle puts the matter still more concisely when he says, "Some men are by nature free, others slaves"; this perfectly expresses the moral aspect. For freedom is by no means an abstract thing, to which every human being has fundamentally a claim; a right to freedom must evidently depend upon capacity for it, and this again presupposes physical and intellectual power. One may make the assertion, that even the mere conception of freedom is quite unknown to most men. Do we not see the *homo syriacus* develop just as well and as happily in the position of slave as of master? Do the Chinese not show us another example of the same nature? Do not all historians tell us that the Semites and half-Semites, in spite of their great intelligence, never succeeded in founding a State that lasted, and that because everyone always endeavored to grasp all power for himself, thus showing that their capabilities were limited to despotism and anarchy, the two opposites of freedom? And here we see at once what great gifts a man must have in order that one may say of him, he is "by nature free," for the first condition of this is the power of creating. Only a State-building race can be free; the gifts which make the individual an artist and philosopher are essentially the same as those which, spread through the whole mass as instinct, found States and give to the individual that which hitherto had remained unknown to all nature: the idea of freedom. As soon as we understand this, the near affinity of the Germanic peoples to the Greeks and Romans strikes us, and at the same time we recognize what separates them. In the case of the Greeks the individualistic creative character predominates, even in the forming of constitutions; in the case of the Romans it is communistic legislation and military authority that predominate; the Germanic races, on the other hand, have individually and collectively perhaps less creative power, but they possess a harmony of qualities, maintaining the balance between the instinct of individual freedom, which finds its highest expression in creative art, and the instinct of public freedom which creates the State; and in this way they prove themselves to be the equals of their great predecessors. Art more perfect in its creations, so far as form is concerned, there may have been, but no art has ever been more powerful in its creations than that which includes the whole range of things human between the winged pen of Shakespeare and the etching-tool of Albrecht Dürer, and which in its own special language—music—penetrates deeper into the heart than any previous attempt to create immortality out of that which is mortal—to transform matter into spirit. And in the meantime the European States, founded by Germanic peoples, in spite of their, so to speak, improvised, always provisional and changeable character—or rather perhaps thanks to this character—proved themselves to be the most enduring as well as the most powerful in the world. In spite of all storms of war, in spite of the deceptions of that ancestral enemy, the chaos of peoples, which carried its poison into the very heart of our nation, freedom and its correlative, the State, remained, through all the ages the creating and saving ideal, even though the balance between the two often seemed to be upset: we recognize that more clearly today than ever.

In order that this might be so, that fundamental and common "Aryan" capacity of free creative power had to be supplemented by another quality, the incomparable and altogether peculiar Germanic loyalty (*Treue*). If that intellectual and physical development which leads to the idea of freedom and which produces on the one hand art, philosophy, science, on the other constitutions (as well as all the phenomena of culture which this word implies), is common to the Hellenes and Romans as well as to the Germanic peoples, so also is the extravagant conception of loyalty a specific characteristic of the Teuton. . . .

A Forward Glance

I, a modest historian, who can neither influence the course of events nor possess the power of looking clearly into the future, must be satisfied if in fulfilling the purpose of this book I have succeeded in showing the distinction between the Germanic and the Non-Germanic. That the Teuton is one of the greatest, perhaps the very greatest power in the history of mankind, no one will wish to deny, but in order to arrive at a correct appreciation of the present time, it behooved us to settle once for all who could and who could not be regarded as Teuton. In the nineteenth century, as in all former centuries, but of course with widely different grouping and with constantly changing relative power, there stood side by side in Europe these "Heirs"—the chaos of half-breeds, relics of the former Roman Empire, the Germanizing of which is falling off—the Jews—and the Germans, whose contamination by mixture with the half-breeds and the descendants of other Non-Aryan races is on the increase. No arguing about "humanity" can alter the fact that this means a struggle. Where the struggle is not waged with cannon-balls, it goes on silently in the heart of society by marriages, by the annihilation of distances which furthers intercourse, by the varying powers of resistance in the different types of mankind, by the shifting of wealth, by the birth of new influences and the disappearance of others, and by many other motive powers. But this struggle, silent though it be, is above all others a struggle for life and death.

Section IV

FASCIST PHILOSOPHY IN ITALY

Twentieth-century fascism originally was an Italian movement. The word *fasciare* means to bind or to envelop, and fascism was intended by its founders as a doctrine that would, once for all, bind the Italian nation into an organic entity, maintaining and expanding the traditions and glories of ancient Rome.

The history of the Italian Fascist movement is neither long nor consistent. It began with the founding of the Fascist Party by Benito Mussolini in 1919, and his rise to power in the "March on Rome" in 1922, and concluded with his inglorious assassination by Italian partisans in 1945. Mussolini originally had been a socialist and an atheist; he became a bitter critic of socialism and a strong supporter of the Roman Catholic Church. He was once in favor of republicanism, but became a monarchist; once a supporter of the principles of laissez faire, but eventually came to demand complete state regulation of all economic activity. And it was characteristic of the antirational philosophy of fascism that, rather than deny these inconsistencies, Mussolini gloried in them. "No dogma! Discipline suffices" was the early slogan of the regime. "My program is action, not thought," said Mussolini; and to all intellectual criticism of the movement his followers learned to reply, "We think with our blood."

Some attempt to expound the philosophy of fascism was eventually undertaken, however, by certain leading members of the Mussolini government. In 1925, the core of the fascist philosophy was laid down by Alfredo Rocco as the theory of a supreme, totalitarian state led by the intuitive genius of an all-powerful ruler. These were the themes upon which Mussolini himself, Giovanni Gentile, and others were later to expand, interweaving with them a glorification of heroism, sacrifice, and war, and presenting the whole with fanatical and inspiring enthusiasm.

332

At last Mussolini could say: "We have created our myth; it is a faith, a passion . . . It is a reality by virtue of being a spur, a source of courage. Our myth is the nation, the greatness of the nation. And to this myth, this grandeur . . . we subordinate all the rest."

40. ALFREDO ROCCO

Alfredo Rocco (1875-1935) was Fascist Minister of Justice, and an intimate adviser and friend to Il Duce. His philosophical views clearly present the bitter opposition of fascism to any form of social atomism, and his conception of an "integral doctrine of sociality." A vigorous admirer of Machiavelli, and a supporter of the supreme power of the organic state, he blended these elements into a philosophy which, he claimed, "was to restore Italian thought in the sphere of political doctrine to its own traditions, which are the traditions of Rome."

The Political Doctrine of Fascism*

Premier Mussolini's Endorsement of Signor Rocco's Speech

The following message was sent by Benito Mussolini, the Premier of Italy, to Signor Rocco after he had delivered his speech at Perugia.

Dear Rocco,

I have just read your magnificent address which I endorse throughout. You have presented in a masterful way the doctrine of Fascism. For Fascism has a doctrine, or, if you will, a particular philosophy with regard to all the questions which beset the human mind today. All Italian Fascists should read your discourse and derive from it both the clear formulation of the basic principles of our program as well as the reasons why Fascism must be systematically, firmly, and rationally inflexible in its uncompromising attitude towards other parties. Thus

* A. Rocco, *The Political Doctrine of Fascism*, 1925. Reprinted from *Readings on Fascism and National Socialism*, selected by members of the philosophy department of the University of Colorado, by permission of the publisher, Alan Swallow, Denver.

and only thus can the word become flesh and the ideas be turned into deeds.

Cordial greetings,

MUSSOLINI.

Fascism as Action, as Feeling, and as Thought

Much has been said, and is now being said for or against this complex political and social phenomenon which in the brief period of six years has taken complete hold of Italian life and, spreading beyond the borders of the Kingdom, has made itself felt in varying degrees of intensity throughout the world. But people have been much more eager to extol or to deplore than to understand—which is natural enough in a period of tumultuous fervor and of political passion. The time has not yet arrived for a dispassionate judgment. For even I, who noticed the very first manifestations of this great development, saw its significance from the start and participated directly in its first doings, carefully watching all its early uncertain and changing developments, even I do not feel competent to pass definite judgment. Fascism is so large a part of myself that it would be both arbitrary and absurd for me to try to dissociate my personality from it, to submit it to impartial scrutiny in order to evaluate it coldly and accurately. What can be done, however, and it seldom is attempted, is to make inquiry into the phenomenon which shall not merely consider its fragmentary and adventitious aspects, but strive to get at its inner essence. The undertaking may not be easy, but it is necessary, and no occasion for attempting it is more suitable than the present one afforded me by my friends of Perugia. Suitable it is in time because, at the inauguration of a course of lectures and lessons principally intended to illustrate that old and glorious trend of the life and history of Italy which takes its name from the humble saint of Assisi, it seemed natural to connect it with the greatest achievement of modern Italy, different in so many ways from the Franciscan movement, but united with it by the mighty common current of Italian History. It is suitable as well in place because at Perugia, which witnessed the growth of our religious ideas, of our political doctrines and of our legal science in the course of the most glorious centuries of our cultural history, the mind is properly disposed and almost oriented towards an investigation of this nature.

First of all let us ask ourselves if there is a political doctrine of

a means for securing, in behalf of the individual, a direct check
[o]n this, the strongest branch, and an indirect check on the entire
[go]vernment of the state. This system of checks and limitations, which
[go]es by the name of constitutional government resulted in a moderate
[an]d measured liberalism. The checking power was exercised only by
[th]ose citizens who were deemed worthy and capable, with the result
[th]at a small élite was made to represent legally the entire body poli-
[tic] for whose benefit this régime was instituted.

It was evident, however, that this moderate system, being funda-
[me]ntally illogical and in contradiction with the very principles from
[wh]ich it proceeded, would soon become the object of serious criti-
[cis]m. For if the object of society and of the state is the welfare of
[ind]ividuals, severally considered, how is it possible to admit that this
[we]lfare can be secured by the individuals themselves only through
[th]e possibilities of such a liberal régime? The inequalities brought
[ab]out both by nature and by social organizations are so numerous
[an]d so serious, that, for the greater part, individuals abandoned to
[th]emselves not only would fail to attain happiness, but would also
[co]ntribute to the perpetuation of their condition of misery and dejec-
[tio]n. The state therefore cannot limit itself to the merely negative
[fun]ction of the defense of liberty. It must become active, in behalf
[of] everybody, for the welfare of the people. It must intervene, when
[ne]cessary, in order to improve the material, intellectual, and moral
[co]nditions of the masses; it must find work for the unemployed,
[ins]truct and educate the people, and care for health and hygiene. For
[if t]he purpose of society and of the state is the welfare of individuals,
[an]d if it is just that these individuals themselves control the attain-
[me]nt of their ends, it becomes difficult to understand why Liberalism
[sho]uld not go the whole distance, why it should see fit to distinguish
[cer]tain individuals from the rest of the mass, and why the functions
[of] the people should be restricted to the exercise of a mere check.
[Th]erefore the state, if it exists for all, must be governed by all, and
[no]t by a small minority: if the state is for the people, sovereignty
[mu]st reside in the people: if all individuals have the right to govern
[the] state, liberty is no longer sufficient; equality must be added:
[an]d if sovereignty is vested in the people, the people must wield all
[so]vereignty and not merely a part of it. The power to check and
[cur]b the government is not sufficient. The people must be the gov-
[ern]ment. Thus, logically developed, Liberalism leads to Democracy,
[for] Democracy contains the promises of Liberalism but oversteps its

Fascism; if there is any ideal content in the Fascist state. For in
order to link Fascism, both as concept and system, with the history
of Italian thought and find therein a place for it, we must first show
that it is thought; that it is a doctrine. Many persons are not quite
convinced that it is either the one or the other; and I am not referring
solely to those men, cultured or uncultured, as the case may be and
very numerous everywhere, who can discern in this political innova-
tion nothing except its local and personal aspects, and who know
Fascism only as the particular manner of behavior of this or that
well-known Fascist, of this or that group of a certain town; who
therefore like or dislike the movement on the basis of their likes and
dislikes for the individuals who represent it. Nor do I refer to those
intelligent and cultivated persons, very intelligent indeed and very
cultivated, who because of their direct or indirect allegiance to the
parties that have been dispossessed by the advent of Fascism, have
a natural cause of resentment against it and are therefore unable to
see, in the blindness of hatred, anything good in it. I am referring
rather to those—and there are many in our ranks too—who know
Fascism as action and feeling but not yet as thought, who therefore
have an intuition but no comprehension of it.

It is true that Fascism is, above all, action and sentiment and that
such it must continue to be. Were it otherwise, it could not keep up
that immense driving force, that renovating power which it now
possesses and would merely be the solitary meditation of a chosen
few. Only because it is feeling and sentiment, only because it is the
unconscious reawakening of our profound racial instinct, has it the
force to stir the soul of the people, and to set free an irresistible current of national will. Only because it is action, and as such actualizes
itself in a vast organization and in a huge movement, has it the
conditions for determining the historical course of contemporary
Italy.

But Fascism is thought as well and it has a theory, which is an
essential part of this historical phenomenon, and which is responsible
in a great measure for the successes that have been achieved. To the
existence of this ideal content of Fascism, to the truth of this Fascist
logic we ascribe the fact that though we commit many errors of
detail, we very seldom go astray on fundamentals, whereas all the
parties of the opposition, deprived as they are of an informing,
animating principle, of a unique directing concept, do very often
wage their war faultlessly in minor tactics, better trained as they are

in parliamentary and journalistic maneuvers, but they constantly break down on the important issues. Fascism, moreover, considered as action, is a typically Italian phenomenon and acquires a universal validity because of the existence of this coherent and organic doctrine. The originality of Fascism is due in great part to the autonomy of its theoretical principles. For even when, in its external behavior and in its conclusions, it seems identical with other political creeds, in reality it possesses an inner originality due to the new spirit which animates it and to an entirely different theoretical approach.

Common Origins and Common Background of Modern Political Doctrines: From Liberalism to Socialism

Modern political thought remained, until recently, both in Italy and outside of Italy under the absolute control of those doctrines which, proceeding from the Protestant Reformation and developed by the adepts of natural law in the seventeenth and eighteenth centuries, were firmly grounded in the institutions and customs of the English, of the American, and of the French Revolutions. Under different and sometimes clashing forms these doctrines have left a determining imprint upon all theories and actions both social and political, of the nineteenth and twentieth centuries down to the rise of Fascism. The common basis of all these doctrines, which stretch from Longuet, from Buchanan, and from Althusen down to Karl Marx, to Wilson and to Lenin is a social and state concept which I shall call mechanical or atomistic.

Society according to this concept is merely a sum total of individuals, a plurality which breaks up into its single components. Therefore the ends of a society, so considered, are nothing more than the ends of the individuals which compose it and for whose sake it exists. An atomistic view of this kind is also necessarily anti-historical, inasmuch as it considers society in its spatial attributes and not in its temporal ones; and because it reduces social life to the existence of a single generation. Society becomes thus a sum of determined individuals, viz., the generation living at a given moment. This doctrine which I call atomistic and which appears to be anti-historical, reveals from under a concealing cloak a strongly materialistic nature. For in its endeavors to isolate the present from the past and the future, it rejects the spiritual inheritance of ideas and sentiments which each generation receives from those preceding and

hands down to the following generation thus destroyin and the spiritual life itself of human society.

This common basis shows the close logical connect between all political doctrines; the substantial solidarity, all the political movements, from Liberalism to Socialisr recently have dominated Europe. For these political s from one another in their methods, but all agree as to be achieved. All of them consider the welfare and happ dividuals to be the goal of society, itself considered as individuals of the present generation. All of them see in in its juridical organization, the state, the mere inst means whereby individuals can attain their ends. They that the methods pursued for the attainment of these en siderably one from the other.

Thus the Liberals insist that the best manner to sec fare of the citizens as individuals is to interfere as little with the free development of their activities and that t essential task of the state is merely to coordinate these sev in such a way as to guarantee their coexistence. Kar without doubt the most powerful and thorough philosoph ism, said, "man, who is the end, cannot be assumed value of an instrument." And again, "justice, of which the specific organ, is the condition whereby the freedo conditioned upon the freedom of others, according to the of liberty."

Having thus defined the task of the state, Liberalism c to the demand of certain guarantees which are to ke from overstepping its functions as general coordinator and from sacrificing the freedom of individuals more t lutely necessary for the accomplishment of its purpose. A are therefore directed to see to it that the ruler, man and entrusted with the realization, through and by lit harmonious happiness of everybody, should never be undue power. Hence the creation of a system of check: tions designed to keep the rulers within bounds; and first and foremost, the principle of the division of powe as a means for weakening the state in its relation to th by making it impossible for the state ever to appear, in with citizens, in the full plenitude of sovereign powe principle of the participation of citizens in the lawma

limitations in that it makes the action of the state positive, proclaims the equality of all citizens through the dogma of popular sovereignty. Democracy therefore necessarily implies a republican form of government even though at times, for reasons of expediency, it temporarily adjusts itself to a monarchical régime.

Once started on this downward grade of logical deductions it was inevitable that this atomistic theory of state and society should pass on to a more advanced position. Great industrial developments and the existence of a huge mass of working men, as yet badly treated and in a condition of semi-servitude, possibly endurable in a régime of domestic industry, became intolerable after the industrial revolution. Hence a state of affairs which towards the middle of the last century appeared to be both cruel and threatening. It was therefore natural that the following question be raised: "If the state is created for the welfare of its citizens, severally considered, how can it tolerate an economic system which divides the population into a small minority of exploiters, the capitalists, on one side, and an immense multitude of exploited, the working people, on the other?" No! The state must again intervene and give rise to a different and less iniquitous economic organization, by abolishing private property, by assuming direct control of all production, and by organizing it in such a way that the products of labor be distributed solely among those who create them, viz., the working classes. Hence we find Socialism, with its new economic organization of society, abolishing private ownership of capital and of the instruments and means of production, socializing the product, suppressing the extra profit of capital, and turning over to the working class the entire output of the productive processes. It is evident that Socialism contains and surpasses Democracy in the same way that Democracy comprises and surpasses Liberalism, being a more advanced development of the same fundamental concept. Socialism in its turn generates the still more extreme doctrine of Bolshevism which demands the violent suppression of the holders of capital, the dictatorship of the proletariat, as means for a fairer economic organization of society and for the rescue of the laboring classes from capitalistic exploitation.

Thus Liberalism, Democracy, and Socialism, appear to be, as they are in reality, not only the offspring of one and the same theory of government, but also logical derivations one of the other. Logically developed Liberalism leads to Democracy; the logical development of Democracy issues into Socialism. It is true that for many years,

and with some justification, Socialism was looked upon as antithetical to Liberalism. But the antithesis is purely relative and breaks
down as we approach the common origin and foundation of the two
doctrines, for we find that the opposition is one of method, not of
purpose. The end is the same for both, viz., the welfare of the individual members of society. The difference lies in the fact that
Liberalism would be guided to its goal by liberty, whereas Socialism
strives to attain it by the collective organization of production. There
is therefore no antithesis nor even a divergence as to the nature and
scope of the state and the relation of individuals to society. There
is only a difference of evaluation of the means for bringing about
these ends and establishing these relations, which difference depends
entirely on the different economic conditions which prevailed at the
time when the various doctrines were formulated. Liberalism arose
and began to thrive in the period of small industry; Socialism grew
with the rise of industrialism and of world-wide capitalism. The dissension therefore between these two points of view, or the antithesis,
if we wish so to call it, is limited to the economic field. Socialism
is at odds with Liberalism only on the question of the organization
of production and of the division of wealth. In religious, intellectual,
and moral matters it is liberal, as it is liberal and democratic in its
politics. Even the anti-liberalism and anti-democracy of Bolshevism
are in themselves purely contingent. For Bolshevism is opposed to
Liberalism only in so far as the former is revolutionary, not in its
socialistic aspect. For if the opposition of the Bolsheviki to liberal
and democratic doctrines were to continue, as now seems more and
more probable, the result might be a complete break between Bolshevism and Socialism notwithstanding the fact that the ultimate
aims of both are identical.

Fascism as an Integral Doctrine of Sociality Antithetical to the Atomism of Liberal, Democratic, and Socialistic Theories

The true antithesis, not to this or that manifestation of the liberal-
democratic-socialistic conception of the state but to the concept itself, is to be found in the doctrine of Fascism. For while the disagreement between Liberalism and Democracy, and between Liberalism
and Socialism lies in a difference of method, as we have said, the
rift between Socialism, Democracy, and Liberalism on one side and

Fascism on the other is caused by a difference in concept. As a matter of fact, Fascism never raises the question of methods, using in its political praxis now liberal ways, now democratic means and at times even socialistic devices. This indifference to method often exposes Fascism to the charge of incoherence on the part of superficial observers, who do not see that what counts with us is the end and that therefore even when we employ the same means we act with a radically different spiritual attitude and strive for entirely different results. The Fascist concept then of the nation, of the scope of the state, and of the relations obtaining between society and its individual components, rejects entirely the doctrine which I said proceeded from the theories of natural law developed in the course of the sixteenth, seventeenth, and eighteenth centuries and which form the basis of the liberal, democratic, and socialistic ideology.

I shall not try here to expound this doctrine but shall limit myself to a brief résumé of its fundamental concepts.

Man—the political animal—according to the definition of Aristotle, lives and must live in society. A human being outside the pale of society is an inconceivable thing—a non-man. Humankind in its entirety lives in social groups that are still, today, very numerous and diverse, varying in importance and organization from the tribes of Central Africa to the great Western Empires. These various societies are fractions of the human species each one of them endowed with a unified organization. And as there is no unique organization of the human species, there is not "one" but there are "several" human societies. Humanity therefore exists solely as a biological concept not as a social one.

Each society on the other hand exists in the unity of both its biological and its social contents. Socially considered it is a fraction of the human species endowed with unity of organization for the attainment of the peculiar ends of the species.

This definition brings out all the elements of the social phenomenon and not merely those relating to the preservation and perpetuation of the species. For man is not solely matter; and the ends of the human species, far from being the materialistic ones we have in common with other animals, are, rather, and predominantly, the spiritual finalities which are peculiar to man and which every form of society strives to attain as well as its stage of social development allows. Thus the organization of every social group is more or less pervaded by the spiritual influxes of: unity of language, of culture, of religion, of tradition, of customs, and in general of feeling and of volition, which are as essential as the material elements: unity of economic interests, of living conditions, and of territory. The definition given above demonstrates another truth, which has been ignored by the political doctrines that for the last four centuries have been the foundations of political systems, viz., that the social concept has a biological aspect, because social groups are fractions of the human species, each one possessing a peculiar organization, a particular rank in the development of civilization with certain needs and appropriate ends, in short, a life which is really its own. If social groups are then fractions of the human species, they must possess the same fundamental traits of the human species, which means that they must be considered as a succession of generations and not as a collection of individuals.

It is evident therefore that as the human species is not the total of the living human beings of the world, so the various social groups which compose it are not the sum of the several individuals which at a given moment belong to it, but rather the infinite series of the past, present, and future generations constituting it. And as the ends of the human species are not those of the several individuals living at a certain moment, being occasionally in direct opposition to them, so the ends of the various social groups are not necessarily those of the individuals that belong to the groups but may even possibly be in conflict with such ends, as one sees clearly whenever the preservation and the development of the species demand the sacrifice of the individual, to wit, in times of war.

Fascism replaces therefore the old atomistic and mechanical state theory which was at the basis of the liberal and democratic doctrines with an organic and historic concept. When I say organic I do not wish to convey the impression that I consider society as an organism after the manner of the so-called "organic theories of the state"; but rather to indicate that the social groups as fractions of the species receive thereby a life and scope which transcend the scope and life of the individuals identifying themselves with the history and finalities of the uninterrupted series of generations. It is irrelevant in this connection to determine whether social groups, considered as fractions of the species, constitute organisms. The important thing is to ascertain that this organic concept of the state gives to society a continuous life over and beyond the existence of the several individuals.

The relations therefore between state and citizens are completely reversed by the Fascist doctrine. Instead of the liberal-democratic formula, "society for the individual," we have, "individuals for society" with this difference however: that while the liberal doctrines eliminated society, Fascism does not submerge the individual in the social group. It subordinates him, but does not eliminate him; the individual as a part of his generation ever remaining an element of society however transient and insignificant he may be. Moreover the development of individuals in each generation, when coordinated and harmonized, conditions the development and prosperity of the entire social unit.

At this juncture the antithesis between the two theories must appear complete and absolute. Liberalism, Democracy, and Socialism look upon social groups as aggregates of living individuals; for Fascism they are the recapitulating unity of the indefinite series of generations. For Liberalism, society has no purposes other than those of the members living at a given moment. For Fascism, society has historical and immanent ends of preservation, expansion, improvement, quite distinct from those of the individuals which at a given moment compose it; so distinct in fact that they may even be in opposition. Hence the necessity, for which the older doctrines make little allowance, of sacrifice, even up to the total immolation of individuals, in behalf of society; hence the true explanation of war, eternal law of mankind, interpreted by the liberal-democratic doctrines as a degenerate absurdity or as a maddened monstrosity.

For Liberalism, society has no life distinct from the life of the individuals, or as the phrase goes: *solvitur in singularitates*. For Fascism, the life of society overlaps the existence of individuals and projects itself into the succeeding generations through centuries and millennia. Individuals come into being, grow, and die, followed by others, unceasingly; social unity remains always identical to itself. For Liberalism, the individual is the end and society the means; nor is it conceivable that the individual, considered in the dignity of an ultimate finality, be lowered to mere instrumentality. For Fascism, society is the end, individuals the means, and its whole life consists in using individuals as instruments for its social ends. The state therefore guards and protects the welfare and development of individuals not for their exclusive interest, but because of the identity of the needs of individuals with those of society as a whole. We can thus accept and explain institutions and practices, which like the death penalty, are condemned by Liberalism in the name of the preeminence of individualism.

The fundamental problem of society in the old doctrines is the question of the rights of individuals. It may be the right to freedom as the Liberals would have it; or the right to the government of the commonwealth as the Democrats claim it, or the right to economic justice as the Socialists contend; but in every case it is the right of individuals, or groups of individuals (classes). Fascism on the other hand faces squarely the problem of the right of the state and of the duty of individuals. Individual rights are only recognized in so far as they are implied in the rights of the state. In this preeminence of duty we find the highest ethical value of Fascism.

The Problems of Liberty, of Government, and of Social Justice in the Political Doctrine of Fascism

This, however, does not mean that the problems raised by the other schools are ignored by Fascism. It means simply that it faces them and solves them differently, as, for example, the problem of liberty.

There is a Liberal theory of freedom, and there is a Fascist concept of liberty. For we, too, maintain the necessity of safeguarding the conditions that make for the free development of the individual; we, too, believe that the oppression of individual personality can find no place in the modern state. We do not, however, accept a bill of rights which tends to make the individual superior to the state and to empower him to act in opposition to society. Our concept of liberty is that the individual must be allowed to develop his personality in behalf of the state, for these ephemeral and infinitesimal elements of the complex and permanent life of society determine by their normal growth the development of the state. But this individual growth must be normal. A huge and disproportionate development of the individual of classes, would prove as fatal to society as abnormal growths are to living organisms. Freedom therefore is due to the citizen and to classes on condition that they exercise it in the interest of society as a whole and within the limits set by social exigencies, liberty being, like any other individual right, a concession of the state. What I say concerning civil liberties applies to economic freedom as well. Fascism does not look upon the doctrine of economic liberty as an absolute dogma. It does not refer economic problems to individual needs, to individual interest, to individual solutions. On the contrary it considers the economic development, and especially the production of wealth, as an eminently social concern, wealth being for society an essential element of power and prosperity. But Fascism maintains that in the ordinary run of events economic liberty serves the social purposes best; that it is profitable to entrust to individual initiative the task of economic development both as to production and as to distribution; that in the economic world individual ambition is the most effective means for obtaining the best social results with the least effort. Therefore, on the question also of economic liberty the Fascists differ fundamentally from the Liberals; the latter see in liberty a principle, the Fascists accept it as a method. By the Liberals, freedom is recognized in the interest of the citizens; the Fascists grant it in the interest of society. In other terms, Fascists make of the individual an economic instrument for the advancement of society, an instrument which they use so long as it functions and which they subordinate when no longer serviceable. In this guise Fascism solves the eternal problem of economic freedom and of state interference, considering both as mere methods which may or may not be employed in accordance with the social needs of the moment.

What I have said concerning political and economic Liberalism applies also to Democracy. The latter envisages fundamentally the problem of sovereignty; Fascism does also, but in an entirely different manner. Democracy vests sovereignty in the people, that is to say, in the mass of human beings. Fascism discovers sovereignty to be inherent in society when it is juridically organized as a state. Democracy therefore turns over the government of the state to the multitude of living men that they may use it to further their own interests; Fascism insists that the government be entrusted to men capable of rising above their own private interests and of realizing the aspirations of the social collectivity, considered in its unity and in its relation to the past and future. Fascism therefore not only rejects the dogma of popular sovereignty and substitutes for it that of state sovereignty, but it also proclaims that the great mass of citizens is not a suitable advocate of social interests for the reason that the capacity to ignore individual private interests in favor of the higher demands of society and of history is a very rare gift and the privilege of the chosen few. Natural intelligence and cultural preparation are of great service in such tasks. Still more valuable perhaps is the intuitiveness of rare great minds, their traditionalism and their inherited qualities. This must not however be construed to mean that the masses are not to be allowed to exercise any influence on the life of the state. On the contrary, among peoples with a great history and with noble traditions, even the lowest elements of society possess an instinctive discernment of what is necessary for the welfare of the race, which in moments of great historical crises reveals itself to be almost infallible. It is therefore as wise to afford to this instinct the means of declaring itself as it is judicious to entrust the normal control of the commonwealth to a selected élite. . . .

Historical Value of the Doctrine of Fascism

. . . At this point it will not be very difficult to assign a fitting place in history to this great trend of thought which is called Fascism and which, in spite of the initial difficulties, already gives clear indication of the magnitude of its developments.

The liberal-democratic speculation both in its origin and in the manner of its development appears to be essentially a non-Italian formation. Its connection with the Middle Ages already shows it to be foreign to the Latin mind, the medieval disintegration being the result of the triumph of Germanic individualism over the political mentality of the Romans. The barbarians, boring from within and hacking from without, pulled down the great political structure raised by Latin genius and put nothing in its place. Anarchy lasted eight centuries during which time only one institution survived and that a Roman one—the Catholic Church. But, as soon as the laborious process of reconstruction was started with the constitution of the great national states backed by the Roman Church the Protestant Reformation set in followed by the individualistic currents of the seventeenth and eighteenth centuries, and the process of disintegration was started anew. This anti-state tendency was the expression of the Germanic spirit and it therefore became predominant among the Germanic peoples and wherever Germanism had left a deep imprint even if afterward superficially covered by a veneer of Latin culture. . . .

While therefore in other countries such as France, England, Germany, and Holland, the general tradition in the social and political sciences worked in behalf of anti-state individualism, and therefore of liberal and democratic doctrines, Italy, on the other hand, clung to the powerful legacy of its past in virtue of which she proclaims the rights of the state, the preeminence of its authority, and the superiority of its ends. The very fact that the Italian political doctrine in the Middle Ages linked itself with the great political writers of antiquity, Plato and Aristotle, who in a different manner but with an equal firmness advocated a strong state and the subordination of individuals to it, is a sufficient index of the orientation of political philosophy in Italy. We all know how thorough and crushing the authority of Aristotle was in the Middle Ages. But for Aristotle the spiritual cement of the state is "virtue" not absolute virtue but political virtue, which is social devotion. His state is made up solely of its citizens, the citizens being either those who defend it with their arms or who govern it as magistrates. All others who provide it with the materials and services it needs are not citizens. They become such only in the corrupt forms of certain democracies. Society is therefore divided into two classes, the free men or citizens who give their time to noble and virtuous occupations and who profess their subjection to the state, and the laborers and slaves who work for the maintenance of the former. No man in this scheme is his own master. The slaves belong to the freemen, and the freemen belong to the state.

It was therefore natural that St. Thomas Aquinas, the greatest political writer of the Middle Ages, should emphasize the necessity of unity in the political field, the harm of plurality of rulers, the dangers and damaging effects of demagogy. The good of the state, says St. Thomas Aquinas, is unity. And who can procure unity more fittingly than he who is himself one? Moreover the government must follow, as far as possible, the course of nature and in nature power is always one. In the physical body only one organ is dominant —the heart; in the spirit only one faculty has sway—reason. Bees have one sole ruler; and the entire universe one sole sovereign—God. Experience shows that the countries, which are ruled by many, perish because of discord while those that are ruled over by one enjoy peace, justice, and plenty. The States which are not ruled by one are troubled by dissensions, and toil unceasingly. On the contrary the states which are ruled over by one king enjoy peace, thrive in justice and are gladdened by affluence.* The rule of the multitudes cannot be sanctioned, for where the crowd rules it oppresses the rich as would a tyrant.† . . .

* De reg. princ. I. c. 2.
† Comm. In Polit. L. III. lectio VIII.

The Roman tradition, which was one of practice but not of theories —for Rome constructed the most solid state known to history with extraordinary statemanship but with hardly any political writings— influenced considerably the founder of modern political science, Niccolo Machiavelli, who was himself in truth not a creator of doctrines but a keen observer of human nature who derived from the study of history practical maxims of political import. He freed the science of politics from the formalism of the scholastic and brought it close to concrete reality. His writings, an inexhaustible mine of practical remarks and precious observations, reveal dominant in him the state idea, no longer abstract but in the full historical concreteness of the national unity of Italy. Machiavelli therefore is not only the greatest of modern political writers, he is also the greatest of our countrymen in full possession of a national Italian consciousness. To liberate Italy, which was in his day "enslaved, torn and pillaged," and to make her more powerful, he would use any means, for to his mind the holiness of the end justified them completely. In this he was sharply rebuked by foreigners who were not as hostile to his means as they were fearful of the end which he propounded. He advocated therefore the constitution of a strong Italian state, supported by the sacrifices and by the blood of the citizens, not defended by mercenary troops; well-ordered internally, aggressive and bent on expansion. . . .

A powerful innovating movement, issuing from the war and of which Fascism is the purest expression, was to restore Italian thought in the sphere of political doctrine to its own traditions which are the traditions of Rome.

This task of intellectual liberation, now slowly being accomplished, is no less important than the political deliverance brought about by the Fascist Revolution. It is a great task which continues and integrates the Risorgimento; it is now bringing to an end, after the cessation of our political servitude, the intellectual dependence of Italy.

Thanks to it, Italy again speaks to the world and the world listens to Italy. It is a great task and a great deed and it demands great efforts. To carry it through, we must, each one of us, free ourselves of the dross of ideas and mental habits which two centuries of foreign intellectualistic tradition have heaped upon us; we must not only take on a new culture but create for ourselves a new soul. We must methodically and patiently contribute something towards the organic and complete elaboration of our doctrine, at the same time supporting it both at home and abroad with untiring devotion. We ask this effort of renovation and collaboration of all Fascists, as well as of all who feel themselves to be Italians. After the hour of sacrifice comes the hour of unyielding efforts. To our work, then, fellow countrymen, for the glory of Italy!

41. BENITO MUSSOLINI

Benito Mussolini (1883-1945) was the founder of the Fascist Party in Italy, and dictator from 1922 until his death in 1945. The following article, which first appeared as a contribution to Enciclopedia Italiana *in 1932, is the most famous statement of that composite known as the philosophy of fascism.*

The Doctrine of Fascism*

(i) Fundamental Ideas

1. Like every sound political conception, Fascism is both practice and thought; action in which a doctrine is immanent, and a doctrine which, arising out of a given system of historical forces, remains embedded in them and works there from within. Hence it has a form correlative to the contingencies of place and time, but it has also a content of thought which raises it to a formula of truth in the higher level of the history of thought. In the world one does not act spiritually as a human will dominating other wills without a conception of the transient and particular reality under which it is necessary to act, and of the permanent and universal reality in which the first has its being and its life. In order to know men it is necessary to know man; and in order to know man it is necessary to know reality and its laws. There is no concept of the State which is not fundamentally a concept of life: philosophy or intuition, a

* Benito Mussolini, *The Doctrine of Fascism, 1932.* This translation is reprinted from *The Social and Political Doctrines of Contemporary Europe,* 1939, edited by Michael Oakeshott, by permission of the Cambridge University Press.

system of ideas which develops logically or is gathered up into a vision or into a faith, but which is always, at least virtually, an organic conception of the world.

2. Thus Fascism could not be understood in many of its practical manifestations as a party organization, as a system of education, as a discipline, if it were not always looked at in the light of its whole way of conceiving life, a spiritualized way. The world seen through Fascism is not this material world which appears on the surface, in which man is an individual separated from all others and standing by himself, and in which he is governed by a natural law that makes him instinctively live a life of selfish and momentary pleasure. The man of Fascism is an individual who is nation and fatherland, which is a moral law, binding together individuals and the generations into a tradition and a mission, suppressing the instinct for a life enclosed within the brief round of pleasure in order to restore within duty a higher life free from the limits of time and space: a life in which the individual, through the denial of himself, through the sacrifice of his own private interests, through death itself, realizes that completely spiritual existence in which his value as a man lies.

3. Therefore it is a spiritualized conception, itself the result of the general reaction of modern times against the flabby materialistic positivism of the nineteenth century. Anti-positivistic, but positive: not sceptical, nor agnostic, nor pessimistic, nor passively optimistic, as are, in general, the doctrines (all negative) that put the center of life outside man, who with his free will can and must create his own world. Fascism desires an active man, one engaged in activity with all his energies: it desires a man virilely conscious of the difficulties that exist in action and ready to face them. It conceives of life as a struggle, considering that it behooves man to conquer for himself that life truly worthy of him, creating first of all in himself the instrument (physical, moral, intellectual) in order to construct it. Thus for the single individual, thus for the nation, thus for humanity. Hence the high value of culture in all its forms (art, religion, science), and the enormous importance of education. Hence also the essential value of work, with which man conquers nature and creates the human world (economic, political, moral, intellectual).

4. This positive conception of life is clearly an ethical conception. It covers the whole of reality, not merely the human activity which controls it. No action can be divorced from moral judgment; there is nothing in the world which can be deprived of the value which belongs

to everything in its relation to moral ends. Life, therefore, as conceived by the Fascist, is serious, austere, religious: the whole of it is poised in a world supported by the moral and responsible forces of the spirit. The Fascist disdains the "comfortable" life.

5. Fascism is a religious conception in which man is seen in his immanent relationship with a superior law and with an objective Will that transcends the particular individual and raises him to conscious membership of a spiritual society. Whoever has seen in the religious politics of the Fascist regime nothing but mere opportunism has not understood that Fascism besides being a system of government is also, and above all, a system of thought.

6. Fascism is a historical conception, in which man is what he is only in so far as he works with the spiritual process in which he finds himself, in the family or social group, in the nation and in the history in which all nations collaborate. From this follows the great value of tradition, in memories, in language, in customs, in the standards of social life. Outside history man is nothing. Consequently Fascism is opposed to all the individualistic abstractions of a materialistic nature like those of the eighteenth century; and it is opposed to all Jacobin utopias and innovations. It does not consider that "happiness" is possible upon earth, as it appeared to be in the desire of the economic literature of the eighteenth century, and hence it rejects all teleological theories according to which mankind would reach a definitive stabilized condition at a certain period in history. This implies putting oneself outside history and life, which is a continual change and coming to be. Politically, Fascism wishes to be a realistic doctrine; practically, it aspires to solve only the problems which arise historically of themselves and that of themselves find or suggest their own solution. To act among men, as to act in the natural world, it is necessary to enter into the process of reality and to master the already operating forces.

7. Against individualism, the Fascist conception is for the State; and it is for the individual in so far as he coincides with the State, which is the conscience and universal will of man in his historical existence. It is opposed to classical Liberalism, which arose from the necessity of reacting against absolutism, and which brought its historical purpose to an end when the State was transformed into the conscience and will of the people. Liberalism denied the State in the interests of the particular individual; Fascism reaffirms the State as the true reality of the individual. And if liberty is to be the

attribute of the real man, and not of that abstract puppet envisaged by individualistic Liberalism, Fascism is for liberty. And for the only liberty which can be a real thing, the liberty of the State and of the individual within the State. Therefore, for the Fascist, everything is in the State, and nothing human or spiritual exists, much less has value, outside the State. In this sense Fascism is totalitarian, and the Fascist State, the synthesis and unity of all values, interprets, develops and gives strength to the whole life of the people.

8. Outside the State there can be neither individuals nor groups (political parties, associations, syndicates, classes). Therefore Fascism is opposed to Socialism, which confines the movement of history within the class struggle and ignores the unity of classes established in one economic and moral reality in the State; and analogously it is opposed to class syndicalism. Fascism recognizes the real exigencies for which the socialist and syndicalist movement arose, but while recognizing them wishes to bring them under the control of the State and give them a purpose within the corporative system of interests reconciled within the unity of the State.

9. Individuals form classes according to the similarity of their interests, they form syndicates according to differentiated economic activities within these interests; but they form first, and above all, the State, which is not to be thought of numerically as the sum-total of individuals forming the majority of a nation. And consequently Fascism is opposed to Democracy, which equates the nation to the majority, lowering it to the level of that majority; nevertheless it is the purest form of democracy if the nation is conceived, as it should be, qualitatively and not quantitatively, as the most powerful idea (most powerful because most moral, most coherent, most true) which acts within the nation as the conscience and the will of a few, even of One, which ideal tends to become active within the conscience and the will of all—that is to say, of all those who rightly constitute a nation by reason of nature, history or race, and have set out upon the same line of development and spiritual formation as one conscience and one sole will. Not a race, nor a geographically determined region, but as a community historically perpetuating itself, a multitude unified by a single idea, which is the will to existence and to power: consciousness of itself, personality.

10. This higher personality is truly the nation in so far as it is the State. It is not the nation that generates the State, as according to the old naturalistic concept which served as the basis of the political

theories of the national States of the nineteenth century. Rather the nation is created by the State, which gives to the people, conscious of its own moral unity, a will and therefore an effective existence. The right of a nation to independence derives not from a literary and ideal consciousness of its own being, still less from a more or less unconscious and inert acceptance of a *de facto* situation, but from an active consciousness, from a political will in action and ready to demonstrate its own rights: that is to say, from a state already coming into being. The State, in fact, as the universal ethical will, is the creator of right.

11. The nation as the State is an ethical reality which exists and lives in so far as it develops. To arrest its development is to kill it. Therefore the State is not only the authority which governs and gives the form of laws and the value of spiritual life to the wills of individuals, but it is also a power that makes its will felt abroad, making it known and respected, in other words, demonstrating the fact of its universality in all the necessary directions of its development. It is consequently organization and expansion, at least virtually. Thus it can be likened to the human will which knows no limits to its development and realizes itself in testing its own limitlessness.

12. The Fascist State, the highest and most powerful form of personality, is a force, but a spiritual force, which takes over all the forms of the moral and intellectual life of man. It cannot therefore confine itself simply to the functions of order and supervision as Liberalism desired. It is not simply a mechanism which limits the sphere of the supposed liberties of the individual. It is the form, the inner standard and the discipline of the whole person; it saturates the will as well as the intelligence. Its principle, the central inspiration of the human personality living in the civil community, pierces into the depths and makes its home in the heart of the man of action as well as of the thinker, of the artist as well as of the scientist: it is the soul of the soul.

13. Fascism, in short, is not only the giver of laws and the founder of institutions, but the educator and promoter of spiritual life. It wants to remake, not the forms of human life, but its content, man, character, faith. And to this end it requires discipline and authority that can enter into the spirits of men and there govern unopposed. Its sign, therefore, is the Lictors' rods, the symbol of unity, of strength and justice.

(ii) Political and Social Doctrine

1. When in the now distant March of 1919 I summoned to Milan, through the columns of the *Popolo d' Italia,* my surviving supporters who had followed me since the constitution of the Fasces of Revolutionary Action, founded in January 1915, there was no specific doctrinal plan in my mind. I had known and lived through only one doctrine, that of the Socialism of 1903-4 up to the winter of 1914, almost ten years. My experience in this had been that of a follower and of a leader, but not that of a theoretician. My doctrine, even in that period, had been a doctrine of action. An unequivocal Socialism, universally accepted, did not exist after 1905, when the Revisionist Movement began in Germany under Bernstein and there was formed in opposition to that, in the see-saw of tendencies, an extreme revolutionary movement, which in Italy never emerged from the condition of mere words, whilst in Russian Socialism it was the prelude to Bolshevism. Reform, Revolution, Centralization—even the echoes of the terminology are now spent; whilst in the great river of Fascism are to be found the streams which had their source in Sorel, Peguy, in the Lagardelle of the *Mouvement Socialiste* and the groups of Italian Syndicalists, who between 1904 and 1914 brought a note of novelty into Italian Socialism, which by that time had been devitalized and drugged by fornication with Giolitti, in *Pagine Libere* of Olivetti, *La Lupa* of Orano and *Divenire Sociale* of Enrico Leone.

In 1919, at the end of the War, Socialism as a doctrine was already dead: it existed only as hatred, it had still only one possibility, especially in Italy, that of revenge against those who had wished for the War and who should be made to expiate it. The *Popolo d' Italia* expressed it in its sub-title—"The Newspaper of Combatants and Producers." The word "producers" was already the expression of a tendency. Fascism was not given out to the wet nurse of a doctrine elaborated beforehand round a table: it was born of the need for action; it was not a party, but in its first two years it was a movement against all parties. The name which I gave to the organization defined its characteristics. Nevertheless, whoever rereads, in the now crumpled pages of the time, the account of the constituent assembly of the *Fasci italiani di Combattimento* will not find a doctrine, but a series of suggestions, of anticipations, of admonitions, which when freed from the inevitable vein of contingency, were destined later, after a few years, to develop into a series of doctrinal attitudes which made of Fascism a self-sufficient political doctrine able to face all others, both past and present. "If the bourgeoisie," I said at that time, "thinks to find in us a lightning-conductor, it is mistaken. We must go forward in opposition to Labor. . . . We want to accustom the working classes to being under a leader, to convince them also that it is not easy to direct an industry or a commercial undertaking successfully. . . . We shall fight against technical and spiritual retrogression. . . . The successors of the present regime still being undecided, we must not be unwilling to fight for it. We must hasten; when the present regime is superseded, we must be the ones to take its place. The right of succession belongs to us because we pushed the country into the War and we lead it to victory. The present method of political representation cannot be sufficient for us, we wish for a direct representation of individual interests. . . . It might be said against this programme that it is a return to the corporations. It doesn't matter! . . . I should like, nevertheless, the Assembly to accept the claims of national syndicalism from the point of view of economics. . . ."

It is not surprising that from the first day in the Piazza San Sepolcro there should resound the word "Corporation" which was destined in the course of the revolution to signify one of the legislative and social creations at the base of the regime?

2. The years preceding the March on Rome were years during which the necessity of action did not tolerate enquiries or complete elaborations of doctrine. Battles were being fought in the cities and villages. There were discussions, but—and this is more sacred and important—there were deaths. People knew how to die. The doctrine —beautiful, well-formed, divided into chapters and paragraphs and surrounded by a commentary—might be missing; but there was present something more decisive to supplant it—Faith. Nevertheless, he who recalls the past with the aid of books, articles, votes in Parliament, the major and the minor speeches, he who knows how to investigate and weigh evidence, will find that the foundations of the doctrine were laid while the battle was raging. It was precisely in these years that Fascist thought armed itself, refined itself, moving towards one organization of its own. The problems of the individual and the State; the problems of authority and liberty; political and social problems and those more specifically national; the struggle against liberal, democratic, socialist, Masonic, demagogic doctrines was carried on at the same time as the "punitive expeditions." But since

the "system" was lacking, adversaries ingenuously denied that Fascism had any power to make a doctrine of its own, while the doctrine rose up, even though tumultuously, at first under the aspect of a violent and dogmatic negation, as happens to all ideas that break new ground, then under the positive aspect of a constructive policy which, during the years 1926, 1927, 1928, was realized in the laws and institutions of the regime.

Fascism is today clearly defined not only as a regime but as a doctrine. And I mean by this that Fascism today, self-critical as well as critical of other movements, has an unequivocal point of view of its own, a criterion, and hence an aim, in face of all the material and intellectual problems which oppress the people of the world.

3. Above all, Fascism, in so far as it considers and observes the future and the development of humanity quite apart from the political considerations of the moment, believes neither in the possibility nor in the utility of perptual peace. It thus repudiates the doctrine of Pacifism—born of a renunciation of the struggle and an act of cowardice in the face of sacrifice. War alone brings up to their highest tension all human energies and puts the stamp of nobility upon the peoples who have the courage to meet it. All other trials are substitutes, which never really put a man in front of himself in the alternative of life and death. A doctrine, therefore, which begins with a prejudice in favor of peace is foreign to Fascism; as are foreign to the spirit of Fascism, even though acceptable by reason of the utility which they might have in given political situations, all internationalistic and socialistic systems which, as history proves, can be blown to the winds when emotional, idealistic and practical movements storm the hearts of peoples. Fascism carries over this anti-pacifist spirit even into the lives of individuals. The proud motto of the *Squadrista, "Me ne frego,"* written on the bandages of a wound is an act of philosophy which is not only stoical, it is the epitome of a doctrine that is not only political: it is education for combat, the acceptance of the risks which it brings; it is a new way of life for Italy. Thus the Fascist accepts and loves life, he knows nothing of suicide and despises it; he looks on life as duty, ascent, conquest: life which must be noble and full: lived for oneself, but above all for those others near and far away, present and future.

4. The "demographic" policy of the regime follows from these premises. Even the Fascist does in fact love his neighbor, but this "neighbor" is not for him a vague and ill-defined concept; love for

one's neighbor does not exclude necessary educational severities, and still less differentiations and distances. Fascism rejects universal concord, and, since it lives in the community of civilized peoples, it keeps them vigilantly and suspiciously before its eyes, it follows their states of mind and the changes in their interests and it does not let itself be deceived by temporary and fallacious appearances.

5. Such a conception of life makes Fascism the precise negation of that doctrine which formed the basis of the so-called Scientific or Marxian Socialism: the doctrine of historical Materialism, according to which the history of human civilizations can be explained only as the struggle of interest between the different social groups and as arising out of change in the means and instruments of production. That economic improvements—discoveries of raw materials, new methods of work, scientific inventions—should have an importance of their own, no one denies, but that they should suffice to explain human history to the exclusion of all other factors is absurd: Fascism believes, now and always, in holiness and in heroism, that is in acts in which no economic motive—remote or immediate—plays a part. With this negation of historical materialism, according to which men would be only by-products of history, who appear and disappear on the surface of the waves while in the depths the real directive forces are at work, there is also denied the immutable and irreparable "class struggle" which is the natural product of this economic conception of history, and above all it is denied that the class struggle can be the primary agent of social changes. Socialism, being thus wounded in these two primary tenets of its doctrine, nothing of it is left save the sentimental aspiration—old as humanity—towards a social order in which the sufferings and the pains of the humblest folk could be alleviated. But here Fascism rejects the concept of an economic "happiness" which would be realized socialistically and almost automatically at a given moment of economic evolution by assuring to all a maximum prosperity. Fascism denies the possibility of the materialistic conception of "happiness" and leaves it to the economists of the first half of the eighteenth century; it denies, that is, the equation of prosperity with happiness, which would transform men into animals with one sole preoccupation: that of being well-fed and fat, degraded in consequence to a merely physical existence.

6. After Socialism, Fascism attacks the whole complex of democratic ideologies and rejects them both in their theoretical premises and in their applications or practical manifestations. Fascism denies

that the majority, through the mere fact of being a majority, can rule human societies; it denies that this majority can govern by means of a periodical consultation; it affirms the irremediable, fruitful and beneficent inequality of men, who cannot be leveled by such a mechanical and extrinsic fact as universal suffrage. By democratic regimes we mean those in which from time to time the people is given the illusion of being sovereign, while true effective sovereignty lies in other, perhaps irresponsible and secret, forces. Democracy is a regime without a king, but with very many kings, perhaps more exclusive, tyrannical and violent than one king even though a tyrant. This explains why Fascism, although before 1922 for reasons of expediency it made a gesture of republicanism, renounced it before the March on Rome, convinced that the question of the political forms of a State is not preeminent to-day, and that studying past and present monarchies, past and present Republics it becomes clear that monarchy and republic are not to be judged *sub specie aeternitatis,* but represent forms in which the political evolution, the history, the tradition, the psychology of a given country are manifested. Now Fascism overcomes the antithesis between monarchy and republic which retarded the movements of democracy, burdening the former with every defect and defending the latter as the regime of perfection. Now it has been seen that there are inherently reactionary and absolutistic republics, and monarchies that welcome the most daring political and social innovations.

7. "Reason, Science," said Renan (who was inspired before Fascism existed) in one of his philosophical Meditations, "are products of humanity, but to expect reason directly from the people and through the people is a chimera. It is not necessary for the existence of reason that everybody should know it. In any case, if such an initiation should be made, it would not be made by means of base democracy, which apparently must lead to the extinction of every difficult culture, and every higher discipline. The principle that society exists only for the prosperity and the liberty of the individuals who compose it does not seem to conform with the plans of nature, plans in which the species alone is taken into consideration and the individual seems to be sacrificed. It is strongly to be feared lest the last word of democracy thus understood (I hasten to say that it can also be understood in other ways) would be a social state in which a degenerate mass would have no other care than to enjoy the ignoble pleasures of vulgar men."

Thus far Renan. Fascism rejects in democracy the absurd conventional lie of political equalitarianism clothed in the dress of collective irresponsibility and the myth of happiness and indefinite progress. But if democracy can be understood in other ways, that is, if democracy means not to relegate the people to the periphery of the State, then Fascism could be defined as an "organized, centralized, authoritarian democracy."

8. In face of Liberal doctrines, Fascism takes up an attitude of absolute opposition both in the field of politics and in that of economics. It is not necessary to exaggerate—merely for the purpose of present controversies—the importance of Liberalism in the past century, and to make of that which was one of the numerous doctrines sketched in that century a religion of humanity for all times, present and future. Liberalism flourished for no more than some fifteen years. It was born in 1830, as a reaction against the Holy Alliance that wished to drag Europe back to what it had been before 1789, and it had its year of splendor in 1848 when even Pius IX was a Liberal. Immediately afterwards the decay set in. If 1848 was a year of light and of poetry, 1849 was a year of darkness and of tragedy. The Republic of Rome was destroyed by another Republic, that of France. In the same year Marx launched the gospel of the religion of Socialism with the famous *Communist Manifesto*. In 1851 Napoleon III carried out his unliberal *coup d'état* and ruled over France until 1870, when he was dethroned by a popular revolt, but as a consequence of a military defeat which ranks among the most resounding that history can relate. The victor was Bismarck, who never knew the home of the religion of liberty or who were its prophets. It is symptomatic that a people of high culture like the Germans should have been completely ignorant of the religion of liberty during the whole of the nineteenth century. It was, there, no more than a parenthesis, represented by what has been called the "ridiculous Parliament of Frankfort" which lasted only a season. Germany has achieved her national unity outside the doctrines of Liberalism, against Liberalism, a doctrine which seems foreign to the German soul, a soul essentially monarchical, while Liberalism is the historical and logical beginning of anarchism. The stages of German unity are the three wars of 1864, 1866 and 1870, conducted by "Liberals" like Moltke and Bismarck. As for Italian unity, Liberalism has had in it a part absolutely inferior to the share of Mazzini and of Garibaldi, who were not Liberals. Without the intervention of the unliberal Napoleon we

should not have gained Lombardy, and without the help of the un-liberal Bismarck at Sadowa and Sedan, very probably we should not have gained Venice in 1866; and in 1870 we should not have entered Rome. From 1870-1915 there occurs the period in which the very priests of the new creed had to confess the twilight of their religion: defeated as it was by decadence in literature, by activism in practice. Activism: that is to say, Nationalism, Futurism, Fascism. The "Liberal" century, after having accumulated an infinity of Gordian knots, tried to untie them by the hecatomb of the World War. Never before has any religion imposed such a cruel sacrifice. Were the gods of Liberalism thirsty for blood? Now Liberalism is about to close the doors of its deserted temples because the peoples feel that its agnosticism in economics, its indifferentism in politics and in morals, would lead, as they have led, the States to certain ruin. In this way one can understand why all the political experiences of the con-temporary world are anti-Liberal, and it is supremely ridiculous to wish on that account to class them outside of history; as if history were a hunting ground reserved to Liberalism and its professors, as if Liberalism were the definitive and no longer surpassable message of civilization.

9. But the Fascist repudiations of Socialism, Democracy, Liberal-ism must not make one think that Fascism wishes to make the world return to what it was before 1789, the year which has been indicated as the year of the beginning of the liberal-democratic age. One does not go backwards. The Fascist doctrine has not chosen De Maistre as its prophet. Monarchical absolutism is a thing of the past and so also is every theocracy. So also feudal privileges and division into im-penetrable and isolated castes have had their day. The theory of Fascist authority has nothing to do with the police State. A party that governs a nation in a totalitarian way is a new fact in history. References and comparisons are not possible. Fascism takes over from the ruins of Liberal Socialistic democratic doctrines those elements which still have a living value. It preserves those that can be called the established facts of history, it rejects all the rest, that is to say the idea of a doctrine which holds good for all times and all peoples. If it is admitted that the nineteenth century has been the century of Socialism, Liberalism and Democracy, it does not follow that the twentieth must also be the century of Liberalism, Socialism and Democracy. Political doctrines pass; peoples remain. It is to be expected that this century may be that of authority, a century of the

"Right," a Fascist century. If the nineteenth was the century of the individual (Liberalism means individualism) it may be expected that this one may be the century of "collectivism" and therefore the century of the State. That a new doctrine should use the still vital elements of other doctrines is perfectly logical. No doctrine is born quite new, shining, never before seen. No doctrine can boast of an absolute "originality." It is bound, even if only historically, to other doctrines that have been, and to develop into other doctrines that will be. Thus the scientific socialism of Marx is bound to the Utopian Socialism of the Fouriers, the Owens and the Saint-Simons; thus the Liberalism of the nineteenth century is connected with the whole "Enlightenment" of the eighteenth century. Thus the doctrines of democracy are bound to the *Encyclopédie*. Every doctrine tends to direct the activity of men towards a determined objective; but the activity of man reacts upon the doctrine, transforms it, adapts it to new necessities or transcends it. The doctrine itself, therefore, must be, not words, but an act of life. Hence, the pragmatic veins in Fascism, its will to power, its will to be, its attitude in the face of the fact of "violence" and of its own courage.

10. The keystone of Fascist doctrine is the conception of the State, of its essence, of its tasks, of its ends. For Fascism the State is an absolute before which individuals and groups are relative. Individuals and groups are "thinkable" in so far as they are within the State. The Liberal State does not direct the interplay and the material and spiritual development of the groups, but limits itself to registering the results; the Fascist State has a consciousness of its own, a will of its own, on this account it is called an "ethical" State. In 1929, at the first quinquennial assembly of the regime, I said: "For Fascism, the State is not the night-watchman who is concerned only with the personal security of the citizens; nor is it an organization for purely material ends, such as that of guaranteeing a certain degree of prosperity and a relatively peaceful social order, to achieve which a council of administration would be sufficient, nor is it a creation of mere politics with no contact with the material and complex reality of the lives of individuals and the life of peoples. The State, as conceived by Fascism and as it acts, is a spiritual and moral fact because it makes concrete the political, juridical, economic organization of the nation and such an organization is, in its origin and in its development, a manifestation of the spirit. The State is the guarantor of internal and external security, but it is also the guardian and the transmitter of

the spirit of the people as it has been elaborated through the centuries in language, custom, faith. The State is not only present, it is also past, and above all future. It is the State which, transcending the brief limit of individual lives, represents the immanent conscience of the nation. The forms in which States express themselves change, but the necessity of the State remains. It is the State which educates citizens for civic virtue, makes them conscious of their mission, calls them to unity; harmonizes their interests in justice; hands on the achievements of thought in the sciences, the arts, in law, in human solidarity; it carries men from the elementary life of the tribe to the highest human expression of power which is Empire; it entrusts to the ages the names of those who died for its integrity or in obedience to its laws; it puts forward as an example and recommends to the generations that are to come the leaders who increased its territory and the men of genius who gave it glory. When the sense of the State declines and the disintegrating and centrifugal tendencies of individuals and groups prevail, national societies move to their decline."

11. From 1929 up to the present day these doctrinal positions have been strengthened by the whole economico-political evolution of the world. It is the State alone that grows in size, in power. It is the State alone that can solve the dramatic contradictions of capitalism. What is called the crisis cannot be overcome except by the State, within the State. Where are the shades of the Jules Simons who, at the dawn of liberalism, proclaimed that "the State must strive to render itself unnecessary and to prepare for its demise"; of the MacCullochs who, in the second half of the last century, affirmed that the State must abstain from too much governing? And faced with the continual, necessary and inevitable interventions of the State in economic affairs what would the Englishman Bentham now say, according to whom industry should have asked of the State only to be left in peace? Or the German Humboldt, according to whom the "idle" State must be considered the best? It is true that the second generation of liberal economists was less extremist than the first, and already Smith himself opened, even though cautiously, the door to State intervention in economics. But when one says liberalism, one says the individual; when one says Fascism, one says the State. But the Fascist State is unique; it is an original creation. It is not reactionary, but revolutionary in that it anticipates the solutions of certain universal problems. These problems are no longer seen in the same light: in the sphere of politics they are removed from party

rivalries, from the supreme power of parliament, from the irresponsibility of assemblies; in the sphere of economics they are removed from the sphere of the syndicates' activities—activities that were ever widening their scope and increasing their power both on the workers' side and on the employers'—removed from their struggles and their designs; in the moral sphere they are divorced from ideas of the need for order, discipline and obedience, and lifted into the plane of the moral commandments of the fatherland. Fascism desires the State to be strong, organic and at the same time founded on a wide popular basis. The Fascist State has also claimed for itself the field of economics and, through the corporative, social and educational institutions which it has created, the meaning of the State reaches out to and includes the farthest off-shoots; and within the State, framed in their respective organizations, there revolve all the political, economic and spiritual forces of the nation. A State founded on millions of individuals who recognize it, feel it, are ready to serve it, is not the tyrannical State of the medieval lord. It has nothing in common with the absolutist States that existed either before or after 1789. In the Fascist State the individual is not suppressed, but rather multiplied, just as in a regiment a soldier is not weakened but multiplied by the number of his comrades. The Fascist State organizes the nation, but it leaves sufficient scope to individuals; it has limited useless or harmful liberties and has preserved those that are essential. It cannot be the individual who decides in this matter, but only the State.

12. The Fascist State does not remain indifferent to the fact of religion in general and to that particular positive religion which is Italian Catholicism. The State has no theology, but it has an ethic. In the Fascist State religion is looked upon as one of the deepest manifestations of the spirit; it is, therefore, not only respected, but defended and protected. The Fascist State does not create a "God" of its own, as Robespierre once, at the height of the Convention's foolishness, wished to do; nor does it vainly seek, like Bolshevism, to expel religion from the minds of men; Fascism respects the God of the ascetics, of the saints, of the heroes, and also God as seen and prayed to by the simple and primitive heart of the people.

13. The Fascist State is a will to power and to government. In it the tradition of Rome is an idea that has force. In the doctrine of Fascism Empire is not only a territorial, military or mercantile expression, but spiritual or moral. One can think of an empire, that is to

say a nation that directly or indirectly leads other nations, without needing to conquer a single square kilometer of territory. For Fascism the tendency to Empire, that is to say, to the expansion of nations, is a manifestation of vitality; its opposite, staying at home, is a sign of decadence: peoples who rise or re-rise are imperialist, peoples who die are renunciatory. Fascism is the doctrine that is most fitted to represent the aims, the states of mind, of a people, like the Italian people, rising again after many centuries of abandonment or slavery to foreigners. But Empire calls for discipline, coordination of forces, duty and sacrifice; this explains many aspects of the practical working of the regime and the direction of many of the forces of the State and the necessary severity shown to those who would wish to oppose this spontaneous and destined impulse of the Italy of the twentieth century, to oppose it in the name of the superseded ideologies of the nineteenth, repudiated wherever great experiments of political and social transformation have been courageously attempted: especially where, as now, peoples thirst for authority, for leadership, for order. If every age has its own doctrine, it is apparent from a thousand signs that the doctrine of the present age is Fascism. That it is a doctrine of life is shown by the fact that it has resuscitated a faith. That this faith has conquered minds is proved by the fact that Fascism has had its dead and its martyrs.

Fascism henceforward has in the world the universality of all of those doctrines which, by fulfilling themselves, have significance in the history of the human spirit.

42. GIOVANNI GENTILE

Giovanni Gentile (1875-1944) was a Neo-Hegelian philosopher and one of the leaders of intellectual affairs in pre-fascist Italy. He became Minister of Education in the Mussolini government, and the chief fascist theoretician. The following passage underscores the totalitarian and anti-intellectual character of the fascist philosophy.

The Philosophic Basis of Fascism*

. . . In the definition of Fascism, the first point to grasp is the comprehensive, or as Fascists say, the "totalitarian" scope of its doctrine, which concerns itself not only with political organization and political tendency, but with the whole will and thought and feeling of the nation.

There is a second and equally important point. Fascism is not a philosophy. Much less is it a religion. It is not even a political theory which may be stated in a series of formulae. The significance of Fascism is not to be grasped in the special theses which it from time to time assumes. When on occasion it has announced a program, a goal, a concept to be realized in action, Fascism has not hesitated to abandon them when in practice these were found to be inadequate or inconsistent with the principle of Fascism. Fascism has never been willing to compromise its future. Mussolini has boasted that he is a *tempista,* that his real pride is in "good timing." He makes decisions and acts on them at the precise moment when all the conditions and considerations which make them feasible and opportune are properly matured. This is a way of saying that Fascism returns to the most rigorous meaning of Mazzini's "Thought and Action," whereby the two terms are so perfectly coincident that no thought has value which is not already expressed in action. The real "views" of the *Duce* are those which he formulates and executes at one and the same time.

Is Fascism therefore "anti-intellectual," as has been so often charged? It is eminently anti-intellectual, eminently Mazzinian, that is, if by intellectualism we mean the divorce of thought from action, of knowledge from life, of brain from heart, of theory from practice. Fascism is hostile to all Utopian systems which are destined never to face the test of reality. It is hostile to all science and all philosophy which remain matters of mere fancy or intelligence. It is not that Fascism denies value to culture, to the higher intellectual pursuits by which thought is invigorated as a source of action. Fascist anti-intellectualism holds in scorn a product peculiarly typical of the educated classes in Italy: the *leterato*—the man who plays with knowledge

* From G. Gentile, *The Philosophic Basis of Fascism,* 1928. Reprinted from *Readings on Fascism and National Socialism,* selected by members of the philosophy department of the University of Colorado, by permission of the publisher. Alan Swallow, Denver.

and with thought without any sense of responsibility for the practical world. It is hostile not so much to culture as to bad culture, the culture which does not educate, which does not make men, but rather creates pedants and aesthetes, egotists in a word, men morally and politically indifferent. It has no use, for instance, for the man who is "above the conflict" when his country or its important interests are at stake.

By virtue of its repugnance for "intellectualism," Fascism prefers not to waste time constructing abstract theories about itself. But when we say that it is not a system or a doctrine we must not conclude that it is a blind praxis or a purely instinctive method. If by system or philosophy we mean a living thought, a principle of universal character daily revealing its inner fertility and significance, then Fascism is a perfect system, with a solidly established foundation and with a rigorous logic in its development; and all who feel the truth and the vitality of the principle work day by day for its development, now doing, now undoing, now going forward, now retracing their steps, according as the things they do prove to be in harmony with the principle or to deviate from it.

And we come finally to a third point.

The Fascist system is not a political system, but it has its center of gravity in politics. Fascism came into being to meet serious problems of politics in post-war Italy. And it presents itself as a political method. But in confronting and solving political problems it is carried by its very nature, that is to say by its method, to consider moral, religious, and philosophical questions and to unfold and demonstrate the comprehensive totalitarian character peculiar to it. It is only after we have grasped the political character of the Fascist principle that we are able adequately to appreciate the deeper concept of life which underlies that principle and from which the principle springs. The political doctrine of Fascism is not the whole of Fascism. It is rather its more prominent aspect and in general its most interesting one.

The politic of Fascism revolves wholly about the concept of the national State; and accordingly it has points of contact with nationalist doctrines, along with distinctions from the latter which it is important to bear in mind.

Both Fascism and nationalism regard the State as the foundation of all rights and the source of all values in the individuals composing it. For the one as for the other the State is not a consequence—it is a principle. But in the case of nationalism, the relation which individualistic liberalism, and for that matter socialism also, assumed between individual and State is inverted. Since the State is a principle, the individual becomes a consequence—he is something which finds an antecedent in the State: the State limits him and determines his manner of existence, restricting his freedom, binding him to a piece of ground whereon he was born, whereon he must live and will die. In the case of Fascism, State and individual are one and the same things, or rather, they are inseparable terms of a necessary synthesis.

Nationalism, in fact, founds the State on the concept of nation, the nation being an entity which transcends the will and the life of the individual because it is conceived as objectively existing apart from the consciousness of individuals, existing even if the individual does nothing to bring it into being. For the nationalist, the nation exists not by virtue of the citizen's will, but as datum, a fact, of nature.

For Fascism, on the contrary, the State is a wholly spiritual creation. It is a national State, because, from the Fascist point of view, the nation itself is a creation of the mind and is not a material presupposition, is not a datum of nature. The nation, says the Fascist, is never really made; neither, therefore, can the State attain an absolute form, since it is merely the nation in the latter's concrete, political manifestation. For the Fascist, the State is always *in fieri*. It is in our hands, wholly; whence our very serious responsibility towards it.

But this State of the Fascists which is created by the consciousness and the will of the citizen, and is not a force descending on the citizen from above or from without, cannot have toward the mass of the population the relationship which was presumed by nationalism.

Nationalism identified State with Nation, and made of the nation an entity preëxisting, which needed not to be created but merely to be recognized or known. The nationalists, therefore, required a ruling class of an intellectual character, which was conscious of the nation and could understand, appreciate and exalt it. The authority of the State, furthermore, was not a product but a presupposition. It could not depend on the people—rather the people depended on the State and on the State's authority as the source of the life which they lived and apart from which they could not live. The nationalistic State was, therefore, an aristocratic State, enforcing itself upon the masses through the power conferred upon it by its origins.

The Fascist State, on the contrary, is a people's state, and, as such, the democratic State *par excellence*. The relationship between State and citizen (not this or that citizen, but all citizens) is accordingly so intimate that the State exists only as, and in so far as, the citizen causes it to exist. Its formation therefore is the formation of a consciousness of it in individuals, in the masses. Hence the need of the Party, and of all the instruments of propaganda and education which Fascism uses to make the thought and will of the *Duce* the thought and will of the masses. Hence the enormous task which Fascism sets itself in trying to bring the whole mass of the people, beginning with the little children, inside the fold of the Party.

On the popular character of the Fascist State likewise depends its greatest social and constitutional reform—the foundation of the Corporations of Syndicates. In this reform Fascism took over from syndicalism the notion of the moral and educational function of the syndicate. But the Corporations of Syndicates were necessary in order to reduce the syndicates to State discipline and make them an expression of the State's organism from within. The Corporations of Syndicates are a device through which the Fascist State goes looking for the individual in order to create itself through the individual's will. But the individual it seeks is not the abstract political individual whom the old liberalism took for granted. He is the only individual who can ever be found, the individual who exists as a specialized productive force, and who, by the fact of his specialization, is brought to unite with other individuals of his same category and comes to belong with them to the one great economic unit which is none other than the nation.

This great reform is already well under way. Toward it nationalism, syndicalism, and even liberalism itself, were already tending in the past. For even liberalism was beginning to criticize the older forms of political representation, seeking some system of organic representation which would correspond to the structural reality of the State.

The Fascist conception of liberty merits passing notice. The *Duce* of Fascism once chose to discuss the theme of "Force or consent?"; and he concluded that the two terms are inseparable, that the one implies the other and cannot exist apart from the other; that, in other words, the authority of the State and the freedom of the citizen constitute a continuous circle wherein authority presupposes liberty and liberty authority. For freedom can exist only within the State, and the State means authority. But the State is not an entity hovering in the air over the heads of its citizens. It is one with the personality of the citizen. Fascism, indeed, envisages the contrast not as between liberty and authority, but as between a true, a concrete liberty which exists, and an abstract, illusory liberty which cannot exist.

Liberalism broke the circle above referred to, setting the individual against the State and liberty against authority. What the liberal desired was liberty as against the State, a liberty which was a limitation of the State; though the liberal had to resign himself, as the lesser of the evils, to a State which was a limitation on liberty. The absurdities inherent in the liberal concept of freedom were apparent to liberals themselves early in the Nineteenth Century. It is no merit of Fascism to have again indicated them. Fascism has its own solution of the paradox of liberty and authority. The authority of the State is absolute. It does not compromise, it does not bargain, it does not surrender any portion of its field to other moral or religious principles which may interfere with the individual conscience. But on the other hand, the State becomes a reality only in the consciousness of its individuals. And the Fascist corporative State supplies a representative system more sincere and more in touch with realities than any other previously devised and is therefore freer than the old liberal State.

43. MARIO PALMIERI

Mario Palmieri published The Philosophy of Fascism *in Chicago in 1936. Unlike the short essays and speeches of some Italian fascists, it is a volume of considerable scope. The following passages present the fascist position on some matters not touched upon in the preceding selections.*

Fascism and the Meaning of Life*

We must never forget that other civilizations of far greater significance than ours from the standpoint of spiritual achievements— the only true standard of comparison possible—have appeared on

* From M. Palmieri, *The Philosophy of Fascism,* 1936.

this earth, flowered forth in magnificent products of spiritual expression and disappeared again, engulfed in the shadows of oblivion and covered by few layers of sand or by the triumphant vegetation of the earth.

A new dark age is still possible, and it will dawn upon us soon enough unless we find again a meaning for life, a different purpose than the satisfaction of the senses, and, finally, a new goal for our efforts, nowadays so implacably frustrated by the emptiness, the vacuity, and the futility of the goal which we try so desperately and still so vainly to reach.

It is the possibility of such a Dark Age which Fascism is trying strenuously and successfully to stave off by teaching us anew the truth that we need to visualize and to worship a deeper reality lying behind and beyond the immediate and closely bound world of the self, if we want to find peace, achieve salvation and restore dignity and purpose to our life.

At this extremely critical time of our history, when the fate of a whole civilization is at stake, Fascism takes up once again the challenge and to the perplexing, ages-old query, it answers emphatically that life *has* a meaning, that it has a purpose and a goal, and that it has worth and dignity and beauty.

When we shall become aware that our individuality is truly and fully realized in those institutions and through those institutions called the Family, the Church, the Nation, and the State, then and only then, we shall realize the great significance and the deep import of the Fascist philosophy of life.

Fascism maintains in effect that the meaning of life is found only in the realization of a full life of the Spirit; that this realization in turn is achieved only when the individual's spiritual needs, aspirations and longings are rooted, integrated and nurtured in the Family, the Church, the Nation and the State; that these institutions, forming the framework of all life of the Spirit, enjoy in turn an existence of their own: timeless and absolute, whose essence partakes of the Spirit itself and is not contingent upon the Will and the actions of man.

In the Fascist philosophy of life Man first rises to the capacity of a true spiritual being when in the Family he finds something in which and through which he can express and realize his first spiritual needs —then in the church, an institution which offers him a new outlet for those spiritual needs not satisfied by the Family. Next, in the Nation, he finds something which expresses the fundamental continuity of his human experience within determinate limits of space, and the fundamental unity which is at the very root of life. Finally, in the State he finds an organism which gives ample scope to the expression of his spiritual life, an organism born of the conscious act of restricting, of his own free will, the full play of his activity and the full extent of his freedom; to allow his own rights, his own liberties, his own opportunities, to those fellow beings bound by the same laws, the same duties, the same authority.

The Family, the Church, the Nation, the State, these are the four cardinal points of the life of man; through them this life can flower forth in an expression of great spiritual achievement; denying them it can only revert to a state of satisfied animal wants unworthy of the name of human. . . .

In conclusion, if man, to achieve salvation, must be led anew to visualize and worship a deeper reality than the immediate and closely bound world of the self, there is one way, and one way only to lead him to the goal, says Fascism, and that way is through the renewed cult of the Family, the Church, the Nation and the State.

This cult will give anew a meaning to life; with this cult life will again find a purpose; through this cult life will finally reach its far off, magnificent goal which is nothing less than the spiritualization of man.

Fascism and the Conduct of Life

The conduct of life must rest upon three great, unalterable principles—Fascism maintains—namely: the principle of Unity, the principle of Authority and the principle of Duty.

One invisible tie binds together the destinies of all the people of one nation. There cannot be any joy or any pain experienced by one single individual, any good or any evil befallen to him which shall not ultimately affect the welfare of the whole nation.

This is the first principle of the Fascist conduct of life, and one whose consequences prove to be the most far-reaching in the life of a nation.

If we have found always, says Fascism, such shifting grounds for the foundations of a durable and satisfactory social life, it is simply because we have forgotten that the good of the whole cannot be dependent upon the material welfare of the individual, that the very life of the individual is dependent upon and is part of the life of an entity much greater and of far deeper meaning than his small ego, namely, the nation of which he is an integral part and which constitutes for him the supreme essence of the race.

Never before, to be sure, had a social and political system advanced such claims upon the inner world of man as this claim of Fascism to determine for him the forms of conduct; never before has that regeneration of social and political life, always dreamed, never effectuated, been so close to realization.

The first principle of the Fascist conduct of life rests upon a mystic belief of the oneness of all living beings; the second principle, the principle of Authority, rests upon another mystic belief: that of the divine essence of the hero. Not the military hero, but hero in the sense meant by Carlyle: hero of the soul.

> Find in any country the ablest man that exists there, raise him to the supreme place and loyalty, reverence him, you have a perfect government for that country; no ballot box, parliamentary eloquence, voting, constitution building or other machinery whatsoever can improve it a whit. It is the perfect State, the ideal Country.

Thus spoke Carlyle in his lecture on the hero as king, delivered the twenty-second of May, 1840. And his words are no less true today than they were a hundred years ago. Nay, still closer to the truth, if that could be possible, and true in a still deeper sense than Carlyle ever thought. Because the ultimate reality of the Universe which lies behind and beyond the deceiving realm of appearances, does not reveal itself indiscriminately and equally to all men.

There is Man in the abstract as a thinking and spiritual being; there are men in the concrete gifted in various degrees with the gifts of these divine elements of thought and soul.

We are all partakers of the divine, but the hero among us is partaker of it in a fuller measure than all. He is in a more direct, more immediate relationship with the fountain-head of all knowledge, all wisdom, all love. What he sees in life we do not see, and it is even useless for us to strive toward a better comprehension of life, a better understanding of nature, because we shall never be able to render asunder the veil of mystery shrouding the ultimate aspect of reality.

Vainly we strive through observation, experimentation, analysis, logic, to reach the core of being. The highest truths are hidden from us. Only that magic flash of a moment of supreme intuition, that flash which renders for an instant man akin to God, can reveal the Truth. And we shall never know the ecstasy of that moment. The supreme gifts of synthesis, intuition, revelation, are denied to us; they belong rightly to the hero and to none other.

And if there is no hero in a country, darkness is upon the land; the darkness originating from the confusion of conflicting ideas, conflicting beliefs, conflicting wills.

It can be realized then at once how utterly impossible it is to conciliate such an article of faith with a naive belief in the wisdom of the mass, the leadership of the many, the supreme worth of Democracy.

The day may come, perhaps, and we all sincerely hope and pray for it, when all men will be heroes, but at the present stage of human evolution, let only the greatest among the great rule and govern, because he sees deeper and further than we shall ever be able to see, because he knows what we shall never be able to know, because he is a gift from God.

But if the principle of Authority recognizes that ultimately there must be a supreme power, it is, nevertheless, not completely exhausted by this recognition. Fascism holds, in fact, that the State must be a social, political, economic, moral and religious organism built as a pyramid at whose vertex is the national hero, the greatest man of his time and his nation, and leading to this national hero by an uninterrupted series of continuously widening powers arranged in hierarchies.

The hierarchy becomes thus the very essence of Authority and the hierarchical arrangement of Society its truest expression in the world of man.

All the recognition of a man's worth is expressed in the place he occupies in the hierarchy; all the functions of a man's social and political life are contained in the functions he must fulfill as a member of the hierarchy.

No man is an outcast in the social system of Fascism, no man is worthless; no man, that is, who belongs to the Fascist nation and to its life.

It is, therefore, not the smallest title of glory of Fascism to have brought about this new realization of the fellowship of man at a time held, by common consent, to be a time of supreme and inevitable moral decadence.

But these two great principles of the unity of all human beings and of devotion to authority as expressed through a scale of human values, cannot be separated—Fascism holds—from the third and greatest principle of all: the principle of Duty.

And it is, perhaps, in this conception of duty as supreme motive power of the actions of man, and in the belief that such a conception can be transformed into living reality, that Fascism reveals most clearly the profound idealism underlying its philosophy. . . .

No more far reaching and revolutionary words than these were ever heard by the modern world:

> Right is the faith of the individual. Duty is the common collective faith. Right can but organize resistance; it may destroy, it cannot found. Duty builds up, associates and unites; it is derived from a general law, whereas, Right is derived only from human will. There is nothing therefore to forbid a struggle against Right; any individual may rebel against any right in another which is injurious to him; and the sole judge left between the adversaries is Force.
>
> Societies based upon Duty would not be compelled to have recourse to Force; Duty, once admitted as the rule excludes the possibility of struggle; and by rendering the individual subject to the general aim, it cuts at the very root of those evils which Right is unable to prevent, and only affects to cure.
>
> The doctrine of Rights puts an end to sacrifice and cancels martyrdom from the world; in every theory of individual rights, interests become the governing and motive power and martyrdom an absurdity, for what interests can endure beyond the tomb!

Life thus, as conceived by Fascism, is "serious, austere, religious, and its development takes place in a world sustained by the moral and responsible forces of the spirit."

This means, in turn, that to be a Fascist is, of all things, the most difficult in the world. He who subscribes to the doctrine of Fascism subscribes also to rules of conduct which make exacting claims upon his will to live a satisfactory sensual life. The life of the Fascist is a life of ascetic self-denial, heroic self-sacrifice, moral abnegation and religious enthusiasm.

The true Fascist works not for himself alone, but for his nation as well; believes not in a godless Universe, but in a universe which exists by the will of God; worships this God not as a remote, abstract entity having no intimate connection with his individual life, but as something from which he parted at birth, to which he can confidently appeal in life and which he shall rejoin at death; the true Fascist forsakes the realization of his rights for the fulfillment of his duties; strives to make of love an expression of the soul rather than an enjoyment of the senses; holds the unity of the family to be a sacred thing and monogamic marriage to be the supreme test and the true end of love; respects that hierarchical arrangement of society which, through successive stages, confers the primary Authority of divine origin to men invested with power to rule over their fellow beings; is willing to sacrifice his personal pleasure for the welfare of his brethren, willing to suffer for the welfare of his family, willing to die for the welfare of his country and, finally, the true Fascist is willing to forego all claims to personal freedom if these claims conflict with the realization of the true goal of life: the spiritualization of man.

Fascism and Liberty

The Fascist conception of life is so radically revolutionary in all its aspects as to justify an extended individual treatment of each one of these aspects in a detailed analysis.

As we have already seen, the general, all-embracing conception is that life is an expression of the soul, and, as such, flowering at its best only when its spiritual claims are fully recognized and satisfied.

Now the nature of these claims is such that they conflict inevitably with all the individual's egotistic aspirations, ambitions and desires.

The Fascist conception of life advances, therefore, demands upon the inner world of man, that the ordinary human being is wary to satisfy. It is from this contrast between the claims of the individual and the claims of the whole that the problem of Liberty arises. Because Fascism finds necessary, at the outset, to take away from the ordinary human being what he has been taught and has grown to cherish the most: personal liberty. And it can be affirmed, without falling into exaggeration, that a curtailment of personal liberty not only has proved to be, but must necessarily be, a fundamental condition of the triumph of Fascism.

Unfortunately, it is just due to such a curtailment that the greatest misunderstanding of Fascism has arisen in the world where personal liberty is made almost the paramount issue of life.

But Fascism holds that personal liberty is not an end to itself.

Personal liberty is simply a means to the realization of a much greater end: namely, the liberty of the Spirit; this last meaning the faculty of the human Soul of rising above the power of outward circumstances and inward needs to devote itself to the cult of those ideals which form the true goal of life.

Two radically different conceptions of Liberty are thus in conflict, and there is no hope that the abyss which separates them can ever be bridged.

In the Fascist conception, to be free, means to be no more a slave to one's own passions, ambitions or desires; means to be free to will what is true, and good and just, at all times, in all cases; means, in other words, to realize here in this world the true mission of man.

In the Individualistic conception, instead, to be free is . . . to follow the call of one's own nature; to worship one's own God; to think, to act, or to speak according to the dictates of one's own mind; to earn, to spend, to save or to hoard at will; to accumulate property and deed it following one's own whims or fancy; to reach all hedonistic goals; wealth, health, happiness or pleasure. In other words, to be unhindered by compulsions, restrictions, prohibitions, rules, codes and laws. . . .

What the Individualistic conception of Liberty implies is thus nothing less than freedom from all those external fetters born of the very fact that man is forced to live in a state of society; a state, that is, which makes fundamental claims over all forms of individual freedoms, a state which places iron-clad restrictions to that form of Liberty which would allow complete expression of his instincts, his desires and his needs. . . .

But it is a fact, a conclusively proved historical fact, that the ordinary human being *does not know* how to use his freedom, or rather he knows simply how to use it for the satisfaction of his instincts and desires.

And it is only because he finds himself compelled to live in a state of society that restrains him from bringing to its logical conclusion his assumption that the individual is the center of the whole universe.

All through the ages his life has been thus a sorry compromise between his desire to self expression and the need of curbing this desire if some kind of social life had to be realized at all.

It is high time, instead, says Fascism, that the individual be brought back to the vision of his true place in the universe; it is high time that he learns how to curb and master his self; it is high time that his freedom be taken away from him if he is to realize the greatest aim of life: the furtherance of the Spirit. . . .

According to Fascism, a true, a great spiritual life cannot take place unless the State has risen to a position of pre-eminence in the world of man. The curtailment of liberty thus becomes justified at once, with this need of raising the State to its rightful position.

As Giovanni Gentile says, in his book— "What is Fascism!"—

Liberty is, to be sure, the supreme end and aim of every human life, but insofar as personal and social education realize it by evoking this common will in the individual, it presents itself as law, and hence as the State. The maximum of liberty coincides with the maximum strength of the State.

. . . Liberty, therefore, cannot be concerned with the individual's claims, but must find its maximum concern in the fullest expression of the nation's life, and of the State which of such a life is the concrete realization. . . .

The Fascist State

Without State there is no Nation. These words reverse the commonly accepted principle of modern political science that without Nation there is no State. They seem at first to run counter to all evidence, but they represent, instead, for Fascism, the expression of a fundamental truth, one of those truths which are at the very basis of the social life of mankind.

To say, in fact, that in the State and through the State a Nation first rises to the consciousness of itself, means that the State gives to the people that political, social and moral unity without which there is no possibility of a true national life. Furthermore, the State is the only organ through which the anonymous will of the people can find the expression of will of a single personality, conscious of its aims, its purposes and its needs.

The State becomes thus invested with the dignity, the attributes and the power of an ethical personality which exists and lives, and develops and progresses or decays, and, finally dies.

Compared to this personality of the State with its characteristics of transcendent values and its problems of momentous magnitude, the personality of the single individual loses all of that importance which it had assumed in the modern times.

It is possible thus for a Fascist writer, G. Corso, to write:

> . . . the liberal idea, the democratic idea and the socialistic idea, start from the common presupposition that the individual must be free because only the individual is real. To such a conception Fascism opposes the other that the individual is to be considered as a highly transitory and apparent thing, when compared to the ethnic reality of the race, the spiritual reality of the Nation, the ethical reality of the State.

Or for Mussolini to state:

> . . . Liberalism denied the State in the interest of the particular individual; Fascism, instead reaffirms the State as the true reality of the individual.

In this shifting of emphasis from the individual to the State, the very functions of the one become part of the life of the other. The State must, therefore, concern itself not only with social order, political organization and economic problems, but with morality and religion as well.

The Fascist State is, in other words, not only the social, political and economic organization of the people of one nation, but is also the outward manifestation of their moral and religious life, and, as such, is therefore an Ethical State.

The Fascist State presupposes that man beside being an individual is also a social being, and therefore, willing and compelled to come under some form of disciplinary authority for the good of the whole.

It presupposes also that the highest law for man is the moral law, and that right or wrong, good or evil, have well defined meanings in this moral law and are beyond the pale of individual likes or dislikes or individual judgment.

It presupposes, finally, that the Nation-State is gifted with an organic life of its own, which far transcends in meaning the life of the individual, and whose development, growth and progress, follow laws which man cannot ignore or modify, but only discover and obey.

Henceforth the State is no longer a word denoting the authority underlying a complex system of relationships between individuals, classes, organizations, etc., but something of far greater import, far greater meaning than that: it is a living entity, it is the highest spiritual entity of the political world. . . .

To bring mankind back to the true vision of the relative worth of the individual and of the nation, that organism of which the single individual is an integral, although accidental and infinitesimal part, needs a truly superhuman effort.

Gone is forever the time when it was possible to find a way to the heart of man through his devotion to higher things than his personal affairs; gone is the time when it was possible to appeal to the mystic side of his nature through a religious commandment; gone, finally, is the time when it was possible to illuminate the reasoning powers of his mind with the light of ideals whose existence and whose reason of being cannot be proved through the powers of reason.

All that remains is an appeal to force, to compulsion; intellectual as well as physical, an appeal to what lies outside of man, to what he fears and with what he must of necessity abide.

Such a forceful appeal is made at present by Fascism which, compelling the elder or educating the younger, is slowly but surely bringing the Italian people to the comprehension of the worth, the beauty and the significance of the National Ideal.

But if the Fascist State is an Ethical State, it is also, and above all, a Sovereign State. Its power, therefore, is not conditional to the will of the people, the parliament, the King, or any other of its constituent elements: it is rather immanent in its very essence.

Once more we find Individualism with its offsprings: the liberal, democratic and radical doctrines, in antithetic contrast to Fascism on an issue of paramount importance for the whole world of man.

Passing from the Liberal doctrine, which had conceded the sovereignty of the State to the people as a whole, to the democratic doctrine, which this sovereignty gave away to the numerical majority and to the socialistic, communistic doctrine which invested it in one small particular class, we find an always greater abdication of the sovereign attributes to an always more restricted constituent element of the nation.

To affirm instead, as Fascism does, that "All is in the State and for the State; nothing outside the State, nothing against the State," means to affirm that the Ideal State is the one which is above individuals, organizations, castes or classes; or above all particularized interests, needs or ambitions.

The rise of Fascism destroys forever, thus, that Gordian Knot of apparently insoluble social problems born from the clash of conflicting interests of individuals within the State. It destroys also the subjection of the welfare of the State to the welfare of any individual, or any group of individuals, or even the totality of all the people. And, as the resort to the Will of God as final authority in all matters which may affect the welfare of the State has lost all meaning in our modern, individualistic, materialistic Society, in the same way the demagogic appeal to the will of the people is to lose all significance in the coming Fascist Society.

The triumph of Fascism means, in fact, that the role of the people is finally brought back to that secondary importance which it assumes when considered in its proper relation to the other elements of the Nation-State.

The Corporative Idea

Fascism, which is the very antithesis of Individualism, stands as the nemesis of all economic doctrines and all economic practice of both the capitalistic and the communistic systems. Fascism holds that:

1. The economic life of man cannot be abstracted and separated from the whole of his spiritual life. In the words of Mussolini: "The economic man does not exist. Man is integral; he is political, economic, religious, saint and warrior at the same time."

2. The economic life of man is influenced, if not actually determined, by idealistic factors.

3. True economic progress can derive only from the concerted effort of individuals who know how to sacrifice their personal egoism and ambitions for the good of the whole.

4. Economic initiatives cannot be left to the arbitrary decisions of private, individual interests.

5. Open competition, if not wisely directed and restricted, actually destroys wealth instead of creating it.

6. The wealth of a community is something intangible which cannot be identified with the sum of riches of single individuals.

7. The proper function of the State in the Fascist system is that of supervising, regulating and arbitrating the relationships of capital and labor, employers and employees, individuals and associations, private interests and national interests.

8. Class war is avoidable and must be avoided. Class war is deleterious to the orderly and fruitful life of the nation, therefore it has no place in the Fascist State.

9. More important than the production of wealth is its right distribution, distribution which must benefit in the best possible way all the classes of the nation, hence, the nation itself.

10. Private wealth belongs not only to the individual, but, in a symbolic sense, to the State as well.

These fundamental tenets of Fascist economy derive in turn from those basic conceptions of the Fascist doctrine of the State which we have expounded in the chapter of the "Fascist State." We have said there, in fact, that the Fascist State is a Sovereign State. This means that there cannot be any single economic interests which are above the general economic interests of the State, no individual, economic initiatives which do not fall under the supervision and regulation of the State, no relationships of the various classes of the nation which are not the concern of the State.

Furthermore, the Fascist State is an Ethical State. This means that all the factors influencing the life of a nation: the economic, the social, the political, etc., are brought into the Fascist State under the dominion of the moral law, which becomes not only the supreme law of the individual, but the supreme law of the State as well.

"One invisible tie binds together all the people of a nation. There cannot be any joy or any pain experienced by one single individual which shall not ultimately affect the welfare of the whole nation."

This is the principle of Fascist Ethics which, translated and applied to the realm of Economics, has transformed the economic organization of the State.

If it is true that one invisible tie binds together the destinies of all the people of one nation, then it is also true that the terms wealthy and pauper, capitalist and worker, landowner and farmer, employer and employee, lose their antagonistic meaning altogether and remain to signify brethren in spirit if not in flesh, engaged from different angles, on different planes, in the arduous task of building up a nation's life.

We see thus the Fascist State resolutely enter the economic field to dictate what shall be from now on the relationship between capital and labor, employer and employee, landowner and farmhand, industrialist and worker. . . .

By delimiting thus the field of action of capital and labor, by harmonizing production and distribution to the actual needs of the nation, the legislation of Fascism has accomplished in the realm of Economics what no legislation of any other political system has ever been able to accomplish; namely, a co-ordination of all the economic forces of the nation so that the material life of the people may be free of struggles, strikes, unemployment, class war, concentrated wealth and widespread misery.

To bring about such a magic transformation of the economic life of the nation, Fascism has made use of the most characteristic phenomenon of the modern era: the syndicalist phenomenon. Originated as an instrument of the war of classes, syndicalism attempted to organize the various categories of workers in syndical organizations having no other goal than the protection of the material welfare of their own members. These organizations were devoted thus to the furthering of supremely particularized interests, ready to set themselves against each other and against the State itself, whenever those interests were menaced or conflicted with others.

The problem which presented itself as an ominous menace upon the horizon of Fascism at the outset of its very life in Italy was, therefore, to bring at once the phenomenon of syndicalism under the authority of the State, and, successively, to transform its original aim of protecting the interests of the proletariat into protecting the interests of the whole nation.

This could be accomplished only by enlarging the narrow form of the original syndicalist organizations into larger forms which would include all the citizens of the nation into an all-comprehensive national manifestation. This manifestation of the Italians of all classes, all professions, all trades and all creeds into the framework of one enormous and far-reaching organization, which has for its end the material welfare of the whole, is called National Syndicalism.

This National Syndicalism represents the first attempt made to bring the egotistic claims of the individual under the discipline of the Sovereign State; for the realization of an aim which transcends the welfare of the individual and identifies itself with the prosperity of the whole nation.

To make this discipline possible, and the sovereignty effective in practice as well as in theory, Fascism has devised the "Corporazione," an instrument of social life destined to exercise the most far-reaching influence upon the economic development of Fascist States. (The Italian word "Corporazione" which is currently translated into English by the apparently analogous word "Corporation," means, more exactly in the Italian language, what the word "Guild" means in English; that is: associations of persons engaged in kindred pursuits. We shall nevertheless follow the general usage to obviate the danger of misunderstandings.)

Within the Corporations the interests of producers and consumers, employers and employees, individuals and associations are interlocked and integrated in a unique and univocal way, while all types of interests are brought under the aegis of the State.

Finally, through these corporations the State may at any time that it deems fit, or that the need requires, intervene within the economic life of the individual to let the supreme interests of the nation have precedence over his private, particular interests, even to the point where his work, his savings, his whole fortune may need to be pledged, and if absolutely necessary, sacrificed. . . .

The corporative principle which is essentially an anti-individualistic principle, becomes thus the true foundation of the anti-individualistic Fascist State.

That organization to which it gives origin in the field of economics, finds its counterpart in the political field where it gives birth to a new and entirely original social formation.

This is possible because the corporative principle is, in the words of Bottai:

> . . . a principal of political-juridical organization, and at the same time, a principle of social life. To give value and to organize the economic categories, to set them in a certain form of hierarchy at whose vertex is the national interest, means, at the same time, to devise not only the special organs which must realize them, but to devise a whole series or principles of subordination of two kinds: political, that is of interests and facts; juridical, that is of rights and laws. And, inasmuch as the parties of the social relationship are always two: the individual and the commonwealth; and, inasmuch as every political or juridical organization is at bottom only a system of relationships among the various individuals and between the single individual and society, it follows that the corporative principle is a principle of complex and progressive subordination of the Individual's economic interests to the greater interests of the various economic categories and the general all-comprehensive national economy.

Whoever thinks of Fascist Economy must think of it, therefore, as of something more than a new form of Economics, because it is first of all, and above all, a translation of Ethics into Economics, an application of Ethical principles to economic facts.

The Legacy of Rome

The historical continuity of political forms, social organization, religious expression and spiritual aspirations, in the life of the Italian people, which had lasted two thousand years and had been broken only in the last few centuries of servitude to foreigners and their foreign ways of living, has been at last restored by Fascism, which is the direct heir of Roman traditions and of Roman ideals.

Fascism means, in fact, the return to Order, to Authority, to Law; the return to the Roman conception of human Society, conception which those centuries of oblivion could obscure but never efface.

Fascism is, in other words, intimately connected to Rome; its mission is the continuation of the mission of Rome; its heritage is the legacy of Rome.

There are some things Rome symbolized in the golden age of its glory which were and still are of supreme significance to mankind; things of the spirit of an eternal and absolute value which Fascism wants restored to their rightful supremacy. . . .

Empire, in the generally accepted meaning, is a political organization whose foundation is always a territorial extension. Empire, in the Fascist meaning of the word denotes, instead, that unification of peoples and nations brought about by the triumph of a universal idea. Hence, the seat of Empire is necessarily there where the realization of this universal idea takes place.

It is not incomprehensible, thus, that Rome has been twice the seat of Empire, and that she has been chosen again by destiny to fill such a role for the third successive time in the twenty-eighth century of her fateful history.

Twice in the past, from Rome, a Universal Idea has sent a message of harmony and unity to divided, warring and ailing mankind. Twice have the seven hills of Rome seen the triumph of this Idea bring about in their midst the realization of Empire.

The triumph of the Idea of Order, of Authority, of equal Justice under Law, saw the Empire of Augustus and of Trajanus give to mankind for the first and only time in human history the life-enhancing blessing of political unity.

The triumph of the Catholic Idea of salvation in Christ and

through Christ and His Church, saw the Empire of the Church give to mankind the life-inspiring blessing of spiritual unity.

The triumph of the Fascist Idea of subjection of all individual life to the life of the Whole will see a new Empire rise on the seven hills of Rome, an empire founded not necessarily upon territorial possessions and political conquests, but primarily upon the generalized belief that Fascism may finally furnish man with the long sought solution of the riddle of life.

A spiritual power generated from those great Italian spirits who have been in the past the assertors of Rome's immortal and eternal right to Empire, and the prophets of Rome's third form of Empire, is the leaven which has brought about that fermentation of spiritual forces called Fascism. . . .

"Del Primato morale e civile degli Italiani" (On the Moral and Civil Primacy of the Italian People)* is one of those books which leave an indelible mark upon the soul of a nation.

But to call the Primato a book is not quite correct, because it is something more than a mere book; it is a message; it is a call and a prophecy. Nowhere else have the claims of Italy and of the Italians to supreme primacy in the moral and social realms—apart from the "De Monarchia" of Dante, which establishes and supports these claims in the political field—found such forceful and thorough expression as in the two large volumes of the Primato.

The main thesis of the Primato is that modern Civilization is built and must rest upon the foundations laid by Christianity and that the true expression of Christianity is found only in Catholicism.

> European Civilization must be re-established a second time by recalling it to its Christian and Catholic origins and extinguishing the heterodoxy which for two centuries reigned in all its parts. . . .

When a civilization is to be rebuilt, a moral center of action must be established where the source of motion may reside and whence the movement may be spread to all its parts as from the center to the circumference.

> History teaches that every civilization has its special seat in one country or city as its base, which becomes morally the capital of the civilized world.
>
> The center of the civilizing process is where the center of Catholicism is. . . . Now, since Italy is center of the latter, it follows that Italy is

* By Vincenzo Gioberti, 1845.—*Ed.*

the true head of civilization and Rome the ideal metropolis of the world.

Providence chose the Italian land for this high destiny, nourishing a spark of divine truth in it "ab antico" and molding there a race wonderfully adapted in genius and intelligence for subjecting the whole world in Christian obedience. . . . Italy is the priestly nation among the great body of redeemed peoples. . . . Nor did the inhabitants of this peninsula give to other peoples merely divine gifts, but also every other civil and human good, and all the great intellects of Europe, who enhanced in any measure the glory of their countries, lit their lamps at the living flame of Italian genius.

Words like these are words of fire, and very little wonder is left, after reading them, at the vision of Italy dreaming once more dreams of glory, dreams of greatness, dreams of empire. . . .

The Hero as Leader

The age of hero-worship appears to us most strange and remote, indeed; the very possibility of a hero appearing in our midst is denied with a vehemence and a finality which reveal our incapacity to understand the true essence of heroism; everything points, in other words, to the low state to which has fallen the cult and the practice of the heroic in man.

But if the age of hero-worship is past forever, it is not true that heroes may not appear in our midst.

What is a hero, the Carlylean hero?

A hero is he who can pierce with the mystic light of an inner vision to the very heart of things; he who can re-discover the greatest and most profound of all truths: viz., that beyond his realm of fugitive appearances there lies, immutable and eternal, what Fichte called the "Divine Idea of the World"; finally, he who, living already in spirit in this realm of timeless and absolute Reality, is able to translate his vision into deeds and to act according to the dictates of an inner voice telling him that ". . . they wrong man greatly who say he is to be seduced by ease. Difficulty, abnegation, martyrdom, death are the allurements that act on the heart of man."

As a god or a prophet, as a saint or a warrior, as a poet or a king; under whatever aspect they might have appeared on this earth, all heroes have always delivered and, for that matter, will ever deliver, the same message to mankind: viz., that man lives a true human life only when his life is devoted to and, if necessary, sacrificed for the triumph of an ideal and that only by living such a life can he ever find happiness on this earth.

And because every age brings forth its own type of hero, the hero as Leader; the new type of hero born of the need of the times, answering the call of history, in delivering anew such a message—a message of hope and trust, of faith and revolt, of abnegation and assertion at the same time—must deliver it not in the form of revealed religion, not in the form of a God-inspired book, of a prophecy, or of a poem encompassing earth and heaven, but in the form of a new way of life: a way of life capable of leading man out of his present unhappy, miserable state

The hero as Leader!

To acknowledge that a man in our midst, a man of flesh and bone, with our vices and our virtues, with our strength and our weaknesses, with our aspirations and our dreams, is truly a hero: the hero as Leader, we must ask of him first of all, and above all, that through his speech, his actions, his influence, his example, his whole life, in short, he live the very message he is delivering to us.

But this is not sufficient; we want to be certain that he is not a quack, a charlatan or an impostor, but a true and sincere man. Sincerity of purpose, that magic touchstone which serves so well to distinguish the gold from the dross in the actions of men—is what we expect to find in the man to be recognized as hero.

And yet, sincerity, however admirable it may be, by itself achieves nothing everlasting if it is not accompanied by courage. Nothing great, nothing of any value, of any meaning whatsoever can ever be accomplished in this world of ours, if all fear of the known and unknown hostile, belittling or derisive forces is not banished from the heart and the mind of man.

Finally, sincerity and courage must be accompanied by belief belief in one's own destiny, belief in the role which one is destined to play on the stage of life, belief in one's own powers if the world is to be actually and effectively changed through one's own efforts.

Underlying this magic trinity of sincerity, courage and faith, there must always exist within the soul's deepest recesses a mystic power of immediate knowledge of the truth through the supreme gift of intuition, if the action of a man must share the finality of an act of God.

Once we find all these qualities within the soul of one man, once we discover that they not only exist there, but have taken complete possession of his inner life, blotting out—so to speak—any other virtue, any other vice, then we may rest assured that we have found a man entitled to our admiration, a true hero worthy of inclusion within the sacred cohort of the Carlylean heroes.

But our skeptical brethren—little men without vision, without faith, without belief—ask for pragmatic proof of his right to our admiration, if not to our worship. Such proof is evidently not needed by those who can recognize the hero when they see him, but is sorely needed by those aware of the bread they eat but blind to the reality of the unseen.

To this category of people, condemned by a mean fate to the worst form of necessity of all, it will be necessary to furnish explanations, it will be necessary to ask them whether an imposter, a quack, a false man could ever bring about the unification of a nation, the resurrection of an empire, the redemption of a land, the regeneration of the moral conscience of a people. What impostor, what quack, what false man has ever accomplished that before? By what miracle of ingenuity, cunning or malice, has he ever been able to fool all the people all of the time? And is that ever possible?

If what was accomplished once is guaranty of what can be accomplished now, if the past is forerunner of the present, if it is true that "Historia magistra vitae," we are forced to acknowledge then that there is here among us on this earth a man marked by Destiny to say a new word to mankind. His words, his deeds, his thoughts, the whole life of this man is a living lesson of heroism for all those timid souls who believe that there is no greater thing on earth than to be satisfied with a routine, commonplace existence.

How deeply, movingly pathetic beyond words it is to see this man, burning with the great flame that he has carried and still carries, deep within; seek here and there and everywhere a refuge, and with the refuge a piece of bread, and with the piece of bread the means to bring forth that inner flame burning deep, deep within. How inspiring to see him follow the call of destiny without being aware of exactly what destiny expected from him; only dimly perceiving in a blurred vision the image of some great thing shaping itself in the mist, and calling to him, leading him, drawing him toward an unknown and perhaps dangerous goal. . . .

But the hour of destiny is calling. Is there no hope left for Italy?

Must Italy renounce forever her glorious past? Must she resign herself to a minor role in world history? Is there no significance in all that which forms the substance of the Idea of a nation, the Italian nation? . . .

Questions like these must have agitated the mind and the heart of that man when the hour of destiny struck its call.

But the mist enveloping the vision haunting his dreams since the early days of his youth is finally lifting, the contours of this vision become finally sharp, clear and distinct. . . . What do they reveal to the inner eye of the seer? They reveal the image of the great mother Italy sunk in the mire, seeking light, pleading for help.

It was then that a true, complete revolution of all thoughts, all feelings, all sensations, took the soul of that man by storm and forced him to examine critically his whole past, revise all his beliefs, fashion for himself a new creed, find within himself the capacity to utter a new word, the *word* that a whole people, a whole continent, the whole western civilization was in need to hear and was waiting to hear.

He had then the intuition that something of tremendous import for mankind was at stake, hung precariously on the decision of his life course; he had the revelation that an issue of far-reaching consequence for the future of mankind had to be settled then. It was a question whether, faced by the decay of the liberal-democratic-capitalistic-materialistic organization of society, man had to embrace communism and abjection or choose another way of life in tune with his soul's aspirations, if not with his animal nature's wants.

It was thus that the dumb, inchoate historical forces which shape the destinies of man found suddenly a voice; it was thus that centuries of thought and action were brought suddenly to a climax by such a voice; it was thus that the people themselves acquired suddenly the voice they so earnestly and yet so vainly had sought; because if Fascism is a creature of the man Benito Mussolini, yet, in truth, it belongs to western civilization itself.

The man was simply the mouthpiece chosen by destiny to utter what needed to be uttered at a crucial time of human history; what he said all people were longing to say; what he did many people, perhaps, were trying to do.

He actually expressed in words what remained unexpressed in the inmost heart of the people; he only translated into action what lay dormant in a potential state within the very nature of the people.

Alone, he could achieve nothing. As a leader he could change, and is changing the aspect of the world. . . .

44. THE NATIONAL FASCIST PARTY AND THE CHARTER OF LABOR

The two short selections which follow are indicative of the way in which the philosophy of fascism was embodied in the laws and principles of Mussolini's regime. The first selection is the preamble to a statute of 1929 and describes the place of the Party in Italian fascism. The second is from The Charter of Labor, *which, though not a legislative act, was established and promulgated by the Fascist Grand Council in April, 1927, and came to be regarded as the organic law of the regime.*

[The National Fascist Party] *

The National Fascist Party is a civil militia for the service of the nation. Its objective: to realize the greatness of the Italian people. From its beginnings, which are indistinguishable from the renaissance of the Italian conscience and the will to victory, until now, the party has always thought of itself as in a state of war, at first in order to combat those who were stifling the will of the nation, today and from henceforth to defend and increase the power of the Italian people. Fascism is not merely an Italian organization connected with a program partly realized and partly still to be realized; it is above all a faith which has had its confessors, and under the impulse of which the new Italians work as soldiers, pledged to achieve victory in the struggle between the nation and its enemies. The Party is an essential part of this new organization, and its function is fundamental and indispensable to the vitality of the regime. In the hour of vigil, its organization was fixed according to the necessities of battle, and the people recognized the Duce by the marks of his will, his strength and

* *The Preamble to the Statute of 20 December 1929.* Reprinted from *The Political and Social Doctrines of Contemporary Europe,* 1939, edited by Michael Oakeshott, by permission of the Cambridge University Press.

his achievements. In that heat of the struggle, action took precedence of law. Every stage was marked by a conquest, and the assemblies were only gatherings of officers and men dominated by the memory of the dead. Without dogmatic formulas or rigid projects, Fascism knows that victory lies in the possibility of its own continuous renewal. Fascism lives today in terms of the future, and regards the new generations as forces destined to achieve the ends appointed by our will. Without order and hierarchy, there can be neither discipline nor effort nor education of the people, which must receive light and guidance from that high place where is to be found the complete vision of rewards, tasks, functions and merits, and where the only guidance is in the general interest.

The Charter of Labor*

I. The Italian nation is an organic whole having life, purposes and means of action superior in power and duration to those of the individuals, single or associated, of which it is composed. It is a moral, political and economic unity, which is realized integrally in the Fascist State.

II. Work in all its forms—intellectual, technical or manual— whether organization or execution—is a social duty. And for this reason only it is regulated by the State. The process of production, from the national point of view, is a single whole, its aims are united and identified with the well-being of the producers and the promotion of national power.

III. Occupational or syndical organization is free; but only the juridically recognized syndicate which submits to the control of State has the right to represent legally the entire category of employers or workers for which it is constituted, in safeguarding its interests vis-à-vis the State and other occupational associations, in making collective contracts of work binding on all the members of the category, in levying contributions and exercising over its members functions delegated to it in the public interest.

IV. In the collective contract of work the solidarity of the various factors of production finds its concrete expression in the reconciliation

* From *The Charter of Labor,* 1927. Reprinted from *The Political and Social Doctrines of Contemporary Europe,* 1939, edited by Michael Oakeshott, by permission of the Cambridge University Press.

of the conflicting interests of employers and employees and in their subordination to the superior interests of production. . . .

45. THE FASCIST DECALOGUE

The Ten Commandments of the Italian soldier under Mussolini provide the essence of the philosophy of fascism in short compass. The following two versions of these commandments constitute one of the best examples of the way in which a political philosophy may be translated into maxims of individual conduct.

The Fascist Decalogue*

(i)

1. Know that the Fascist and in particular the soldier, must not believe in perpetual peace.

2. Days of imprisonment are always deserved.

3. The nation serves even as a sentinel over a can of petrol.

4. A companion must be a brother, first, because he lives with you, and secondly because he thinks like you.

5. The rifle and cartridge belt, and the rest, are confided to you not to rust in leisure, but to be preserved in war.

6. Do not ever say "The Government will pay . . ." because it is *you* who pay; and the Government is that which you willed to have, and for which you put on a uniform.

7. Discipline is the soul of armies; without it there are no soldiers, only confusion and defeat.

8. Mussolini is always right.

9. For a volunteer there are no extenuating circumstances when he is disobedient.

10. One thing must be dear to you above all: the life of the Duce.

1934

* Reprinted from *The Political and Social Doctrines of Contemporary Europe,* 1939, edited by Michael Oakeshott, by permission of the Cambridge University Press.

(ii)

1. Remember that those who fell for the revolution and for the empire march at the head of your columns.

2. Your comrade is your brother. He lives with you, thinks with you, and is at your side in the battle.

3. Service to Italy can be rendered at all times, in all places, and by every means. It can be paid with toil and also with blood.

4. The enemy of Fascism is your enemy. Give him no quarter.

5. Discipline is the sunshine of armies. It prepares and illuminates the victory.

6. He who advances to the attack with decision has victory already in his grasp.

7. Conscious and complete obedience is the virtue of the Legionary.

8. There do not exist things important and things unimportant. There is only duty.

9. The Fascist revolution has depended in the past and still depends on the bayonets of its Legionaries.

10. Mussolini is always right.

1938

Section V

FASCIST PHILOSOPHY IN GERMANY

The culmination of the philosophy of fascism was reached in Germany with the development of the National Socialist (Nazi) Party, under the leadership of Adolf Hitler, from 1921 to 1945. The history of the Nazi Party is one of cruelty, ruthlessness, and slaughter; it need not be detailed here.

Philosophically, the German fascists added little to the principles of fascist organization that had already been laid down in Italy. They did succeed in carrying out these principles more effectively and in developing more fully a deliberately irrational totalitarianism.

In some respects German and Italian fascists differed. Mussolini, in order to justify his imperialism in Africa, argued that the state is fundamental and creates the nation. Hitler and his associates claimed that the nation, or people, was primary, and that the state was its instrument, to justify their claims upon German-speaking areas in France and Czechoslovakia. It is also obvious that the myth of Roman grandeur could not suit the purposes of the German fascists. Their own myth was that of the Aryan super race, from which all that was valuable in Europe derived, and of which the Germans were the last pure representatives—Jews, Negroes, and Marxists being the chief corrupters of a pure Germanic civilization. Despite its apparent absurdity, this myth of Germanic superiority proved extremely effective, and received enthusiastic and widespread support.

Particularly characteristic of the German development of fascist philosophy was its intensely irrational character, which resulted in its intolerant racism, the inhuman persecution of minorities, and the onset of the most catastrophic war in history.

46. HERMANN GÖRING

Hermann Göring (1893-1946) was one of Hitler's closest associates. Prime Minister of Prussia, and commander of the German air forces during the Second World War. The following passage from Germany Reborn *is representative of fascist hero worship, and also of the Nazi claim that they were the last bulwark of Europe against Soviet Communism.*

[Swastika Versus Star] *

May the other peoples realize that the Leader in Germany is the first guarantor of European peace. For the task which Hitler has taken over, and the fight which he is waging at home, does not only concern Germany. Hitler's mission is of importance for the history of the whole world, because he took up a war to the death against Communism and therewith raised a bulwark for the other European nations. Many times before in world history have mighty spiritual struggles been decided on German territory. It is our solemn belief that if, in the mighty struggle between Communism and National Socialism, the former had won, then the deadly bacillus would have spread from Communist Germany to the other European countries. The day will come when the other countries will begin to realize this, and on that day France, England and other peoples will be thankful that at the critical moment there was an Adolf Hitler in Germany.

The great struggle on the outcome of which the future not only of Germany, but of Europe and the whole world, depended was the struggle between the Swastika and Soviet Star. If the Soviet Star had been victorious, Germany would have perished in a bloody Communist reign of terror, and the whole of the western world would have followed Germany into the abyss. The victory of the Swastika has at any rate averted this terrible danger, and for that we must give thanks to God. Once more it has become possible for Ger-

---

* From H. Göring, *Germany Reborn*, 1934. Reprinted by permission of George Allen & Unwin Ltd., London.

many to rise again and for us to create a healthy Germany. But Germany is, and will remain, the heart of Europe, and Europe can only be healthy and live in peace when its heart is healthy and intact. The German people has arisen and Germany will again be healthy. For that we have the guarantor who is Adolf Hitler, the Chancellor of the German people and the protector of their honor and freedom.

47. ALFRED ROSENBERG

Alfred Rosenberg (1893-1946) was the leading apologist for German racism, elaborating at length upon the myth of blood, and Volk, *and* Aryan *superiority. After lengthy trial at Nürnberg, in 1946, he was convicted and hanged as a war criminal. Appropriately, his chief work was entitled* The Myth of the Twentieth Century.

[Race and History] *

Racial history is thus at the same time natural history and soul-*mystique.* The history of the religion of blood is, conversely, the great world-narrative of the rise and decline of peoples, their heroes and thinkers, their inventors and artists. . . .

The "meaning of world history" has radiated out from the north over the whole world, borne by a blue-eyed blond race which in several great waves determined the spiritual face of the world . . . These wander-periods were the legendary migration of the Atlantides across north Africa, the migration of the Aryans into India and Persia; the migration of the Dorians, Macedonians, Latins; the migration of the Germanic tribes; the colonization of the world by the Germanic occident. . . .

* From A. Rosenberg, *The Myth of the Twentieth Century,* 1930. These passages are reprinted from selections appearing in *National Socialism,* a report prepared by the Division of European Affairs, U.S. Department of State; United States Government Printing Office, Washington, 1943.

[The Myth of Nordic Blood]

We stand today before a definitive decision. Either through a new experience and cultivation of the old blood, coupled with an enhanced fighting will, we will rise to a purificatory action, or the last Germanic-western values of morality and state-culture shall sink away in the filthy human masses of the big cities, become stunted on the sterile burning asphalt of a bestialized inhumanity, or trickle away as a morbific agent in the form of emigrants, bastardizing themselves in South America, China, Dutch East India, Africa. . . .

A *new* faith is arising today: the myth of the blood, the faith, to defend with the blood the divine essence of man. The faith, embodied in clearest knowledge, that the Nordic blood represents that *mysterium* which has replaced and overcome the old sacraments. . . .

The new real struggle today is concerned not so much with external changes in power, along with an internal compromise as hitherto, but, conversely, with the new rebuilding of the soul-cells of the Nordic peoples, for the sake of the re-institution in their sovereign rights [*Herrscherrechte*] of those ideals and values from which originates everything which signifies culture to us, and for the sake of the preservation of the racial substance itself. . . .

[German National Honor]

A German religious movement, which would like to develop into a folk-church, will have to declare that the ideal of neighborly love is unconditionally to be subordinated to the idea of national honor, that no act of a German church may be approved which does not primarily serve the safeguarding of the *Volkstum*. . . .

The idea of honor, national honor, is for us the beginning and end of our entire thinking and doing. It does not admit of any equal-valued center of force alongside of it, no matter of what kind, neither Christian love, nor the Masonic humanity, nor the Roman philosophy. . . .

The essence of the contemporary world revolution lies in the awakening of the racial types. Not in Europe alone but on the whole planet. This awakening is the organic counter movement against the last chaotic remnants of the liberal economic imperialism, whose ob-

ject of exploitation out of desperation has fallen into the snare of
Bolshevik Marxism, in order to complete what democracy had begun,
the extirpation of the racial and national consciousness. . . .

[State and Folk]

The state is nowadays no longer an independent idol, before which
everything must bow down; the state is not even an end but is only
a means for the preservation of the folk . . . Forms of the state
change, and the laws of the state pass away; the folk remains. From
this alone follows that the nation is the first and *last,* that to which
everything else has to be subordinated. . . .

The new thought puts folk and race higher than the state and its
forms. It declares protection of the folk more important than protection of a religious denomination, a class, the monarchy, or the republic; it sees in treason against the folk a greater crime than high
treason against the state. . . .

No folk of Europe is racially unified, including Germany. In
accordance with the newest researches, we recognize five races, which
exhibit noticeably different types. Now it is beyond question true
that the Nordic race primarily has borne the genuine cultural fruits
of Europe. The great heroes, artists, founders of states have come
from this race . . . Nordic blood created *German* life above all
others. Even those sections, in which only a small part today is pure
Nordic, have their basic stock from the Nordic race. Nordic is German and has functioned so as to shape the culture and human types
of the *westisch, dinarisch,* and *ostisch-Baltisch* races. Also a type
which is predominantly *dinarisch* has often been innerly formed in a
Nordic mode. This emphasis on the Nordic race does not mean a
sowing of "race-hatred" in Germany but, on the contrary, the conscious acknowledgment of a kind of racial cement within our nationality . . . On the day when Nordic blood should completely dry up,
Germany would fall to ruin, would decline into a characterless chaos.
That many forces are consciously working toward this, has been discussed in detail. For this they rely primarily on the Alpine lower
stratum, which, without any value of its own, has remained essentially
superstitious and slavish despite all Germanization. Now that the
external bond of the old idea of the Reich has fallen away, this blood
is active, together with other bastard phenomena, in order to put itself

in the service of a magic faith or in the service of the democratic chaos, which finds its herald in the parasitic but energetic Judaism. . . .

The foundation for the arising of a *new aristocracy* lies in those men who have stood—in a spiritual, political, and military sense—in the foremost positions in the struggle for the coming Reich. It will appear thereby with inner necessity that up to 80 percent of these men will also externally approach the Nordic type, since the fulfillment of the demanded values lies on a line with the highest values of this blood. With the others the inheritance, which exhibits itself in actions, outweighs personal appearance. . . .

[Nordic Europe]

Europe's states have all been founded and preserved by the Nordic man. This Nordic man through alcohol, the World War, and Marxism has partially degenerated, partially been uprooted . . . In order to preserve Europe, the Nordic energies of Europe must first be revitalized, strengthened. That means then Germany, Scandinavia with Finland, and England. . . .

Nordic Europe is the fated future, with a *German* central Europe. Germany as racial and national state, as central power of the continent, safeguarding the south and southeast; the Scandinavian states with Finland as a second group, safeguarding the northeast; and Great Britain, safeguarding the west and overseas at those places where required in the interest of the Nordic man. . . .

48. ERNST R. HUBER

Ernst R. Huber (1903-   ) was one of the foremost theoreticians of the Third German Reich. In the following passages he develops the three central concepts of German fascism: the Volk *or people, the* Führer *or leader, and the Nazi Party, which represents the State.*

[The People] *

There is no people without an objective unity, but there is also none without a common consciousness of unity. A people is determined by a number of different factors: by racial derivation and by the character of its land, by language and other forms of life, by religion and history, but also by the common consciousness of its solidarity and by its common will to unity. For the concrete concept of a people, as represented by the various peoples of the earth, it is of decisive significance which of these various factors they regard as determinants for the nature of the people. The new German Reich proceeds from the concept of the political people, determined by the natural characteristics and by the historical idea of a closed community. The political people is formed through the uniformity of its natural characteristics. Race is the natural basis of the people . . . As a political people the natural community becomes conscious of its solidarity and strives to form itself, to develop itself, to defend itself, to realize itself. "Nationalism" is essentially this striving of a people which has become conscious of itself toward self-direction and self-realization, toward a deepening and renewing of its natural qualities.

This consciousness of self, springing from the consciousness of a historical idea, awakens in a people its will to historical formation: the will to action. The political people is no passive, sluggish mass, no mere object for the efforts of the state at government or protective welfare work . . . The great misconception of the democracies is that they can see the active participation of the people only in the form of plebiscites according to the principle of majority. In a democracy the people does not act as a unit but as a complex of unrelated individuals who form themselves into parties . . . The new Reich is based on the principle that real action of a self-determining people is only possible according to the principle of leadership and following. . . .

In the theory of the nationalistic [*völkisch*] Reich, people and state are conceived as an inseparable unity. The people is the pre-

* From E. Huber, *Constitutional Law of the Greater German Reich,* 1939. These passages are reprinted from selections appearing in *National Socialism,* a report prepared by the Division of European Affairs, U.S. Department of State, U.S. Government Printing Office, Washington, 1943.

requisite for the entire political order; the state does not form the people but the people molds the state out of itself as the form in which it achieves historical permanence . . . The state is a function of the people, but it is not therefore a subordinate secondary machine which can be used or laid aside at will. It is the form in which the people attains to historical reality. It is the bearer of the historical continuity of the people which remains the same in the center of its being in spite of all changes, revolutions, and transformations. . . .

[The Führer]

The Führer Reich of the [German] people is founded on the recognition that the true will of the people cannot be disclosed through parliamentary votes and plebiscites but that the will of the people in its pure and uncorrupted form can only be expressed through the Führer. Thus a distinction must be drawn between the supposed will of the people in a parliamentary democracy, which merely reflects the conflict of the various social interests, and the true will of the people in the Führer-state, in which the collective will of the real political unit is manifested . . .

The Führer is the bearer of the people's will; he is independent of all groups, associations, and interests, but he is bound by laws which are inherent in the nature of his people. In this twofold condition: independence of all factional interests but unconditional dependence of the people, is reflected the true nature of the Führer principle. Thus the Führer has nothing in common with the functionary, the agent, or the exponent who exercises a mandate delegated to him and who is bound to the will of those who appoint him. The Führer is no "representative" of a particular group whose wishes he must carry out. He is no "organ" of the state in the sense of a mere executive agent. He is rather himself the bearer of the collective will of the people. In his will the will of the people is realized. He transforms the mere feelings of the people into a conscious will . . . Thus it is possible for him, in the name of the true will of the people which he serves, to go against the subjective opinions and convictions of single individuals within the people if these are not in accord with the objective destiny of the people . . . He shapes the collective will of the people within himself and he embodies the political unity and entirety of the people in opposition to individual interests . . .

But the Führer, even as the bearer of the people's will, is not arbitrary and free of all responsibility. His will is not the subjective, individual will of a single man, but the collective national will is embodied within him in all its objective, historical greatness . . . Such a collective will is not a fiction, as is the collective will of the democracies, but it is a political reality which finds its expression in the Führer. The people's collective will has its foundation in the political idea which is given to a people. It is present in the people, but the Führer raises it to consciousness and discloses it . . .

In the Führer are manifested also the natural laws inherent in the people: It is he who makes them into a code governing all national activity. In disclosing these natural laws he sets up the great ends which are to be attained and draws up the plans for the utilization of all national powers in the achievement of the common goals. Through his planning and directing he gives the national life its true purpose and value. This directing and planning activity is especially manifested in the lawgiving power which lies in the Führer's hand. The great change in significance which the law has undergone is characterized therein that it no longer sets up the limits of social life, as in liberalistic times, but that it drafts the plans and the aims of the nation's actions . . .

The Führer principle rests upon unlimited authority but not upon mere outward force. It has often been said, but it must constantly be repeated, that the Führer principle has nothing in common with arbitrary bureaucracy and represents no system of brutal force, but that it can only be maintained by mutual loyalty which must find its expression in a free relation. The Führer-order depends upon the responsibility of the following, just as it counts on the responsibility and loyalty of the Führer to his mission and to his following . . . There is no greater responsibility than that upon which the Führer principle is grounded. . . .

The office of the Führer developed out of the National Socialist movement. It was originally not a state office; this fact can never be disregarded if one is to understand the present legal and political position of the Führer. The office of the Führer first took root in the structure of the Reich when the Führer took over the powers of the Chancelor, and then when he assumed the position of the Chief of State. But his primary significance is always as leader of the movement; he has absorbed within himself the two highest offices of the political leadership of the Reich and has created thereby the new

office of "Führer of the people and the Reich." That is not a superficial grouping together of various offices, functions, and powers . . .
It is not a union of offices but a unity of office. The Führer does not
unite the old offices of Chancelor and President side by side within
himself, but he fills a new, unified office. . . .

The Führer unites in himself all the sovereign authority of the
Reich; all public authority in the state as well as in the movement is
derived from the authority of the Führer. We must speak not of the
state's authority but of the Führer's authority if we wish to designate
the character of the political authority within the Reich correctly. The
state does not hold political authority as an impersonal unit but receives it from the Führer as the executor of the national will. The
authority of the Führer is complete and all-embracing; it unites in
itself all the means of political direction; it extends into all fields of
national life; it embraces the entire people, which is bound to the
Führer in loyalty and obedience. The authority of the Führer is not
limited by checks and controls, by special autonomous bodies or individual rights, but it is free and independent, all-inclusive and unlimited. It is not, however, self-seeking or arbitrary and its ties are
within itself. It is derived from the people; that is, it is entrusted to
the Führer by the people. It exists for the people and has its justification in the people; it is free of all outward ties because it is in its
innermost nature firmly bound up with the fate, the welfare, the
mission, and the honor of the people. . . .

[The National Socialist Party]

On July 14, 1933 was issued the law against the formation of new
parties which raised the NSDAP to the only political party in Germany . . . The overthrow of the old party-state was accompanied
by the construction of the new movement-state [*Bewegungsstaat*]. Out
of a political fighting organization the NSDAP grew to a community
capable of carrying the state and the nation. This process was accomplished step by step in the first months after the National Socialist
seizure of power. The assumption of the office of Chancelor by the
Führer of the movement formed the basis for this development.
Various party leaders were appointed as *Reichsminister;* the governors
of the provinces were national leaders or *Gauleiter* of the party, such
as General von Epp; the Prussian government officials are as a rule

Gauleiter of the party; the Prussian police chiefs are mostly high-ranking SA leaders. By this system of a union of the personnel of the party and state offices the unity of party and state was achieved. . . .

The aim of the National Socialist movement is the nationalistic Reich: that is, a state of which the nature and development is determined by the idea of the people, for which the people is the substance of political unity, of which the inward and outward strength is drawn from the whole peopl , and which is supported by the whole people . . . The people and the party in the National Socialist Reich are a unit, not in the sense that every citizen must be a member of the party, but in the sense that the movement is only possible as the visible embodiment and realization of the all-embracing unity of the people. The totality of National Socialism is not to be explained therein that all fields of life are penetrated by the political will of the movement but that all members of the people are expected to take part in the common political life and to share in the determination of the common political fate. . . .

[The Individual and the Reich]

Not until the nationalistic political philosophy had become dominant could the liberalistic idea of basic rights be really overcome. The concept of personal liberties of the individual as opposed to the authority of the state had to disappear; it is not to be reconciled with the principle of the nationalistic Reich. There are no personal liberties of the individual which fall outside of the realm of the state and which must be respected by the state. The member of the people, organically connected with the whole community, has replaced the isolated individual; he is included in the totality of the political people and is drawn into the collective action. There can no longer be any question of a private sphere, free of state influence, which is sacred and untouchable before the political unity. The constitution of the nationalistic Reich is therefore not based upon a system of inborn and inalienable rights of the individual. . . .

The legal position of the individual member of the people forms an entirely new concept which is indispensable for the construction of a nationalistic order. The legal position of the individual is always related to the community and conditioned by duty. It is developed not for the sake of the individual but for the community, which can only be filled with life, power, and purpose when a suitable field of action is insured for the individual member. Without a concrete determination of the individual's legal position there can be no real community. This legal position represents the organic fixation of the individual in the living order. Rights and obligations arise from the application of this legal position to specific individual relationships . . . But all rights must be regarded as duty-bound rights. Their exercise is always dependent upon the fulfillment by the individual of those duties to which all rights are subordinate . . .

It is a mistake to claim that the citizen of the Reich has no rights but only duties; that there is no right of choice but only a duty of acclamation. There are, of course, no inborn, inalienable political rights which are inherent in the individual himself and which would tend to limit and hamper the leadership of the Reich. But in every true political community the individual has his legal position which he receives from the Führer and which makes him a true follower. . . .

49. ADOLF HITLER

Adolf Hitler (1889-1945) became Chancellor of Germany in 1933, and shortly thereafter the absolute power in the Third German Reich. As a dictator pursuing policies of external expansion, terrorization, and war, he has had no real equal in all history. An impassioned orator with the power to inspire an almost hysterical enthusiasm, he best revealed the character of his philosophy, such as it was, in his speeches to the German nation.

[Might Makes Right] *

The Strong over the Weak

Wars supposedly are not necessary among civilized peoples. The supposition is that disputes among nations are no longer necessary,

* From *Hitler's Words, the Speeches of Adolph Hitler from 1923-1943*, edited by G. W. Prange and reprinted by permission of the Public Affairs Press, Washington.

for they are represented to be merely the expression of the oppression of one class by the particular bourgeois group dominating at the time. In the case of actual differences of opinion between nations, a court of arbitration is supposed to decide. The question, however, whether the judges of this court would have the power to bring the respective parties before the bar remains unanswered. Would a state be able to bring an accused into court if it did not have the police behind it? It is the same in the life of nations, and in the final analysis it is always a sort of divine ordeal that decides. The power which nations can bring to bear is the decisive factor. It is evident that the stronger has the right before God and the world to enforce his will. History shows that the right as such does not mean a thing, unless it is backed up by great power. If one does not have the power to enforce his right, that right alone will profit him absolutely nothing. The stronger have always been victorious. The whole of nature is a continuous struggle between strength and weakness, an eternal victory of the strong over the weak. All nature would be full of decay if it were otherwise. And the states which do not wish to recognize this law will decay. If you need an example of this kind of decay, look at the present German Reich. (Munich, April 13, 1923; *Völkischer Boebachter,* April 15/16, 1923.)

Only Force Rules

The fundamental motif through all the centuries has been the principle that force and power are the determining factors. All development is struggle. Only force rules. Force is the first law. A struggle has already taken place between original man and his primeval world. Only through struggle have states and the world become great. If one should ask whether this struggle is gruesome, then the only answer could be: For the weak, yes, for humanity as a whole, no.

World history proves that in the struggle between nations, that race has always won out whose drive for self-preservation was the more pronounced, the stronger. . . . Unfortunately, the contemporary world stresses internationalism instead of the innate values of race, democracy and the majority instead of the worth of the great leader. Instead of everlasting struggle the world preaches cowardly pacifism, and everlasting peace. These three things, considered in the light of their ultimate consequences, are the causes of the downfall of all humanity. The practical result of conciliation among nations is the renunciation of a people's own strength and their voluntary enslavement. (Essen, Nov. 22, 1926; *Völkischer Beobachter,* Nov. 26, 1926.)

The Nonsense of Humanitarianism

The inventions of mankind are the result of eternal struggle. Never would aviation have progressed so remarkably had it not been for the war, had not countless thousands sacrificed their lives in this cruel struggle against nature. The struggle against the great beasts is ended, but it is being inexorably carried on against the tiny creatures—against bacteria and bacilli. There is no Marxian reconciliation on this score; it is either you or I, life or death, either extermination or servitude.

From [various] examples we arrive at the fundamental conclusion that there is no humanitarianism but only an eternal struggle, a struggle which is the prerequisite for the development of all humanity.

The borderline between man and the animal is established by man himself. The position which man enjoys today is his own accomplishment. We see before us the Aryan race which is manifestly the bearer of all culture, the true representative of all humanity. All inventions in the field of transportation must be credited to the members of a particular race. Our entire industrial science is without exception the work of the Nordics. All great composers from Beethoven to Richard Wagner are Aryans, even though they were born in Italy or France. Do not say that art is international. The tango, the shimmy, and the jazzband are international but they are not art. Man owes everything that is of any importance to the principle of struggle and to one race which has carried itself forward successfully. Take away the Nordic Germans and nothing remains but the dance of apes. . . . Because we recognize the fact that our people can endure only through struggle, we National Socialists are fighters. (Munich, April 2, 1927; *Völkischer Beobachter,* April 5, 1927.)

Struggle—The Source of Strength

Politics is nothing else than the struggle of a people for its existence in this world; it is the eternal battle of a people, for better or for worse, for its existence on this planet. How does this struggle take place? Great men of world history have described it. Frederick the Great said that politics is the art of serving one's people with all the means at one's disposal; according to Bismarck, politics is the art of the possible. . . . Clemenceau declared that the politics of peace was nothing else than the continuation of war with other means. Clausewitz asserted that war was nothing else than the continuation of politics with other weapons. In reality, then, politics is the struggle of a people with all weapons to the limit of its power for its existence on this earth.

With what question is struggle primarily related? It is the drive for self-preservation which leads to struggle—that is, the question of love and hunger. These are the two fundamental primitive forces around which everything on this earth centers. The total space on which life is carried on is circumscribed. This leads to a struggle of one against the other for this limited area. In addition, this area is more restricted for certain groups than for others so that their existence is dependent upon the preservation of the particular region which they inhabit.

Thus, the struggle for daily bread becomes in reality a struggle for the soil which produces this daily bread; that is, for space itself. It is an iron principle: the weak fall in order that the strong may live. . . . From all the innumerable creatures a complete species rises and becomes the master of the rest. Such a one is man—the most brutal, the most resolute creature on earth. He knows nothing but the extermination of his enemies in the world. . . . This struggle, this battle has not been carried on by all men in the same way. Certain species stand out, and at the top of the list is the Aryan. The Aryan has forged the weapons with which mankind has made itself master of the animal world. There is scarcely anything in existence which when traced back to its origin cannot claim an Aryan as its creator. . . . Never have votes and majorities added one iota to the culture of mankind. Every accomplishment is solely the result of the work and energy of great men, and as such, a flaming protest against the inertia of the masses.

How does this process then take place? It is an eternal struggle. Every achievement is nothing else than the result of a struggle of give-and-take. Every new invention is a triumph over an old one. Every record is a struggle against that which exists. Every championship performance is a conquest of that which prevailed previously.

Hence the following principles result: The value of man is determined in the first place by his inner racial virtues; second, by the ability of the race to bring forth men who in turn become leaders in the struggle for advancement; third, this entire process takes places in the form of eternal struggle. As a consequence struggle is the father of all things in this world. (Munich, Nov. 21, 1927; *Völkischer Beobachter,* Nov. 23, 1927.)

Originality plus Brutality

The will to live leads beyond the limitations of the present to the struggle for the prerequisites of life. Struggle is the impulse of self-preservation in nature. Man has become great through struggle.

The first fundamental of any rational *Weltanschauung* is the fact that on earth and in the universe force alone is decisive. Whatever goal man has reached is due to his originality plus his brutality. Whatever man possesses today in the field of culture is the culture of the Aryan race. The Aryan has stamped his character on the whole world. The basis for all development is the creative urge of the individual, not the vote of majorities. The genius of the individual is decisive, not the spirit of the masses. All life is bound up in three theses: Struggle is the father of all things, virtue lies in blood, leadership is primary and decisive.

Because the German people has forgotten this, it has collapsed. And if the German people does not again acquire power, that is, power in the sense of values and will, then no other choice is left the German people but to perish. There will never be a solution of the German problem until we return to the three fundamental principles which control the existence of every nation: The concept of struggle, the purity of blood, and the ingenuity of the individual. (Chemnitz, April 2, 1928; *Völkischer Beobachter,* April 7, 1928.)

Peace by the Sword

Politics is history in the making. History is the story of a people's struggle for survival. There is no distinction between war and peace. Struggle is ever present. A latent peace is only possible when one is either a free lord or a slave. The final decision lies with the sword.

In the power of the sword lies the vital strength of a nation. There is, therefore, no difference between domestic policy and foreign policy. The one is the support of the other and in turn presupposes the existence of the other. Politics cannot be carried out without the recognition of certain fundamental principles: the principle of struggle, the purity of blood, and the ideal of the leader. (Munich, May 2, 1928; *Völkischer Beobachter,* May 4, 1928.)

Man Must Kill

If men wish to live, then they are forced to kill others. The entire struggle for survival is a conquest of the means of existence which in turn results in the elimination of others from these same sources of subsistence. As long as there are peoples on this earth, there will be nations against nations and they will be forced to protect their vital rights in the same way as the individual is forced to protect his rights.

There is in reality no distinction between peace and war. Life, no matter in what form, is a process which always leads to the same result. Self-preservation will always be the goal of every individual. Struggle is ever-present and will remain. This signifies a constant willingness on the part of man to sacrifice to the utmost. Weapons, methods, instruments, formations, these may change, but in the end the struggle for survival remains. . . .

One is either the hammer or the anvil. We confess that it is our purpose to prepare the German people again for the role of the hammer. For ten years we have preached, and our deepest concern is: How can we again achieve power? We admit freely and openly that, if our Movement is victorious, we will be concerned day and night with the question of how to produce the armed forces which are forbidden us by the peace treaty. We solemnly confess that we consider everyone a scoundrel who does not try day and night to figure out a way to violate this treaty, for we have never recognized this treaty.

We admit, therefore, that as far as we are concerned the German army in its present form is not permanent. For us it will serve only as a great cadre army, that is, as a source of sergeants and officers. And in the meantime we will be continuously at work filling in the ranks. We will take every step which strengthens our arms, which augments the number of our forces, and which increases the strength of our people.

We confess further that we will dash anyone to pieces who should dare to hinder us in this undertaking. . . . Our rights will never be represented by others. Our rights will be protected only when the

German Reich is again supported by the point of the German dagger. (Munich, March 15, 1929; *Völkischer Beobachter,* March 17, 1929.)

[Nationalism Versus Internationalism]

Long Live Fanatical Nationalism

Our entire work consists of enlightening our people, of reshaping its mentality. It consists in the creation of a new Movement which will reform our people from top to bottom even reaching into the soul of the common German man, a new Movement which establishes three great postulates without which foreign policy cannot be carried out in the future.

In the first place, our people must be delivered from the hopeless confusion of international convictions, and educated consciously and systematically to fanatical nationalism. We will not declare that our goal is to have the German people sing German songs again in the future. No, our goal is that the German people should again acquire honor and conviction, that it should again bow in adoration before its own history, that it should respect those things which formerly gave it significance, and that it should curse that which damaged its honor. We recognize only two Gods: A God in Heaven and a God on earth and that is our Fatherland.

Second, insofar as we educate the people to fight against the delirium of democracy and bring it again to the recognition of the necessity of authority and of leadership, we tear it away from the nonsense of parliamentarianism; thereby we deliver it from the atmosphere of irresponsibility and lead it to responsibility and to a recognition of duty on the part of the individual person.

Third, insofar as we deliver the people from the atmosphere of pitiable belief in possibilities which lie outside the bounds of one's own strength—such as the belief in reconciliation, understanding, world peace, the League of Nations, and international solidarity— we destroy these ideas. There is only one right in this world and this right is one's own strength.

The people must recognize that its future will not be molded through cowardly belief in the help of others but through faithful devotion to one's own task. Out of this devotion deliverance must one day come—freedom and happiness and life. (Munich, Sept. 22, 1928; *Völkische. Beobachter,* Sept. 23, 1928.)

Racial and National Regeneration

He who shows his fist to the German people, his fist we will break open, and we will force him to be our brother. He who does not want to be a German has no place in our ranks. We are going to see to it that in this state there will be 60,000,000 who will not say in the first line of their political creed: "I am a democrat," or "I am a member of the People's Party," but who will say "I am a German."

Racial degeneration continues apace. The bastardization of great states has begun. The Negroization of culture, of customs—not only of blood—strides forward. The world becomes democratized. The value of the individual declines. The masses apparently are gaining the victory over the idea of the great leader. Numbers are chosen as the new God.

The poison of pacifism is again scattered about. The world forgets that struggle is the father of all things. State upon state is becoming intoxicated with ideas that must lead to the obliteration of a people. When the bastard, however, stands against the thoroughbred, and the Negro stands against the white man, the one who from the racial standpoint is the strongest, will be victorious. The individual is creative and has given culture to the world. When cowardice is pitted against courage and pacifism against daring, courage and daring gain the victory. That state will be victorious which does not fall prey to the vice of cowardice and pacifism. The people who opposed pacifism with the idea of struggle will with mathematical certainty become the master of its fate.

A people who opposes the bastardization of its spirit and its blood can be saved. The German people has its specific value and cannot be placed on the same level as 70,000,000 Negroes. If the German people will recognize its value it can mold the forces which will lead to victory.

Negro music is now the rage. But if we put the shimmy alongside a Beethoven symphony, then the triumph is clear. Let us think about the German soul, and then faith, creative power, and tenacity will not fail. Our people has always found men who conquered distress. Now it is believed, however, that leaders can be dispensed with; and at present world history is not being made, but, rather, the history of submission. Out of our strong faith will come the strength to help ourselves against this bastardization.

The goal which the National Socialist German Workers Party has set up for itself is to divest the terms nationalism and socialism of their former meaning. A nationalist can only be he who stands for his people, and a socialist can only be he who intercedes for the rights of his people—also in the field of foreign affairs. . . . This Movement begins a gigantic struggle against internationalism with all its effects to the left as well as to the right. All peoples on this earth are a matter of indifference to us, but in relation to one people we are full of passionate love, namely, in relation to our own people. . . . We fight against the idea of numbers and the delirium of the masses. We want to see those who are superior take the reins of government in their hands. There are 100,000 among us for whom voting is of no consequence—only the authority of the leader. And these 100,000 know that democracy in itself is a deception. (Berlin, Nov. 17, 1928; *Völkischer Beobachter,* Nov. 21, 1928.)

[England and France]

The Balkanization of Germany

Two Powers play a decisive role in the future development of Europe: England and France. England has the one and everlasting aim of Balkanizing Europe and of establishing a balance of power in Europe so that her position in the world will not be threatened. She is not, in principle, an enemy of Germany, but she is rather the power that tries to gain the first place in Europe. France is the outright enemy of Germany. Just as England needs the Balkanization of Europe, France needs the Balkanization of Germany in order to dominate Europe. After four and one-half years of hard struggle, victory, thanks to the Revolution, fell to the coalition of these two Powers. The result was as follows. France was confronted with this question. Was she to bring her eternal war aim to full realization or not, that is, could she destroy Germany, and rob her of all the means of subsistence? Today France is nearing the fulfillment of this age-old plan. It makes no difference which government is in power in France. The Supreme goal will remain—the destruction of Germany, the annihilation of 20,000,000 Germans and the dissolution of Germany into small states. (Munich, March 27, 1924; *Allgemeine Zeitung,* March 28, 1924.)

Alliance with the Devil

I was an opponent of France my entire life because I see in France the deadly enemy of my people. . . . May the people come to recognize that which is necessary, namely, not to come to terms with France but to organize general European opposition to France. If today Satan would come along and offer to be my ally against France, I would give him my hand, and I would march with him. For I know one thing: As long as France is not displaced from her position of hegemony in Europe, Germany will never acquire that which is necessary for her existence. I see two states which can never have an interest in this hegemony of France. They are Germany and Italy, and perhaps also England, which cannot wish to see France become an all-powerful state. (Munich, May 23, 1928; *Völkischer Beobachter,* May 25, 1928.)

Always Against France

There can be only one pole-star for German foreign policy: How can we again acquire power? For this purpose France has to be completely eliminated. France is not only the enemy of a German Government, she is not only the enemy of the form of the German State or of a certain mentality, the French people is the hereditary enemy of the German people. And if a Communist today says: Class against class—my dear friend, if the world becomes too small, no longer will class be against class, but people against people and the primeval struggle will again come to life in all its violence. Then your ridiculous class concepts will break apart as though they were nothing and all that will be left will be people against people. Thus the motto for every possible German foreign policy is: Always against France. Never will a German government succeed in coming to an understanding with France. . . . If one has grasped the magnitude of the task of German foreign policy, it must be clear that it will never be solved with the phrase about the restitution of any German boundary. Boundary problems are not what are at stake but the existence of the German nation in its entirety. . . . (Munich, Sept. 22, 1928; *Völkischer Beobachter,* Sept. 23/24, 1928.)

[The Jew]

The Jewish Peril

Is there still a racial problem in this "modern" world? The yellow race is denied the permission to settle in America. But this peril, ·comparatively speaking, is not nearly so great as the peril which today stretches its hand over the entire world—the Jewish peril. Many people do not regard the Jews as a race, but is there another people that is as determined to perpetuate its race everywhere in the world as the Jews? As a matter of fact, the Jew can never become a German. If he wanted to become a German he would have to give up being a Jew. That he cannot do. The Jew cannot become a German at heart for a number of reasons: First, because of his blood, second, because of his character; third, because of his will; and fourth, because of his actions. His actions remain Jewish and he works for the "greater idea" of the Jewish people. Since that is so and cannot be otherwise, the mere existence of the Jew is a colossal lie. The Jew is a past master at lying, for his existence as such in the organism of other peoples is only possible because of falsehood. This already was the opinion of the great Arthur Schopenhauer. The Jew lies to the other peoples when he pretends to be German, French, or the like.

What are the aims of the Jews? They aim to expand their invisible state as a supreme tyranny over the whole world. The Jew is therefore a destroyer of nations. In order to realize his domination over peoples he has to work in two directions. Economically he dominates the peoples, politically and morally he subjugates them. Politically he accomplishes his aims through the propagation of the principles of democracy and the doctrine of Marxism, which makes the proletarian a terrorist in domestic matters and a pacifist in foreign policy. From the ethical point of view the Jew destroys the peoples in respect to religious and moral considerations. Anyone who is willing to see that, can see it; and no one can help the person who refuses to see it. The Jew, voluntarily or involuntarily, consciously or unconsciously, undermines the foundation on which alone a nation can exist.

Thus, the following question comes up: Are we still in a position to resist an enemy who is our deadly enemy? The prime consideration is whether we want to save Germany. If so, then we must first save her from her destroyer. I confess, it is a severe struggle that must be fought out on this score. We National Socialists, however, occupy an extreme position in this regard. We know only one people for which we fight, and that is our own people. We may be inhuman, but if we save Germany we will have achieved the greatest thing on earth. We may do wrong, but if we save Germany, we will have righted the greatest wrong on earth. We may be immoral, but if we save our people, morality will have been given a new lease on life.

It is said that we are only making a lot of noise about anti-Semitism. Yes indeed, we want to stir up a storm. The people must not sleep, they should know that a storm is gathering. We have therefore laid down the principle in our program that only Germans can be citizens of the state. We could tolerate Jews only as guests, providing they did us no harm. But they are harmful. (Munich, April 20, 1923; *Völkischer Beobachter,* April 22/23, 1923.)

The Rightness of Racial Instinct

There were times when there was no danger of a Jewish bastardization of the people. A Goethe still had the natural instinct to say: Marriage between a Jew and a Gentile seems to me something against nature; it is impossible and cannot be. For generations, therefore, no laws concerning this question were necessary. Racial instinct protected the people; the odor of that race deterred Gentiles from marrying Jews. At present, in these days of perfume, where any dandy can assume the same odor as anyone else, the feeling for these finer distinctions between peoples is being lost. The Jew counts on that. The eye also becomes accustomed to differences between peoples. In this respect, knowledge must come to our aid. What generations once did instinctively, we must by necessity do consciously, lest we perish. And with that we come to the basic principle of our *Weltanschauung.* Instinct is the sound *Weltanschauung* of the primitive man reared in nature. As long as his instinct remains sound, his *Weltanschauung* is sound. Instinct keeps him from the wrong ways of thinking. (Munich, Nov. 29, 1929; *Völkischer Beobachter,* Dec. 3, 1929.)

Destroyer of Civilization

The Jew became the founder of the Social Democratic Movement, at that time. He succeeded with exceptional cleverness in securing the leadership more and more by means of two measures. He applied one measure on the Right, the other measure on the Left, for he had his apostles in both camps. As regards the Right, he tried to exaggerate all existing shortcomings to such an extent that through the emphasis on those things which necessarily antagonize the common man, the poor devil, the latter would be aroused as much as possible. It was the Jew who caused the greed for money to increase to an extreme. It was he who finally preached that unscrupulousness in the attainment of business ends was a matter of course. It was he who forced others to use the same methods because of his competition. It was he who became so heartless in the attainment of his ends that the saying, "Business, too, marches over corpses," became generally accepted. It was the Jew in particular whose repulsive insolence aroused the deadly hatred of the great masses. While the Jew on the one hand corrupted people by his bad example, he polluted their blood by systematic bastardization. More and more Jews filtered into the upper families, and it was from the Jews that the latter took their wives. The result was that in a short time it was precisely the leading class of the nation that had become completely estranged from its own people.

This was the prerequisite for the Jew's work on the Left. He made good use of this prerequisite. On the Left he was the common demagogue. Two measures were sufficient for him to drive the national intelligentsia from the leadership of the working class. First, there was the international approach. The Jew knew only too well that the moment he convinced the working class of the necessity of the international approach in his life and struggle, the national intelligentsia would drop out of the working class movement. For it would not continue under such circumstances. The national intelligentsia is willing to make the greatest sacrifices, to do everything for its people, but it cannot be so insane as to believe that a people can be made happy and prosperous by renouncing the existence of that people, by renouncing its own rights, and by abolishing national resistance toward foreign elements. The national intelligentsia could not do that and so it stayed away. Then there was the Jew's second measure— Marxist theory. The moment the statement is made that private property as such is theft, that is, in other words, as soon as one forsakes the self-evident formula that only natural resources can and should be common property, but that everything that anyone earns honestly should be his, from that moment too the economic intelligentsia with national ideals could no longer cooperate, for it realized that this theory would lead to the collapse of all human culture. Thus the Jew succeeded in isolating this new movement [of the workers] from all national elements. Furthermore, the Jew succeeded, by an ingenious exploitation of the press, in influencing the masses to such an extent that the faults of the Left appeared to the Right as the faults of the German worker, and the faults of the Right at the same time appeared to the German worker as the faults of the German middle class. Neither of the two groups realized that the faults of both sides were the result of a scheme, planned by devilish foreign agitators. This alone explains how the greatest farce in history was possible, namely, how the Jews of the stock exchange could become the leaders of the German Workers Movement. It is a gigantic fraud, the like of which is seldom seen in world history. . . .

In all this one can see again and again how well they work together, the Jew from the stock exchange and the leader of the workers; the newspaper of the stock exchange and the organ of the workers. . . . While the business agent Moses Cohn persuades his company to react most unfavorably to the demands of the workers, his brother Isaac Cohn, the labor leader, stands in the factory yard, arouses the masses and shouts: Just look at them, they only want to oppress you; throw off your chains. And upstairs his brother sees to it that those chains are well forged. On the one hand is the organ of the stock exchange, intent on encouraging ever-greater speculation. The prices of grain and all foods are driven higher and higher at an unprecedented rate. On the other hand there is the organ of the workers which arouses the masses by telling them: Bread has gone up; one thing and another has increased in price; do not tolerate it any longer; awake, proletarian. . . .

How long can this process go on? For it implies the annihilation of the economic system as well as the annihilation of a whole people. It is quite evident that this fourth estate [the workers] was not organized by the Jew just to safeguard the interests of that class. It is clear that the Jew Isaac Cohn does not stand in the factory out of love for the workers. It is self-evident that all those apostles who are talking themselves blue in the face on behalf of the workers, but at the same time patronize the Hotel Excelsior, ride in express trains, and spend their vacations in Nice, are not exerting themselves for the sake of the people. No, the people is not to derive any benefits from all this. The people is supposed to destroy the backbone of its own independence, its own economic system so it will all the more certainly sink into the golden fetters of the everlasting interest-slavery of the Jewish race. . . .

How long can this continue? It will continue until suddenly from out of the masses someone comes forth who will seize the leadership, find more comrades, and gradually cause the anger that has long been restrained to break loose against the deceivers. This is the great lurking danger which confronts the Jew; and he has only one safeguard against it, namely, to do away with this evil national intelligentsia. This is the irrevocable and ultimate aim of the Jewish revolution. And he must pursue this aim. He knows full well that his system is no blessing, that he is no master race (*Herrenvolk*), that he is an exploiter, that the Jews are a people of robbers. The Jew has never yet founded a civilization, but he has destroyed hundreds. He can show nothing of his own creation. Everything that he has is stolen. He has foreign people, foreign workers build his temples; foreigners create and work for him; foreigners shed their blood for him. He knows no "people's army" (*Volksheer*) but only paid mercenaries, who are ready to risk their lives for him. He has no art of his own, everything has either been stolen from other peoples or imitated. He does not even know how to preserve these costly possessions. In his hands they turn immediately to filth and dung. He also knows that he cannot maintain any state for any length of time. There is a difference between him and the Aryan. It is true that the Aryan has also dominated inferior peoples. But how? He went about his task, cleared the forests, transformed the wilderness into civilizations, and he did not use the inferior peoples for his own purposes but he integrated them into the state in accordance with their abilities. It was through the Aryan that art and science flourished. It was he alone who, in the final analysis, knew how to establish states.

The Jew is incapable of all this. His revolutions, therefore, must be "international." They must spread like a disease. For the Jew is incapable of building a state and saying: Look, here it is, a model for all. Imitate us! He has to see to it that the epidemic does not abate, that it is not confined to any one place, because it might otherwise consume itself there. Thus he has to spread everything internationally. And how long? Until the whole world falls in ruins and brings him down with it in the midst of the ruins. (Munich, July 28, 1922; *Völkischer Beobachter,* Aug. 16, 1922.)

[To the German Youth]

"Obedience Über Alles"

German Youth! For the third time you have answered this call, you who are more than 50,000 representatives of a community that is growing from year to year. The importance of that community which you embody here each year becomes increasingly greater. Not only in numbers, no; we see it, but also in quality. When I think back on the first call, and on the second one, and compare them with that of today, then I see the same development that we now notice in all phases of German life. Our people becomes noticeably more disciplined, more upright and stronger, and our youth is setting the pace. The ideal of manhood even among our people has not always been the same. There were times—and they seem far away and we can hardly understand them—when the fellow who could hold his liquor was the ideal of the young German. Today we are happy to see the youth resistant to any hardship of the weather, the hardy youth, in place of the fellow who knows how to drink. For it does not only depend on how many glasses of beer he can drink, but on how much he can endure; not on how many nights in a row he can gallivant, but on how many kilometers he can march. Today we no longer see the ideal of the German people in the beer drinker of former days, but in men and women who are healthy to the core, who are sturdy.

The things we want from our youth are different from what was wanted in the past. In our eyes the German youth of the future should be slim and lithe, fast as greyhounds, tough as leather, and hard as Krupp steel. We must bring up a new type of man, so that our people will not succumb to the symptoms of degeneracy of the times.

We do not talk, we act. We undertook to give this people a new type of education, an education that is to begin with our youth and will never end. In the future our young men will pass from one school into the other. It starts with the child and ends with the old fighter of the Movement. No one shall say that there is any time when he can be left entirely to his own devices. It is the duty of everyone to serve his people. Everyone has the duty to prepare himself for this service, to harden himself physically and to prepare and strengthen himself spiritually. The earlier this preparation begins, the better. In the future we will not permit ten or fifteen years to go by in German education and then be forced to make up what unfortunately has previously been spoiled. It is our intent and unshakable determination to instill already into the hearts of youth the spirit which we regard as the only one possible in this great Germany, the spirit which we want to see perpetuated in the future. . . .

The time will come when the German people will look with real joy upon its youth; then all of us will peacefully and confidently spend our old age in the firm and happy conviction, in the happy knowledge that our struggle was not in vain. Behind us someone is already following in our footsteps, someone with our spirit, our determination, our hardiness, the representatives of the life of our race.

We will harden ourselves to such an extent that any storm will find us strong. We will never forget that the sum total of all virtues and all strength can be effective only when it is subservient to one will and to one command. We are standing here now not by mere chance, not because each one of you did as he pleased, but because you were called here by the order of your youth leader, and because that order became a thousand separate orders. And as each of these orders was obeyed, millions of German boys in Germany became one organization; and out of tens of thousands of comrades living in Germany came this demonstration, this present roll call. Nothing is possible unless one will commands, a will which has to be obeyed by others, beginning at the top and ending only at the very bottom. Beside physical training and education, this is our second great task.

We are a following (*Gefolgschaft*) but as the word itself indicates, following means to follow, it means to be a loyal member of a following. We must train our people so that whenever someone has been appointed to command, the others will recognize it as their duty to obey him, for it can happen that an hour later they will be called upon to command, and they can do it then only if others in turn obey. This is the expression of an authoritarian state—not of a weak, babbling democracy—of an authoritarian state where everyone is proud to obey, because he knows: I will likewise be obeyed when I must take command. Germany is no chicken house where everyone runs about at random, cackling and crowing, but we are a people that from its infancy on learns how to be disciplined. If others do not understand us, that is all the same to us. . . . We did not sit back with our hands in our laps and say: It is not given to us to solve the problem, there is nothing we can do about it. No. Something could be done about it, and we did it. You, my boys and girls, are the living proof of the success of this work. You are the proof that this idea has come to life in the German Reich. You are the proof of how this idea has become reality. Believe me, the day will come when German youth will once again have a wonderful healthy and glowing appearance, healthy, frank, sincere, brave, and peace loving. We are no ruffians. If the rest of the world misunderstands us in our discipline, that is not our fault. From this discipline fewer quarrels will develop for the world than from the parliamentary-democratic confusion of the present day. We go our own way and we do not wish to cross the path of anyone else. Let the others leave our course undisturbed. The only requirement we have to set up for our love of peace is to harm no one and to tolerate no harm to us.

If we plan and define the way of life for the German people in this fashion, then eventually I believe there will develop among other nations an understanding for such a decent attitude and that perhaps here and there out of this understanding a few will extend to us the hand of brotherhood. But we must never forget that only the strong deserve friendship and only the strong grant friendship. We want, therefore, to make ourselves strong—that is our motto. You are responsible to me for making this come true. You are the future of the nation, the future of the German Reich. (Nürnberg, Sept. 14, 1935; *Völkischer Beobachter,* Sept. 15, 1935.)

Part Three

DEMOCRACY

Democracy is many things. It is a form of government in which we presently take pride; it is a set of ideals toward which we earnestly strive. It is a way of attaining objectives held in common and a process for the resolution of conflicts among men. Democracy is a set of institutions—the secret ballot, the nominating convention, the representative parliament; it is also an attitude, a temper of thought, a way of looking at society and its problems. Democracy is truly a way of life.

The varied and changing character of the many facets of democratic philosophy will emerge throughout this part. There is no straightforward doctrine universally acknowledged to be *the* philosophy of democracy. There is no man, or group of men, to whom the democrat can refer as the ultimate authority. There is no body of writings that can serve as democratic gospel; there may be dogmatic democrats, but there is little if anything that can pass for democratic dogma.

Does this mean that democratic philosophers have been inconsistent, one with another? It does; and much of this inconsistency will be disclosed in the ensuing selections. But one should not conclude from this inconsistency that democratic philosophers have been no more than apologists for particular political movements. For while these thinkers often worked actively for concrete political objectives, it was not the rationalization of a previously held policy, but the deepest of philosophical principles that generally served as their motivation.

If there is any single principle or attitude held in common by all democratic philosophers, it is a confidence in the capacity of human beings, living together, to govern themselves justly. There is no finer statement of this confidence, and of the character and ideals to which it gives birth, than the funeral oration of the Athenian, Pericles, delivered over two

423

thousand years ago. That oration is presented here as the best possible
introduction to the philosophy of democracy.*

". . . But before I praise the dead, I should like to point out by what
principles of action we rose to power, and under what institutions and
through what manner of life our empire became great. For I conceive
that such thoughts are not unsuited to the occasion, and that this numerous assembly of citizens and strangers may profitably listen to them.

"Our form of government does not enter into rivalry with the institutions of others. We do not copy our neighbours, but are an example to
them. It is true that we are called a democracy, for the administration is
in the hands of the many and not of the few. But while the law secures
equal justice to all alike in their private disputes, the claim of excellence
is also recognized; and when a citizen is in any way distinguished, he is
preferred to the public service, not as a matter of privilege, but as the
reward of merit. Neither is poverty a bar, but a man may benefit his
country whatever be the obscurity of his condition. There is no exclusiveness in our public life, and in our private intercourse we are not suspicious
of one another, nor angry with our neighbor if he does what he likes; we
do not put on sour looks at him which, though harmless, are not pleasant.
While we are thus unconstrained in our private intercourse, a spirit of
reverence pervades our public acts; we are prevented from doing wrong
by respect for authority and for the laws, having an especial regard to
those which are ordained for the protection of the injured as well as to
those unwritten laws which bring upon the transgressor of them the
reprobation of the general sentiment.

"And we have not forgotten to provide for our weary spirits many
relaxations from toil; we have regular games and sacrifices throughout
the year; at home the style of our life is refined; and the delight which
we daily feel in all these things helps to banish melancholy. Because of
the greatness of our city the fruits of the whole earth flow in upon us;
so that we enjoy the goods of other countries as freely as of our own.

"Then, again, our military training is in many respects superior to
that of our adversaries. Our city is thrown open to the world, and we
never expel a foreigner or prevent him from seeing or learning anything
of which the secret if revealed to an enemy might profit him. We rely not
upon management or trickery, but upon our own hearts and hands. And
in the matter of education, whereas they from early youth are always
undergoing laborious exercises which are to make them brave, we live
at ease, and yet are equally ready to face the perils which they face. And
here is the proof. The Lacedaemonians come into Attica not by them-

---

* This oration, delivered in 430 B.C., was reported by Thucydides in his his-
'ory of the Peloponnesian War. The translation used here is by Benjamin
Jowett, originally published in 1881, at the Clarendon Press, Oxford.

selves, but with their whole confederacy following; we go alone into a neighbor's country; and although our opponents are fighting for their homes and we on a foreign soil, we have seldom any difficulty in overcoming them. Our enemies have never yet felt our united strength; the care of a navy divides our attention, and on land we are obliged to send our own citizens everywhere. But they, if they meet and defeat a part of our army, are as proud as if they had routed us all, and when defeated they pretend to have been vanquished by us all.

"If then we prefer to meet danger with a light heart but without laborious training, and with a courage which is gained by habit and not enforced by law, are we not greatly the gainers? Since we do not anticipate the pain, although, when the hour comes, we can be as brave as those who never allow themselves to rest; and thus too our city is equally admirable in peace and in war. For we are lovers of the beautiful, yet simple in our tastes, and we cultivate the mind without loss of manliness. Wealth we employ, not for talk and ostentation, but when there is a real use for it. To avow poverty with us is no disgrace; the true disgrace is in doing nothing to avoid it. An Athenian citizen does not neglect the state because he takes care of his own household; and even those of us who are engaged in business have a very fair idea of politics. We alone regard a man who takes no interest in public affairs, not as a harmless, but as a useless character; and if few of us are originators, we are all sound judges of a policy. The great impediment to action is, in our opinion, not discussion, but the want of that knowledge which is gained by discussion preparatory to action. For we have a peculiar power of thinking before we act and of acting too, whereas other men are courageous from ignorance but hesitate upon reflection. And they are surely to be esteemed the bravest spirits who, having the clearest sense both of the pains and pleasures of life, do not on that account shrink from danger. In doing good, again, we are unlike others; we make our friends by conferring, not by receiving favors. Now he who confers a favor is the firmer friend, because he would fain by kindness keep alive the memory of an obligation; but the recipient is colder in his feelings, because he knows that in requiting another's generosity he will not be winning gratitude but only paying a debt. We alone do good to our neighbors not upon a calculation of interest, but in the confidence of freedom and in a frank and fearless spirit. To sum up: I say that Athens is the school of Hellas, and that the individual Athenian in his own person seems to have the power of adapting himself to the most varied forms of action with the utmost versatility and grace. This is no passing and idle word, but truth and fact; and the assertion is verified by the position to which these qualities have raised the state. For in the hour of trial Athens alone among her contemporaries is superior to the r⌒port of her. No enemy who comes against her is indignant at the reverses which he sustains at the hands of such a city; no subject complains that his masters are unworthy of him. And we shall assuredly not be without witnesses; there are mighty monuments of our power which will make us the wonder of this and of succeeding ages; we shall not need the praises of Homer or of any other panegyrist whose poetry may please for the moment, although his representation of the facts will not bear the light of day. For we have compelled every land and every sea to open a path for our valor, and have everywhere planted eternal memorials of our friendship and of our enmity. Such is the city for whose sake these men nobly fought and died; they could not bear the thought that she might be taken from them; and every one of us who survive should gladly toil on her behalf.

"I have dwelt upon the greatness of Athens because I want to show you that we are contending for a higher prize than those who enjoy none of these privileges, and to establish by manifest proof the merit of these men whom I am now commemorating. Their loftiest praise has been already spoken. For in magnifying the city I have magnified them, and men like them whose virtues made her glorious. And of how few Hellenes can it be said as of them, that their deeds when weighed in the balance have been found equal to their fame! Methinks that a death such as theirs has been given the true measure of a man's worth; it may be the first revelation of his virtues, but is at any rate their final seal. For even those who come short in other ways may justly plead the valor with which they have fought for their country; they have blotted out the evil with the good, and have benefited the state more by their public services than they have injured her by their private actions. None of these men were enervated by wealth or hesitated to resign the pleasures of life; none of them put off the evil day in the hope, natural to poverty, that a man, though poor, may one day become rich. But, deeming that the punishment of their enemies was sweeter than any of these things, and that they could fall in no nobler cause, they determined at the hazard of their lives to be honorably avenged, and to leave the rest. They resigned to hope their unknown chance of happiness; but in the face of death they resolved to rely upon themselves alone. And when the moment came they were minded to resist and suffer, rather than to fly and save their lives; they ran away from the word of dishonor, but on the battlefield their feet stood fast, and in an instant, at the height of their fortune, they passed away from the scene, not of their fear, but of their glory. . . ."

Section I

NATURAL RIGHTS DEMOCRACY

The oldest forms of systematic democratic thought are those based upon the existence of a law of nature, from which the inalienable rights of every citizen are derived. According to these views, the foundations of democracy are usually held to have been laid down by God, whose laws, open to the scrutiny of all mankind, decree a universal citizenship and a universal code of right and justice. Since all are equal under God, all have an equal claim to freedom, and to participation in government. This time-honored theme remains a viable and influential tradition in contemporary democratic thought.

Several consequences of great importance derive directly from this theory of natural right. First, since the highest law and the rights that it prescribes come directly from the Supreme Being, this law must be prior to any government in time and superior at all times to any governmental authority. Indeed, according to this view, the chief end for which governments are devised is the protection of the rights and freedoms with which man is naturally endowed. "We hold these truths to be self-evident," Jefferson wrote, "that all men are created equal; that they are endowed by their Creator with certain unalienable Rights . . . That to secure these rights, Governments are instituted among Men, deriving their just powers from the consent of the governed."

Second, since the laws of a civil society supplement the laws of nature, but cannot alter them, these civil laws are to be obeyed only when they are consistent with the higher principles to which they are subordinate. Thus emerges the right to resist an illegitimate power—the philosophical foundation upon which a series of democratic rebellions was based, including the American Revolution of 1776. "Rebellion to tyrants," said the fathers of that revolution, "is obedience to God."

50. MARCUS TULLIUS CICERO

Marcus Tullius Cicero (106-43 B.C.) was one of the great statesmen and orators of ancient Rome. A Stoic, he formulated one of the earliest statements of the theory of natural law—law universal in application and grasped directly by the human reason. Upon this natural law, he argued, all real justice is founded, and from it all man-made laws derive their authority.

[The Source of Law] *

M.† My opinions? Well then, I believe that there have been most eminent men in our State whose customary function it was to interpret the law to the people and answer questions in regard to it, but that these men, though they have made great claims, have spent their time on unimportant details. What subject indeed is so vast as the law of the State? But what is so trivial as the task of those who give legal advice? It is, however, necessary for the people. But, while I do not consider that those who have applied themselves to this profession have lacked a conception of universal law, yet they have carried their studies of this civil law, as it is called, only far enough to accomplish their purpose of being useful to the people. Now all this amounts to little so far as learning is concerned, though for practical purposes it is indispensable. What subject is it, then, that you are asking me to expound? To what task are you urging me? Do you want me to write a treatise on the law of eaves and house-walls? Or to compose formulas for contracts and court procedure? These subjects have been carefully treated by many writers, and are of a humbler character, I believe, than what is expected of me.

A. Yet if you ask what I expect of you, I consider it a logical thing that, since you have already written a treatise on the constitu-

---

* From Cicero, *De Legibus*. This and the following passages are from a translation by C. W. Keyes, Loeb Classical Library, 1928. Reprinted by permission of The Harvard University Press.

† In these conversations, M.'s opinions represent the views of Cicero.—*Ed.*

tion of the ideal State, you should also write one on its laws. For I note that this was done by your beloved Plato, whom you admire, revere above all others, and love above all others.

M. Is it your wish, then, that, as he discussed the institutions of States and the ideal laws with Clinias and the Spartan Megillus in Crete on a summer day amid the cypress groves and forest paths of Cnossus, sometimes walking about, sometimes resting—you recall his description—we, in like manner, strolling or taking our ease among these stately poplars on the green and shady river bank, shall discuss the same subjects along somewhat broader lines than the practice of the courts calls for?

A. I should certainly like to hear such a conversation.

M. What does Quintus say?

Q. No other subject would suit me better.

M. And you are wise, for you must understand that in no other kind of discussion can one bring out so clearly what Nature's gifts to man are, what a wealth of most excellent possessions the human mind enjoys, what the purpose is, to strive after and accomplish which we have been born and placed in this world, what it is that unites men, and what natural fellowship there is among them. For it is only after all these things have been made clear that the origin of Law and Justice can be discovered.

A. Then you do not think that the science of law is to be derived from the praetor's edict, as the majority do now, or from the Twelve Tables, as people used to think, but from the deepest mysteries of philosophy?

M. Quite right; for in our present conversation, Pomponius, we are not trying to learn how to protect ourselves legally, or how to answer clients' questions. Such problems may be important, and in fact they are; for in former times many eminent men made a specialty of their solution, and at present one person performs this duty with the greatest authority and skill. But in our present investigation we intend to cover the whole range of universal Justice and Law in such a way that our own civil law, as it is called, will be confined to a small and narrow corner. For we must explain the nature of Justice, and this must be sought for in the nature of man; we must also consider the laws by which States ought to be governed; then we must deal with the enactments and decrees of nations which are already formulated and put in writing; and among these the civil law, as it is called, of the Roman people will not fail to find a place.

Q. You probe deep, and seek, as you should, the very fountain-head, to find what we are after, brother. And those who teach the civil law in any other way are teaching not so much the path of justice as of litigation.

M. There you are mistaken, Quintus, for it is rather ignorance of the law than knowledge of it that leads to litigation. But that will come later; now let us investigate the origins of Justice.

[Law is Right Reason]

M. Well then, the most learned men have determined to begin with Law, and it would seem that they are right if, according to their definition, Law is the highest reason, implanted in Nature, which commands what ought to be done and forbids the opposite. This reason, when firmly fixed and fully developed in the human mind, is Law. And so they believe that Law is intelligence, whose natural function it is to command right conduct and forbid wrongdoing. They think that this quality has derived its name in Greek from the idea of grant-ing to every man his own, and in our language I believe it has been named from the idea of choosing. For as they have attributed the idea of fairness to the word law, so we have given it that of selection, though both ideas properly belong to Law. Now if this is correct, as I think it to be in general, then the origin of Justice is to be found in Law, for Law is a natural force; it is the mind and reason of the intelligent man, the standard by which Justice and Injustice are measured. But since our whole discussion has to do with the reason-ing of the populace, it will sometimes be necessary to speak in the popular manner, and give the name of law to that which in written form decrees whatever it wishes, either by command or prohibition. For such is the crowd's definition of law. But in determining what Justice is, let us begin with that supreme Law which had its origin ages before any written law existed or any State had been established.

Q. Indeed that will be preferable and more suitable to the charac-ter of the conversation we have begun.

M. Well, then, shall we seek the origin of Justice itself at its fountainhead? For when that is discovered we shall undoubtedly have a standard by which the things we are seeking may be tested.

Q. I think that is certainly what we must do.

A. Put me down also as agreeing with your brother's opinion.

M. Since, then, we must retain and preserve that constitution of the State which Scipio proved to be the best in the six books devoted to the subject, and all our laws must be fitted to that type of State, and since we must also inculcate good morals, and not prescribe everything in writing, I shall seek the root of Justice in Nature, under whose guidance our whole discussion must be conducted.

A. Quite right. Surely with her as our guide, it will be impossible for us to go astray.

M. Do you grant us, then, Pomponius (for I am aware of what Quintus thinks), that it is by the might of the immortal gods, or by their nature, reason, power, mind, will, or any other term which may make my meaning clearer, that all Nature is governed? For if you do not admit it, we must begin our argument with this problem before taking up anything else.

A. Surely I will grant it, if you insist upon it, for the singing of the birds about us and the babbling of the streams relieve me from all fear that I may be overheard by any of my comrades in the School.*

M. Yet you must be careful; for it is their way to become very angry at times, as virtuous men will; and they will not tolerate your treason, if they hear of it, to the opening passage of that excellent book, in which the author† has written, "God troubles himself about nothing, neither his own concerns nor those of others."

A. Continue, if you please, for I am eager to learn what my admission will lead to.

M. I will not make the argument long. Your admission leads us to this: that animal which we call man, endowed with foresight and quick intelligence, complex, keen, possessing memory, full of reason and prudence, has been given a certain distinguished status by the supreme God who created him; for he is the only one among so many different kinds and varieties of living beings who has a share in reason and thought, while all the rest are deprived of it. But what is more divine, I will not say in man only, but in all heaven and earth, than reason? And reason, when it is full grown and perfected, is rightly called wisdom. Therefore, since there is nothing better than reason, and since it exists both in man and God, the first common possession of man and God is reason. But those who have reason in common must also have right reason in common. And since right reason is Law, we must believe that men have Law also in common

---

* The speaker, Atticus, was an Epicurean.—*Ed.*
† Epicurus—*Ed.*

with the gods. Further, those who share Law must also share Justice; and those who share these are to be regarded as members of the same commonwealth. If indeed they obey the same authorities and powers, this is true in a far greater degree; but as a matter of fact they do obey this celestial system, the divine mind, and the God of transcendent power. Hence we must now conceive of this whole universe as one commonwealth of which both gods and men are members. . . .

[Right is Based upon Nature]

A. Ye immortal gods, how far back you go to find the origins of Justice! And you discourse so eloquently that I not only have no desire to hasten on to the consideration of the civil law, concerning which I was expecting you to speak, but I should have no objection to your spending even the entire day on your present topic; for the matters which you have taken up, no doubt, merely as preparatory to another subject, are of greater import than the subject itself to which they form an introduction.

M. The points which are now being briefly touched upon are certainly important: but out of all the material of the philosophers' discussions, surely there comes nothing more valuable than the full realization that we are born for Justice, and that right is based, not upon men's opinions, but upon Nature. This fact will immediately be plain if you once get a clear conception of man's fellowship and union with his fellow-men. For no single thing is so like another, so exactly its counterpart, as all of us are to one another. Nay, if bad habits and false beliefs did not twist the weaker minds and turn them in whatever direction they are inclined, no one would be so like his own self as all men would be like all others. And so, however we may define man, a single definition will apply to all. This is a sufficient proof that there is no difference in kind between man and man; for if there were, one definition could not be applicable to all men; and indeed reason, which alone raises us above the level of the beasts and enables us to draw inferences, to prove and disprove, to discuss and solve problems, and to come to conclusions, is certainly common to us all, and, though varying in what it learns, at least in the capacity to learn it is invariable. For the same things are invariably perceived by the senses, and those things which stimulate the senses, stimulate them in the same way in all men; and those rudimentary beginnings of intelligence to which I have referred, which are imprinted on our minds, are imprinted on all minds alike; and speech, the mind's interpreter, though differing in the choice of words, agrees in the sentiments expressed. In fact, there is no human being of any race who, if he finds a guide, cannot attain to virtue.

The similarity of the human race is clearly marked in its evil tendencies as well as in its goodness. For pleasure also attracts all men; and even though it is an enticement to vice, yet it has some likeness to what is naturally good. For it delights us by its lightness and agreeableness; and for this reason, by an error of thought, it is embraced as something wholesome. It is through a similar misconception that we shun death as though it were a dissolution of nature, and cling to life because it keeps us in the sphere in which we were born; and that we look upon pain as one of the greatest of evils, not only because of its cruelty, but also because it seems to lead to the destruction of nature. In the same way, on account of the similarity between moral worth and renown, those who are publicly honored are considered happy, while those who do not attain fame are thought miserable. Troubles, joys, desires, and fears haunt the minds of all men without distinction, and even if different men have different beliefs, that does not prove, for example, that it is not the same quality of superstition that besets those races which worship dogs and cats as gods, as that which torments other races. But what nation does not love courtesy, kindliness, gratitude, and remembrance of favors bestowed? What people does not hate and despise the haughty, the wicked, the cruel, and the ungrateful? Inasmuch as these considerations prove to us that the whole human race is bound together in unity, it follows, finally, that knowledge of the principles of right living is what makes men better.

If you approve of what has been said, I will go on to what follows. But if there is anything that you care to have explained, we will take that up first.

A. We have no questions, if I may speak for both of us.

M. The next point, then, is that we are so constituted by Nature as to share the sense of Justice with one another and to pass it on to all men. And in this whole discussion I want it understood that what I shall call Nature is [that which is implanted in us by Nature]; that, however, the corruption caused by bad habits is so great that the sparks of fire, so to speak, which Nature has kindled in us are extinguished by this corruption, and the vices which are their opposites spring up and are established. But if the judgments of men were in agreement with Nature, so that, as the poet says, they considered "nothing alien to them which concerns mankind," then Justice would be equally observed by all. For those creatures who have received the gift of reason from Nature have also received right reason, and therefore they have also received the gift of Law, which is right reason applied to command and prohibition. And if they have received Law, they have received Justice also. Now all men have received reason; therefore all men have received Justice. Consequently Socrates was right when he cursed, as he often did, the man who first separated utility from Justice; for this separation, he complained, is the source of all mischief. For what gave rise to Pythagoras' famous words about friendship? . . . From this it is clear that, when a wise man shows toward another endowed with equal virtue the kind of benevolence which is so widely diffused among men, that will then have come to pass which, unbelievable as it seems to some, is after all the inevitable result—namely, that he loves himself no whit more than he loves another. For what difference can there be among things which are all equal? But if the least distinction should be made in friendship, then the very name of friendship would perish forthwith; for its essence is such that, as soon as either friend prefers anything for himself, friendship ceases to exist.

Now all this is really a preface to what remains to be said in our discussion, and its purpose is to make it more easily understood that Justice is inherent in Nature. After I have said a few words more on this topic, I shall go on to the civil law, the subject which gives rise to all this discourse.

Q. You certainly need to say very little more on that head, for from what you have already said, Atticus is convinced, and certainly I am, that Nature is the source of Justice.

A. How can I help being convinced, when it has just been proved to us, first, that we have been provided and equipped with what we may call the gifts of the gods; next, that there is only one principle by which men may live with one another, and that this is the same for all, and possessed equally by all; and, finally, that all men are bound together by a certain natural feeling of kindliness and good-will, and also by a partnership in Justice? Now that we have admitted the truth of these conclusions, and rightly, I think, how can we separate Law and Justice from Nature? . . .

[Natural and Conventional Justice Distinguished]

M. But the most foolish notion of all is the belief that everything is just which is found in the customs or laws of nations. Would that be true, even if these laws had been enacted by tyrants? If the well-known Thirty had desired to enact a set of laws at Athens, or if the Athenians without exception were delighted by the tyrants' laws, that would not entitle such laws to be regarded as just, would it? No more, in my opinion, should that law be considered just which a Roman interrex proposed, to the effect that a dictator might put to death with impunity any citizen he wished, even without a trial. For Justice is one; it binds all human society, and is based on one Law, which is right reason applied to command and prohibition. Whoever knows not this Law, whether it has been recorded in writing anywhere or not, is without Justice.

But if Justice is conformity to written laws and national customs, and if, as the same persons claim, everything is to be tested by the standard of utility, then anyone who thinks it will be profitable to him will, if he is able, disregard and violate the laws. It follows that Justice does not exist at all, if it does not exist in Nature, and if that form of it which is based on utility can be overthrown by that very utility itself. And if Nature is not to be considered the foundation of Justice, that will mean the destruction [of the virtues on which human society depends]. For where then will there be a place for generosity, or love of country, or loyalty, or the inclination to be of service to others or to show gratitude for favors received? For these virtues originate in our natural inclination to love our fellow-men, and this is the foundation of Justice. Otherwise not merely consideration for men but also rites and pious observances in honor of the gods are done away with; for I think that these ought to be maintained, not through fear, but on account of the close relationship which exists between man and God. But if the principles of Justice were founded on the decrees of peoples, the edicts of princes, or the decisions of judges, then Justice would sanction robbery and adultery and forgery of wills, in case these acts were approved by the votes or decrees of the populace. But if so great a power belongs to the decisions and decrees of fools that the laws of Nature can be changed by their votes, then why do they not ordain that what is bad and baneful shall be considered good and salutary? Or, if a law can make Justice out of Injustice, can it not also make good out of bad? But in fact we can perceive the difference between good laws and bad by referring them to no other standard than Nature; indeed, it is not merely Justice and Injustice which are distinguished by Nature, but also and without exception things which are honorable and dishonorable. For since an intelligence common to us all makes things known to us and formulates them in our minds, honorable actions are ascribed by us to virtue, and dishonorable actions to vice; and only a madman would conclude that these judgments are matters of opinion, and not fixed by Nature. . . .

51. JOHN LOCKE

John Locke (1632-1704) is the most important figure in the tradition of natural rights democracy. Although the central ideas of democratic theory were by no means original with him, his Second Treatise of Government, *in which the principles of individualism and natural law were carefully interwoven, is one of the most influential political treatises of all time. Upon a foundation of universal and natural rights, Locke develops a theory of government as the deliberate product of a social contract, which, when broken, justifies the creation, by the people, of a new and better instrument for the protection of their lives, liberties, and estates.*

Of the State of Nature*

To understand political power right, and derive it from its original, we must consider what state all men are naturally in, and that is, a state of perfect freedom to order their actions and dispose of their possessions and persons as they think fit, within the bounds of the law of nature, without asking leave or depending upon the will of any other man.

A state also of equality, wherein all the power and jurisdiction is

* From J. Locke, *Second Treatise of Government,* 1690. These passages are from an edition of Locke's works published in London, by Thomas Tegg and others, in 1823.

reciprocal, no one having more than another; there being nothing more evident than that creatures of the same species and rank, promiscuously born to all the same advantages of nature and the use of the same faculties, should also be equal one among another without subordination or subjection; unless the Lord and Master of them all should, by any manifest declaration of his will, set one above another, and confer on him, by an evident and clear appointment, an undoubted right to dominion and sovereignty. . . .

But though this be a state of liberty, yet it is not a state of license; though man in that state have an uncontrollable liberty to dispose of his person or possessions, yet he has not liberty to destroy himself, or so much as any creature in his possession, but where some nobler use than its bare preservation calls for it. The state of nature has a law of nature to govern it, which obliges everyone; and reason, which is that law, teaches all mankind who will but consult it that being all equal and independent, no one ought to harm another in his life, health, liberty, or possessions; for men being all the workmanship of one omnipotent and infinitely wise Maker—all the servants of one sovereign Master, sent into the world by his order, and about his business—they are his property, whose workmanship they are, made to last during his, not one another's pleasure; and being furnished with like faculties, sharing all in one community of nature, there cannot be supposed any such subordination among us that may authorize us to destroy another, as if we were made for one another's uses, as the inferior ranks of creatures are for ours. Everyone, as he is bound to preserve himself, and not to quit his station willfully, so by the like reason, when his own preservation comes not in competition, ought he, as much as he can, to preserve the rest of mankind, and may not, unless it be to do justice to an offender, take away or impair the life (or what tends to the preservation of life) the liberty, health, limb, or goods of another.

And that all men may be restrained from invading others' rights, and from doing hurt to one another, and the law of nature be observed, which wills the peace and preservation of all mankind, the execution of the law of nature is, in that state, put into every man's hands, whereby everyone has a right to punish the transgressors of that law to such a degree as may hinder its violation; for the law of nature would, as all other laws that concern men in this world, be in vain, if there were nobody that in that state of nature had a power to execute that law and thereby preserve the innocent and restrain offenders. And if anyone in the state of nature may punish another for any evil he has done, everyone may do so; for in that state of perfect equality, where naturally there is no superiority or jurisdiction of one over another, what any may do in prosecution of that law everyone must needs have a right to do. . . .

It is often asked as a mighty objection, "Where are or ever were there any men in such a state of nature?" To which it may suffice as an answer at present, that since all princes and rulers of independent governments all through the world are in a state of nature, it is plain the world never was, nor ever will be, without numbers of men in that state. I have named all governors of independent communities, whether they are, or are not, in league with others; for it is not every compact that puts an end to the state of nature between men, but only this one of agreeing together mutually to enter into one community, and make one body politic; other promises and compacts men may make one with another, and yet still be in the state of nature; . . . for truth and keeping of faith belongs to men as men, and not as members of society.

To those that say there were never any men in the state of nature, I will not only oppose the authority of the judicious Hooker,* *Eccl. Pol.,* lib. i., sect. 10, where he says:

> The laws which have been hitherto mentioned [i.e., the laws of nature] do bind men absolutely, even as they are men, although they have never any settled fellowship, never any solemn agreement among themselves what to do, or not to do; but forasmuch as we are not by ourselves sufficient to furnish ourselves with competent store of things, needful for such a life as our nature doth desire, a life fit for the dignity of man; therefore to supply those defects and imperfections which are in us, as living singly and solely by ourselves, we are naturally induced to seek communion and fellowship with others. This was the cause of men's uniting themselves at first in politic societies.

But I moreover affirm that all men are naturally in that state and remain so till by their own consents they make themselves members of some politic society; and I doubt not in the sequel of this discourse to make it very clear.

---

* Richard Hooker was an important sixteenth century political theorist, and author of *The Laws of Ecclesiastical Polity.* Through his work the medieval tradition of limited government had great influence upon Locke.—*Ed.*

Of the State of War

The state of war is a state of enmity and destruction; and therefore declaring by word or action, not a passionate and hasty, but a sedate, settled design upon another man's life, puts him in a state of war with him against whom he has declared such an intention, and so has exposed his life to the other's power to be taken away by him, or anyone that joins with him in his defense and espouses his quarrel; it being reasonable and just I should have a right to destroy that which threatens me with destruction; for, by the fundamental law of nature, man being to be preserved as much as possible, when all cannot be preserved, the safety of the innocent is to be preferred; and one may destroy a man who makes war upon him, or has discovered an enmity to his being, for the same reason that he may kill a wolf or a lion; because such men are not under the ties of the common law of reason, have no other rule but that of force and violence, and so may be treated as beasts of prey, those dangerous and noxious creatures that will be sure to destroy him whenever he falls into their power.

And hence it is that he who attempts to get another man into his absolute power, does thereby put himself into a state of war with him; it being to be understood as a declaration of a design upon his life; for I have reason to conclude that he who would get me into his power without my consent would use me as he pleased when he got me there, and destroy me too when he had a fancy to it; for nobody can desire to have me in his absolute power, unless it be to compel me by force to that which is against the right of my freedom, i.e., make me a slave. To be free from such force is the only security of my preservation; and reason bids me look on him as an enemy to my preservation, who would take away that freedom which is the fence to it; so that he who makes an attempt to enslave me thereby puts himself into a state of war with me. He that, in the state of nature, would take away the freedom that belongs to anyone in that state, must necessarily be supposed to have a design to take away everything else, that freedom being the foundation of all the rest; as he that, in the state of society, would take away the freedom belonging to those of that society or commonwealth, must be supposed to design to take away from them everything else, and so be looked on as in a state of war. . . .

And here we have the plain "difference between the state of nature and the state of war," which, however some men have confounded [them],* are as far distant as a state of peace, good-will, mutual assistance and preservation, and state of enmity, malice, violence, and mutual destruction, are one from another. Men living together according to reason, without a common superior on earth with authority to judge between them, is properly the state of nature. But force, or a declared design of force, upon the person of another, where there is no common superior on earth to appeal to for relief, is the state of war; and it is the want of such an appeal [that] gives a man the right of war even against an aggressor, though he be in society, and a fellow subject. Thus a thief, whom I cannot harm but by appeal to the law, for having stolen all that I am worth, I may kill when he sets on me to rob me but of my horse or coat; because the law, which was made for my preservation, where it cannot interpose to secure my life from present force, which, if lost, is capable of no reparation, permits me my own defense, and the right of war, a liberty to kill the aggressor, because the aggressor allows not time to appeal to our common judge, nor the decision of the law, for remedy in a case where the mischief may be irreparable. Want of a common judge with authority puts all men in a state of nature; force without right upon a man's person makes a state of war both where there is and is not a common judge. . . .

To avoid this state of war (wherein there is no appeal but to Heaven, and wherein every least difference is apt to end, where there is no authority to decide between the contenders) is one great reason of men's putting themselves into society and quitting the state of nature; for where there is an authority, a power on earth from which relief can be had by appeal, there the continuance of the state of war is excluded, and the controversy is decided by that power. . . .

Of Political or Civil Society

Man being born, as has been proved, with a title to perfect freedom and uncontrolled enjoyment of all the rights and privileges of the law of nature equally with any other man or number of men in the world, has by nature a power not only to preserve his property

* The reference is almost certainly to Thomas Hobbes.—*Ed.*

—that is, his life, liberty, and estate—against the injuries and attempts of other men, but to judge of and punish the breaches of that law in others as he is persuaded the offense deserves, even with death itself in crimes where the heinousness of the fact in his opinion requires it. But because no political society can be, nor subsist, without having in itself the power to preserve the property and, in order thereunto, punish the offenses of all those of that society, there and there only is political society where every one of the members has quitted his natural power, resigned it up into the hands of the community in all cases that exclude him not from appealing for protection to the law established by it. And thus all private judgment of every particular member being excluded, the community comes to be umpire by settled standing rules, indifferent and the same to all parties; and by men having authority from the community for the execution of those rules decides all the differences that may happen between any members of that society concerning any matter of right; and punishes those offenses which any member has committed against the society, with such penalties as the law has established; whereby it is easy to discern who are, and who are not, in political society together. Those who are united into one body, and have a common established law and judicature to appeal to, with authority to decide controversies between them, and punish offenders, are in civil society one with another; but those who have no such common appeal, I mean on earth, are still in the state of nature, each being, where there is no other, judge for himself, and executioner, which is, as I have before shown it, the perfect state of nature.

And thus the commonwealth comes by a power to set down what punishment shall belong to the several transgressions which they think worthy of it, committed among the members of that society (which is the power of making laws) as well as it has the power to punish any injury done unto any of its members, by anyone that is not of it (which is the power of war and peace): and all this for the preservation of the property of all the members of that society as far as is possible. But though every man who has entered into civil society, and is become a member of any commonwealth, has thereby quitted his power to punish offenses against the law of nature, in prosecution of his own private judgment; yet, with the judgment of offenses, which he has given up to the legislative in all cases, where he can appeal to the magistrate, he has given a right to the commonwealth to employ his force for the execution of the judgments of the commonwealth, whenever he shall be called to it; which, indeed, are his own judgments, they being made by himself or his representative. And herein we have the original of the legislative and executive power of civil society, which is to judge by standing laws how far offenses are to be punished when committed within the commonwealth, and also to determine, by occasional judgments founded on the present circumstances of the fact, how far injuries from without are to be vindicated; and in both these to employ all the force of all the members, when there shall be need.

Whenever, therefore, any number of men are so united into one society, as to quit every one his executive power of the law of nature, and to resign it to the public, there and there only is a political or civil society. And this is done wherever any number of men, in the state of nature, enter into society to make one people, one body politic, under one supreme government; or else when any one joins himself to, and incorporates with, any government already made; for hereby he authorizes the society or, which is all one, the legislative thereof, to make laws for him, as the public good of the society shall require, to the execution whereof his own assistance (as to his own decrees) is due. And this puts men out of a state of nature into that of a commonwealth by setting up a judge on earth, with authority to determine all the controversies, and redress the injuries that may happen to any member of the commonwealth; which judge is the legislative, or magistrate appointed by it. And wherever there are any number of men, however associated, that have no such decisive power to appeal to, there they are still in the state of nature.

Hence it is evident that absolute monarchy, which by some men is counted the only government in the world, is indeed inconsistent with civil society, and so can be no form of civil government at all; for the end of civil society being to avoid and remedy those inconveniences of the state of nature which necessarily follow from every man being judge in his own case, by setting up a known authority, to which everyone of that society may appeal upon any injury received or controversy that may arise, and which everyone of the society ought to obey. Wherever any persons are who have not such an authority to appeal to for the decision of any difference between them, there those persons are still in the state of nature; and so is every absolute prince, in respect of those who are under his dominion.

For he being supposed to have all, both legislative and executive power in himself alone, there is no judge to be found, no appeal lies open to anyone who may fairly and indifferently and with authority decide, and from whose decision relief and redress may be expected of any injury or inconvenience that may be suffered from the prince, or by his order; so that such a man, however entitled, "czar," or "grand seignior," or how you please, is as much in the state of nature with all under his dominion, as he is with the rest of mankind; for wherever any two men are who have no standing rule, and common judge to appeal to on earth, for the determination of controversies of right betwixt them, there they are still in the state of nature, and under all the inconveniences of it, with only this woeful difference to the subject, or rather slave, of an absolute prince: that whereas in the ordinary state of nature he has a liberty to judge of his right and, according to the best of his power to maintain it; now, whenever his property is invaded by the will and order of his monarch, he has not only no appeal as those in society ought to have but, as if he were degraded from the common state of rational creatures, is denied a liberty to judge of, or to defend his right; and so is exposed to all the misery and inconveniences that a man can fear from one who, being in the unrestrained state of nature, is yet corrupted with flattery and armed with power. . . .

Of the Beginning of Political Societies

Men, being, as has been said, by nature all free, equal, and independent, no one can be put out of this estate and subjected to the political power of another without his own consent. The only way whereby anyone divests himself of his natural liberty and puts on the bonds of civil society is by agreeing with other men to join and unite into a community for their comfortable, safe, and peaceable living one among another, in a secure enjoyment of their properties and a greater security against any that are not of it. This any number of men may do, because it injures not the freedom of the rest; they are left as they were in the liberty of the state of nature. When any number of men have so consented to make one community or government, they are thereby presently incorporated and make one body politic wherein the majority have a right to act and conclude the rest.

For when any number of men have, by the consent of every individual, made a community, they have thereby made that community one body, with a power to act as one body, which is only by the will and determination of the majority; for that which acts any community being only the consent of the individuals of it, and it being necessary to that which is one body to move one way, it is necessary the body should move that way whither the greater force carries it, which is the consent of the majority; or else it is impossible it should act or continue one body, one community, which the consent of every individual that united into it agreed that it should; and so everyone is bound by that consent to be concluded by the majority. And therefore we see that in assemblies impowered to act by positive laws, where no number is set by that positive law which impowers them, the act of the majority passes for the act of the whole, and of course determines, as having by the law of nature and reason the power of the whole.

And thus every man, by consenting with others to make one body politic under one government, puts himself under an obligation to everyone of that society to submit to the determination of the majority, and to be concluded by it; or else this original compact, whereby he with others incorporates into one society, would signify nothing, and be no compact, if he be left free, and under no other ties than he was in before in the state of nature. For what appearance would there be of any compact? What new engagement if he were no further tied by any decrees of the society than he himself thought fit and did actually consent to? This would be still as great a liberty as he himself had before his compact, or anyone else in the state of nature has, who may submit himself and consent to any acts of it if he thinks fit.

For if the consent of the majority shall not, in reason, be received as the act of the whole, and conclude every individual, nothing but the consent of every individual can make anything to be the act of the whole; but such a consent is next to impossible ever to be had if we consider the infirmities of health and avocations of business, which in a number, though much less than that of a commonwealth, will necessarily keep many away from the public assembly. To which, if we add the variety of opinions and contrariety of interests which unavoidably happen in all collections of men, the coming into society upon such terms would be only like Cato's coming into the theater only to go out again. Such a constitution as this would make the mighty leviathan of a shorter duration than the feeblest creatures, and not let it outlast the day it was born in; which cannot be supposed till we can think that rational creatures should desire and constitute societies only to be dissolved; for where the majority cannot conclude the rest, there they cannot act as one body, and consequently will be immediately dissolved again.

Whosoever, therefore, out of a state of nature unite into a community must be understood to give up all the power necessary to the ends for which they unite into society to the majority of the community, unless they expressly agreed in any number greater than the majority. And this is done by barely agreeing to unite into one political society, which is all the compact that is, or needs be, between the individuals that enter into or make up a commonwealth. And thus that which begins and actually constitutes any political society is nothing but the consent of any number of freemen capable of a majority to unite and incorporate into such a society. And this is that, and that only, which did or could give beginning to any lawful government in the world.

To this I find two objections made:

First, "That there are no instances to be found in story of a company of men independent and equal one among another, that met together, and in this way began and set up a government."

Secondly, "It is impossible of right, that men should do so, because all men being born under government, they are to submit to that, and are not at liberty to begin a new one."

To the first there is this to answer: that it is not at all to be wondered that history gives us but a very little account of men that lived together in the state of nature. The inconveniences of that condition, and the love and want of society, no sooner brought any number of them together, but they presently united and incorporated if they designed to continue together. And if we may not suppose men ever to have been in the state of nature, because we hear not much of them in such a state, we may as well suppose the armies of Salmanasser or Xerxes were never children, because we hear little of them till they were men and embodied in armies. Government is everywhere antecedent to records, and letters seldom come in among a people till a long continuation of civil society has, by other more necessary arts, provided for their safety, ease, and plenty; and then they begin to look after the history of their founders and search into their original, when they have outlived the memory of it; for it is with commonwealths as with particular persons—they are commonly ignorant of their own births and infancies; and if they know anything of their original, they are beholden for it to the accidental records that others have kept of it. And those that we have of the beginning of any politics in the world, excepting that of the Jews, where God himself immediately interposed, and which favors not at all paternal dominion, are all either plain instances of such a beginning as I have mentioned, or at least have manifest footsteps of it. . . .

But to conclude, reason being plain on our side, that men are naturally free, and the examples of history showing that the governments of the world, that were begun in peace, had their beginning laid on that foundation, and were made by the consent of the people, there can be little room for doubt, either where the right is, or what has been the opinion or practice of mankind about the first erecting of governments. . . .

The other objection I find urged against the beginning of politics in the way I have mentioned is this:

"That all men being born under government, some or other, it is impossible any of them should ever be free and at liberty to unite together and begin a new one, or ever be able to erect a lawful government."

If this argument be good, I ask, how came so many lawful monarchies into the world? For if anybody, upon this supposition, can show me any one man in any age of the world free to begin a lawful monarchy, I will be bound to show him ten other free men at liberty at the same time to unite and begin a new government under a regal or any other form, it being demonstration that if anyone, born under the dominion of another, may be so free as to have a right to command others in a new and distinct empire, everyone that is born under the dominion of another may be so free, too, and may become a ruler, or subject of a distinct separate government. And so, by this their own principle, either all men, however born, are free, or else there is but one lawful prince, one lawful government in the world. And then they have nothing to do, but barely to show us which that is; which, when they have done, I doubt not but all mankind will easily agree to pay obedience to him.

Though it be a sufficient answer to their objection, to show that it involves them in the same difficulties that it does those they use it against, yet I shall endeavor to discover the weakness of this argument a little further. "All men," say they, "are born under government, and therefore they cannot be at liberty to begin a new one. Everyone is born a subject to his father, or his prince, and is therefore under the perpetual tie of subjection and allegiance." It is plain mankind never owned nor considered any such natural subjection that they were born in, to one or to the other, that tied them without their own consents, to a subjection to them and their heirs.

For there are no examples so frequent in history, both sacred and profane, as those of men withdrawing themselves, and their obedience, from the jurisdiction they were born under, and the family or community they were bred up in, and setting up new governments in other places; from whence sprang all that number of petty commonwealths in the beginning of ages, and which always multiplied as long as there was room enough, till the stronger or more fortunate swallowed the weaker, and those great ones, again breaking to pieces, dissolved into lesser dominions. All which are so many testimonies against paternal sovereignty, and plainly prove that it was not the natural right of the father descending to his heirs that made governments in the beginning, since it was impossible, upon that ground, there should have been so many little kingdoms; all must have been but only one universal monarchy, if men had not been at liberty to separate themselves from their families and the government, be it what it will, that was set up in it, and go and make distinct commonwealths and other governments, as they thought fit. . . .

Every man being, as has been shown, naturally free, and nothing being able to put him into subjection to any earthly power but only his own consent, it is to be considered what shall be understood to be a sufficient declaration of a man's consent to make him subject to the laws of any government. There is a common distinction of an express and a tacit consent, which will concern our present case. Nobody doubts but an express consent of any man entering into any society makes him a perfect member of that society, a subject of that government. The difficulty is, what ought to be looked upon as a tacit consent, and how far it binds—i.e., how far anyone shall be looked upon to have consented and thereby submitted to any government, where he has made no expressions of it at all. And to this I say that every man that has any possessions or enjoyment of any part of the dominions of any government does thereby give his tacit consent, and is as far forth obliged to obedience to the laws of that government, during such enjoyment, as anyone under it; whether this his possession be of land to him and his heirs forever, or a lodging only for a week, or whether it be barely traveling freely on the highway; and, in effect, it reaches as far as the very being of anyone within the territories of that government.

To understand this the better, it is fit to consider that every man, when he at first incorporates himself into any commonwealth, he, by his uniting himself thereunto, annexes also, and submits to the community those possessions which he has, or shall acquire, that do not already belong to any other government; for it would be a direct contradiction for anyone to enter into society with others for the securing and regulating of property, and yet to suppose his land, whose property is to be regulated by the laws of the society, should be exempt from the jurisdiction of that government to which he himself, the proprietor of the land, is a subject. By the same act therefore, whereby anyone unites his person, which was before free, to any commonwealth, by the same he unites his possessions, which were before free, to it also; and they become, both of them, person and possession, subject to the government and dominion of that commonwealth as long as it has a being. Whoever, therefore, from thenceforth by inheritance, purchase, permission, or otherwise, enjoys any part of the land so annexed to, and under the government of that commonwealth, must take it with the condition it is under— that is, of submitting to the government of the commonwealth, under whose jurisdiction it is, as far forth as any subject of it.

But since the government has a direct jurisdiction only over the land, and reaches the possessor of it (before he has actually incorporated himself in the society) only as he dwells upon and enjoys that, the obligation anyone is under by virtue of such enjoyment, to submit to the government, begins and ends with the enjoyment; so that whenever the owner, who has given nothing but such a tacit consent to the government, will, by donation, sale, or otherwise, quit the said possession, he is at liberty to go and incorporate himself into any other commonwealth, or to agree with others to begin a new one, *in vacuis locis,* in any part of the world they can find free and unpossessed. Whereas he that has once, by actual agreement, and any express declaration, given his consent to be of any commonwealth, is perpetually and indispensably obliged to be and remain unalterably a subject to it, and can never be again in the liberty of the state of nature, unless, by any calamity, the government he was under comes to be dissolved, or else by some public act, cuts him off from being any longer a member of it.

But submitting to the laws of any country, living quietly, and enjoying privileges and protection under them, makes not a man a member of that society; this is only a local protection and homage due to and from all those who, not being in a state of war, come within the territories belonging to any government, to all parts whereof the force of its laws extends. But this no more makes a man a member of that society, a perpetual subject of that commonwealth, than it would make a man a subject to another, in whose family he found it convenient to abide for some time, though, while he continued in it, he were obliged to comply with the laws, and submit to the government he found there. And thus we see that foreigners, by living all their lives under another government, and enjoying the privileges and protection of it, though they are bound, even in conscience, to submit to its administration, as far forth as any denizen, yet do not thereby come to be subjects or members of that commonwealth. Nothing can make any man so but his actually entering into it by positive engagement, and express promise and compact. That is that which I think concerning the beginning of political societies, and that consent which makes anyone a member of any commonwealth.

Of the Ends of Political Society and Government

If man in the state of nature be so free as has been said; if he be absolute lord of his own person and possessions, equal to the greatest, and subject to nobody, why will he part with his freedom, why will he give up his empire, and subject himself to the dominion and control of any other power? To which it is obvious to answer that though in the state of nature he has such a right, yet the enjoyment of it is very uncertain, and constantly exposed to the invasion of others; for all being kings as much as he, every man his equal, and the greater part no strict observers of equity and justice, the enjoyment of the property he has in this state is very unsafe, very unsecure. This makes him willing to quit a condition which, however free, is full of fears and continual dangers; and it is not without reason that he seeks out and is willing to join in society with others who are already united, or have a mind to unite, for the mutual preservation of their lives, liberties, and estates, which I call by the general name "property."

The great and chief end, therefore, of men's uniting into commonwealths and putting themselves under government is the preservation of their property. To which in the state of nature there are many things wanting:

First, there wants an established, settled, known law, received and allowed by common consent to be the standard of right and wrong, and the common measure to decide all controversies between them; for though the law of nature be plain and intelligible to all rational creatures, yet men being biased by their interest, as well as ignorant for want of studying it, are not apt to allow of it as a law binding to them in the application of it to their particular cases.

Secondly, in the state of nature there wants a known and indifferent judge, with authority to determine all differences according to the established law; for everyone in that state being both judge and executioner of the law of nature, men being partial to themselves, passion and revenge is very apt to carry them too far and with too much heat in their own cases, as well as negligence and unconcernedness to make them too remiss in other men's.

Thirdly, in the state of nature there often wants power to back and support the sentence when right, and to give it due execution. They who by any injustice offend, will seldom fail, where they are able, by force to make good their injustice; such resistance many times makes the punishment dangerous, and frequently destructive to those who attempt it.

Thus mankind, notwithstanding all the privileges of the state of nature, being but in an ill condition while they remain in it, are quickly driven into society. Hence it comes to pass that we seldom find any number of men live any time together in this state. The inconveniences that they are therein exposed to, by the irregular and uncertain exercise of the power every man has of punishing the transgressions of others, make them take sanctuary under the established laws of government and therein seek the preservation of their property. It is this makes them so willingly give up every one his single power of punishing, to be exercised by such alone as shall be appointed to it among them; and by such rules as the community, or those authorized by them to that purpose, shall agree on. And in this we have the original right of both the legislative and executive power, as well as of the governments and societies themselves.

For in the state of nature, to omit the liberty he has of innocent delights, a man has two powers:

The first is to do whatsoever he thinks fit for the preservation of himself and others within the permission of the law of nature, by which law, common to them all, he and all the rest of mankind are one community, make up one society, distinct from all other creatures. And, were it not for the corruption and viciousness of degenerate men, there would be no need of any other, no necessity that men should separate from this great and natural community, and by positive agreements combine into smaller and divided associations.

The other power a man has in the state of nature is the power to punish the crimes committed against that law. Both these he gives up when he joins in a private, if I may so call it, or particular politic society and incorporates into any commonwealth separate from the rest of mankind.

The first power, viz., of doing whatsoever he thought fit for the preservation of himself and the rest of mankind, he gives up to be regulated by laws made by the society, so far forth as the preservation of himself and the rest of that society shall require; which laws of the society in many things confine the liberty he had by the law of nature.

Secondly, the power of punishing he wholly gives up, and engages his natural force (which he might before employ in the execution of the law of nature, by his own single authority, as he thought fit) to assist the executive power of the society, as the law thereof shall require; for being now in a new state, wherein he is to enjoy many conveniences from the labor, assistance, and society of others in the same community as well as protection from its whole strength, he is to part also with as much of his natural liberty, in providing for himself, as the good, prosperity, and safety of the society shall require, which is not only necessary, but just, since the other members of the society do the like.

But though men when they enter into society, give up the equality, liberty, and executive power they had in the state of nature, into the hands of the society, to be so far disposed of by the legislative as the good of the society shall require; yet it being only with an intention in everyone the better to preserve himself, his liberty and property (for no rational creature can be supposed to change his condition with an intention to be worse), the power of the society, or legislative constituted by them, can never be supposed to extend farther than the common good, but is obliged to secure everyone's property by providing against those three defects above-mentioned that made the state of nature so unsafe and uneasy. And so whoever has the legislative or supreme power of any commonwealth is bound to govern by established standing laws, promulgated and known to the people, and not by extemporary decrees; by indifferent and upright judges who are to decide controversies by those laws; and to employ the force of the community at home only in the execution of such laws, or abroad to prevent or redress foreign injuries, and secure the community from inroads and invasion. And all this to be directed to no other end but the peace, safety, and public good of the people. . . .

Of the Extent of the Legislative Power

The great end of men's entering into society being the enjoyment of their properties in peace and safety, and the great instrument and means of that being the laws established in that society, the first and fundamental positive law of all commonwealths is the establishing of the legislative power; as the first and fundamental natural law, which is to govern even the legislative itself, is the preservation of the society, and (as far as will consist with the public good) of every person in it. This legislative is not only the supreme power of the commonwealth, but sacred and unalterable in the hands where the community have once placed it; nor can any edict of anybody else, in what form soever conceived or by what power soever backed, have the force and obligation of a law, which has not its sanction from that legislative which the public has chosen and appointed; for without this the law could not have that which is absolutely necessary to its being a law: the consent of the society over whom nobody can have a power to make laws, but by their own consent, and by authority received from them.* And therefore all the obedience,

* "The lawful power of making laws to command whole politic societies of men, belonging so properly unto the same entire societies, that for any prince or potentate of what kind soever upon earth, to exercise the same of himself, and not by express commission immediately and personally received from God, or else by authority derived at the first from their consent, upon whose persons

which by the most solemn ties anyone can be obliged to pay, ultimately terminates in this supreme power, and is directed by those laws which it enacts; nor can any oaths to any foreign power whatsoever, or any domestic subordinate power, discharge any member of the society from his obedience to the legislative acting pursuant to their trust, nor oblige him to any obedience contrary to the laws so enacted, or farther than they do allow; it being ridiculous to imagine one can be tied ultimately to obey any power in the society which is not supreme.

Though the legislative, whether placed in one or more, whether it be always in being, or only by intervals, though it be the supreme power in every commonwealth; yet:

First, it is not, nor can possibly be absolutely arbitrary over the lives and fortunes of the people; for it being but the joint power of every member of the society given up to that person or assembly which is legislator, it can be no more than those persons had in a state of nature before they entered into society and gave up to the community; for nobody can transfer to another more power than he has in himself, and nobody has an absolute arbitrary power over himself, or over any other, to destroy his own life, or take away the life or property of another. A man, as has been proved, cannot subject himself to the arbitrary power of another; and having in the state of nature no arbitrary power over the life, liberty, or possession of another, but only so much as the law of nature gave him for the preservation of himself and the rest of mankind, this is all he does or can give up to the commonwealth, and by it to the legislative power, so that the legislative can have no more than this. Their power, in the utmost bounds of it, is limited to the public good of the society. It is a power that has no other end but preservation, and therefore can never have a right to destroy, enslave, or designedly to impoverish the subjects. The obligations of the law of nature cease not in society but only in many cases are drawn closer and

---

they impose laws, it is no better than mere tyranny. Laws they are not, therefore, which public approbation hath not made so" (Hooker's *Eccl. Pol.* lib. i. sect. 10).

"Of this point, therefore, we are to note, that such men naturally have no full and perfect power to command whole politic multitudes of men, therefore utterly without our consent, we could in such sort be at no man's commandment living. And to be commanded we do consent, when that society, whereof we be a part, hath at any time before consented, without revoking the same by the like universal agreement. Laws therefore human, of what kind soever, are available by consent" (*Ibid.*).

have by human laws known penalties annexed to them to enforce their observation. Thus the law of nature stands as an eternal rule to all men, legislators as well as others. The rules that they make for other men's actions must, as well as their own and other men's actions be conformable to the law of nature, i.e., to the will of God, of which that is a declaration, and the fundamental law of nature being the preservation of mankind, no human sanction can be good or valid against it.

Secondly, the legislative or supreme authority cannot assume to itself a power to rule by extemporary, arbitrary decrees, but is bound to dispense justice, and to decide the rights of the subject by promulgated, standing laws, and known authorized judges. For the law of nature being unwritten, and so nowhere to be found but in the minds of men, they who through passion or interest shall miscite or misapply it, cannot so easily be convinced of their mistake where there is no established judge; and so it serves not, as it ought, to determine the rights and fence the properties of those that live under it, especially where everyone is judge, interpreter, and executioner of it too, and that in his own case; and he that has right on his side, having ordinarily but his own single strength, has not force enough to defend himself from injuries or to punish delinquents. To avoid these inconveniences which disorder men's properties in the state of nature, men unite into societies that they may have the united strength of the whole society to secure and defend their properties, and may have standing rules to bound it by which everyone may know what is his. To this end it is that men give up all their natural power to the society which they enter into, and the community put the legislative power into such hands as they think fit with this trust, that they shall be governed by declared laws, or else their peace, quiet, and property will still be at the same uncertainty as it was in the state of nature.

Absolute arbitrary power or governing without settled standing laws can neither of them consist with the ends of society and government which men would not quit the freedom of the state of nature for, and tie themselves up under, were it not to preserve their lives, liberties, and fortunes, and by stated rules of right and property to secure their peace and quiet. It cannot be supposed that they should intend, had they a power so to do, to give to any one, or more, an absolute arbitrary power over their persons and estates, and put a force into the magistrate's hand to execute his unlimited will arbitrarily upon them. This were to put themselves into a worse condition than the state of nature, wherein they had a liberty to defend their right against the injuries of others, and were upon equal terms of force to maintain it, whether invaded by a single man or many in combination. Whereas, by supposing they have given up themselves to the absolute arbitrary power and will of a legislator, they have disarmed themselves, and armed him, to make a prey of them when he pleases; he being in a much worse condition who is exposed to the arbitrary power of one man, who has the command of 100,000, than he that is exposed to the arbitrary power of 100,000 single men, nobody being secure that his will, who has such a command, is better than that of other men, though his force be 100,000 times stronger. And therefore, whatever form the commonwealth is under, the ruling power ought to govern by declared and received laws and not by extemporary dictates and undetermined resolutions; for then mankind will be in a far worse condition than in the state of nature if they shall have armed one or a few men with the joint power of a multitude, to force them to obey at pleasure the exorbitant and unlimited decrees of their sudden thoughts, or unrestrained, and till that moment unknown wills, without having any measures set down which may guide and justify their actions. For all the power the government has being only for the good of the society, as it ought not to be arbitrary and at pleasure, so it ought to be exercised by established and promulgated laws; that both the people may know their duty and be safe and secure within the limits of the law; and the rulers, too, kept within their bounds, and not be tempted by the power they have in their hands to employ it to such purposes and by such measures as they would not have known, and own not willingly.

Thirdly, the supreme power cannot take from any man part of his property without his own consent; for the preservation of property being the end of government, and that for which men enter into society, it necessarily supposes and requires, that the people should have property; without which they must be supposed to lose that, by entering into society, which was the end for which they entered into it—too gross an absurdity for any man to own. Men, therefore, in society having property, they have such right to the goods, which by the law of the community are theirs, that nobody has a right to take their substance or any part of it from them, without their own consent; without this they have no property at all; for I have truly no property in that which another can by right take from me when he pleases, against my consent. Hence it is a mistake to think that the supreme or legislative power of any commonwealth can do what it will and dispose of the estates of the subject arbitrarily, or take any part of them at pleasure. This is not much to be feared in governments where the legislative consists, wholly or in part, in assemblies which are variable, whose members, upon the dissolution of the assembly, are subjects under the common laws of their country, equally with the rest. But in governments where the legislative is in one lasting assembly always in being, or in one man, as in absolute monarchies, there is danger still that they will think themselves to have a distinct interest from the rest of the community, and so will be apt to increase their own riches and power by taking what they think fit from the people; for a man's property is not at all secure, though there be good and equitable laws to set the bounds of it between him and his fellow subjects, if he who commands those subjects have power to take from any private man what part he pleases of his property and use and dispose of it as he thinks good.

But government, into whatsoever hands it is put, being, as I have before shown, entrusted with this condition, and for this end, that men might have and secure their properties; the prince, or senate, however, it may have power to make laws for the regulating of property between the subjects one among another, yet can never have a power to take to themselves the whole or any part of the subject's property without their own consent; for this would be in effect to leave them no property at all. And to let us see that even absolute power, where it is necessary, is not arbitrary by being absolute, but is still limited by that reason and confined to those ends, which required it in some cases to be absolute, we need look no farther than the common practice of martial discipline; for the preservation of the army, and in it of the whole commonwealth, requires an absolute obedience to the command of every superior officer, and it is justly death to disobey or dispute the most dangerous or unreasonable of them; but yet we see, that neither the sergeant, that could command a soldier to march up to the mouth of a cannon, or stand in a breach where he is almost sure to perish, can command that soldier to give him one penny of his money; nor the general, that can condemn him to death for deserting his post, or for not obeying the most desperate orders, can yet, with all his absolute power of life and death, dispose of one farthing of that soldier's estate or seize one jot of his goods, whom yet he can command anything, and hang for the least disobedience. Because such a blind obedience is necessary to that end for which the commander has his power, viz., the preservation of the rest; but the disposing of his goods has nothing to do with it.

It is true, governments cannot be supported without great charge, and it is fit everyone who enjoys his share of the protection should pay out of his estate his proportion for the maintenance of it. But still it must be with his own consent, i.e., the consent of the majority, giving it either by themselves or their representatives chosen by them. For if anyone shall claim a power to lay and levy taxes on the people, by his own authority and without such consent of the people, he thereby invades the fundamental law of property and subverts the end of government; for what property have I in that which another may by right take, when he pleases, to himself?

Fourthly, the legislative cannot transfer the power of making laws to any other hands; for it being but a delegated power from the people, they who have it cannot pass it over to others. The people alone can appoint the form of the commonwealth, which is by constituting the legislative and appointing in whose hands that shall be. And when the people have said, we will submit to rules and be governed by laws made by such men, and in such forms, nobody else can say other men shall make laws for them; nor can the people be bound by any laws but such as are enacted by those whom they have chosen and authorized to make laws for them. The power of the legislative being derived from the people by a positive voluntary grant and institution, can be no other than what that positive grant conveyed, which being only to make laws, and not to make legislators, the legislative can have no power to transfer their authority of making laws and place it in other hands.

These are the bounds which the trust that is put in them by the society, and the law of God and nature, have set to the legislative power of every commonwealth, in all forms of government:

First, they are to govern by promulgated established laws, not to be varied in particular cases, but to have one rule for rich and poor, for the favorite at court and the countryman at plow.

Secondly, these laws also ought to be designed for no other end ultimately, but the good of the people.

Thirdly, they must not raise taxes on the property of the people without the consent of the people, given by themselves or their deputies. And this properly concerns only such governments where the legislative is always in being, or at least where the people have not reserved any part of the legislative to deputies to be from time to time chosen by themselves.

Fourthly, the legislative neither must nor can transfer the power of making laws to anybody else, or place it anywhere but where the people have.

Of the Legislative, Executive, and Federative Power of the Commonwealth

The legislative power is that which has a right to direct how the force of the commonwealth shall be employed for preserving the community and the members of it. But because those laws which are constantly to be executed, and whose force is always to continue, may be made in a little time, therefore there is no need that the legislative should be always in being, not having always business to do. And because it may be too great a temptation to human frailty, apt to grasp at power, for the same persons who have the power of making laws to have also in their hands the power to execute them, whereby they may exempt themselves from obedience to the laws they make, and suit the law, both in its making and execution, to their own private advantage, and thereby come to have a distinct interest from the rest of the community, contrary to the end of society and government; therefore, in well ordered commonwealths, where the good of the whole is so considered, as it ought, the legislative power is put into the hands of diverse persons, who, duly assembled, have by themselves, or jointly with others, a power to make laws; which when they have done, being separated again, they are themselves subject to the laws they have made, which is a new and near tie upon them to take care that they make them for the public good.

But because the laws that are at once and in a short time made have a constant and lasting force and need a perpetual execution, or an attendance thereunto; therefore, it is necessary there should be a power always in being which should see to the execution of the laws that are made and remain in force. And thus the legislative and executive power come often to be separated.

There is another power in every commonwealth which one may

call natural, because it is that which answers to the power every man naturally had before he entered into society; for though in a commonwealth, the members of it are distinct persons still in reference to one another, and as such are governed by the laws of the society, yet, in reference to the rest of mankind, they make one body which is, as every member of it before was, still in the state of nature with the rest of mankind. Hence it is, that the controversies that happen between any man of the society with those that are out of it are managed by the public, and an injury done to a member of their body engages the whole in the reparation of it. So that, under this consideration, the whole community is one body in the state of nature, in respect of all other states or persons out of its community.

This therefore contains the power of war and peace, leagues and alliances, and all the transactions with all persons and communities without the commonwealth, and may be called "federative," if anyone pleases. So the thing be understood, I am indifferent as to the name. . . .

Though, as I said, the executive and federative power of every community be really distinct in themselves, yet they are hardly to be separated and placed at the same time in the hands of distinct persons; for both of them requiring the force of the society for their exercise, it is almost impracticable to place the force of the commonwealth in distinct and not subordinate hands, or that the executive and federative power should be placed in persons that might act separately, whereby the force of the public would be under different commands, which would be apt some time or other to cause disorder and ruin.

Of the Subordination of the Powers of the Commonwealth

Though in a constituted commonwealth, standing upon its own basis, and acting according to its own nature, that is, acting for the preservation of the community, there can be but one supreme power, which is the legislative, to which all the rest are and must be subordinate; yet, the legislative being only a fiduciary power to act for certain ends, there remains still in the people a supreme power to remove or alter the legislative, when they find the legislative act contrary to the trust reposed in them; for all power given with trust for the attaining an end, being limited by that end; whenever that end is manifestly neglected or opposed, the trust must necessarily be forfeited and the power devolve into the hands of those that gave it, who may place it anew where they shall think best for their safety and security. And thus the community perpetually retains a supreme power of saving themselves from the attempts and designs of anybody, even of their legislators, whenever they shall be so foolish or so wicked as to lay and carry on designs against the liberties and properties of the subject; for no man, or society of men, having a power to deliver up their preservation, or consequently the means of it, to the absolute will and arbitrary dominion of another, whenever anyone shall go about to bring them into such a slavish condition, they will always have a right to preserve what they have not a power to part with, and to rid themselves of those who invade this fundamental, sacred, and unalterable law of self-preservation, for which they entered into society. And thus the community may be said in this respect to be always the supreme power, but not as considered under any form of government, because this power of the people can never take place till the government be dissolved.

In all cases, while the government subsists, the legislative is the supreme power; for what can give laws to another must needs be superior to him; and since the legislative is not otherwise legislative of the society, but by the right it has to make laws for all the parts and for every member of the society, prescribing rules to their actions, and giving power of execution where they are transgressed, the legislative must needs be the supreme, and all other powers in any members or parts of the society, derived from and subordinate to it.

In some commonwealths, where the legislative is not always in being, and the executive is vested in a single person who has also a share in the legislative, there that single person in a very tolerable sense may also be called supreme; not that he has in himself all the supreme power, which is that of lawmaking, but because he has in him the supreme execution, from whom all inferior magistrates derive all their several subordinate powers, or at least the greatest part of them. Having also no legislative superior to him, there being no law to be made without his consent which cannot be expected should ever subject him to the other part of the legislative, he is properly enough in this sense supreme. But yet it is to be observed that though oaths of allegiance and fealty are taken to him, it is not to him as supreme legislator, but as supreme executor of the law made by a joint power of him with others; allegiance being nothing but an obedience according to law, which when he violates, he has no right to obedience, nor can claim it otherwise than as the public person invested with the power of the law, and so is to be considered as the image, phantom, or representative of the commonwealth, acted by the will of the society, declared in its laws; and thus he has no will, no power, but that of the law. But when he quits this representation, this public will, and acts by his own private will, he degrades himself and is but a single private person without power and without will that has no right to obedience—the members owing no obedience but to the public will of the society.

The executive power, placed anywhere but in a person that has also a share in the legislative, is visibly subordinate and accountable to it and may be at pleasure changed and displaced, so that it is not the supreme executive power that is exempt from subordination, but the supreme executive power vested in one, who having a share in the legislative, has no distinct superior legislative to be subordinate and accountable to, farther than he himself shall join and consent; so that he is no more subordinate than he himself shall think fit, which one may certainly conclude will be but very little. Of other ministerial and subordinate powers in a commonwealth we need not speak, they being so multiplied with infinite variety, in the different customs and constitutions of distinct commonwealths, that it is impossible to give a particular account of them all. Only thus much, which is necessary to our present purpose, we may take notice of concerning them, that they have no manner of authority, any of them, beyond what is by positive grant and commission delegated to them, and are all of them accountable to some other power in the commonwealth.

It is not necessary, no, nor so much as convenient, that the legislative should be always in being; but absolutely necessary that the executive power should, because there is not always need of new laws to be made, but always need of execution of the laws that are made. When the legislative has put the execution of the laws they make into other hands, they have a power still to resume it out of those hands, when they find cause, and to punish for any maladministration against the laws. The same holds also in regard of the federative power, that and the executive being both ministerial and subordinate to the legislative which, as has been shown, in a constituted commonwealth is the supreme. . . .

The power of assembling and dismissing the legislative, placed in the executive, gives not the executive a superiority over it, but is a fiduciary trust placed in him for the safety of the people, in a case where the uncertainty and variableness of human affairs could not bear a steady fixed rule; for it not being possible that the first framers of the government should, by any foresight, be so much masters of future events as to be able to prefix so just periods of return and duration to the assemblies of the legislative, in all times to come, that might exactly answer all the exigencies of the commonwealth, the best remedy could be found for this defect was to trust this to the prudence of one who was always to be present and whose business it was to watch over the public good. Constant, frequent meetings of the legislative, and long continuations of their assemblies without necessary occasion, could not but be burdensome to the people and must necessarily in time produce more dangerous inconveniences, and yet the quick turn of affairs might be sometimes such as to need their present help. Any delay of their convening might endanger the public; and sometimes, too, their business might be so great that the limited time of their sitting might be too short for their work, and rob the public of that benefit which could be had only from their mature deliberation. What then could be done in this case to prevent the community from being exposed, some time or other, to eminent hazard, on one side or the other, by fixed intervals and periods, set to the meeting and acting of the legislative, but to entrust it to the prudence of some who, being present and acquainted with the state of public affairs, might make use of this prerogative for the public good? And where else could this be so well placed as in his hands who was entrusted with the execution of the laws for the same end? Thus supposing the regulation of times for the assembling and sitting of the legislative not settled by the original constitution, it naturally fell into the hands of the executive, not as an arbitrary power depending on his good pleasure, but with this trust always to have it exercised only for the public weal, as the occurrences of times and change of affairs might require. Whether settled periods of their convening, or a liberty left to the prince for convoking the legislative, or perhaps a mixture of both, has the least inconvenience attending it, it is not my business here to inquire; but only to show, that though the executive power may have the prerogative of convoking and dis-

solving such conventions of the legislative, yet it is not thereby superior
to it. . . .

Of the Dissolution of Government

He that will with any clearness speak of the dissolution of government, ought in the first place to distinguish between the dissolution of
the society and the dissolution of the government. That which makes
the community and brings men out of the loose state of nature into
one politic society is the agreement which everyone has with the rest
to incorporate and act as one body, and so be one distinct commonwealth. The usual, and almost only, way whereby this union is dissolved is the inroad of foreign force making a conquest upon them;
for in that case (not being able to maintain and support themselves
as one entire and independent body) the union belonging to that body
which consisted therein must necessarily cease, and so everyone return to the state he was in before, with a liberty to shift for himself
and provide for his own safety, as he thinks fit, in some other society.
Whenever the society is dissolved, it is certain the government of
that society cannot remain. Thus conquerors' swords often cut up
governments by the roots and mangle societies to pieces, separating
the subdued or scattered multitude from the protection of, and dependence on, that society which ought to have preserved them from
violence. The world is too well instructed in, and too forward to allow
of, this way of dissolving of governments to need any more to be
said of it; and there wants not much argument to prove, that where
the society is dissolved, the government cannot remain—that being
as impossible as for the frame of a house to subsist when the materials
of it are scattered and dissipated by a whirlwind, or jumbled into a
confused heap by an earthquake.

Besides this overturning from without, governments are dissolved
from within.

First, when the legislative is altered. Civil society being a state of
peace among those who are of it, from whom the state of war is
excluded by the umpirage which they have provided in their legislative for the ending all differences that may arise among any of
them; it is in their legislative that the members of a commonwealth
are united and combined together into one coherent living body. This

is the soul that gives form, life, and unity to the commonwealth; from hence the several members have their mutual influence, sympathy, and connection; and, therefore, when the legislative is broken or dissolved, dissolution and death follows; for the essence and union of the society consisting in having one will, the legislative, when once established by the majority, has the declaring and, as it were, keeping of that will. The constitution of the legislative is the first and fundamental act of society, whereby provision is made for the continuation of their union under the direction of persons and bonds of laws made by persons authorized thereunto by the consent and appointment of the people, without which no one man, or number of men, among them can have authority of making laws that shall be binding to the rest. When any one, or more, shall take upon them to make laws, whom the people have not appointed so to do, they make laws without authority, which the people are not therefore bound to obey; by which means they come again to be out of subjection and may constitute to themselves a new legislative as they think best, being in full liberty to resist the force of those who without authority would impose anything upon them. Everyone is at the disposure of his own will when those who had, by the delegation of the society, the declaring of the public will are excluded from it, and others usurp the place, who have no such authority or delegation. . . .

There is therefore, secondly, another way whereby governments are dissolved, and that is when the legislative or the prince, either of them, act contrary to their trust.

First, the legislative acts against the trust reposed in them, when they endeavor to invade the property of the subject, and to make themselves, or any part of the community, masters or arbitrary disposers of the lives, liberties, or fortunes of the people.

The reason why men enter into society is the preservation of their property; and the end why they choose and authorize a legislative is that there may be laws made, and rules set, as guards and fences to the properties of all the members of the society, to limit the power, and moderate the dominion of every part and member of the society; for since it can never be supposed to be the will of the society that the legislative should have a power to destroy that which everyone designs to secure by entering into society, and for which the people submitted themselves to legislators of their own making. Whenever the legislators endeavor to take away and destroy the property of the people, or to reduce them to slavery under arbitrary power, they put themselves into a state of war with the people, who are thereupon absolved from any further obedience, and are left to the common refuge which God has provided for all men against force and violence. Whensoever therefore the legislative shall transgress this fundamental rule of society, and either by ambition, fear, folly, or corruption, endeavor to grasp themselves, or put into the hands of any other, an absolute power over the lives, liberties, and estates of the people, by this breach of trust they forfeit the power the people had put into their hands for quite contrary ends, and it devolves to the people, who have a right to resume their original liberty, and, by the establishment of a new legislative, such as they shall think fit, provide for their own safety and security, which is the end for which they are in society. What I have said here concerning the legislative in general holds true also concerning the supreme executor, who having a double trust put in him, both to have a part in the legislative and the supreme execution of the law, acts against both when he goes about to set up his own arbitrary will as the law of the society. He acts also contrary to his trust when he either employs the force, treasure, and offices of the society to corrupt the representatives and gain them to his purposes, or openly pre-engages the electors and prescribes to their choice such whom he has by solicitations, threats, promises, or otherwise won to his designs, and employs them to bring in such who have promised beforehand what to vote and what to enact. Thus to regulate candidates and electors, and new-model the ways of election, what is it but to cut up the government by the roots, and poison the very fountain of public security? For the people having reserved to themselves the choice of their representatives, as the fence to their properties, could do it for no other end but that they might always be freely chosen, and, so chosen, freely act and advise as the necessity of the commonwealth and the public good should, upon examination and mature debate, be judged to require. This, those who give their votes before they hear the debate and have weighed the reasons on all sides are not capable of doing. To prepare such an assembly as this, and endeavor to set up the declared abettors of his own will for the true representatives of the people and the lawmakers of the society, is certainly as great a breach of trust and as perfect a declaration of a design to subvert the government as is possible to be met with. To which if one shall add rewards and punishments visibly employed to the same end, and all the arts of perverted law made use of to take off and destroy all that stand in the way of such a design, and will not comply and consent to betray the liberties of their country, it will be past doubt what is doing. What power they ought to have in the society, who thus employ it contrary to the trust that went along with it in its first institution, is easy to determine; and one cannot but see that he who has once attempted any such thing as this cannot any longer be trusted.

To this perhaps it will be said, that the people being ignorant, and always discontented, to lay the foundation of government in the unsteady opinion and uncertain humor of the people, is to expose it to certain ruin; and no government will be able long to subsist if the people may set up a new legislative, whenever they take offense at the old one. To this I answer: Quite the contrary. People are not so easily got out of their old forms as some are apt to suggest. They are hardly to be prevailed with to amend the acknowledged faults in the frame they have been accustomed to. And if there be any original defects, or adventitious ones introduced by time or corruption, it is not an easy thing to get them changed, even when all the world sees there is an opportunity for it. This slowness and aversion in the people to quit their old constitutions has, in the many revolutions which have been seen in this kingdom, in this and former ages, still kept us to, or after some interval of fruitless attempts still brought us back again to, our old legislative of king, lords, and commons; and whatever provocations have made the crown be taken from some of our princes' heads, they never carried the people so far as to place it in another line.

But it will be said this hypothesis lays a ferment for frequent rebellion. To which I answer:

First, no more than any other hypothesis; for when the people are made miserable, and find themselves exposed to the ill-usage of arbitrary power, cry up their governors as much as you will for sons of Jupiter, let them be sacred or divine, descended or authorized from heaven, give them out for whom or what you please, the same will happen. The people generally ill-treated, and contrary to right, will be ready upon any occasion to ease themselves of a burden that sits heavy upon them. They will wish and seek for the opportunity, which in the change, weakness, and accidents of human affairs seldom delays long to offer itself. He must have lived but a little while in the world who has not seen examples of this in his time, and he must have read very little who cannot produce examples of it in all sorts of governments in the world.

Secondly, I answer, such revolutions happen not upon every little mismanagement in public affairs. Great mistakes in the ruling part, many wrong and inconvenient laws, and all the slips of human frailty will be borne by the people without mutiny or murmur. But if a long train of abuses, prevarications, and artifices, all tending the same way, make the design visible to the people, and they cannot but feel what they lie under, and see whither they are going, it is not to be wondered that they should then rouse themselves and endeavor to put the rule into such hands which may secure to them the ends for which government was at first erected, and without which ancient names and specious forms are so far from being better that they are much worse than the state of nature or pure anarchy—the inconveniences being all as great and as near, but the remedy farther off and more difficult.

Thirdly, I answer that this doctrine of a power in the people of providing for their safety anew by a new legislative, when their legislators have acted contrary to their trust by invading their property, is the best fence against rebellion, and the probablest means to hinder it; for rebellion being an opposition, not to persons, but authority which is founded only in the constitutions and laws of the government, those, whoever they be, who by force break through, and by force justify their violation of them, are truly and properly rebels; for when men, by entering into society and civil government, have excluded force and introduced laws for the preservation of property, peace, and unity among themselves, those who set up force again in opposition to the laws do *rebellare,* that is, bring back again the state of war, and are properly rebels; which they who are in power (by the pretense they have to authority, the temptation of force they have in their hands, and the flattery of those about them), being likeliest to do, the properest way to prevent the evil is to show them the danger and injustice of it who are under the greatest temptation to run into it.

In both the forementioned cases, when either the legislative is changed, or the legislators act contrary to the end for which they were constituted, those who are guilty are guilty of rebellion; for if anyone by force takes away the established legislative of any society, and the laws of them made pursuant to their trust, he thereby takes away the umpirage which everyone had consented to for a peaceable decision of all their controversies, and a bar to the state of war among them. They who remove or change the legislative take away this decisive power which nobody can have but by the appointment and consent of the people, and so destroying the authority which the people did, and nobody else can, set up, and introducing a power which the people has not authorized, they actually introduce a state of war which is that of force without authority; and thus, by removing the legislative established by the society (in whose decisions the people acquiesced and united as to that of their own will), they untie the knot and expose the people anew to the state of war. And if those, who by force take away the legislative, are rebels, the legislators themselves, as has been shown, can be no less esteemed so, when they who were set up for the protection and preservation of the people, their liberties and properties, shall by force invade and endeavor to take them away; and so they putting themselves into a state of war with those who made them the protectors and guardians of their peace, are properly, and with the greatest aggravation, *rebellantes,* rebels.

But if they who say "it lays a foundation for rebellion" mean that it may occasion civil wars or intestine broils, to tell the people they are absolved from obedience when illegal attempts are made upon their liberties or properties, and may oppose the unlawful violence of those who were their magistrates when they invade their properties contrary to the trust put in them, and that therefore this doctrine is not to be allowed, being so destructive to the peace of the world; they may as well say, upon the same ground, that honest men may not oppose robbers or pirates because this may occasion disorder or bloodshed. If any mischief come in such cases, it is not to be charged upon him who defends his own right, but on him that invades his neighbor's. If the innocent honest man must quietly quit all he has, for peace's sake, to him who will lay violent hands upon it, I desire it may be considered, what a kind of peace there will be in the world, which consists only in violence and rapine, and which is to be maintained only for the benefit of robbers and oppressors. Who would not think it an admirable peace betwixt the mighty and the mean when the lamb without resistance yielded his throat to be torn by the imperious wolf? Polyphemus' den gives us a perfect pattern of such a peace and such a government, wherein Ulysses and his companions had nothing to do but quietly to suffer themselves to be devoured. And no doubt Ulysses, who was a prudent man, preached up passive obedience, and exhorted them to a quiet submission by representing to them of what concernment peace was to mankind, and by showing the inconveniences which might happen if they should offer to resist Polyphemus, who had now the power over them.

The end of government is the good of mankind. And which is best for mankind: that the people should be always exposed to the boundless will of tyranny, or that the rulers should be sometimes liable to be opposed when they grow exorbitant in the use of their power and employ it for the destruction and not the preservation of the properties of their people?

Nor let anyone say that mischief can arise from hence as often as it shall please a busy head, or turbulent spirit, to desire the alteration of the government. It is true such men may stir whenever they please, but it will be only to their own just ruin and perdition; for till the mischief be grown general, and the ill designs of the rulers become visible, or their attempts sensible to the greater part, the people, who are more disposed to suffer than right themselves by resistance, are not apt to stir. The examples of particular injustice or oppression of here and there an unfortunate man moves them not. But if they universally have a persuasion, grounded upon manifest evidence, that designs are carrying on against their liberties, and the general course and tendency of things cannot but give them strong suspicions of the evil intention of their governors, who is to be blamed for it? Who can help it if they who might avoid it bring themselves into this suspicion? Are the people to be blamed if they have the sense of rational creatures and can think of things no otherwise than as they find and feel them? And is it not rather their fault who put things into such a posture that they would not have them thought to be as they are? I grant that the pride, ambition, and turbulence of private men have sometimes caused great disorders in commonwealths, and factions have been fatal to states and kingdoms. But whether the mischief has oftener begun in the people's wantonness and a desire to cast off the lawful authority of their rulers, or in the rulers' insolence and endeavors to get and exercise an arbitrary power over their people—whether oppression or disobedience gave the first rise to the disorder, I leave it to impartial history to determine. This I am sure: whoever, either ruler or subject, by force goes about to invade the rights of either prince or people and lays the foundation for overturning the constitution and frame of any just government is highly guilty of the greatest crime I think a man is capable of—being to answer for all those mischiefs of blood, rapine, and desolation, which the breaking to pieces of governments bring on a country. And he who does it is justly to be esteemed the common enemy and pest of mankind, and is to be treated accordingly.

That subjects or foreigners, attempting by force on the properties of any people, may be resisted with force, is agreed on all hands. But that magistrates doing the same thing may be resisted, has of late been denied; as if those who had the greatest priviliges and advantages by the law, had thereby a power to break those laws by which alone they were set in a better place than their brethren; whereas their offense is thereby the greater, both as being ungrateful for the greater share they have by the law, and breaking also that trust which is put into their hands by their brethren.

Whosoever uses force without right, as everyone does in society who does it without law, puts himself into a state of war with those against whom he so uses it; and in that state all former ties are canceled, all other rights cease, and everyone has a right to defend himself and to resist the aggressor. . . .

Here, it is like, the common question will be made: Who shall be judge whether the prince or legislative act contrary to their trust? This, perhaps, ill-affected and factious men may spread among the people, when the prince only makes use of his due prerogative. To this I reply: The people shall be judge; for who shall be judge whether his trustee or deputy acts well and according to the trust reposed in him, but he who deputes him, and must, by having deputed him, have still a power to discard him when he fails in his trust? If this be reasonable in particular cases of private men, why should it be otherwise in that of the greatest moment, where the welfare of millions is concerned, and also where the evil, if not prevented, is greater, and the redress very difficult, dear, and dangerous?

But further, this question, "Who shall be judge?" cannot mean that there is no judge at all; for where there is no judicature on earth, to decide controversies among men, God in heaven is Judge. He alone, it is true, is Judge of the right. But every man is judge for himself, as in all other cases, so in this, whether another has put himself into a state of war with him, and whether he should appeal to the Supreme Judge, as Jephthah did.

If a controversy arise betwixt a prince and some of the people in a matter where the law is silent or doubtful, and the thing be of great consequence, I should think the proper umpire, in such a case, should be the body of the people; for in cases where the prince has a trust reposed in him and is dispensed from the common ordinary rules of the law, there, if any men find themselves aggrieved, and think the prince acts contrary to or beyond that trust, who so proper to judge as the body of the people (who, at first, lodged that trust in him) how far they meant it should extend? But if the prince, or whoever they be in the administration, decline that way of determination, the appeal then lies nowhere but to Heaven; force between either persons who have no known superior on earth, or which permits no appeal to a judge on earth, being properly a state of war, wherein the appeal lies only to Heaven; and in that state the injured party must judge for himself, when he will think fit to make use of that appeal, and put himself upon it.

To conclude, the power that every individual gave the society when he entered into it can never revert to the individuals again as long as the society lasts, but will always remain in the community, because without this there can be no community, no commonwealth, which is contrary to the original agreement; so also when the society has placed the legislative in any assembly of men, to continue in them and their successors, with direction and authority for providing such successors, the legislative can never revert to the people while that government lasts; because having provided a legislative with power to continue forever, they have given up their political power to the legislative and cannot resume it. But if they have set limits to the duration of their legislative, and made this supreme power in any person or assembly, only temporary, or else, when by the miscarriages of those in authority it is forfeited, upon the forfeiture, or at the determination of the time set, it reverts to the society, and the people have a right to act as supreme and continue the legislative in themselves, or erect a new form, or under the old form place it in new hands, as they think good

52. JEAN JACQUES ROUSSEAU

Jean Jacques Rousseau (1712-1778), like Locke, developed the theory of the social contract, but in quite a different way. Rather than interpreting it as an agreement between ruler and ruled, Rousseau viewed the contract as the original and constitutive instrument which makes possible a genu-

inely unified society. In describing and defending this great unity, he crystallized and dramatized the ideals of the coming French Revolution. Liberty through the sovereignty of the people, equality of all citizens united by original compact, and fraternity resulting from each giving himself to all—these were the principles which motivated him, and which through him motivated a nation and an age. Although adherents of other political theories have claimed to find support in Rousseau's work, these ideals of liberty, equality, and fraternity have remained among the highest aims of all modern democracies.

The Social Contract*

Man is born free, and everywhere he is in chains. Many a man believes himself to be the master of others who is, no less than they, a slave. How did this change take place? I do not know. What can make it legitimate? To this question I hope to be able to furnish an answer.

Were I considering only force and the effects of force, I should say: "So long as a People is constrained to obey, and does, in fact, obey, it does well. So soon as it can shake off its yoke, and succeeds in doing so, it does better. The fact that it has recovered its liberty by virtue of that same right by which it was stolen, means either that it is entitled to resume it, or that its theft by others was, in the first place, without justification." But the social order is a sacred right which serves as a foundation for all other rights. This right, however, since it comes not by nature, must have been built upon conventions. To discover what these conventions are is the matter of our inquiry.

Of the Right of the Strongest

However strong a man, he is never strong enough to remain master always, unless he transform his Might into Right, and Obedience into Duty. Hence we have come to speak of the Right of the Strongest, a right which, seemingly assumed in irony, has, in fact, become established in principle. But the meaning of the phrase has never been adequately explained. Strength is a physical attribute, and I fail to

---

* From J. J. Rousseau, *The Social Contract,* 1762. Reprinted from a translation by Gerard Hopkins in *Social Contract: Essays by Locke, Hume, and Rousseau,* edited by Sir Ernest Barker. By permission of the Oxford University Press, New York, 1947.

see how any moral sanction can attach to its effects. To yield to the strong is an act of necessity, not of will. At most it is the result of a dictate of prudence. How, then, can it become a duty?

Let us assume for a moment that some such Right does really exist. The only deduction from this premise is inexplicable gibberish. For to admit that Might makes Right is to reverse the process of effect and cause. The mighty man who defeats his rival becomes heir to his Right. So soon as we can disobey with impunity, disobedience becomes legitimate. And, since the Mightiest is always right, it merely remains for us to become possessed of Might. But what validity can there be in a Right which ceases to exist when Might changes hands? If a man be constrained by Might to obey, what need has he to obey by Duty? And if he is not constrained to obey, there is no further obligation on him to do so. It follows, therefore, that the word Right adds nothing to the idea of Might. It becomes, in this connection, completely meaningless.

Obey the Powers that be. If that means Yield to Force, the precept is admirable but redundant. My reply to those who advance it is that no case will ever be found of its violation. All power comes from God. Certainly, but so do all ailments. Are we to conclude from such an argument that we are never to call in the doctor? If I am waylaid by a footpad at the corner of a wood, I am constrained by force to give him my purse. But if I can manage to keep it from him, is it my duty to hand it over? His pistol is also a symbol of Power. It must, then, be admitted that Might does not create Right, and that no man is under an obligation to obey any but the legitimate powers of the State. And so I continually come back to the question I first asked.

Of Slavery

Since no man has natural authority over his fellows, and since Might can produce no Right, the only foundation left for legitimate authority in human societies is Agreement.

If a private citizen, says Grotius, can alienate his liberty and make himself another man's slave, why should not a whole people do the same, and subject themselves to the will of a King? The argument contains a number of ambiguous words which stand in need of explanation. But let us confine our attention to one only—*alienate*. To alienate means to give or to sell. Now a man who becomes the slave of another does not give himself. He sells himself in return for bare subsistence, if for nothing more. But why should a whole people sell themselves? So far from furnishing subsistence to his subjects, a King draws his own from them, and from them alone. According to Rabelais, it takes a lot to keep a King. Do we, then, maintain that a subject surrenders his person on condition that his property be taken too? It is difficult to see what he will have left.

It will be said that the despot guarantees civil peace to his subjects. So be it. But how are they the gainers if the wars to which his ambition may expose them, his insatiable greed, and the vexatious demands of his Ministers cause them more loss than would any outbreak of internal dissension? How do they benefit if that very condition of civil peace be one of the causes of their wretchedness? One can live peacefully enough in a dungeon, but such peace will hardly, of itself, ensure one's happiness. The Greeks imprisoned in the cave of Cyclops lived peacefully while awaiting their turn to be devoured.

To say that a man gives himself for nothing is to commit oneself to an absurd and inconceivable statement. Such an act of surrender is illegitimate, null, and void by the mere fact that he who makes it is not in his right mind. To say the same thing of a whole People is tantamount to admitting that the People in question are a nation of imbeciles. Imbecility does not produce Right.

Even if a man can alienate himself, he cannot alienate his children. They are born free, their liberty belongs to them, and no one but themselves has a right to dispose of it. Before they have attained the age of reason their father may make, on their behalf, certain rules with a view to ensuring their preservation and well-being. But any such limitation of their freedom of choice must be regarded as neither irrevocable nor unconditional, for to alienate another's liberty is contrary to the natural order, and is an abuse of the father's rights. It follows that an arbitrary government can be legitimate only on condition that each successive generation of subjects is free either to accept or to reject it, and if this is so, then the government will no longer be arbitrary.

When a man renounces his liberty he renounces his essential manhood, his rights, and even his duty as a human being. There is no compensation possible for such complete renunciation. It is incompatible with man's nature, and to deprive him of his free will is to deprive his actions of all moral sanction. The convention, in short, which sets up on one side an absolute authority, and on the other an obligation to obey without question, is vain and meaningless. Is it not obvious that where we can demand everything we owe nothing? Where there is no mutual obligation, no interchange of duties, it must, surely, be clear that the actions of the commanded cease to have any moral value? For how can it be maintained that my slave has any "right" against me when everything that he has is my property? His right being *my* right, it is absurd to speak of it as ever operating to my disadvantage. . . .

That We Must Always Go Back to an Original Compact

Even were I to grant all that I have so far refuted, the champions of despotism would not be one whit the better off. There will always be a vast difference between subduing a mob and governing a social group. No matter how many isolated individuals may submit to the enforced control of a single conqueror, the resulting relationship will ever be that of Master and Slave, never of People and Ruler. The body of men so controlled may be an agglomeration; it is not an association. It implies neither public welfare nor a body politic. An individual may conquer half the world, but he is still only an individual. His interests, wholly different from those of his subjects, are private to himself. When he dies his empire is left scattered and disintegrated. He is like an oak which crumbles and collapses in ashes so soon as the fire consumes it.

"A People," says Grotius, "may give themselves to a king." His argument implies that the said People were already a People before this act of surrender. The very act of gift was that of a political group and presupposed public deliberation. Before, therefore, we consider the act by which a People chooses their king, it were well if we considered the act by which a People is constituted as such. For it necessarily precedes the other, and is the true foundation on which all Societies rest.

Had there been no original compact, why, unless the choice were unanimous, should the minority ever have agreed to accept the decision of the majority? What right have the hundred who desire a master to vote for the ten who do not? The institution of the franchise is, in itself, a form of compact, and assumes that, at least once in its operation, complete unanimity existed.

Of the Social Pact

I assume, for the sake of argument, that a point was reached in the history of mankind when the obstacles to continuing in a state of Nature were stronger than the forces which each individual could employ to the end of continuing in it. The original state of Nature, therefore, could no longer endure, and the human race would have perished had it not changed its manner of existence.

Now, since men can by no means engender new powers, but can only unite and control those of which they are already possessed, there is no way in which they can maintain themselves save by coming together and pooling their strength in a way that will enable them to withstand any resistance exerted upon them from without. They must develop some sort of central direction and learn to act in concert.

Such a concentration of powers can be brought about only as the consequence of an agreement reached between individuals. But the self-preservation of each single man derives primarily from his own strength and from his own freedom. How, then, can he limit these without, at the same time, doing himself an injury and neglecting that care which it is his duty to devote to his own concerns? This difficulty, in so far as it is relevant to my subject, can be expressed as follows:

"Some form of association must be found as a result of which the whole strength of the community will be enlisted for the protection of the person and property of each constituent member, in such a way that each, when united to his fellows, renders obedience to his own will, and remains as free as he was before." That is the basic problem of which the Social Contract provides the solution.

The clauses of this Contract are determined by the Act of Association in such a way that the least modification must render them null and void. Even though they may never have been formally enunciated, they must be everywhere the same, and everywhere tacitly admitted and recognized. So completely must this be the case that, should the social compact be violated, each associated individual would at once resume all the rights which once were his, and regain his natural liberty, by the mere fact of losing the agreed liberty for which he renounced it.

It must be clearly understood that the clauses in question can be reduced, in the last analysis, to one only, to wit, the complete alienation by each associate member to the community of *all his rights*. For, in the first place, since each has made surrender of himself without reservation, the resultant conditions are the same for all: and, because they are the same for all, it is in the interest of none to make them onerous to his fellows.

Furthermore, this alienation having been made unreservedly, the union of individuals is as perfect as it well can be, none of the associated members having any claim against the community. For should there be any rights left to individuals, and no common authority be empowered to pronounce as between them and the public, then each, being in some things his own judge, would soon claim to be so in all. Were that so, a state of Nature would still remain in being, the conditions of association becoming either despotic or ineffective.

In short, whoso gives himself to all gives himself to none. And, since there is no member of the social group over whom we do not acquire precisely the same rights as those over ourselves which we have surrendered to him, it follows that we gain the exact equivalent of what we lose, as well as an added power to conserve what we already have.

If, then, we take from the social pact everything which is not essential to it, we shall find it to be reduced to the following terms: "each of us contributes to the group his person and the powers which he wields as a person, and we receive into the body politic each individual as forming an indivisible part of the whole."

As soon as the act of association becomes a reality, it substitutes for a person of each of the contracting parties a moral and collective body made up of as many members as the constituting assembly has votes, which body receives from this very act of constitution its unity, its dispersed *self,* and its will. The public person thus formed by the union of individuals was known in the old days as a *City,* but now as the *Republic* or *Body Politic. . . .*

Of the Civil State

The passage from the state of nature to the civil state produces a truly remarkable change in the individual. It substitutes justice for instinct in his behavior, and gives to his actions a moral basis which formerly was lacking. Only when the voice of duty replaces physical impulse and the cravings of appetite does the man who, till then, was concerned solely with himself, realize that he is under compulsion to obey quite different principles, and that he must now consult his reason and not merely respond to the promptings of desire. Although he may find himself deprived of many advantages which were his in a state of nature, he will recognize that he has gained others which are of far greater value. By dint of being exercised, his faculties will develop, his ideas take on a wider scope, his sentiments become ennobled, and his whole soul be so elevated, that, but for the fact that misuse of the new conditions still, at times, degrades him to a point below that from which he has emerged, he would unceasingly bless the day which freed him for ever from his ancient state, and turned him from a limited and stupid animal into an intelligent being and a Man.

Let us reduce all this to terms which can be easily comprehended. What a man loses as a result of the Social Contract is his natural liberty and his unqualified right to lay hands on all that tempts him, provided only that he can compass its possession. What he gains is civil liberty and the ownership of what belongs to him. That we may labor under no illusion concerning these compensations, it is well that we distinguish between natural liberty which the individual enjoys so long as he is strong enough to maintain it, and civil liberty which is curtailed by the general will. Between possessions which derive from physical strength and the right of the first-comer, and ownership which can be based only on a positive title.

To the benefits conferred by the status of citizenship might be added that of Moral Freedom, which alone makes a man his own master. For to be subject to appetite is to be a slave, while to obey the laws laid down by society is to be free. . . .

Of the Limits of the Sovereign Power

If the State or the City is nothing but a moral person the life of which consists in the union of its members, and if the most important of its concerns is the maintenance of its own being, then it follows that it must have at its disposition a power of compulsion covering the whole field of its operations in order that it may be in a position to shift and adjust each single part in a way that shall be most beneficial to the whole. As nature gives to each man complete power over his limbs, so, too, the social compact gives to the body politic complete power over its members: and it is this power, directed by the general will, which, as I have already pointed out, bears the name of sovereignty.

But we have to consider not only the State as a public person, but those individual persons, too, who compose it, and whose lives and liberties are, in nature, independent of it. It is important, therefore, that we carefully distinguish between the rights of the citizens and the rights of the sovereign, between the duties which the former owe as subjects, and the natural rights which, as men, they are entitled to enjoy.

It is agreed that what, as a result of the social compact, each man alienates of power, property, and liberty is only so much as concerns the well-being of the community. But, further, it must be admitted that the sovereign alone can determine how much, precisely, this is.

Such services as the citizen owes to the State must be rendered by him whenever the sovereign demands. But the sovereign cannot lay upon its subjects any burden not necessitated by the well-being of the community. It cannot even wish to do so, for in the realm of reason, as of nature, nothing is ever done without cause.

The undertakings which bind us to the Commonwealth are obligatory only because they are mutual: their nature being such that we cannot labor for others without, at the same time, laboring for ourselves. For how can the general will be always right, and how can all constantly will the happiness of each, if every single individual does not include himself in that word *each*, so that in voting for the general interest he may feel that he is voting for his own? Which goes to show that the equality of rights and the idea of justice which it produces derive from the preference which each man has for his own concerns—in other words, from human nature: that the general will, if it be deserving of its name, must be general, not in its origins only, but in its objects, applicable to all as well as operated *by* all, and that it loses its natural validity as soon as it is concerned to achieve a merely individual and limited end, since, in that case, we, pronouncing judgment on something outside ourselves, cease to be possessed of that true principle of equity which is our guide.

In fact, as soon as issue is joined on some *particular* point, on some *specific* right arising out of a situation which has not previously been regulated by some form of general agreement, we are in the realm of debate. The matter becomes a trial in which certain interested individuals are ranged against the public, but where there is no certainty about what law is applicable nor about who can rightly act as judge. It would be absurd in such a case to demand an *ad hoc* decision of the general will, since the general will would then be the decision of one of the parties only. To the other it would appear in the guise of a pronouncement made by some outside power, sectarian in its nature, tending to injustice in the particular instance, and subject to error. Thus, just as the will of the individual cannot represent the general will, so, too, the general will changes its nature when called upon to pronounce upon a particular object. In so far as it is general, it cannot judge of an individual person or an isolated fact. When, for instance, the people of Athens appointed or removed their leaders, according honors to one and penalties to another: when, in other words, using the machinery supplied by a multiplicity of specific decrees, they exercised, in a muddled sort of way, all the functions of government, they ceased, strictly speaking, to have any general will at all, and behaved not as sovereign so much as magistrate. This statement may seem to be at variance with generally accepted ideas. I ask only that I may be granted time in which to develop my own. What makes the will general is not the number of citizens concerned but the common interest by which they are united. For in the sort of community with which I am dealing, each citizen necessarily submits to the conditions which he imposes on his neighbors. Whence comes that admirable identity of interest and justice which gives to the common deliberations of the People a complexion of equity. When, however, discussion turns on specific issues, this complexion vanishes, because there is no longer any common interest uniting and identifying the pronouncement of the judge with that of the interested party.

No matter by what way we return to our general principle, the conclusion must always be the same, to wit, that the social compact establishes between all the citizens of a State a degree of equality such that all undertake to observe the same obligations and to claim the same rights. Consequently, by the very nature of the pact, every act of Sovereignty—that is to say, every authentic act of the general will— lays the same obligations and confers the same benefits on all. The sovereign knows only the nation as a whole and does not distinguish between the individuals who compose it.

What, then, is a true act of sovereignty? It is not a convention established between a superior and an inferior, but between the body politic and each of its members: a convention having the force of law because it is based upon the social contract: equitable, because it affects all alike: useful, because its sole object is the general good: firm, because it is backed by public force and the supreme power. So long as the subjects of a State observe only conventions of this kind, they are obeying not a single person, but the decision of their own wills. To ask what are the limits of the respective rights of sovereign and citizens is merely to ask to what extent the latter can enter into an undertaking with themselves, each in relation to all, and all in relation to each. . . .

53. THOMAS JEFFERSON

Thomas Jefferson (1743-1826) was a careful student of the philosophy of Locke and Rousseau, and the most eloquent proponent of the theory of natural rights democracy. When Locke wrote his Second Treatise, *he was thinking chiefly of the Glorious Revolution of 1688 which had just ended. Jefferson applied the same principles to America in the eighteenth century. The result was the Declaration of Independence.*

The Declaration of Independence

When in the Course of human events it becomes necessary for one people to dissolve the political bands which have connected them with another, and to assume among the powers of the earth, the separate and equal station to which the Laws of Nature and of Nature's God entitle them, a decent respect to the opinions of mankind requires that they should declare the causes which impel them to the separation.

We hold these truths to be self-evident, that all men are created equal, that they are endowed by their Creator with certain unalienable Rights, that among these are Life, Liberty and the pursuit of Happiness.—That to secure these rights, Governments are instituted among Men, deriving their just powers from the consent of the governed.—That whenever any Form of Government becomes destructive of these ends, it is the Right of the People to alter or to abolish it, and to institute new Government, laying its foundation on such principles, and organizing its powers in such form, as to them shall seem most likely to effect their Safety and Happiness. Prudence, indeed, will dictate that Governments long established should not be changed for light and transient causes; and accordingly all experience hath shewn, that mankind are more disposed to suffer, while evils are sufferable, than to right themselves by abolishing the forms to which they are accustomed. But when a long train of abuses and usurpations, pursuing invariably the same Object, evinces a design to reduce them under absolute Despotism, it is their right, it is their duty, to throw off such Government, and to provide new Guards for their future security.—Such has been the patient sufferance of these Colonies; and such is now the necessity which constrains them to alter their former Systems of Government. The history of the present King of Great Britain is a history of repeated injuries and usurpations, all having in direct object the establishment of an absolute Tyranny over these States. To prove this, let Facts be submitted to a candid world. . . .

In every stage of these Oppressions We have Petitioned for Redress in the most humble terms: Our repeated Petitions have been answered only by repeated injury. A Prince, whose character is thus marked by every act which may define a Tyrant, is unfit to be the ruler of a free people.

Nor have We been wanting in attentions to our British brethren. We have warned them from time to time of attempts by their legislature to extend an unwarrantable jurisdiction over us. We have reminded them of the circumstances of our emigration and settlement here. We have appealed to their native justice and magnanimity, and we have conjured them by the ties of our common kindred to disavow these usurpations, which would inevitably interrupt our connections and correspondence. They too have been deaf to the voice of justice and of consanguinity. We must, therefore, acquiesce in the necessity, which denounces our Separation, and hold them, as we hold the rest of mankind, Enemies in War, in Peace Friends.

We, therefore, the Representatives of the united States of America, in General Congress, Assembled, appealing to the Supreme Judge of the world for the rectitude of our intentions, do, in the Name, and by Authority of the good People of these Colonies solemnly publish and declare, That these United Colonies are, and of Right ought to be Free and Independent States; that they are Absolved from all

Allegiance to the British Crown, and that all political connection between them and the State of Great Britain, is and ought to be totally dissolved; and that as Free and Independent States, they have full Power to levy War, conclude Peace, contract Alliances, establish Commerce, and to do all other Acts and Things which Independent States may of right do.

And for the support of this Declaration, with a firm reliance on the protection of divine Providence, we mutually pledge to each other our Lives, our Fortunes and our sacred Honor.

[On Rebellion] *

God forbid we should ever be twenty years without such a rebellion [Shays's Rebellion]. The people cannot be all, and always, well-informed. The part which is wrong will be discontented in proportion to the importance of the facts they misconceive. If they remain quiet under such misconceptions, it is a lethargy, the forerunner of death to the public liberty. We have had thirteen States independent for eleven years. There has been one rebellion. That comes to one rebellion in a century and a half for each State. What country before ever existed a century and a half without a rebellion? And what country can preserve its liberties if its rulers are not warned from time to time that this people preserve the spirit of resistance? Let them take arms. The remedy is to set them right as to facts, pardon and pacify them. What signify a few lives lost in a century or two? The tree of liberty must be refreshed from time to time with the blood of patriots and tyrants. It is its natural manure.

To William S. Smith, Paris, November 13, 1787.

[On Monarchy and America]

So much for the blessings of having kings, and magistrates who would be kings. From these events, our young republic may learn useful lessons: never to call on foreign powers to settle their differences; to guard against hereditary magistrates; to prevent their

* This and the following selections from the letters of Jefferson are from *The Political Writings of Thomas Jefferson,* edited by Edward Dumbauld, New York, 1955. Reprinted by permission of the publishers, The Liberal Arts Press, Inc.

citizens from becoming so established in wealth and power as to be thought worthy of alliance by marriage with the nieces, sisters, etc., of kings; and, in short, to besiege the throne of heaven with eternal prayers, to extirpate from creation this class of human lions, tigers, and mammoths called kings, from whom let him perish who does not say "good Lord deliver us."

To David Humphreys, Paris, August 14, 1787.

I was much an enemy to monarchies before I came to Europe. I am ten thousand times more so since I have seen what they are. There is scarcely an evil known in these countries which may not be traced to their king as its source, nor a good which is not derived from the small fibers of republicanism existing among them. I can further say, with safety, there is not a crowned head in Europe whose talents or merits would entitle him to be elected a vestryman by the people of any parish in America.

To George Washington, Paris, May 2, 1788.

With all the defects of our constitutions, whether general or particular, the comparison of our governments with those of Europe is like a comparison of heaven and hell. England, like the earth, may be allowed to take the intermediate station. And yet I hear there are people among you who think the experience of our governments has already proved that republican governments will not answer. Send those gentry here to count the blessings of monarchy.

To Joseph Jones, Paris, August 14, 1787.

We may say with confidence that the worst of the American constitutions is better than the best which ever existed before in any other country.

To Thomas M. Randolph, Jr., Paris, July 6, 1787.

I am sensible that there are defects in our federal government, yet they are so much lighter than those of monarchies that I view them with much indulgence. I rely, too, on the good sense of the people for remedy, whereas the evils of monarchical government are beyond remedy. If any of our countrymen wish for a king, give them Aesop's fable of the frogs who asked for a king; if this does not cure them, send them to Europe. They will go back good republicans.

To David Ramsay, Paris, August 4, 1787.

I sincerely wish you may find it convenient to come here; the pleasure of the trip will be less than you expect, but the utility greater. It will make you adore your own country—its soil, its climate, its equality, liberty, laws, people, and manners. My God! how little do my countrymen know what precious blessings they are in possession of and which no other people on earth enjoy. I confess I had no idea of it myself. While we shall see multiplied instances of Europeans going to live in America, I will venture to say no man now living will ever see an instance of an American removing to settle in Europe and continuing there. Come, then, and see the proofs of this, and on your return add your testimony to that of every thinking American in order to satisfy our countrymen how much it is their interest to preserve, uninfected by contagion, those peculiarities in their government and manners to which they are indebted for those blessings.

To James Monroe, Paris, June 17, 1785.

[On Government by the People]

I have no fear but that the result of our experiment will be that men may be trusted to govern themselves without a master. Could the contrary of this be proved, I should conclude either that there is no God or that he is a malevolent being.

To David Hartley, Paris, July 2, 1787.

I consider the people who constitute a society or nation as the source of all authority in that nation; as free to transact their common concerns by any agents they think proper; to change these agents individually or the organization of them in form or function whenever they please; that all the acts done by these agents under the authority of the nation are the acts of the nation, are obligatory on them and enure to their use, and can in no wise be annulled or affected by any change in the form of the government, or of the persons administering it.

Cabinet Opinion, April 28, 1793.

In every country where man is free to think and to speak, differences of opinion will arise from difference of perception and the imperfection of reason; but these differences, when permitted, as in this happy country, to purify themselves by free discussion, are but as passing clouds overspreading our land transiently and leaving our horizon more bright and serene. That love of order and obedience to the laws, which so remarkably characterize the citizens of the United States, are sure pledges of internal tranquility; and the elective franchise, if guarded as the ark of our safety, will peaceably dissipate all combinations to subvert a Constitution dictated by the wisdom and resting on the will of the people. That will is the only legitimate foundation of any government, and to protect its free expression should be our first object.

> To Benjamin Waring, Washington, March 23, 1801.

The first principle of republicanism is that the *lex majoris partis* is the fundamental law of every society of individuals of equal rights; to consider the will of the society enounced by the majority of a single vote as sacred as if unanimous is the first of all lessons in importance, yet the last which is thoroughly learnt. This law once disregarded, no other remains but that of force, which ends necessarily in military despotism.

> To Alexander Humboldt, Monticello, June 13, 1817.

[On Education]

And say, finally, whether peace is best preserved by giving energy to the government or information to the people. This last is the most certain and the most legitimate engine of government. Educate and inform the whole mass of the people. Enable them to see that it is their interest to preserve peace and order, and they will preserve them. And it requires no very high degree of education to convince them of this. They are the only sure reliance for the preservation of our liberty.

> To James Madison, Paris, December 20, 1787.

I know of no safe depository of the ultimate powers of the society but the people themselves, and if we think them not enlightened enough to exercise their control with a wholesome discretion, the remedy is not to take it from them but to inform their discretion by education.

> To William C. Jarvis, Monticello, September 28, 1820.

It is an axiom in my mind that our liberty can never be safe but in the hands of the people themselves, and that, too, of the people with a certain degree of instruction. This it is the business of the state to effect and on a general plan.

To George Washington, Paris, January 4, 1786.

If a nation expects to be ignorant and free in a state of civilization, it expects what never was and never will be. The functionaries of every government have propensities to command at will the liberty and property of their constituents. There is no safe deposit for these but with the people themselves, nor can they be safe with them without information. Where the press is free and every man able to read, all is safe.

To Charles Yancey, Monticello, January 6, 1816.

Section II

DEMOCRATIC LIBERALISM

During the nineteenth century the United States and much of Europe experienced a period of steadily increasing democratization and liberalization. The ideals of maximal freedom and self-government were proposed and defended anew, but the arguments in their favor came to be founded upon principles quite different from those of the natural-rights theorists.

The political philosophers turned from alleged inalienable rights to the well-being and happiness of all members of a society. Democratic ideals were supported as those best suited for the achievement of the greatest good for the greatest number. Men must be free and equal, not because it had been preordained, but because only freedom and equality could lead to the kind of government and the kind of man considered ideal by all.

Philosophical treatises about democracy took the form of well-reasoned arguments, the aim of which was to demonstrate, on largely utilitarian principles, the advantages of enlarging democracy and the superior results that only democratic forms could bring about. "I forgo any advantage," J. S. Mill wrote, "which could be derived to my argument from the idea of abstract right, as a thing independent of utility. I regard utility as the ultimate appeal on all ethical questions, but it must be utility in the largest sense. . . ."

Although not all the philosophers represented in this section were strictly utilitarian, they were all primarily concerned with the operation of democracy, and with changes in its laws and institutions that would have the optimum consequences. They were concerned about the possible tyranny of the majority and how it could be prevented within a democracy; they were troubled about the conflicts of interest into which

488

excessive liberty could lead; and they tried to develop principles upon which freedoms could be safely extended and, when necessary, justly restricted. For the most part, these philosophers of democratic liberalism were intensely active in political affairs; they knew how democracy worked in practice, recognized its shortcomings, and strove constantly to improve it.

54. JEREMY BENTHAM

Jeremy Bentham (1748-1832) was the founder of the utilitarian movement, and the most influential English philosopher of his day. It was he who formulated the goal of the greatest happiness for the greatest number, where happiness was understood as the increase of pleasure and the decrease of pain. With this "principle of utility" he provided the ethical foundation for a great part of the political and economic reform which was to take place during the nineteenth century. "Between two opposite modes of action, would you know to which the preference is due? Calculate the effects, in good and ill, and decide for that which promises the greatest amount of happiness."

Of the Principle of Utility*

The happiness of the people ought to be the aim of the Legislator; *general utility* ought to be the principle of reasoning in legislation. To know what is good for the community whose welfare is at stake, constitutes the science; to find the means of producing that good, constitutes the art.

The principle of *Utility,* when vaguely taught, provokes little contradiction; it is even regarded as a common field in morals and in politics. But this almost universal assent is only apparent. People do not all attach the same ideas to the word; they do not all give it the same

* From Jeremy Bentham, *Principles of Legislation*, 1802. These passages are selected from an edition of Bentham's work by Stephen Dumont, his personal friend, in which several of Bentham's manuscripts are combined, and the ethical, legal, and political elements of his theory are carefully integrated.

value; and from it there is therefore no consequent and uniform flow of reasoning. . . .

Nature has subjected man to the dominion of *pleasure* and *pain*. To them we are indebted for all our ideas. To them we refer all our opinions, and every judgment we give. He who pretends to be free from their influence, knows not what he says; at the very instant when he appears to avoid the greatest pleasure, and to seek the greatest pain, his ultimate object is to find pleasure and avoid pain. This eternal and irresistible propensity ought to be the chief study of the moralist and the legislator. The *principle of utility* refers every thing to these two motives.

Utility is an abstract term. It expresses the suitableness, or the tendency of a thing to preserve from some evil, or to procure some good. *Evil* is pain, or the cause of pain. *Good* is pleasure, or the cause of pleasure. What is conformable to utility, or to the interest of an individual, is whatever tends to augment the sum-total of his happiness. What is conformable to utility, or to the interest of a community, is whatever tends to augment the sum-total of the happiness of the individuals composing that community.

A *principle* is a first idea, which we take for the commencement or foundation of our reasoning. Or to make it more sensible to the understanding, it may be regarded as a fixed object to which the first link of a chain is attached. The principle should be evident. To cause it to be received for truth, it should be enough to *explain* it. It is like an axiom in mathematics; it need not be formally proved; it is enough to show that by rejecting it we fall into absurdity.

The *logic of utility* consists in setting out from the calculation or comparison of pains with pleasures in all the operations of the judgment, and in excluding every other idea.

I am a partisan of the principle of utility, when I measure my approbation or my disapprobation of an act, whether public or private, by its tendency to produce pains and pleasures; when I employ the terms *just, unjust, moral, immoral, good, bad,* as collective terms, which express ideas of certain pleasures, or of certain pains, without any other meaning. Be it understood that I take the words *pain* and *pleasure* in their common acceptation, without inventing arbitrary definitions, either to exclude certain pleasures; or to deny certain pains. No subtility, no metaphysics; we need not consult Plato nor Aristotle. *Pain* and *pleasure* are what everybody feels them to be;

the peasant as well as the prince, the uneducated-man as well as the philosopher.

To the partisan of the *Principle of Utility* virtue itself is good, only because of the pleasures which are derived from it; and vice an evil, only because of its tendency to produce pain. Moral good is a *good* only because of its tendency to produce physical good; moral evil is bad only because of its tendency to produce physical evil. But by *physical,* I understand the pleasure and pains of the mind, as well as the pains and pleasures of sense. I look to man as he is by nature and by constitution.

If the partisan of the *Principle of Utility* should find in the common catalogue of the virtues, an action from which results more pain than pleasure, he would not fail to regard such pretended virtue as a vice. He would not suffer himself to be carried away by the general error; nor would he lightly believe that false virtues may be lawfully employed in support of the true.

If he should find moreover in the common catalogue of offenses, some indifferent action, or innocent pleasure, he would not scruple to remove the pretended offense to the class of legitimate acts; he would feel pity for the pretended criminals, and reserve his indignation for the pretended virtuous, who persecuted them.

Objections Answered

We may raise trifling objections to the principle of Utility, we may attack it with small verbal criticism, but there is no room for serious or decided objections.

How would it be possible indeed to attack the principle, but by reasons drawn from the principle itself? To say it is dangerous were to say that it would be contrary to utility to consult utility.

The difficulty of the question arises from a sort of perversity in the language. We are accustomed to speak of *virtue* in opposition to *Utility.* Virtue, says someone, is the sacrifice of our interest to our duties.—To express ourselves clearly, we should say, that there are different degrees of interests, and that divers interests under certain circumstances are incompatible. Virtue is the sacrifice of a lesser interest to a greater; of a momentary interest to a durable interest; of a doubtful interest to a certain interest. Every idea of virtue not derived from that notion is as obscure as the motive is precarious.

They who, for convenience, would distinguish politics from morality, and refer the first to the principle of Utility, and the second to that of justice, have but a confused idea of the truth. The whole difference between politics and morals is, that one directs the operations of government, while the other regulates the doings of individuals; but their common object is happiness. What is politically good, cannot be morally bad, unless the rules of arithmetic, which are good for a large number, are bad for a small one.

We may go wrong, while we persuade ourselves that we are following the principle of Utility. A weak and limited understanding may deceive itself, by taking into view only a small part of the good and evil, which result from a given act. A passionate man may deceive himself by attaching an excessive value to some good, which hinders him from seeing the evil connected with it. What constitutes wickedness is a habit of indulging in pleasures that are hurtful to others; but even that supposes the absence of many kinds of pleasure. But we are not to charge the principle with the faults which are contrary to it, and which alone might serve to regulate it. If a man calculates ill, it is not arithmetic that is in fault; it is himself. If the reproaches that are heaped on Machiavel are just, his errors do not proceed from his not having consulted the *principle of Utility,* but from his having made false applications of it. The author of *Anti-Machiavel* saw this clearly: he refutes the *Prince* by showing that his maxims are pernicious, and that bad faith is bad policy.

Those who, after reading Cicero's Offices, and the Platonic moralists, have a confused notion of Utility as opposed to honesty, often quote the saying of Aristides upon the project, which Themistocles would explain only to him. "The project of Themistocles is *very advantageous,*" said Aristides, to the assembled Athenians; "but *it is very unjust.*" People imagine that they see here a decided opposition of the just to the useful; they are mistaken: it is but a comparison of good and evil. *Unjust* is a term which presents the collective idea of all the mischief resulting from a situation, in which men could no longer trust one another. Aristides might have said, "The project of Themistocles would be useful for a moment, and hurtful for ages; what it would give, is nothing to what it would take away." . . .

But says another, "Every man constitutes himself the judge of Utility for himself: Every obligation will cease whenever it does not accord with his own interest."

Every man constitutes himself the judge of Utility *for* himself. So it is, and so it should be; otherwise man would not be a reasonable agent. He who is not a judge of what is good for himself, is less than an infant—he is an idiot. Obligation which holds men to their engagements, is nothing but the sense of an interest of a higher class which prevails over a subordinate interest. Men are not held by the particular utility of this or that engagement; but in a case where the engagement is an evil to one of the parties, he is held by the general utility of engagements; by the confidence which every enlightened man wishes to have placed in his word, in order that he may be considered as a man of good faith, and enjoy the advantages attached to probity and to esteem. It is not the engagement itself which constitutes the obligation; for there are unlawful and void engagements; And why? Because they are considered hurtful. It is then the utility of the contract which gives it force.

One might easily reduce every act of exalted virtue to a calculation of good and evil. It is neither to degrade it, nor to weaken it, to represent it as the effect of reason, and to explain it in an intelligible and simple manner.

We perceive now into what a circle they are led who refuse to acknowledge the principle of Utility. I ought to keep my promise. Why? Because I am commanded to do so by my conscience. How do you know that you are commanded to do so by your conscience? Because I have the inward feeling. Why ought you to obey your conscience? Because God is the author of my nature, and to obey my conscience is to obey God. Why ought you to obey God? Because it is my first duty. How know you this? Because my conscience tells me so, &c. Such is the everlasting circle out of which we are never to escape; such the source of obstinacy and of invincible error. For if we judge of everything by sentiment, there is no means of distinguishing between the injunctions of an enlightened conscience, and those of a blind conscience. All persecutors have the same title: all fanatics the same right.

If you would reject the principle of Utility, because it may be misapplied, what would you substitute for it? What rule have you discovered that one cannot abuse? Where is that infallible guide?

Will you substitute for it some despotic principle, which orders men to act in such or such a way, without knowing why, from pure obedience?

Will you substitute for it some chaotic, vague and capricious principle, founded only upon your inward and peculiar sentiments?

In this case what are the inducements you would offer to persuade men to follow you? Would they be independent of their interest? If they do not agree with you, how will you reason with them, how contrive to conciliate them? Whither will you summon all the sects, all the opinions, all the contradictions that fill the world, if not to the tribunal of a common interest?

The most obstinate adversaries of the principle of utility are those who establish themselves upon what they call the *religious principle*. They profess to take the will of God for the only rule of good and evil. It is the only rule say they, which has all the characteristics required, being infallible, universal sovereign, &c. &c.

I answer that the religious principle is not a distinct principle; it is not one of those treated of, under another form. What is called the will of God, can be (at the best) but his presumed will, since God does not explain himself to us by immediate acts, nor by particular revelations. But how can a man presume to know the will of God? By his own will. But his own will is always directed by one of the three principles above mentioned. How do you know that God does not desire such or such a thing? Because it would be prejudicial to the happiness of man, answers the partisan of utility. Because it contains a gross and sensual pleasure which God reproves, answers the ascetic. Because it wounds the conscience, is contrary to our natural sentiments, and because we ought to detest it without permitting ourselves to examine it. Such is the language of antipathy.

But revelation, says another, is the direct expression of the will of God. There is nothing arbitrary there. It is a guide which ought to prevail over all human reason.

I will not answer indirectly that revelation is not universal; that even among christians themselves, many individuals do not admit it, and that a common principle of reasoning is required for all mankind.

But I answer that revelation is not a system of politics nor of morals; that all its precepts require to be explained, modified and limited one by another; that taken in the literal sense, they would overthrow the world, annihilate self-defense, industry, commerce, and reciprocal attachment; that the ecclesiastical history is a proof incontestable of the dreadful mischief that has resulted from religious maxims ill-understood.

Of the Value of Pleasures and Pains

To multiply pleasures, to diminish pains—such is the whole business of the legislator. Their value should be well known, therefore. Pleasures and pains are the only instruments that can be employed: Their power should be well studied, therefore.

If we examine the *value* of a pleasure considered in itself, and with relation to one single individual, we shall find it to depend on four circumstances.

1. Its *intensity*.
2. Its *duration*.
3. Its *certainty*.
4. Its *proximity*.

The value of a pain depends upon the same circumstances.

But, in fact, it is not enough to examine the value of pains, or of pleasures, as if they were isolated and independent: pains and pleasures may have consequences, which will be in their turn, pains and pleasures. If therefore, we wish to calculate the *tendency* of an act from which results an immediate pain or pleasure, we must take into view two other circumstances.

5. Its *fruitfulness*.
6. Its *purity*.

Fruitful pleasure: that which has a chance to be followed by pleasures of the same sort.

Fruitful pain: that which has a chance of being followed with pains of the same sort.

Pure pleasure: that which has no chance of producing pain.

Pure pain: that which has no chance of producing pleasure.

When the above estimation is to refer to a collection of individuals, we are to add another circumstance.

7. *Extent:* that is to say, the number of persons who are afflicted by such pain or pleasure.

Would one estimate the value of an action? He must follow in detail the operations that have just been described. They are the elements of the moral calculation, and legislation becomes a matter of arithmetic. The *evil* caused is the expense: the *good* that one produces is the profit. The rules for this calculation are the same as in every other.*

It is a slow but sure way: What is called *sentiment* is more rapid but liable to go astray. But we are not obliged to renew the whole process on every occasion: When we are familiar with it, when we have acquired the judgment which results from such familiarity with it, we compare the sum-total of good, and the sum-total of mischief, with so much promptitude as not to perceive the items of the reasoning. We do the sum without knowing it. The analytical method becomes necessary whenever a new or complicated operation is to be performed, or when it is necessary to clear up a contested point, to teach or demonstrate a truth to the ignorant.

This theory of moral calculation has never been fully explained; but it has always been followed in practice; at least, wherever men have had a clear idea of their own interest. What constitutes the value of a lot of ground? It is not the amount of pleasure to be drawn from it? And does not that value vary according to the greater or less duration that we are able to promise ourselves in the enjoyment of it?—according to the proximity or distance of the period, when we are to enter into the enjoyment?—according to the certainty or uncertainty of the possession?

Errors in the moral conduct of men, or in legislation, may always be referred to some circumstances which have been unknown, forgotten, or badly appreciated in the calculation of good and evil.

Of Political Good and Evil

It is with government, as with medicine. They have both but a choice of evils. Every law is an evil, for every law is an infraction of liberty: And I repeat that government has but a choice of evils: In making this choice, what ought to be the object of the legislator? He ought to assure himself of two things; 1st, that in every case, the

* In his *Introduction to the Principles of Morals and Legislation,* Bentham added, in a footnote, the following lines as an aid to the memory:
   "Intense, long, certain, speedy, fruitful, pure;
   These marks in pleasures and in pains endure.
   Such pleasures seek, if private be thy end;
   If it be public, wide let them extend.
   Such pains avoid, whichever be thy view;
   If pains must come, let them extend to few." [*Ed.*]

incidents which he tries to prevent are really evils; and 2ndly, that if evils, they are greater than those which he employs to prevent them.

There are then two things to be regarded; the evil of the offense and the evil of the law; the evil of the malady and the evil of the remedy.

An evil comes rarely alone. A lot of evil cannot well fall upon an individual without spreading itself about him, as about a common center. In the course of its progress we see it take different shapes: we see evil of one kind issue from evil of another kind; evil proceed from good and good from evil. All these changes, it is important to know and to distinguish; in this, in fact, consists the essence of legislation. . . .

Of the Limits Which Separate Morals from Legislation

Morality in general is the act of directing the actions of men, so as to produce the greatest possible amount of happiness.

Legislation ought to have precisely the same object in view.

But although these two arts, or these two sciences have the same end in view, they differ much in their extent. All actions, whether public or private, are the springs of morals. It is a guide which may conduct an individual, as it were by the hand, through all the details of life, through all the relationships of society. Legislation cannot do this, and if it could, it ought not to exercise a continual and direct interference with the conduct of men. Morality prescribes to each individual to do whatever is advantageous to himself and to the community. But as there are many acts useful to the community which the legislator ought never to command: So are there many hurtful acts, which he ought not to forbid, although morality may. Legislation in a word has much the same center as morality, though not the same circumference.

There are two reasons for the difference: 1. Legislation cannot secretly influence the conduct of men but by punishment: these punishments are so many evils, which are no further justifiable, than as they produce a greater sum of good. But in many cases where we might wish to strengthen a moral precept by a penalty, the evil of the fault would be less than the evil of the penalty; the means necessary for securing the execution of the law would be of a nature to spread a degree of alarm more hurtful than the evil that we might wish to prevent.

2. Legislation is often stopped by the fear of including the innocent while striving to reach the guilty. Whence comes the danger? From the difficulty of defining the offense, of giving a clear and precise idea of it. For example, severity, ingratitude, perfidy, and other vices which the popular sanction punishes, cannot come within the supervision of the law, for we cannot give an exact definition of them, as of robbery, homicide, perjury, etc. . . .

General Rule. Leave to individuals the greatest possible latitude, in every case where they can only injure themselves, for they are the best judges of their own interests. If they deceive themselves, the moment they perceive their error, it is to be presumed they will not persist. Do not suffer the power of the law to interfere, unless to prevent their injuring each other. It is there that law is necessary; it is there that the application of punishment is truly useful, since the rigor shown toward one may ensure the safety of all. . . .

Conclusion

I shall finish with a general observation. The language of error is always obscure, feeble, and changeable. A great abundance of words only serves to hide the poverty and falsity of ideas. The more the terms are varied, the more easy it is to lead people astray. The language of truth is uniform and simple: the same ideas, the same terms. All these refer to pleasures and to pains. We avoid all that may hide or intercept that familiar notion.—*From such or such an act, results such or such an impression of pain or pleasure.* Do not trust to me; trust to experience; and above all, to your own. *Between two opposite modes of action, would you know to which the preference is due? Calculate the effects, in good and ill, and decide for that which promises the greatest amount of happiness.*

55. JOHN STUART MILL

John Stuart Mill (1806-1873) was a leading utilitarian philosopher, a vigorous reformer, and a champion of individual liberty of thought and *action.* In* Considerations on Representative Government, *from which the following selection is taken, he argues painstakingly and forcefully that, since self-government best promotes the good management of social affairs and is, at the same time, most effective in improving the character and abilities of the citizens, democracy is "the ideally best polity."*

The Ideally Best Polity†

There is no difficulty in showing that the ideally best form of government is that in which the sovereignty, or supreme controlling power in the last resort, is vested in the entire aggregate of the community, every citizen not only having a voice in the exercise of the ultimate sovereignty, but being, at least occasionally, called on to take an actual part in the government by the personal discharge of some public function, local or general.

To test this proposition, it has to be examined in reference to the two branches into which, as pointed out in the last chapter, the inquiry into the goodness of a government conveniently divides itself, namely, how far it promotes the good management of the affairs of society by means of the existing faculties, moral, intellectual, and active, of its various members, and what is its effect in improving or deteriorating those faculties.

The ideally best form of government, it is scarcely necessary to say, does not mean one which is practicable or eligible in all states of civilization, but the one which, in the circumstances in which it is practicable and eligible, is attended with the greatest amount of beneficial consequences, immediate and prospective. A completely popular government is the only polity which can make out any claim to this character. It is pre-eminent in both the departments between which the excellence of a political Constitution is divided. It is both more favorable to present good government, and promotes a better and higher form of national character than any other polity whatsoever.

Its superiority in reference to present well-being rests upon two principles, of as universal truth and applicability as any general

---

* Selections from *On Liberty,* in which the Utilitarian arguments for individual freedoms are presented, will be found later in this volume, pp. 547 ff.

† From J. S. Mill, *Considerations on Representative Government,* 1861. These passages are reprinted from an edition published by Harper and Brothers, New York, 1862.

propositions which can be laid down respecting human affairs. The first is that the rights and interests of every or any person are only secure from being disregarded when the person interested is himself able, and habitually disposed, to stand up for them. The second is, that the general prosperity attains a greater height, and is more widely diffused, in proportion to the amount and variety of the personal energies enlisted in promoting it.

Putting these two propositions into a shape more special to their present application—human beings are only secure from evil at the hands of others in proportion as they have the power of being, and are, self-*protecting;* and they only achieve a high degree of success in their struggle with Nature in proportion as they are self-*dependent,* relying on what they themselves can do, either separately or in concert, rather than on what others do for them.

The former proposition—that each is the only safe guardian of his own rights and interests—is one of those elementary maxims of prudence which every person capable of conducting his own affairs implicitly acts upon wherever he himself is interested. Many, indeed, have a great dislike to it as a political doctrine, and are fond of holding it up to obloquy as a doctrine of universal selfishness. To which we may answer, that whenever it ceases to be true that mankind, as a rule, prefer themselves to others, and those nearest to them to those more remote, from that moment Communism is not only practicable, but the only defensible form of society, and will, when that time arrives, be assuredly carried into effect. For my own part, not believing in universal selfishness, I have no difficulty in admitting that Communism would even now be practicable among the *élite* of mankind, and may become so among the rest. But as this opinion is anything but popular with those defenders of existing institutions who find fault with the doctrine of the general predominance of self-interest, I am inclined to think they do in reality believe that most men consider themselves before other people. It is not, however, necessary to affirm even thus much in order to support the claim of all to participate in the sovereign power. We need not suppose that when power resides in an exclusive class, that class will knowingly and deliberately sacrifice the other classes to themselves: it suffices that, in the absence of its natural defenders, the interest of the excluded is always in danger of being overlooked; and, when looked at, is seen with very different eyes from those of the persons whom it directly concerns. In this country, for example, what are called the working classes may be considered as excluded from all direct participation in the government. I do not believe that the classes who do participate in it have in general any intention of sacrificing the working classes to themselves. They once had that intention; witness the persevering attempts so long made to keep down wages by law. But in the present day their ordinary disposition is the very opposite: they willingly make considerable sacrifices, especially of their pecuniary interest, for the benefit of the working classes, and err rather by too lavish and indiscriminating beneficence; nor do I believe that any rulers in history have been actuated by a more sincere desire to do their duty toward the poorer portion of their countrymen. Yet does Parliament, or almost any of the members composing it, ever for an instant look at any question with the eyes of a working man? When a subject arises in which the laborers as such have an interest, is it regarded from any point of view but that of the employers of labor? I do not say that the working men's view of these questions is in general nearer to the truth than the other, but it is sometimes quite as near; and in any case it ought to be respectfully listened to, instead of being, as it is, not merely turned away from, but ignored. On the question of strikes, for instance, it is doubtful if there is so much as one among the leading members of either House who is not firmly convinced that the reason of the matter is unqualifiedly on the side of the masters, and that the men's view of it is simply absurd. Those who have studied the question know well how far this is from being the case, and in how different, and how infinitely less superficial a manner the point would have to be argued if the classes who strike were able to make themselves heard in Parliament.

It is an inherent condition of human affairs that no intention, however sincere, of protecting the interests of others can make it safe or salutary to tie up their own hands. Still more obviously true is it that by their own hands only can any positive and durable improvement of their circumstances in life be worked out. Through the joint influence of these two principles, all free communities have both been more exempt from social injustice and crime, and have attained more brilliant prosperity than any others, or than they themselves after they lost their freedom. Contrast the free states of the world, while their freedom lasted, with the contemporary subjects of monarchical or oligarchical despotism: the Greek cities with the Persian satrapies, the Italian republics, and the free towns of Flanders and Germany, with the feudal monarchies of Europe; Switzerland, Holland, and England with Austria or ante-revolutionary France. Their superior prosperity was too obvious ever to have been gainsaid; while their superiority in good government and social relations is proved by the prosperity, and is manifest besides in every page of history. If we compare, not one age with another, but the different governments which coexisted in the same age, no amount of disorder which exaggeration itself can pretend to have existed amidst the publicity of the free states can be compared for a moment with the contemptuous trampling upon the mass of the people which pervaded the whole life of the monarchical countries, or the disgusting individual tyranny which was of more than daily occurrence under the systems of plunder which they called fiscal arrangements, and in the secrecy of their frightful courts of justice.

It must be acknowledged that the benefits of freedom, so far as they have hitherto been enjoyed, were obtained by the extension of its privileges to a part only of the community, and that a government in which they are extended impartially to all is a desideratum still unrealized. But, though every approach to this has an independent value, and in many cases more than an approach could not, in the existing state of general improvement, be made, the participation of all in these benefits is the ideally perfect conception of free government. In proportion as any, no matter who, are excluded from it, the interests of the excluded are left without the guaranty accorded to the rest, and they themselves have less scope and encouragement than they might otherwise have to that exertion of their energies for the good of themselves and of the community, to which the general prosperity is always proportioned.

Thus stands the case as regards present well-being—the good management of the affairs of the existing generation. If we now pass to the influence of the form of government upon character, we shall find the superiority of popular government over every other to be, if possible, still more decided and indisputable.

This question really depends upon a still more fundamental one, viz., which of two common types of character, for the general good of humanity, it is most desirable should predominate—the active or the passive type; that which struggles against evils or that which endures them; that which bends to circumstances, or that which endeavors to make circumstances bend to itself.

The commonplaces of moralists and the general sympathies of

mankind, are in favor of the passive type. Energetic characters may be admired, but the acquiescent and submissive are those which most men personally prefer. The passiveness of our neighbors increases our own sense of security, and plays into the hands of our willfulness. Passive characters, if we do not happen to need their activity, seem an obstruction the less in our own path. A contented character is not a dangerous rival. Yet nothing is more certain than that improvement in human affairs is wholly the work of the uncontented characters; and, moreover, that it is much easier for an active mind to acquire the virtues of patience, than for a passive one to assume those of energy. . . .

The striving, go-ahead character of England and the United States is only a fit subject of disapproving criticism on account of the very secondary objects on which it commonly expends its strength. In itself it is the foundation of the best hopes for the general improvement of mankind. It has been acutely remarked, that whenever anything goes amiss, the habitual impulse of French people is to say, "Il faut de la patience"; and of English people, "What a shame." The people who think it a shame when anything goes wrong—who rush to the conclusion that the evil could and ought to have been prevented, are those who, in the long run, do most to make the world better. If the desires are low placed, if they extend to little beyond physical comfort, and the show of riches, the immediate results of the energy will not be much more than the continual extension of man's power over material objects; but even this makes room, and prepares the mechanical appliances for the greatest intellectual and social achievements; and while the energy is there, some persons will apply it, and it will be applied more and more, to the perfecting not of outward circumstances alone, but of man's inward nature. Inactivity, unaspiringness, absence of desire, is a more fatal hindrance to improvement than any misdirection of energy, and is that through which alone, when existing in the mass, any very formidable misdirection by an energetic few becomes possible. It is this, mainly, which retains in a savage or semi-savage state the great majority of the human race.

Now there can be no kind of doubt that the passive type of character is favored by the government of one or a few, and the active self-helping type by that of the many. Irresponsible rulers need the quiescence of the ruled more than they need any activity but that which they can compel. Submissiveness to the prescriptions of men as necessities of nature is the lesson inculcated by all governments upon those who are wholly without participation in them. The will of superiors, and the law as the will of superiors, must be passively yielded to. But no men are mere instruments or materials in the hands of their rulers who have will, or spirit, or a spring of internal activity in the rest of their proceedings, and any manifestation of these qualities, instead of receiving encouragement from despots, has to get itself forgiven by them. Even when irresponsible rulers are not sufficiently conscious of danger from the mental activity of their subjects to be desirous of repressing it, the position itself is a repression. Endeavor is even more effectually restrained by the certainty of its impotence than by any positive discouragement. Between subjection to the will of others and the virtues of self-help and self-government, there is a natural incompatibility. This is more or less complete, according as the bondage is strained or relaxed. Rulers differ very much in the length to which they carry the control of the free agency of their subjects, or the suppression of it by managing their business for them. But the difference is in degree, not in principle; and the best despots often go the greatest lengths in chaining up the free agency of their subjects. A bad despot, when his own personal indulgences have been provided for, may sometimes be willing to let the people alone; but a good despot insists on doing them good by making them do their own business in a better way than they themselves know of. . . .

Very different is the state of the human faculties where a human being feels himself under no other external restraint than the necessities of nature, or mandates of society which he has his share in imposing, and which it is open to him, if he thinks them wrong, publicly to dissent from, and exert himself actively to get altered. No doubt, under a government partially popular, this freedom may be exercised even by those who are not partakers in the full privileges of citizenship; but it is a great additional stimulus to anyone's self-help and self-reliance when he starts from even ground, and has not to feel that his success depends on the impression he can make upon the sentiments and dispositions of a body of whom he is not one. It is a great discouragement to an individual, and a still greater one to a class, to be left out of the constitution; to be reduced to plead from outside the door to the arbiters of their destiny, not taken into consultation within. The maximum of the invigorating effect of freedom upon the character is only obtained when the person acted on either is, or is looking forward to become a citizen as fully privileged as any other. What is still more important than even this matter of feeling is the practical discipline which the character obtains from the occasional demand made upon the citizens to exercise, for a time and in their turn, some social function. It is not sufficiently considered how little there is in most men's ordinary life to give any largeness either to their conceptions or to their sentiments. Their work is a routine; not a labor of love, but of self-interest in the most elementary form, the satisfaction of daily wants; neither the thing done, nor the process of doing it, introduces the mind to thoughts or feelings extending beyond individuals; if instructive books are within their reach, there is no stimulus to read them; and, in most cases, the individual has no access to any person of cultivation much superior to his own. Giving him something to do for the public supplies, in a measure, all these deficiencies. If circumstances allow the amount of public duty assigned him to be considerable, it makes him an educated man. Notwithstanding the defects of the social system and moral ideas of antiquity, the practice of the dicastery and the ecclesia raised the intellectual standard of an average Athenian citizen far beyond anything of which there is yet an example in any other mass of men, ancient or modern. The proofs of this are apparent in every page of our great historian of Greece; but we need scarcely look further than to the high quality of the addresses which their great orators deemed best calculated to act with effect on their understanding and will. A benefit of the same kind, though far less in degree, is produced on Englishmen of the lower middle class by their liability to be placed on juries and to serve parish offices, which, though it does not occur to so many, nor is so continuous, nor introduces them to so great a variety of elevated considerations as to admit of comparison with the public education which every citizen of Athens obtained from her democratic institutions, makes them nevertheless very different beings, in range of ideas and development of faculties, from those who have done nothing in their lives but drive a quill, or sell goods over a counter. Still more salutary is the moral part of the instruction afforded by the participation of the private citizen, if even rarely, in public functions. He is called upon, while so engaged, to weigh interests not his own; to be guided, in case of conflicting claims, by another rule than his private partialities; to apply, at every turn, principles and maxims which have for their reason of existence the general good; and he usually finds associated with him in the same work minds more familiarized than his own with these ideas and operations, whose study it will be to supply reason to his understanding, and stimulation to his feeling for the general good. He is made to feel himself one of the public, and whatever is their interest to be his interest. Where this school of public spirit does not exist, scarcely any sense is entertained that private persons, in no eminent social situation, owe any duties to society except to obey the laws and submit to the government. There is no unselfish sentiment of identification with the public. Every thought or feeling, either of interest or of duty, is absorbed in the individual and in the family. The man never thinks of any collective interest, of any objects to be pursued jointly with others, but only in competition with them, and in some measure at their expense. A neighbor, not being an ally or an associate, since he is never engaged in any common undertaking for joint benefit, is therefore only a rival. Thus even private morality suffers, while public is actually extinct. Were this the universal and only possible state of things, the utmost aspirations of the lawgiver or the moralist could only stretch to make the bulk of the community a flock of sheep innocently nibbling the grass side by side.

From these accumulated considerations, it is evident that the only government which can fully satisfy all the exigencies of the social state is one in which the whole people participate; that any participation, even in the smallest public function, is useful; that the participation should everywhere be as great as the general degree of improvement of the community will allow; and that nothing less can be ultimately desirable than the admission of all to a share in the sovereign power of the state. But since all cannot, in a community exceeding a single small town, participate personally in any but some very minor portions of the public business, it follows that the ideal type of a perfect government must be representative.

56. JOHN C. CALHOUN

John C. Calhoun (1782-1850) was Secretary of War, and then Vice-President of the United States—which office he resigned to become U.S.

*Senator from the state of South Carolina. He was a vigorous advocate
of the Southern cause in the years prior to the Civil War, and in this
context developed his theory of the concurrent majority, which provided,
he claimed, the only constitutional arrangement within a democracy that
could properly protect the interests of large minorities. He argued that the
great distinction in governments lay between those which were constitutional and those which were absolute. The conservative principle of the
latter, he contended, was force, while that of the former was compromise.
No one had a better understanding of the origins of conflict within a
democracy than Calhoun, and he believed that the only salvation of this
form of government was a "disposition to harmonize" on the part of all
interests.*

[Man and Government] *

In order to have a clear and just conception of the nature and
object of government, it is indispensable to understand correctly
what that constitution or law of our nature is, in which government
originates; or to express it more fully and accurately—that law, without which government would not, and with which it must necessarily
exist. Without this, it is as impossible to lay any solid foundation for
the science of government as it would be to lay one for that of
astronomy, without a like understanding of that constitution or law
of the material world according to which the several bodies composing the solar system mutually act on each other and by which
they are kept in their respective spheres. The first question, accordingly, to be considered is, What is that constitution or law of our
nature, without which government would not exist, and with which
its existence is necessary?

In considering this, I assume, as an incontestable fact, that man
is so constituted as to be a social being. His inclinations and wants,
physical and moral, irresistibly impel him to associate with his kind;
and he has, accordingly, never been found, in any age or country,
in any state other than the social. In no other, indeed, could he exist;
and in no other—were it possible for him to exist—could he attain
to a full development of his moral and intellectual faculties, or raise

---

* From J. C. Calhoun, *A Disquisition on Government.* These passages are
from the text of the first edition of the *Disquisition,* published under the direction of the General Assembly of the State of South Carolina, Columbia, S.C.,
1851.

himself, in the scale of being, much above the level of the brute creation.

I next assume also, as a fact not less incontestable, that, while man is so constituted as to make the social state necessary to his existence and the full development of his faculties, this state itself cannot exist without government. The assumption rests on universal experience. In no age or country has any society or community ever been found, whether enlightened or savage, without government of some description.

Having assumed these as unquestionable phenomena of our nature, I shall, without further remark, proceed to the investigation of the primary and important question, What is that constitution of our nature which, while it impels man to associate with his kind, renders it impossible for society to exist without government?

The answer will be found in the fact (not less incontestable than either of the others) that, while man is created for the social state, and is accordingly so formed as to feel what affects others as well as what affects himself, he is, at the same time, so constituted as to feel more intensely what affects him directly, than what affects him indirectly through others; or, to express it differently, he is so constituted that his direct or individual affections are stronger than his sympathetic or social feelings. I intentionally avoid the expression "*selfish* feelings" as applicable to the former, because, as commonly used, it implies an unusual excess of the individual over the social feelings, in the person to whom it is applied and, consequently, something depraved and vicious. My object is to exclude such inference, and to restrict the inquiry exclusively to facts in their bearings on the subject under consideration, viewed as mere phenomena appertaining to our nature—constituted as it is; and which are as unquestionable as is that of gravitation, or any other phenomenon of the material world.

In asserting that our individual are stronger than our social feelings, it is not intended to deny that there are instances, growing out of peculiar relations—as that of a mother and her infant—or resulting from the force of education and habit over peculiar constitutions, in which the latter have overpowered the former; but these instances are few and always regarded as something extraordinary. The deep impression they make, whenever they occur, is the strongest proof that they are regarded as exceptions to some general and well-understood law of our nature; just as some of the minor powers of the material world are apparently to gravitation.

I might go farther and assert this to be a phenomenon, not of our nature only, but of all animated existence, throughout its entire range, so far as our knowledge extends. It would, indeed, seem to be essentially connected with the great law of self-preservation which pervades all that feels, from man down to the lowest and most insignificant reptile or insect. In none is it stronger than in man. His social feelings may, indeed, in a state of safety and abundance, combined with high intellectual and moral culture, acquire great expansion and force, but not so great as to overpower this all-pervading and essential law of animated existence.

But that constitution of our nature which makes us feel more intensely what affects us directly than what affects us indirectly through others necessarily leads to conflict between individuals. Each, in consequence, has a greater regard for his own safety or happiness, than for the safety or happiness of others; and, where these come in opposition, is ready to sacrifice the interests of others to his own. And hence the tendency to a universal state of conflict between individual and individual, accompanied by the connected passions of suspicion, jealousy, anger, and revenge—followed by insolence, fraud, and cruelty—and, if not prevented by some controlling power, ending in a state of universal discord and confusion, destructive of the social state and the ends for which it is ordained. This controlling power, wherever vested or by whomsoever exercised, is *Government*.

It follows, then, that man is so constituted that government is necessary to the existence of society, and society to his existence and the perfection of his faculties. It follows, also, that government has its origin in this twofold constitution of his nature; the sympathetic or social feelings constituting the remote, and the individual or direct the proximate, cause.

If man had been differently constituted in either particular—if, instead of being social in his nature, he had been created without sympathy for his kind, and independent of others for his safety and existence; or if, on the other hand, he had been so created as to feel more intensely what affected others than what affected himself (if that were possible), or even had this supposed interest been equal—it is manifest that, in either case, there would have been no necessity for government, and that none would ever have existed. But although society and government are thus intimately connected with and dependent on each other—of the two, society is the greater. It is the first in the order of things, and in the dignity of its object; that of society being primary—to preserve and perfect our race—and that of government secondary and subordinate—to preserve and perfect society. Both are, however, necessary to the existence and well-being of our race, and equally of divine ordination. . . .

[Government and Constitution]

But government, although intended to protect and preserve society, has itself a strong tendency to disorder and abuse of its powers, as all experience and almost every page of history testify. The cause is to be found in the same constitution of our nature which makes government indispensable. The powers which it is necessary for government to possess, in order to repress violence and preserve order, cannot execute themselves. They must be administered by men in whom, like others, the individual are stronger than the social feelings. And hence the powers vested in them to prevent injustice and oppression on the part of others will, if left unguarded, be by them converted into instruments to oppress the rest of the community. That by which this is prevented, by whatever name called, is what is meant by *constitution,* in its most comprehensive sense, when applied to *government.*

Having its origin in the same principle of our nature, *constitution* stands to *government,* as *government* stands to *society;* and, as the end for which society is ordained, would be defeated without government, so that for which government is ordained would, in a great measure, be defeated without constitution. But they differ in this striking particular. There is no difficulty in forming government. It is not even a matter of choice, whether there shall be one or not. Like breathing, it is not permitted to depend on our volition. Necessity will force it on all communities in some one form or another. Very different is the case as to constitution. Instead of a matter of necessity, it is one of the most difficult tasks imposed on man to form a constitution worthy of the name; while, to form a perfect one—one that would completely counteract the tendency of government to oppression and abuse, and hold it strictly to the great ends for which it is ordained—has thus far exceeded human wisdom, and possibly ever will. From this, another striking difference results. Constitution is the contrivance of man, while government is of divine ordination. Man is left to perfect what the wisdom of the Infinite ordained as necessary to preserve the race.

With these remarks I proceed to the consideration of the important and difficult question: How is this tendency of government to be counteracted? Or, to express it more fully, How can those who are invested with the powers of government be prevented from employing them as the means of aggrandizing themselves instead of using them to protect and preserve society? It cannot be done by instituting a higher power to control the government and those who administer it. This would be but to change the seat of authority, and to make this higher power, in reality, the government, with the same tendency, on the part of those who might control its powers, to pervert them into instruments of aggrandizement. Nor can it be done by limiting the powers of government, so as to make it too feeble to be made an instrument of abuse; for, passing by the difficulty of so limiting its powers without creating a power higher than the government itself to enforce the observance of the limitations, it is a sufficient objection that it would, if practicable, defeat the end for which government is ordained, by making it too feeble to protect and preserve society. The powers necessary for this purpose will ever prove sufficient to aggrandize those who control it, at the expense of the rest of the community. . . .

In answering the important question under consideration, it is not necessary to enter into an examination of the various contrivances adopted by these celebrated governments to counteract this tendency to disorder and abuse, nor to undertake to treat of constitution in its most comprehensive sense. What I propose is far more limited: to explain on what principles government must be formed, in order to resist, by its own interior structure—or, to use a single term, *organism*—the tendency to abuse of power. This structure, or organism, is what is meant by constitution, in its strict and more usual sense; and it is this which distinguishes what are called "constitutional" governments from "absolute." It is in this strict and more usual sense that I propose to use the term hereafter.

How government, then, must be constructed, in order to counteract, through its organism, this tendency on the part of those who make and execute the laws to oppress those subject to their operation, is the next question which claims attention.

There is but one way in which this can possibly be done; and that is, by such an organism as will furnish the ruled with the means of resisting successfully this tendency on the part of the rulers to oppression and abuse. Power can only be resisted by power—and tendency by tendency. Those who exercise power and those subject to its exercise—the rulers and the ruled—stand in antagonistic relations to each other. The same constitution of our nature which leads rulers to oppress the ruled—regardless of the object for which government is ordained—will, with equal strength, lead the ruled to resist, when possessed of the means of making peaceable and effective resistance. Such an organism, then, as will furnish the means by which resistance may be systematically and peaceably made on the part of the ruled, to oppression and abuse of power on the part of the rulers, is the first and indispensable step toward *forming* a constitutional government. And as this can only be effected by or through the right of suffrage—the right on the part of the ruled to choose their rulers at proper intervals, and to hold them thereby responsible for their conduct—the responsibility of the rulers to the ruled, through the right of suffrage, is the indispensable and primary principle in the *foundation* of a constitutional government. When this right is properly guarded, and the people sufficiently enlightened to understand their own rights and the interests of the community, and duly to appreciate the motives and conduct of those appointed to make and execute the laws, it is all-sufficient to give to those who elect effective control over those they have elected.

I call the right of suffrage the indispensable and primary principle; for it would be a great and dangerous mistake to suppose, as many do, that it is, of itself, sufficient to form constitutional governments. To this erroneous opinion may be traced one of the causes why so few attempts to form constitutional governments have succeeded, and why, of the few which have, so small a number have had durable existence. It has led, not only to mistakes in the attempts to form such governments, but to their overthrow when they have, by some good fortune, been correctly formed. So far from being, of itself, sufficient—however well guarded it might be, and however enlightened the people—it would, unaided by other provisions, leave the government as absolute as it would be in the hands of irresponsible rulers; and with a tendency, at least as strong, toward oppression and abuse of its powers, as I shall next proceed to explain.

The right of suffrage, of itself, can do no more than give complete control to those who elect, over the conduct of those they have elected. In doing this, it accomplishes all it possibly can accomplish. This is its aim—and when this is attained, its end is fulfilled. It can do no more, however enlightened the people, or however extended or well guarded the right may be. The sum total, then, of its effects, when most successful, is to make those elected the true and faithful representatives of those who elected them—instead of irresponsible rulers, as they would be without it; and thus, by converting it into an agency, and the rulers into agents, to divest government of all claims to sovereignty, and to retain it unimpaired to the community. But it is manifest that the right of suffrage, in making these changes transfers, in reality, the actual control over the government, from those who make and execute the laws, to the body of the community, and thereby places the powers of the government as fully in the mass of the community as they would be if they, in fact, had assembled, made, and executed the laws themselves, without the intervention of representatives or agents. The more perfectly it does this, the more perfectly it accomplishes its ends; but in doing so, it only changes the seat of authority, without counteracting, in the least, the tendency of the government to oppression and abuse of its powers.

If the whole community had the same interests, so that the interests of each and every portion would be so affected by the action of the government that the laws which oppressed or impoverished one portion would necessarily oppress and impoverish all others— or the reverse—then the right of suffrage, of itself, would be all-sufficient to counteract the tendency of the government to oppression and abuse of its powers, and, of course, would form, of itself, a perfect constitutional government. The interest of all being the same, by supposition, as far as the action of the government was concerned, all would have like interests as to what laws should be made, and how they should be executed. All strife and struggle would cease as to who should be elected to make and execute them. The only question would be, who was most fit, who the wisest and most capable of understanding the common interest of the whole. This decided, the election would pass off quietly, and without party discord, as no one portion could advance its own peculiar interest without regard to the rest by electing a favorite candidate.

But such is not the case. On the contrary, nothing is more difficult than to equalize the action of the government, in reference to the various and diversified interests of the community; and nothing more easy than to pervert its powers into instruments to aggrandize and enrich one or more interests by oppressing and impoverishing the others; and this too, under the operation of laws couched in general terms—and which, on their face, appear fair and equal. Nor is this the case in some particular communities only. It is so in all—the small and the great, the poor and the rich—irrespective of pursuits, productions, or degrees of civilization; with, however, this difference, that the more extensive and populous the country, the more diversified the condition and pursuits of its population, and the richer, more luxurious, and dissimilar the people, the more difficult is it to equalize the action of the government, and the more easy for one portion of the community to pervert its powers to oppress and plunder the other.

Such being the case, it necessarily results that the right of suffrage, by placing the control of the government in the community, must, from the same constitution of our nature which makes government necessary to preserve society, lead to conflict among its different interests—each striving to obtain possession of its powers, as the means of protecting itself against the others, or of advancing its respective interests regardless of the interests of others. For this purpose, a struggle will take place between the various interests to obtain a majority in order to control the government. If no one interest be strong enough, of itself, to obtain it, a combination will be formed between those whose interests are most alike—each conceding something to the others until a sufficient number is obtained to make a majority. The process may be slow, and much time may be required before a compact, organized majority can be thus formed, but formed it will be in time, even without preconcert or design, by the sure workings of that principle or constitution of our nature in which government itself originates. When once formed, the community will be divided into two great parties—a major and minor—between which there will be incessant struggles on the one side to retain, and on the other to obtain the majority, and, thereby, the control of the government and the advantages it confers.

So deeply seated, indeed, is this tendency to conflict between the different interests or portions of the community, that it would result from the action of the government itself, even though it were possible to find a community where the people were all of the same pursuits, placed in the same condition of life, and in every respect so situated, as to be without inequality of condition or diversity of interests. The advantages of possessing the control of the powers of the government, and, thereby, of its honors and emoluments, are, of themselves, exclusive of all other considerations, ample to divide even such a community into two great hostile parties.

In order to form a just estimate of the full force of these advantages, without reference to any other consideration, it must be remembered that government—to fulfill the ends for which it is ordained, and more especially that of protection against external dangers—must, in the present condition of the world, be clothed with powers sufficient to call forth the resources of the community, and be prepared, at all times, to command them promptly in every emergency which may possibly arise. For this purpose large establishments are necessary, both civil and military (including naval, where, from situation, that description of force may be required), with all the means necessary for prompt and effective action, such as fortifications, fleets, armories, arsenals, magazines, arms of all descriptions, with well-trained forces, in sufficient numbers to wield them with skill and energy, whenever the occasion requires it. The administration and management of a government with such vast establishments must necessarily require a host of employees, agents, and officers—of whom many must be vested with high and responsible trusts, and occupy exalted stations accompanied with much influence and patronage. To meet the necessary expenses, large sums must be collected and disbursed; and, for this purpose, heavy taxes must be imposed, requiring a multitude of officers for their collection and disbursement. The whole united must necessarily place under the control of government an amount of honors and emoluments sufficient to excite profoundly the ambition of the aspiring and the cupidity of the avaricious, and to lead to the formation of hostile parties, and violent party conflicts and struggles to obtain the control of the government. And what makes this evil remediless through the right of suffrage of itself, however modified or carefully guarded or however enlightened the people, is the fact that, as far as the honors and emoluments of the government and its fiscal action are concerned, it is impossible to equalize it. The reason is obvious. Its honors and emoluments, however great, can fall to the lot of but a few, compared to the entire number of the community and the multitude who will seek to participate in them. . . .

That it [the power of government] *will* be so used, unless prevented, is, from the constitution of man, just as certain as that it *can* be so used; and that, if not prevented, it must give rise to two parties, and to violent conflicts and struggles between them, to obtain the control of the government, is, for the same reason, not less certain.

Nor is it less certain, from the operation of all these causes, that the dominant majority, for the time, would have the same tendency to oppression and abuse of power which, without the right of suffrage, irresponsible rulers would have. No reason, indeed, can be assigned, why the latter would abuse their power, which would not apply, with equal force, to the former. The dominant majority, for the time, would, in reality, through the right of suffrage, be the rulers—the controlling, governing, and irresponsible power; and those who make and execute the laws would, for the time, be, in reality but *their* representatives and agents.

Nor would the fact that the former would constitute a majority of the community, counteract a tendency originating in the constitution of man, and which, as such, cannot depend on the number by whom the powers of the government may be wielded. Be it greater or smaller, a majority or minority, it must equally partake of an attribute inherent in each individual composing it; and, as in each the individual is stronger than the social feelings, the one would have the same tendency as the other to oppression and abuse of power. The reason applies to government in all its forms—whether it be that of the one, the few, or the many. In each there must, of necessity, be a governing and a governed—a ruling and a subject portion. The one implies the other; and in all, the two bear the same relation to each other—and have, on the part of the governing portion, the same tendency to oppression and abuse of power. Where the majority is that portion, it matters not how its powers may be exercised—whether directly by themselves, or indirectly, through representatives or agents. Be it which it may, the minority, for the time, will be as much the governed or subject portion, as are the people in an aristocracy, or the subjects in a monarchy. The only difference in this respect is, that in the government of a majority the minority may become the majority, and the majority the minority, through the right of suffrage, and thereby change their relative positions without the intervention of force and revolution. But the duration, or uncertainty of the tenure, by which power is held, cannot, of itself, counteract the tendency inherent in government to oppression and abuse of power. On the contrary, the very uncertainty of the tenure, combined with the violent party warfare which must ever precede a change of parties under such governments, would rather tend to increase than diminish the tendency to oppression.

[The Concurrent Majority]

As, then, the right of suffrage, without some other provision, cannot counteract this tendency of government, the next question for consideration is, What is that other provision? This demands the most serious consideration; for of all the questions embraced in the science of government, it involves a principle, the most important, and the least understood, and when understood, the most difficult of application in practice. It is, indeed, emphatically, that principle which *makes* the constitution, in its strict and limited sense.

From what has been said, it is manifest, that this provision must be of a character calculated to prevent any one interest, or combination of interests, from using the powers of government to aggrandize itself at the expense of the others. Here lies the evil: and just in proportion as it shall prevent, or fail to prevent it, in the same degree it will effect, or fail to effect, the end intended to be accomplished. There is but one certain mode in which this result can be secured; and that is, by the adoption of some restriction or limitation which shall so effectually prevent any one interest, or combination of interests, from obtaining the exclusive control of the government, as to render hopeless all attempts directed to that end. There is, again, but one mode in which this can be effected; and that is, by taking the sense of each interest or portion of the community, which may be unequally and injuriously affected by the action of the government, separately, through its own majority, or in some other way by which its voice may be fairly expressed, and to require the consent of each interest, either to put or to keep the government in action. This, too, can be accomplished only in one way, and that is, by such an organism of the government—and, if necessary for the purpose, of the community also—as will, by dividing and distributing the powers of government, give to each division or interest, through its appropriate organ, either a concurrent voice in making and executing the laws, or a veto on their execution. It is only by such an organism that the assent of each can be made necessary to put the government in motion, or the power made effectual to arrest its action when put in motion; and it is only by the one or the other that the different interests, orders, classes, or portions into which the community may be divided can be protected, and all conflict and struggle between them prevented—by rendering it impossible to put or to keep it in action, without the concurrent consent of all.

Such an organism as this, combined with the right of suffrage, constitutes, in fact, the elements of constitutional government. The one, by rendering those who make and execute the laws responsible to those on whom they operate, prevents the rulers from oppressing the ruled; and the other, by making it impossible for any one interest or combination of interests, or class, or order, or portion of the community, to obtain exclusive control, prevents any one of them from oppressing the other. It is clear, that oppression and abuse of power must come, if at all, from the one or the other quarter. From no other can they come. It follows, that the two, suffrage and proper organism combined, are sufficient to counteract the tendency of government to oppression and abuse of power, and to restrict it to the fulfillment of the great ends for which it is ordained.

In coming to this conclusion, I have assumed the organism to be perfect, and the different interests, portions, or classes of the community, to be sufficiently enlightened to understand its character and object, and to exercise, with due intelligence, the right of suffrage. To the extent that either may be defective, to the same extent the government would fall short of fulfilling its end. But this does not impeach the truth of the principles on which it rests. In reducing them to proper form, in applying them to practical uses, all elementary principles are liable to difficulties; but they are not, on this account, the less true or valuable. Where the organism is perfect, every interest will be truly and fully represented, and of course the whole community must be so. It may be difficult, or even impossible, to make a perfect organism—but, although this be true, yet even when, instead of the sense of each and of all, it takes that of a few great and prominent interests only, it would still, in a great measure, if not altogether, fulfill the end intended by a constitution. For, in such case, it would require so large a portion of the community, compared with the whole, to concur, or acquiesce in the action of the government, that the number to be plundered would be too few, and the number to be aggrandized too many, to afford adequate motives to oppression and the abuse of its powers. Indeed, however imperfect the organism, it must have more or less effect in diminishing such tendency.

It may be readily inferred, from what has been stated, that the effect of organism is neither to supersede nor diminish the importance of the right of suffrage, but to aid and perfect it. The object of the latter is, to collect the sense of the community. The more fully and perfectly it accomplishes this, the more fully and perfectly it fulfills its end. But the most it can do, of itself, is to collect the sense of the greater number; that is, of the stronger interests or combination of interests, and to assume this to be the sense of the community. It is only when aided by a proper organism that it can collect the sense of the entire community, of each and all its interests: of each, through its appropriate organ, and of the whole, through all of them united. This would truly be the sense of the entire community; for whatever diversity each interest might have within itself —as all would have the same interest in reference to the action of the government—the individuals composing each would be fully and truly represented by its own majority or appropriate organ, regarded in reference to the other interests. In brief, every individual of every interest might trust, with confidence, its majority or appropriate organ, against that of every other interest.

[Numerical and Concurrent Majorities Distinguished]

It results, from what has been said, that there are two different modes in which the sense of the community may be taken: one, simply by the right of suffrage, unaided; the other, by the right through a proper organism. Each collects the sense of the majority. But one regards numbers only, and considers the whole community as a unit, having but one common interest throughout, and collects the sense of the greater number of the whole, as that of the community. The other, on the contrary, regards interests as well as numbers—considering the community as made up of different and conflicting interests, as far as the action of the government is concerned —and takes the sense of each, through its majority or appropriate organ, and the united sense of all, as the sense of the entire community. The former of these I shall call the numerical, or absolute majority; and the latter, the concurrent, or constitutional majority.

I call it the constitutional majority because it is an essential element in every constitutional government, be its form what it may. So great is the difference, politically speaking, between the two majorities, that they cannot be confounded without leading to great and fatal errors; and yet the distinction between them has been so entirely overlooked, that when the term "majority" is used in political discussions, it is applied exclusively to designate the numerical—as if there were no other. Until this distinction is recognized, and better understood, there will continue to be great liability to error in properly constructing constitutional governments, especially of the popular form, and of preserving them when properly constructed. Until then, the latter will have a strong tendency to slide, first, into the government of the numerical majority, and, finally, into absolute government of some other form. To show that such must be the case, and at the same time to mark more strongly the difference between the two, in order to guard against the danger of overlooking it, I propose to consider the subject more at length.

The first and leading error which naturally arises from overlooking the distinction referred to is to confound the numerical majority with the people, and this so completely as to regard them as identical. This is a consequence that necessarily results from considering the numerical as the only majority. All admit that a popular government, or democracy, is the government of the people, for the terms imply this. A perfect government of the kind would be one which would embrace the consent of every citizen or member of the community; but as this is impracticable, in the opinion of those who regard the numerical as the only majority, and who can perceive no other way by which the sense of the people can be taken, they are compelled to adopt this as the only true basis of popular government, in contradistinction to governments of the aristocratical or monarchical form. Being thus constrained, they are, in the next place, forced to regard the numerical majority as, in effect, the entire people; that is, the greater part as the whole, and the government of the greater part as the government of the whole. It is thus the two come to be confounded, and a part made identical with the whole. And it is thus, also, that all the rights, powers, and immunities of the whole people come to be attributed to the numerical majority— and, among others, the supreme, sovereign authority of establishing and abolishing governments at pleasure.

This radical error, the consequence of confounding the two and of regarding the numerical as the only majority, has contributed more than any other cause to prevent the formation of popular constitutional governments, and to destroy them even when they have been formed. It leads to the conclusion that, in their formation and establishment, nothing more is necessary than the right of suffrage, and the allotment to each division of the community a representation in the government in proportion to numbers. If the numerical majority were really the people, and if to take its sense truly were to take the sense of the people truly, a government so constituted would be a true and perfect model of a popular constitutional government; and every departure from it would detract from its excellence. But, as such is not the case, as the numerical majority, instead of being the people, is only a portion of them, such a government, instead of being a true and perfect model of the people's government, that is, a people self-governed, is but the government of a part over a part—the major over the minor portion.

But this misconception of the true elements of constitutional government does not stop here. It leads to others equally false and fatal, in reference to the best means of preserving and perpetuating them, when, from some fortunate combination of circumstances, they are correctly formed. For they who fall into these errors regard the restrictions which organism imposes on the will of the numerical majority as restrictions on the will of the people, and, therefore, as not only useless, but wrongful and mischievous. And hence they endeavor to destroy organism, under the delusive hope of making government more democratic.

Such are some of the consequences of confounding the two, and of regarding the numerical as the only majority. And in this may be found the reason why so few popular governments have been properly constructed, and why, of these few, so small a number have proved durable. Such must continue to be the result, so long as these errors continue to be prevalent. . . .

[The Concurrent Majority and Constitutional Government]

I shall next proceed to explain, more fully, why the concurrent majority is an indispensable element in forming constitutional governments, and why the numerical majority, of itself, must, in all cases, make governments absolute.

The necessary consequence of taking the sense of the community by the concurrent majority is, as has been explained, to give to each interest or portion of the community a negative on the others. It is this mutual negative among its various conflicting interests, which invests each with the power of protecting itself, and places the rights and safety of each where only they can be securely placed, under its own guardianship. Without this there can be no systematic, peaceful, or effective resistance to the natural tendency of each to come into conflict with the others; and without this there can be no constitution. It is this negative power—the power of preventing or arresting the action of the government, be it called by what term it may, veto, interposition, nullification, check, or balance of power—which, in fact, forms the constitution. They are all but different names for the negative power. In all its forms, and under all its names, it results from the concurrent majority. Without this there can be no negative; and without a negative, no constitution. The assertion is true in reference to all constitutional governments, be their forms what they may. It is, indeed, the negative power which makes the constitution, and the positive which makes the government. The one is the power of acting; and the other the power of preventing or arresting action. The two, combined, make constitutional governments.

But as there can be no constitution without the negative power, and no negative power without the concurrent majority, it follows, necessarily, that where the numerical majority has the sole control of the government, there can be no constitution, as constitution implies limitation or restriction—and, of course, is inconsistent with the idea of sole or exclusive power. And hence, the numerical, unmixed with the concurrent, majority necessarily forms, in all cases, absolute government.

It is, indeed, the single or *one power* which excludes the negative, and constitutes absolute government, and not the *number* in whom the power is vested. The numerical majority is as truly a *single power* —and excludes the negative as completely as the absolute government of one, or of the few. The former is as much the absolute government of the democratic, or popular form, as the latter of the monarchical or aristocratical. It has, accordingly, in common with them, the same tendency to oppression and abuse of power.

Constitutional governments, of whatever form, are, indeed, much more similar to each other, in their structure and character, than they are, respectively, to the absolute governments, even of their own class. All constitutional governments, of whatever class they may be, take the sense of the community by its parts—each through its appropriate organ—and regard the sense of all its parts as the sense of the whole. They all rest on the right of suffrage and the responsibility of rulers, directly or indirectly. On the contrary, all absolute governments, of whatever form, concentrate power in one uncontrolled and irresponsible individual or body, whose will is regarded as the sense of the community. And hence the great and broad distinction between governments is not that of the one, the few, or the many, but of the constitutional and the absolute.

From this there results another distinction which, although secondary in its character, very strongly marks the difference between these forms of government. I refer to their respective conservative principle—that is, the principle by which they are upheld and preserved. This principle in constitutional governments is *compromise;* and in absolute governments is *force,* as will be next explained.

It has been already shown, that the same constitution of man which leads those who govern to oppress the governed, if not prevented, will, with equal force and certainty, lead the latter to resist oppression when possessed of the means of doing so peaceably and successfully. But absolute governments, of all forms, exclude all other means of resistance to their authority, than that of force, and, of course, leave no other alternative to the governed but to acquiesce in oppression, however great it may be, or to resort to force to put down the government. But the dread of such a resort must necessarily lead the government to prepare to meet force in order to protect itself, and hence, of necessity, force becomes the conservative principle of all such governments.

On the contrary, the government of the concurrent majority, where the organism is perfect, excludes the possibility of oppression, by giving to each interest, or portion, or order—where there are established classes—the means of protecting itself, by its negative, against all measures calculated to advance the peculiar interests of others at its expense. Its effect, then, is to cause the different interests, portions, or orders, as the case may be, to desist from attempting to adopt any measure calculated to promote the prosperity of one, or more, by sacrificing that of others; and thus to force them to unite in such measures only as would promote the prosperity of all, as the only means to prevent the suspension of the action of the government, and, thereby, to avoid anarchy, the greatest of all evils. It is by means of such authorized and effectual resistance that oppression is prevented, and the necessity of resorting to force superseded, in governments of the concurrent majority; and hence compromise, instead of force, becomes their conservative principle.

It would, perhaps, be more strictly correct to trace the conservative principle of constitutional governments to the necessity which compels the different interests, or portions, or orders to compromise —as the only way to promote their respective prosperity and to avoid anarchy—rather than to the compromise itself. No necessity can be more urgent and imperious, than that of avoiding anarchy. It is the same as that which makes government indispensable to preserve society, and is not less imperative than that which compels obedience to superior force. Traced to this source, the voice of a people— uttered under the necessity of avoiding the greatest of calamities, through the organs of a government so constructed as to suppress the expression of all partial and selfish interests, and to give a full and faithful utterance to the sense of the whole community, in reference to its common welfare—may, without impiety, be called *the voice of God*. To call any other so would be impious. . . .

[Objections and Replies]

Such are the many and striking advantages of the concurrent over the numerical majority. Against the former but two objections can be made. The one is that it is difficult of construction, which has already been sufficiently noticed; and the other that it would be impracticable to obtain the concurrence of conflicting interests, where they were numerous and diversified; or, if not, that the process for this purpose would be too tardy to meet, with sufficient promptness, the many and dangerous emergencies to which all communities are exposed. This objection is plausible, and deserves a fuller notice than it has yet received.

The diversity of opinion is usually so great, on almost all questions of policy, that it is not surprising, on a slight view of the subject, it should be thought impracticable to bring the various conflicting interests of a community to unite on any one line of policy, or that a government founded on such a principle would be too slow in its movements and too weak in its foundation to succeed in practice. But plausible as it may seem at the first glance, a more deliberate view will show that this opinion is erroneous. It is true that, when there is no urgent necessity, it is difficult to bring those who differ to agree on any one line of action. Each will naturally insist on taking the course he may think best, and, from pride of opinion, will be unwilling to yield to others. But the case is different when there is an urgent necessity to unite on some common course of action, as reason and experience both prove. When something *must* be done—and when it can be done only by the united consent of all—the necessity of the case will force to a compromise, be the case of that necessity what it may. On all questions of acting, necessity, where it exists, is the overruling motive; and where, in such cases, compromise among the parties is an indispensable condition to acting, it exerts an overruling influence in predisposing them to acquiesce in some one opinion or course of action. Experience furnishes many examples in confirmation of this important truth. Among these, the trial by jury is the most familiar, and on that account, will be selected for illustration.

In these, twelve individuals, selected without discrimination, must unanimously concur in opinion—under the obligations of an oath to find a true verdict according to law and evidence, and this, too, not unfrequently under such great difficulty and doubt that the ablest and most experienced judges and advocates differ in opinion, after careful examination. And yet, as impracticable as this mode of trial would seem to a superficial observer, it is found, in practice, not only to succeed, but to be the safest, the wisest, and the best that human ingenuity has ever devised. When closely investigated, the cause will be found in the necessity, under which the jury is placed, to agree unanimously in order to find a verdict. This necessity acts as the predisposing cause of concurrence in some common opinion, and with such efficacy, that a jury rarely fails to find a verdict.

Under its potent influence, the jurors take their seats with the disposition to give a fair and impartial hearing to the arguments on both sides—meet together in the jury-room, not as disputants, but calmly to hear the opinions of each other, and to compare and weigh the arguments on which they are founded, and finally to adopt that which, on the whole, is thought to be true. Under the influence of this *disposition to harmonize,* one after another falls into the same opinion until unanimity is obtained. Hence its practicability—and hence also its peculiar excellence. Nothing, indeed, can be more favorable to the success of truth and justice, than this predisposing influence caused by the necessity of being unanimous. It is so much so as to compensate for the defect of legal knowledge and a high degree of intelligence on the part of those who usually compose juries. If the necessity of unanimity were dispensed with, and the finding of a jury made to depend on a bare majority, jury trial, instead of being one of the greatest improvements in the judicial department of government, would be one of the greatest evils that could be inflicted on the community. It would be, in such case, the conduit through which all the factious feelings of the day would enter and contaminate justice at its source.

But the same cause would act with still greater force in predisposing the various interests of the community to agree in a well-organized government, founded on the concurrent majority. The necessity for unanimity, in order to keep the government in motion, would be far more urgent, and would act under circumstances still more favorable to secure it. It would be superfluous, after what has been stated, to add other reasons in order to show that no necessity, physical or moral, can be more imperious than that of government. It is so much so that, to suspend its action altogether, even for an inconsiderable period, would subject the community to convulsions and anarchy. But in governments of the concurrent majority such fatal consequences can only be avoided by the unanimous concurrence or acquiescence of the various portions of the community. Such is the imperious character of the necessity which impels to compromise under governments of this description.

But to have a just conception of the overpowering influence it would exert, the circumstances under which it would act must be taken into consideration. These will be found, on comparison, much more favorable than those under which juries act. In the latter case there is nothing besides the necessity of unanimity in finding a verdict, and the inconvenience to which they might be subjected in the event of division, to induce juries to agree, except the love of truth and justice, which, when not counteracted by some improper motive or bias, more or less influences all, not excepting the most depraved. In the case of governments of the concurrent majority, there is, besides these, the love of country, than which, if not counteracted by the unequal and oppressive action of government, or other causes, few motives exert a greater sway. It comprehends, indeed, within itself, a large portion both of our individual and social feelings; and hence its almost boundless control when left free to act. But the government of the concurrent majority leaves it free, by preventing abuse and oppression, and, with them, the whole train of feelings and passions which lead to discord and conflict between different portions of the community. Impelled by the imperious necessity of preventing the suspension of the action of government, with the fatal consequences to which it would lead, and by the strong additional impulse derived from an ardent love of country, each portion would regard the sacrifice it might have to make by yielding its peculiar interest to secure the common interest and safety of all, including its own, as nothing compared to the evils that would be inflicted on all, including its own, by pertinaciously adhering to a different line of action. So powerful, indeed, would be the motives for concurring, and, under such circumstances, so weak would be those opposed to it, the wonder would be, not that there should, but that there should not be a compromise.

But to form a juster estimate of the full force of this impulse to compromise, there must be added that, in governments of the concurrent majority, each portion, in order to advance its own peculiar interests, would have to conciliate all others by showing a disposition to advance theirs; and, for this purpose, each would select those to represent it whose wisdom, patriotism, and weight of character would command the confidence of the others. Under its influence—and with representatives so well qualified to accomplish the object for which they were selected—the prevailing desire would be to promote the common interests of the whole; and hence the competition would be, not which should yield the least to promote the common good, but which should yield the most. It is thus that concession would cease to be considered a sacrifice—would become a free-will offering on the altar of the country and lose the name of compromise. And herein is to be found the feature which distinguishes governments of the concurrent majority so strikingly from those of the numerical. In the latter, each faction, in the struggle to obtain the control of the government, elevates to power the designing, the artful, and unscrupulous, who in their devotion to party—instead of aiming at the good of the whole—aim exclusively at securing the ascendency of party.

When traced to its source, this difference will be found to originate in the fact that in governments of the concurrent majority individual feelings are, from its organism, necessarily enlisted on the side of the social, and made to unite with them in promoting the interests of the whole, as the best way of promoting the separate interests of each; while, in those of the numerical majority, the social are necessarily enlisted on the side of the individual and made to contribute to the interest of parties, regardless of that of the whole. To effect the former —to enlist the individual on the side of the social feelings to promote the good of the whole—is the greatest possible achievement of the science of government; while to enlist the social on the side of the individual to promote the interest of parties at the expense of the good of the whole is the greatest blunder which ignorance can possibly commit.

To this, also, may be referred the greater solidity of foundation on which governments of the concurrent majority repose. Both, ultimately, rest on necessity; for force, by which those of the numerical majority are upheld, is only acquiesced in from necessity—in a necessity not more imperious, however, than that which compels the different portions, in governments of the concurrent majority, to acquiesce in compromise. There is, however, a great difference in the motive, the feeling, the aim which characterize the act in the two cases. In the one, it is done with that reluctance and hostility ever incident to enforced submission to what is regarded as injustice and oppression, accompanied by the desire and purpose to seize on the first favorable opportunity for resistance; but in the other, willingly and cheerfully, under the impulse of an exalted patriotism, impelling all to acquiesce in whatever the common good requires. . . .

57. ALEXIS DE TOCQUEVILLE

Alexis de Tocqueville (1805-1859) was a French lawyer and states-man who came to the United States in 1831-32 on an official mission and, upon his return, wrote a penetrating analysis of American democracy. Aristocratic in family and temperament, de Tocqueville wrote sharply and at length of the faults of democracy; but as a cool-headed observer, he foresaw the inevitable advance of popular government, and the real advantages that, with an intelligent and vigorous citizenry, democracy could bring.

The Real Advantages of a Democracy*

Before entering upon the present chapter, I must remind the reader of what I have more than once observed in this book. The political Constitution of the United States appears to me to be one of the forms of government that a democracy may adopt; but I do not regard the American Constitution as the best, or as the only one, that a democratic people may establish. In showing the advantages which the Americans derive from the government of democracy, I am therefore very far from affirming, or believing, that similar advantages can be obtained only from the same laws.

1. General Tendency of the Laws

The defects and weaknesses of a democratic government may readily be discovered; they can be proved by obvious facts, whereas their healthy influence becomes evident in ways which are not obvious and are, so to speak, hidden. A glance suffices to detect its faults, but its good qualities can be discerned only by long observation. The laws of the American democracy are frequently defective or incomplete; they sometimes attack vested rights, or sanction others which are dangerous to the community; and even if they were good, their frequency would still be a great evil. How comes it, then, that the American republics prosper and continue?

In the consideration of laws, a distinction must be carefully observed between the end at which they aim, and the means by which they pursue that end; between their absolute and their relative excellence. If it be the intention of the legislator to favor the interests of the minority at the expense of the majority, and if the measures he takes are so combined as to accomplish the object he has in view with the least possible expense of time and exertion, the law may be well drawn up, although its purpose is bad; and the more efficacious it is, the more dangerous it will be.

Democratic laws generally tend to promote the welfare of the greatest possible number; for they emanate from the majority of the

* From A. de Tocqueville, *Democracy in America*, 1835. These passages are reprinted from a translation by Henry Reeve, revised by Francis Bowen, and further corrected and edited by Phillips Bradley, by permission of the publisher, Alfred A. Knopf, Inc., New York, and Vintage Books, Inc. Copyright 1945 by Alfred A. Knopf, Inc.

citizens, who are subject to error, but who cannot have an interest opposed to their own advantage. The laws of an aristocracy tend, on the contrary, to concentrate wealth and power in the hands of the minority; because an aristocracy, by its very nature, constitutes a minority. It may therefore be asserted, as a general proposition, that the purpose of a democracy in its legislation is more useful to humanity than that of an aristocracy. This, however, is the sum total of its advantages.

Aristocracies are infinitely more expert in the science of legislation than democracies ever can be. They are possessed of a self-control that protects them from the errors of temporary excitement; and they form far-reaching designs, which they know how to mature till a favorable opportunity arrives. Aristocratic government proceeds with the dexterity of art; it understands how to make the collective force of all its laws converge at the same time to a given point. Such is not the case with democracies, whose laws are almost always ineffective or inopportune. The means of democracy are therefore more imperfect than those of aristocracy, and the measures that it unwittingly adopts are frequently opposed to its own cause; but the object it has in view is more useful.

Let us now imagine a community so organized by nature or by its constitution that it can support the transitory action of bad laws, and that it can await, without destruction, the general tendency of its legislation: we shall then conceive how a democratic government, notwithstanding its faults, may be best fitted to produce the prosperity of this community. This is precisely what has occurred in the United States; and I repeat what I have before remarked, that the great advantage of the Americans consists in their being able to commit faults which they may afterwards repair.

An analogous observation may be made respecting public officers. It is easy to perceive that American democracy frequently errs in the choice of the individuals to whom it entrusts the power of the administration; but it is more difficult to say why the state prospers under their rule. In the first place, it is to be remarked that if, in a democratic state, the governors have less honesty and less capacity than elsewhere, the governed are more enlightened and more attentive to their interests. As the people in democracies are more constantly vigilant in their affairs and more jealous of their rights, they prevent their representatives from abandoning that general line of conduct which their own interest prescribes. In the second place, it must be remembered that if the democratic magistrate is more apt to misuse his power, he possesses it for a shorter time. But there is yet another reason which is still more general and conclusive. It is no doubt of importance to the welfare of nations that they should be governed by men of talents and virtue; but it is perhaps still more important for them that the interests of those men should not differ from the interests of the community at large; for if such were the case, their virtues might become almost useless and their talents might be turned to a bad account. I have said that it is important that the interests of the persons in authority should not differ from or oppose the interests of the community at large; but I do not insist upon their having the same interests as the *whole* population, because I am not aware that such a state of things ever existed in any country.

No political form has hitherto been discovered that is equally favorable to the prosperity and the development of all the classes into which society is divided. These classes continue to form, as it were, so many distinct communities in the same nation; and experience has shown that it is no less dangerous to place the fate of these classes exclusively in the hands of any one of them than it is to make one people the arbiter of the destiny of another. When the rich alone govern, the interest of the poor is always endangered; and when the poor make the laws, that of the rich incurs very serious risks. The advantage of democracy does not consist, therefore, as has sometimes been asserted, in favoring the prosperity of all, but simply in contributing to the well-being of the greatest number.

The men who are entrusted with the direction of public affairs in the United States are frequently inferior, in both capacity and morality, to those whom an aristocracy would raise to power. But their interest is identified and mingled with that of the majority of their fellow citizens. They may frequently be faithless and frequently mistaken; but they will never systematically adopt a line of conduct hostile to the majority; and they cannot give a dangerous or exclusive tendency to the government.

The maladministration of a democratic magistrate, moreover, is an isolated fact, which has influence only during the short period for which he is elected. Corruption and incapacity do not act as common interests which may connect men permanently with one another. A corrupt or incapable magistrate will not combine his measures with another magistrate simply because the latter is as corrupt and incapable as himself; and these two men will never unite their endeavors to promote the corruption and inaptitude of their remote posterity. The ambition and the maneuvers of the one will serve, on the contrary, to unmask the other. The vices of a magistrate in democratic states are usually wholly personal.

But under aristocratic governments public men are swayed by the interest of their order, which, if it is sometimes confused with the interests of the majority, is very frequently distinct from them. This interest is the common and lasting bond that unites them; it induces them to coalesce and combine their efforts to attain an end which is not always the happiness of the greatest number; and it serves not only to connect the persons in authority with one another, but to unite them with a considerable portion of the community, since a numerous body of citizens belong to the aristocracy without being invested with official functions. The aristocratic magistrate is therefore constantly supported by a portion of the community as well as by the government of which he is a member.

The common purpose which in aristocracies connects the interest of the magistrates with that of a portion of their contemporaries identifies it also with that of future generations; they labor for the future as well as for the present. The aristocratic magistrate is urged at the same time towards the same point by the passions of the community, by his own, and, I may almost add, by those of his posterity. Is it, then, wonderful that he does not resist such repeated impulses? And, indeed, aristocracies are often carried away by their class spirit without being corrupted by it; and they unconsciously fashion society to their own ends and prepare it for their own descendants.

The English aristocracy is perhaps the most liberal that has ever existed, and no body of men has ever, uninterruptedly, furnished so many honorable and enlightened individuals to the government of a country. It cannot escape observation, however, that in the legislation of England the interests of the poor have often been sacrificed to the advantages of the rich, and the rights of the majority to the privileges of a few. The result is that England at the present day combines the extremes of good and evil fortune in the bosom of her society; and the miseries and privations of her poor almost equal her power and renown.

In the United States, where public officers have no class interests to promote, the general and constant influence of the government is beneficial, although the individuals who conduct it are frequently unskillful and sometimes contemptible. There is, indeed, a secret tendency in democratic institutions that makes the exertions of the citizens subservient to the prosperity of the community in spite of their vices and mistakes; while in aristocratic institutions there is a secret bias which, notwithstanding the talents and virtues of those who conduct the government, leads them to contribute to the evils that oppress their fellow creatures. In aristocratic governments public men may frequently do harm without intending it; and in democratic states they bring about good results of which they have never thought.

2. Public Spirit

There is one sort of patriotic attachment which principally arises from that instinctive, disinterested, and undefinable feeling which connects the affections of man with his birthplace. This natural fondness is united with a taste for ancient customs and a reverence for traditions of the past; those who cherish it love their country as they love the mansion of their fathers. They love the tranquillity that it affords them; they cling to the peaceful habits that they have contracted within its bosom; they are attached to the reminiscences that it awakens; and they are even pleased by living there in a state of obedience. This patriotism is sometimes stimulated by religious enthusiasm, and then it is capable of making prodigious efforts. It is in itself a kind of religion: it does not reason, but it acts from the impulse of faith and sentiment. In some nations the monarch is regarded as a personification of the country; and, the fervor of patriotism being converted into the fervor of loyalty, they take a sympathetic pride in his conquests, and glory in his power. There was a time under the ancient monarchy when the French felt a sort of satisfaction in the sense of their dependence upon the arbitrary will of their king; and they were wont to say with pride: "We live under the most powerful king in the world."

But, like all instinctive passions, this kind of patriotism incites great transient exertions, but no continuity of effort. It may save the state in critical circumstances, but often allows it to decline in times of peace. While the manners of a people are simple and its faith unshaken, while society is steadily based upon traditional institutions whose legitimacy has never been contested, this instinctive patriotism is wont to endure.

But there is another species of attachment to country which is more rational than the one I have been describing. It is perhaps less generous and less ardent, but it is more fruitful and more lasting: it springs from knowledge; it is nurtured by the laws; it grows by the exercise of civil rights; and, in the end, it is confounded with the personal interests of the citizen. A man comprehends the influence which the well-being of his country has upon his own; he is aware that the laws permit him to contribute to that prosperity, and he labors to promote it, first because it benefits him, and secondly because it is in part his own work.

But epochs sometimes occur in the life of a nation when the old customs of a people are changed, public morality is destroyed, religious belief shaken, and the spell of tradition broken, while the diffusion of knowledge is yet imperfect and the civil rights of the community are ill secured or confined within narrow limits. The country then assumes a dim and dubious shape in the eyes of the citizens; they no longer behold it in the soil which they inhabit, for that soil is to them an inanimate clod; nor in the usages of their forefathers, which they have learned to regard as a debasing yoke; nor in religion, for of that they doubt; nor in the laws, which do not originate in their own authority; nor in the legislator, whom they fear and despise. The country is lost to their senses; they can discover it neither under its own nor under borrowed features, and they retire into a narrow and unenlightened selfishness. They are emancipated from prejudice without having acknowledged the empire of reason; they have neither the instinctive patriotism of a monarchy nor the reflecting patriotism of a republic; but they have stopped between the two in the midst of confusion and distress.

In this predicament to retreat is impossible, for a people cannot recover the sentiments of their youth any more than a man can return to the innocent tastes of childhood; such things may be regretted, but they cannot be renewed. They must go forward and accelerate the union of private with public interests, since the period of disinterested patriotism is gone by forever.

I am certainly far from affirming that in order to obtain this result the exercise of political rights should be immediately granted to all men. But I maintain that the most powerful and perhaps the only means that we still possess of interesting men in the welfare of their country is to make them partakers in the government. At the present time civic zeal seems to me to be inseparable from the exercise of political rights; and I think that the number of citizens will be found to augment or decrease in Europe in proportion as those rights are extended.

How does it happen that in the United States, where the inhabitants have only recently immigrated to the land which they now occupy, and brought neither customs nor traditions with them there; where they met one another for the first time with no previous acquaintance; where, in short, the instinctive love of country can scarcely exist; how does it happen that everyone takes as zealous an interest in the affairs of his township, his county, and the whole state as if they were his own? It is because everyone, in his sphere, takes an active part in the government of society.

The lower orders in the United States understand the influence exercised by the general prosperity upon their own welfare; simple as this observation is, it is too rarely made by the people. Besides, they are accustomed to regard this prosperity as the fruit of their own exertions. The citizen looks upon the fortune of the public as his own, and he labors for the good of the state, not merely from a sense of pride or duty, but from what I venture to term cupidity.

It is unnecessary to study the institutions and the history of the Americans in order to know the truth of this remark, for their manners render it sufficiently evident. As the American participates in all that is done in his country, he thinks himself obliged to defend whatever may be censured in it; for it is not only his country that is then attacked, it is himself. The consequence is that his national pride resorts to a thousand artifices and descends to all the petty tricks of personal vanity.

Nothing is more embarrassing in the ordinary intercourse of life than this irritable patriotism of the Americans. A stranger may be well inclined to praise many of the institutions of their country, but he begs permission to blame some things in it, a permission that is inexorably refused. America is therefore a free country in which, lest anybody should be hurt by your remarks, you are not allowed to speak freely of private individuals or of the state, of the citizens or of the authorities, of public or of private undertakings, or, in short, of anything at all except, perhaps, the climate and the soil; and even then Americans will be found ready to defend both as if they had co-operated in producing them.

In our times we must choose between the patriotism of all and the government of a few; for the social force and activity which the first confers are irreconcilable with the pledges of tranquillity which are given by the second.

3. Respect for Right

After the general idea of virtue, I know no higher principle than that of right; or rather these two ideas are united in one. The idea of right is simply that of virtue introduced into the political world. It was the idea of right that enabled men to define anarchy and tyranny, and that taught them how to be independent without arrogance and to obey without servility. The man who submits to violence is debased by his compliance; but when he submits to that right of authority which he acknowledges in a fellow creature, he rises in some measure above the person who gives the command. There are no great men without virtue; and there are no great nations—it may almost be added, there would be no society—without respect for right; for what is a union of rational and intelligent beings who are held together only by the bond of force?

I am persuaded that the only means which we possess, at the present time of inculcating the idea of right and of rendering it, as it were, palpable to the senses is to endow all with the peaceful exercise of certain rights: this is very clearly seen in children, who are men without the strength and the experience of manhood. When a child begins to move in the midst of the objects that surround him, he is instinctively led to appropriate to himself everything that he can lay his hands upon; he has no notion of the property of others; but as he gradually learns the value of things, and begins to perceive that he may in his turn be despoiled, he becomes more circumspect, and he ends by respecting those rights in others which he wishes to have respected in himself. The principle which the child derives from the possession of his toys is taught to the man by the objects which he may call his own. In America, the most democratic of nations, those complaints against property in general, which are so frequent in Europe, are never heard, because in America there are no paupers. As everyone has property of his own to defend, everyone recognizes the principle upon which he holds it.

The same thing occurs in the political world. In America, the lowest classes have conceived a very high notion of political rights, because they exercise those rights; and they refrain from attacking the rights of others in order that their own may not be violated. While in Europe the same classes sometimes resist even the supreme power, the American submits without a murmur to the authority of the pettiest magistrate.

This truth appears even in the trivial details of national life. In France few pleasures are exclusively reserved for the higher classes; the poor are generally admitted wherever the rich are received; and they consequently behave with propriety, and respect whatever promotes the enjoyments that they themselves share. In England, where wealth has a monopoly of amusement as well as of power, complaints are made that whenever the poor happen to enter the places reserved for the pleasures of the rich, they do wanton mischief: can this be wondered at, since care has been taken that they should have nothing to lose?

The government of a democracy brings the notion of political rights to the level of the humblest citizens, just as the dissemination of wealth brings the notion of property within the reach of all men; to my mind, this is one of its greatest advantages. I do not say it is easy to teach men how to exercise political rights, but I maintain that, when it is possible, the effects which result from it are highly important; and I add that, if there ever was a time at which such an attempt ought to be made, that time is now. Do you not see that religious belief is shaken and the divine notion of right is declining, that morality is debased and the notion of moral right is therefore fading away? Argument is substituted for faith, and calculation for the impulses of sentiment. If, in the midst of this general disruption, you do not succeed in connecting the notion of right with that of private interest, which is the only immutable point in the human heart, what means will you have of governing the world except by fear? When I am told that the laws are weak and the people are turbulent, that passions are excited and the authority of virtue is paralyzed, and therefore no measures must be taken to increase the rights of the democracy, I reply that for these very reasons some measures of the kind ought to be taken; and I believe that governments are still more interested in taking them than society at large, for governments may perish, but society cannot die.

But I do not wish to exaggerate the example that America furnishes. There the people were invested with political rights at a time when they could not be abused, for the inhabitants were few in number and simple in their manners. As they have increased, the Americans have not augmented the power of the democracy; they have rather extended its domain.

It cannot be doubted that the moment at which political rights are granted to a people that had before been without them is a very critical one, that the measure, though often necessary, is always dangerous. A child may kill before he is aware of the value of life; and he may deprive another person of his property before he is aware that his own may be taken from him. The lower orders, when they are first invested with political rights, stand in relation to those rights in the same position as the child does to the whole of nature; and the celebrated adage may then be aplied to them: *Homo puer robustus.* This truth may be perceived even in America. The states in which the citizens have enjoyed their rights longest are those in which they make the best use of them.

It cannot be repeated too often that nothing is more fertile in prodigies than the art of being free; but there is nothing more arduous than the apprenticeship of liberty. It is not so with despotism: despotism often promises to make amends for a thousand previous ills; it supports the right, it protects the oppressed, and it maintains public order. The nation is lulled by the temporary prosperity that it produces, until it is roused to a sense of its misery. Liberty, on the contrary, is generally established with difficulty in the midst of storms; it is perfected by civil discord; and its benefits cannot be appreciated until it is already old.

4. Respect for Law

It is not always feasible to consult the whole people, either directly or indirectly, in the formation of law; but it cannot be denied that, when this is possible, the authority of law is much augmented. This popular origin, which impairs the excellence and the wisdom of legislation, contributes much to increase its power. There is an amazing strength in the expression of the will of a whole people; and when it declares itself, even the imagination of those who would wish to contest it is overawed. The truth of this fact is well known by parties, and they consequently strive to make out a majority whenever they can. If they have not the greater number of voters on their side, they assert that the true majority abstained from voting; and if they are foiled even there, they have recourse to those persons who had no right to vote.

In the United States, except slaves, servants, and paupers supported by the townships, there is no class of persons who do not exercise the elective franchise and who do not indirectly contribute to make the laws. Those who wish to attack the laws must consequently either change the opinion of the nation or trample upon its decision.

A second reason, which is still more direct and weighty, may be adduced: in the United States everyone is personally interested in enforcing the obedience of the whole community to the law; for as the minority may shortly rally the majority to its principles, it is interested in professing that respect for the decrees of the legislator which it may soon have occasion to claim for its own. However irksome an enactment may be, the citizen of the United States complies with it, not only because it is the work of the majority, but because it is his own, and he regards it as a contract to which he is himself a party.

In the United States, then, that numerous and turbulent multitude does not exist who, regarding the law as their natural enemy, look upon it with fear and distrust. It is impossible, on the contrary, not to perceive that all classes display the utmost reliance upon the legislation of their country and are attached to it by a kind of parental affection.

I am wrong, however, in saying all classes; for as in America the European scale of authority is inverted, there the wealthy are placed in a position analogous to that of the poor in the Old World, and it is the opulent classes who frequently look upon law with suspicion. I have already observed that the advantage of democracy is not, as has been sometimes asserted, that it protects the interests of all, but simply that it protects those of the majority. In the United States, where the poor rule, the rich have always something to fear from the abuse of their power. This natural anxiety of the rich may produce a secret dissatisfaction; but society is not disturbed by it, for the same reason that withholds the confidence of the rich from the legislative authority makes them obey its mandates: their wealth, which prevents them from making the law, prevents them from withstanding it. Among civilized nations, only those who have nothing to lose ever revolt; and if the laws of a democracy are not always worthy of respect, they are always respected; for those who usually infringe the laws cannot fail to obey those which they have themselves made and by which they are benefited; while the citizens who might be interested in their infraction are induced, by their character and station, to submit to the decisions of the legislature, whatever they may be. Besides, the people in America obey the law, not only because it is their own work, but because it may be changed if it is harmful; a law is observed because, first, it is a self-imposed evil, and, secondly, it is an evil of transient duration.

5. All-Pervading Political Activity

On passing from a free country into one which is not free the traveler is struck by the change; in the former all is bustle and activity; in the latter everything seems calm and motionless. In the one, amelioration and progress are the topics of inquiry; in the other, it seems as if the community wished only to repose in the enjoyment of advantages already acquired. Nevertheless, the country which exerts itself so strenuously to become happy is generally more wealthy and prosperous than that which appears so contented with its lot; and when we compare them, we can scarcely conceive how so many new wants are daily felt in the former, while so few seem to exist in the latter.

If this remark is applicable to those free countries which have preserved monarchical forms and aristocratic institutions, it is still more so to democratic republics. In these states it is not a portion only of the people who endeavor to improve the state of society, but the whole community is engaged in the task; and it is not the exigencies and convenience of a single class for which provision is to be made, but the exigencies and convenience of all classes at once.

It is not impossible to conceive the surprising liberty that the Americans enjoy; some idea may likewise be formed of their extreme equality; but the political activity that pervades the United States must be seen in order to be understood. No sooner do you set foot upon American ground than you are stunned by a kind of tumult; a confused clamor is heard on every side, and a thousand simultaneous voices demand the satisfaction of their social wants. Everything is in motion around you; here the people of one quarter of a town are met to decide upon the building of a church; there the election of a representative is going on; a little farther, the delegates of a district are hastening to the town in order to consult upon some local improvements; in another place, the laborers of a village quit their plows to deliberate upon the project of a road or a public school. Meetings are called for the sole purpose of declaring their disapprobation of the conduct of the government; while in other assemblies citizens salute the authorities of the day as the fathers of their country. Societies are formed which regard drunkenness as the principal cause of the evils of the state, and solemnly bind themselves to give an example of temperance.

The great political agitation of American legislative bodies, which is the only one that attracts the attention of foreigners, is a mere episode, or a sort of continuation, of that universal movement which originates in the lowest classes of the people and extends successively to all the ranks of society. It is impossible to spend more effort in the pursuit of happiness.

It is difficult to say what place is taken up in the life of an inhabitant of the United States by his concern for politics. To take a hand in the regulation of society and to discuss it is his biggest concern and, so to speak, the only pleasure an American knows. This feeling pervades the most trifling habits of life; even the women frequently attend public meetings and listen to political harangues as a recreation from their household labors. Debating clubs are, to a certain extent, a substitute for theatrical entertainments: an American cannot converse, but he can discuss, and his talk falls into a dissertation. He speaks to you as if he was addressing a meeting; and if he should chance to become warm in the discussion, he will say "Gentlemen" to the person with whom he is conversing.

In some countries the inhabitants seem unwilling to avail themselves of the political privileges which the law gives them; it would seem that they set too high a value upon their time to spend it on the interests of the community; and they shut themselves up in a narrow selfishness, marked out by four sunk fences and a quickset hedge. But if an American were condemned to confine his activity to his own affairs, he would be robbed of one half of his existence; he would feel an immense void in the life which he is accustomed to lead, and his wretchedness would be unbearable. I am persuaded that if ever a despotism should be established in America, it will be more difficult to overcome the habits that freedom has formed than to conquer the love of freedom itself.

This ceaseless agitation which democratic government has introduced into the political world influences all social intercourse. I am not sure that, on the whole, this is not the greatest advantage of democracy; and I am less inclined to applaud it for what it does than for what it causes to be done.

It is incontestable that the people frequently conduct public business very badly; but it is impossible that the lower orders should take a part in public business without extending the circle of their ideas and quitting the ordinary routine of their thoughts. The humblest individual who cooperates in the government of society acquires a certain degree of self-respect; and as he possesses authority, he can command the services of minds more enlightened than his own. He is canvassed by a multitude of applicants, and in seeking to deceive him in a thousand ways, they really enlighten him. He takes a part in political undertakings which he did not originate, but which give him a taste for undertakings of the kind. New improvements are daily pointed out to him in the common property, and this gives him the desire of improving that property which is his own. He is perhaps neither happier nor better than those who came before him, but he is better informed and more active. I have no doubt that the democratic institutions of the United States, joined to the physical constitution of the country, are the cause (not the direct, as is so often asserted, but the indirect cause) of the prodigious commercial activity of the inhabitants. It is not created by the laws, but the people learn how to promote it by the experience derived from legislation.

When the opponents of democracy assert that a single man performs what he undertakes better than the government of all, it appears to me that they are right. The government of an individual, supposing an equality of knowledge on either side, is more consistent, more persevering, more uniform, and more accurate in details than that of a multitude, and it selects with more discrimination the men whom it employs. If any deny this, they have never seen a democratic government, or have judged upon partial evidence. It is true that, even when local circumstances and the dispositions of the people allow democratic institutions to exist, they do not display a regular and methodical system of government. Democratic liberty is far from accomplishing all its projects with the skill of an adroit despotism. It frequently abandons them before they have borne their fruits, or risks them when the consequences may be dangerous; but in the end it produces more than any absolute government; if it does fewer things well, it does a greater number of things. Under its sway the grandeur is not in what the public administration does, but in what is done without it or outside of it. Democracy does not give the people sight of the Creator and Preserver of men. What appears to me to be man's decline is, to His eye, advancement; what afflicts me is acceptable to Him. A state of equality is perhaps less elevated, but it is more just: and its justice constitutes its greatness and its beauty. I would strive, then, to raise myself to this point of the divine contemplation and thence to view and to judge the concerns of men.

No man on the earth can as yet affirm, absolutely and generally, that the new state of the world is better than its former one; but it is already easy to perceive that this state is different. Some vices and some virtues were so inherent in the constitution of an aristocratic nation and are so opposite to the character of a modern people that they can never be infused into it; some good tendencies and some bad propensities which were unknown to the former are natural to the latter; some ideas suggest themselves spontaneously to the imagination of the one which are utterly repugnant to the mind of the other. They are like two distinct orders of human beings, each of which has its own merits and defects, its own advantages and its own evils. Care must therefore be taken not to judge the state of society that is now coming into existence by notions derived from a state of society that no longer exists; for as these states of society are exceedingly different in their structure, they cannot be submitted to a just or fair comparison. It would be scarcely more reasonable to require of our contemporaries the peculiar virtues which originated in the social conditions of their forefathers, since that social condition is itself fallen and has drawn into one promiscuous ruin the good and evil that belonged to it.

But as yet these things are imperfectly understood. I find that a great number of my contemporaries undertake to make a selection from among the institutions, the opinions, and the ideas that originated in the aristocratic constitution of society as it was; a portion of these elements they would willingly relinquish, but they would keep the remainder and transplant them into their new world. I fear that such men are wasting their time and their strength in virtuous but unprofitable efforts. The object is, not to retain the peculiar advantages which the inequality of conditions bestows upon mankind, but to secure the new benefits which equality may supply. We have not to seek to make ourselves like our progenitors but to strive to work out that species of greatness and happiness which is our own.

For myself, who now look back from this extreme limit of my task and discover from afar, but at once, the various objects which

the most skillful government, but it produces what the ablest governments are frequently unable to create: namely, an all-pervading and restless activity, a superabundant force, and an energy which is inseparable from it and which may, however unfavorable circumstances may be, produce wonders. These are the true advantages of democracy.

In the present age, when the destinies of Christendom seem to be in suspense, some hasten to assail democracy as a hostile power while it is yet growing; and others already adore this new deity which is springing forth from chaos. But both parties are imperfectly acquainted with the object of their hatred or their worship; they strike in the dark and distribute their blows at random.

We must first understand what is wanted of society and its government. Do you wish to give a certain elevation to the human mind and teach it to regard the things of this world with generous feelings, to inspire men with a scorn of mere temporal advantages, to form and nourish strong convictions and keep alive the spirit of honorable devotedness? Is it your object to refine the habits, embellish the manners, and cultivate the arts, to promote the love of poetry, beauty, and glory? Would you constitute a people fitted to act powerfully upon all other nations, and prepared for those high enterprises which, whatever be their results, will leave a name forever famous in history? If you believe such to be the principal object of society, avoid the government of the democracy, for it would not lead you with certainty to the goal.

But if you hold it expedient to divert the moral and intellectual activity of man to the production of comfort and the promotion of general well-being; if a clear understanding be more profitable to man than genius; if your object is not to stimulate the virtues of heroism, but the habits of peace; if you had rather witness vices than crimes, and are content to meet with fewer noble deeds, provided offenses be diminished in the same proportion; if, instead of living in the midst of a brilliant society, you are contented to have prosperity around you; if, in short, you are of the opinion that the principal object of a government is not to confer the greatest possible power and glory upon the body of the nation, but to ensure the greatest enjoyment and to avoid the most misery to each of the individuals who compose it—if such be your desire, then equalize the conditions of men and establish democratic institutions.

But if the time is past at which such a choice was possible, and if some power superior to that of man already hurries us, without consulting our wishes, towards one or the other of these two governments, let us endeavor to make the best of that which is allotted to us and, by finding out both its good and its evil tendencies, be able to foster the former and repress the latter to the utmost.

General Survey of the Subject

Before finally closing the subject that I have now discussed, I should like to take a parting survey of all the different characteristics of modern society and appreciate at last the general influence to be exercised by the principle of equality upon the fate of mankind; but I am stopped by the difficulty of the task, and, in presence of so great a theme, my sight is troubled and my reason fails.

The society of the modern world, which I have sought to delineate and which I seek to judge, has but just come into existence. Time has not yet shaped it into perfect form; the great revolution by which it has been created is not yet over; and amid the occurrences of our time it is almost impossible to discern what will pass away with the revolution itself and what will survive its close. The world that is rising into existence is still half encumbered by the remains of the world that is waning into decay; and amid the vast perplexity of human affairs none can say how much of ancient institutions and former customs will remain or how much will completely disappear.

Although the revolution that is taking place in the social condition, the laws, the opinions, and the feelings of men is still very far from being terminated, yet its results already admit of no comparison with anything that the world has ever before witnessed. I go back from age to age up to the remotest antiquity, but I find no parallel to what is occurring before my eyes; as the past has ceased to throw its light upon the future, the mind of man wanders in obscurity.

Nevertheless, in the midst of a prospect so wide, so novel, and so confused, some of the more prominent characteristics may already be discerned and pointed out. The good things and the evils of life are more equally distributed in the world: great wealth tends to disappear, the number of small fortunes to increase; desires and gratifications are multiplied, but extraordinary prosperity and irremediable penury are alike unknown. The sentiment of ambition is universal, but the scope of ambition is seldom vast. Each individual stands apart in

solitary weakness, but society at large is active, provident, and powerful; the performances of private persons are insignificant, those of the state immense.

There is little energy of character, but customs are mild and laws humane. If there are few instances of exalted heroism or of virtues of the highest, brightest, and purest temper, men's habits are regular, violence is rare, and cruelty almost unknown. Human existence becomes longer and property more secure; life is not adorned with brilliant trophies, but it is extremely easy and tranquil. Few pleasures are either very refined or very coarse, and highly polished manners are as uncommon as great brutality of tastes. Neither men of great learning nor extremely ignorant communities are to be met with; genius becomes more rare, information more diffused. The human mind is impelled by the small effort of all mankind combined together, not by the strenuous activity of a few men. There is less perfection, but more abundance, in all the productions of the arts. The ties of race, of rank, and of country are relaxed; the great bond of humanity is strengthened.

If I endeavor to find out the most general and most prominent of all these different characteristics, I perceive that what is taking place in men's fortunes manifests itself under a thousand other forms. Almost all extremes are softened or blunted: all that was most prominent is superseded by some middle term, at once less lofty and less low, less brilliant and less obscure, than what before existed in the world.

When I survey this countless multitude of beings, shaped in each other's likeness, amid whom nothing rises and nothing falls, the sight of such universal uniformity saddens and chills me and I am tempted to regret that state of society which has ceased to be. When the world was full of men of great importance and extreme insignificance, of great wealth and extreme poverty, of great learning and extreme ignorance, I turned aside from the latter to fix my observation on the former alone, who gratified my sympathies. But I admit that this gratification arose from my own weakness; it is because I am unable to see at once all that is around me that I am allowed thus to select and separate the objects of my predilection from among so many others. Such is not the case with that Almighty and Eternal Being whose gaze necessarily includes the whole of created things and who surveys distinctly, though all at once, mankind and man.

We may naturally believe that it is not the singular prosperity of the few, but the greater well-being of all that is most pleasing in

have attracted my more attentive investigation upon my way, I am full of apprehensions and of hopes. I perceive mighty dangers which it is possible to ward off, mighty evils which may be avoided or alleviated; and I cling with a firmer hold to the belief that for democratic nations to be virtuous and prosperous, they require but to will it.

I am aware that many of my contemporaries maintain that nations are never their own masters here below, and that they necessarily obey some insurmountable and unintelligent power, arising from anterior events, from their race, or from the soil and climate of their country. Such principles are false and cowardly; such principles can never produce aught but feeble men and pusillanimous nations. Providence has not created mankind entirely independent or entirely free. It is true that around every man a fatal circle is traced beyond which he cannot pass; but within the wide verge of that circle he is powerful and free; as it is with man, so with communities. The nations of our time cannot prevent the conditions of men from becoming equal, but it depends upon themselves whether the principle of equality is to lead them to servitude or freedom, to knowledge or barbarism, to prosperity or wretchedness.

58. JOHN STUART MILL

On Liberty is probably the most stirring and most powerfully presented defense of individual freedom in the English language. Although the arguments were presented over one hundred years ago, they are applicable still to contemporary democratic society. This essay is one of the outstanding classics of democratic philosophy.

Introductory*

The subject of this Essay is not the so-called Liberty of the Will, so unfortunately opposed to the misnamed doctrine of Philosophical

* From J. S. Mill, *On Liberty*, 1859. These passages are reprinted from an edition published by Ticknor and Fields, Boston, 1863.

Necessity; but Civil, or Social Liberty: the nature and limits of the power which can be legitimately exercised by society over the individual. A question seldom stated, and hardly ever discussed, in general terms, but which profoundly influences the practical controversies of the age by its latent presence, and is likely soon to make itself recognized as the vital question of the future. It is so far from being new, that, in a certain sense, it has divided mankind, almost from the remotest ages; but in the stage of progress into which the more civilized portions of the species have now entered, it presents itself under new conditions, and requires a different and more fundamental treatment.

The struggle between Liberty and Authority is the most conspicuous feature in the portions of history with which we are earliest familiar, particularly in that of Greece, Rome, and England. But in old times this contest was between subjects, or some classes of subjects, and the Government. By liberty, was meant protection against the tyranny of the political rulers. The rulers were conceived (except in some of the popular governments of Greece) as in a necessarily antagonistic position to the people whom they ruled. They consisted of a governing One, or a governing tribe or caste, who derived their authority from inheritance or conquest, who, at all events, did not hold it at the pleasure of the governed, and whose supremacy men did not venture, perhaps did not desire, to contest, whatever precautions might be taken against its oppressive exercise. Their power was regarded as necessary, but also as highly dangerous; as a weapon which they would attempt to use against their subjects, no less than against external enemies. To prevent the weaker members of the community from being preyed upon by innumerable vultures, it was needful that there should be an animal of prey stronger than the rest, commissioned to keep them down. But as the king of the vultures would be no less bent upon preying on the flock than any of the minor harpies, it was indispensable to be in a perpetual attitude of defense against his beak and claws. The aim, therefore, of patriots was to set limits to the power which the ruler should be suffered to exercise over the community; and this limitation was what they meant by liberty. . . .

A time, however, came, in the progress of human affairs, when men ceased to think it a necessity of nature that their governors should be an independent power, opposed in interest to themselves. It appeared to them much better that the various magistrates of the State should be their tenants or delegates, revocable at their pleasure.

In that way alone, it seemed, could they have complete security that the powers of government would never be abused to their disadvantage. By degrees this new demand for elective and temporary rulers became the prominent object of the exertions of the popular party, wherever any such party existed; and superseded, to a considerable extent, the previous efforts to limit the power of rulers. As the struggle proceeded for making the ruling powers emanate from the periodical choice of the ruled, some persons began to think that too much importance had been attached to the limitation of the power itself. *That* (it might seem) was a resource against rulers whose interests were habitually opposed to those of the people. What was now wanted was, that the rulers should be identified with the people; that their interest and will should be the interest and will of the nation. The nation did not need to be protected against its own will. There was no fear of its tyrannizing over itself. Let the rulers be effectually responsible to it, promptly removable by it, and it could afford to trust them with power of which it could itself dictate the use to be made. Their power was but the nation's own power, concentrated, and in a form convenient for exercise. . . .

[The Tyranny of the Majority]

But, in political and philosophical theories, as well as in persons, success discloses faults and infirmities which failure might have concealed from observation. The notion, that the people have no need to limit their power over themselves, might seem axiomatic, when popular government was a thing only dreamed about, or read of as having existed at some distant period of the past. . . .

In time, however, a democratic republic came to occupy a large portion of the earth's surface, and made itself felt as one of the most powerful members of the community of nations; and elective and responsible government became subject to the observations and criticisms which wait upon a great existing fact. It was now perceived that such phrases as "self-government," and "the power of the people over themselves," do not express the true state of the case. The "people" who exercise the power are not always the same people with those over whom it is exercised; and the "self-government" spoken of is not the government of each by himself, but of each by all the rest. The will of the people, moreover, practically means the will of the most numerous or the most active *part* of the people; the majority, or those who succeed in making themselves accepted as the majority; the people, consequently, *may* desire to oppress a part of their number; and precautions are as much needed against this as against any other abuse of power. The limitation, therefore, of the power of government over individuals loses none of its importance when the holders of power are regularly accountable to the community, that is, to the strongest party therein. This view of things, recommending itself equally to the intelligence of thinkers and to the inclination of those important classes in European society to whose real or supposed interests democracy is adverse, has had no difficulty in establishing itself; and in political speculations "the tyranny of the majority" is now generally included among the evils against which society requires to be on its guard.

Like other tyrannies, the tyranny of the majority was at first, and is still vulgarly, held in dread, chiefly as operating through the acts of the public authorities. But reflecting persons perceived that when society is itself the tyrant—society collectively, over the separate individuals who compose it—its means of tyrannizing are not restricted to the acts which it may do by the hands of its political functionaries. Society can and does execute its own mandates: and if it issues wrong mandates instead of right, or any mandates at all in things with which it ought not to meddle, it practices a social tyranny more formidable than many kinds of political oppression, since, though not usually upheld by such extreme penalties, it leaves fewer means of escape, penetrating much more deeply into the details of life, and enslaving the soul itself. Protection, therefore, against the tyranny of the magistrate is not enough: there needs protection also against the tyranny of the prevailing opinion and feeling; against the tendency of society to impose, by other means than civil penalties, its own ideas and practices as rules of conduct on those who dissent from them; to fetter the development, and, if possible, prevent the formation, of any individuality not in harmony with its ways, and compel all characters to fashion themselves upon the model of its own. There is a limit to the legitimate interference of collective opinion with individual independence: and to find that limit, and maintain it against encroachment, is as indispensable to a good condition of human affairs, as protection against political despotism. . . .

[The Domain of Human Liberty]

The object of this Essay is to assert one very simple principle, as entitled to govern absolutely the dealings of society with the individual in the way of compulsion and control, whether the means used be physical force in the form of legal penalties, or the moral coercion of public opinion. That principle is, that the sole end for which mankind are warranted, individually or collectively, in interfering with the liberty of action of any of their number, is self-protection. That the only purpose for which power can be rightfully exercised over any member of a civilized community, against his will, is to prevent harm to others. His own good, either physical or moral, is not a sufficient warrant. He cannot rightfully be compelled to do or forbear because it will be better for him to do so, because it will make him happier, because, in the opinions of others, to do so would be wise, or even right. These are good reasons for remonstrating with him, or reasoning with him, or persuading him, or entreating him, but not for compelling him, or visiting him with any evil in case he do otherwise. To justify that, the conduct from which it is desired to deter him, must be calculated to produce evil to someone else. The only part of the conduct of anyone, for which he is amenable to society, is that which concerns others. In the part which merely concerns himself, his independence is, of right, absolute. Over himself, over his own body and mind, the individual is sovereign. . . .

It is proper to state that I forgo any advantage which could be derived to my argument from the idea of abstract right, as a thing independent of utility. I regard utility as the ultimate appeal on all ethical questions; but it must be utility in the largest sense, grounded on the permanent interests of man as a progressive being. Those interests, I contend, authorize the subjection of individual spontaneity to external control, only in respect to those actions of each, which concern the interest of other people. . . .

But there is a sphere of action in which society, as distinguished from the individual, has, if any, only an indirect interest; comprehending all that portion of a person's life and conduct which affects only himself, or if it also affects others, only with their free, voluntary, and undeceived consent and participation. When I say only himself, I mean directly, and in the first instance: for whatever affects himself, may affect others through himself; and the objection which may be grounded on this contingency will receive consideration in the sequel. This, then, is the appropriate region of human liberty. It comprises, first, the inward domain of consciousness; demanding liberty of conscience, in the most comprehensive sense; liberty of thought and feeling; absolute freedom of opinion and sentiment on all subjects, practical or speculative, scientific, moral, or theological. The liberty of expressing and publishing opinions may seem to fall under a different principle, since it belongs to that part of the conduct of an individual which concerns other people; but, being almost of as much importance as the liberty of thought itself, and resting in great part on the same reasons, is practically inseparable from it. Secondly, the principle requires liberty of tastes and pursuits; of framing the plan of our life to suit our own character; of doing as we like, subject to such consequences as may follow: without impediment from our fellow creatures, so long as what we do does not harm them, even though they should think our conduct foolish, perverse, or wrong. Thirdly, from this liberty of each individual, follows the liberty, within the same limits, of combination among individuals; freedom to unite, for any purpose not involving harm to others: the persons combining being supposed to be of full age, and not forced or deceived.

No society in which these liberties are not, on the whole, respected, is free, whatever may be its form of government; and none is completely free in which they do not exist absolute and unqualified. The only freedom which deserves the name, is that of pursuing our own good in our own way, so long as we do not attempt to deprive others of theirs, or impede their efforts to obtain it. Each is the proper guardian of his own health, whether bodily, or mental and spiritual. Mankind are greater gainers by suffering each other to live as seems good to themselves, than by compelling each to live as seems good to the rest. . . .

Apart from the peculiar tenets of individual thinkers, there is also in the world at large an increasing inclination to stretch unduly the powers of society over the individual, both by the force of opinion and even by that of legislation: and as the tendency of all the changes taking place in the world is to strengthen society, and diminish the power of the individual, this encroachment is not one of the evils which tend spontaneously to disappear, but, on the contrary, to grow more and more formidable. The disposition of mankind, whether as rulers or as fellow citizens, to impose their own opinions and inclinations as a rule of conduct on others, is so energetically supported by some of the best and by some of the worst feelings incident to human nature, that it is hardly ever kept under restraint by anything but want of power; and as the power is not declining, but growing, unless a strong barrier of moral conviction can be raised against the mischief, we must expect, in the present circumstances of the world, to see it increase.

It will be convenient for the argument, if, instead of at once entering upon the general thesis, we confine ourselves in the first instance to a single branch of it, on which the principle here stated is, if not fully, yet to a certain point, recognized by the current opinions. This one branch is the Liberty of Thought: from which it is impossible to separate the cognate liberty of speaking and of writing. Although these liberties, to some considerable amount, form part of the political morality of all countries which profess religious toleration and free institutions, the grounds, both philosophical and practical, on which they rest, are perhaps not so familiar to the general mind, nor so thoroughly appreciated by many even of the leaders of opinion, as might have been expected. Those grounds, when rightly understood, are of much wider application than to only one division of the subject, and a thorough consideration of this part of the question will be found the best introduction to the remainder. . . .

Of the Liberty of Thought and Discussion

The time, it is to be hoped, is gone by, when any defense would be necessary of the "liberty of the press" as one of the securities against corrupt or tyrannical government. No argument, we may suppose, can now be needed, against permitting a legislature or an executive, not identified in interest with the people, to prescribe opinions to them, and determine what doctrines or what arguments they shall be allowed to hear. This aspect of the question, besides, has been so often and so triumphantly enforced by preceding writers, that it needs not be specially insisted on in this place. . . . Let us suppose, therefore, that the government is entirely at one with the people, and never thinks of exerting any power of coercion unless in agreement with what it conceives to be their voice. But I deny the right of the people to exercise such coercion, either by themselves or by their government. The power itself is illegitimate. The best government has no more title to it than the worst. It is as noxious, or more noxious, when exerted in accordance with public opinion, than when in opposition to it. If all mankind minus one, were of one opinion, and only one person were of the contrary opinion, mankind would be no more justified in silencing that one person, than he, if he had the power, would be justified in silencing mankind. Were an opinion a personal possession of no value except to the owner; if to be obstructed in the enjoyment of it were simply a private injury, it would make some difference whether the injury was inflicted only on a few persons or on many. But the peculiar evil of silencing the expression of an opinion is, that it is robbing the human race; posterity as well as the existing generation; those who dissent from the opinion, still more than those who hold it. If the opinion is right, they are deprived of the opportunity of exchanging error for truth: if wrong, they lose, what is almost as great a benefit, the clearer perception and livelier impression of truth, produced by its collision with error.

It is necessary to consider separately these two hypotheses, each of which has a distinct branch of the argument corresponding to it. We can never be sure that the opinion we are endeavoring to stifle is a false opinion; and if we were sure, stifling it would be an evil still.

First: the opinion which it is attempted to suppress by authority may possibly be true. Those who desire to suppress it, of course deny its truth; but they are not infallible. They have no authority to decide the question for all mankind, and exclude every other person from the means of judging. To refuse a hearing to an opinion, because they are sure that it is false, is to assume that *their* certainty is the same thing as *absolute* certainty. All silencing of discussion is an assumption of infallibility. Its condemnation may be allowed to rest on this common argument, not the worse for being common.

Unfortunately for the good sense of mankind, the fact of their fallibility is far from carrying the weight in their practical judgment, which is always allowed to it in theory; for while everyone well knows himself to be fallible, few think it necessary to take any precautions against their own fallibility, or admit the supposition that any opinion, of which they feel very certain, may be one of the examples of the error to which they acknowledge themselves to be liable. Absolute princes, or others who are accustomed to unlimited deference, usually feel this complete confidence in their own opinions on nearly all subjects. People more happily situated, who sometimes hear their opinions disputed, and are not wholly unused to be set right when they are wrong, place the same unbounded reliance only on such of their opinions as are shared by all who surround them, or to whom they habitually defer: for in proportion to a man's want of confidence in his own solitary judgment, does he usually repose, with implicit trust, on the infallibility of "the world" in general. And the world, to each individual, means the part of it with which he comes in contact; his party, his sect, his church, his class of society: the man may be called, by comparison, almost liberal and large-minded to whom it means anything so comprehensive as his own country or his own age. Nor is his faith in this collective authority at all shaken by his being aware that other ages, countries, sects, churches, classes, and parties have thought, and even now think, the exact reverse. He devolves upon his own world the responsibility of being in the right against the dissentient worlds of other people; and it never troubles him that mere accident has decided which of these numerous worlds is the object of his reliance, and that the same causes which make him a Churchman in London, would have made him a Buddhist or a Confucian in Pekin. Yet it is as evident in itself, as any amount of argument can make it, that ages are no more infallible than individuals; every age having held many opinions which subsequent ages have deemed not only false but absurd; and it is as certain that many opinions, now general, will be rejected by future ages, as it is that many, once general, are rejected by the present.

The objection likely to be made to this argument would probably take some such form as the following. There is no greater assumption of infallibility in forbidding the propagation of error, than in any other thing which is done by public authority on its own judgment and responsibility. Judgment is given to men that they may use it. Because it may be used erroneously, are men to be told that they ought not to use it at all? To prohibit what they think pernicious, is not claiming exemption from error, but fulfilling the duty incumbent on them, although fallible, of acting on their conscientious conviction. If we were never to act on our opinions, because those opinions may be wrong, we should leave all our interests uncared for, and all our duties unperformed. An objection which applies to all conduct, can be no valid objection to any conduct, in particular. It is the duty of governments, and of individuals, to form the truest opinions they can; to form them carefully, and never impose them upon others unless they are quite sure of being right. But when they are sure (such reasoners may say), it is not conscientiousness but cowardice to shrink from acting on their opinions, and allow doctrines which they honestly think dangerous to the welfare of mankind, either in this life or in another, to be scattered abroad without restraint, because other people, in less enlightened times, have persecuted opinions now believed to be true. Let us take care, it may be said, not to make the same mistake: but governments and nations have made mistakes in other things, which are not denied to be fit subjects for the exercise of authority: they have laid on bad taxes, made unjust wars. Ought we therefore to lay on no taxes, and, under whatever provocation, make no wars? Men, and governments, must act to the best of their ability. There is no such thing as absolute certainty, but there is assurance sufficient for the purposes of human life. We may, and must, assume our opinion to be true for the guidance of our own conduct: and it is assuming no more when we forbid bad men to pervert society by the propagation of opinions which we regard as false and pernicious.

I answer, that it is assuming very much more. There is the greatest difference between presuming an opinion to be true, because, with every opportunity for contesting it, it has not been refuted, and assuming its truth for the purpose of not permitting its refutation. Complete liberty of contradicting and disproving our opinion, is the very condition which justifies us in assuming its truth for purposes of action; and on no other terms can a being with human faculties have any rational assurance of being right.

When we consider either the history of opinion, or the ordinary conduct of human life, to what is it to be ascribed that the one and the other are no worse than they are? Not certainly to the inherent force of the human understanding; for, on any matter not self-evident, there are ninety-nine persons totally incapable of judging of it, for one who is capable; and the capacity of the hundredth person is only comparative; for the majority of the eminent men of every past generation held many opinions now known to be erroneous, and did or approved numerous things which no one will now justify. Why is it, then, that there is on the whole a preponderance among mankind of rational opinions and rational conduct? If there really is this preponderance—which there must be unless human affairs are, and have always been, in an almost desperate state—it is owing to a quality of the human mind, the source of everything respectable in man either as an intellectual or as a moral being, namely, that his errors are corrigible. He is capable of rectifying his mistakes, by discussion and experience. Not by experience alone. There must be discussion, to show how experience is to be interpreted. Wrong opinions and practices gradually yield to fact and argument: but facts and arguments, to produce any effect on the mind, must be brought before it. Very few facts are able to tell their own story, without comments to bring out their meaning. The whole strength and value, then, of human judgment, depending on the one property, that it can be set right when it is wrong, reliance can be placed on it only when the means of setting it right are kept constantly at hand. In the case of any person whose judgment is really deserving of confidence, how has it become so? Because he has kept his mind open to criticism of his opinions and conduct. Because it has been his practice to listen to all that could be said against him; to profit by as much of it as was just, and expound to himself, and upon occasion to others, the fallacy of what was fallacious. Because he has felt, that the only way in which a human being can make some approach to knowing the whole of a subject, is by hearing what can be said about it by persons of every variety of opinion, and studying all modes in which it can be looked at by every character of mind. No wise man ever acquired his wisdom in any mode but this; nor is it in the nature of human intellect to become wise in any other manner. The steady habit of correcting and completing his own opinion by collating it with those of others, so far from causing doubt and hesitation in carrying it into practice, is the only stable foundation for a just reliance on it: for, being cognizant of all that can, at least obviously, be said against him, and having taken up his position against all gainsayers—knowing that he has sought for objections and difficulties, instead of avoiding them, and has shut out no light which can be thrown upon the subject from any quarter—he has a right to think his judgment better than that of any person, or any multitude, who have not gone through a similar process.

It is not too much to require that what the wisest of mankind, those who are best entitled to trust their own judgment, find necessary to warrant their relying on it, should be submitted to by that miscellaneous collection of a few wise and many foolish individuals, called the public. The most intolerant of churches, the Roman Catholic Church, even at the canonization of a saint, admits, and listens patiently to, a "devil's advocate." The holiest of men, it appears, cannot be admitted to posthumous honors, until all that the devil could say against him is known and weighed. If even the Newtonian philosophy were not permitted to be questioned, mankind could not feel as complete assurance of its truth as they now do. The beliefs which we have most warrant for, have no safeguard to rest on, but a standing invitation to the whole world to prove them unfounded. If the challenge is not accepted, or is accepted and the attempt fails, we are far enough from certainty still; but we have done the best that the existing state of human reason admits of; we have neglected nothing that could give the truth a chance of reaching us: if the lists are kept open, we may hope that if there be a better truth, it will be found when the human mind is capable of receiving it; and in the meantime we may rely on having attained such approach to truth, as is possible in our own day. This is the amount of certainty attainable by a fallible being, and this the sole way of attaining it.

Strange it is, that men should admit the validity of the arguments for free discussion, but object to their being "pushed to an extreme"; not seeing that unless the reasons are good for an extreme case, they are not good for any case. Strange that they should imagine that they are not assuming infallibility, when they acknowledge that there should be free discussion on all subjects which can possibly be *doubtful,* but think that some particular principle or doctrine should be forbidden to be questioned because it is so *certain,* that is, because *they are certain* that it is certain. To call any proposition certain, while there is any one who would deny its certainty if permitted, but who is not permitted, is to assume that we ourselves, and those who agree with us, are the judges of certainty, and judges without hearing the other side.

In the present age—which has been described as "destitute of faith, but terrified at scepticism"—in which people feel sure, not so much that their opinions are true, as that they should not know what to do without them—the claims of an opinion to be protected from public attack are rested not so much on its truth, as on its importance to society. There are, it is alleged, certain beliefs, so useful, not to say indispensable to well-being, that it is as much the duty of governments to uphold those beliefs, as to protect any other of the interests of society. In a case of such necessity, and so directly in the line of their duty, something less than infallibility may, it is maintained, warrant, and even bind, governments, to act on their own opinion, confirmed by the general opinion of mankind. It is also often argued, and still oftener thought, that none but bad men would desire to weaken these salutary beliefs; and there can be nothing wrong, it is thought, in restraining bad men, and prohibiting what only such men would wish to practice. This mode of thinking makes the justification of restraints on discussion not a question of the truth of doctrines, but of their usefulness; and flatters itself by that means to escape the responsibility of claiming to be an infallible judge of opinions. But those who thus satisfy themselves, do not perceive that the assumption of infallibility is merely shifted from one point to another. The usefulness of an opinion is itself matter of opinion: as disputable, as open to discussion, and requiring discussion as much, as the opinion itself. There is the same need of an infallible judge of opinions to decide an opinion to be noxious, as to decide it to be false, unless the opinion condemned has full opportunity of defending itself. And it will not do to say that the heretic may be allowed to maintain the utility or harmlessness of his opinion, though forbidden to maintain its truth. The truth of an opinion is part of its utility. If we would know whether or not it is desirable that a proposition should be believed, is it possible to exclude the consideration of whether or not it is true? In the opinion, not of bad men, but of the best men, no belief which is contrary to truth can be really useful: and can you prevent such men from urging that plea, when they are charged with culpability for denying some doctrine which they are told is useful, but which they believe to be false? Those who are on the side of received opinions, never fail to take all possible advantage of this plea; you do not find *them* handling the question of utility as if it could be completely abstracted from that of truth: on the contrary, it is, above all, because their doctrine is the "truth," that the knowledge or the belief of it is held to be so indispensable. There can be no fair discussion of the question of usefulness, when an argument so vital may be employed on one side, but not on the other. And in point of fact, when law or public feeling do not permit the truth of an opinion to be disputed, they are just as little tolerant of a denial of its usefulness. The utmost they allow is an extenuation of its absolute necessity, or of the positive guilt of rejecting it.

In order more fully to illustrate the mischief of denying a hearing to opinions because we, in our own judgment, have condemned them, it will be desirable to fix down the discussion to a concrete case; and I choose, by preference, the cases which are least favorable to me—in which the argument against freedom of opinion, both on the score of truth and on that of utility, is considered the strongest. Let the opinions impugned be the belief in a God and in a future state, or any of the commonly received doctrines of morality. To fight the battle on such ground, gives a great advantage to an unfair antagonist; since he will be sure to say (and many who have no desire to be unfair will say it internally), Are these the doctrines which you do not deem sufficiently certain to be taken under the protection of law? Is the belief in a God one of the opinions, to feel sure of which, you hold to be assuming infallibility? But I must be permitted to observe, that it is not the feeling sure of a doctrine (be it what it may) which I call an assumption of infallibility. It is the undertaking to decide that question *for others,* without allowing them to hear what can be said on the contrary side. And I denounce and reprobate this pretension not the less, if put forth on the side of my most solemn convictions. However positive anyone's persuasion may be, not only of the falsity but of the pernicious consequences —not only of the pernicious consequences, but (to adopt expressions which I altogether condemn) the immorality and impiety of an opinion; yet if, in pursuance of that private judgment, though backed by the public judgment of his country or his cotemporaries, he prevents the opinion from being heard in its defense, he assumes infallibility. And so far from the assumption being less objectionable or less dangerous because the opinion is called immoral or impious, this is the case of all others in which it is most fatal. These are exactly the occasions on which the men of one generation commit those dreadful mistakes, which excite the astonishment and horror of posterity. It is among such that we find the instances memorable in history, when the arm of the law has been employed to root out the best men and the noblest doctrines; with deplorable success as to the men, though some of the doctrines have survived to be (as if in mockery) invoked, in defense of similar conduct towards those who dissent from *them,* or from their received interpretation.

Mankind can hardly be too often reminded, that there was once a man named Socrates, between whom and the legal authorities and public opinion of his time, there took place a memorable collision. Born in an age and country abounding in individual greatness, this man has been handed down to us by those who best knew both him and the age, as the most virtuous man in it; while *we* know him as the head and prototype of all subsequent teachers of virtue, the source equally of the lofty inspiration of Plato and the judicious utilitarianism of Aristotle, *"i maëstri di color che sanno,"* the two headsprings of ethical as of all other philosophy. This acknowledged master of all the eminent thinkers who have since lived—whose fame, still growing after more than two thousand years, all but outweighs the whole remainder of the names which make his native city illustrious—was put to death by his countrymen, after a judicial conviction, for impiety and immorality. Impiety, in denying the gods recognized by the State; indeed his accuser asserted (see the *Apologia*) that he believed in no gods at all. Immorality, in being, by his doctrines and instructions, a "corruptor of youth." Of these charges the tribunal, there is every ground for believing, honestly found him guilty, and condemned the man who probably of all then born had deserved best of mankind, to be put to death as a criminal.

To pass from this to the only other instance of judicial iniquity, the mention of which, after the condemnation of Socrates, would not be an anti-climax: the event which took place on Calvary rather more than eighteen hundred years ago. The man who left on the memory of those who witnessed his life and conversation, such an impression of his moral grandeur, that eighteen subsequent centuries have done homage to him as the Almighty in person, was ignominiously put to death, as what? As a blasphemer. Men did not merely mistake their benefactor; they mistook him for the exact contrary of what he was, and treated him as that prodigy of impiety, which they themselves are now held to be, for their treatment of him. The feelings with which mankind now regard these lamentable transactions, especially the later of the two, render them extremely unjust in their judgment of the unhappy actors. These were, to all appearance, not bad men—not worse than men commonly are, but rather the contrary; men who possessed in a full, or somewhat more than a full measure, the religious, moral, and patriotic feelings of their time and people: the very kind of men who, in all times, our own included, have every chance of passing through life blameless and respected. The high-priest who rent his garments when the words were pronounced, which, according to all the ideas of his country, constituted the blackest guilt, was in all probability quite as sincere in his horror and indignation, as the generality of respectable and pious men now are in the religious and moral sentiments they profess; and most of those who now shudder at his conduct, if they had lived in his time, and been born Jews, would have acted precisely as he did. Orthodox Christians who are tempted to think that those who stoned to death the first martyrs must have been worse men than they themselves are, ought to remember that one of those persecutors was Saint Paul.

Let us add one more example, the most striking of all, if the impressiveness of an error is measured by the wisdom and virtue of him who falls into it. If ever anyone, possessed of power, had grounds for thinking himself the best and most enlightened among his contemporaries, it was the Emperor Marcus Aurelius. Absolute monarch of the whole civilized world, he preserved through life not only the most unblemished justice, but what was less to be expected from his Stoical breeding, the tenderest heart. The few failings which are attributed to him, were all on the side of indulgence: while his writings, the highest ethical product of the ancient mind, differ scarcely perceptibly, if they differ at all, from the most characteristic teachings of Christ. This man, a better Christian in all but the dogmatic sense of the word, than almost any of the ostensibly Christian sovereigns who have since reigned, persecuted Christianity. Placed at the summit of all the previous attainments of humanity, with an open, unfettered intellect, and a character which led him of himself to embody in his moral writings the Christian ideal, he yet failed to see that Christianity was to be a good and not an evil to the world, with his duties to which he was so deeply penetrated. Existing society he knew to be in a deplorable state. But such as it was, he saw, or thought he saw, that it was held together, and prevented from being worse, by belief and reverence of the received divinities. As a ruler of mankind, he deemed it his duty not to suffer society to fall in pieces; and saw not how, if its existing ties were removed, any others could be formed which could again knit it together. The new religion openly aimed at dissolving these ties: unless, therefore, it was his duty to adopt that religion, it seemed to be his duty to put it down. Inasmuch then as the theology of Christianity did not appear to him true or of divine origin; inasmuch as this strange history of a crucified God was not credible to him, and a system which purported to rest entirely upon a foundation to him so wholly unbelievable, could not be foreseen by him to be that renovating agency which, after all abatements, it has in fact proved to be; the gentlest and most amiable of philosophers and rulers, under a solemn sense of duty, authorized the persecution of Christianity. To my mind this is one of the most tragical facts in all history. It is a bitter thought, how different a thing the Christianity of the world might have been, if the Christian faith had been adopted as the religion of the empire under the auspices of Marcus Aurelius instead of those of Constantine. But it would be equally unjust to him and false to truth, to deny, that no one plea which can be urged for punishing anti-Christian teaching, was wanting to Marcus Aurelius for punishing, as he did, the propagation of Christianity. No Christian more firmly believes that Atheism is false, and tends to the dissolution of society, than Marcus Aurelius believed the same things of Christianity; he who, of all men then living, might have been thought the most capable of appreciating it. Unless anyone who approves of punishment for the promulgation of opinions, flatters himself that he is a wiser and better man than Marcus Aurelius—more deeply versed in the wisdom of his time, more elevated in his intellect above it—more earnest in his search for truth, or more singleminded in his devotion to it when found—let him abstain from that assumption of the joint infallibility of himself and the multitude, which the great Antoninus made with so unfortunate a result. . . .

But, indeed, the dictum that truth always triumphs over persecution, is one of those pleasant falsehoods which men repeat after one another till they pass into commonplaces, but which all experience refutes. History teems with instances of truth put down by persecution. If not suppressed forever, it may be thrown back for centuries. To speak only of religious opinions: the Reformation broke out at least twenty times before Luther, and was put down. Arnold of Brescia was put down. Fra Dolcino was put down. Savonarola was put down. The Albigeois were put down. The Vaudois were put down. The Lollards were put down. The Hussites were put down. Even after the era of Luther, wherever persecution was persisted in, it was successful. In Spain, Italy, Flanders, the Austrian empire, Protestantism was rooted out; and, most likely, would have been so in England, had Queen Mary lived, or Queen Elizabeth died. Persecution has always succeeded, save where the heretics were too strong a party to be effectually persecuted. No reasonable person can doubt that Christianity might have been extirpated in the Roman Empire. It spread, and became predominant, because the persecutions were only occasional, lasting but a short time, and separated by long intervals of almost undisturbed propagandism. It is a piece of idle sentimentality that truth, merely truth, has any inherent power denied to error, of prevailing against the dungeon and the stake. Men are not more zealous for truth than they often are for error, and a sufficient application of legal or even of social penalties will generally succeed in stopping the propagation of either. The real advantage which truth has, consists in this, that when an opinion is true, it may be extinguished once, twice, or many times, but in the course of ages there will generally be found persons to rediscover it, until some one of its reappearances falls on a time when from favorable circumstances it escapes persecution until it has made such head as to withstand all subsequent attempts to suppress it.

It will be said, that we do not now put to death the introducers of new opinions: we are not like our fathers who slew the prophets, we even build sepulchers to them. It is true we no longer put heretics to death; and the amount of penal infliction which modern feeling would probably tolerate, even against the most obnoxious opinions, is not sufficient to extirpate them. But let us not flatter ourselves that we are yet free from the stain even of legal persecution. Penalties for opinion, or at least for its expression, still exist by law; and their enforcement is not, even in these times, so unexampled as to make it at all incredible that they may some day be revived in full force. In the year 1857, at the summer assizes of the county of Cornwall, an unfortunate man,* said to be of unexceptionable conduct in all relations of life, was sentenced to twenty-one months' imprisonment, for uttering, and writing on a gate, some offensive words concerning Christianity. Within a month of the same time, at the Old Bailey, two persons, on two separate occasions,† were rejected as jurymen, and one of them grossly insulted by the judge and by one of the counsel, because they honestly declared that they had no theological belief; and a third, a foreigner,‡ for the same reason, was denied justice against a thief. This refusal of redress took place in virtue of the legal doctrine, that no person can be allowed to give evidence in a court of justice, who does not profess belief in a God (any god is sufficient) and in a future state; which is equivalent to declaring such persons to be outlaws, excluded from the protection of the tribunals; who may not only be robbed or assaulted with impunity, if no one but themselves, or persons of similar

---

* Thomas Pooley, Bodmin Assizes, July 31, 1857. In December following, he received a free pardon from the Crown.

† George Jacob Holyoake, August 17, 1857; Edward Truelove, July, 1857.

‡ Baron de Gleichen, Marlborough-street Police Court, August 4, 1857.

opinions, be present, but anyone else may be robbed or assaulted with impunity, if the proof of the fact depends on their evidence. The assumption on which this is grounded is that the oath is worthless, of a person who does not believe in a future state; a proposition which betokens much ignorance of history in those who assent to it (since it is historically true that a large proportion of infidels in all ages have been persons of distinguished integrity and honor); and would be maintained by no one who had the smallest conception how many of the persons in greatest repute with the world, both for virtues and for attainments, are well known, at least to their intimates, to be unbelievers. The rule, besides, is suicidal, and cuts away its own foundation. Under pretense that atheists must be liars, it admits the testimony of all atheists who are willing to lie, and rejects only those who brave the obloquy of publicly confessing a detested creed rather than affirm a falsehood. A rule thus self-convicted of absurdity so far as regards its professed purpose, can be kept in force only as a badge of hatred, a relic of persecution; a persecution, too, having the peculiarity, that the qualification for undergoing it, is the being clearly proved not to deserve it. The rule, and the theory it implies, are hardly less insulting to believers than to infidels. For if he who does not believe in a future state, necessarily lies, it follows that they who do believe are only prevented from lying, if prevented they are, by the fear of hell. We will not do the authors and abettors of the rule the injury of supposing, that the conception which they have formed of Christian virtue is drawn from their own consciousness.

These, indeed, are but rags and remnants of persecution, and may be thought to be not so much an indication of the wish to persecute, as an example of that very frequent infirmity of English minds, which makes them take a preposterous pleasure in the assertion of a bad principle, when they are no longer bad enough to desire to carry it really into practice. But unhappily there is no security in the state of the public mind, that the suspension of worse forms of legal persecution, which has lasted for about the space of a generation, will continue. In this age the quiet surface of routine is as often ruffled by attempts to resuscitate past evils, as to introduce new benefits. What is boasted of at the present time as the revival of religion, is always, in narrow and uncultivated minds, at least as much the revival of bigotry; and where there is the strong permanent leaven of intolerance in the feelings of a people, which at all times abides in

the middle classes of this country, it needs but little to provoke them
into actively persecuting those whom they have never ceased to think
proper objects of persecution. For it is this—it is the opinions men
entertain, and the feelings they cherish, respecting those who disown
the beliefs they deem important, which makes this country not a
place of mental freedom. For a long time past, the chief mischief
of the legal penalties is that they strengthen the social stigma. It is
that stigma which is really effective, and so effective is it, that the
profession of opinions which are under the ban of society is much
less common in England, than is, in many other countries, the avowal
of those which incur risk of judicial punishment. . . . Our merely
social intolerance kills no one, roots out no opinions, but induces
men to disguise them, or to abstain from any active effort for their
diffusion. With us, heretical opinions do not perceptibly gain, or even
lose, ground in each decade or generation; they never blaze out far
and wide, but continue to smolder in the narrow circles of thinking
and studious persons among whom they originate, without ever
lighting up the general affairs of mankind with either a true or a
deceptive light. And thus is kept up a state of things very satisfactory
to some minds, because, without the unpleasant process of fining
or imprisoning anybody, it maintains all prevailing opinions out-
wardly undisturbed, while it does not absolutely interdict the exercise of reason by dissentients afflicted with the malady of thought. A
convenient plan for having peace in the intellectual world, and keeping all things going on therein very much as they do already. But
the price paid for this sort of intellectual pacification, is the sacrifice
of the entire moral courage of the human mind. A state of things in
which a large portion of the most active and inquiring intellects find
it advisable to keep the general principles and grounds of their convictions within their own breasts, and attempt, in what they address
to the public, to fit as much as they can of their own conclusions
to premises which they have internally renounced, cannot send forth
the open, fearless characters, and logical, consistent intellects who
once adorned the thinking world. The sort of men who can be looked
for under it, are either mere conformers to commonplace, or time-
servers for truth, whose arguments on all great subjects are meant
for their hearers, and are not those which have convinced themselves. Those who avoid this alternative, do so by narrowing their
thoughts and interest to things which can be spoken of without ven-
turing within the region of principles, that is, to small practical mat-

ters, which would come right of themselves, if but the minds of mankind were strengthened and enlarged, and which will never be made effectually right until then: while that which would strengthen and enlarge men's minds, free and daring speculation on the highest subjects, is abandoned.

Those in whose eyes this reticence on the part of heretics is no evil, should consider in the first place, that in consequence of it there is never any fair and thorough discussion of heretical opinions; and that such of them as could not stand such a discussion, though they may be prevented from spreading, do not disappear. But it is not the minds of heretics that are deteriorated most, by the ban placed on all inquiry which does not end in the orthodox conclusions. The greatest harm done is to those who are not heretics, and whose whole mental development is cramped, and their reason cowed, by the fear of heresy. Who can compute what the world loses in the multitude of promising intellects combined with timid characters, who dare not follow out any bold, vigorous, independent train of thought, lest it should land them in something which would admit of being considered irreligious or immoral? Among them we may occasionally see some man of deep conscientiousness, and subtle and refined understanding, who spends a life in sophisticating with an intellect which he cannot silence, and exhausts the resources of ingenuity in attempting to reconcile the promptings of his conscience and reason with orthodoxy, which yet he does not, perhaps, to the end succeed in doing. No one can be a great thinker who does not recognize, that as a thinker it is his first duty to follow his intellect to whatever conclusions it may lead. Truth gains more even by the errors of one who, with due study and preparation, thinks for himself, than by the true opinions of those who only hold them because they do not suffer themselves to think. Not that it is solely, or chiefly, to form great thinkers, that freedom of thinking is required. On the contrary, it is as much and even more indispensable, to enable average human beings to attain the mental stature which they are capable of. There have been, and may again be, great individual thinkers, in a general atmosphere of mental slavery. But there never has been, nor ever will be, in that atmosphere, an intellectually active people. When any people has made a temporary approach to such a character, it has been because the dread of heterodox speculation was for a time suspended. Where there is a tacit convention that principles are not to be disputed; where the discussion of the greatest questions which can occupy humanity is considered to be closed, we cannot hope to find that generally high scale of mental activity which has made some periods of history so remarkable. . . .

Let us now pass to the second division of the argument, and dismissing the supposition that any of the received opinions may be false, let us assume them to be true, and examine into the worth of the manner in which they are likely to be held, when their truth is not freely and openly canvassed. However unwillingly a person who has a strong opinion may admit the possibility that his opinion may be false, he ought to be moved by the consideration that however true it may be, if it is not fully, frequently, and fearlessly discussed, it will be held as a dead dogma, not a living truth.

There is a class of persons (happily not quite so numerous as formerly) who think it enough if a person assents undoubtingly to what they think true, though he has no knowledge whatever of the grounds of the opinion, and could not make a tenable defense of it against the most superficial objections. Such persons, if they can once get their creed taught from authority, naturally think that no good, and some harm, comes of its being allowed to be questioned. Where their influence prevails, they make it nearly impossible for the received opinion to be rejected wisely and considerately, though it may still be rejected rashly and ignorantly; for to shut out discussion entirely is seldom possible, and when it once gets in, beliefs not grounded on conviction are apt to give way before the slightest semblance of an argument. Waiving, however, this possibility—assuming that the true opinion abides in the mind, but abides as a prejudice, a belief independent of, and proof against, argument—this is not the way in which truth ought to be held by a rational being. This is not knowing the truth. Truth, thus held, is but one superstition the more accidentally clinging to the words which enunciate a truth.

If the intellect and judgment of mankind ought to be cultivated, a thing which Protestants at least do not deny, on what can these faculties be more appropriately exercised by anyone, than on the things which concern him so much that it is considered necessary for him to hold opinions on them? If the cultivation of the understanding consists in one thing more than in another, it is surely in learning the grounds of one's own opinions. Whatever people believe, on subjects on which it is of the first importance to believe rightly, they ought to be able to defend against at least the common objections. But, some one may say, "Let them be *taught* the grounds of their opinions. It does not follow that opinions must be merely parroted because they are never heard controverted. Persons who learn geometry do not simply commit the theorems to memory, but understand and learn likewise the demonstrations; and it would be absurd to say that they remain ignorant of the grounds of geometrical truths, because they never hear anyone deny, and attempt to disprove them." Undoubtedly: and such teaching suffices on a subject like mathematics, where there is nothing at all to be said on the wrong side of the question. The peculiarity of the evidence of mathematical truths is, that all the argument is on one side. There are no objections, and no answers to objections. But on every subject on which difference of opinion is possible, the truth depends on a balance to be struck between two sets of conflicting reasons. Even in natural philosophy, there is always some other explanation possible of the same facts; some geocentric theory instead of heliocentric, some phlogiston instead of oxygen; and it has to be shown why that other theory cannot be the true one: and until this is shown, and until we know how it is shown, we do not understand the grounds of our opinion. But when we turn to subjects infinitely more complicated, to morals, religion, politics, social relations, and the business of life, three-fourths of the arguments for every disputed opinion consist in dispelling the appearances which favor some opinion different from it. The greatest orator, save one, of antiquity, has left it on record that he always studied his adversary's case with as great, if not with still greater, intensity than even his own. What Cicero practiced as the means of forensic success, requires to be imitated by all who study any subject in order to arrive at the truth. He who knows only his own side of the case, knows little of that. His reasons may be good, and no one may have been able to refute them. But if he is equally unable to refute the reasons on the opposite side; if he does not so much as know what they are, he has no ground for preferring either opinion. The rational position for him would be suspension of judgment, and unless he contents himself with that, he is either led by authority, or adopts, like the generality of the world, the side to which he feels most inclination. Nor is it enough that he should hear the arguments of adversaries from his own teachers, presented as they state them, and accompanied by what they offer as refutations. That is not the way to do justice to the arguments, or bring them into real contact with his own mind. He must be able to hear them from persons who actually believe them; who defend them in earnest, and do their very utmost for them. He must know them in their most plausible and persuasive form; he must feel the whole force of the difficulty which the true view of the subject has to encounter and dispose of, else he will never really possess himself of the portion of truth which meets and removes that difficulty. Ninety-nine in a hundred of what are called educated men are in this condition; even of those who can argue fluently for their opinions. Their conclusion may be true, but it might be false for anything they know: they have never thrown themselves into the mental position of those who think differently from them, and considered what such persons may have to say; and consequently they do not, in any proper sense of the word, know the doctrine which they themselves profess. They do not know those parts of it which explain and justify the remainder; the considerations which show that a fact which seemingly conflicts with another is reconcilable with it, or that, of two apparently strong reasons, one and not the other ought to be preferred. All that part of the truth which turns the scale, and decides the judgment of a completely informed mind, they are strangers to; nor is it ever really known, but to those who have attended equally and impartially to both sides, and endeavored to see the reasons of both in the strongest light. So essential is this discipline to a real understanding of moral and human subjects, that if opponents of all important truths do not exist, it is indispensable to imagine them, and supply them with the strongest arguments which the most skillful devil's advocate can conjure up.

To abate the force of these considerations, an enemy of free discussion may be supposed to say, that there is no necessity for mankind in general to know and understand all that can be said against or for their opinions by philosophers and theologians. That it is not needful for common men to be able to expose all the misstatements or fallacies of an ingenious opponent. That it is enough if there is always somebody capable of answering them, so that nothing likely to mislead uninstructed persons remains unrefuted. That simple minds, having been taught the obvious grounds of the truths inculcated in them, may trust to authority for the rest, and being aware that they have neither knowledge nor talent to resolve every difficulty which can be raised, may repose in the assurance that all those which have been raised have been or can be answered, by those who are specially trained to the task.

Conceding to this view of the subject the utmost that can be claimed for it by those most easily satisfied with the amount of understanding of truth which ought to accompany the belief of it; even so, the argument for free discussion is no way weakened. For even this doctrine acknowledges that mankind ought to have a rational assurance that all objections have been satisfactorily answered; and how are they to be answered if that which requires to be answered is not spoken? or how can the answer be known to be satisfactory, if the objectors have no opportunity of showing that it is unsatisfactory? If not the public, at least the philosophers and theologians who are to resolve the difficulties, must make themselves familiar with those difficulties in their most puzzling form; and this cannot be accomplished unless they are freely stated, and placed in the most advantageous light which they admit of. The Catholic Church has its own way of dealing with this embarrassing problem. It makes a broad separation between those who can be permitted to receive its doctrines on conviction, and those who must accept them on trust. Neither, indeed, are allowed any choice as to what they will accept; but the clergy, such at least as can be fully confided in, may admissibly and meritoriously make themselves acquainted with the arguments of opponents, in order to answer them, and may, therefore, read heretical books; the laity, not unless by special permission, hard to be obtained. This discipline recognizes a knowledge of the enemy's case as beneficial to the teachers, but finds means, consistent with this, of denying it to the rest of the world: thus giving to the *élite* more mental culture, though not more mental freedom, than it allows to the mass. By this device it succeeds in obtaining the kind of mental superiority which its purposes require; for though culture without freedom never made a large and liberal mind, it can make a clever *nisi prius* advocate of a cause. But in countries professing Protestantism, this resource is denied; since Protestants hold, at least in theory, that the responsibility for the choice of a religion must be borne by each for himself, and cannot be thrown off upon teachers. Besides, in the present state of the world, it is practically impossible that writings which are read by the instructed can be kept from the uninstructed. If the teachers of mankind are to be cognizant of all that they ought to know, everything must be free to be written and published without restraint.

If, however, the mischievous operation of the absence of free discussion, when the received opinions are true, were confined to leaving men ignorant of the grounds of those opinions, it might be thought that this, if an intellectual, is no moral evil, and does not affect the worth of the opinions, regarded in their influence on the character. The fact, however, is, that not only the grounds of the opinion are forgotten in the absence of discussion, but too often the meaning of the opinion itself. The words which convey it, cease to suggest ideas, or suggest only a small portion of those they were originally employed to communicate. Instead of a vivid conception and a living belief, there remain only a few phrases retained by rote; or, if any part, the shell and husk only of the meaning is retained, the finer essence being lost. The great chapter in human history which this fact occupies and fills, cannot be too earnestly studied and meditated on.

It is illustrated in the experience of almost all ethical doctrines and religious creeds. They are all full of meaning and vitality to those who originate them, and to the direct disciples of the originators. Their meaning continues to be felt in undiminished strength, and is perhaps brought out into even fuller consciousness, so long as the struggle lasts to give the doctrine or creed an ascendancy over other creeds. At last it either prevails, and becomes the general opinion, or its progress stops; it keeps possession of the ground it has gained, but ceases to spread further. When either of these results has become apparent, controversy on the subject flags, and gradually dies away. The doctrine has taken its place, if not as a received opinion, as one of the admitted sects or divisions of opinion: those who hold it have generally inherited, not adopted it; and conversion from one of these doctrines to another, being now an exceptional fact, occupies little place in the thoughts of their professors. Instead of being, as at first, constantly on the alert either to defend themselves against the world, or to bring the world over to them, they have subsided into acquiescence, and neither listen, when they can help it, to arguments against their creed, nor trouble dissentients (if there be such) with arguments in its favor. From this time may usually be dated the decline in the living power of the doctrine. We often hear the teachers of all creeds lamenting the difficulty of keeping up in the minds of believers a lively apprehension of the truth which they nominally recognize, so that it may penetrate the feelings, and acquire a real mastery over the conduct. No such difficulty is complained of while the creed is still fighting for its existence: even the weaker combatants then know and feel what they are fighting for, and the difference between it and other doctrines; and in that period of every creed's existence, not a few persons may be found, who have realized its fundamental principles in all the forms of thought, have weighed and considered them in all their important bearings, and have experienced the full effect on the character, which belief in that creed ought to produce in a mind thoroughly imbued with it. But when it has come to be an hereditary creed, and to be received passively, not actively—when the mind is no longer compelled, in the same degree as at first, to exercise its vital powers on the questions which its belief presents to it, there is a progressive tendency to forget all of the belief except the formularies, or to give it a dull and torpid assent, as if accepting it on trust dispensed with the necessity of realizing it in consciousness, or testing it by personal experience; until it almost ceases to connect itself at all with the inner life of the human being. Then are seen the cases, so frequent in this age of the world as almost to form the majority, in which the creed remains as it were outside the mind, encrusting and petrifying it against all other influences addressed to the higher parts of our nature; manifesting its power by not suffering any fresh and living conviction to get in, but itself doing nothing for the mind or heart, except standing sentinel over them to keep them vacant.

To what an extent doctrines intrinsically fitted to make the deepest impression upon the mind may remain in it as dead beliefs, without being ever realized in the imagination, the feelings, or the understanding, is exemplified by the manner in which the majority of believers hold the doctrines of Christianity. By Christianity I here mean what is accounted such by all churches and sects—the maxims and precepts contained in the New Testament. These are considered sacred, and accepted as laws, by all professing Christians. Yet it is scarcely too much to say that not one Christian in a thousand guides or tests his individual conduct by reference to those laws. The standard to which he does refer it, is the custom of his nation, his class, or his religious profession. He has thus, on the one hand, a collection of ethical maxims, which he believes to have been vouchsafed to him by infallible wisdom as rules for his government; and on the other, a set of everyday judgments and practices, which go a certain length with some of those maxims, not so great a length with others, stand in direct opposition to some, and are, on the whole, a compromise between the Christian creed and the interests and suggestions of worldly life. To the first of these standards he gives his

homage; to the other his real allegiance. All Christians believe that
the blessed are the poor and humble, and those who are ill-used by
the world; that it is easier for a camel to pass through the eye of a
needle than for a rich man to enter the kingdom of heaven; that they
should judge not, lest they be judged; that they should swear not at
all; that they should love their neighbor as themselves; that if one
take their cloak, they should give him their coat also; that they
should take no thought for the morrow; that if they would be perfect,
they should sell all that they have and give it to the poor. They are
not insincere when they say that they believe these things. They do
believe them, as people believe what they have always heard lauded
and never discussed. But in the sense of that living belief which regulates conduct, they believe these doctrines just up to the point to
which it is usual to act upon them. The doctrines in their integrity
are serviceable to pelt adversaries with; and it is understood that they
are to put forward (when possible) as the reasons for whatever people do that they think laudable. But anyone who reminded them
that the maxims require an infinity of things which they never even
think of doing, would gain nothing but to be classed among those
very unpopular characters who affect to be better than other people.
The doctrines have no hold on ordinary believers—are not a power
in their minds. They have an habitual respect for the sound of them,
but no feeling which spreads from the words to the things signified,
and forces the mind to take *them* in, and make them conform to the
formula. Whenever conduct is concerned, they look round for Mr.
A and B to direct them how far to go in obeying Christ.

Now we may be well assured that the case was not thus, but far
otherwise, with the early Christians. Had it been thus, Christianity
never would have expanded from an obscure sect of the despised
Hebrews into the religion of the Roman empire. When their enemies
said, "See how these Christians love one another" (a remark not
likely to be made by anybody now), they assuredly had a much
livelier feeling of the meaning of their creed than they have ever had
since. And to this cause, probably, it is chiefly owing that Christianity
now makes so little progress in extending its domain, and after
eighteen centuries, is still nearly confined to Europeans and the
descendants of Europeans. Even with the strictly religious, who are
much in earnest about their doctrines, and attach a greater amount
of meaning to many of them than people in general, it commonly
happens that the part which is thus comparatively active in their

minds is that which was made by Calvin, or Knox, or some such person much nearer in character to themselves. The sayings of Christ co-exist passively in their minds, producing hardly any effect beyond what is caused by mere listening to words so amiable and bland. There are many reasons, doubtless, why doctrines which are the badge of a sect retain more of their vitality than those common to all recognized sects, and why more pains are taken by teachers to keep their meaning alive; but one reason certainly is, that the peculiar doctrines are more questioned, and have to be oftener defended against open gainsayers. Both teachers and learners go to sleep at their post, as soon as there is no enemy in the field.

The same thing holds true, generally speaking, of all traditional doctrines—those of prudence and knowledge of life, as well as morals or religion. All languages and literatures are full of general observations on life, both as to what it is, and how to conduct oneself in it; observations which everybody knows, which everybody repeats, or hears with acquiescence, which are received as truisms, yet of which most people first truly learn the meaning, when experience, generally of a painful kind, has made it a reality to them. How often, when smarting under some unforeseen misfortune or disappointment, does a person call to mind some proverb or common saying, familiar to him all his life, the meaning of which, if he had ever before felt it as he does now, would have saved him from the calamity. There are indeed reasons for this, other than the absence of discussion: there are many truths of which the full meaning *cannot* be realized, until personal experience has brought it home. But much more of the meaning even of these would have been understood, and what was understood would have been far more deeply impressed on the mind, if the man had been accustomed to hear it argued *pro* and *con* by people who did understand it. The fatal tendency of mankind to leave off thinking about a thing when it is no longer doubtful, is the cause of half their errors. A contemporary author has well spoken of "the deep slumber of a decided opinion."

But what! (it may be asked) Is the absence of unanimity an indispensable condition of true knowledge? Is it necessary that some part of mankind should persist in error, to enable any to realize the truth? Does a belief cease to be real and vital as soon as it is generally received—and is a proposition never thoroughly understood and felt unless some doubt of it remains? As soon as mankind have unanimously accepted a truth, does the truth perish within them? The highest aim and best result of improved intelligence, it has hitherto been thought, is to unite mankind more and more in the acknowledgment of all important truths: and does the intelligence only last as long as it has not achieved its object? Do the fruits of conquest perish by the very completeness of the victory?

I affirm no such thing. As mankind improve, the number of doctrines which are no longer disputed or doubted will be constantly on the increase: and the well-being of mankind may almost be measured by the number and gravity of the truths which have reached the point of being uncontested. The cessation, on one question after another, of serious controversy, is one of the necessary incidents of the consolidation of opinion; a consolidation as salutary in the case of true opinions, as it is dangerous and noxious when the opinions are erroneous. But though this gradual narrowing of the bounds of diversity of opinion is necessary in both senses of the term, being at once inevitable and indispensable, we are not therefore obliged to conclude that all its consequences must be beneficial. The loss of so important an aid to the intelligent and living apprehension of a truth, as is afforded by the necessity of explaining it to, or defending it against, opponents, though not sufficient to outweigh, is no trifling drawback from, the benefit of its universal recognition. Where this advantage can no longer be had, I confess I should like to see the teachers of mankind endeavoring to provide a substitute for it; some contrivance for making the difficulties of the question as present to the learner's consciousness, as if they were pressed upon him by a dissentient champion, eager for his conversion.

But instead of seeking contrivances for this purpose, they have lost those they formerly had. The Socratic dialectics, so magnificently exemplified in the dialogues of Plato, were a contrivance of this description. They were essentially a negative discussion of the great questions of philosophy and life, directed with consummate skill to the purpose of convincing anyone who had merely adopted the commonplaces of received opinion, that he did not understand the subject—that he as yet attached no definite meaning to the doctrines he professed; in order that, becoming aware of his ignorance, he might be put in the way to attain a stable belief, resting on a clear apprehension both of the meaning of doctrines and of their evidence. The school disputations of the middle ages had a somewhat similar object. They were intended to make sure that the pupil understood his own opinion, and (by necessary correlation) the opinion opposed to it, and could enforce the grounds of the one and confute those of the other. These last-mentioned contests had indeed the incurable defect, that the premises appealed to were taken from authority, not from reason; and, as a discipline to the mind, they were in every respect inferior to the powerful dialectics which formed the intellects of the *"Socratici viri":* but the modern mind owes far more to both than it is generally willing to admit, and the present modes of education contain nothing which in the smallest degree supplies the place either of the one or of the other. A person who derives all his instruction from teachers or books, even if he escape the besetting temptation of contenting himself with cram, is under no compulsion to hear both sides; accordingly it is far from a frequent accomplishment, even among thinkers, to know both sides; and the weakest part of what everybody says in defense of his opinion, is what he intends as a reply to antagonists. It is the fashion of the present time to disparage negative logic—that which points out weaknesses in theory or errors in practice, without establishing positive truths. Such negative criticism would indeed be poor enough as an ultimate result; but as a means to attaining any positive knowledge or conviction worthy the name, it cannot be valued too highly; and until people are again systematically trained to it, there will be few great thinkers, and a low general average of intellect, in any but the mathematical and physical departments of speculation. On any other subject no one's opinions deserve the name of knowledge, except so far as he has either had forced upon him by others, or gone through of himself, the same mental process which would have been required of him in carrying on an active controversy with opponents. That, therefore, which when absent, it is so indispensable, but so difficult, to create, how worse than absurd it is to forego, when spontaneously offering itself! If there are any persons who contest a received opinion, or who will do so if law or opinion will let them, let us thank them for it, open our minds to listen to them, and rejoice that there is someone to do for us what we otherwise ought, if we have any regard for either the certainty or the vitality of our convictions, to do with much greater labor for ourselves.

It still remains to speak of one of the principal causes which make diversity of opinion advantageous, and will continue to do so until mankind shall have entered a stage of intellectual advancement which at present seems at an incalculable distance. We have hitherto considered only two possibilities: that the received opinion may be false, and some other opinion, consequently, true; or that, the received opinion being true, a conflict with the opposite error is essential to a clear apprehension and deep feeling of its truth. But there is a commoner case than either of these; when the conflicting doctrines, instead of being one true and the other false, share the truth between them; and the nonconforming opinion is needed to supply the remainder of the truth, of which the received doctrine embodies only a part. Popular opinions, on subjects not palpable to sense, are often true, but seldom or never the whole truth. They are a part of the truth; sometimes a greater, sometimes a smaller part, but exaggerated, distorted, and disjoined from the truths by which they ought to be accompanied and limited. Heretical opinions, on the other hand, are generally some of these suppressed and neglected truths, bursting the bonds which kept them down, and either seeking reconciliation with the truth contained in the common opinion, or fronting it as enemies, and setting themselves up, with similar exclusiveness, as the whole truth. The latter case is hitherto the most frequent, as, in the human mind, one-sidedness has always been the rule, and many-sidedness the exception. Hence, even in revolutions of opinion, one part of the truth usually sets while another rises. Even progress, which ought to superadd, for the most part only substitutes, one partial and incomplete truth for another; improvement consisting chiefly in this, that the new fragment of truth is more wanted, more adapted to the needs of the time, than that which it displaces. Such being the partial character of prevailing opinions, even when resting on a true foundation, every opinion which embodies somewhat of the portion of truth which the common opinion omits, ought to be considered precious, with whatever amount of error and confusion that truth may be blended. No sober judge of human affairs will feel bound to be indignant because those who force on our notice truths which we should otherwise have overlooked, overlook some of those which we see. Rather, he will think that so long as popular truth is one-sided, it is more desirable than otherwise that unpopular truth should have one-sided asserters too; such being usually the most energetic, and the most likely to compel reluctant attention to the fragment of wisdom which they proclaim as if it were the whole. . . .

In politics, again, it is almost a commonplace, that a party of order or stability, and a party of progress or reform, are both necessary elements of a healthy state of political life; until the one or the other shall have so enlarged its mental grasp as to be a party equally of order and of progress, knowing and distinguishing what is fit to be preserved from what ought to be swept away. Each of these modes of thinking derives its utility from the deficiencies of the other; but it is in a great measure the opposition of the other that keeps each within the limits of reason and sanity. Unless opinions favorable to democracy and to aristocracy, to property and to equality, to co-operation and to competition, to luxury and to abstinence, to sociality and individuality, to liberty and discipline, and all the other standing antagonisms of practical life, are expressed with equal freedom, and enforced and defended with equal talent and energy, there is no chance of both elements obtaining their due; one scale is sure to go up, and the other down. Truth, in the great practical concerns of life, is so much a question of the reconciling and combining of opposites, that very few have minds sufficiently capacious and impartial to make the adjustment with an approach to correctness, and it has to be made by the rough process of a struggle between combatants fighting under hostile banners. On any of the great open questions just enumerated, if either of the two opinions has a better claim than the other, not merely to be tolerated, but to be encouraged and countenanced, it is the one which happens at the particular time and place to be in a minority. That is the opinion which, for the time being, represents the neglected interests, the side of human well-being which is in danger of obtaining less than its share. I am aware that there is not, in this country, any intolerance of differences of opinion on most of these topics. They are adduced to show, by admitted and multiplied examples, the universality of the fact, that only through diversity of opinion is there, in the existing state of human intellect, a chance of fair play to all sides of the truth. When there are persons to be found, who form an exception to the apparent unanimity of the world on any subject, even if the world is in the right, it is always probable that dissentients have something worth hearing to say for themselves, and that truth would lose something by their silence. . . .

I do not pretend that the most unlimited use of the freedom of enunciating all possible opinions would put an end to the evils of religious or philosophical sectarianism. Every truth which men of narrow capacity are in earnest about, is sure to be asserted, inculcated, and in many ways even acted on, as if no other truth existed in the world, or at all events none that could limit or qualify the first. I acknowledge that the tendency of all opinions to become sectarian is not cured by the freest discussion, but is often heightened and exacerbated thereby; the truth which ought to have been, but was not, seen, being rejected all the more violently because proclaimed by persons regarded as opponents. But it is not on the impassioned partisan, it is on the calmer and more disinterested bystander, that this collision of opinions works its salutary effect. Not the violent conflict between parts of the truth, but the quiet suppression of half of it, is the formidable evil; there is always hope when people are forced to listen to both sides; it is when they attend only to one that errors harden into prejudices, and truth itself ceases to have the effect of truth, by being exaggerated into falsehood. And since there are few mental attributes more rare than that judicial faculty which can sit in intelligent judgment between two sides of a question, of which only one is represented by an advocate before it, truth has no chance but in proportion as every side of it, every opinion which embodies any fraction of the truth, not only finds advocates, but is so advocated as to be listened to.

We have now recognized the necessity to the mental well-being of mankind (on which all their other well-being depends) of freedom of opinion, and freedom of the expression of opinion, on four distinct grounds; which we will now briefly recapitulate.

First, if any opinion is compelled to silence, that opinion may, for aught we can certainly know, be true. To deny this is to assume our own infallibility.

Secondly, though the silenced opinion be an error, it may, and very commonly does, contain a portion of truth; and since the general or prevailing opinion of any subject is rarely or never the whole truth, it is only by the collision of adverse opinions that the remainder of the truth has any chance of being supplied.

Thirdly, even if the received opinion be not only true, but the whole truth; unless it is suffered to be, and actually is, vigorously and earnestly contested, it will, by most of those who receive it, be held in the manner of a prejudice, with little comprehension or feeling of its rational grounds. And not only this, but, fourthly, the meaning of the doctrine itself will be in danger of being lost, or enfeebled, and deprived of its vital effect on the character and conduct: the dogma becoming a mere formal profession, inefficacious for good, but cumbering the ground, and preventing the growth of any real and heartfelt conviction, from reason or personal experience.

Before quitting the subject of freedom of opinion, it is fit to take some notice of those who say, that the free expression of all opinions should be permitted, on condition that the manner be temperate, and do not pass the bounds of fair discussion. Much might be said on the impossibility of fixing where these supposed bounds are to be placed; for if the test be offense to those whose opinion is attacked, I think experience testifies that this offense is given whenever the attack is telling and powerful, and that every opponent who pushes them hard, and whom they find it difficult to answer, appears to them, if he shows any strong feeling on the subject, an intemperate opponent. But this, though an important consideration in a practical point of view, merges in a more fundamental objection. Undoubtedly the manner of asserting an opinion, even though it be a true one, may be very objectionable, and may justly incur severe censure. But the principal offenses of the kind are such as it is mostly impossible, unless by accidental self-betrayal, to bring home to conviction. The gravest of them is, to argue sophistically, to suppress facts or arguments, to misstate the elements of the case, or misrepresent the opposite opinion. But all this, even to the most aggravated degree, is so continually done in perfect good faith, by persons who are not considered, and in many other respects may not deserve to be considered, ignorant or incompetent, that it is rarely possible on adequate grounds conscientiously to stamp the misrepresentation as morally culpable; and still less could law presume to interfere with this kind of controversial misconduct. With regard to what is commonly meant by intemperate discussion, namely invective, sarcasm, personality, and the like, the denunciation of these weapons would deserve more sympathy if it were ever proposed to interdict them equally to both sides; but it is only desired to restrain the employment of them against the prevailing opinion: against the unprevailing they may not only be used without general disapproval, but will be likely to obtain for him who uses them the praise of honest zeal and righteous indignation. Yet whatever mischief arises from their use, is greatest when they are employed against the comparatively defenseless; and whatever unfair advantage can be derived by any opinion from this mode of asserting it, accrues almost exclusively to received opinions. The worst offense of this kind which can be committed by a polemic, is to stigmatize those who hold the contrary opinion as bad and immoral men. To calumny of this sort, those who hold any unpopular opinion are peculiarly exposed, because they are in general few and uninfluential, and nobody but themselves feels much interested in seeing justice done them; but this weapon is, from the nature of the case, denied to those who attack a prevailing opinion: they can neither use it with safety to themselves, nor, if they could, would it do anything but recoil on their own cause. In general, opinions contrary to those commonly received can only obtain a hearing by studied moderation of language, and the most cautious avoidance of unnecessary offense, from which they hardly ever deviate even in a slight degree without losing ground: while unmeasured vituperation employed on the side of the prevailing opinion, really does deter people from professing contrary opinions, and from listening to those who profess them. For the interest, therefore, of truth and justice, it is far more important to restrain this employment of vituperative language than the other; and, for example, if it were necessary to choose, there would be much more need to discourage offensive attacks on infidelity, than on religion. It is, however, obvious that law and authority have no business with restraining either, while opinion ought, in every instance, to determine its verdict by the circumstances of the individual case; condemning everyone, on whichever side of the argument he places himself, in whose mode of advocacy either want of candor, or malignity, bigotry, or intolerance of feeling manifest themselves; but not inferring these vices from the side which a person takes, though it be the contrary side of the question to our own: and giving merited honor to everyone, whatever opinion he may hold, who has calmness to see and honesty to state what his opponents and their opinions really are, exaggerating nothing to their discredit, keeping nothing back which tells, or can be supposed to tell, in their favor. This is the real morality of public discussion: and if often violated, I am happy to think that there are many controversialists who to a great extent observe it, and a still greater number who conscientiously strive towards it.

Section III

THE FORMS OF CONTEMPORARY DEMOCRACY

The task of democratic philosophers, in recent years, has been to formulate a restatement of traditional ideals that would do justice to the demand for the freedom and equality of individuals and, at the same time, recognize the critical role of state activity in modern social life. By the end of the nineteenth century, liberal thinkers had pointed to the need for positive as well as negative freedoms. It came to be generally agreed that in a modern democracy the state must play an active part in providing the conditions—schools, business regulation, social welfare—that the full development and protection of all citizens makes necessary.

But how greatly is the role of the state to be thus enlarged? Is freedom of individual enterprise an outworn shibboleth in a democracy or a necessary condition for its preservation? Two trends may be distinguished in the replies given to these questions: one trend, democratic socialism, emphasizing the need for radical social reconstruction, presses for a greater range of state activity, and the coöperative determination of planned economic objectives; the other, democratic capitalism, while recognizing the need for some state activity, emphasizes the primacy of individual liberty and presents a more conservative defense of the freedom of enterprise.

Both these forms of government and most of their many variants have retained their traditional commitments to democratic ideals and procedures. The recent aim of both democratic capitalism and democratic socialism has been to reinterpret these ideals and procedures in terms of institutions that are practicable in a highly industrialized, densely populated, and rapidly changing society. Whether democracy in the future will be manifested in one of these forms, or in some other not yet developed, will probably depend upon the outcome of present democratic experiments and the will of the citizens concerned.

59. THOMAS HILL GREEN

Thomas Hill Green (1836-1882) was a Neo-Hegelian philosopher, and leader of liberal thought in the late nineteenth century. Like his predecessors, he was deeply concerned about the liberty of the individual; but he thought that such liberty could best be protected and extended when the state was used as a positive instrument in support of the well-being of its citizens. True liberty comes, he argued, not merely with absence of restraint, but only when, in addition, the minimal conditions of human well-being are actively developed by society. What, then, is the principle which should determine when the democratic state may legislatively restrict some liberties for the preservation of others? Such social action is legitimate, Green maintained, only when the state can thereby remove some real obstacles to the self-fulfillment of its individual members.

[Negative and Positive Freedom] *

We shall probably all agree that freedom, rightly understood, is the greatest of blessings; that its attainment is the true end of all our efforts as citizens. But when we thus speak of freedom, we should consider carefully what we mean by it. We do not mean merely freedom from restraint or compulsion. We do not mean merely freedom to do as we like irrespectively of what it is that we like. We do not mean a freedom that can be enjoyed by one man or one set of men at the cost of a loss of freedom to others. When we speak of freedom as something to be so highly prized, we mean a positive power or capacity of doing or enjoying something worth doing or enjoying, and that, too, something that we do or enjoy in common with others. We mean by it a power which each man exercises through

* From T. H. Green, *Liberal Legislation and Freedom of Contract*, 1880. This passage is reprinted from *The Works of Thomas Hill Green*, Volume 3, published by Longmans, Green and Co., London, 1888.

the help or security given him by his fellow-men, and which he in turn helps to secure for them. When we measure the progress of a society by its growth in freedom, we measure it by the increasing development and exercise on the whole of those powers of contributing to social good with which we believe the members of the society to be endowed; in short, by the greater power on the part of the citizens as a body to make the most and best of themselves. Thus, though of course there can be no freedom among men who act not willingly but under compulsion, yet on the other hand the mere removal of compulsion, the mere enabling a man to do as he likes, is in itself no contribution to true freedom. In one sense no man is so well able to do as he likes as the wandering savage. He has no master. There is no one to say him nay. Yet we do not count him really free, because the freedom of savagery is not strength, but weakness. The actual powers of the noblest savage do not admit of comparison with those of the humblest citizen of a law-abiding state. He is not the slave of man, but he is the slave of nature. Of compulsion by natural necessity he has plenty of experience, though of restraint by society none at all. Nor can he deliver himself from that compulsion except by submitting to this restraint. So to submit is the first step in true freedom, because the first step towards the full exercise of the faculties with which man is endowed. But we rightly refuse to recognize the highest development on the part of an exceptional individual or exceptional class, as an advance towards the true freedom of man, if it is founded on a refusal of the same opportunity to other men. The powers of the human mind have probably never attained such force and keenness, the proof of what society can do for the individual has never been so strikingly exhibited, as among the small groups of men who possessed civil privileges in the small republics of antiquity. The whole framework of our political ideas, to say nothing of our philosophy, is derived from them. But in them this extraordinary efflorescence of the privileged class was accompanied by the slavery of the multitude. That slavery was the condition on which it depended, and for that reason it was doomed to decay. There is no clearer ordinance of that supreme reason, often dark to us, which governs the course of men's affairs, than that no body of men should in the long run be able to strengthen itself at the cost of others' weakness. The civilization and freedom of the ancient world were shortlived because they were partial and exceptional. If the ideal of true freedom is the maximum of power for all members of human society alike to make the best of themselves, we are right in refusing to ascribe the glory of freedom to a state in which the apparent elevation of the few is founded on the degradation of the many, and in ranking modern society, founded as it is on free industry, with all its confusion and ignorant licence and waste of effort, above the most splendid of ancient republics.

If I have given a true account of that freedom which forms the goal of social effort, we shall see that freedom of contract, freedom of all the forms of doing what one will with one's own, is valuable only as a means to an end. That end is what I call freedom in the positive sense: in other words, the liberation of the powers of all men equally for contributions to a common good. No one has a right to do what he will with his own in such a way as to contravene this end. It is only through the guarantee which society gives him that he has property at all, or, strictly speaking, any right to his possessions. This guarantee is founded on a sense of common interest. Every one has an interest in securing to every one else the free use and enjoy-ment and disposal of his possessions, so long as that freedom on the part of one does not interfere with a like freedom on the part of others, because such freedom contributes to that equal development of the faculties of all which is the highest good for all. This is the true and the only justification of rights of property. Rights of property, how-ever, have been and are claimed which cannot thus be justified. We are all now agreed that men cannot rightly be the property of men. The institution of property being only justifiable as a means to the free exercise of the social capabilities of all, there can be no true right to property of a kind which debars one class of men from such free exercise altogether. We condemn slavery no less when it arises out of a voluntary agreement on the part of the enslaved person. A contract by which anyone agreed for a certain consideration to become the slave of another we should reckon a void contract. Here, then, as a limitation upon freedom of contract which we all recognize as rightful. No contract is valid in which human persons, willingly or unwillingly, are dealt with as commodities, because such contracts of necessity defeat the end for which alone society enforces contracts at all.

Are there no other contracts which, less obviously perhaps but really, are open to the same objection? In the first place, let us con-sider contracts affecting labor. Labor, the economist tells us, is a commodity exchangeable like other commodities. This is in a certain sense true, but it is a commodity which attaches in a peculiar manner to the person of man. Hence restrictions may need to be placed on the sale of this commodity which would be unnecessary in other cases, in order to prevent labor from being sold under conditions which make it impossible for the person selling it ever to become a free contributor to social good in any form. This is most plainly the case when a man bargains to work under conditions fatal to health, in an unventilated factory. Every injury to the health of the individual is, so far as it goes, a public injury. It is an impediment to the general freedom; so much deduction from our power, as members of society, to make the best of ourselves. Society is, therefore, plainly within its right when it limits freedom of contract for the sale of labor, so far as is done by our laws for the sanitary regulations of factories, workshops, and mines. It is equally within its right in prohibiting the labor of women and young persons beyond certain hours. If they work beyond those hours, the result is demonstrably physical deterioration; which, as demonstrably, carries with it a lowering of the moral forces of society. For the sake of that general freedom of its members to make the best of themselves, which it is the object of civil society to secure, a prohibition should be put by law, which is the deliberate voice of society, on all such contracts of service as in a general way yield such a result. The purchase or hire of un-wholesome dwellings is properly forbidden on the same principle. Its application to compulsory education may not be quite so obvious, but it will appear on a little reflection. Without a command of certain elementary arts and knowledge, the individual in modern society is as effectually crippled as by the loss of a limb or a broken constitution. He is not free to develop his faculties. With a view to securing such freedom among its members it is as certainly within the province of the state to prevent children from growing up in that kind of ignorance which practically excludes them from a free career in life, as it is within its province to require the sort of building and drainage necessary for public health.

Our modern legislation then with reference to labor, and education, and health, involving as it does manifold interference with freedom of contract, is justified on the ground that it is the business of the state, not indeed directly to promote moral goodness, for that, from the very nature of moral goodness, it cannot do, but to maintain the conditions without which a free exercise of the human faculties is impossible. It does not indeed follow that it is advisable for the state to do all which it is justified in doing. We are often warned now-a-days against the danger of over-legislation; or, as I heard it put in a speech of the present home secretary in the days when he was sowing his political wild oats, of "grandmotherly government." There may be good ground for the warning, but at any rate we should be quite clear what we mean by it. The outcry against state interference is often raised by men whose real objection is not to state interference but to centralization, to the constant aggression of the central executive upon local authorities. As I have already pointed out, compulsion at the discretion of some elected municipal board proceeds just as much from the state as does compulsion exercised by a government office in London. No doubt, much needless friction is avoided, much is gained in the way of elasticity and adjustment to circumstances, by the independent local administration of general laws; and most of us would agree that of late there has been a dangerous tendency to override municipal discretion by the hard and fast rules of London "departments." But centralization is one thing: over-legislation, or the improper exercise of the power of the state, quite another. It is one question whether of late the central government has been unduly trenching on local government, and another question whether the law of the state, either as administered by central or by provincial authorities, has been unduly interfering with the discretion of individuals. We may object most strongly to advancing centralization, and yet wish that the law should put rather more than less restraint on those liberties of the individual which are a social nuisance. But there are some political speculators whose objection is not merely to centralization, but to the extended action of the law altogether. They think that the individual ought to be left much more to himself than has of late been the case. Might not our people, they ask, have been trusted to learn in time for themselves to eschew unhealthy dwellings, to refuse dangerous and degrading employment, to get their children the schooling necessary for making their way in the world? Would they not for their own comfort, if not from more chivalrous feeling, keep their wives and daughters from overwork? Or, failing this, ought not women, like men, to learn to protect themselves? Might not all the rules, in short, which legislation of the kind we have been discussing is intended to attain, have been attained without it; not so quickly, perhaps, but without tampering so dangerously with the independence and self-reliance of the people?

Now, we shall probably all agree that a society in which the public health was duly protected, and necessary education duly provided for, by the spontaneous action of individuals, was in a higher condition than one in which the compulsion of law was needed to secure those ends. But we must take men as we find them. Until such a condition of society is reached, it is the business of the state to make the best security it can for the young citizens' growing up in such health and with so much knowledge as is necessary for their real freedom. In so doing it need not at all interfere with the independence and self-reliance of those whom it requires to do what they would otherwise do for themselves. The man who, of his own right feeling, saves his wife from overwork and sends his children to school, suffers no moral degradation from a law which, if he did not do this for himself, would seek to make him do it. Such a man does not feel the law as constraint at all. To him it is simply a powerful friend. It gives him security for that being done efficiently which, with the best wishes, he might have much trouble in getting done efficiently if left to himself. No doubt it relieves him from some of the responsibility which would otherwise fall to him as head of a family, but, if he is what we are supposing him to be, in proportion as he is relieved of responsibilities in one direction he will assume them in another. The security which the state gives him for the safe housing and sufficient schooling of his family will only make him the more careful for their well-being in other respects, which he is left to look after for himself. We need have no fear, then, of such legislation having an ill-effect on those who, without the law, would have seen to that being done, though probably less efficiently, which the law requires to be done. But it was not their case that the laws we are considering were especially meant to meet. It was the overworked women, the ill-housed and untaught families, for whose benefit they were intended. And the question is whether without these laws the suffering classes could have been delivered quickly or slowly from the condition they were in. Could the enlightened self-interest or benevolence of individuals, working under a system of unlimited freedom of contract, have ever brought them into a state compatible with the free development of the human faculties? No one considering the facts can have any doubt as to the answer to this question. Left to itself, or to the operation of casual benevolence, a degraded population perpetuates and increases itself. Read any of the authorized accounts, given before royal or parliamentary commissions, of the state of the laborers, especially of the women and children, as they were in our great industries before the law was first brought to bear on them, and before freedom of contract was first interfered with in them. Ask yourself what chance there was of a generation, born and bred under such conditions, ever contracting itself out of them. Given a certain standard of moral and material well-being, people may be trusted not to sell their labor, or the labor of their children, on terms which would not allow that standard to be maintained. But with large masses of our population, until the laws we have been considering took effect, there was no such standard. There was nothing on their part, in the way either of self-respect or established demand for comforts, to prevent them from working and living, or from putting their children to work and live, in a way in which no one who is to be a healthy and free citizen can work and live. No doubt there were many high-minded employers who did their best for their work-people before the days of state-interference, but they could not prevent less scrupulous hirers of labor from hiring it on the cheapest terms. It is true that cheap labor is in the long run dear labor, but it is so only in the long run, and eager traders do not think of the long run. If labor is to be had under conditions incompatible with the health or decent housing or education of the laborer, there will always be plenty of people to buy it under those conditions, careless of the burden in the shape of rates and taxes which they may be laying up for posterity. Either the standard of well-being on the part of the sellers of labor must prevent them from selling their labor under those conditions, or the law must prevent it. With a population such as ours was forty years ago, and still largely is, the law must prevent it and continue the prevention for some generations, before the sellers will be in a state to prevent it for themselves. . . .

60. LEONARD T. HOBHOUSE

Leonard T. Hobhouse (1864-1929) was a leading journalist and social philosopher in Britain in the early twentieth century. Contending that the fullest liberty and development of each citizen is possible only within a community in which each actively furthers the development of all, Hobhouse tried to reëstablish, within a framework of democratic liberal principles, the need for an organic conception of society. The ideals of nineteenth century liberalism are here reinterpreted in a new liberalism, of which the heart is the freeing of individual energies within this organic community.

The Heart of Liberalism*

The teaching of Mill brings us close to the heart of Liberalism. We learn from him, in the first place, that liberty is no mere formula of law, or of the restriction of law. There may be a tyranny of custom, a tyranny of opinion, even a tyranny of circumstance, as real as any tyranny of government and more pervasive. Nor does liberty rest on the self-assertion of the individual. There is scope abundant for Liberalism and illiberalism in personal conduct. Nor is liberty opposed to discipline, to organization, to strenuous conviction as to what is true and just. Nor is it to be identified with tolerance of opposed opinions. The Liberal does not meet opinions which he conceives to be false with toleration, as though they did not matter. He meets them with justice, and exacts for them a fair hearing as though they mattered just as much as his own. He is always ready to put his own convictions to the proof, not because he doubts them, but because he believes in them. For, both as to that which he holds for true and as to that which he holds for false, he believes that one final test applies. Let error have free play, and one of two things will happen. Either as it develops, as its implications and consequences become clear, some elements of truth will appear within it. They will separate themselves out; they will go to enrich the stock of human ideas; they will add something to the truth which he himself mistakenly took as final; they will serve to explain the root of the error; for error itself is generally a truth misconceived, and it is only when it is explained that it is finally and satisfactorily confuted. Or, in the alternative, no element of truth will appear. In that case the more fully the error is understood, the more patiently it is followed up in all the windings of its implications and consequences, the more thoroughly will it refute itself. The cancerous growth cannot be extirpated by the knife. The root is always left, and it is only the evolution of the self-protecting anti-toxin that works the final cure. Exactly parallel is the logic of truth. The more the truth is developed in all

* From L. T. Hobhouse, *Liberalism,* 1911. This selection is reprinted by permission of the publisher, The Oxford University Press, London.

its implications, the greater is the opportunity of detecting any element of error that it may contain; and, conversely, if no error appears, the more completely does it establish itself as the whole truth and nothing but the truth. Liberalism applies the wisdom of Gamaliel in no spirit of indifference, but in the full conviction of the potency of truth. If this thing be of man, i.e. if it is not rooted in actual verity, it will come to naught. If it be of God, let us take care that we be not found fighting against God.

Divergences of opinion of character, of conduct are not unimportant matters. They may be most serious matters, and no one is called on in the name of Liberalism to overlook their seriousness. There are, for example, certain disqualifications inherent in the profession of certain opinions. It is not illiberal to recognize such disqualifications. It is not illiberal for a Protestant in choosing a tutor for his son to reject a conscientious Roman Catholic who avows that all his teaching is centered on the doctrine of his Church. It would be illiberal to reject the same man for the specific purpose of teaching arithmetic, if he avowed that he had no intention of using his position for the purpose of religious propagandism. For the former purpose the divergence of religious opinion is an inherent disqualification. It negates the object propounded, which is the general education of the boy on lines in which the father believes. For the latter purpose the opinion is no disqualification. The devout Catholic accepts the multiplication table, and can impart his knowledge without reference to the infallibility of the Pope. To refuse to employ him is to impose an extraneous penalty on his convictions. It is not illiberal for an editor to decline the services of a member of the opposite party as a leader writer, or even as a political reviewer or in any capacity in which his opinions would affect his work. It is illiberal to reject him as a compositor or as a clerk, or in any capacity in which his opinions would not affect his work for the paper. It is not illiberal to refuse a position of trust to the man whose record shows that he is likely to abuse such a trust. It is illiberal—and this the "moralist" has yet to learn—to punish a man who has done a wrong in one relation by excluding him from the performance of useful social functions for which he is perfectly fitted, by which he could at once serve society and re-establish his own self-respect. There may, however, yet come a time when Liberalism, already recognized as a duty in religion and in politics, will take its true place at the center of our ethical conceptions, and will be seen to have its application not only to him whom we conceive to be the teacher of false opinions, but to the man whom we hold a sinner.

The ground of Liberalism so understood is certainly not the view that a man's personal opinions are socially indifferent, nor that his personal morality matters nothing to others. So far as Mill rested his case on the distinction between self-regarding actions and actions that affect others, he was still dominated by the older individualism. We should frankly recognize that there is no side of a man's life which is unimportant to society, for whatever he is, does, or thinks may affect his own well-being, which is and ought to be matter of common concern, and may also directly or indirectly affect the thought, action, and character of those with whom he comes in contact. The underlying principle may be put in two ways. In the first place, the man is much more than his opinions and his actions. Carlyle and Sterling did not differ "except in opinion." To most of us that is just what difference means. Carlyle was aware that there was something much deeper, something that opinion just crassly formulates, and for the most part formulates inadequately, that is the real man. The real man is something more than is ever adequately expressed in terms which his fellows can understand; and just as his essential humanity lies deeper than all distinctions of rank, and class, and color, and even, though in a different sense, of sex, so also it goes far below those comparatively external events which make one man figure as a saint and another as a criminal. This sense of ultimate oneness is the real meaning of equality, as it is the foundation of social solidarity and the bond which, if genuinely experienced, resists the disruptive force of all conflict, intellectual, religious, and ethical.

But, further, while personal opinions and social institutions are l ke crystallized results, achievements that have been won by certain definite processes of individual or collective effort, human personality is that which lives and grows, which can be destroyed but cannot be made, which cannot be taken to pieces and repaired, but can be placed under conditions in which it will flourish and expand, or, if it is diseased, under conditions in which it will heal itself by its own recuperative powers. The foundation of liberty is the idea of growth. Life is learning, but whether in theory or practice what a man genuinely learns is what he absorbs, and what he absorbs depends on the energy which he himself puts forth in response to his surroundings. Thus, to come at once to the real crux, the question of moral discipline, it is of course possible to reduce a man to order and prevent him from being a nuisance to his neighbors by arbitrary control and harsh punishment. This may be to the comfort of the neighbors, as is admitted, but regarded as a moral discipline it is a contradiction in terms. It is doing less than nothing for the character of the man himself. It is merely crushing him, and unless his will is killed the effect will be seen if ever the superincumbent pressure is by chance removed. It is also possible, though it takes a much higher skill, to teach the same man to discipline himself, and this is to foster the development of will, of personality, of self-control, or whatever we please to call that central harmonizing power which makes us capable of directing our own lives. Liberalism is the belief that society can safely be founded on this self-directing power of personality, that it is only on this foundation that a true community can be built, and that so established its foundations are so deep and so wide that there is no limit that we can place to the extent of the building. Liberty then becomes not so much a right of the individual as a necessity of society. It rests not on the claim of A to be let alone by B, but on the duty of B to treat A as a rational being. It is not right to let crime alone or to let error alone, but it is imperative to treat the criminal or the mistaken or the ignorant as beings capable of right and truth, and to lead them on instead of merely beating them down. The rule of liberty is just the application of rational method. It is the opening of the door to the appeal of reason, of imagination, of social feeling; and except through the response to this appeal there is no assured progress of society.

Now, I am not contending that these principles are free from difficulty in application. At many points they suggest difficulties both in theory and in practice, with some of which I shall try to deal later on. Nor, again, am I contending that freedom is the universal solvent, or the idea of liberty the sole foundation on which a true social philosophy can be based. On the contrary, freedom is only one side of social life. Mutual aid is not less important than mutual forbearance, the theory of collective action no less fundamental than the theory of personal freedom. But, in an inquiry where all the elements are so closely interwoven as they are in the field of social life, the point of departure becomes almost indifferent. Wherever we start we shall, if we are quite frank and consistent, be led on to look at the whole from some central point, and this, I think, has happened to us in working with the conception of "liberty." For, beginning with the right of the individual, and the antithesis between personal freedom

and social control, we have been led on to a point at which we regard
liberty as primarily a matter of social interest, as something flowing
from the necessities of continuous advance in those regions of truth
and of ethics which constitute the matters of highest social concern.
At the same time, we have come to look for the effect of liberty in the
firmer establishment of social solidarity, as the only foundation on
which such solidarity can securely rest. We have, in fact, arrived by
a path of our own at that which is ordinarily described as the organic
conception of the relation between the individual and society—a
conception towards which Mill worked through his career, and which
forms the starting-point of T. H. Green's philosophy alike in ethics
and in politics.

The term organic is so much used and abused that it is best to
state simply what it means. A thing is called organic when it is made
up of parts which are quite distinct from one another, but which are
destroyed or vitally altered when they are removed from the whole.
Thus, the human body is organic because its life depends on the
functions performed by many organs, while each of these organs
depends in turn on the life of the body, perishing and decomposing if
removed therefrom. Now, the organic view of society is equally
simple. It means that, while the life of society is nothing but the
life of individuals as they act one upon another, the life of the individual in turn would be something utterly different if he could be
separated from society. A great deal of him would not exist at all.
Even if he himself could maintain physical existence by the luck and
skill of a Robinson Crusoe, his mental and moral being would, if it
existed at all, be something quite different from anything that we
know. By language, by training, by simply living with others, each of
us absorbs into his system the social atmosphere that surrounds us.
In particular, in the matter of rights and duties which is cardinal for
Liberal theory, the relation of the individual to the community is
everything. His rights and his duties are alike defined by the common good. What, for example, is my right? On the face of it, it is
something that I claim. But a mere claim is nothing. I might claim
anything and everything. If my claim is of right it is because it is
sound, well grounded, in the judgment of an impartial observer. But
an impartial observer will not consider me alone. He will equally
weigh the opposed claims of others. He will take us in relation to
one another, that is to say, as individuals involved in a social relationship. Further, if his decision is in any sense a rational one, it must

rest on a principle of some kind; and again, as a rational man, any principle which he asserts he must found on some good result which it serves or embodies, and as an impartial man he must take the good of everyone affected into account. That is to say, he must found his judgment on the common good. An individual right, then, cannot conflict with the common good, nor could any right exist apart from the common good.

The argument might seem to make the individual too subservient to society. But this is to forget the other side of the original supposition. Society consists wholly of persons. It has no distinct personality separate from and superior to those of its members. It has, indeed, a certain collective life and character. The British nation is a unity with a life of its own. But the unity is constituted by certain ties that bind together all British subjects, which ties are in the last resort feelings and ideas, sentiments of patriotism, of kinship, a common pride, and a thousand more subtle sentiments that bind together men who speak a common language, have behind them a common history, and understand one another as they can understand no one else. The British nation is not a mysterious entity over and above the forty odd millions of living souls who dwell together under a common law. Its life is their life, its well-being or ill-fortune their well-being or ill-fortune. Thus, the common good to which each man's rights are subordinate is a good in which each man has a share. This share consists in realizing his capacities of feeling, of loving, of mental and physical energy, and in realizing these he plays his part in the social life, or, in Green's phrase, he finds his own good in the common good.

Now, this phrase, it must be admitted, involves a certain assumption, which may be regarded as the fundamental postulate of the organic view of society. It implies that such a fulfillment or full development of personality is practically possible not for one man only but for all members of a community. There must be a line of development open along which each can move in harmony with others. Harmony in the full sense would involve not merely absence of conflict but actual support. There must be for each, then, possibilities of development such as not merely to permit but actively to further the development of others. Now, the older economists conceived a natural harmony, such that the interests of each would, if properly understood and unchecked by outside interference, inevitably lead him in courses profitable to others and to society at large. We saw that this assumption was too optimistic. The conception which we have now reached does not assume so much. It postulates, not that there is an actually existing harmony requiring nothing but prudence and coolness of judgment for its effective operation, but only that there is a possible ethical harmony, to which, partly by discipline, partly by the improvement of the conditions of life, men might attain, and that in such attainment lies the social ideal. To attempt the systematic proof of this postulate would take us into the field of philosophical first principles. It is the point at which the philosophy of politics comes into contact with that of ethics. It must suffice to say here that, just as the endeavor to establish coherent system in the world of thought is the characteristic of the rational impulse which lies at the root of science and philosophy, so the impulse to establish harmony in the world of feeling and action—a harmony which must include all those who think and feel—is of the essence of the rational impulse in the world of practice. To move towards harmony is the persistent impulse of the rational being, even if the goal lies always beyond the reach of accomplished effort.

These principles may appear very abstract, remote from practical life, and valueless for concrete teaching. But this remoteness is of the nature of first principles when taken without the connecting links that bind them to the details of experience. To find some of these links let us take up again our old Liberal principles, and see how they look in the light of the organic, or, as we may now call it, the harmonic conception. We shall readily see, to begin with, that the old idea of equality has its place. For the common good includes every individual. It is founded on personality, and postulates free scope for the development of personality in each member of the community. This is the foundation not only of equal rights before the law, but also of what is called equality of opportunity. It does not necessarily imply actual equality of treatment for all persons any more than it implies original equality of powers.* It does, I think, imply that whatever inequality of actual treatment, of income, rank, office, consideration, there be in a good social system, it would rest, not on the interest of the favored individual as such, but on the common good. If the existence of millionaires on the one hand and of paupers on the other is just, it must be because such contrasts are the result of an economic system which upon the whole works out for the common good, the good of the pauper being included therein as well as the good of the

---

* An absurd misconception fostered principally by opponents of equality for controversial purposes.

millionaire; that is to say, that when we have well weighed the good and the evil of all parties concerned we can find no alternative open to us which could do better for the good of all. I am not for the moment either attacking or defending any economic system. I point out only that this is the position which according to the organic or harmonic view of society must be made good by any rational defense of grave inequality in the distribution of wealth. In relation to equality, indeed, it appears, oddly enough, that the harmonic principle can adopt wholesale, and even expand, one of the "Rights of Man" as formulated in 1789—"Social distinctions can only be founded upon common utility." If it is really just that A should be superior to B in wealth or power or position, it is only because when the good of all concerned is considered, among whom B is one, it turns out that there is a net gain in the arrangement as compared with any alternative that we can devise.

If we turn from equality to liberty, the general lines of argument have already been indicated, and the discussion of difficulties in detail must be left for the next chapter. It need only be repeated here that on the harmonic principle the fundamental importance of liberty rests on the nature of the "good" itself, and that whether we are thinking of the good of society or the good of the individual. The good is something attained by the development of the basal factors of personality, a development proceeding by the widening of ideas, the awakening of the imagination, the play of affection and passion, the strengthening and extension of rational control. As it is the development of these factors in each human being that makes his life worth having, so it is their harmonious interaction, the response of each to each, that makes of society a living whole. Liberty so interpreted cannot, as we have seen, dispense with restraint; restraint, however, is not an end but a means to an end, and one of the principal elements in that end is the enlargement of liberty.

But the collective activity of the community does not necessarily proceed by coercion or restraint. The more securely it is founded on freedom and general willing assent, the more it is free to work out all the achievements in which the individual is feeble or powerless while combined action is strong. Human progress, on whatever side we consider it, is found to be in the main social progress, the work of conscious or unconscious co-operation. In this work voluntary association plays a large and increasing part. But the State is one form of association among others, distinguished by its use of coercive power, by its supremacy, and by its claim to control all who dwell within its geographical limits. What the functions of such a form of association are to be we shall have to consider a little further in connection with the other questions which we have already raised. But that, in general, we are justified in regarding the State as one among many forms of human association for the maintenance and improvement of life is the general principle that we have to point out here, and this is the point at which we stand furthest from the older Liberalism. We have, however, already seen some reason for thinking that the older doctrines led, when carefully examined, to a more enlarged conception of State action than appeared on the surface; and we shall see more fully before we have done that the "positive" conception of the State which we have now reached not only involves no conflict with the true principle of personal liberty, but is necessary to its effective realization.

There is, in addition, one principle of historic Liberalism with which our present conception of the State is in full sympathy. The conception of the common good as it has been explained can be realized in its fullness only through the common will. There are, of course, elements of value in the good government of a benevolent despot or of a fatherly aristocracy. Within any peaceful order there is room for many good things to flourish. But the full fruit of social progress is only to be reaped by a society in which the generality of men and women are not only passive recipients but practical contributors. To make the rights and responsibilities of citizens real and living, and to extend them as widely as the conditions of society allow, is thus an integral part of the organic conception of society, and the justification of the democratic principle. It is, at the same time, the justification of nationalism so far as nationalism is founded on a true interpretation of history. For, inasmuch as the true social harmony rests on feeling and makes use of all the national ties of kinship, of neighborliness, of congruity of character and belief, and of language and mode of life, the best, healthiest, and most vigorous political unit is that to which men are by their own feelings strongly drawn. Any breach of such unity, whether by forcible disruption or by compulsory inclusion in a larger society of alien sentiments and laws, tends to mutilate—or, at lowest, to cramp—the spontaneous development of social life. National and personal freedom are growths of the same root, and their historic connection rests on no accident, but on ultimate identity of idea.

Thus in the organic conception of society each of the leading ideas of historic Liberalism has its part to play. The ideal society is conceived as a whole which lives and flourishes by the harmonious growth of its parts, each of which in developing on its own lines and in accordance with its own nature tends on the whole to further the development of others. There is some elementary trace of such harmony in every form of social life that can maintain itself, for if the conflicting impulses predominated society would break up, and when they do predominate society does break up. At the other extreme, true harmony is an ideal which it is perhaps beyond the power of man to realize, but which serves to indicate the line of advance. But to admit this is to admit that the lines of possible development for each individual or, to use a more general phrase, for each constituent of the social order are not limited and fixed. There are many possibilities, and the course that will in the end make for social harmony is only one among them, while the possibilities of disharmony and conflict are many. The progress of society like that of the individual depends, then, ultimately on choice. It is not "natural," in the sense in which a physical law is natural, that is, in the sense of going forward automatically from stage to stage without backward turnings, deflections to the left, or fallings away on the right. It is natural only in this sense, that it is the expression of deep-seated forces of human nature which come to their own only by an infinitely slow and cumbersome process of mutual adjustment. Every constructive social doctrine rests the conception of human progress. The heart of Liberalism is the understanding that progress is not a matter of mechanical contrivance, but of the liberation of living spiritual energy. Good mechanism is that which provides the channels wherein such energy can flow unimpeded, unobstructed by its own exuberance of output, vivifying the social structure, expanding and ennobling the life of mind.

61. HERBERT C. HOOVER

Herbert C. Hoover (1874- 1965) was President of the United States from 1929 to 1933. A lifelong supporter of democratic capitalism, and the freedom of private enterprise essential to it, he has argued that many programs which have recently been called liberalism do not genuinely deserve the name; for in advocating central administration, and the entrance of the state into economic affairs, they have moved toward the ultimate restriction, not enlargement, of liberty.

What is Real Liberalism? *

We hear much as to who is a Tory, a Reactionary, a Conservative, a Liberal, or a Radical. These terms when used honestly reflect an attitude of mind. The political use of them was imported from England. They do not fit well in America. However, they have certain advantages. You can elect yourself to any one of these groups if you say it often enough. If you do not like anybody you can consign him to the one which is most hated by your listener.

Taking a compound of definitions coming out of Washington, the impression would be that the Tories do the money-changing. The Reactionaries are members of well-warmed and well-stocked clubs. The Conservatives are greedily trying to keep their jobs and their savings. The Liberals have the exclusive right to define the opinions of others. The Radicals do not know what to do but do it in every direction.

As a matter of serious fact, these terms have been used mostly for camouflage and for political assassination.

The natural choice of youth is toward true liberalism. True liberalism seeks all legitimate freedom first, in the confident belief that without such freedom the pursuit of other blessings is in vain. Liberalism is a force true of the spirit, proceeding from the deep realization that economic freedom cannot be sacrificed if political freedom is to be preserved.

It is a false liberalism that interprets itself into dictation by government. Every step in that direction crushes the very roots of liberalism. It is the road not to liberty but to less liberty. The spirit of liberalism is to create free men. It is not the regimentation of men. It is not the extension of bureaucracy. You cannot extend the mastery of government over the daily life of a people without somewhere making it master of people's souls and thoughts.

* From H. C. Hoover, *Addresses upon the American Road*, 1933-1938. Reprinted by permission of the publisher, Charles Scribner's Sons, New York. This passage is from a speech delivered in Colorado Springs, Colo., March 7, 1936.

Today, however, the term Liberal is claimed by every sect that would limit human freedom and stagnate the human soul—whether they be Fascists, Socialists, Communists, Epics, or New Dealers.

This misuse of English political terms is used to cover the confusion of thought that pumps from the New Deal. Yet our American problems cut squarely across such muddy classifications.

If an open mind, free to search for the truth and apply it in government, is liberal, then you should be liberal.

If belief in open opportunity and equal opportunity has become conservative, then you should be conservative.

If belief that this can be held only in a society of orderly individual initiative and enterprise is conservative, then you should be conservative.

If opposition to those things which abuse and limit equal opportunity, such as privilege, monopolies, exploitation, or oppression whether in business or in government, is liberal, then you should be liberal.

If opposition to managed economy whether of the Socialist, Fascist, or New Deal pattern is Tory, then you should be Tory.

If the humane action to eliminate such abominations as slum squalor, child labor, and sweated labor, to give greater protection from unemployment and old age is radical, then you should be radical.

If the use of all the powers of the government to relieve our people from hunger and cold in calamity is radical, then you should be radical.

If belief in the old-fashioned virtues of self-reliance, thrift, government economy, of a balanced budget, of a stable currency, of fidelity of government to its obligations is reactionary, then you should be reactionary.

If holding to the Bill of Rights with its safeguards of the balance of powers and local government is Tory, then you should be Tory.

If demand that change in the Constitution be by open submission to the people and not by subterfuge constitutes reaction, then again you should be reactionary.

If demand that we have a government of laws and not of bureaucrats is conservative, then you should be conservative.

If you agree with all this, then you have shed yourselves of many "isms" or you have melted them into plain Americanism.

If you add to that a belief in decency of Americans, a conception of spiritual prosperity, and a faith in the greatness of America, you will have lifted these realities to the realms of idealism.

But it all sums up to this—whether the choice of youth will be to carry on that liberty for which Americans have died upon a thousand battlefields. . . .

The Fifth Freedom*

The President of the United States on January 6, 1942, stated that we seek "everywhere in the world" the four old freedoms: freedom of speech and expression, freedom of religion, freedom from fear, freedom from want.

Soon thereafter I called attention to the fact that there is a Fifth Freedom—economic freedom—without which none of the other four freedoms will be realized.

I have stated many times over the years that to be free, men must choose their jobs and callings, bargain for their own wages and salaries, save and provide by private property for their families and old age. And they must be free to engage in enterprise so long as each does not injure his fellowmen. And that requires laws to prevent abuse. And when I use the term "Fifth Freedom," I use it in this sense only, not in the sense of laissez faire or economic exploitation. Exploitation is the negation of freedom. The Fifth Freedom does not mean going back to abuses.

Laws to prevent men doing economic injury to their fellows were universal in civilized countries long before the first World War. In the United States, for example, the State and Federal Governments had established regulation of banks, railroads, utilities, coinage; prevention of combinations to restrain trade; government support to credit in times of stress; public works; tariffs; limitations on hours of labor and in other directions.

The key of such government action to economic freedom is that government must not destroy but promote freedom. When Governments exert regulation of economic life, they must do so by definite statutory rules of conduct imposed by legislative bodies that all men may read as they run and in which they may have at all times the

* From H. C. Hoover, *Addresses upon the American Road,* 1941-1945. Reprinted by permission of the publisher, D. Van Nostrand Company, New York.

protection of the courts. No final judicial or legislative authority must be delegated to bureaucrats, or at once tyranny begins.

When Government violates these principles, it sooner or later weakens constitutional safeguards of personal liberty and representative government.

When Government goes into business in competition with citizens, bureaucracy always relies upon tyranny to win. And bureaucracy never develops that competence in management which comes from the mills of competition. Its conduct of business inevitably lowers the living standards of the people. Nor does bureaucracy ever discover or invent. A Millikan, Ford, or Edison never came from a bureaucracy.

And inherent in bureaucracy is the grasping spirit of more and more power. It always resents criticism and sooner or later begins directly or indirectly to limit free speech and free press. Intellectual and spiritual freedom will not long survive the passing of economic freedom. One of the illusions of our time is that we can have totalitarian economics and the personal freedoms. Ten nations on the Continent of Europe tried it and wound up with dictators and no liberty.

The first trench in the battle for the five freedoms is to maintain them in America. That rests upon fidelity not only to the letter, but to the spirit of constitutional government. Failure of Congress to assert its responsibilities or for the Executive to take steps beyond the authority of Congress is a direct destruction of the safeguards of freedom. We badly need a complete overhaul of our governmental relations to the Fifth Freedom if it is to be preserved.

The Fifth Freedom in no way inhibits social reforms and social advancement. In fact, it furnishes the increasing resources upon which such progress can be built. And itself flourishes upon the advancing social aspirations of our people. Social advancement was part of the whole American concept during the whole of our national life. The greatest of all social advances was free education. Next came concern for public health. We have always held it an obligation to prevent suffering from misfortune, to care for widows, orphans, and old age, and those upon whom disaster falls.

The methods have gradually improved from the ancient workhouse, the asylum, and the county hospital to more systematic and more inclusive action. And that more inclusive action has only been possible with the growing wealth born from the Fifth Freedom. For many years in the United States our States and the nation have been gradually developing protection to children, to women, limitation of hours, and safeguards of health in industry. From these 48 laboratories we have seen the development of such actions as public health control, hospitalization, care of children, workmen's compensation, unemployment and health insurance, old-age, widows', and orphans' pensions. They are not new ideas. As we expand in these purposes, there are safeguards to liberty that can and must be preserved.

One of these safeguards is where personal insurance for any purpose is given by the Government it must be contributory. Even where subsidized by the Federal Government it should be administered by the States to limit the growth of centralized bureaucracy and political action.

Liberty has its greatest protection from local not centralized government.

Another concept in all social insurance or pensions must be that the responsibility of the people as a whole is to provide only a reasonable subsistence basis. Beyond that the citizen must look after himself if initiative and self-respect are to be maintained. Today our measures in these matters badly need vigorous overhauling to make them comport with these fundamental principles; to put them upon a "pay-as-you-go" basis; to make them inclusive of everybody; and to make them synchronize and not destroy private institutions and efforts.

A system devoted to development of individuality and personal freedom is a complicated business. It can destroy its own purposes by foolish action.

Today we are faced with the relation of personal liberty to total war. Our people must be mobilized for that immediate purpose.

We must sacrifice much economic freedom to win the war. That is economic Fascism, for Fascist economics were born of just these measures in the last war. But there are two vast differences in the application of this sort of economic system at the hands of democracies or at the hands of dictators. First, in democracies we strive to keep free speech, free press, free worship, trial by jury, and the other personal liberties alive. And, second, we want so to design our actions that these Fascist economic measures are not frozen into life, but shall thaw out after the war.

Even the temporary suspension of economic liberty creates grave dangers because liberty rapidly atrophies from disuse. Vested interests and vested habits grow around its restrictions. It would be a vain thing to fight the war and lose our own liberties. If we would have them return, we must hold furiously to the ideals of economic liberty. We must challenge every departure from them. There are just two tests: "Is this departure necessary to win the war?" "How are we going to restore these freedoms after the war?"

We have no right to complain of necessary sacrifices. Our soldiers and sailors are deprived of all their freedoms except the right to grouse a little. But they will expect their freedoms back when they come home.

Under the stress of reconstruction after the war, our liberties will be slow in coming back, but the essential thing in this sort of question is the direction in which we travel. We must establish the direction now.

62. FRIEDRICH A. HAYEK

Friedrich A. Hayek (1899-   ) is one of the most vigorous critics of the tendency toward increased state control of economic activity. In a democracy, he argues, the attempt to engage in long-range economic planning forces the society to make decisions which are not really within the power of its elected assembly—thereby paving the way for the elevation of economic "experts" who become, eventually, economic dictators. He contends that planned economy and a democratic society are, of necessity, incompatible. The case for the essential relation between political democracy and individual economic freedom is effectively presented in his book, The Road to Serfdom, *from which the following passages are taken.*

Planning and Democracy*

The common features of all collectivist systems may be described, in a phrase ever dear to socialists of all schools, as the deliberate organization of the labors of society for a definite social goal. That our present society lacks such "conscious" direction toward a single

* From F. Hayek, *The Road to Serfdom,* 1944. © 1944 by the University of Chicago Press. Reprinted by permission of the University of Chicago Press and of Routledge and Kegan Paul, Ltd.

aim, that its activities are guided by the whims and fancies of irresponsible individuals, has always been one of the main complaints of its socialist critics.

In many ways this puts the basic issue very clearly. And it directs us at once to the point where the conflict arises between individual freedom and collectivism. The various kinds of collectivism, communism, fascism, etc., differ among themselves in the nature of the goal toward which they want to direct the efforts of society. But they all differ from liberalism and individualism in wanting to organize the whole of society and all its resources for this unitary end and in refusing to recognize autonomous spheres in which the ends of the individuals are supreme. In short, they are totalitarian in the true sense of this new word which we have adopted to describe the unexpected but nevertheless inseparable manifestations of what in theory we call collectivism.

The "social goal," or "common purpose," for which society is to be organized is usually vaguely described as the "common good," the "general welfare," or the "general interest." It does not need much reflection to see that these terms have no sufficiently definite meaning to determine a particular course of action. The welfare and the happiness of millions cannot be measured on a single scale of less and more. The welfare of a people, like the happiness of a man, depends on a great many things that can be provided in an infinite variety of combinations. It cannot be adequately expressed as a single end, but only as a hierarchy of ends, a comprehensive scale of values in which every need of every person is given its place. To direct all our activities according to a single plan presupposes that every one of our needs is given its rank in an order of values which must be complete enough to make it possible to decide among all the different courses which the planner has to choose. It presupposes, in short, the existence of a complete ethical code in which all the different human values are allotted their due place.

The conception of a complete ethical code is unfamiliar, and it requires some effort of imagination to see what it involves. We are not in the habit of thinking of moral codes as more or less complete. The fact that we are constantly choosing between different values without a social code prescribing how we ought to choose does not surprise us and does not suggest to us that our moral code is incomplete. In our society there is neither occasion nor reason why people should develop common views about what should be done in such situations. But where all the means to be used are the property of society and are to be used in the name of society according to a unitary plan, a "social" view about what ought to be done must guide all decisions. In such a world we should soon find that our moral code is full of gaps.

We are not concerned here with the question whether it would be desirable to have such a complete ethical code. It may merely be pointed out that up to the present the growth of civilization has been accompanied by a steady diminution of the sphere in which individual actions are bound by fixed rules. The rules of which our common moral code consists have progressively become fewer and more general in character. From the primitive man, who was bound by an elaborate ritual in almost every one of his daily activities, who was limited by innumerable taboos, and who could scarcely conceive of doing things in a way different from his fellows, morals have more and more tended to become merely limits circumscribing the sphere within which the individual could behave as he liked. The adoption of a common ethical code comprehensive enough to determine a unitary economic plan would mean a complete reversal of this tendency.

The essential point for us is that no such complete ethical code exists. The attempt to direct all economic activity according to a single plan would raise innumerable questions to which the answer could be provided only by a moral rule, but to which existing morals have no answer and where there exists no agreed view on what ought to be done. People will have either no definite views or conflicting views in such questions, because in the free society in which we have lived there has been no occasion to think about them and still less to form common opinions about them.

Not only do we not possess such an all-inclusive scale of values: it would be impossible for any mind to comprehend the infinite variety of different needs of different people which compete for the available resources and to attach a definite weight to each. For our problem it is of minor importance whether the ends for which any person cares comprehend only his own individual needs, or whether they include the needs of his closer or even those of his more distant fellows—that is, whether he is egoistic or altruistic in the ordinary senses of these words. The point which is so important is the basic fact that it is impossible for any man to survey more than a limited field, to be aware of the urgency of more than a limited number of needs. Whether his interests center round his own physical needs, or whether he takes a warm interest in the welfare of every human being he knows, the ends about which he can be concerned will always be only an infinitesimal fraction of the needs of all men.

This is the fundamental fact on which the whole philosophy of individualism is based. It does not assume, as is often asserted, that man is egoistic or selfish or ought to be. It merely starts from the indisputable fact that the limits of our powers of imagination make it impossible to include in our scale of values more than a sector of the needs of the whole society, and that, since, strictly speaking, scales of value can exist only in individual minds, nothing but partial scales of values exist—scales which are inevitably different and often inconsistent with each other. From this the individualist concludes that the individuals should be allowed, within defined limits, to follow their own values and preferences rather than somebody else's; that within these spheres the individual's system of ends should be supreme and not subject to any dictation by others. It is this recognition of the individual as the ultimate judge of his ends, the belief that as far as possible his own views ought to govern his actions, that forms the essence of the individualist position.

This view does not, of course, exclude the recognition of social ends, or rather of a coincidence of individual ends which makes it advisable for men to combine for their pursuit. But it limits such common action to the instances where individual views coincide; what are called "social ends" are for it merely identical ends of many individuals—or ends to the achievement of which individuals are willing to contribute in return for the assistance they receive in the satisfaction of their own desires. Common action is thus limited to the fields where people agree on common ends. Very frequently these common ends will not be ultimate ends to the individuals but means which different persons can use for different purposes. In fact, people are most likely to agree on common action where the common end is not an ultimate end to them but a means capable of serving a great variety of purposes.

When individuals combine in a joint effort to realize ends they have in common, the organizations, like the state, that they form for this purpose are given their own system of ends and their own means. But any organization thus formed remains one "person" among others, in the case of the state much more powerful than any of the others, it is true, yet still with its separate and limited sphere in which alone its ends are supreme. The limits of this sphere

are determined by the extent to which the individuals agree on particular ends; and the probability that they will agree on a particular
course of action necessarily decreases as the scope of such action
extends. There are certain functions of the state on the exercise of
which there will be practical unanimity among its citizens; there will
be others on which there will be agreement of a substantial majority;
and so on, until we come to fields where, although each individual
might wish the state to act in some way, there will be almost as
many views about what the government should do as there are different people.

We can rely on voluntary agreement to guide the action of the
state only so long as it is confined to spheres where agreement exists.
But not only when the state undertakes direct control in fields
where there is no such agreement is it bound to suppress individual
freedom. We can unfortunately not indefinitely extend the sphere of
common action and still leave the individual free in his own sphere.
Once the communal sector, in which the state controls all the means,
exceeds a certain proportion of the whole, the effects of its actions
dominate the whole system. Although the state controls directly the
use of only a large part of the available resources, the effects of its
decisions on the remaining part of the economic system become so
great that indirectly it controls almost everything. Where, as was,
for example, true in Germany as early as 1928, the central and local
authorities directly control the use of more than half the national
income (according to an official German estimate then, 53 per cent),
they control indirectly almost the whole economic life of the nation.
There is, then, scarcely an individual end which is not dependent for
its achievement on the action of the state, and the "social scale of
values" which guides the state's action must embrace practically all
individual ends.

It is not difficult to see what must be the consequences when
democracy embarks upon a course of planning which in its execution
requires more agreement than in fact exists. The people may have
agreed on adopting a system of directed economy because they have
been convinced that it will produce great prosperity. In the discussions
leading to the decision, the goal of planning will have been described
by some such term as "common welfare," which only conceals the
absence of real agreement on the ends of planning. Agreement will
in fact exist only on the mechanism to be used. But it is a mechanism
which can be used only for a common end; and the question of the

precise goal toward which all activity is to be directed will arise as soon as the executive power has to translate the demand for a single plan into particular plan. Then it will appear that the agreement on the desirability of planning is not supported by agreement on the ends the plan is to serve. The effect of the people's agreeing that there must be central planning, without agreeing on the ends, will be rather as if a group of people were to commit themselves to take a journey together without agreeing where they want to go: with the result that they may all have to make a journey which most of them do not want at all. That planning creates a situation in which it is necessary for us to agree on a much larger number of topics than we have been used to, and that in a planned system we cannot confine collective action to the tasks on which we can agree but are forced to produce agreement on everything in order that any action can be taken at all, is one of the features which contributes more than most to determining the character of a planned system.

It may be the unanimously expressed will of the people that its parliament should prepare a comprehensive economic plan, yet neither the people nor its representatives need therefore be able to agree on any particular plan. The inability of democratic assemblies to carry out what seems to be a clear mandate of the people will inevitably cause dissatisfaction with democratic institutions. Parliaments come to be regarded as ineffective "talking shops," unable or incompetent to carry out the tasks for which they have been chosen. The conviction grows that if efficient planning is to be done, the direction must be "taken out of politics" and placed in the hands of experts—permanent officials or independent autonomous bodies.

The difficulty is well known to socialists. It will soon be half a century since the Webbs began to complain of "the increased incapacity of the House of Commons to cope with its work." * More recently, Professor Laski has elaborated the argument:

"It is common ground that the present parliamentary machine is quite unsuited to pass rapidly a great body of complicated legislation. The National Government, indeed, has in substance admitted this by implementing its economy and tariff measures not by detailed debate in the House of Commons but by a wholesale system of delegated legislation. A Labour Government would, I presume, build upon the amplitude of this precedent. It would confine the House of Commons to the two functions it can properly perform: the ventilation

* Sidney and Beatrice Webb, *Industrial Democracy* (1897), p. 800 n.

of grievances and the discussion of general principles of its measures. Its Bills would take the form of general formulae conferring wide powers on the appropriate government departments; and those powers would be exercised by Order in Council which could, if desired, be attacked in the House by means of a vote of no confidence. The necessity and value of delegated legislation has recently been strongly reaffirmed by the Donoughmore Committee; and its extension is inevitable if the process of socialisation is not to be wrecked by the normal methods of obstruction which existing parliamentary procedure sanctions."

And to make it quite clear that a socialist government must not allow itself to be too much fettered by democratic procedure, Professor Laski at the end of the same article raised the question "whether in a period of transition to Socialism, a Labour Government can risk the overthrow of its measures as a result of the next general election"—and left it significantly unanswered.*

It is important clearly to see the causes of this admitted ineffectiveness of parliaments when it comes to a detailed administration of the economic affairs of a nation. The fault is neither with the individual representatives nor with parliamentary institutions as such but with the contradictions inherent in the task with which they are charged. They are not asked to act where they can agree, but to produce agreement on everything—the whole direction of the resources of the nation. For such a task the system of majority decision is, however, not suited. Majorities will be found where it is a choice between limited alternatives; but it is a superstition to believe that there must be a majority view on everything. There is no reason why there should be a majority in favor of any one of the different possible courses of positive action if their number is legion. Every

---

* H. J. Laski, "Labour and the Constitution," *New Statesman and Nation*, No. 81 (new ser.), September 10, 1932, p. 277. In a book (*Democracy in Crisis* [1933], particularly p. 87) in which Professor Laski later elaborated these ideas, his determination that parliamentary democracy must not be allowed to form an obstacle to the realization of socialism is even more plainly expressed: not only would a socialist government "take vast powers and legislate under them by ordinance and decree" and "suspend the classic formulae of normal opposition" but the "continuance of parliamentary government would depend on its [i.e., the Labour government's] possession of guarantees from the Conservative Party that its work of transformation would not be disrupted by repeal in the event of its defeat at the polls" ;

As Professor Laski invokes the authority of the Donoughmore Committee, it may be worth recalling that Professor Laski was a member of that committee and presumably one of the authors of its report.

member of the legislative assembly might prefer some particular plan for the direction of economic activity to no plan, yet no one plan may appear preferable to a majority to no plan at all.

Nor can a coherent plan be achieved by breaking it up into parts and voting on particular issues. A democratic assembly voting and amending a comprehensive economic plan clause by clause, as it deliberates on an ordinary bill, makes nonsense. An economic plan, to deserve the name, must have a unitary conception. Even if a parliament could, proceeding step by step, agree on some scheme, it would certainly in the end satisfy nobody. A complex whole in which all the parts must be most carefully adjusted to each other cannot be achieved through a compromise between conflicting views. To draw up an economic plan in this fashion is even less possible than, for example, successfully to plan a military campaign by democratic procedure. As in strategy it would become inevitable to delegate the task to the experts.

Yet the difference is that, while the general who is put in charge of a campaign is given a single end to which, for the duration of the campaign, all the means under his control have to be exclusively devoted, there can be no such single goal given to the economic planner, and no similar limitation of the means imposed upon him. The general has not got to balance different independent aims against each other; there is for him only one supreme goal. But the ends of an economic plan, or of any part of it, cannot be defined apart from the particular plan. It is the essence of the economic problem that the making of an economic plan involves the choice between conflicting or competing ends—different needs of different people. But which ends do so conflict, which will have to be sacrificed if we want to achieve certain others, in short, which are the alternatives between which we must choose, can only be known to those who know all the facts; and only they, the experts, are in a position to decide which of the different ends are to be given preference. It is inevitable that they should impose their scale of preferences on the community for which they plan. . . .

The argument by which the planners usually try to reconcile us with this development is that, so long as democracy retains ultimate control, the essentials of democracy are not affected. Thus Karl Mannheim writes:

"The only [*sic*] way in which a planned society differs from that of the nineteenth century is that more and more spheres of social life, and ultimately each and all of them, are subjected to state control. But if a few controls can be held in check by parliamentary sovereignty, so can many. . . . In a democratic state sovereignty can be boundlessly strengthened by plenary powers without renouncing democratic control." *

This belief overlooks a vital distinction. Parliament can, of course, control the execution of tasks where it can give definite directions, where it has first agreed on the aim and merely delegates the working-out of the detail. The situation is entirely different when the reason for the delegation is that there is no real agreement on the ends, when the body charged with the planning has to choose between ends of whose conflict parliament is not even aware, and when the most that can be done is to present to it a plan which has to be accepted or rejected as a whole. There may and probably will be criticism; but as no majority can agree on an alternative plan, and the parts objected to can almost always be represented as essential parts of the whole, it will remain quite ineffective. Parliamentary discussion may be retained as a useful safety valve and even more as a convenient medium through which the official answers to complaints are disseminated. It may even prevent some flagrant abuses and successfully insist on particular shortcomings being remedied. But it cannot direct. It will at best be reduced to choosing the persons who are to have practically absolute power. The whole system will tend toward that plebiscitarian dictatorship in which the head of the government is from time to time confirmed in his position by popular vote, but where he has all the powers at his command to make certain that the vote will go in the direction he desires.

It is the price of democracy that the possibilities of conscious control are restricted to the fields where true agreement exists and that in some fields things must be left to chance. But in a society which for its functioning depends on central planning this control cannot be made dependent on a majority's being able to agree; it will often be necessary that the will of a small minority be imposed upon the people, because this minority will be the largest group able to agree among themselves on the question at issue. Democratic government has worked successfully where, and so long as, the functions of government were, by a widely accepted creed, restricted to fields where agreement among a majority could be achieved by free discussion; and it is the great merit of the liberal creed that it reduced

* *Man and Society in an Age of Reconstruction* (1940), p. 340.

the range of subjects on which agreement was necessary to one on which it was likely to exist in a society of free men. It is now often said that democracy will not tolerate "capitalism." If "capitalism" means here a competitive system based on free disposal over private property, it is far more important to realize that only within this system is democracy possible. When it becomes dominated by a collectivist creed, democracy will inevitably destroy itself.

We have no intention, however, of making a fetish of democracy. It may well be true that our generation talks and thinks too much of democracy and too little of the values which it serves. It cannot be said of democracy, as Lord Acton truly said of liberty, that it "is not a means to a higher political end. It is itself the highest political end. It is not for the sake of a good public administration that it is required, but for the security in the pursuit of the highest objects of civil society, and of private life." Democracy is essentially a means, a utilitarian device for safeguarding internal peace and individual freedom. As such it is by no means infallible or certain. Nor must we forget that there has often been much more cultural and spiritual freedom under an autocratic rule than under some democracies—and it is at least conceivable that under the government of a very homogeneous and doctrinaire majority democratic government might be as oppressive as the worst dictatorship. Our point, however, is not that dictatorship must inevitably extirpate freedom but rather that planning leads to dictatorship because dictatorship is the most effective instrument of coercion and the enforcement of ideals and, as such, essential if central planning on a large scale is to be possible. The clash between planning and democracy arises simply from the fact that the latter is an obstacle to the suppression of freedom which the direction of economic activity requires. But in so far as democracy ceases to be a guaranty of individual freedom, it may well persist in some form under a totalitarian regime. A true "dictatorship of the proletariat," even if democratic in form, if it undertook centrally to direct the economic system, would probably destroy personal freedom as completely as any autocracy has ever done.

The fashionable concentration on democracy as the main value threatened is not without danger. It is largely responsible for the misleading and unfounded belief that, so long as the ultimate source of power is the will of the majority, the power cannot be arbitrary.

The false assurance which many people derive from this belief is an important cause of the general unawareness of the dangers which we face. There is no justification for the belief that, so long as power is conferred by democratic procedure, it cannot be arbitrary; the contrast suggested by this statement is altogether false: it is not the source but the limitation of power which prevents it from being arbitrary. Democratic control *may* prevent power from becoming arbitrary, but it does not do so by its mere existence. If democracy resolves on a task which necessarily involves the use of power which cannot be guided by fixed rules, it must become arbitrary power.

63. SOCIALISM: A NEW STATEMENT OF PRINCIPLES

The new statement of democratic socialist principles, from which the following passages are taken, was written by a left-wing group within the Labour Party in Great Britain, and represents the views of a large segment of that Party. It clearly discloses the ethical idealism of British socialism, as well as its active drive for social reconstruction, within a democratic framework.

The Distinctive Features of Socialism*

These ideals,† so dear to socialists, are by no means confined to socialists alone. They have a long and venerable history and have commanded the devotion of many different schools of thought. In every age they have inspired movements for social progress; they are no one's monopoly. What then, has distinguished socialists from other strivers for a better world?

In seeking the answer let us turn for a moment to history. The

* From *Socialism: A New Statement of Principles*, 1958. Reprinted by permission of Socialist Commentary Publications, London.

† The preceding chapter had been devoted to the three basic ideals which underlie socialist activity: equality, freedom, and fellowship.—*Ed.*

industrial countries of the nineteenth century were the cradle of socialism. The class structure of society, as it took shape in that particular environment, was seen as the fount of evil, the daily violator of every noble ideal. Not the improvidence of workers, nor the cupidity of employers, nor even some divine dispensation had brought this misery to man, but the class system. The first thing to be done, then, was to abolish it. The recognition that social injustice could be removed only by transforming the economic structure gave the socialist movement its special character.

This great task could only be accomplished by the independent organisation of the workers, and circumstances gave the workers their opportunity to organise. Herded together as they were in towns and factories, the very conditions of their existence helped to make them aware of their common suffering and their common need for organisation if they were to improve their lot. They formed trade unions for defence and joined in political agitation to extend their social influence; step by step organised labour became the main vehicle for radical reform. On this practical foundation the modern socialist movement was built.

But these conditions in Western Europe a century ago were neither permanent nor universal. In Britain itself the class structure has been transformed. Our society is no longer split into two distinct classes with a chasm between them. Today power is based on function as well as on ownership of wealth. Managers, administrators, even trade union officials, hold key positions, and privilege has clothed itself in new forms. The composition of the labour movement has also shifted. The organised manual workers are still the hard core, but other underprivileged groups are now embraced as well, and there are many middle-class adherents. The very nature of the Labour Party has changed to reflect these new circumstances. It is no longer a "class" party in the old sense, representing manual workers only; it is a national party in which many diverse interests find a home.

Other countries have other settings. The cleavages may not be between "capital" and "labour," and there may not be the conditions for nation-wide working-class organisation. In less developed lands the class structure may rest on slavery, or feudalism or landlordism. The United States, with its large farming community and dominant "middle-class," has a structure all its own. Does this mean that socialism has no place in these different environments?

If we think of socialism in its particular nineteenth century European form, then it can of course have no universal application. But these special features are not its essentials. Some kind of socialist movement has its place in every class society. In most countries there are three main reform movements in democratic political life. The first wishes to conserve the existing order; reforms are necessary but only as grudging concessions to maintain the political influence of the privileged. The second is composed of those genuine reformers, who, while their consciences are outraged by social evils, believe that these can be cured without endangering the class structure. The third are the socialists, who, in view of their analysis of society, take their stand on the need to change the "system"—in the famous phrase of the Irish socialist, James Connolly, to bring "the axe to the root." For them, political action based on the organisation of the underprivileged classes—whether industrial workers, or peasants, or serfs—is necessary, because ideals do not realise themselves; power must be met by power.

Nearly every country has a movement for social reform of this third kind. It may not call itself socialist; conditions may require of it a programme only distantly related to our own. But all these movements are our allies as long as they have the same broad identity of purpose. So in Britain, as long as a class structure persists and is challenged by political action, we as socialists will have our distinctive character, however our detailed policies may change with changing circumstances.

Two Misleading Dogmas

Just because we have not always recognised that socialist programmes may vary in time and place, and even in name, the belief took root that there is somewhere, even if only in our imaginations, a "socialist system" with its own unique set of institutions. For European socialists in the nineteenth century the position seemed simple. Capitalism was to be overthrown; something known as socialism would naturally replace it. A straight choice was proclaimed between two clear-cut antithetical systems—destroy the one and the other would supersede it.

Today we know that this is a myth. There are no two distinct and opposing systems, only an infinite series of gradations. No one defines British society today as "socialism," yet it is also not nineteenth century capitalism. All the changes we have seen in our lifetime—full employment, planning, controls, housing programmes, social security, the national health service, progressive taxation—have produced a structure to which no ready-made label can be tagged. It may be said that these changes are a part of the transition to socialism. But have any of us knowledge of a system of institutions which would mark the end of the transition? And if we had, would there be any agreement on their nature?

Obviously no such knowledge and no such agreement exists. Our agreement lies deeper—in our ideals, and in a readiness to take the axe to the root causes of social injustice. The essence of socialism is the perpetual struggle to realise its ideals, whenever and wherever possible. From this one statement a number of vital truths flow. Ideals, by their very nature, are never fully realised, but we can strive all the time for their fuller realisation. What is more, just because they are ideals involving the human spirit, their fulfilment cannot depend only upon changes in the social structure; there must be changes in human attitudes and relationships as well. Further, since institutions are means to an end, their exact form will certainly vary in time and place. No one pattern is sacrosanct. Nor can we ever assert the inevitable success of any new institution; it must always be subject to trial and error. In other words, we must come to the making of institutions with an empirical and not a doctrinaire attitude, for there is no accepted institutional blueprint called "socialism."

Are these statements mere platitudes? Although no one of them is original, yet taken together they may dispel some of the anxieties which cloud socialist thinking today. They deny the dogmas of the past, the failure of which has sapped our confidence. They glorify no particular institution which is bound, like all human creations, to be imperfect. They save us from the disillusionment which is the price of a faith in panaceas. And they show us, with an unflinching certainty, where our own tasks lie. Our first responsibility is to be aware of the implications of our own ideals, and to try to shape society and human attitudes accordingly. After all, society is always in a state of transition. Socialists should strive, unremittingly, for its betterment and not shirk current problems by waiting for the miraculous arrival of a Utopia.

Just as the myth of a "socialist system" took hold of men's minds, so did the illusion that to achieve it the "class struggle" must be intensified. Class struggle is an inevitable feature of class society, but its elevation into the supreme rule of socialist action is another of those doctrines which have not stood the test of events. It served, at one time, to drive home to the workers the important lesson that "no saviour from on high delivers," and so was a dynamic idea helping to bring the organised labour movement into being. But Marxism turned it into a dogma, decreeing that growing class conflict would hasten the great day of the successful, creative revolution. The proletariat was sanctified; it could do no wrong except when misled by its class enemies. The emancipation of the working class was the task of workers alone.

The class struggle is no more a fixed pattern of action for the achievement of socialism than socialism itself is a fixed set of institutions. It is true that those who suffer from the class structure are more likely to fight against it than those to whom it brings advantages. But members of the privileged classes have also played an important part in the struggle for a better society; and some of the underprivileged have, at times, rebelled only in order to gain new privileges for themselves. Classes cannot be divided off into sheep and goats. Even if they could, to pit class against class in the end leads to a naked struggle for power and advantage, destroying the very values which socialists wish most to uphold.

Do we even wish, in a democratic country, deliberately to foster class hatred? There are dangers enough in this sort of hostility, as socialists have experienced in office. Democracy demands a willingness to compromise, an attempt to reconcile conflicting interests. Some common standards of behaviour must be accepted. In any community, interests conflict and power may determine the outcome. But what socialists want are civilised methods for resolving conflicts; power alone must not be the arbiter. Strike action was used to gain recognition and respect for the trade unions, but industrial conflict is not an end in itself. On the contrary, the unions have consistently tried to avoid it through agreed and peaceful methods of settling disputes. The concept of advancing towards our ideal society through hatred and schism has already, at least in this country, been largely discarded in practice.

The Duality of the Labour Movement

With all the comforting myths destroyed, we turn back on our own resources. We are not provided, as many socialists have believed, with a ready-made guidebook in our struggles. All we have is the compass of our ideals. Each new set of circumstances is unmapped terrain; each situation demands special treatment. Constant thought and adaptation, and an undogmatic flexibility in solving problems as they arise, are asked of us. We have not the support of a guarantee of success; everything depends wholly on us; there is no escape from our responsibilities. But this does not mean that the individual must bear his responsibility alone. Society cannot be changed without the effort of an organised movement. Power must be won, and the labour movement remains the main vehicle in the battle.

In twentieth century Britain little distinction is made between the labour and socialist movements. The Labour Party was first called the Socialist Party by its opponents who thought that the name would lose its votes, and socialists were happy enough to carry this burden. Yet it creates confusion, for there is a real difference between the labour movement as a whole and its socialist part.

The labour movement has grown through its ability to meet the natural desire of workers to better their conditions. Immediate, tangible results have increased the membership of the trade unions and the Labour Party, and many workers have supported particular socialist measures for the sake of the advantages they would bring to them. But this is only one side of the medal. Behind the daily struggle for "more and more, here and now" there has been a bigger purpose—the desire for just treatment and for self-determination. As producers in trade unions the workers have not only bargained for better wages, they have wanted control over their working conditions and a share in the direction of industry. As consumers in co-operative societies they have been attracted by the "divi" but also by the idea of independence from capitalist monopolies. As citizens in their local parties they have been concerned not only with class measures, such as taxing the rich, but with the broadening of democracy through education and the vote. These deeper purposes in the labour movement have made it receptive to socialist ideas, and brought about the present identification of labour with socialism, even though there may be many trade unionists, co-operators and members of the Party whose interest in socialist goals is slight, if there at all.

Socialists as such—and this is the key difference—cannot be guided by the immediate interests of one class alone. They identify themselves with the manual workers as the underprivileged of our society, but the main dynamic has not been and could not be a drive for material gain. How else could we explain the struggles of the pioneers, the solidarity, loyalty and sacrifice on which the movement still depends, or the sense of common purpose with which it is permeated? The driving-force has come from convictions, ethical convictions as to what is right and good, and should prevail.

The labour movement, in other words, has its materialist and its idealist aspects, its body and its spirit, and sometimes they conflict. A trade union may, for instance, be able to do better for its own members if it rides roughshod over the interests of other workers. Whether it yields to this temptation depends on the spirit of solidarity within its ranks. On the whole the British labour movement, because of its origins, its structure and its leadership, has maintained its larger, social aspirations. But its very success, the power and influence it has achieved, increase the danger that the ideals, which played so great a part in the early stages, may be submerged in a growing materialism. Trade unions may, as experience elsewhere has shown, become nothing more than sectional pressure groups, bodies without a spirit, "business unions" to use the apt term familiar in the United States.

There is no inevitability about the link between the labour movement and socialism, any more than there is that socialism will one day be achieved. All that we can say with certainty is that socialists must uphold their ideals persistently, day by day, within the movement—not as abstractions, not as the decorative dressing to occasional flights of oratory, but in application to policy and in daily life.

Ideals and Realities

The principles of socialism will not of themselves give us a programme for the next General Election, nor map out our path for the next fifty years. This would require, in addition, a thorough analysis of all the facets of social life, which it is not our intention to attempt here. But principles are something more than pious abstractions. They can be given life and meaning by proving their immediate relevance. Our purpose now is to show that they alone can offer a sure guide through the complexity of the world we live in; in the confusing decisions which press on us daily, they are the only trustworthy criterion for determining our choice.

Let us, then, summarise these principles and their implications:

(1) The socialist goal is a society so organised as to provide each one of its members with an equal opportunity for the development and expression of his personality. This is the right of everyone, and institutions should be shaped accordingly. But the human personality will not find its full expression unless men are able to live in freedom and fellowship, that is in the exercise of responsibility and in the spirit of service. These are ideals which give value to human existence and the degree to which they are expressed will determine the quality of the society we hope to build.

(2) This conception of society has from the start been the ethical inspiration of the socialist movement, the deeper reason for its opposition to the exploitation of man by man. It is, of course, a conception of an ideal society which will never be wholly attained. But providing we make it our conscious goal and are not content to regard its coming as inevitable, we can advance towards it. To achieve this advance is the essence of socialist action.

(3) Socialism, in this sense, cannot be expressed in any single pattern of institutions; nor does its realisation depend on any one line of political strategy. It does, however, involve a continuous struggle in various ways to change the class structure of society and the power relationships on which the class structure rests. In this struggle the labour movement, composed mainly of the organisations of the under-privileged classes, is the natural vehicle.

These are the fundamentals of our approach. But today two problems command our immediate attention—peace and economic survival. What point is there, it may be asked, in thinking of an ideal society, when we live under the threat of bankruptcy in a divided and insecure world? War is with us in all but name and what we do at home will hardly survive a new cataclysm. The two world wars we have endured in half a century have already seriously shaken our economic stability. Surely the only realistic aim for this island at the present time is to secure peace and increase productivity?

Socialists cannot formulate their tasks so simply. The immediate threats must of course be overcome, but is it to be at the cost of everything else we care for? We may be carried even further from our real goal if we concentrate only on avoiding war and achieving an economic equilibrium. We have to find a way of meeting these dangers which is in accord with socialist principles, so that in the very act of countering them our values will be yet more firmly established.

The Price of Peace

As soon as one considers the problem of peace or war, these thoughts become pertinent. Anyone who prizes human well-being must look upon war with horror. War destroys life and more than life; it reduces justice to a mockery, and the very things we fight to save may be lost in the battle. At bottom we all know that war will not be abolished as long as world anarchy prevails, with separate nations clinging to their sovereignty and maintaining independent armed forces. Our objective must always be to extend the rule of law beyond national frontiers, through every method that holds out hope. So great an ideal is worthy of the heaviest sacrifice. Yet in the state of things today, world government and all its institutions lie beyond our horizon, and in the meanwhile what price are we prepared to pay for peace? There are times when people prefer the tragic suffering and risks of war to the certain loss of freedom; they may rate their ideals higher than their lives.

Today, once again, there is the possibility that democratic society may be destroyed by totalitarianism. Are we as a people prepared to take a negative pacifist or neutralist line seeing nation after nation succumbing, and in the end going down in darkness ourselves, for the sake of peace? All we will have attained will be the peace of the graveyard where our ideals lie buried. This course was rejected in 1939, and we cannot endorse it now. Whatever may be the merits of a personal pacifist conviction, the vast majority of us do not accept pacifism as a practical political policy and disagree with its assumptions.

But even the most aggressive state will not lightly provoke a world-wide conflict today, for modern war brings terrible destruction to both sides and its outcome can never be certain. The best insurance in existing circumstances lies, then, in bringing home the certain knowledge that aggressive acts will be met with the whole strength of the free world. For this reason we are compelled, however reluctantly, to rearm.

Our natural reluctance, as socialists, to divert resources into instruments of destruction can only be overcome if there is a clear understanding of what is at stake. Totalitarianism reduces life to the negation of everything we consider good. It is no answer to say that dictatorship is only a "transition stage" in the communist countries, or that they are after all "socialist" states because they have adopted the economic institutions of state ownership. It is not only the economic institutions which make a country "socialist" but also the values which these express. The values we cherish most are now suppressed in communist countries, and there is not the slightest sign of their being revived. They will be destroyed with the same relentlessness in our own or any other land which falls under totalitarian sway.

But is understanding the issues involved and advocating military preparedness to counter aggression the limit of what socialists in this country can do? The forces which will decide for peace or war are not wholly under British control. Yet something more than resignation and readiness for the worst is left us. The cold war is as much a conflict of ideas as a conflict between states. If we have something convincing to offer the world—and can offer it sincerely and effectively—we may yet turn the scales. A resolute stand on behalf of our ideals may yet influence world opinion.

This stand can be taken in many fields of international policy. Our attitude must, in the first place, always distinguish between countries in the grip of suppression and countries all of whose citizens are free to decide their own destiny. Our international socialist ideals would be betrayed if we ignored the submerged cravings for freedom which undoubtedly continue to exist everywhere. We can show, on every possible occasion, our complete opposition to oppressive regimes, be they communist, fascist or racialist.

It is perhaps in the undeveloped areas of the world that our socialist principles have the most direct application; it is there that the conflict of ideologies is most open. With some exceptions, the democratic powers have been unimaginative in helping forward the great changes which are revolutionising these regions. We are still tainted by imperialist traditions, and are niggardly in extending economic assistance. Great schemes of World Mutual Aid are planned, but little emerges because we fight shy of sacrifices. Even socialists are unready to project the ideal of equality on to a world-wide scale. When help is offered the personal approach is crude and inept, just because we have not learnt to respect fully the dignity of individuals of other races. To approach them in the spirit of fellowship requires that we should identify ourselves with their feelings, and the secret of such an attitude too often eludes us. The result is that even our best actions are greeted with cool suspicion. We have not yet explored—with some rare exceptions—how to apply socialist ideals in international relations. India has been one of the exceptions, and no one can deny the success with which the new policy there was crowned, nor the influence which this one act of liberation has had on the attitude of the East towards the West.

One fallacy must be shed—that by helping the backward countries to raise their standards of living they will automatically create democratic societies, which will turn to us in friendship. Something more is required; we need to extend our help and intimate association to all the progressive forces in these lands, particularly to the socialists there, so as to bring them into our common effort for enlarging the free area of the world.

In general we should insist that Britain gives a more forceful moral leadership in international councils. There are more opportunities than is often assumed. At the one extreme we could associate ourselves wholeheartedly with the constructive work that the United Nations is doing in many fields and, as a country, contribute generously to the needed funds. At the other, we could display a greater readiness to welcome foreign workers on our soil. Above all, we could offer to renounce something of our national sovereignty and of our standard of living, not only to help Western Europe out of her present difficulties, but to advance to that world order which is the condition of a lasting peace. . . .

Socialist Action

The difficulty with which socialists contend today is that their programmes, their ways of thought, their very language, have all grown out of the discontents of the past, and were designed to meet the injustices of a past age. They were directly concerned with economic exploitation and the resulting inequalities. Today capitalist exploitation is no longer the burning question that it was. The class struggle has, it is true, not disappeared—its prosecution may sometimes still be necessary in face of the selfish action of the privileged —but it is clearly no longer the main path of progress.

To have the inspiration of the good society on the one hand, and the knowledge of what is wrong on the other, is still not enough. Out of the marriage of inspiration and knowledge must come a clear line of action. The leading task of the movement today and the duty of each individual socialist must be clearly and freshly defined. The historical significance of the *Communist Manifesto* was not the theory on which it was based, but the fact that it reduced the bewildering complex of social problems to a straight-forward, categorical imperative: Workers of the world, unite! It called upon the workers in all countries to recognise their common cause, to take up the struggle against capitalism and to establish their own independent organisations and political parties. Whatever may have been the errors of Marxism, in 1848 Marx and Engels influenced the course of history.

What emerges now as the leading task for socialists? The old struggle for political power to eradicate the remaining evils of a class society must go on. The ground that has been won is again being threatened and large areas still stand unconquered. But more and more must this attack on the bad be matched by a new, and in some ways more difficult struggle to establish the good. What does this involve? The answer, if it is to be brief, can be summed up in a phrase—to arouse *responsible participation*. All that we have said of the pressing problems of our time, the world conflict and the need to raise productivity, all our analysis of the dangers and discontents in our society, point to this conclusion.

In international affairs, for example, the whole of the people are involved to an unprecedented extent: grave decisions have to be faced which transcend more than ever the details of diplomacy. These great decisions of peace or war, of sacrifice to help others, cannot be taken by statesmen and politicians alone, they are to some extent in the hands of every individual citizen. The strongest sense of responsibility is asked for in taking them. In the same way, every citizen is involved when it comes to building up the material basis for international action and for the further unfolding of social policies at home. How are we to succeed unless workers and management alike accept their new responsibilities?

The dangers of the managerial society flow out of apathy and the lack of responsible participation from below. There is a deplorable tendency to leave the choice of aims to the "experts," whose only qualification is the technical knowledge which enables them to advise on the means. The counterpart of this acquiescent attitude are those discontents to which we have referred. They will only be overcome when men are themselves able to give shape to the creative tasks of citizenship. Then, only, will they know the joy which comes from making a contribution to the lives of others, and from the development of their own potentialities.

Thus, every citizen must be encouraged to play a more responsible part in shaping his own and his neighbour's environment, through all the institutions that link them together—in their locality, their job, their political action or their leisure activities. Mere participation is not sufficient. One may participate in the consultative committee at work without mastering the problems or caring greatly about the results. One may be an active member of a trade union without thinking much about the policy one advocates. One may vote in an election without trying to understand the issues at stake, and then grumble when things go wrong. Responsible participation is something quite different. It demands knowledge and effort, an awareness of the interests of others and a readiness to accept the consequences of one's actions, which is the real meaning of freedom of choice.

But the will to participate does not grow of its own accord; it must be developed. It depends on the opportunities which open up for the individual, and this depends in turn on the structure of institutions. In a totalitarian society the opportunities to play a responsible part in social affairs are either trivial or non-existent. In a democracy they can exist in varying degrees, and the right to vote is only one small expression. A socialist programme should now aim at deliberately shaping all the institutions of our society in the light of their effects on the individual.

If this had been the criterion in the past, the institutions which socialists have laboured and struggled so hard to create would now have a very different appearance. The aim in the nationalised industries, for example, would have been to make them a model, not merely of economic efficiency, but of wholesome human relations of a kind to cause the workers in them to point to them with pride, as examples of happiness, dignity and good fellowship in work. The social services, again, would have been regarded not as mere palliatives mitigating the evils of poverty and insecurity, but as the expression in institutions of a spirit of social solidarity bent on creating a nobler life for all. In planning education, we would have put less stress on the competitive struggle at the foot of the ladder of opportunity, and more on the introduction of the whole of the rising generation to a common enjoyment of man's achievements in letters, art and science. Every institution should be seen as a means of broadening the opportunities for each participant to make his contribution.

But the effects of institutional change have their limits, and socialists have sometimes erred in ignoring them. Too much emphasis has been placed on forms of organisation and too little on changing, directly, the attitudes of people. "Men's characters," wrote Robert Owen in 1814, "are made for them and not by them." At that time it was necessary to cry out against the degradation of man into the helpless product of his environment. But in fighting for the recognition of this truth, the socialist movement has tended to the other extreme. There is still a deep-rooted belief that, given only the right sort of machinery—in government, in industrial organisation and in social life generally—the good society would come into being.

We can no longer afford to act on that assumption. However excellently conceived a piece of legislation, however perfectly shaped an institution, much still depends on the response which can be drawn from the men and women whose lives are caught up in the various forms of social organisation, whether they are factories, or schools, or local government or welfare services. The state can achieve no more than establish minimum standards of behaviour, unless it indulges in intolerable coercion. And even if, through an unlimited use of power, it could compel people to refrain from harming others, they cannot—no matter what powers are used—be coerced into acting out of respect and consideration, let alone love for each other.

To work for this change in attitude is the special task of education in general, and of socialist leadership in particular. What is needed most of all is education designed deliberately in order to foster the will for responsible participation. In part this depends on the spirit in our schools, on the values which are held before children, and the opportunities given every child to contribute according to his capacities. But the labour movement, if it is in earnest about this aspect of its work, must lead the way. In its own organisations, in the Labour Party, in the trade unions and in the co-operative societies, it must pursue the type of education which will help members to be responsible participants, both in the organisations themselves and on the outside bodies where they are represented. We have used the term "education" very broadly to include any deliberate effort to change the minds and hearts of men. In this sense it includes propaganda and training; it includes also the force of personal example, which is the essence of leadership.

This brings us to our final word. In all these efforts socialists have to give resolute leadership. To exert such leadership and to believe that people are prepared to respond demands, it is true, a certain conviction. It has often been said that most people do not wish to exercise responsibility. In the nineteenth century, socialists were told that the common man was not interested in politics, economics and education; that, given food and shelter, he was at bottom content with his lot. This they steadfastly refused to accept; they held their fellow-men in greater esteem.

We will not abandon that conviction now. We continue to believe that all men are able to recognise and act upon the ultimate values which give life meaning. There would otherwise be no basis left for further struggle. We could content ourselves with full employment, social security and a minimum standard for all, supplemented by more refrigerators and television sets. The very fact that men are not content with this alone points to the pent-up idealism within them. Socialism has in its trust the key which will release the great creative energies still so often dormant in humanity.

Section IV

DEMOCRACY AS A WAY OF LIFE

Within the context of continuing efforts to develop the forms and institutions of successful democracy in the twentieth century, some philosophers have sought once again to plumb the depths of this political philosophy. Their aim has been to formulate the essentials of the democratic way of life with a generality that would render their theories applicable to democratic societies of every age.

Characteristic of these reformulations has been an emphasis upon the open-mindedness and open-endedness of the democratic philosophy. The fallibility of every individual and every group of individuals has been taken into account, and with it the consequent need for an unending reëvaluation of policies and principles. Free inquiry in every domain is held to be the essence of democracy.

Largely, democracy is an approach to the problems of society that prescribes the general processes of reaching ends freely selected through maximal participation, but that does not fix the particular ends sought. Democracy may thus be embodied in differing sets of institutions, depending upon the size of the group concerned, and the special problems it may confront. But democracy, itself, will be more than any set of political institutions or goals; it will be the way of life within which such institutions and goals are conceived and encouraged. Democracy, Ernest Barker writes, "is not a solution, but a way of seeking solutions—not a form of State devoted to this or that particular end (whether private enterprise or public management), but a form of State devoted, whatever its end may be, to a single means and method of determining that end. The core of democracy is choice, and not something chosen; choice among a number of ideas, and choice, too, of the scheme on which these ideas are eventually composed."

64. ZEVEDEI BARBU

Zevedei Barbu is a Rumanian-born lecturer in social psychology at the University of Glasgow. By means of an empirical study of concrete cases, he has tried to discover the sociological and psychological patterns which accompany all democratic forms. Fundamental among these patterns he finds to be certain attitudes and tendencies which constitute the "frame of mind" of the democrat.

Democracy as a Frame of Mind *

Democracy as a political concept can be described in terms of methods or techniques of government. "We are called a Democracy," says Pericles in his funeral speech, "for the administration is in the hands of the many, and not of the few." Formulae such as government of, by, and for the people, the sovereignty of the people, universal suffrage, popular and responsible government, and others are often used for the description of democracy.

But in spite of this rich and colourful collection of formulae, anyone attempting to define democracy has an almost impossible task. The reason for this lies in the fact that the validity of all fundamental concepts normally involved in such a definition has been seriously challenged by the various historical conditions in which democracy has been realized. Even Aristotle, while agreeing that the main feature of democracy consists in "the election of magistrates by all, out of all," becomes involved in a discussion about the meaning of the concept of "the many." Finally he has to specify that the many who rule in a democracy "are also poor," while the rich, who govern in aristocracy, are "at the same time few in number."

Today it would be easy to prove that decisions taken by "the many"—who are also poor—are not necessarily democratic. During the last century some absolutist monarchs were in favour of extend-

* From Z. Barbu, *Democracy and Dictatorship*, 1956. Reprinted by permission of the Grove Press, New York. Copyright, 1956 by Grove Press.

ing the right to vote to the propertyless classes in the hope that they would be more conservative, i.e., more in favour of the absolutist régime, than the well-to-do classes.

The results of a series of modern "plebiscites" lead inevitably to the conclusion that universal suffrage, or decisions taken by majorities, are but political instruments which can serve democracy as well as other forms of government. One has therefore to take into account a number of factors influencing the behaviour of the people in political matters in order to specify under what conditions the majority act democratically. Thus one has to specify first of all that the concept of majority enters into the definition of democracy only to the extent to which the many possess, and know how to make use of, political power in their community. This obviously means something more than a simple political equality contained in the formula "one man one vote."

Self-government is undoubtedly an essential feature of democracy. Alexis de Tocqueville, amongst others, lays particular stress on this. In the people's interest and participation in the life of their community, in their wish and capacity to conduct their own affairs, he sees not only the spring, but also the main guarantee of democracy. On this point he goes so far as to distinguish between self-government and good government, i.e., government carried on by an enlightened group in the best interest of the people. A democratic reform, or democratic action in general, has to "be brought about not only with the assent of the people, but by their hand."

Now this is obviously true, but it requires certain qualifications. In order to make their society "by their hand" the members of a group have to possess considerable experience in, and knowledge of, public administration. They need also certain institutions which allow them to take a share in the making of their society. But they need something more than this: they need a specific *frame of mind,* that is, certain experiences, attitudes, prejudices and beliefs shared by them all, or by a large majority.

1. One of the basic traits of the democratic frame of mind can be described as the feeling of change. The feeling shared by the members of a community that their personal and their communal life as well are in a state of permanent transformation and readjustment forms, so to speak, the first category of the democratic frame of mind. Owing to this the individual regards his society as an *open* structure, ready to keep pace with the process of general change, and

with the changes taking place in its members in the first place. We classify this trait of the democratic frame of mind as a feeling, because of its general and undifferentiated nature. Considering its origins one can call it also a habit of mind, that particular habit of mind, shared by the majority of the members of a group, to adjust themselves, and to adjust the structure of their society, to the ever-changing conditions of life.

It is obvious that individuals could not have acquired such a habit had they not lived through periods of considerable historical change. Thus democratic régimes are normally preceded by periods of great change which affect the structure of society as a whole. Greek democracies followed a period of radical transformation in the structure of Greek societies. During the eighth and seventh centuries B.C. there took place the transition from the primitive patriarchal to an aristocratic social organization. A period of great change started then, which culminated with Cleisthenes' political reforms. New colonies and big cities were founded, new classes and ways of life made their appearance. A similar historical pattern applies to the Western world in the period preceding the rise of modern democracies. The Renaissance is but the apex of a long process of change. High above all new forms of life stands the capitalist economy which, because of its rapid development, induces in many individuals—in the inhabitants of the town in particular—the feeling of change, novelty and social growth. There was a flow of new things, new ideas, new aspirations and new forms of life for which one needed not only an open mind, but an open and fluid social pattern to integrate them all.

It is this feeling of change and social dynamism which formed the basic element in the mind of the first emigrants to America who, after cutting off all their connexions with the old society, made full use of it in building up the first modern democracy. In France there was needed a revolution before this frame of mind, of which the feeling of permanent change and transformation was a component, found expression in new social institutions. In England the process was slow, but obviously in the same direction.

The individual belonging to post-Renaissance societies had to develop to a maximum his capacity for adjustment to change and novelty. It is because of this that the feeling of change becomes a fundamental category of his mind. Sometimes the effects of this feeling remain unconscious, at other times they are projected at the conscious level as a theoretical construct. Thus the same feeling of change which was a basic trait of the democratic frame of mind, became articulated in a theory of evolution or a philosophy of progress. It is easy to prove the existence of such a phenomenon in modern culture-patterns, for there is no other period in human history in which a greater concern is shown with the rational formulation of the phenomena of change and evolution. In the early stage of this period Vico made an attempt towards the articulation of this deep mental category of modern man in a philosophy of history; later on, Condorcet, in a philosophy of progress, and later still, Hegel did the same thing by laying the foundation of a logic of change and evolution. Though it is generally held that the Greeks were less aware of the changeable character of things, one can hardly say that their mind remained completely unaffected by the feeling of change. The philosophical doctrine of Heraclitus and Thucydides' profound sense of history are characteristic from this point of view.

On the social plane the feeling of change is articulated in the conviction, and in the social behaviour resulting from it, that society is an open structure in a state of permanent readiness for change. "Our city is thrown open to the world" says Pericles about his democratic Athens.

2. The feeling of change cannot be regarded as an isolated trait; the social and cultural behaviour generated by it is moulded by other categories of the democratic frame of mind. Thus, the feeling of change and any other category of the democratic frame of mind are parts of a whole.

The individuals who create or live in a democracy not only hold the belief that their society is in perpetual change, but also that this change is the direct result of their own activities. Consequently the feeling that society grows from within, by the activity of its members, individuals and corporate bodies, can be considered as another category of the democratic frame of mind.

Like the feeling of change, the feeling that the growth of society is determined from within rests on a series of habits of mind formed in certain communities by a long historical process. The first condition leading to the formation of these habits of mind in some ancient Greek communities is to be found in that complex of factors which make up the so-called genius of the race. Suffice it to mention the Greeks' fondness for public meetings, and their creative capacity in the field of social relations, in order to prove this point. But there were a series of other, more concrete, factors which contributed to the formation of these habits of mind. Most important of all is the rise and development of the middle classes in Athens, which was accomplished by the beginning of the fifth century. To these classes belonged individuals who reached and preserved their position in the existing society by their work and intelligence; moreover it was due primarily to the specific activities carried on by these individuals that new forms of life appeared in the midst of an old patriarchal society. It was therefore only natural for these individuals to possess in a higher degree than others the feeling that society on the whole grows from within by the activities of its own members. The kind of activity they led awakened in them earlier than in other sub-groups the conviction that they are the creators of their society.

There is another aspect of the Greek society of that period that contributed towards the formation of the belief that the structure of society is based on the participation of its members. This consists in the need and the effective experience of social co-operation which stood at the origin of the type of organization known as the *Polis*. The *Polis* arose as the union of several rural settlements representing tribal groups and families. This would have been impossible without a long and successful experience in co-operation and co-ordinated social action, which, we presume, resulted in the feeling that society was in a high degree a matter of common activity and agreements dictated by the nature of common interests and experience.

In European societies, the source of these habits of mind is to be found in the experience gained by the inhabitants of the towns in the administration of their common affairs. The administrative autonomy of the towns is a characteristic feature of Western medieval society. In England the system of local autonomy was preserved throughout the modern era. It is therefore little wonder that the "bourgeois" played such an important part in the building up of Western democratic societies. For, like the Greek member of the middle classes, the modern bourgeois possesses in a high degree the feeling that he can, not only conduct, but even create his own society.

It is not too difficult to find how the belief that society is a matter of co-operation originated in the mind of modern man. The need for, and the experience of co-operation among various social groups, divided and antagonized by a system of privileges, against an autocratic monarch formed in fact an important feature in the rise of modern societies and states. This was noticed throughout the rise of the British modern state, and formed at the same time the central motive in the prelude to the French Revolution. In the example of co-operation between the "three orders" set forth in 1787, by the province of Dauphine, can be grasped the pattern of a new society resulting from the common activity of and agreements among its components, that is, of a society which builds up its form from within. It is this social pattern that lurked in the minds of the Pilgrim Fathers leaving the old Continent. When they settled down in America they put it into practice in its purest form. There was no constituted body or class within their small group; the individual had to be not only a soldier in the protection of his own society, but also a pioneer in the making of it. Later, the French Revolution repeated the same pattern when breaking down the old social order into its basic unity, the individuals, and subsequently trying to build up a new society from the network of individual relationships. The conviction that each individual is a maker of his own society constitutes a basic trait of a democratic frame of mind.

At the cultural level, this trait is articulated in various forms. In the feeling that each individual is, in his own way, an agent in the making of his society lies the seed of both the doctrine of equality and that of freedom. With regard to the former, we are only too aware that, in its most radical form as total equality, it is not necessarily a feature of democratic society. We cannot, however, help noticing that certain equalitarian conceptions arose in the culture-pattern of every community in process of democratization. In some communities, whose members showed particular inclinations towards rational thinking, such as the Athenian and the French communities, equality was worked out into an ideal concept and considered as specific to a democratic way of life. Equalitarian tendencies formed also a specific feature in the early American society. There they crystallized in the doctrine of equal rights, or more recently, in the concept of equal opportunities. Movements such as that initiated by the Levellers show clearly that the ideal of equality formed an important feature in the early stages in the democratization of the British community. The lure of such an ideal was, however, short-lived, owing mainly to the native inclination of the British people to empirical thinking. Equality was considered as an "abstract right."

As for the doctrine of freedom one can say that it can be found in every democratic culture-pattern. Its origins lie, as stated before, in the conviction that the structure of society is not based on a permanent and fixed order, and that, on the contrary, it results from the activity of each of its members, from their common experiences, from their interactions, deliberations and agreements. This conviction itself grows from a great variety of experiences in self-government which certain communities, or certain parts of a community, had gained. In Athens, the doctrine of freedom crystallized, at various stages of social evolution, in concepts such as: *isegoria* (equality of speech), *isonomia* (equality before the law), *isocratia* (political equality), *parrhesia* (equality and freedom of speech). In Western society its most typical crystallization is seen in the doctrine of economic liberalism, and in the conception that society is ultimately a matter of "contract" which formed one of the basic ideological prerequisites in the process of democratization of modern societies.

3. From what has been said so far one can easily infer that a democratic frame of mind contains also a specific attitude towards authority, as one of its categories. To start with, one can say that the basic element of this attitude consists in a feeling of the instability and relativity of power and authority. This aspect of the democratic frame of mind would perhaps be better understood if it were described as the awareness, present in various degrees in the members of a certain community, that the holding of power and authority implies the concession made by one part to another part of the community. In other words it implies a process of delegation.

As for the historical context of this trait one can say that the feeling of the unstable and relative character of political power was certainly aroused by those periods of rapid transformation and social unrest preceding some democracies. The contest of power between the Eupatrids and the kings, on the one hand, and among the Eupatrids themselves, on the other, had certainly something to do with the presence of this feeling in the minds of the Athenians. The same can be said about the struggle between the European aristocracy and monarchy, and between the Church and State. But this is not all. On the contrary, it would be easy to prove that in certain circumstances the contests of power, and social instability do not necessarily lead to the feeling of the relative character of authority. The formation of this specific attitude towards authority in Western man is in fact determined by a complex of circumstances. Most important of all is the process of secularization which, as will be shown later, shook the foundation of absolute authority in the mind of modern man.

Interpreting the process of democratization as it took place on the Continent—in France in particular—one is often inclined to believe that the feeling of the relative character of power and authority, so characteristic of modern man, comes mainly as a reaction from the absolutist régime preceding the democratic era. Thus the early meaning of democracy was "no more than opposition to the privileges of the old powers, the clergy and the feudal nobility; hence the negation of those values which served to uphold their position." * In fact, the reaction against permanent and absolutist power constitutes only one element in the composition of the democratic attitude towards authority and power. This lies at the basis of that aspect of the democratic attitude towards authority which has been called "negative freedom," and which is in fact a natural outcome of the struggle for liberation from an authoritarian régime. In this respect one has to recognize that the democratic attitude towards power and authority contains the seeds of anarchy which may grow into trees wherever the soil is favourable. There is no need to prove this by examples.

But, as just stated, this is only one aspect—the negative one—of the democratic attitude towards authority. The social experience leading towards the rise of modern democracies shows clearly that the attitude towards authority could not be exclusively negative. The authority based on absolute power was undoubtedly negated, but another type of authority took its place. This is the internal authority of reason and conscience. One can speak in this case about a displacement of authority which is characteristic of modern man; the confidence in, and reliance on external and divine authority was gradually transformed into confidence in, and reliance on the powers of human reason and conscience.

But human reason and conscience are not social authority in themselves. Here comes an important point in the formation of that aspect of the democratic frame of mind which refers to the nature of social authority. The experiences in self-government, in building up new social forms and groups, characteristic of some modern Western communities, implanted in the individual the conviction that the authority based on the principles of the human mind—logical and moral—can be imparted to other individuals by deliberation. The same experiences implanted also the conviction that the authority founded on the in-

* A. von Martin, *The Sociology of the Renaissance*. Kegan Paul, London 1945, p. 4.

dividual's reason can be concentrated by an act of common will, and conferred as such upon a man, a party, or an institution. In other words, authority can be represented.

Therefore, the essence of the democratic attitude towards authority consists in the concept of inner and individualized authority. This authority can be concentrated by agreement and conferred upon a representative. Hence the social order is a representative order. It ought also to be said that authority is conferred, yet never entirely transferred. This is due to the conviction shared by every individual member of a democratic community, that he himself is an agent in the making of his society; hence the exercise of social power is to him an act of agreement by deliberation, rather than an act of assenting. Whenever a community of people is ready to transfer power and authority to a leader or a party there is an obvious proof that they lack the democratic frame of mind, even when this transfer is carried out by impeccable democratic methods. The best example of this kind is furnished by the German people of today. They once transferred the power to Hitler, and the great numbers of votes given to Adenauer in September 1953 give us ground to believe that they are ready to repeat the act. It is either the people's lack of confidence that they can create their own society "by their hand," or the existence of other factors that make it difficult for them to resist the transference of power and its concentration in the hands of a few.

The articulation on the social plane of the feeling of the relative and representative character of power and authority is seen in the doctrine and practice of the division and balance of power, in the decentralization and minimization of power which are, in one form or another, present in all modern democracies.

4. The last category of the democratic frame of mind can be described as an attitude of confidence in reason. But before saying anything on this account we have to recognize the fact that we are aware of the existence of a widespread opinion according to which a democratic way of life must necessarily be rooted in an empirical attitude to life. It would follow from this that the organization of social life according to a rational order is the very opposite of democracy. British society is often mentioned as an example which proves the close connexion between empirical thinking and democracy.

But when we speak about the democratic frame of mind we are only secondarily interested in the cultural or ideological aspect of democracy. It is true that some democratic nations are addicted to an empirical and some others to a rational way of thinking. But this difference is not as deep as is often thought. For the action of a free individual in a flexible society is always carried out on the deep—often unconscious—presupposition that this action will be finally adjusted to an harmonious social pattern based on reason. This is what we mean here by the feeling of confidence in reason; it is a constitutional element of the individual's mind which sometimes is manifested—at the cultural level—as the cult of reason, at other times as a strong conviction that "an invisible hand" leads man on to the right path. Very often it appears as blind confidence in order, the very opposite of the fear of instability and chaos.

Since we have to come back later to the problem of the relationship between reason and democracy, we must try now to answer the question: How did this category of the democratic frame of mind originate in modern society? While we retain a purely psychological point of view, it is necessary to start by saying that the feeling of confidence in reason is necessary as a balancing factor in the mind of the individual who has to adjust himself to a world of change and novelty; it is necessary for this individual to develop the belief that there is an order and stability behind the change, and that there are certain regulative principles which put a check upon change. Therefore free individual action and flexible, open, and even atomized society are for this type of man not only possible but even safe since they obey a certain fundamental order. Whatever the change may be, certain basic principles, certain "fundamental human rights" have to be respected. This deep conviction is knit into the ideological pattern of many democracies. British democracy seems to be an exception. But in the light in which we here regard the democratic frame of mind, this exception seems to be only apparent. For, while in other communities the individuals show their confidence in a set of principles expressed by a rational doctrine, in the British community they place their confidence in a form of practical reason, in a set of norms, traditions, "prejudices" and "prescriptions." While in the former case the change is checked and guided by the order of reason, in the latter, the "expediency" has to compromise with the "permanent" order stored in a body of prejudices and prescriptions. It is the confidence in this order that compensates for the need to adjust to a world of change and novelty. If one replaces the expression "confidence in reason" by "confidence in a fundamental order,"

this often overstressed difference between British and other democratic frames of mind becomes considerably diminished.

Individuals living in a world of rapid change, and in a dynamic
social structure in particular, develop, apart from the feeling of
confidence in a fundamental order, habits of mind which facilitate
an adequate adjustment to a changeable environment. This is another
important source of the need for reason in modern man. For reason
is that complex of mental functions or habits by which the individual
is able to grasp the unity in diversity, and the order in change.
Reason presupposes a high degree of mental flexibility which enables
the individual to compare things, to establish differences and identities,
and finally to compromise. New events demand new relations, and
consequently readjustment.

At the root of this type of adjustment one can certainly find the
belief that there is a certain order in the nature of things. This belief
was, as we have seen, displayed by both the Greek and modern man.
On the other hand, this type of adjustment would hardly have been
possible without the feeling of confidence in the ability of humankind, and without a strong feeling of security, both individual and
collective.

To account for the feeling of security one has to start from the
fact that the historical periods leading to democratization are periods
of progress and prosperity. There is no need to bring proofs in the
support of this assertion with regard to Athenian, British and
American societies. And though the same thing can be said about
Western society as a whole, during the post-Renaissance period,
many people are still inclined to think that the economic frustration
of the French lower class was one of the main factors leading to the
democratic changes initiated by the Revolution. This is not, however,
the opinion held by Tocqueville—and he was followed by many
others—who proves that the period immediately preceding the Revolution was on the whole marked by considerable prosperity. It can
therefore be safely said that it was this general state of prosperity
that first aroused in man confidence in himself and in his society.

There is a strong sense of security, both individual and collective,
involved in any process of democratization. This will come out
clearly from what we have to say at a later stage. For the moment it
will be enough to point out that this sense of security is aroused by
the expanding character of society, and by the conviction, shared by
many individuals, that the human mind is flexible enough to organize

the experience in any field of reality. This flexible character of the mind is expressed by a particular structure whose function it is to relate the data of environment, to compromise between their various aspects, to organize them so as to make adjustment possible. This structure has been called reason; today one can speak about intelligence, or the ego, as fulfilling approximately the same functions. We shall see later that the mental structures which can be called reason, intelligence, or the ego have gradually come into the foreground of the mental life of modern man. They are the most suitable tools for adjustment to a flexible society, and to a changeable universe.

The confidence in reason being a basic category of the democratic frame of mind is manifested in a great variety of forms at the social and cultural levels. Most aspects of the democratic culture-pattern are deeply affected by rational thinking. Even more striking is the fact that any democratic period is marked by a general tendency towards rationalizing the field of social relations. In any democratic community the conviction is widely spread that society can be organized rationally, that the people meeting together and deliberating upon their own interests can find common goals and ways of action which make an equal appeal to every one of them. It can further be said that every democratic community is founded on the conviction of its capacity for self-legislation, the conviction that any diversity of interests can finally be solved in a compromise, that any new experience can be dealt with in a general scheme of action. The first Puritans landing on the barren coast of New England (1620) had the strong conviction that, by their combination into a "body politick," they could "enact, constitute, and frame such just and equal laws, ordinances and acts, constitutions and offices, *from time to time,* as shall be thought most meet and convenient for the general good of the Colony . . ."

65. E. F. M. DURBIN

E. F. M. Durbin (1906-   ) is a British socialist who argues that there are three absolute essentials of political democracy: the ability of a people to choose their government; the freedom of the people to oppose the government once chosen; and, most crucial of all, the implicit understanding among all who contend for power that, once attained, it will not be abused. "Mutual toleration is the keystone of the arch and the cornerstone of the building."

The Essence of Democracy*

If the method of dictatorship is an unlikely way to secure social justice, what alternative method is open to us?

I wish to argue that the only conceivable route to a better social order lies in the pathway of democracy, and that the political method of democratic government is an essential principle, not an accidental accompaniment, of any just society.

If by the "socialist commonwealth" we mean a society in which a larger measure of social justice has been established through the instrumentality of a planned economy, then I believe that the democratic method is an inherent part of socialism, and cannot be separated from it—any more than batting can be separated from cricket or love from life. They are all necessary parts of a complex whole.

I am now concerned to argue the validity of this contention; but before I do so, it is necessary to make clear the sense in which I use the term "democracy."

Democracy is an ambiguous term in political discussion. Many people use it in such a way as to make it synonymous with the phrase "the good society." A community is a "true" democracy only if all cause for sighing and weeping have passed away. Before such persons will call any society a democracy, it must be completely free from social inequalities and economic insecurity. J. A. Hobson uses the term in this sense when he says "effective political democracy is unattainable without economic equality." In this use the term "democracy" becomes identified with the conception of a social justice itself, and is therefore remote from the political practice of any present society.

By using the word in this way it is possible to say, quite rightly, that we have not got "democracy" in Britain, or America, or France, or Sweden. In none of these countries has inequality, or insecurity, or

* From E. F. M. Durbin, *The Politics of Democratic Socialism*, 1940. Reprinted by permission of the publishers, Routledge and Kegan Paul Ltd., London.

class antagonism, passed wholly away. Democracy, in its Utopian sense, does not yet exist within these nations. They only possess "capitalist democracy," or "*political* democracy." They do not possess "economic democracy" or "true democracy" or "real democracy."

Now it is perfectly open to anyone to use terms as they please. If some people choose to mean by "democracy" what other people mean by "Utopia" there is nothing to stop them doing so. The moon will still be the moon even if we call it the sun. Utopia by any other name will smell as sweet, and look as remote. But it is not in Utopia, nor in the perfect society, that I am, for the moment, interested. I wish to discuss a narrower thing, a single political habit, a method of taking political decisions, a practicable and actual condition of certain societies. In short, what I want to consider is the significance or value of what the Utopian "democrats" would call "mere political democracy." In what does that consist? Of what value is it? By what arguments can it be justified or criticized?

It is obvious that the institution of "mere political democracy" must exist in some real sense, even in a capitalist society, since it is possible to distinguish "capitalist democracies" from "capitalist dictatorships." Even in his most fanatical moments the Communist has not denied the *possibility* of making the distinction, although he used to deny the *importance* of making it. There must be therefore some sense in which democracy is compatible with capitalism and consequently with economic inequality. It is with this limited form of political democracy, its meaning and value, that I am here concerned.

In what does "democracy" in this sense consist?

I believe the correct answer to this question to be that political democracy consists in the possession by any society of *three* characteristic habits or institutions:

1. The *first* and most typical of these characteristics is the ability of the people to choose a government.

Disagreement between individuals is of the very essence of human personality. As long as we are different persons, there will be some of us who like one thing and some who do not, some who desire one order of society and some another, some who believe justice to be realized in one set of circumstances and some who disagree with that judgment.

Now the course of action taken at any moment, and the form of society thus brought slowly into existence, are determined largely by the decisions of the Government. The Government has its hands upon the controls of the "apparatus of coercion," and is therefore the *immediate* authority determining social policy. The nature of the decisions taken by the Government will depend upon the character of the persons forming it. Consequently there can be no control of the form of society by us, the common people, unless it is possible to change the personnel of the Government and of the legislature. That is the first and most obvious characteristic of political democracy —the existence of a government responsible to the people, and the dependence of it and of the membership of the legislative assembly upon the free vote of the people.

In our own history we have found that the essential thing to attain and preserve is the power of the people to *dismiss* a government from office. This negative power is in reality an important positive power, because ordinary men and women are moved more deeply by the disapproval of measures they dislike in practice, than by their less definite conception of what they desire in the future. Political change in democracies is more frequently induced by a slow accumulation of resentment against an existing government or institution, than by the growth of a positive idea of new social forms. Experience is more real than imagination, to unimaginative people.

Every practising politician appreciates this fact. The enthusiasts composing the party machine through which he has to work may be animated by the clear vision of a new society, but they are, at the best, a small minority of the surrounding electoral masses, and the masses are rarely inspired by Christian's clear vision, from a great distance, of the Celestial City. This is not to say that constructive social imagination is not powerful in the affairs of men, but only that democracies proceed to realize the prophets' vision by careful processes of empirical test. By the slow testing of ideas and of institutional experiments, by rejecting all those of which they disapprove and insisting upon the gradual extension of the things they find by experience that they like, an intelligent electorate unconsciously constructs a society that in large measure contents it. Little as we reformists of the Left may like it, the absence of a reforming or revolutionary zeal in our communities is a tribute to the fundamental, and often unrecognizable, ways in which society has been adapted to suit the unconscious, but essential, requirements of the people composing it.

Of this I shall have more to say presently. For the moment I wish only to insist upon the importance of the negative power to destroy a government as part of the broader right to choose a government.

It is the continuous retention of this power that I shall call the "maintenance of democracy."

2. But the continued existence of this right implies and requires the existence of a *second,* and less obvious, political institution. If liberty is to exist, if the dependence of government upon the will of the people is to be real, there must always be a real choice before the people. This implies the steady maintenance of a critical and essential institution—that of *freedom to oppose the Government of the day.* Unless the electorate has more than one possible government before it; unless there is more than one party able to place its views before the country; unless, that is to say, the opposition is free to prepare itself to take over power, and the Government to surrender it peacefully after an electoral decision against it; there is no choice before the people. Their choice is Hobson's choice—they may walk or go upon their legs, they may die or cease to live, they may eat bread or bread. The range of choice is no greater.

This obvious reflection reveals at once the sharp absurdity of the electoral practices of modern dictatorships. Modern dictatorships pay to the institutions of democracy the sincerest form of flattery—that of imitation. They copy the device of the "General Election." But it is an empty and silly imitation—like that of an ape reading a newspaper or a baboon playing on a violin. It deceives no one, except those who wish to be deceived. Of course, no amount of electoral machinery, nor platform eloquence, nor secret balloting, nor "equal voting," has the slightest real significance if there is finally nothing to vote about, no choice before the voters. The contemporary German and Russian elections, in which one Party receives 98 per cent or 99 per cent of the votes polled, may be a tribute to the efficiency of the terror by which these unfortunate peoples are governed; but they have no more political significance than the jabbering of a school of marmosets or the senseless and uniform hissing of a gaggle of geese.

This we can see at once by asking the critical question: *What is the choice before the German or Russian electorate?* There is only one party in the election. There is only one government that can be formed. There may be a choice of individuals, but there is no choice of party, no choice of government, no choice of policy. The alternative before the German people is the choice between Führer Hitler or Führer Hitler; before the Russian people Comrade Stalin or Comrade Stalin. They may choose in the one country, the National-Socialist Party or the National-Socialist Party; in the other, the Communist

Party or the Communist Party. As Herr Goebbels said, "All we National-Socialists are convinced that we are right, and we cannot bear with anyone who maintains that he is right. For either, if he is right, he must be a National-Socialist, or, if he is not a National-Socialist, then he is not right." Comrade Stalin thinks very much the same. It is only odd that both these self-righteous regimes consider it worth while to spend so much time and money in marching the adult population mechanically and idiotically through the polling booths to affirm a meaningless slogan.

Here then is the acid test of democracy. Democracy may be defined by the toleration of opposition. In so far as it is tolerated— in so far as alternative governments are allowed to come into existence and into office—democracy, in my sense, exists. In so far as opposition is persecuted, rendered illegal, or stamped out of existence, democracy is not present, and either has never existed or is in process of being destroyed.

Obviously this is not a simple test. There are varying degrees of freedom permitted to those in opposition to the Government of the day in the various political systems of the world. In the older democracies, like our own, there is complete legal freedom for parties in opposition to the Government. Their rights in respect of political agitation are the *same* as those of the Government. From this extreme there is an almost infinite gradation of liberty, through the milder dictatorships of Poland and even Italy, to the savage and ruthless insistence upon uniformity that characterizes Germany and Russia. There is no precise line at which it is possible to say that all the communities on this side of it are democracies, and all on the other side of it are dictatorships. But, although the test is quantitative and complicated, it is nevertheless an acid test. The suppression of opposition, as distinct from sedition,* is the proof of dictatorial ambition. It is by our judgment of that condition in society that we shall judge democracy itself.†

3. But there is a *third,* and still less obvious, characteristic necessary to the existence of democracy. Both the previous characteristics —those of responsible government and of legal opposition—are the definitive properties of democracy, but they are not the causes of

---

* The advocacy of the *violent* overthrow of the Government.

† Of course I am not arguing the proposition that "the more Parties there are the better." The institutions of democracy clearly work best with a very small number of Parties.

democracy. When these conditions are present in a society, democracy in my sense is present also; when they are absent democracy in my sense is dead. But they do not cause democracy to become present; they simply define democracy. What then *causes* democracy to appear? What is the substantial social condition guaranteeing its existence and continuance?

Now I shall go on to argue, before this Part is finished, that the ultimate cause of stable democratic habits among a people is the possession by them of a certain type of emotional character. I shall argue that democracy is the epiphenomenon of a certain emotional balance in the individuals composing a nation, and I shall try to describe the kind of personality that, in my view, alone makes democracy possible. But there is a simpler and more immediate description of the *result* of the predominance of such persons in any society; and that is, in my submission, the most essential condition for the existence and maintenance of democracy. It is the existence of *an implicit undertaking between the Parties contending for power in the State not to persecute each other.** It is upon that agreement that I believe democracy can alone be securely founded. Mutual toleration is the keystone of the arch and the cornerstone of the building.

It is obvious, upon a moment's reflection, why this should be so. Let us imagine for a moment that this condition is not fulfilled. Let us suppose that the Conservative Party now in power in Great Britain has reason to believe that the Labour opposition has never accepted, or does not now accept, the obligations of this informal compact of toleration. The Government has reason to think that, if and when the Labour Party comes to power, it will use that power not merely to carry out its programme, but to break up and destroy the Conservative Party as a political organization, and to stamp out, by persecution, conservatism as an idea. That is to say, it is the known intention of the Labour Party—as it is now the known intention of the Communist and Fascist Parties—to use the apparatus of coercion, control over which is vested in them as the Government, to "liquidate" the Parties that will then be in opposition to them. What will then follow? I suggest that in these circumstances the continuance of democracy is inconceivable. It is not even necessary that one of the large Parties in the community should intend to resort to physical cruelty. It may be certain that they will be forced to do so by the

---

* Or any other minority—such as a racial or religious minority within the state.

attempt to liquidate their opponents; but even if this is not the case, the mere desire on their part to prevent the other Party, by force, from ever holding office again is sufficient to make the maintenance of democracy impossible. Why is this so? Because the Party so threatened will never surrender power peacefully. There is every reason why it should not do so. To hand over the reins of government to the victorious Opposition is to court political death, to put a noose around one's own neck, to hand over the gun to a murderer. There would be no sense in such a procedure. Why should I present a knife to a man who is going to stab me in the back with it? Who would willingly hand over a machine-gun to a lunatic or a gangster?

Indeed, it may very well be the duty of a political leader not to hand over the control of government voluntarily to a persecutor. The leaders of the Conservative Party, in the case that we are imagining, are the responsible leaders of a certain section of the community. They have been entrusted with the guardianship of certain interests and certain ideas. It may be their duty not to step aside, even in the face of the popular will, to give places of power to persecutors and tormentors. By so doing they sell the men and women they represent into slavery. They betray the ideas, for which they stood trustee, to destruction. It may be their duty to fight, to meet force with force, and not to yield. Only the extreme pacifist contends that it is our certain duty to allow ourselves to be tortured and persecuted and killed. In any case it is certain that most people will not do it—even were it their duty to do so.

These moral dilemmas need not delay us now, as we shall return to them before the end of this Part. I am merely trying to elucidate the conditions necessary for the existence of democracy as I have defined it. Democracy requires the peaceful alternation of Parties in government. This is impossible if the Government believes that the Opposition intends to liquidate them if and when they, the Opposition, attain power. The Government is not likely in these circumstances to surrender power peacefully. Even if they did, democracy would nevertheless cease to exist, since the victorious Opposition would then proceed, by the persecution of those who disagreed with them, to the destruction of democracy itself. Political liberty or democracy, in my sense, depends then, first and last, now and in the future, upon mutual toleration between opposing Parties.

It will be noticed that, in my description of democracy, there is no reference to social equality or distributive justice, or to any characteristic of the ideal society. It is therefore perfectly open to anyone to suggest that it is not a valuable institution. It is possible to say: "If that is all you mean by democracy, I am not interested in it. It does not appear to me to be a particularly important or valuable political habit. I see no necessity to trouble myself greatly over its preservation." We are therefore brought, at once, to a consideration of the advantages and disadvantages of this method of government. What are the arguments for democracy? What are the arguments against it? What are the forces that support or undermine it?

66. HENRY B. MAYO

Henry Mayo (1911-   ) is an American philosopher who has developed a coherent and comprehensive theory of democracy. Mayo believes that by the use of a small set of interrelated operational principles common to all democracies, the presence of genuine democracy is more readily identified, and the ideals of democracy more clearly understood. His is one of the few contemporary efforts to construct a universal democratic theory in practical terms.

The Theory of Democracy Outlined *

The approach taken in this study is to regard democracy as a political system with a theory to explain and justify it. The first problem is, then, to identify the working principles of the political system generally called democratic.

In order to arrive at these distinguishing principles, several starting points are possible. We could, for example, begin with some of the older classic statements of democracy, or with a contemporary definition, or with the institutions of one of the existing democratic systems. Although all these sources will be tapped from time to time, I shall take as the starting point the Athenian example. . . . This need not be misleading if we do take it as no more than a starting

* From H. B. Mayo, *An Introduction to Democratic Theory*, 1960. Reprinted by permission of the Oxford University Press, New York. © 1960 by Oxford University Press, Inc.

point, and do not regard Athens and its unique institutional features as a small scale model of contemporary democracies.

The original democratic system of Athens could be described in one phrase as "rule by the people," if "people" was construed narrowly to mean adult male citizens, comprising a small proportion of the total persons in a small state. This definitive operating principle, traced out into secondary principles and institutions, made it easy for Athenians—and for us—to distinguish the democracy from other ancient political systems. Such a principle was both accurately descriptive and quite workable, given the scale of operations. But the principle is neither descriptive of nor feasible in any modern state. It makes sense to say that one person rules, or that a few persons do, no matter how large the state; but it makes almost no sense to say that the people rule in any modern state, in any ordinary sense of the word "rule." (In this sense "rule" means to make directly the binding political decisions—or the major ones, including the decision as to what is major—and to receive the obedience.) In Gladstone's words:

> No people of a magnitude to be called a nation has ever, in strictness, governed itself; the utmost which appears to be attainable, under the conditions of human life, is that it should choose its governors, and that it should on select occasions bear directly on their action.*

Or as MacIver was always concerned to put it:

> Democracy is not a way of governing, whether by majority or otherwise, but primarily a way of determining who shall govern and, broadly, to what ends . . . The people, let us repeat, do not and cannot govern; they control the government.†

The only exception to this is the occasional use of "direct democratic devices" such as the referendum.

Democracy, then, as a political system must have identifiable features other than the people's actually "governing," to distinguish it from other methods of making public policies. The problem is to separate the accidental features from the characteristic. Some political features, such as whether the government is federal or unitary, presidential or parliamentary, unicameral or bicameral, republican or

---

* *Nineteenth Century Opinion,* ed. Michael Goodwin, Harmondsworth, Middlesex, 1951, p. 226.

† R. M. MacIver, *The Web of Government,* New York, 1947, p. 198. *The Ramparts We Guard,* New York, 1950, p. 51.

monarchical, are by general agreement accidental variations from a common type. So, too, is the kind of economic system with which the political system is associated—although this is more debatable. These and other features are not necessarily related, either in logic or practice, with features of the political system ordinarily listed as democratic. Since one cannot analyze all of a system, except perhaps in a treatise on comparative democratic systems, we seek here only the differentiating features or principles of organization typical of all democracies and not typical of any other systems.

What, then, in any contemporary state corresponds to the "rule by the people" in the Athenian system? We are inevitably driven to conclude, I think, that such a corresponding factor lies in the effectiveness of the popular control over the rulers or decision-makers. In short, a political system is democratic to the extent that the decision-makers are under effective popular control. (One should perhaps add: to the extent to which decisions are *influenced* by the people, but this is a more amorphous concept, for which allowance will be made later.)

Plainly however, this, although in the spirit of the Athenian democracy, is a much vaguer test to apply than the Athenian. To distinguish ancient democracy from other types of the Greek *polis* was easy, and there could scarcely be dispute about it. But when the test is the extent of effective popular control, then the existence of democracy in any system is obviously a matter of degree. At one extreme will be the absolute ruler—a Hitler, a Stalin, a Peron—who, however despotic, must sometimes take popular sentiment into account (but who will endeavor, through education, censorship, propaganda, and other means, to engineer the popular sentiment which he wishes), and whose elections and plebiscites, if they are held at all, are carefully "rigged." At the other will be an elected government anxious to be re-elected, and an opposition anxious to become the government, both of them therefore sensitive to public opinion, with a wide range of political freedoms through which continuing influence as well as periodic control can be exercised.

Popular control of policy-makers is then the basic feature or principle, and political systems can be classified as more or less democratic according to a number of criteria associated with popular control and designed to make it effective; only if a particular system meets the tests of a substantial number of these criteria do we, by common consent, agree to call it democratic. But although the existence of democracy then becomes a matter of degree, the distinction is valid enough as we shall see, and the criteria will enable us to say in what respects and to what extent a system is democratic.

It must now be our purpose to try to make this somewhat vague language more precise. Accordingly I shall first sketch what I take to be a consistent and coherent theory of democracy in the form of the minimum number of distinguishing principles. At the same time, the outline will be reasonably close to contemporary usage, and is recognizably approximated by a number of existing democracies. The analysis and justification of these principles and of the system as a whole, together with the chief questions or problems which arise, will be given in later chapters.

Distinguishing Principles of a Democratic System

Influence over decision-makers and hence over public policies may be exercised in many ways, even in a non-democratic system. The policies of an absolute ruler or of an oligarchy, for instance, may be affected by palace intrigue and court favorites, or by careful calculation of what the subjects will stand in the way of taxes and the like; it is possible to conceive of a benevolent autocrat who will in fact keep his ear to the ground and often graciously accede to public demands. But popular influence, although necessary, is not enough even if institutionalized to make a political system democratic.

1. *Popular control of policy-makers,* however, is a democratic stigmatum, and this is our first and most general principle. The one institutional embodiment of the principle universally regarded as indispensable in modern democracies is that of choosing the policy-makers (representatives) at elections held at more or less regular intervals. This is as close as we usually get—which is not very close—to imitating the making and control of decisions in the Athenian *ecclesia.*

Other methods of choosing and authorizing representatives—e.g. by lot or heredity—have died out, except for remnants of the lot such as are left in the choice of a jury. Even the Soviet type of "democracy" pays tribute to the method of electing representatives, although their practice of it is quite different from that in other kinds of democracies. In this as in other respects, the Soviet Union has borrowed some of the forms and language of democracy and stripped them of their spirit and meaning.

Three riders must be added to our general principle at the outset in order to avoid misunderstanding:

(a) On the whole, no democratic system operates on the principle that voters directly decide public policies at elections. The control over policy is much more indirect—through the representatives. This will be made clear later . . . but if we accept provisionally that voters choose representatives at elections and do not normally decide policies, then the usual criticism aimed at modern democracies on grounds of the incompetence of voters to judge policies is wide of the mark, however true it may have been of Athens where the citizens did decide directly.

(b) The popular influence upon policies, as distinct from control over policy-makers, goes on all the time and may take many institutionalized and legitimate forms. The extent of such influence, however, cannot be reduced to any public test which can be incorporated at the present time into a general theory. The reason is that popular influence and consultation take such an infinity of forms —of which interest or pressure groups are perhaps the best known— that hardly any general principle can as yet be enunciated. What gives popular influence its sanction is that it can affect the chances of a representative at election time, or, more accurately, the representative's estimate of his chances.

(c) Popular control by means of modern elections has only a faint resemblance to the old principle that, in some sense, authority stems from the people, and to old practices such as an elective monarchy. The assumption or belief that authority *should* derive from the people —sometimes called the doctrine of popular sovereignty—does of course underlie the practice of popular elections, but our immediate concern is with the translation of the assumption into an operating principle or institutional practice.

2. The second principle of democracy is that of *political equality,* which in turn is institutionalized as the equality of all adult citizens in voting.

It makes little difference whether we think of this principle as coordinate with the first, or derivative—a widening of the meaning of "popular." Political equality is a principle common to Athenian and modern democracies. There is, of course, more to citizenship than voting, and hence other ways in which political equality or inequality can prevail, but it is not debatable today that in any democracy the principle of equality of voting is taken for granted.

Although the general principle may be cast in the Athenian form, the modern expression of it is quite different. For one thing, equality of voting is not, as in Athens, an equal share directly over the decisions; the share in the decisions is indirect—only the share in the control of the decision-makers is direct. For another, political equality today covers a wider range of citizens and voters than the Athenian, and in this respect we should call modern democracies more democratic than Athens.

Political equality is complex, like all general principles, and may be broken down into several elements, consisting at least of the following:

(a) Every adult should have the vote—the familiar device of the universal adult suffrage. Popular control defines the "people" as all adult citizens, although there are of course minor differences in the definitions of an "adult."

(b) One person should have one vote—that is, there should be no plural voting.

(c) Each vote should count equally—that is, votes are not weighted in any way.

In terms of representation, the belief in equal voting is expressed in the old slogan of "representation by population" or in Bentham's formula regarding happiness, that "everybody is to count for one, nobody for more than one." In terms of control over policy-makers, it is expressed by saying that every vote should have an equal share in that control.

(d) If every vote is to count equally, the corollary follows that the number of representatives elected should be directly proportional to the number of votes cast for them. If we assume, for simplicity of argument, a two-party system, then the number of representatives elected from each party will be proportional to the number of votes cast for that party. Thus, in a two-party system, if party A gets 60 per cent of the popular vote it will get 60 per cent of the seats, and party B will get 40 per cent. Any other result would not be counting each vote equally.* It is just at this point, however, as we shall see, that the practice of many democracies diverges from

---

* Note that the reference is in terms of actual votes, not in terms of eligible adults—a point to which fuller reference is made later.

this aspect of political equality, and often does so for very good reasons.

A little reflection will show that equality of voting, even if followed to the letter, is not enough of itself to distinguish a democratic system from an elected dictatorship. The belief and indeed the practice of equal voting are both official in the Soviet Union. Equality of voting, with its corollary, may thus be regarded as a necessary, but not a sufficient, principle of democracy. Is there, then, anything else about political equality and the franchise to distinguish a democratic political system? The answer must lie in the fact that voting alone does not ensure the reality of popular control; the mechanism may be manipulated to prevent such control.

3. The third principle may be stated either in terms of the *effectiveness of the popular control* or in terms of *political freedoms*.

Again, it makes little difference whether we regard "effectiveness" as part of the first principle (popular control) or as specifying the conditions of effective control. Can one set of decision-makers be turned out of office at elections and another set installed? Is there a free choice among alternatives, whether independent candidates or parties? That is, is the voting merely ritual, or does it effectively (freely) control the decision makers?

This again is a very general statement of what prevails in a democracy. To make the general standard specific enough to test in practice, we must once more break it into components.

(a) To say that the voting must be effective is to say that there must be free choice, without coercion or intimidation of the voters. This in turn drives us back upon the secrecy of the ballot, whether we draw the conclusion from reflecting on human nature—that we live in an imperfect world of imperfect people—or from reflecting upon the historical experience of many countries with open voting. Yet the condition of the secret ballot alone is not enough to ensure free choice, since even a Soviet election may provide the voter with privacy in the voting booth.

(b) In order that voting may be effective, it must, then, be free in another sense, i.e. at least two candidates for each position must be able to come forward if they wish. This minimum in itself is also not enough, because it could be cleverly imitated even in the Soviet Union by the simple device of putting forward more official candidates than seats to be filled.

An effective choice for the voter entails freedom for candidates to stand for election outside of the single party, not deterred by legal obstacles. (The question of *de facto* obstacles such as poverty is explored later.) At this point we come close to the most characteristic feature of a modern democracy: the meaningful choice or control when candidates are free to run for office, when they and their supporters are free to press their claims publicly, to put forward alternative policies, to criticize the present decision-makers and other candidates; in short, when there is what Schumpeter has called a competitive bidding for votes.

The effectiveness of popular control thus entails a range of political freedoms. Among them are certainly the freedoms of speech, assembly, and organization, as well as the freedom to run for office. These widespread political liberties were characteristic of the Athenian form of democracy, and are likewise typical of all other historical versions, though lacking in the Soviet system.

These formal rules or conditions or devices of effective choice— secret ballot, freedom to run for office, and freedom to speak, assemble, and organize for political purposes—are procedural political freedoms, necessary if there is to be any meaningful choice at the polls, if the voters are to control the decision-makers at election times and through them indirectly to sanction the decisions. Or they may be looked upon as the rules which insure free competition for office, men being what they are and the world being what it is.

Among those political freedoms, that of organization leads almost inevitably (as we shall see later) to the formation of political parties, with different sets of candidates and sometimes with different outlooks and policy alternatives. The pure theory, of itself, will hardly tell us whether or not political parties will make their appearance in a democracy. They are not, so to speak, logically entailed as part of popular control, of effective choice in free and equal voting, and they do not always appear at local levels of government. Experience and history, however, give an enormous weight of evidence to show that political parties invariably do appear, despite the early, and mostly non-democratic, objection to "factions."

The existence and extent of these political liberties, as manifested above all in political opposition, is perhaps the most crucial test of the extent of democracy within a country. They are often summed up in the single concept "freedom to oppose." The touchstone of a democratic system is political freedoms, opposition, and parties. Not one of the indispensable freedoms, nor the open and legitimate opposition which is always the consequence of freedoms, is present, for example, in the Soviet Union, despite the noble language of liberty embalmed in the Soviet constitution of 1936. For that reason we are fully justified in saying there is no effective choice or popular control of the decision-makers in the Soviet Union.

The result of political activity taking place within these rules— equality of voting and political liberties—is to enable the effective choice of representatives to take place, i.e. to ensure the popular control of decision-makers at election time, and to keep the channels open to legitimate influence at all times. From the viewpoint of the individual voter, the vote is the formal means by which he takes his share in political power. It scarcely needs pointing out that other implications also follow, for instance that the outvoted citizens accept the verdict of the polls with fortitude if not with gladness.

Although equality of voting within the context of political freedoms is a basic part of a democratic system, it is not all. Another essential part, already implicit, is that the policy decisions are made by the elected representatives, since only these are susceptible to popular control. The policies are not made, for instance, by others behind the scenes—as Marxists allege—nor by any non-elected body, such as a hereditary upper house. Insofar as they are made elsewhere, to that extent we say democracy is lacking. (To say this, however, is not to ignore the political reality of executive or Cabinet leadership.)

It is plain that we cannot expect the representatives to be unanimous, any more than we can expect the electorate to be so. Political systems are devised *because* there is conflict and disagreement. There must, then, be a principle or rule according to which decisions are made among the representatives themselves.

4. The fourth principle is that *when the representatives are divided, the decision of the majority prevails.*

This is, in fact, the nearly universal rule for decision-making in all legislatures. Let us be clear how it links with the previous principles. Equality of voting, in a context of political freedoms, turns up representatives who are authorized to make the policies for the time being. This may be loosely called "consent of the governed" in the sense that there is a choice and one set of representatives rather than another is chosen. But "consent" is a slippery term, and it is better to think of election results as authorizing the successful candidates to make decisions, or in other words, as investing the government and its policies with legitimacy.

The common assumption is that with an electoral system based on equality of voting a majority of the representatives have been chosen by a majority of the voters, and hence the majority rule in the legislature yields decisions as legitimate "as if" they had been made directly by a majority of the voters, and indeed by a majority of all the adult citizens. That is why this fourth principle is sometimes called "majority rule." In fact, however, if governments depended for their legitimacy on this strict relation of votes to representatives, half the democratic governments of the world could at times claim no rightful authority from the "people."

The principle of decision-making by a majority of representatives is much disputed, and is examined *in extenso* later, particularly the justification for the majority principle. The case *against* may be put in a nutshell: that it is both necessary and feasible to maintain legal limits upon a majority of the decision-makers (and hence by implication upon a majority of the citizens), and by so doing we may achieve the best of all possible systems: a "wise" minority veto of "unwise" majority decisions. Democracy would then be identical with ideal government, and the historic search for a government with power to rule wisely, but powerless to do wrong, would be over. To state the case is almost enough to refute it.

From this method of policy-making there follow certain implications, which may be called the rules of the game for representatives.

First, the majority of the representatives makes the policy decisions within the framework of the political freedoms mentioned earlier. These freedoms are taken as given, as part of the formal principles or essential conditions of democracy. Whatever else the majority may do —and it may mete very ill treatment through some of its decisions— it does not shut up the opposition, the critics, the dissenters, whether these are within or without the legislature. Opponents may be coerced into obedience to law, but not abolished or silenced or shorn of their political liberties: this is the one inhibition upon the majority decisions so long as a democracy exists. When the political liberties and the legitimate opposition are gone, so, too, is democracy.

Second, the minority of representatives and their supporters among the public obey even though under protest, while working either to alter the policy to which they object or to dislodge the government and if possible to become a majority—by all peaceful political means, but only by these. . . .

Third, when the opposition in its turn has grown into a majority and attains office, the play begins all over again with different actors in the roles of government and opposition. The minority also agrees beforehand that they, too, will extend the same political freedoms and follow the same rules of the game should they arrive in the seats of office. The problem which arises here is that created by the existence of a minority party which uses the political freedoms in order to abolish democracy.

Many social conditions are, of course, necessary if the majority principle is to work well, but those formal conditions just stated are the minimum rules of the game for majorities and minorities in the legislature if democracy is to work *at all*. Moreover, in any functioning democracy, regardless of the niceties of the electoral system, the rules apply in those common cases where the majority of representatives happen to be elected by the minority of voters. No identity of voters and representatives need be assumed as long as the unwritten constitution does not require it, although there is, I think, an obligation to reduce the likelihood of wide discrepancies by eliminating abuses from the electoral system and thus closely approximating the principle of political equality.

The foregoing is a simplified, formal, abstract sketch of a democratic political system—its essential principles of operation for political policy-making. It concentrates upon how the binding decisions, related to government and arising from conflict and dispute, are made in the context of political freedoms. In other terms, the outline concentrates upon the ways in which policy-makers get their power and authorization—their legitimacy, always a prime concern to any political theory. The principles are close enough to common usage, and to some political systems in existence, to warrant the description democratic.

Each of the principles can be cast in operational terms. This has the great advantage of giving us practical tests which, taken together, enable us to distinguish democratic from non-democratic systems, and also to identify democracies empirically as more or less democratic, in this or that respect. One need not attempt, however, to solve the impossible problem of exact summation—of trying to construct a single index number which will register all the tests for democracy. Some criteria are more important than others, and all are a matter of degree.*

Each of the principles can also be cast in normative (moral) terms —for example, that political equality *should* prevail—and in this form they constitute the moral justification of a theory of democracy. They are moral beliefs for which a case can be made, and which may be traced further back until we lay bare the "ultimates" or postulates to which the principles commit us.

Considered in both operational and normative terms, the principles may thus fairly be described as making up a democratic political theory which both explains and justifies a democratic political system.

A working definition may be constructed from the above: a democratic political system is one in which public policies are made, on a majority basis, by representatives subject to effective popular control at periodic elections which are conducted on the principle of political equality and under conditions of political freedom. The definition is hardly remarkable; others of a similar kind have frequently been constructed.†

I am aware that the bare outline bristles with questions, as any model does when it is made up of an abstraction of formal principles. Moreover, even when the skeleton has been given flesh and blood, there are a number of other far-reaching queries which at once suggest themselves, among them; what values (if any) inhere in a political system operating on such principles? What case can be made for the system as a whole other than that involved in the justification of the separate principles?

Again—and this will be the question of chief concern to many— what of the kind or quality of decisions thus made and authorized? Must we assume that the content of democratic decisions will take

---

* See Russell H. Fitzgibbon, "A Statistical Evaluation of Latin-American Democracy," *Western Political Quarterly,* IX, September 1956, pp. 607ff., for an attempt to measure (in "a crude and groping way," as the author says) which countries of Latin America are more democratic. At that time, Uruguay, Costa Rica, and Chile were at the top of the list.

† For instance, John Morley's: Democracy is "the name for a form of government by which the ultimate control of the machinery of government is committed to a numerical majority of the community." *Oracles on Man and Government,* London, 1923, p. 29. Or again: Democracy is "government of the whole, by the majority, generally through representatives elected by secret ballot of adults." E. F. Carritt, *Ethical and Political Thinking,* Oxford, 1957, p. 150.

care of itself, or has the theory any implicit purposes to which the system is committed? What kind of case can be made against such a system and against its theory by the critics? What of the social, economic, and other conditions which may be needed in order that a democratic system may work at all, or work well? What are the prospects for such a system in the world today? What application has the theory to international politics?

For the time being, these wider questions will be put aside for later consideration, and I turn now to an examination of the empirical and the normative beliefs involved in the principles listed, and of how existing democracies deviate from the practice of these principles.

67. ERNEST BARKER

Ernest Barker (1874-   ) is one of the leading British political philosophers of the twentieth century. A profound student of Plato and Aristotle, he has tried to embody the political ideals of ancient Greece in a theory of contemporary democracy. In the following passage he contends that only a democratic state is true to the character of the society out of which it emerges, for only in a democracy is the possibility of genuine interplay among ideas actually realized.

[Democracy and the Plurality of Ideas] *

If the State can be regarded as mediating social thought about justice to its members, and as expressing in its law the product of such thought, we may draw from that premiss the conclusion that the State should itself correspond, in its own nature and operation, to the process of social thought which it mediates, and should thus be a broad open channel for the flow of the product which it expresses. The process of social thought is a process in which all the members of Society can freely share, and to which they can all contribute freely. It follows that, if there is to be correspondence and a broad open

* From E. Barker, *Principles of Social and Political Theory*, 1951. Reprinted by permission of the Clarendon Press, Oxford.

flow, the process of the activity of the State should also be a process in which all its members can freely share and to which they can all freely contribute. We may argue that this demand is satisfied, and satisfied only, by the democratic State. Indeed we may argue that it is satisfied doubly by the democratic State; first in the form of its constitution and the way of its coming into being, and next in its method of government and the way of its operation.

In their actual coming into being, as has already been noted, States are historical products of very various patterns, due to a variety of historical causes. But the question before us here is not a question of the far-off origins, back in the mists of time, of the States we know today in their changed and developed form as the modern States of our Western world. It is a question of the basis and *raison d'être* of the modern State *as we know it now,* in the form which it has now assumed in the world in which we now live. What set of ideas, and what motions of the mind, have formed and brought into being the State we now know in the form it now has? Some answer to that question has already been given; and it is only necessary to summarize briefly the heads of the answer. A national Society, in the course of a process of social thought, creates and sustains an idea and ideal of a right of order relations between its members: an idea and ideal of justice. But it cannot attain its ends, or turn the idea into fact and the ideal into reality, without an organized system for the declaration and enforcement of the dictates of justice. We must therefore conceive the society as making itself, or "constituting" itself, an organized system *for this purpose,* or, in other words, as forming itself into a *legal* association or State, while still continuing to exist and act as a Society, and still continuing, as such, to maintain and develop that process of social thought which is continually fertilizing the idea and ideal of justice. This act of the "constitution" of a State by the members of a national Society results, and expresses itself, in a "constitution" in another and further sense of the word: the Constitution with a capital C; the articles of association (both written and unwritten) which warrant, authorize, and control the actions and the organs of the legal association. We may say that this Constitution, or set of articles of association, is of the nature of a contract, which we may call the political contract; and in that sense, as has already been noted, we may say that the State has a contractual basis. We may also say that the constitution of a State by a national Society and by all the members of that Society, or in other words by the people, is the first stage and the foundation of the democratic method of government. In it, and by it, the people have given themselves the basis of political action by a first democratic act of creation. Will they not then go on, still following the same path, and give themselves a method of government and a way of permanent operation in which they are equally active? *

To find a firm basis for a theory of the democratic method of government in the modern State, we must go back to the process of social thought from which the State issues and to which it always remains attached. The process of social thought is naturally and necessarily a process of discussion. Ideas emerge here and there: each emergent idea becomes a magnet which attracts a clustering group of adherents: the various ideas, and the various groups they attract, must either engage in a war of competition with one another to achieve a victory, or attempt a method of composition which fuses and blends them together in peace. The military idea of a war of competition between ideas is prominent in the philosophy of Hegel. His dialectical idealism (which Marx turned upside down, or as he preferred to say "right side up again," in his dialectical materialism) assumes a war of ideas, in which "one shrewd thought devours another": a battle of thesis and antithesis, in which each side fights for itself. But even Hegel's military conception of the war of ideas ends in a sort of composition between thesis and antithesis; or, more exactly, it ends by producing the synthesis of a higher truth in which the partial truths of the thesis and the antithesis are abolished and transcended. It has thus, after all, some approach to the principle of discussion; but Hegel's theory of discussion is rather that of a logical process inside a solitary mind (even if that mind be conceived as the "objective" mind of a whole Society) than that of a social process among and

---

* To avoid misunderstanding, and to make the argument clear, it should be noted that the argument here advanced is simply, and only, an argument that the modern State is the product of a shift of ideas, which may be traced in England from the beginning of the Civil War to the Revolution of 1688 and the Hanoverian settlement; which showed itself in North America and France in the last quarter of the eighteenth century; and which spread over Western Europe, South America, and the countries of the British Commonwealth, during the nineteenth century. Whatever the State may hitherto have been, it became, with this shifting of ideas, a specifically legal association, created by the sentiment and action of the national Society, and based on a constitution which is of the nature of a contract. It would be a folly to argue that the State (in the sense of all States, at all times) is based upon contract. It is not a folly to argue that the modern State, in all the parts of the world which have been stirred by this shift of ideas, is so based.

between a number of minds. The theory which is implied in Aristotle's *Politics* is much nearer to the idea of such a social process. Instead of assuming a war of two conflicting ideas, to be ended by a transcendent and triumphant synthesis, he assumes a plurality of social ideas, to be fused and blended together in a "scheme of composition." Just as it takes all sorts of men to make a world, so it takes all sorts of ideas to produce a "catholic" and all-round view. Aristotle applies this conception to the field of culture and the province of artistic judgment: here, he says, "some appreciate one aspect, and some another, but all together appreciate all." But he also applies it generally to the whole field of social thought; and he applies it, in particular, to matters of political judgment. The Many, he holds, "when they meet together," and put their minds fairly to one another, can achieve a composition of ideas which gives their judgment a general validity.

If we follow the guidance of Aristotle, we shall say that social thought proceeds by the way of a plurality of ideas, by the way of debate and discussion between the different ideas, "when they meet together" and come into contact with one another and by the way of a composition of ideas attained through such debate and discussion. We shall also say that this social way must also be, and also is, the political way: in other words it must also be, and also is, the method of the State's government and the way of the State's operation. This is not only because the State should be true to the Society from which it comes and on which it continues to rest: it is also because the way of Society (the way of plurality of ideas, debate among them, and composition of them) is right in itself and universally right—right for Society, right for the State, and right wherever men are gathered together and have to act together. The one way to get at practical truth, the right thing to do, the straight line of action, is, in any form of group, the way of thinking things over together and talking them over together, with a view to finding some composition of the different threads of thought. It is the way of the Friends, when they seek what they call "the sense of the meeting." It is the way of democracy, which is not a solution, but a way of seeking solutions— not a form of State devoted to this or that particular end (whether private enterprise or public management), but a form of State devoted, whatever its end may be, to a single means and method of determining that end. The core of democracy is choice, and not something chosen; choice among a number of ideas, and choice, too, of the scheme on which those ideas are eventually composed. Democracy is incompatible with any form of one-idea State, because its essence is hospitality to a plurality of ideas, and because its method (which is also its essence) consists in holding together a number of different ideas with a view to comparison and composition of their difference. The democratic criticism of the one-idea State is not a criticism of its object (which may also be the object of the democratic State, or at any rate part of its object): it is a criticism of its whole process of life.

This last phrase, "process of life," suggests a further consideration which is of vital importance in the theory of democracy. One of the archbishops of Canterbury, Frederic Temple, once said that there were two schools of political thought: one which held that politics existed for the production of a result, or the *ergon* school; and another which held that politics was valuable in itself as a process of activity, or the *energeia* school. The school of production judged politics by the results which it produced: the school of process preferred to judge on a different basis, and it was content, and more than content, if the process of the political life of a community elicited and enlisted for its operation the minds and wills of its members, thus aiding, and indeed in its measure constituting, the development of their capacities as persons. The distinction here suggested, which goes back to Aristotle,* is a just and pregnant distinction. We are naturally apt to think of politics in terms of making, rather than of doing, as if our political activity were directed wholly to achieving an object outside itself (and not immanent in itself), such as a scheme of legal order, or an adjustment of economic relations, or some other similar structure. But this is not the whole of the matter, or even the greater part. It is certainly true, and indeed it has already been urged in the course of our argument, that the State as a legal association must necessarily produce a result: it must produce a scheme of declared and enforced law which gives expression to the idea of justice. But there are two other things which must also be borne in mind. First, the ultimate purpose behind justice, and therefore behind law, is the development of the capacities of human personality in as many persons as possible to the greatest possible extent. That is the final result which the State must produce—or rather help

---

* The distinction between production (*poiesis*) and action (*praxis*) is discussed in the *Ethics*, Book VI, cc. iii-v. The gist of the argument is that "Production has an end other than itself: action cannot have; for good action is itself its own end."

to produce; for the result produces itself in each person through his own internal activity, even if it needs help, in the way of removal of hindrances and the offering of opportunities, in order to produce itself fully. This first reflection naturally leads to the second. If we hold that behind and beyond the *production* of law by the State there is a *process* of personal activity and personal development in its members, we may go on to say that the production should itself be drawn into the process. In other words we may argue that the productive effort of the State, the effort of declaring and enforcing a system of law, should also be a process in which, and through which, each member of the State is spurred into personal development, because he is drawn into free participation in one of the greatest of all our secular human activities.

These reflections suggest a second main justification of the democratic system. Not only is it justified, as we saw at the beginning of this section, by the fact that it makes the State true to the method of general discussion and composition of ideas which is the method of Society; it is also justified, as we now see, by the fact that it makes the State, in the very process of its own operation, true to the fundamental purpose which lies behind its operation, the purpose of the development in action of the capacities of personality.

68. JOHN DEWEY

John Dewey (1859-1952) is properly known as the philosopher of democracy. Throughout his long life he was a tireless supporter of democratic principles not only as embodied in American government, but as rightfully ruling every sphere of human social action. The spirit of democracy ought, he argued, to govern the conduct of the society of nations, just as it ought to govern the relations of individuals in the home, the school, and the community. Dewey was dedicated to liberal democracy; he held it to be the only political system which could do justice to the wholeness and complexity of human experience, and the only system through which, at the same time, the methods of intelligent inquiry could be applied to man's social life.

Philosophy and Democracy*

There has been, roughly speaking, a coincidence in the development of modern experimental science and of democracy. Philosophy has no more important question than a consideration of how far this may be mere coincidence, and how far it marks a genuine correspondence. Is democracy a comparatively superficial human expedient, a device of petty manipulation, or does nature itself, as that is uncovered and understood by our best contemporaneous knowledge, sustain and support our democratic hopes and aspirations? Or, if we choose to begin arbitrarily at the other end, if to construct democratic institutions is our aim, how then shall we construe and interpret the natural environment and natural history of humanity in order to get an intellectual warrant for our endeavors, a reasonable persuasion that our undertaking is not contradicted by what science authorizes us to say about the structure of the world? How shall we read what we call reality (that is to say the world of existence accessible to verifiable inquiry) so that we may essay our deepest political and social problems with a conviction that they are to a reasonable extent sanctioned and sustained by the nature of things? Is the world as an object of knowledge at odds with our purposes and efforts? Is it merely neutral and indifferent? Does it lend itself equally to all our social ideals, which means that it gives itself to none, but stays aloof, ridiculing as it were the ardor and earnestness with which we take our trivial and transitory hopes and plans? Or is its nature such that it is at least willing to coöperate, that it not only does not say us nay, but gives us an encouraging nod?

Is not this, you may ask, taking democracy too seriously? Why not ask the question about say presbyterianism or free verse? Well, I would not wholly deny the pertinency of similar questions about such movements. All deliberate action of mind is in a way an experiment with the world to see what it will stand for, what it will promote and what frustrate. The world is tolerant and fairly hospitable. It permits and even encourages all sorts of experiments. But in the long run some are more welcomed and assimilated than others. Hence

* From J. Dewey, *Characters and Events,* Volume II, 1929, edited by Joseph Ratner. Reprinted by permission of the publisher, Henry Holt and Co., New York. This passage was originally part of an address delivered at the University of California, November 29, 1918.

there can be no difference save one of depth and scope between the questions of the relation of the world to a scheme of conduct in the form of church government or a form of art and that of its relation to democracy. If there be a difference, it is only because democracy is a form of desire and endeavor which reaches further and condenses into itself more issues.

This statement implies a matter of definition. What is meant by democracy? It can certainly be defined in a way which limits the issue to matters which if they bear upon philosophy at all affect it only in limited and technical aspects. Anything that can be said in the way of definition in the remaining space must be, and confessedly is, arbitrary. The arbitrariness may however, be mitigated by linking up the conception with the historic formula of the greatest liberal movement of history—the formula of liberty, equality and fraternity. In referring to this, we only exchange arbitrariness for vagueness. It would be hard indeed to arrive at any consensus of judgment about the meaning of any one of the three terms inscribed on the democratic banner. Men did not agree in the eighteenth century and subsequent events have done much to accentuate their differences. Do they apply purely politically, or do they have an economic meaning?—to refer to one great cleavage which in the nineteenth century broke the liberal movement into two factions, now opposed to one another as liberal and conservative were once opposed.

Let us then take frank advantage of the vagueness and employ the terms with a certain generosity and breadth. What does the demand for liberty imply for philosophy, when we take the idea of liberty as conveying something of decided moral significance? Roughly speaking, there are two typical ideas of liberty. One of them says that freedom is action in accord with the consciousness of fixed law; that men are free when they are rational, and they are rational when they recognize and consciously conform to the necessities which the universe exemplified. As Tolstoi says, even the ox would be free if it recognized the yoke about its neck and took the yoke for the law of its own action instead of engaging in a vain task of revolt which escapes no necessity but only turns it in the direction of misery and destruction. This is a noble idea of freedom embodied, both openly and disguisedly, in classic philosophies. It is the only view consistent with any form of absolutism whether materialistic or idealistic, whether it considers the necessary relations which form the universe to be physical in character or spiritual. It holds of any view which says that reality exists under the form of eternity, that it is, to use a technical term, a *simul totum,* an all at once and forever affair, no matter whether the all at once be of mathematical-physical laws and structures, or a comprehensive and exhaustive divine consciousness. Of such a conception one can only say that however noble, it is not one which is spontaneously congenial to the idea of liberty in a society which has set its heart on democracy.

A philosophy animated, be it unconsciously or consciously, by the strivings of men to achieve democracy will construe liberty as meaning a universe in which there is real uncertainty and contingency, a world which is not all in, and never will be, a world which in some respects is incomplete and in the making, and which in these respects may be made this way or that according as men judge, prize, love and labor. To such a philosophy any notion of a perfect or complete reality, finished, existing always the same without regard to the vicissitudes of time, will be abhorrent. It will think of time not as that part of reality which for some strange reason has not yet been traversed, but as a genuine field of novelty, of real and unpredictable increments to existence, a field for experimentation and invention. It will indeed recognize that there is in things a grain against which we cannot successfully go, but it will also insist that we cannot even discover what that grain is except as we make this new experiment and that fresh effort, and that consequently the mistake, the effort which is frustrated in direct execution, is as true a constituent of the world as is the act which most carefully observes law. For it is the grain which is rubbed the wrong way which more clearly stands out. It will recognize that in a world where discovery is genuine, error is an inevitable ingredient of reality, and that man's business is not to avoid it—or to cultivate the illusion that it is mere appearance—but to turn it to account, to make it fruitful. Nor will such a philosophy be mealy-mouthed in admitting that where contingency is real and experiment is required, good fortune and bad fortune are facts. It will not construe all accomplishment in terms of merit and virtue, and all loss and frustration in terms of demerit and just punishment. Because it recognizes that contingency coöperates with intelligence in the realization of every plan, even the one most carefully and wisely thought out, it will avoid conceit and intellectual arrogance. It will not fall into the delusion that consciousness is or can be everything as a determiner of events. Hence it will be humbly grateful that a world in which the most extensive and accurate thought and reason can only take advantage of events is also a world which gives room to move about in, and which offers the delights of consummations that are new revelations, as well as those defeats that are admonishments to conceit.

The evident contrast of equality is inequality. Perhaps it is not so evident that inequality means practically inferiority and superiority. And that this relation works out practically in support of a régime of authority or feudal hierarchy in which each lower or inferior element depends upon, holds from, one superior from which it gets direction and to which it is responsible. Let one bear this idea fully in mind and he will see how largely philosophy has been committed to a metaphysics of feudalism. By this I mean it has thought of things in the world as occupying certain grades of value, or as having fixed degrees of truth, ranks of reality.

The traditional conception of philosophy to which I referred at the outset, which identifies it with insight into supreme reality or ultimate and comprehensive truth, shows how thoroughly philosophy has been committed to a notion that inherently some realities are superior to others, are better than others. Now any such philosophy inevitably works in behalf of a régime of authority, for it is only right that the superior should lord it over the inferior. The result is that much of philosophy has gone to justifying the particular scheme of authority in religion or social order which happened to exist at a given time. It has become unconsciously an apologetic for the established order, because it has tried to show the rationality of this or that existent hierarchical grading of values and schemes of life. Or when it has questioned the established order it has been a revolutionary search for some rival principle of authority.

How largely indeed has historic philosophy been a search for an indefeasible seat of authority! Greek philosophy began when men doubted the authority of custom as a regulator of life; it sought in universal reason or in the immediate particular, in being or in flux, a rival source of authority, but one which as a rival was to be as certain and definite as ever custom had been. Medieval philosophy was frankly an attempt to reconcile authority with reason, and modern philosophy began when man doubting the authority of revelation began a search for some authority which should have all the weight, certainty and inerrancy previously ascribed to the will of God embodied in the divinely instituted church.

Thus for the most part the democratic practice of life has been at an immense intellectual disadvantage. Prevailing philosophies have unconsciously discountenanced it. They have failed to furnish it with articulation, with reasonableness, for they have at bottom been committed to the principle of a single, final and unalterable authority from which all lesser authorities are derived. The men who questioned the divine right of kings did so in the name of another absolute. The voice of the people was mythologized into the voice of God. Now a halo may be preserved about the monarch. Because of his distance, he can be rendered transcendentally without easy detection. But the people are too close at hand, too obviously empirical, to be lent to deification. Hence democracy has ranked for the most part as an intellectual anomaly, lacking philosophical basis and logical coherency, but upon the whole to be accepted because somehow or other it works better than other schemes and seems to develop a more kindly and humane set of social institutions. For when it has tried to achieve a philosophy it has clothed itself in an atomistic individualism, as full of defects and inconsistencies in theory as it was charged with obnoxious consequences when an attempt was made to act upon it.

Now whatever the idea of equality means for democracy, it means, I take it, that the world is not to be construed as a fixed order of species, grades or degrees. It means that every existence deserving the name of existence has something unique and irreplaceable about it, that it does not exist to illustrate a principle, to realize a universal or to embody a kind or class. As philosophy it denies the basic principle of atomistic individualism as truly as that of rigid feudalism. For the individualism traditionally associated with democracy makes equality quantitative, and hence individuality something external and mechanical rather than qualitative and unique.

In social and moral matters, equality does not mean mathematical equivalence. It means rather the inapplicability of considerations of greater and less, superior and inferior. It means that no matter how great the quantitative differences of ability, strength, position, wealth, such differences are negligible in comparison with something else— the fact of individuality, the manifestation of something irreplaceable. It means, in short, a world in which an existence must be reckoned with on its own account, not as something capable of equation with and transformation into something else. It implies, so to speak, a metaphysical mathematics of the incommensurable in which each speaks for itself and demands consideration on its own behalf.

If democratic equality may be construed as individuality, there is nothing forced in understanding fraternity as continuity, that is to say, as association and interaction without limit. Equality, individuality, tends to isolation and independence. It is centrifugal. To say that what is specific and unique can be exhibited and become forceful or actual only in relationship with other like beings is merely, I take it, to give a metaphysical version to the fact that democracy is concerned not with freaks or geniuses or heroes or divine leaders but with associated individuals in which each by intercourse with others somehow makes the life of each more distinctive.

All this, of course, is but by way of intimation. In spite of its form it is not really a plea for a certain kind of philosophizing. For if democracy be a serious, important choice and predilection it must in time justify itself by generating its own child of wisdom, to be justified in turn by its children, better institutions of life. It is not so much a question as to whether there will be a philosophy of this kind as it is of just who will be the philosophers associated with it. . . .

[The Foundation of Democracy] *

Democracy is much broader than a special political form, a method of conducting government, of making laws and carrying on governmental administration by means of popular suffrage and elected officers. It is that, of course. But it is something broader and deeper than that. The political and governmental phase of democracy is a means, the best means so far found, for realizing ends that lie in the wide domain of human relationships and the development of human personality. It is, as we often say, though perhaps without appreciating all that is involved in the saying, a way of life, social and individual. The keynote of democracy as a way of life may be expressed, it seems to me, as the necessity for the participation of every mature human being in formation of the values that regulate the living of men together: which is necessary from the standpoint of both the general social welfare and the full development of human beings as individuals.

* From J. Dewey, *Democracy and Educational Administration,* an address before the National Education Association, Feb. 22, 1937. Reprinted from *Intelligence in the Modern World,* edited by Joseph Ratner, and published by The Modern Library, Random House, New York, 1939.

Universal suffrage, recurring elections, responsibility of those who are in political power to the voters, and the other factors of democratic government are means that have been found expedient for realizing democracy as the truly human way of living. They are not a final end and a final value. They are to be judged on the basis of their contribution to end. It is a form of idolatry to erect means into the end which they serve. Democratic political forms are simply the best means that human wit has devised up to a special time in history. But they rest back upon the idea that no man or limited set of men is wise enough or good enough to rule others without their consent; the positive meaning of this statement is that all those who are affected by social institutions must have a share in producing and managing them. The two facts that each one is influenced in what he does and enjoys and in what he becomes by the institutions under which he lives, and that therefore he shall have, in a democracy, a voice in shaping them, are the passive and active sides of the same fact.

The development of political democracy came about through substitution of the method of mutual consultation and voluntary agreement for the method of subordination of the many to the few enforced from above. Social arrangements which involve fixed subordination are maintained by coercion. The coercion need not be physical. There have existed, for short periods, benevolent despotisms. But coercion of some sort there has been; perhaps economic, certainly psychological and moral. The very fact of exclusion from participation is a subtle form of suppression. It gives individuals no opportunity to reflect and decide upon what is good for them. Others who are supposed to be wiser and who in any case have more power decide the question for them and also decide the methods and means by which subjects may arrive at the enjoyment of what is good for them. This form of coercion and suppression is more subtle and more effective than are overt intimidation and restraint. When it is habitual and embodied in social institutions, it seems the normal and natural state of affairs. The mass usually become unaware that they have a claim to a development of their own powers. Their experience is so restricted that they are not conscious of restriction. It is part of the democratic conception that they as individuals are not the only sufferers, but that the whole social body is deprived of the potential resources that should be at its service. The individuals of the submerged mass may not be very wise. But there is one thing they are wiser about than anybody else can be, and that is where the shoe pinches, the troubles they suffer from.

The foundation of democracy is faith in the capacities of human nature; faith in human intelligence and in the power of pooled and coöperative experience. It is not belief that these things are complete but that if given a show they will grow and be able to generate progressively the knowledge and wisdom needed to guide collective action. Every autocratic and authoritarian scheme of social action rests on a belief that the needed intelligence is confined to a superior few, who because of inherent natural gifts are endowed with the ability and the right to control the conduct of others; laying down principles and rules and directing the ways in which they are carried out. It would be foolish to deny that much can be said for this point of view. It is that which controlled human relations in social groups for much the greater part of human history. The democratic faith has emerged very, very recently in the history of mankind. Even where democracies now exist, men's minds and feelings are still permeated with ideas about leadership imposed from above, ideas that developed in the long early history of mankind. After democratic political institutions were nominally established, beliefs and ways of looking at life and of acting that originated when men and women were externally controlled and subjected to arbitrary power, persisted in the family, the church, business and the school, and experience shows that as long as they persist there, political democracy is not secure.

Belief in equality is an element of the democratic credo. It is not, however, belief in equality of natural endowments. Those who proclaimed the idea of equality did not suppose they were enunciating a psychological doctrine, but a legal and political one. All individuals are entitled to equality of treatment by law and in its administration. Each one is affected equally in quality if not in quantity by the institutions under which he lives and has an equal right to express his judgment, although the weight of his judgment may not be equal in amount when it enters into the pooled result to that of others. In short, each one is equally an individual and entitled to equal opportunity of development of his own capacities, be they large or small in range. Moreover, each has needs of his own, as significant to him as those of others are to them. The very fact of natural and psychological inequality is all the more reason for establishment by law of equality of opportunity, since otherwise the former becomes a means of oppression of the less gifted.

While what we call intelligence may be distributed in unequal amounts, it is the democratic faith that it is sufficiently general so that each individual has something to contribute, and the value of each contribution can be assessed only as it enters into the final pooled intelligence constituted by the contributions of all. Every authoritarian scheme, on the contrary, assumes that its value may be assessed by some *prior* principle, if not of family and birth or race and color or possession of material wealth, then by the position and rank a person occupies in the existing social scheme. The democratic faith in equality is the faith that each individual shall have the chance and opportunity to contribute whatever he is capable of contributing and that the value of his contribution be decided by its place and function in the organized total of similar contributions, not on the basis of prior status of any kind whatever.

I have emphasized in what precedes the importance of the effective release of intelligence in connection with personal experience in the democratic way of living. I have done so purposely because democracy is so often and so naturally associated in our minds with freedom of *action,* forgetting the importance of freed intelligence which is necessary to direct and to warrant freedom of action. Unless freedom of individual action has intelligence and informed conviction back of it, its manifestation is almost sure to result in confusion and disorder. The democratic idea of freedom is not the right of each individual to *do* as he pleases, even if it be qualified by adding "provided he does not interfere with the same freedom on the part of others." While the idea is not always, not often enough, expressed in words, the basic freedom is that of freedom of *mind* and of whatever degree of freedom of action and experience is necessary to produce freedom of intelligence. The modes of freedom guaranteed in the Bill of Rights are all of this nature: Freedom of belief and conscience, of expression of opinion, of assembly for discussion and conference, of the press as an organ of communication. They are guaranteed because without them individuals are not free to develop and society is deprived of what they might contribute.

The Future of Liberalism*

The emphasis of earlier liberalism upon individuality and liberty
defines the focal points in discussion of the philosophy of liberalism
today. This earlier liberalism was itself an outgrowth, in the late
eighteenth and nineteenth centuries, of the earlier revolt against
oligarchical government, one which came to its culmination in the
"glorious revolution" of 1688. The latter was fundamentally a demand for freedom of the taxpayer from government arbitrary action
in connection with a demand for confessional freedom in religion by
the Protestant churches. In the later liberalism, expressly so called,
the demand for liberty and individual freedom of action came primarily
from the rising industrial and trading class and was directed against
restrictions placed by government, in legislation, common law and
judicial action, and other institutions having connection with the
political state, upon freedom of economic enterprise. In both cases,
governmental action and the desired freedom were placed in antithesis
to each other. This way of conceiving liberty has persisted; it was
strengthened in this country by the revolt of the colonies and by
pioneer conditions.

Nineteenth-century philosophic liberalism added, more or less because of its dominant economic interest, the conception of natural
laws to that of natural rights of the Whig movement. There are natural laws, it held, in social matters as well as in physical, and these
natural laws are economic in character. Political laws, on the other
hand, are man-made and in that sense artificial. Governmental intervention in industry and exchange was thus regarded as a violation
not only of inherent individual liberty but also of natural laws—of
which supply and demand is a sample. The proper sphere of governmental action was simply to prevent and to secure redress for in-
fringement by one, in the exercise of his liberty, of like and equal
liberty of action on the part of others.

Nevertheless, the demand for freedom in initiation and conduct
of business enterprise did not exhaust the content of earlier liberalism.
In the minds of its chief promulgators there was included an equally
strenuous demand for the liberty of mind, freedom of thought and

* From J. Dewey, *The Future of Liberalism*. Reprinted from *The Journal of
Philosophy*, Vol. 32, No. 9, April 25, 1935, by permission of the publishers.

its expression in speech, writing, print, and assemblage. The earlier interest in confessional freedom was generalized, and thereby deepened as well as broadened. This demand was a product of the rational enlightenment of the eighteenth century and of the growing importance of science. The great tide of reaction that set in after the defeat of Napoleon, the demand for order and discipline, gave the agitation for freedom of thought and its expression plenty of cause and plenty of opportunity.

The earlier liberal philosophy rendered valiant service. It finally succeeded in sweeping away, especially in its home, Great Britain, an innumerable number of abuses and restrictions. The history of social reforms in the nineteenth century is almost one with the history of liberal social thought. It is not, then, from ingratitude that I shall emphasize its defects, for recognition of them is essential to an intelligent statement of the elements of liberal philosophy for the present and any nearby future. The fundamental defect was lack of perception of historic relativity. This lack is expressed in the conception of the individual as something given, complete in itself, and of liberty as a ready-made possession of the individual, only needing the removal of external restrictions in order to manifest itself. The individual of earlier liberalism was a Newtonian atom having only external time and space relations to other individuals, save that each social atom was equipped with inherent freedom. These ideas might not have been especially harmful if they had been merely a rallying cry for practical movements. But they formed part of a philosophy and of a philosophy in which these particular ideas of individuality and freedom were asserted to be absolute and eternal truths; good for all times and all places.

This absolutism, this ignoring and denial of temporal relativity, is one great reason why the earlier liberalism degenerated so easily into pseudo-liberalism. For the sake of saving time, I shall identify what I mean by this spurious liberalism, the kind of social ideas represented by the "Liberty League" and ex-President Hoover. I call it a pseudo-liberalism because it ossified and narrowed generous ideas and aspirations. Even when words remain the same, they mean something very different when they are uttered by a minority struggling against repressive measures and when expressed by a group that, having attained power, then uses ideas that were once weapons of emancipation as instruments for keeping the power and wealth it has obtained. Ideas that at one time are means of producing social

change assume another guise when they are used as means of preventing further social change. This fact is itself an illustration of historic
relativity, and an evidence of the evil that lay in the assertion by
earlier liberalism of the immutable and eternal character of their
ideas. Because of this latter fact, the *laissez-faire* doctrine was held
by the degenerate school of liberals to express the very order of
nature itself. The outcome was the degradation of the idea of individuality, until in the minds of many who are themselves struggling
for a wider and fuller development of individuality, individualism has
become a term of hissing and reproach, while many can see no remedy
for the evils that have come from the use of socially unrestrained
liberty in business enterprise, save change produced by violence. The
historic tendency to conceive the whole question of liberty as a
matter in which individual and government are opposed parties has
borne bitter fruit. Born of despotic government, it has continued to
influence thinking and action after government had become popular
and *in theory* the servant of the people.

I pass now to what the social philosophy of liberalism becomes
when its inheritance of absolutism is eliminated. In the first place such
liberalism knows that an individual is nothing fixed, given ready-
made. It is something achieved, and achieved not in isolation, but
the aid and support of conditions, cultural and physical, including
in "cultural" economic, legal, and political institutions as well as
science and art. Liberalism knows that social conditions may restrict,
distort, and almost prevent the development of individuality. It therefore takes an active interest in the working of social institutions that
have a bearing, positive or negative, upon the growth of individuals
who shall be rugged in fact and not merely in abstract theory. It is as
much interested in the positive construction of favorable institutions,
legal, political, and economic, as it is in the work of removing abuses
and overt oppressions.

In the second place, liberalism is committed to the idea of historic
relativity. It knows that the content of the individual and freedom
change with time; that this is as true of social change as it is of
individual development from infancy to maturity. The positive counterpart of opposition to doctrinal absolutism is experimentalism. The
connection between historic relativity and experimental method is
intrinsic. Time signifies change. The significance of individuality
with respect to social policies alters with change of the conditions in
which individuals live. The earlier liberalism in being absolute was

also unhistoric. Underlying it there was a philosophy of history which assumed that history, like time in the Newtonian scheme, means only modification of external relations; that it is quantitative, not equalitative and internal. The same thing is true of any theory that assumes, like the one usually attributed to Marx, that temporal changes in society are inevitable—that is to say, are governed by a law that is not itself historical. The fact is that the historicism and the evolutionism of nineteenth-century doctrine were only half-way doctrines. They assumed that historical and developmental processes were subject to some law or formula outside temporal processes.

The commitment of liberalism to experimental procedure carries with it the idea of continuous reconstruction of the ideas of individuality and of liberty in intimate connection with changes in social relations. It is enough to refer to the changes in productivity and distribution since the time when the earlier liberalism was formulated, and the effect of these transformations, due to science and technology, upon the terms on which men associate together. An experimental method is the recognition of this temporal change in ideas and policies so that the latter shall coördinate with the facts instead of being opposed to them. Any other view maintains a rigid conceptualism and implies that facts should conform to concepts that are framed independently of temporal or historical change.

The two things essential, then, to thorough-going social liberalism are, first, realistic study of existing conditions in their movement, and, secondly, leading ideas, in the form of policies for dealing with these conditions in the interest of development of increased individuality and liberty. The first requirement is so obviously implied that I shall not elaborate it. The second point needs some amplification. Experimental method is not just messing around nor doing a little of this and a little of that in the hope that things will improve. Just as in the physical sciences, it implies a coherent body of ideas, a theory, that gives direction to effort. What is implied, in contrast to every form of absolutism, is that the ideas and theory be taken as methods of action tested and continuously revised by the consequences they produce in actual social conditions. Since they are operational in nature, they modify conditions, while the first requirement, that of basing them upon realistic study of actual conditions, brings about their continuous reconstruction.

It follows finally that there is no opposition in principle between liberalism as social philosophy and radicalism in action, if by rad-

icalism is signified the adoption of policies that bring about drastic instead of piece-meal social changes. It is all a question of what kind of
procedures the intelligent study of changing conditions discloses. These
changes have been so tremendous in the last century, yes, in the last
forty years, that it looks to me as if radical methods were now necessary. But all that the argument here requires is recognition of the
fact that there is nothing in the nature of liberalism that makes it a
milk-water doctrine, committed to compromise and minor "reforms."
It is worth noting that the earlier liberals were regarded in their day
as subversive radicals.

What has been said should make it clear that the question of
method in formation and execution of policies is the central thing
in liberalism. The method indicated is that of maximum reliance
upon intelligence. This fact determines its opposition to those forms
of radicalism that place chief dependence upon violent overthrow of
existing institutions as the method of effecting desired social change.
A genuine liberal will emphasize as crucial the complete correlation
between the means used and the consequences that follow. The same
principle which makes him aware that the means employed by pseudo-
liberalism only perpetuate and multiply the evils of existing conditions,
makes him also aware that dependence upon sheer massed force as
the means of social change decides the kind of consequences that
actually result. Doctrines, whether proceeding from Mussolini or
from Marx, which assume that because certain ends are desirable
therefore those ends and nothing else will result from the use of force
to attain them is but another example of the limitations put upon
intelligence by any absolute theory. In the degree in which mere
force is resorted to, actual consequences are themselves so compro-
mised that the ends originally in view have in fact to be worked out
afterwards by the method of experimental intelligence.

In saying this, I do not wish to be understood as meaning that
radicals of the type mentioned have any monopoly of the use of force.
The contrary is the case. The reactionaries are in possession of force,
in not only the army and police, but in the press and the schools. The
only reason they do not advocate the use of force is the fact that they
are already in possession of it, so their policy is to cover up its existence with idealistic phrases—of which their present use of individual
initiative and liberty is a striking example.

These facts illustrate the essential evil of reliance upon sheer force.
Action and reaction are equal and in opposite directions, and force as

such is physical. Dependence upon force sooner or later calls out force on the other side. The whole problem of the relation of intelligence to force is much too large to go into here. I can only say that when the forces in possession are so blind and stubborn as to throw all their weight against the use of liberty of inquiry and of communication, of organization to effect social change, they not only encourage the use of force by those who want social change, but they give the latter the most justification they ever have. The emphasis of liberalism upon the method of intelligence does not commit it to unqualified pacificism, but to the unremitting use of every method of intelligence that conditions permit, and to search for all that are possible.

In conclusion, I wish to emphasize one point implied in the early part of the paper. The question of the practical significance of liberty is much wider than that of the relation of government to the individual, to say nothing of the monstrosity of the doctrine that assumes that under all conditions governmental action and individual liberty are found in separate and independent spheres. Government is one factor and an important one. But it comes into the picture only in relation to other matters. At present, these other matters are economic and cultural. It is absurd to conceive liberty as that of the business entrepreneur and ignore the immense regimentation to which workers are subjected, intellectual as well as manual workers. Moreover, full freedom of the human spirit and of individuality can be achieved only as there is effective opportunity to share in the cultural resources of civilization. No economic state of affairs is merely economic. It has a profound effect upon presence or absence of cultural freedom. Any liberalism that does not make full cultural freedom supreme and that does not see the relation between it and genuine industrial freedom as a way of life is a degenerate and delusive liberalism.

Creative Democracy—The Task Before Us*

Under present circumstances I cannot hope to conceal the fact that I have managed to exist eighty years. Mention of the fact may

* J. Dewey, *Creative Democracy—The Task Before Us* from *The Philosopher of the Common Man,* Essays in Honor of John Dewey to Celebrate His Eightieth Birthday. Copyright 1940 by the Conference on Methods in Philosophy. Reprinted by permission of G. P. Putnam's Sons, publishers.

suggest to you a more important fact—namely, that events of the utmost significance for the destiny of this country have taken place during the past four-fifths of a century, a period that covers more than half of its national life in its present form. For obvious reasons I shall not attempt a summary of even the more important of these events. I refer here to them because of their bearing upon the issue to which this country committed itself when the nation took shape— the creation of democracy, an issue which is now as urgent as it was a hundred and fifty years ago when the most experienced and wisest men of the country gathered to take stock of conditions and to create the political structure of a self-governing society.

For the net import of the changes that have taken place in these later years is that ways of life and institutions which were once the natural, almost the inevitable, product of fortunate conditions have now to be won by conscious and resolute effort. Not all the country was in a pioneer state eighty years ago. But it was still, save perhaps in a few large cities, so close to the pioneer stage of American life that the traditions of the pioneer, indeed of the frontier, were active agencies in forming the thoughts and shaping the beliefs of those who were born into its life. In imagination at least the country was still having an open frontier, one of unused and unappropriated resources. It was a country of physical opportunity and invitation. Even so, there was more than a marvelous conjunction of physical circumstances involved in bringing to birth this new nation. There was in existence a group of men who were capable of readapting older institutions and ideas to meet the situations provided by new physical conditions—a group of men extraordinarily gifted in political inventiveness.

At the present time, the frontier is moral, not physical. The period of free lands that seemed boundless in extent has vanished. Unused resources are now human rather than material. They are found in the waste of grown men and women who are without the chance to work, and in the young men and young women who find doors closed where there was once opportunity. The crisis that one hundred and fifty years ago called out social and political inventiveness is with us in a form which puts a heavier demand on human creativeness.

At all events this is what I mean when I say that we now have to re-create by deliberate and determined endeavor the kind of democracy which in its origin one hundred and fifty years ago was largely the product of a fortunate combination of men and circumstances.

We have lived for a long time upon the heritage that came to us from the happy conjunction of men and events in an earlier day. The present state of the world is more than a reminder that we have now to put forth every energy of our own to prove worthy of our heritage. It is a challenge to do for the critical and complex conditions of today what the men of an earlier day did for simpler conditions.

If I emphasize that the task can be accomplished only by inventive effort and creative activity, it is in part because the depth of the present crisis is due in considerable part to the fact that for a long period we acted as if our democracy were something that perpetuated itself automatically; as if our ancestors had succeeded in setting up a machine that solved the problem of perpetual motion in politics. We acted as if democracy were something that took place mainly at Washington and Albany—or some other state capital—under the impetus of what happened when men and women went to the polls once a year or so—which is a somewhat extreme way of saying that we have had the habit of thinking of democracy as a kind of political mechanism that will work as long as citizens were reasonably faithful in performing political duties.

Of late years we have heard more and more frequently that this is not enough; that democracy is a way of life. This saying gets down to hard pan. But I am not sure that something of the externality of the old idea does not cling to the new and better statement. In any case we can escape from this external way of thinking only as we realize in thought and act that democracy is a *personal* way of individual life; that it signifies the possession and continual use of certain attitudes, forming personal character and determining desire and purpose in all the relations of life. Instead of thinking of our own dispositions and habits as accommodated to certain institutions we have to learn to think of the latter as expressions, projections, and extensions of habitually dominant personal attitudes.

Democracy as a personal, an individual, way of life involves nothing fundamentally new. But when applied it puts a new practical meaning in old ideas. Put into effect it signifies that powerful present enemies of democracy can be successfully met only by the creation of personal attitudes in individual human beings; that we must get over our tendency to think that its defense can be found in any external means whatever, whether military or civil, if they are separated from individual attitudes so deep-seated as to constitute personal character.

Democracy is a way of life controlled by a working faith in the possibilities of human nature. Belief in the Common Man is a familiar article in the democratic creed. That belief is without basis and significance save as it means faith in the potentialities of human nature as that nature is exhibited in every human being irrespective of race, color, sex, birth, and family, of material or cultural wealth. This faith may be enacted in statutes, but it is only on paper unless it is put in force in the attitudes which human beings display to one another in all the incidents and relations of daily life. To denounce Naziism for intolerance, cruelty and stimulation of hatred amounts to fostering insincerity if, in our personal relations to other persons, if, in our daily walk and conversation, we are moved by racial, color, or other class prejudice; indeed, by anything save a generous belief in their possibilities as human beings, a belief which brings with it the need for providing conditions which will enable these capacities to reach fulfillment. The democratic faith in human equality is belief that every human being, independent of the quantity or range of his personal endowment, has the right to equal opportunity with every other person for development of whatever gifts he has. The democratic belief in the principle of leadership is a generous one. It is universal. It is belief in the capacity of every person to lead his own life free from coercion and imposition by others provided right conditions are supplied.

Democracy is a way of personal life controlled not merely by faith in human nature in general but by faith in the capacity of human beings for intelligent judgment and action if proper conditions are furnished. I have been accused more than once and from opposed quarters of an undue, a utopian, faith in the possibilities of intelligence and in education as a correlate of intelligence. At all events I did not invent this faith. I acquired it from my surroundings as far as those surroundings were animated by the democratic spirit. For what is the faith of democracy in the rôle of consultation, of conference, of persuasion, of discussion, in formation of public opinion, which in the long run is self-corrective, except faith in the capacity of the intelligence of the common man to respond with common sense to the free play of facts and ideas which are secured by effective guarantees of free inquiry, free assembly, and free communication? I am willing to leave to upholders of totalitarian states of the right and the left the view that faith in the capacities of intelligence is utopian. For the faith is so deeply embedded in the methods which are intrinsic to democracy that when a professed democrat denies the faith he convicts himself of treachery to his profession.

When I think of the conditions under which men and women are living in many foreign countries today, fear of espionage, with danger hanging over the meeting of friends for friendly conversation in private gatherings, I am inclined to believe that the heart and final guarantee of democracy is in free gatherings of neighbors on the street corner to discuss back and forth what is read in uncensored news of the day, and in gatherings of friends in the living rooms of houses and apartments to converse freely with one another. Intolerance, abuse, calling of names because of differences of opinion about religion or politics or business, as well as because of differences of race, color, wealth, or degree of culture, are treason to the democratic way of life. For everything which bars freedom and fullness of communication sets up barriers that divide human beings into sets and cliques, into antagonistic sects and factions, and thereby undermines the democratic way of life. Merely legal guarantees of the civil liberties of free belief, free expression, free assembly are of little avail if in daily life freedom of communication, the give and take of ideas, facts, experiences, is choked by mutual suspicion, by abuse, by fear and hatred. These things destroy the essential condition of the democratic way of living even more effectually than open coercion, which—as the example of totalitarian states proves—is effective only when it succeeds in breeding hate, suspicion, intolerance in the minds of individual human beings.

Finally, given the two conditions just mentioned, democracy as a way of life is controlled by personal faith in personal day-by-day working together with others. Democracy is the belief that even when needs and ends or consequences are different for each individual, the habit of amicable co-operation—which may include, as in sport, rivalry and competition—is itself a priceless addition to life. To take as far as possible every conflict which arises—and they are bound to arise—out of the atmosphere and medium of force, of violence as a means of settlement, into that of discussion and of intelligence, is to treat those who disagree—even profoundly—with us as those from whom we may learn, and in so far, as friends. A genuinely democratic faith in peace is faith in the possibility of conducting disputes, controversies, and conflicts as co-operative undertakings in which both parties learn by giving the other a chance to express itself, instead of having one party conquer by forceful suppression of the other—a suppression which is none the less one of violence when it takes place by psychological means of ridicule, abuse, intimidation, instead of by overt imprisonment or in concentration camps. To co-operate by giving differences a chance to show themselves because of the belief that the expression of difference is not only a right of the other persons but is a means of enriching one's own life-experience, is inherent in the democratic personal way of life.

If what has been said is charged with being a set of moral commonplaces, my only reply is that that is just the point in saying them. For to get rid of the habit of thinking of democracy as something institutional and external and to acquire the habit of treating it as a way of personal life is to realize that democracy is a moral ideal and so far as it becomes a fact is a moral fact. It is to realize that democracy is a reality only as it is indeed a commonplace of living.

Since my adult years have been given to the pursuit of philosophy, I shall ask your indulgence if in concluding I state briefly the democratic faith in the formal terms of a philosophic position. So stated, democracy is belief in the ability of human experience to generate the aims and methods by which further experience will grow in ordered richness. Every other form of moral and social faith rests upon the idea that experience must be subjected at some point or other to some form of external control; to some "authority" alleged to exist outside the processes of experience. Democracy is the faith that the process of experience is more important than any special result attained, so that special results achieved are of ultimate value only as they are used to enrich and order the ongoing process. Since the process of experience is capable of being educative, faith in democracy is all one with faith in experience and education. All ends and values that are cut off from the ongoing process become arrests, fixations. They strive to fixate what has been gained instead of using it to open the road and point the way to new and better experiences.

If one asks what is meant by experience in this connection, my reply is that it is that free interaction of individual human beings with surrounding conditions, especially the human surroundings, which develops and satisfies need and desire by increasing knowledge of things as they are. Knowledge of conditions as they are is the only solid ground for communication and sharing; all other communication means the subjection of some persons to the personal opinion of other persons. Need and desire—out of which grow purpose and direction of energy—go beyond what exists, and hence beyond knowledge, beyond science. They continually open the way into the unexplored and unattained future.

Democracy as compared with other ways of life is the sole way of living which believes wholeheartedly in the process of experience as end and as means; as that which is capable of generating the science which is the sole dependable authority for the direction of further experience and which releases emotions, needs, and desires so as to call into being the things that have not existed in the past. For every way of life that fails in its democracy limits the contacts, the exchanges, the communications, the interactions by which experience is steadied while it is also enlarged and enriched. The task of this release and enrichment is one that has to be carried on day by day. Since it is one that can have no end till experience itself comes to an end, the task of democracy is forever that of creation of a freer and more humane experience in which all share and to which all contribute.

INDEX